WILEY **PLUS**

www.wileyplus.com

This online teaching and learning environment integrates the entire digital textbook with the most effective instructor and student resources to fit every learning style.

With **WileyPLUS:**

D0178888

○ Students achieve concept mastery in a rich, structured environment that's available 24/7

○ Instructors personalize and manage their course more effectively with assessment, assignments, grade tracking, and more

- manage time better
- study smarter
- save money

From multiple study paths, to self-assessment, to a wealth of interactive visual and audio resources, *WileyPLUS* gives you everything you need to personalize the teaching and learning experience.

≫Find out how to MAKE IT YOURS≫

www.wiley**plus**.com

ALL THE HELP, RESOURCES, AND PERSONAL SUPPORT YOU AND YOUR STUDENTS NEED!

2-Minute Tutorials and all
of the resources you & your
students need to get started
www.wileyplus.com/firstday

Student support from an
experienced student user
Ask your local representative
for details!

Collaborate with your colleagues,
find a mentor, attend virtual and live
events, and view resources
www.WhereFacultyConnect.com

Pre-loaded, ready-to-use
assignments and presentations
www.wiley.com/college/quickstart

Technical Support 24/7
FAQs, online chat,
and phone support
www.wileyplus.com/support

Your WileyPLUS
Account Manager
Training and implementation support
www.wileyplus.com/accountmanager

www.wileyplus.com

MAKE IT YOURS!

Java 6th edition

Concepts

INTERNATIONAL STUDENT VERSION

Java

Concepts

INTERNATIONAL STUDENT VERSION

Cay Horstmann SAN JOSE STATE UNIVERSITY

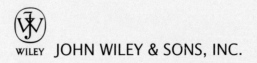

WILEY JOHN WILEY & SONS, INC.

PREFACE

This book is an introductory text in computer science, focusing on the principles of programming and software engineering. Here are its key features:

- Teach objects gradually.

  In Chapter 2, students learn how to use objects and classes from the standard library. The chapter then shows the mechanics of implementing classes *from a given specification*. Students then use simple objects as they master branches, loops, and arrays. Object-oriented design starts in Chapter 7. This gradual approach allows students to use objects throughout their study of the core algorithmic topics, without teaching bad habits that must be un-learned later.

- Reinforce sound engineering practices.

  A focus on test-driven development encourages students to test their programs systematically. A multitude of useful tips on software quality and common errors encourage the development of good programming habits.

- Help students with guidance and worked examples.

  Beginning programmers often ask "How do I start? Now what do I do?" Of course, an activity as complex as programming cannot be reduced to cookbook-style instructions. However, step-by-step guidance is immensely helpful for building confidence and providing an outline for the task at hand. The book contains a large number of "How To" guides for common tasks, with pointers to additional worked examples on the Web.

- Focus on the essentials while being technically accurate.

  An encyclopedic coverage is not helpful for a beginning programmer, but neither is the opposite—reducing the material to a list of simplistic bullet points that give an illusion of knowledge. In this book, the essentials of each subject are presented in digestible chunks, with separate notes that go deeper into good practices or language features when the reader is ready for the additional information.

- Use standard Java.

  The book teaches the standard Java language—not a specialized "training wheels" environment. The Java language, library, and tools are presented at a depth that is sufficient to solve real-world programming problems.

- Provide an optional graphics track.

  Graphical shapes are splendid examples of objects. Many students enjoy writing programs that create drawings or use graphical user interfaces. If desired, these topics can be integrated into the course by using the materials at the end of Chapters 2, 8, and 9.

New in This Edition

This is the fourth edition of *Big Java,* and the book has once again been carefully revised and updated. The new and improved features include:

More Help for Beginning Programmers

- The How To sections have been updated and expanded, and four new ones have been added. Fifteen new Worked Examples (on the companion web site and in WileyPLUS) walk students through the steps required for solving complex and interesting problems.
- The treatment of algorithm design, planning, and the use of pseudocode has been enhanced. Students learn to use pseudocode to define the solution algorithm in Chapter 1.
- Chapters have been revised to focus each section on a specific learning objective. These learning objectives also organize the chapter summary to help students assess their progress.

Annotated Examples

- Syntax diagrams now call out features of typical example code to draw student attention to the key elements of the syntax. Additional annotations point out special cases, common errors, and good practice associated with the syntax.
- New example tables clearly present a variety of typical and special cases in a compact format. Each example is accompanied by a brief note explaining the usage shown and the values that result from it.
- The gradual introduction of objects has been further improved by providing additional examples and insights in the early chapters.

Updated for Java 7

- Features introduced in Java 7 are covered as Special Topics so that students can prepare for them. In this edition, we use Java 5 or 6 for the main discussion.

More Opportunities for Practice

- The test bank has been greatly expanded and improved. (See page xi.)
- A new set of lab assignments enables students to practice solving complex problems one step at a time.
- The LabRat code evaluation feature, enhanced for this edition, gives students instant feedback on their programming assignments. (See page xvi.)

A Tour of the Book

The book can be naturally grouped into four parts, as illustrated by Figure 1. The organization of chapters offers the same flexibility as the previous edition; dependencies among the chapters are also shown in the figure.

Part A: Fundamentals (Chapters 1–6)

Chapter 1 contains a brief introduction to computer science and Java programming. Chapter 2 shows how to manipulate objects of predefined classes, then how to build your own simple classes from given specifications.

Fundamental data types, branches, loops, and arrays are covered in Chapters 3–6.

Part B: Object-Oriented Design (Chapters 7–11)

Chapter 7 takes up the subject of class design in a systematic fashion, and it introduces a very simple subset of the UML notation.

The discussion of polymorphism and inheritance is split into two chapters. Chapter 8 covers interfaces and polymorphism, whereas Chapter 9 covers inheritance. Introducing interfaces before inheritance pays off in an important way: Students immediately see polymorphism before getting bogged down with technical details such as superclass construction.

Exception handling and basic file input/output are covered in Chapter 10. The exception hierarchy gives a useful example for inheritance.

Chapter 11 contains an introduction to object-oriented design, including two significant case studies.

Part C: Data Structures and Algorithms (Chapters 12–14)

Chapters 12 through 14 contain an introduction to algorithms and basic data structures, covering recursion, sorting and searching, and linked lists, stacks, and queues. These topics can be covered as desired after Chapter 6 (see Figure 1).

Recursion is introduced from an object-oriented point of view: An object that solves a problem recursively constructs another object of the same class that solves a simpler problem. The idea of having the other object do the simpler job is more intuitive than having a function call itself.

Chapter 13 covers the fundamental sorting algorithms and gives a gentle introduction to big-Oh analysis. Chapter 14 introduces linked lists, stacks, and queues, both as abstract data types and as they appear in the standard Java library.

Part D: Advanced Topics (Chapters 15–17)

Chapter 15 covers advanced data structures: hash tables, binary search trees, and heaps. Chapter 16 introduces Java generics. This chapter is suitable for advanced students who want to implement their own generic classes and methods. Chapter 17 completes the graphics track coverage of user interfaces with a discussion of layout management and Swing components. These chapters are available on the Web at www.wiley.com/go/global/horstmann, or in the WileyPLUS course for this book.

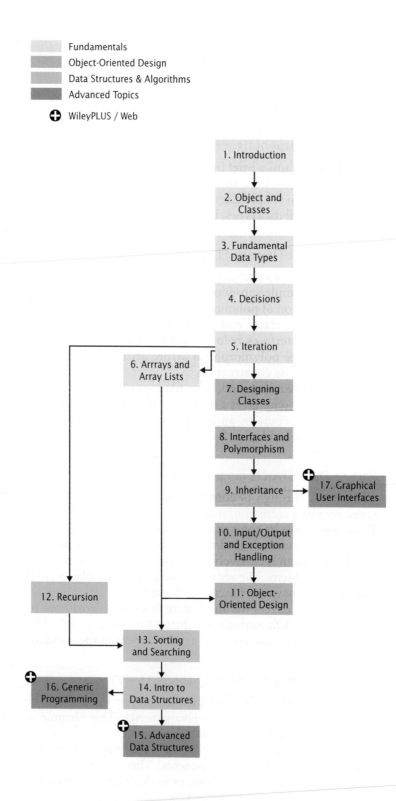

Figure 1 Chapter Dependencies

Appendices

Appendix A lists character escape sequences and the Basic Latin and Latin-1 subsets of Unicode. Appendices B and C summarize Java reserved words and operators. Appendix D documents all of the library methods and classes used in this book.

In addition, Appendices E–L are available on the Web and contain quick references on Java syntax, HTML, Java tools, binary numbers, and UML.

Appendix L contains a style guide for use with this book. Many instructors find it highly beneficial to require a consistent style for all assignments. If this style guide conflicts with instructor sentiment or local customs, however, it is available in electronic form so that it can be modified.

Web Resources

This book is complemented by a complete suite of online resources and a robust WileyPLUS course.

Go to www.wiley.com/go/global/horstmann to visit the online companion site, which includes

- Source code for all examples in the book.
- Worked Examples that apply the problem-solving steps in the book to other realistic examples.
- Laboratory exercises (and solutions for instructors only).
- Lecture presentation slides (in HTML and PowerPoint formats).
- Solutions to all review and programming exercises (for instructors only).
- A test bank that focuses on skills, not just terminology (for instructors only).

WileyPLUS is an online teaching and learning environment that integrates the digital textbook with instructor and student resources. See page xvi for details.

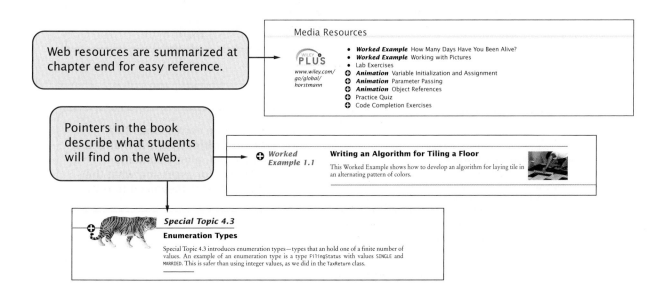

Web resources are summarized at chapter end for easy reference.

Media Resources

PLUS
www.wiley.com/
go/global/
horstmann

- *Worked Example* How Many Days Have You Been Alive?
- *Worked Example* Working with Pictures
- Lab Exercises
- *Animation* Variable Initialization and Assignment
- *Animation* Parameter Passing
- *Animation* Object References
- Practice Quiz
- Code Completion Exercises

Pointers in the book describe what students will find on the Web.

Worked Example 1.1

Writing an Algorithm for Tiling a Floor

This Worked Example shows how to develop an algorithm for laying tile in an alternating pattern of colors.

Special Topic 4.3

Enumeration Types

Special Topic 4.3 introduces enumeration types—types that an hold one of a finite number of values. An example of an enumeration type is a type FilingStatus with values SINGLE and MARRIED. This is safer than using integer values, as we did in the TaxReturn class.

A Walkthrough of the Learning Aids

The pedagogical elements in this book work together to make the book accessible to beginners as well as those learning Java as a second language.

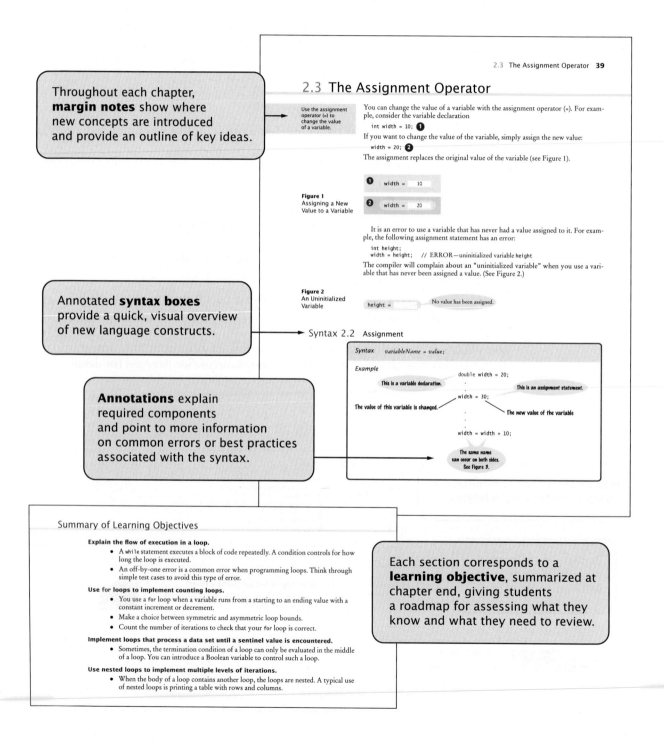

Throughout each chapter, **margin notes** show where new concepts are introduced and provide an outline of key ideas.

Annotated **syntax boxes** provide a quick, visual overview of new language constructs.

Annotations explain required components and point to more information on common errors or best practices associated with the syntax.

Each section corresponds to a **learning objective**, summarized at chapter end, giving students a roadmap for assessing what they know and what they need to review.

2.3 The Assignment Operator **39**

2.3 The Assignment Operator

Use the assignment operator (=) to change the value of a variable.

You can change the value of a variable with the assignment operator (=). For example, consider the variable declaration

```
int width = 10; ❶
```

If you want to change the value of the variable, simply assign the new value:

```
width = 20; ❷
```

The assignment replaces the original value of the variable (see Figure 1).

Figure 1
Assigning a New Value to a Variable

❶ width = 10

❷ width = 20

It is an error to use a variable that has never had a value assigned to it. For example, the following assignment statement has an error:

```
int height;
width = height;   // ERROR—uninitialized variable height
```

The compiler will complain about an "uninitialized variable" when you use a variable that has never been assigned a value. (See Figure 2.)

Figure 2
An Uninitialized Variable

height = No value has been assigned.

Syntax 2.2 Assignment

Syntax   variableName = value;

Example

This is a variable declaration.   double width = 20;   This is an assignment statement.

The value of this variable is changed.   width = 30;   The new value of the variable

width = width + 10;

The same name can occur on both sides. See Figure 5.

Summary of Learning Objectives

Explain the flow of execution in a loop.
- A while statement executes a block of code repeatedly. A condition controls for how long the loop is executed.
- An off-by-one error is a common error when programming loops. Think through simple test cases to avoid this type of error.

Use for loops to implement counting loops.
- You use a for loop when a variable runs from a starting to an ending value with a constant increment or decrement.
- Make a choice between symmetric and asymmetric loop bounds.
- Count the number of iterations to check that your for loop is correct.

Implement loops that process a data set until a sentinel value is encountered.
- Sometimes, the termination condition of a loop can only be evaluated in the middle of a loop. You can introduce a Boolean variable to control such a loop.

Use nested loops to implement multiple levels of iterations.
- When the body of a loop contains another loop, the loops are nested. A typical use of nested loops is printing a table with rows and columns.

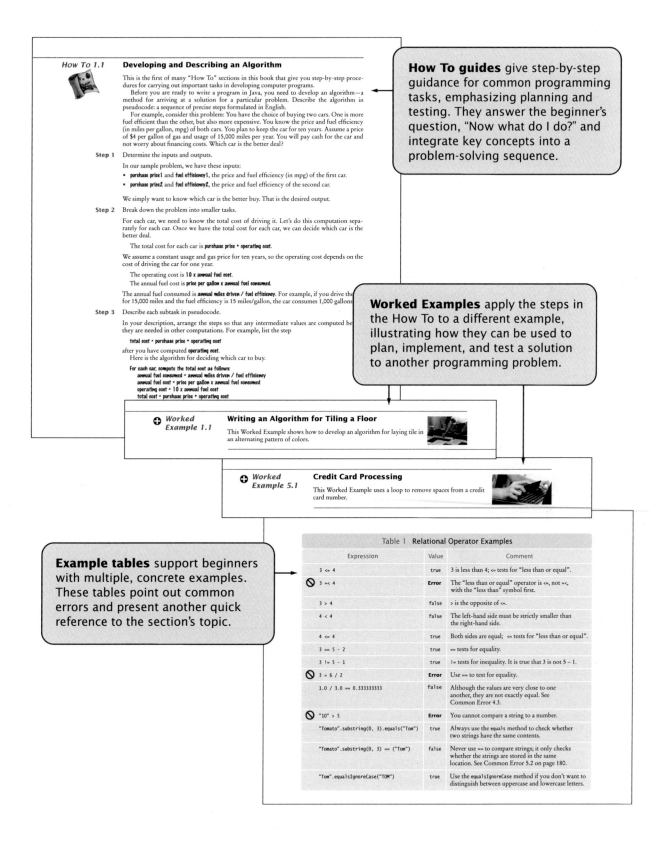

How To 1.1   **Developing and Describing an Algorithm**

This is the first of many "How To" sections in this book that give you step-by-step procedures for carrying out important tasks in developing computer programs.

Before you are ready to write a program in Java, you need to develop an algorithm—a method for arriving at a solution for a particular problem. Describe the algorithm in pseudocode: a sequence of precise steps formulated in English.

For example, consider this problem: You have the choice of buying two cars. One is more fuel efficient than the other, but also more expensive. You know the price and fuel efficiency (in miles per gallon, mpg) of both cars. You plan to keep the car for ten years. Assume a price of $4 per gallon of gas and usage of 15,000 miles per year. You will pay cash for the car and not worry about financing costs. Which car is the better deal?

Step 1   Determine the inputs and outputs.

In our sample problem, we have these inputs:

- purchase price1 and fuel efficiency1, the price and fuel efficiency (in mpg) of the first car.
- purchase price2 and fuel efficiency2, the price and fuel efficiency of the second car.

We simply want to know which car is the better buy. That is the desired output.

Step 2   Break down the problem into smaller tasks.

For each car, we need to know the total cost of driving it. Let's do this computation separately for each car. Once we have the total cost for each car, we can decide which car is the better deal.

The total cost for each car is purchase price + operating cost.

We assume a constant usage and gas price for ten years, so the operating cost depends on the cost of driving the car for one year.

The operating cost is 10 x annual fuel cost.

The annual fuel cost is price per gallon x annual fuel consumed.

The annual fuel consumed is annual miles driven / fuel efficiency. For example, if you drive the for 15,000 miles and the fuel efficiency is 15 miles/gallon, the car consumes 1,000 gallons

Step 3   Describe each subtask in pseudocode.

In your description, arrange the steps so that any intermediate values are computed be they are needed in other computations. For example, list the step

        total cost = purchase price + operating cost

after you have computed operating cost.
Here is the algorithm for deciding which car to buy.

    For each car, compute the total cost as follows:
        annual fuel consumed = annual miles driven / fuel efficiency
        annual fuel cost = price per gallon x annual fuel consumed
        operating cost = 10 x annual fuel cost
        total cost = purchase price + operating cost

How To guides give step-by-step guidance for common programming tasks, emphasizing planning and testing. They answer the beginner's question, "Now what do I do?" and integrate key concepts into a problem-solving sequence.

Worked Examples apply the steps in the How To to a different example, illustrating how they can be used to plan, implement, and test a solution to another programming problem.

⊕ *Worked Example 1.1*   **Writing an Algorithm for Tiling a Floor**

This Worked Example shows how to develop an algorithm for laying tile in an alternating pattern of colors.

⊕ *Worked Example 5.1*   **Credit Card Processing**

This Worked Example uses a loop to remove spaces from a credit card number.

Example tables support beginners with multiple, concrete examples. These tables point out common errors and present another quick reference to the section's topic.

Table 1 Relational Operator Examples

Expression	Value	Comment
3 <= 4	true	3 is less than 4; <= tests for "less than or equal".
⊘ 3 =< 4	**Error**	The "less than or equal" operator is <=, not =<, with the "less than" symbol first.
3 > 4	false	> is the opposite of <=.
4 < 4	false	The left-hand side must be strictly smaller than the right-hand side.
4 <= 4	true	Both sides are equal; <= tests for "less than or equal".
3 == 5 - 2	true	== tests for equality.
3 != 5 - 1	true	!= tests for inequality. It is true that 3 is not 5 – 1.
⊘ 3 = 6 / 2	**Error**	Use == to test for equality.
1.0 / 3.0 == 0.333333333	false	Although the values are very close to one another, they are not exactly equal. See Common Error 4.3.
⊘ "10" > 5	**Error**	You cannot compare a string to a number.
"Tomato".substring(0, 3).equals("Tom")	true	Always use the equals method to check whether two strings have the same contents.
"Tomato".substring(0, 3) == ("Tom")	false	Never use == to compare strings; it only checks whether the strings are stored in the same location. See Common Error 5.2 on page 180.
"Tom".equalsIgnoreCase("TOM")	true	Use the equalsIgnoreCase method if you don't want to distinguish between uppercase and lowercase letters.

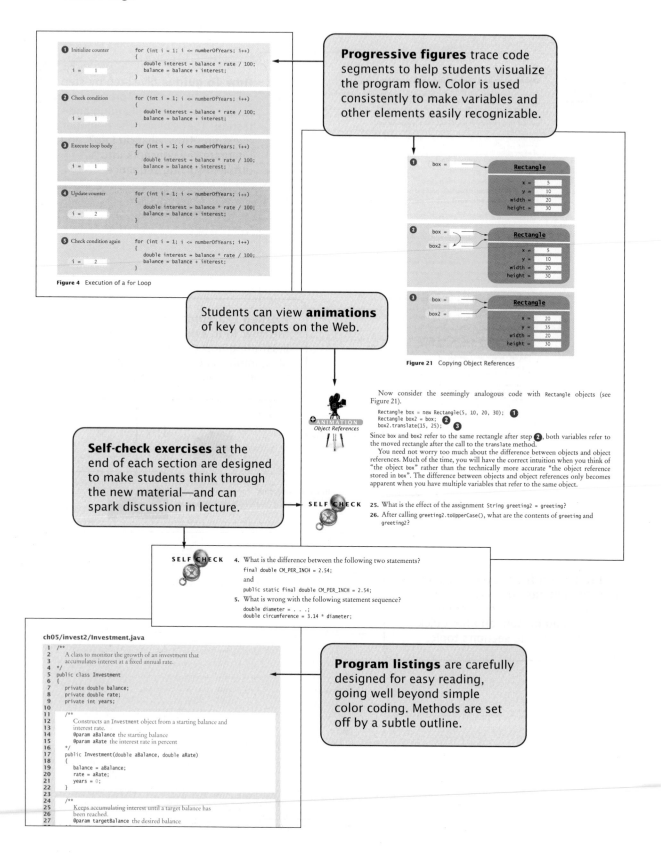

① Initialize counter

```
for (int i = 1; i <= numberOfYears; i++)
{
    double interest = balance * rate / 100;
    balance = balance + interest;
}
```
i = 1

② Check condition

```
for (int i = 1; i <= numberOfYears; i++)
{
    double interest = balance * rate / 100;
    balance = balance + interest;
}
```
i = 1

③ Execute loop body

```
for (int i = 1; i <= numberOfYears; i++)
{
    double interest = balance * rate / 100;
    balance = balance + interest;
}
```
i = 1

④ Update counter

```
for (int i = 1; i <= numberOfYears; i++)
{
    double interest = balance * rate / 100;
    balance = balance + interest;
}
```
i = 2

⑤ Check condition again

```
for (int i = 1; i <= numberOfYears; i++)
{
    double interest = balance * rate / 100;
    balance = balance + interest;
}
```
i = 2

Figure 4 Execution of a for Loop

Progressive figures trace code segments to help students visualize the program flow. Color is used consistently to make variables and other elements easily recognizable.

Students can view **animations** of key concepts on the Web.

❶ box =

Rectangle
x =	5
y =	10
width =	20
height =	30

❷ box =
box2 =

Rectangle
x =	5
y =	10
width =	20
height =	30

❸ box =
box2 =

Rectangle
x =	20
y =	35
width =	20
height =	30

Figure 21 Copying Object References

Now consider the seemingly analogous code with Rectangle objects (see Figure 21).

```
Rectangle box = new Rectangle(5, 10, 20, 30);    ❶
Rectangle box2 = box;    ❷
box2.translate(15, 25);    ❸
```

Since box and box2 refer to the same rectangle after step ❷, both variables refer to the moved rectangle after the call to the translate method.

You need not worry too much about the difference between objects and object references. Much of the time, you will have the correct intuition when you think of "the object box" rather than the technically more accurate "the object reference stored in box". The difference between objects and object references only becomes apparent when you have multiple variables that refer to the same object.

Self-check exercises at the end of each section are designed to make students think through the new material—and can spark discussion in lecture.

+ ANIMATION
Object References

SELF CHECK

25. What is the effect of the assignment String greeting2 = greeting?

26. After calling greeting2.toUpperCase(), what are the contents of greeting and greeting2?

SELF CHECK

4. What is the difference between the following two statements?
```
final double CM_PER_INCH = 2.54;
```
and
```
public static final double CM_PER_INCH = 2.54;
```

5. What is wrong with the following statement sequence?
```
double diameter = . . .;
double circumference = 3.14 * diameter;
```

ch05/invest2/Investment.java

```
1   /**
2       A class to monitor the growth of an investment that
3       accumulates interest at a fixed annual rate.
4   */
5   public class Investment
6   {
7       private double balance;
8       private double rate;
9       private int years;
10
11      /**
12          Constructs an Investment object from a starting balance and
13          interest rate.
14          @param aBalance the starting balance
15          @param aRate the interest rate in percent
16      */
17      public Investment(double aBalance, double aRate)
18      {
19          balance = aBalance;
20          rate = aRate;
21          years = 0;
22      }
23
24      /**
25          Keeps accumulating interest until a target balance has
26          been reached.
27          @param targetBalance the desired balance
```

Program listings are carefully designed for easy reading, going well beyond simple color coding. Methods are set off by a subtle outline.

Common Errors describe the kinds of errors that students often make, with an explanation of why the errors occur, and what to do about them.

Common Error 6.3

Length and Size

Unfortunately, the Java syntax for determining the number of elements in an array, an array list, and a string is not at all consistent. It is a common error to confuse these. You just have to remember the correct syntax for every data type.

Data Type	Number of Elements
Array	a.length
Array list	a.size()
String	a.length()

Quality Tips explain good programming practices. These notes carefully motivate the reason behind the advice, and explain why the effort will be repaid later.

Quality Tip 3.1

Do Not Use Magic Numbers

A magic number is a numeric constant that appears in your code without explanation. For example, consider the following scary example that actually occurs in the Java library source:

```
h = 31 * h + ch;
```

Why 31? The number of days in January? One less than the number of bits in an integer? Actually, this code computes a "hash code" from a string—a number that is derived from the characters in such a way that different strings are likely to yield different hash codes. The value 31 turns out to scramble the character values nicely.
 A better solution is to use a named constant:

```
final int HASH_MULTIPLIER = 31;
h = HASH_MULTIPLIER * h + ch;
```

You should never use magic numbers in your code. Any number that is not completely self-explanatory should be declared as a named constant. Even the most reasonable cosmic constant is going to change one day. You think there are 365 days in a year? Your customers on Mars are going to be pretty unhappy about your silly prejudice. Make a constant

```
final int DAYS_PER_YEAR = 365;
```

By the way, the device

```
final int THREE_HUNDRED_AND_SIXTY_FIVE = 365;
```

Productivity Hints teach students how to use their time and tools more effectively. They encourage students to be more productive with tips and techniques such as hand-tracing.

Productivity Hint 5.1

Hand-Tracing Loops

In Productivity Hint 4.2, you learned about the method of hand tracing. This method is particularly effective for understanding how a loop works.
 Consider this example loop. What value is displayed?

```
int n = 1729;     ①
int sum = 0;
while (n > 0)     ②
{
    int digit = n % 10;   ③ ④ ⑤ ⑥
    sum = sum + digit;
    n = n / 10;
}
System.out.println(sum);   ⑦
```

1. There are three variables: n, sum, and digit. The first two variables are initialized with 1729 and 0 before the loop is entered.

n	sum	digit
1729	0	

Special Topics present optional topics and provide additional explanation of others. New features of Java 7 are also covered in these notes.

Special Topic 6.2

ArrayList Syntax Enhancements in Java 7

Java 7 introduces several convenient syntax enhancements for array lists.
 When you declare and construct an array list, you need not repeat the type parameter in the constructor. That is, you can write

```
ArrayList<String> names = new ArrayList<>();
```

instead of

```
ArrayList<String> names = new ArrayList<String>();
```

Random Facts provide historical and social information on computing—for interest and to fulfill the "historical and social context" requirements of the ACM/IEEE curriculum guidelines.

Random Fact 5.1

The First Bug

According to legend, the first bug was one found in 1947 in the Mark II, a huge electro-mechanical computer at Harvard University. It really was caused by a bug—a moth was trapped in a relay switch. Actually, from the note that the operator left in the log book next to the moth (see the figure), it appears as if the term "bug" had already been in active use at the time.

The First Bug

 The pioneering computer scientist Maurice Wilkes wrote: "Somehow, at the Moore School and afterwards, one had always assumed there would be no particular difficulty in getting programs right. I can remember the exact instant in time at which it dawned on me

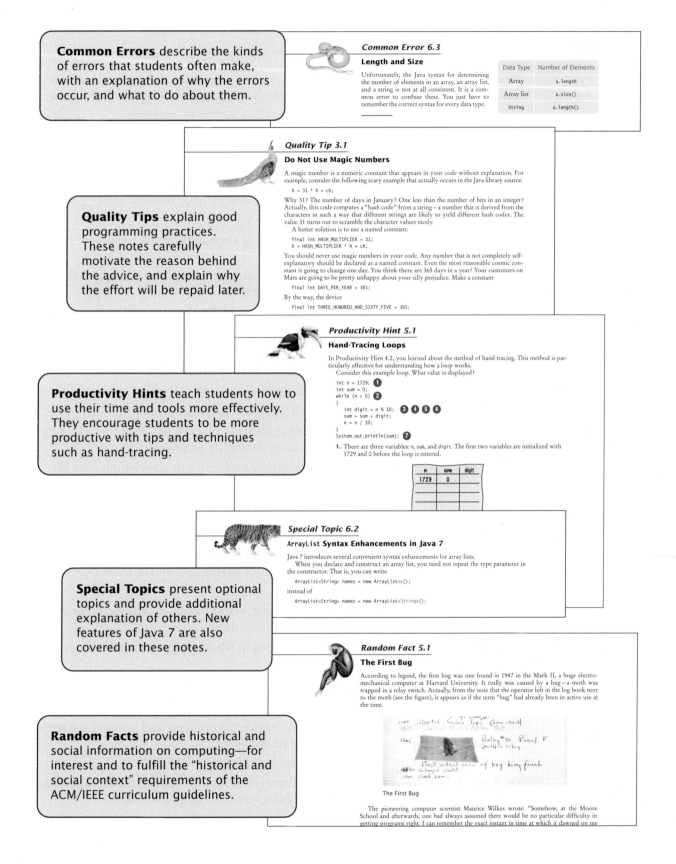

WileyPLUS

WileyPLUS is an online environment that supports students and instructors. This book's WileyPLUS course can complement the printed text or replace it altogether.

For Students

Different learning styles, different levels of proficiency, different levels of preparation—each student is unique. WileyPLUS empowers all students to take advantage of their individual strengths.

Integrated, multi-media resources—including audio and visual exhibits and demonstration problems—encourage active learning and provide multiple study paths to fit each student's learning preferences.

- Worked Examples apply the problem-solving steps in the book to another realistic example.
- Screencast Videos present the author explaining the steps he is taking and showing his work as he solves a programming problem.
- Animations of key concepts allow students to replay dynamic explanations that instructors usually provide on a whiteboard.

Self-assessments are linked to relevant portions of the text. Students can take control of their own learning and practice until they master the material.

- Practice quizzes can reveal areas where students need to focus.
- Lab exercises can be assigned for self-study or for use in the lab.
- "Code completion" questions enable students to practice programming skills by filling in small code snippets and getting immediate feedback.
- LabRat provides instant feedback on student solutions to all programming exercises in the book.

For Instructors

WileyPLUS includes all of the instructor resources found on the companion site, and more.

WileyPLUS gives you tools for identifying those students who are falling behind, allowing you to intervene accordingly, without having to wait for them to come to office hours.

- Practice quizzes for pre-reading assessment, self-quizzing, or additional practice can be used as-is or modified for your course needs.
- Multi-step laboratory exercises can be used in lab or assigned for extra student practice.

WileyPLUS simplifies and automates student performance assessment, making assignments, and scoring student work.

- An extensive set of multiple-choice questions for quizzing and testing have been developed to focus on skills, not just terminology.
- "Code completion" questions can also be added to online quizzes.
- LabRat can track student work on all programming exercises in the book, adding the student solution and a record of completion to the gradebook.
- Solutions to all review and programming exercises are provided..

With WileyPLUS ...

Students can read the book online and take advantage of searching and cross-linking.

Instructors can assign drill-and-practice questions to check that students did their reading and grasp basic concepts.

Students can practice programming by filling in small code snippets and getting immediate feedback.

Students can play and replay dynamic explanations of concepts and program flow.

Students can check that their programming assignments fulfill the specifications.

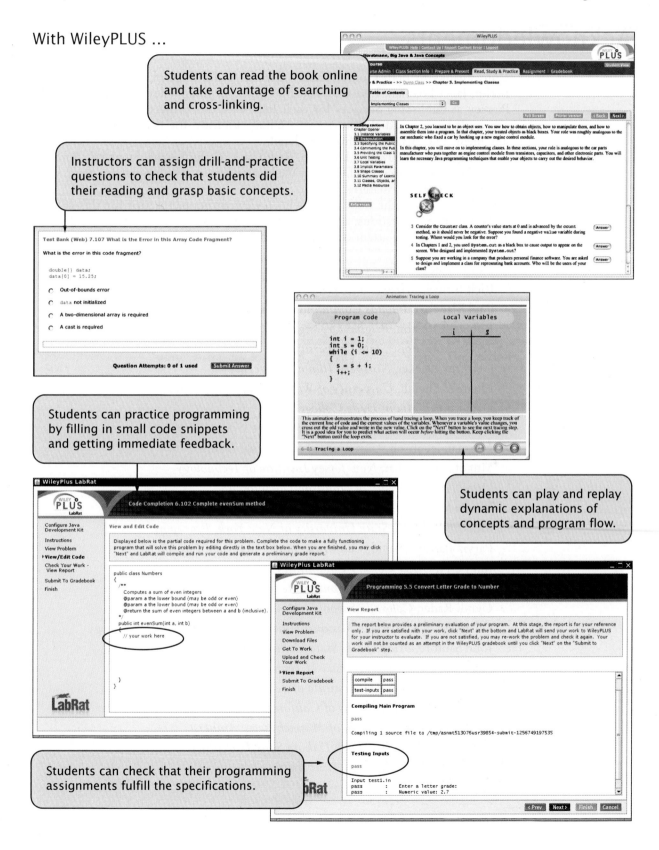

Acknowledgments

Many thanks to Beth Golub, Lauren Sapira, Andre Legaspi, Don Fowley, Mike Berlin, Janet Foxman, Lisa Gee, and Bud Peters at John Wiley & Sons, and Vickie Piercey at Publishing Services for their help with this project. An especially deep acknowledgment and thanks goes to Cindy Johnson for her hard work, sound judgment, and amazing attention to detail.

I am grateful to Suzanne Dietrich, Rick Giles, Kathy Liszka, Stephanie Smullen, Julius Dichter, Patricia McDermott-Wells, and David Woolbright, for their work on the supplemental material.

Many thanks to the individuals who reviewed the manuscript for this edition, made valuable suggestions, and brought an embarrassingly large number of errors and omissions to my attention. They include:

Ian Barland, *Radford University*

Rick Birney, *Arizona State University*

Paul Bladek, *Edmonds Community College*

Robert P. Burton, *Brigham Young University*

Teresa Cole, *Boise State University*

Geoffrey Decker, *Northern Illinois University*

Eman El-Sheikh, *University of West Florida*

David Freer, *Miami Dade College*

Ahmad Ghafarian, *North Georgia College & State University*

Norman Jacobson, *University of California, Irvine*

Mugdha Khaladkar, *New Jersey Institute of Technology*

Hong Lin, *University of Houston, Downtown*

Jeanna Matthews, *Clarkson University*

Sandeep R. Mitra, *State University of New York, Brockport*

Parviz Partow-Navid, *California State University, Los Angeles*

Jim Perry, *Ulster County Community College*

Kai Qian, *Southern Polytechnic State University*

Cyndi Rader, *Colorado School of Mines*

Chaman Lal Sabharwal, *Missouri University of Science and Technology*

John Santore, *Bridgewater State College*

Stephanie Smullen, *University of Tennessee, Chattanooga*

Monica Sweat, *Georgia Institute of Technology*

Shannon Tauro, *University of California, Irvine*

Russell Tessier, *University of Massachusetts, Amherst*

Jonathan L. Tolstedt, *North Dakota State University*

David Vineyard, *Kettering University*

Lea Wittie, *Bucknell University*

Every new edition builds on the suggestions and experiences of prior reviewers and users. I am grateful for the invaluable contributions these individuals have made to this book:

Tim Andersen, *Boise State University*

Ivan Bajic, *San Diego State University*

Ted Bangay, *Sheridan Institute of Technology*

George Basham, *Franklin University*

Sambit Bhattacharya, *Fayetteville State University*

Joseph Bowbeer, *Vizrea Corporation*

Timothy A. Budd, *Oregon State University*

Frank Butt, *IBM*

Jerry Cain, *Stanford University*

Adam Cannon, *Columbia University*

Nancy Chase, *Gonzaga University*

Archana Chidanandan, *Rose-Hulman Institute of Technology*

Vincent Cicirello, *The Richard Stockton College of New Jersey*

Deborah Coleman, *Rochester Institute of Technology*

Valentino Crespi, *California State University, Los Angeles*

Jim Cross, *Auburn University*

Russell Deaton, *University of Arkansas*

H. E. Dunsmore, *Purdue University*

Robert Duvall, *Duke University*

Henry A. Etlinger, *Rochester Institute of Technology*

John Fendrich, *Bradley University*

John Fulton, *Franklin University*

David Geary, *Sabreware, Inc.*

Margaret Geroch, *Wheeling Jesuit University*

Rick Giles, *Acadia University*

Stacey Grasso, *College of San Mateo*

Jianchao Han, *California State University, Dominguez Hills*

Lisa Hansen, *Western New England College*

Elliotte Harold

Eileen Head, *Binghamton University*

Cecily Heiner, *University of Utah*

Brian Howard, *Depauw University*

Lubomir Ivanov, *Iona College*

Curt Jones, *Bloomsburg University*

Aaron Keen, *California Polytechnic State University, San Luis Obispo*

Elliot Koffman, *Temple University*

Kathy Liszka, *University of Akron*

Hunter Lloyd, *Montana State University*

Youmin Lu, *Bloomsburg University*

John S. Mallozzi, *Iona College*

John Martin, *North Dakota State University*

Scott McElfresh, *Carnegie Mellon University*

Joan McGrory, *Christian Brothers University*

Carolyn Miller, *North Carolina State University*

Teng Moh, *San Jose State University*

John Moore, *The Citadel*

Faye Navabi, *Arizona State University*

Kevin O'Gorman, *California Polytechnic State University, San Luis Obispo*

Michael Olan, *Richard Stockton College*

Kevin Parker, *Idaho State University*

Cornel Pokorny, *California Polytechnic State University, San Luis Obispo*

Roger Priebe, *University of Texas, Austin*

C. Robert Putnam, *California State University, Northridge*

Neil Rankin, *Worcester Polytechnic Institute*

Brad Rippe, *Fullerton College*

Pedro I. Rivera Vega, *University of Puerto Rico, Mayaguez*

Daniel Rogers, *SUNY Brockport*

Carolyn Schauble, *Colorado State University*

Christian Shin, *SUNY Geneseo*

Jeffrey Six, *University of Delaware*

Don Slater, *Carnegie Mellon University*

Ken Slonneger, *University of Iowa*

Peter Stanchev, *Kettering University*

Ron Taylor, *Wright State University*

Joseph Vybihal, *McGill University*

Xiaoming Wei, *Iona College*

Todd Whittaker, *Franklin University*

Robert Willhoft, *Roberts Wesleyan College*

David Womack, *University of Texas at San Antonio*

Catherine Wyman, *DeVry University*

Arthur Yanushka, *Christian Brothers University*

Salih Yurttas, *Texas A&M University*

CONTENTS

✛ Available online in WileyPLUS and at www.wiley.com/go/global/horstmann.

ALPHABETICAL LIST OF SYNTAX BOXES

✚ Available online in WileyPLUS and at www.wiley.com/go/global/horstmann.

Productivity Hints

Special Topics

Random Facts

Chapter 1

Introduction

CHAPTER GOALS

- To understand the activity of programming
- To learn about the architecture of computers
- To learn about machine code and high-level programming languages
- To become familiar with the structure of simple Java programs
- To compile and run your first Java program
- To recognize compile-time and run-time errors
- To write pseudocode for simple algorithms

The purpose of this chapter is to familiarize you with the concepts of programming and program development. It reviews the architecture of a computer and discusses the difference between machine code and high-level programming languages. You will see how to compile and run your first Java program, and how to diagnose errors that may occur when a program is compiled or executed. Finally, you will learn how to formulate simple algorithms using pseudocode notation.

CHAPTER CONTENTS

1.1 What Is Programming?

You have probably used a computer for work or fun. Many people use computers for everyday tasks such as balancing a checkbook or writing a term paper. Computers are good for such tasks. They can handle repetitive chores, such as totaling up numbers or placing words on a page, without getting bored or exhausted. Computers also make good game machines because they can play sequences of sounds and pictures, involving the human user in the process.

The flexibility of a computer is quite an amazing phenomenon. The same machine can balance your checkbook, print your term paper, and play a game. In contrast, other machines carry out a much narrower range of tasks—a car drives and a toaster toasts.

> A computer must be programmed to perform tasks. Different tasks require different programs.

To achieve this flexibility, the computer must be *programmed* to perform each task. A computer itself is a machine that stores data (numbers, words, pictures), interacts with devices (the monitor screen, the sound system, the printer), and executes programs. Programs are sequences of instructions and decisions that the computer carries out to achieve a task. One program balances checkbooks; a different program, perhaps designed and constructed by a different company, processes words; and a third program, probably from yet another company, plays a game.

> A computer program executes a sequence of very basic instructions in rapid succession.

Today's computer programs are so sophisticated that it is hard to believe that they are all composed of extremely primitive instructions. A typical instruction may be one of the following:

- Put a red dot onto this screen position.
- Get a number from this location in memory.
- Add up two numbers.
- If this value is negative, continue the program at that instruction.

> A computer program contains the instruction sequences for all tasks that it can execute.

A computer program tells a computer, in minute detail, the sequence of steps that are needed to complete a task. A program contains a huge number of simple instructions, and the computer executes them at great speed. The computer has no intelligence—it simply executes instruction sequences that have been prepared in advance.

2

To use a computer, no knowledge of programming is required. When you write a term paper with a word processor, that computer program has been developed by the manufacturer and is ready for you to use. That is only to be expected—you can drive a car without being a mechanic and toast bread without being an electrician.

A primary purpose of this book is to teach you how to design and implement computer programs. You will learn how to formulate instructions for all tasks that your programs need to execute.

Keep in mind that programming a sophisticated computer game or word processor requires a team of many highly skilled programmers, graphic artists, and other professionals. Your first programming efforts will be more mundane. The concepts and skills you learn in this book form an important foundation, but you should not expect to immediately produce professional software. A typical college degree in computer science or software engineering takes four years to complete; this book is intended as a text for an introductory course in such a program.

Many students find that there is an immense thrill even in simple programming tasks. It is an amazing experience to see the computer carry out a task precisely and quickly that would take you hours of drudgery.

SELF CHECK

1. What is required to play a music CD on a computer?
2. Why is a CD player less flexible than a computer?
3. Can a computer program develop the initiative to execute tasks in a better way than its programmers envisioned?

1.2 The Anatomy of a Computer

To understand the programming process, you need to have a rudimentary understanding of the building blocks that make up a computer. This section will describe a personal computer. Larger computers have faster, larger, or more powerful components, but they have fundamentally the same design.

At the heart of the computer lies the central processing unit (CPU).

At the heart of the computer lies the **central processing unit (CPU)** (see Figure 1). It consists of a single *chip* (integrated circuit) or a small number of chips. A computer chip is a component with a plastic or metal housing, metal connectors,

Figure 1
Central Processing Unit

Figure 2
A Memory Module with
Memory Chips

and inside wiring made principally from silicon. For a CPU chip, the inside wiring is enormously complicated. For example, the Intel Core processor (a popular CPU for inexpensive laptops at the time of this writing) contains several hundred million structural elements called *transistors*—the elements that enable electrical signals to control other electrical signals, making automatic computing possible. The CPU locates and executes the program instructions; it carries out arithmetic operations such as addition, subtraction, multiplication, and division; and it fetches data from storage and input/output devices and sends data back.

Data and programs are stored in primary storage (memory) and secondary storage (such as a hard disk).

The computer keeps data and programs in *storage.* There are two kinds of storage. *Primary storage,* also called *random-access memory* (RAM) or simply *memory,* is fast but expensive; it is made from memory chips (see Figure 2). Primary storage loses all its data when the power is turned off. *Secondary storage,* usually a *hard disk* (see Figure 3), provides less expensive storage that persists without electricity. A hard disk consists of rotating platters, which are coated with a magnetic material, and read/write heads, which can detect and change the patterns of varying magnetic flux on the platters.

Some computers are self-contained units, whereas others are interconnected through *networks.* Home computers are usually intermittently connected to the Internet via a dialup or broadband connection. The computers in your computer lab are probably permanently connected to a local area network. Through the network cabling, the computer can read programs from central storage locations or send data to other computers. For the user of a networked computer, it may not even be obvious which data reside on the computer itself and which are transmitted through the network.

Most computers have *removable storage* devices that can access data or programs on media such as memory sticks or optical disks.

To interact with a human user, a computer requires other peripheral devices. The computer transmits information to the user through a display screen, loudspeakers, and printers. The user can enter information and directions to the computer by using a keyboard or a pointing device such as a mouse.

Figure 3 A Hard Disk

The CPU, the RAM, and the electronics controlling the hard disk and other devices are interconnected through a set of electrical lines called a *bus*. Data travel along the bus from the system memory and peripheral devices to the CPU and back. Figure 4 shows a *motherboard*, which contains the CPU, the RAM, and connectors to peripheral devices.

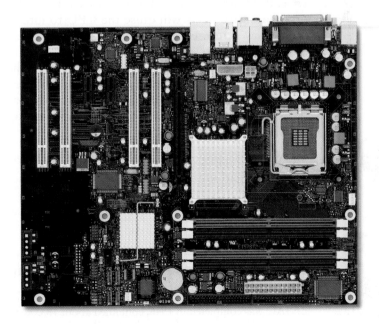

Figure 4 A Motherboard

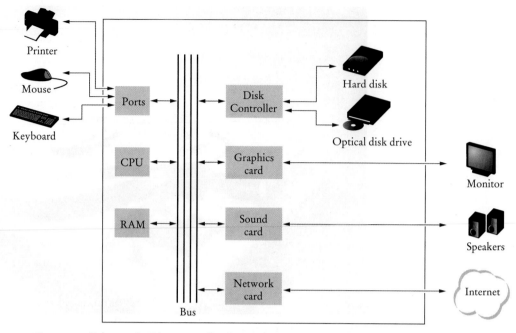

Figure 5 Schematic Diagram of a Computer

The CPU reads machine instructions from memory. The instructions direct it to communicate with memory, secondary storage, and peripheral devices.

Figure 5 gives a schematic overview of the architecture of a computer. Program instructions and data (such as text, numbers, audio, or video) are stored on the hard disk, on an optical disk (such as a DVD), or on a network. When a program is started, it is brought into memory where it can be read by the CPU. The CPU reads the program one instruction at a time. As directed by these instructions, the CPU reads data, modifies it, and writes it back to RAM or to secondary storage. Some program instructions will cause the CPU to interact with the devices that control the display screen or the speaker. Because these actions happen many times over and at great speed, the human user will perceive images and sound. Similarly, the CPU can send instructions to a printer to mark the paper with patterns of closely spaced dots, which a human recognizes as text characters and pictures. Some program instructions read user input from the keyboard or mouse. The program analyzes these inputs and then executes the next appropriate instructions.

SELF CHECK

4. Where is a program stored when it is not currently running?
5. Which part of the computer carries out arithmetic operations, such as addition and multiplication?

Random Fact 1.1

The ENIAC and the Dawn of Computing

Random Fact 1.1 tells the story of the ENIAC, the first usable electronic computer. The ENIAC was completed in 1946, contained about 18,000 vacuum tubes, and filled a large room.

1.3 Translating Human-Readable Programs to Machine Code

On the most basic level, computer instructions are extremely primitive. The processor executes *machine instructions.* CPUs from different vendors, such as the Intel Pentium or the Sun SPARC, have different sets of machine instructions. To enable Java applications to run on different CPUs without modification, Java programs contain machine instructions for a so-called "Java virtual machine" (JVM), an idealized CPU that is simulated by a program run on the actual CPU.

Instructions for actual and virtual machines are very simple and can be executed very quickly. A typical sequence of machine instructions is

1. Load the contents of memory location 40.
2. Load the value 100.
3. If the first value is greater than the second value, continue with the instruction that is stored in memory location 240.

> Generally, machine code depends on the CPU type. However, the instruction set of the Java virtual machine (JVM) can be executed on different CPUs.

Actually, machine instructions are encoded as numbers so that they can be stored in memory. On the Java virtual machine, this sequence of instructions is encoded as the sequence of numbers

```
21 40
16 100
163 240
```

When the virtual machine fetches this sequence of numbers, it decodes them and executes the associated sequence of commands.

How can you communicate the command sequence to the computer? The most direct method is to place the actual numbers into the computer memory. This is, in fact, how the very earliest computers worked. However, a long program is composed of thousands of individual commands, and it is tedious and error-prone to look up the numeric codes for all commands and manually place the codes into memory. As we said before, computers are really good at automating tedious and error-prone activities, and it did not take long for computer programmers to realize that computers could be harnessed to help in the programming process.

> Because machine instructions are encoded as numbers, it is difficult to write programs in machine code.

In the mid-1950s, *high-level* programming languages began to appear. In these languages, the programmer expresses the idea behind the task that needs to be performed, and a special computer program, called a **compiler**, translates the high-level description into machine instructions for a particular processor.

> High-level languages allow you to describe tasks at a higher conceptual level than machine code.

For example, in Java, the high-level programming language that you will use in this book, you might give the following instruction:

```
if (intRate > 100)
    System.out.println("Interest rate error");
```

This means, "If the interest rate is over 100, display the message *Interest rate error*". It is then the job of the compiler program to look at the sequence of characters `if (intRate > 100) . . .` and translate that into

> A compiler translates programs written in a high-level language into machine code.

```
21 40 16 100 163 240 . . .
```

Compilers are quite sophisticated programs. They translate logical statements, such as the if statement, into sequences of computations, tests, and jumps. They assign memory locations for **variables**—items of information identified by symbolic names—like intRate. In this course, we will generally take the existence of a compiler for granted. If you decide to become a professional computer scientist, you may well learn more about compiler-writing techniques later in your studies.

SELF CHECK

6. What is the code for the Java virtual machine instruction "Load the contents of memory location 100"?
7. Does a person who uses a computer for office work ever run a compiler?

1.4 The Java Programming Language

Java was originally designed for programming consumer devices, but it was first used successfully to write Internet applets.

In 1991, a group led by James Gosling and Patrick Naughton at Sun Microsystems designed a programming language that they code-named "Green" for use in consumer devices, such as intelligent television "set-top" boxes. The language was designed to be simple and architecture neutral, so that it could be executed on a variety of hardware. No customer was ever found for this technology.

Gosling recounts that in 1994 the team realized, "We could write a really cool browser. It was one of the few things in the client/server mainstream that needed some of the weird things we'd done: architecture neutral, real-time, reliable, secure." Java was introduced to an enthusiastic crowd at the SunWorld exhibition in 1995.

Java was designed to be safe and portable, benefiting both Internet users and students.

Since then, Java has grown at a phenomenal rate. Programmers have embraced the language because it is simpler than its closest rival, C++. In addition, Java has a rich *library* that makes it possible to write portable programs that can bypass proprietary operating systems—a feature that was eagerly sought by those who wanted to be independent of those proprietary systems and was bitterly fought by their vendors. A "micro edition" and an "enterprise edition" of the Java library make Java programmers at home on hardware ranging from smart cards and cell phones to the largest Internet servers.

Because Java was designed for the Internet, it has two attributes that make it very suitable for beginners: safety and portability. If you visit a web page that contains Java code (so-called *applets*—see Figure 6 for an example), the code automatically starts running. It is important that you can trust that applets are inherently safe. If an applet could do something evil, such as damaging data or reading personal information on your computer, then you would be in real danger every time you browsed the Web—an unscrupulous designer might put up a web page containing dangerous code that would execute on your machine as soon as you visited the page. The Java language has an assortment of security features that guarantees that no malicious applets can run on your computer. As an added benefit, these features also help you to learn the language faster. The Java virtual machine can catch many kinds of beginners' mistakes and report them accurately. (In contrast, many beginners' mistakes in the C++ language merely produce programs that act in random and confusing ways.) The other benefit of Java is portability. The same Java program will run, without change, on Windows, UNIX, Linux, or the Macintosh. This too is a requirement for applets. When you visit a web page, the web server that serves up the page contents has no idea what computer you are using to browse the Web. It simply returns the portable code that was generated by the Java compiler.

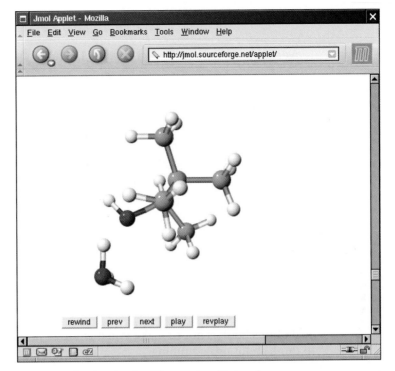

Figure 6 An Applet for Visualizing Molecules
Running in a Browser (*http://jmol.sourceforge.net/applet/*)

The virtual machine on your computer executes that portable code. Again, there is a benefit for the student. You do not have to learn how to write programs for different platforms.

At this time, Java is firmly established as one of the most important languages for general-purpose programming as well as for computer science instruction. However, although Java is a good language for beginners, it is not perfect, for three reasons.

Because Java was not specifically designed for students, no thought was given to making it really simple to write basic programs. You must master a certain amount of technical detail to write even the simplest Java program. This is not a problem for professional programmers, but it is a drawback for beginning students. As you learn how to program in Java, there will be times when you will be asked to be satisfied with a preliminary explanation and wait for complete information in a later chapter.

Java was revised and extended many times during its life—see Table 1 on page 10. In this book, we assume that you have Java version 5 or later.

Finally, you cannot hope to learn all of Java in one term. The Java language itself is relatively simple, but Java has a vast library with support for graphics, user interface design, cryptography, networking, sound, database storage, and many other purposes. Even expert Java programmers cannot hope to know the contents of the entire library—they just use those parts that they need for particular projects.

Using this book, you should expect to learn a good deal about the Java language and about the most important parts of the Java library. Keep in mind that the central

> Java has a very large library. Focus on learning those parts of the library that you need for your programming projects.

Table 1 Java Versions		
Version	Year	Important New Features
1.0	1996	
1.1	1997	Inner classes
1.2	1998	Swing, Collections framework
1.3	2000	Performance enhancements
1.4	2002	Assertions, XML support
5	2004	Generic classes, enhanced for loop, auto-boxing, enumerations, annotations
6	2006	Library improvements
7	2010	Small language changes and library improvements

goal of this book is not to make you memorize Java minutiae, but to teach you how to think about programming.

SELF CHECK

8. What are the two most important benefits of the Java language?

9. How long does it take to learn the entire Java library?

1.5 The Structure of a Simple Program

When learning a new programming language, it is traditional to start with a "Hello, World!" program—a program that displays a greeting. Here is this program in Java:

ch01/hello/HelloPrinter.java

```java
1  public class HelloPrinter
2  {
3     public static void main(String[] args)
4     {
5        // Display a greeting in the console window
6
7        System.out.println("Hello, World!");
8     }
9  }
```

Program Run

```
Hello, World!
```

In the next section, you will see how to compile and run this program. But let us first understand how it is structured.

The line,

```
public class HelloPrinter
```

Classes are the fundamental building blocks of Java programs.

starts a new **class**. Classes are a fundamental concept in Java, and you will begin to study them in Chapter 2. In Java, every program consists of one or more classes.

The word `public` denotes that the class is usable by the "public", that is, everywhere in your program. You will later encounter `private` features.

In Java, every source file can contain at most one public class, and the name of the public class must match the name of the file containing the class. For example, the class `HelloPrinter` *must* be contained in a file named `HelloPrinter.java`.

The construction

```
public static void main(String[] args)
{
    . . .
}
```

Every Java application contains a class with a main method. When the application starts, the instructions in the main method are executed.

declares a **method** called `main`. A method contains a collection of programming instructions that describe how to carry out a particular task. Every Java application must have a `main` method. Most Java programs contain other methods besides `main`, and you will see in Chapter 2 how to write other methods.

We will fully explain the word `static` and the declaration `String[] args` in Chapters 7 and 10. At this time, you should simply consider

```
public class ClassName
{
    public static void main(String[] args)
    {
        . . .
    }
}
```

as a part of the "plumbing" that is required to write any Java program.

The first line inside the `main` method is a **comment**:

```
// Display a greeting in the console window
```

Use comments to help human readers understand your program.

This comment is purely for the benefit of the human reader, to explain in more detail what the next statement does. Any text enclosed between `//` and the end of the line is completely ignored by the compiler. Comments are used to explain the program to other programmers or to yourself.

The instructions or **statements** in the *body* of the `main` method—that is, the statements inside the curly brackets ({})—are executed one by one. Each statement ends in a semicolon (;). Our method has a single statement:

```
System.out.println("Hello, World!");
```

This statement prints a line of text, namely "Hello, World!". However, there are many places where a program can send that text: to a window, to a file, or to a networked computer on the other side of the world. You need to specify that the destination is the *system output*—that is, a console window. The console window is represented in Java by an object called `System.out`. An **object** is an entity that you manipulate in your programs.

In Java, each object belongs to a class, and the class declares methods that specify what you can do with the objects. The `System.out` object belongs to the `PrintStream` class. The `PrintStream` class has a method called `println` for printing a line of text.

Figure 7
Calling a Method

Object Method Parameters

`System.out.println("Hello, World!")`

You do not have to implement this method—the programmers who wrote the Java library already did that for us—but you do need to *call* the method.

Whenever you call a method in Java, you need to specify three items (see Figure 7):

> **A method is called by specifying an object, the method name, and the method parameters.**

1. The object that you want to use (in this case, `System.out`).
2. The name of the method you want to use (in this case, `println`).
3. A pair of parentheses, containing any other information the method needs (in this case, `"Hello, World!"`). The technical term for this information is a **parameter**.

A sequence of characters enclosed in double quotation marks

`"Hello, World!"`

> **A string is a sequence of characters enclosed in quotation marks.**

is called a **string**. You must enclose the contents of the string inside quotation marks so that the compiler knows you literally mean `"Hello, World!"`. There is a reason for this requirement. Suppose you need to print the word *main*. By enclosing it in quotation marks, `"main"`, the compiler knows you mean the sequence of characters m a i n, not the method named `main`. The rule is simply that you must enclose all text strings in quotation marks, so that the compiler considers them plain text and does not try to interpret them as program instructions.

You can also print numerical values. For example, the statement

`System.out.println(3 + 4);`

displays the number 7.

The `println` method prints a string or a number and then starts a new line. For example, the sequence of statements

```
System.out.println("Hello");
System.out.println("World!");
```

Syntax 1.1 Method Call

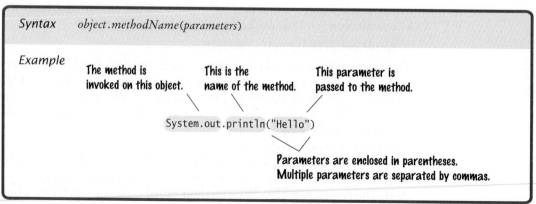

Syntax *object.methodName(parameters)*

Example

The method is invoked on this object.

This is the name of the method.

This parameter is passed to the method.

`System.out.println("Hello")`

Parameters are enclosed in parentheses.
Multiple parameters are separated by commas.

prints two lines of text:

```
Hello
World!
```

There is a second method, called `print`, that you can use to print an item without starting a new line. For example, the output of the two statements

```
System.out.print("00");
System.out.println(3 + 4);
```

is the single line

```
007
```

SELF CHECK

10. How would you modify the `HelloPrinter` program to print the words "Hello," and "World!" on two lines?

11. Would the program continue to work if you omitted the line starting with `//`?

12. What does the following set of statements print?

```
System.out.print("My lucky number is");
System.out.println(3 + 4 + 5);
```

Common Error 1.1

Omitting Semicolons

In Java every statement must end in a semicolon. Forgetting to type a semicolon is a common error. It confuses the compiler, because the compiler uses the semicolon to find where one statement ends and the next one starts. The compiler does not use line breaks or closing braces to recognize the end of statements. For example, the compiler considers

```
System.out.println("Hello")
System.out.println("World!");
```

a single statement, as if you had written

```
System.out.println("Hello") System.out.println("World!");
```

Then it doesn't understand that statement, because it does not expect the word `System` following the closing parenthesis after `"Hello"`. The remedy is simple. Scan every statement for a terminating semicolon, just as a writer would check that every English sentence ends in a period.

Special Topic 1.1

Alternative Comment Syntax

In Java there are two methods for writing comments. You already learned that the compiler ignores anything that you type between `//` and the end of the current line. The compiler also ignores any text between a `/*` and `*/`.

```
/* A simple Java program */
```

The `//` comment is easier to type if the comment is only a single line long. If you have a comment that is longer than a line, then the `/* . . . */` comment is simpler:

```
/*
    This is a simple Java program that you can use to try out
    your compiler and virtual machine.
*/
```

It would be somewhat tedious to add the // at the beginning of each line and to move them around whenever the text of the comment changes.

In this book, we use // for comments that will never grow beyond a line, and /* . . . */ for longer comments. If you prefer, you can always use the // style. The readers of your code will be grateful for *any* comments, no matter which style you use.

1.6 Compiling and Running a Java Program

Set aside some time to become familiar with the computer system and the Java compiler that you will use for your class work.	Many students find that the tools that they need as programmers are very different from the software with which they familiar. You should spend some time making yourself familiar with your programming environment. Instructions for several popular environments are available in WileyPLUS.

Some Java development environments are very convenient to use. Enter the code in one window, click on a button to compile, and click on another button to execute your program. Error messages show up in a second window, and the program runs in a third window. With such an environment you are completely shielded from the details of the compilation process. On other systems you must carry out every step manually, by typing commands into a console window.

An editor is a program for entering and modifying text, such as a Java program.

No matter which development environment you use, you begin your activity by typing in the program statements. The program that you use for entering and modifying the program text is called an *editor*. The first step for creating a Java program, such as the HelloPrinter program of the preceding section, is to start your editor. Make a new program file and call it HelloPrinter.java. (If your environment requires that you supply a project name in addition to the file name, use the name hello for the project.) Enter the program instructions exactly as they are given above. Alternatively, locate an electronic copy and paste it into your editor.

Java is case sensitive. You must be careful about distinguishing between upper- and lowercase letters.

Java is **case sensitive**. You must enter upper- and lowercase letters in the same way as they appear in the program listing. You cannot type MAIN or PrintLn. If you are not careful, you will run into problems—see Common Error 1.2 on page 19. On the other hand, Java has *free-form layout*. You can use any number of spaces and line breaks to separate words. You can cram as many words as possible into each line,

```
public class HelloPrinter{public static void main(String[]
args){// Display a greeting in the console window
System.out.println("Hello, World!");}}
```

Lay out your programs so that they are easy to read.

Of course, this is not a good idea. It is important to format your programs neatly so that you and other programmers can read them easily. We will give you recommendations for good layout throughout this book. Appendix L contains a summary of our recommendations.

Now find out how to run the test program. The message

```
Hello, World!
```

will appear somewhere on the screen (see Figures 8 and 9). The exact location depends on your programming environment.

Figure 8
Running the `HelloPrinter`
Program in a Console Window

The Java compiler
translates source
code into class files
that contain
instructions for the
Java virtual machine.

Running your program takes two steps. (Some development environments automatically carry out both steps when you ask to run a program.)

The first step is to *compile* your program. The compiler translates the Java **source code** (that is, the statements that you wrote) into *class files*, which consist of virtual machine instructions and other information that is required for execution. The class files have the extension `.class`. For example, the virtual machine instructions for the `HelloPrinter` program are stored in a file `HelloPrinter.class`. Note that the compiler does not produce a class file if it has found errors in your program.

The class file contains merely the translation of the instructions that you wrote. That is not enough to actually run the program. To display a string in a window, quite a bit of low-level activity is necessary. The authors of the `System` and

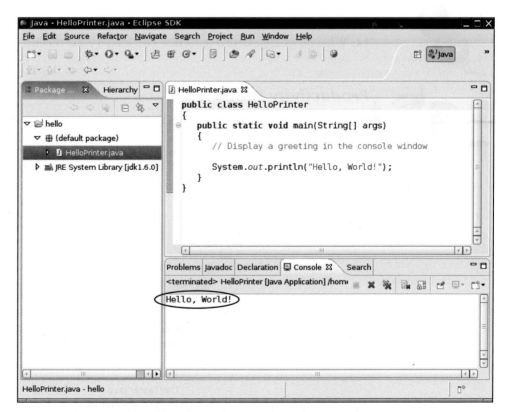

Figure 9 Running the `HelloPrinter` Program in an Integrated
Development Environment

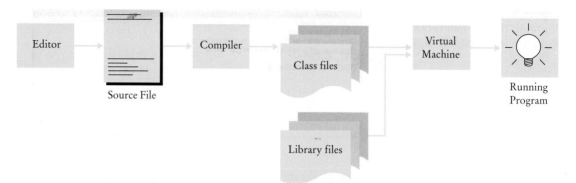

Figure 10 From Source Code to Running Program

PrintStream classes (which declare the out object and the println method) have implemented all necessary actions and placed the required class files into a **library**. A library is a collection of code that has been programmed and translated by someone else, ready for you to use in your program.

> The Java virtual machine loads program instructions from class files and library files.

The Java virtual machine loads the instructions for the program that you wrote, starts your program, and loads the necessary library files as they are required.

The steps of compiling and running your program are outlined in Figure 10.

SELF CHECK

13. Can you use a word processor for writing Java programs?

14. What do you expect to see when you load a class file into your text editor?

Productivity Hint 1.1

Understand the File System

In recent years, computers have become easier to use for home or office users. Many inessential details are now hidden from casual users. For example, many users simply place all their work inside a default folder (such as "Home" or "My Documents") and are blissfully ignorant about details of the file system.

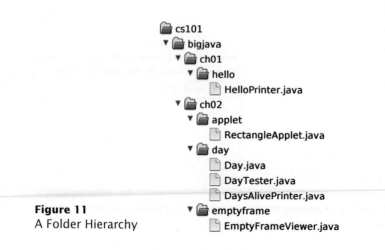

Figure 11
A Folder Hierarchy

For your programming work, you need to understand that files are stored in *folders* or **directories**, and that these file containers can be *nested*. That is, a folder can contain not only files but also other folders, which themselves can contain more files and folders (see Figure 11).

You need to know how to impose an organization on the data that you create. You also need to be able to locate files and inspect their contents.

If you are not comfortable with files and folders, be sure to set aside some time to learn about these concepts.

Productivity Hint 1.2

Have a Backup Strategy

Productivity Hint 1.2 discusses strategies for backing up your programming work so that you won't lose data if your computer malfunctions.

1.7 Errors

Experiment a little with the `HelloPrinter` program. What happens if you make a typing error such as

```
System.ou.println("Hello, World!");
System.out.println("Hello, Word!");
```

A compile-time error is a violation of the programming language rules that is detected by the compiler.

In the first case, the compiler will complain. It will say that it has no clue what you mean by ou. The exact wording of the error message is dependent on the compiler, but it might be something like "Cannot find symbol *ou*". This is a **compile-time error**, also called a *syntax error*. Something is wrong according to the language rules and the compiler finds it. When the compiler finds one or more errors, it refuses to translate the program to Java virtual machine instructions, and as a consequence you have no program that you can run. You must fix the error and compile again. In fact, the compiler is quite picky, and it is common to go through several rounds of fixing compile-time errors before compilation succeeds for the first time.

If the compiler finds an error, it will not simply stop and give up. It will try to report as many errors as it can find, so you can fix them all at once.

Sometimes, an error throws the compiler off track. Suppose, for example, you forget the quotation marks around a string: `System.out.println(Hello, World!)`. The compiler will not complain about the missing quotation marks. Instead, it will report "Cannot find symbol Hello". It is up to you to realize that you need to enclose strings in quotation marks.

The error in the second line is of a different kind. The program will compile and run, but its output will be wrong. It will print

```
Hello, Word!
```

This is a **run-time error**, also called a *logic error*. The program is syntactically correct and does something, but it doesn't do what it is supposed to do.

> A run-time error causes a program to take an action that the programmer did not intend.

This particular run-time error did not include an error message. It simply produced the wrong output. Some kinds of run-time errors are so severe that they generate an *exception*: an error message from the Java virtual machine. For example, if your program includes the statement

```
System.out.println(1/0);
```

you will get a run-time error message "Division by zero".

During program development, errors are unavoidable. Once a program is longer than a few lines, it requires superhuman concentration to enter it correctly without slipping up once. You will find yourself omitting semicolons or quotes more often than you would like, but the compiler will track down these problems for you.

Run-time errors are more troublesome. The compiler will not find them—in fact, the compiler will cheerfully translate any program as long as its syntax is correct—but the resulting program will do something wrong. It is the responsibility of the program author to test the program and find any run-time errors. Testing programs is an important topic that you will encounter many times in this book. Another important aspect of good craftsmanship is *defensive programming:* structuring programs and development processes in such a way that an error in one part of a program does not trigger a disastrous response.

The error examples that you saw so far were not difficult to diagnose or fix, but as you learn more sophisticated programming techniques, there will also be much more room for error. It is an uncomfortable fact that locating all errors in a program is very difficult. Even if you can observe that a program exhibits faulty behavior, it may not at all be obvious what part of the program caused it and how you can fix it. Special software tools (so-called **debuggers**) let you trace through a program to find *bugs*—that is, run-time errors. In Chapter 5 you will learn how to use a debugger effectively.

Note that these errors are different from the types of errors that you are likely to make in calculations. If you total up a column of numbers, you may miss a minus sign or accidentally drop a carry, perhaps because you are bored or tired. Computers do not make these kinds of errors.

This book uses a three-part error management strategy. First, you will learn about common errors and how to avoid them. Then you will learn defensive programming strategies to minimize the likelihood and impact of errors. Finally, you will learn testing and debugging strategies to flush out those errors that remain.

SELF CHECK

15. Suppose you omit the `//` characters from the `HelloPrinter.java` program but not the remainder of the comment. Will you get a compile-time error or a run-time error?

16. When you used your computer, you may have experienced a program that "crashed" (quit spontaneously) or "hung" (failed to respond to your input). Is that behavior a compile-time error or a run-time error?

17. Why can't you test a program for run-time errors when it has compiler errors?

Common Error 1.2

Misspelling Words

If you accidentally misspell a word, then strange things may happen, and it may not always be completely obvious from the error messages what went wrong. Here is a good example of how simple spelling errors can cause trouble:

```java
public class HelloPrinter
{
    public static void Main(String[] args)
    {
        System.out.println("Hello, World!");
    }
}
```

This class declares a method called `Main`. The compiler will not consider this to be the same as the `main` method, because `Main` starts with an uppercase letter and the Java language is case sensitive. Upper- and lowercase letters are considered to be completely different from each other, and to the compiler `Main` is no better match for `main` than `rain`. The compiler will cheerfully compile your `Main` method, but when the Java virtual machine executes the compiled file, it will complain about the missing `main` method and refuse to run the program. Of course, the message "missing main method" should give you a clue where to look for the error.

If you get an error message that seems to indicate that the compiler is on the wrong track, it is a good idea to check for spelling and capitalization. If you misspell the name of a symbol (for example, `ou` instead of `out`), the compiler will produce an error message such as "Cannot find symbol ou". That error message is usually a good clue that you made a spelling error.

1.8 Algorithms

You will soon learn how to program calculations and decision making in Java. But before we look at the mechanics of implementing computations in the next chapter, let's consider the planning process that precedes implementation.

You may have run across advertisements that encourage you to pay for a computerized service that matches you up with a love partner. Think how this might work. You fill out a form and send it in. Others do the same. The data are processed by a computer program. Is it reasonable to assume that the computer can perform the task of finding the best match for you? Suppose your younger brother, not the computer, had all the forms on his desk. What instructions could you give him? You can't say, "Find the best-looking person who likes inline skating and browsing the Internet". There is no objective standard for good looks, and your brother's opinion (or that of a computer program analyzing the digitized photo) will likely be different from yours. If you can't give written instructions for someone to solve the problem, there is no way the computer can magically find the right solution. The computer can only do what you tell it to do. It just does it faster, without getting bored or exhausted.

For that reason, a computerized match-making service cannot guarantee to find the optimal match for you. Instead, it may present a set of potential partners who share common interests with you. That is a task that a computer program can solve.

Now consider the following investment problem:

> You put $10,000 into a bank account that earns 5 percent interest per year. How many years does it take for the account balance to be double the original?

Could you solve this problem by hand? Sure, you could. You figure out the balance as follows:

year	balance
0	10000
1	10000.00 x 1.05 = 10500.00
2	10500.00 x 1.05 = 11025.00
3	11025.00 x 1.05 = 11576.25
4	11576.25 x 1.05 = 12155.06

You keep going until the balance is at least $20,000. Then the last number in the year column is the answer.

Of course, carrying out this computation is intensely boring to you or your younger brother. But computers are very good at carrying out repetitive calculations quickly and flawlessly. What is important to the computer is a description of the steps for finding the solution. Each step must be clear and unambiguous, requiring no guesswork. Here is such a description:

Start with a year value of 0 and a balance of $10,000.

year	balance
0	10000

Repeat the following steps while the balance is less than $20,000.
    Add 1 to the year value.
    Multiply the balance value by 1.05 (a 5 percent increase).

year	balance
0	10000
1	10500
14	19799.32
(15)	20789.28

Report the final year value as the answer.

Of course, these steps are not yet in a language that a computer can understand, but you will soon learn how to formulate them in Java. This informal description is called **pseudocode**.

There are no strict requirements for pseudocode because it is read by human readers, not a computer program. Here are the kinds of pseudocode statements that we will use in this book:

Pseudocode is an informal description of a sequence of steps for solving a problem.

- Use statements such as the following to describe how a value is set or changed:

  total cost = purchase price + operating cost

  or

  Multiply the balance value by 1.05.

  or

  Remove the first and last character from the word.

- Describe decisions and repetitions as follows:

  If total cost 1 < total cost 2

  or

  While the balance is less than $20,000

  or

  For each picture in the sequence

  Use indentation to indicate which statements should be selected or repeated.

  For each car
      operating cost = 10 x annual fuel cost
      total cost = purchase price + operating cost

  Here, the indentation indicates that both statements should be executed for each car.

- Indicate results with statements such as

  Choose car 1.
  Report the final year value as the answer.

The exact wording is not important. What is important is that the pseudocode describes a sequence of steps that is

- Unambiguous
- Executable
- Terminating

The step sequence is *unambiguous* when there are precise instructions for what to do at each step and where to go next. There is no room for guesswork or personal opinion. A step is *executable* when it can be carried out in practice. Had we asked to use the actual interest rate that will be charged in years to come, and not a fixed rate of 5 percent per year, that step would not have been executable, because there is no way for anyone to know what that interest rate will be. A sequence of steps is *terminating* if it will eventually come to an end. In our example, it requires a bit of thought to see that the sequence will not go on forever: With every step, the balance goes up by at least $500, so eventually it must reach $20,000.

A sequence of steps that is unambiguous, executable, and terminating is called an **algorithm**. We have found an algorithm to solve our investment problem, and thus we can find the solution by programming a computer. The existence of an algorithm is an essential prerequisite for programming a task. You need to first discover and describe an algorithm for the task that you want to solve before you start programming (see Figure 12).

An algorithm for solving a problem is a sequence of steps that is unambiguous, executable, and terminating.

Figure 12
The Program Development Process

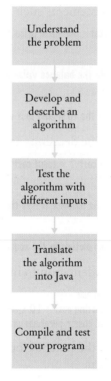

Understand
the problem

Develop and
describe an
algorithm

Test the
algorithm with
different inputs

Translate
the algorithm
into Java

Compile and test
your program

SELF CHECK

18. Suppose the interest rate was 20 percent. How long would it take for the investment to double?

19. Suppose your cell phone carrier charges you $29.95 for up to 300 minutes of calls, and $0.45 for each additional minute, plus 12.5 percent taxes and fees. Give an algorithm to compute the monthly charge for a given number of minutes.

How To 1.1

Developing and Describing an Algorithm

This is the first of many "How To" sections in this book that give you step-by-step procedures for carrying out important tasks in developing computer programs.

Before you are ready to write a program in Java, you need to develop an algorithm—a method for arriving at a solution for a particular problem. Describe the algorithm in pseudocode: a sequence of precise steps formulated in English.

For example, consider this problem: You have the choice of buying two cars. One is more fuel efficient than the other, but also more expensive. You know the price and fuel efficiency (in miles per gallon, mpg) of both cars. You plan to keep the car for ten years. Assume a price of $4 per gallon of gas and usage of 15,000 miles per year. You will pay cash for the car and not worry about financing costs. Which car is the better deal?

Step 1 Determine the inputs and outputs.

In our sample problem, we have these inputs:

- **purchase price1** and **fuel efficiency1**, the price and fuel efficiency (in mpg) of the first car.
- **purchase price2** and **fuel efficiency2**, the price and fuel efficiency of the second car.

We simply want to know which car is the better buy. That is the desired output.

Step 2 Break down the problem into smaller tasks.

For each car, we need to know the total cost of driving it. Let's do this computation separately for each car. Once we have the total cost for each car, we can decide which car is the better deal.

The total cost for each car is **purchase price + operating cost.**

We assume a constant usage and gas price for ten years, so the operating cost depends on the cost of driving the car for one year.

The operating cost is **10 x annual fuel cost.**

The annual fuel cost is **price per gallon x annual fuel consumed.**

The annual fuel consumed is **annual miles driven / fuel efficiency.** For example, if you drive the car for 15,000 miles and the fuel efficiency is 15 miles/gallon, the car consumes 1,000 gallons.

Step 3 Describe each subtask in pseudocode.

In your description, arrange the steps so that any intermediate values are computed before they are needed in other computations. For example, list the step

total cost = purchase price + operating cost

after you have computed **operating cost.**

Here is the algorithm for deciding which car to buy.

For each car, compute the total cost as follows:
    annual fuel consumed = annual miles driven / fuel efficiency
    annual fuel cost = price per gallon x annual fuel consumed
    operating cost = 10 x annual fuel cost
    total cost = purchase price + operating cost
If total cost1 < total cost2
    Choose car1.
Else
    Choose car2.

Step 4 Test your pseudocode by working problems.

We will use these sample values:

Car 1: $25,000, 50 miles/gallon
Car 2: $20,000, 30 miles/gallon

Here is the calculation for the cost of the first car.

annual fuel consumed = annual miles driven / fuel efficiency = 15000 / 50 = 300
annual fuel cost = price per gallon x annual fuel consumed = 4 x 300 = 1200
operating cost = 10 x annual fuel cost = 10 x 1200 = 12000
total cost = purchase price + operating cost = 25000 + 12000 = 37000

Similarly, the total cost for the second car is $40,000. Therefore, the output of the algorithm is to choose car 1.

⊕ *Worked Example 1.1*

Writing an Algorithm for Tiling a Floor

This Worked Example shows how to develop an algorithm for laying tile in an alternating pattern of colors.

Summary of Learning Objectives

Define "computer program" and "programming".

- A computer must be programmed to perform tasks. Different tasks require different programs.
- A computer program executes a sequence of very basic instructions in rapid succession.
- A computer program contains the instruction sequences for all tasks that it can execute.

Describe the components of a computer.

- At the heart of the computer lies the central processing unit (CPU).
- Data and programs are stored in primary storage (memory) and secondary storage (such as a hard disk).
- The CPU reads machine instructions from memory. The instructions direct it to communicate with memory, secondary storage, and peripheral devices.

Describe the process of translating high-level languages to machine code.

- Generally, machine code depends on the CPU type. However, the instruction set of the Java virtual machine (JVM) can be executed on different CPUs.
- Because machine instructions are encoded as numbers, it is difficult to write programs in machine code.
- High-level languages allow you to describe tasks at a higher conceptual level than machine code.
- A compiler translates programs written in a high-level language into machine code.

Describe the history and design principles of the Java programming language.

- Java was originally designed for programming consumer devices, but it was first used successfully to write Internet applets.
- Java was designed to be safe and portable, benefiting both Internet users and students.
- Java has a very large library. Focus on learning those parts of the library that you need for your programming projects.

Describe the building blocks of a simple program and the structure of a method call.

- Classes are the fundamental building blocks of Java programs.
- Every Java application contains a class with a main method. When the application starts, the instructions in the main method are executed.
- Use comments to help human readers understand your program.
- A method is called by specifying an object, the method name, and the method parameters.
- A string is a sequence of characters enclosed in quotation marks.

Use your programming environment to write and run Java programs.

- Set aside some time to become familiar with the computer system and the Java compiler that you will use for your class work.
- An editor is a program for entering and modifying text, such as a Java program.

- Java is case sensitive. You must be careful about distinguishing between upper- and lowercase letters.
- Lay out your programs so that they are easy to read.
- The Java compiler translates source code into class files that contain instructions for the Java virtual machine.
- The Java virtual machine loads program instructions from class files and library files.
- Develop a strategy for keeping backup copies of your work before disaster strikes.

Classify program errors as compile-time and run-time errors.

- A compile-time error is a violation of the programming language rules that is detected by the compiler.
- A run-time error causes a program to take an action that the programmer did not intend.

Write pseudocode for simple algorithms.

- Pseudocode is an informal description of a sequence of steps for solving a problem.
- An algorithm for solving a problem is a sequence of steps that is unambiguous, executable, and terminating.

Classes, Objects, and Methods Introduced in this Chapter

Here is a list of all classes, objects, and methods introduced in this chapter. Turn to the documentation in Appendix D for more information.

```
java.io.PrintStream          java.lang.System
    print                        out
    println
```

Media Resources

www.wiley.com/ go/global/ horstmann

- ***Worked Example*** Writing an Algorithm for Tiling a Floor
- ➕ Practice Quiz
- ➕ Code Completion Exercises

Review Exercises

★ **R1.1** Explain the difference between using a computer program and programming a computer.

★ **R1.2** What distinguishes a computer from a typical household appliance?

★★ **R1.3** Describe *exactly* what steps you would take to back up your work after you have typed in the HelloPrinter.java program.

★★ **R1.4** On your own computer or on a lab computer, find the exact location (folder or directory name) of

    a. The sample file HelloPrinter.java, which you wrote with the editor.

    b. The Java program launcher java.exe or java.

    c. The library file rt.jar that contains the run-time library.

★ **R1.5** How do you discover syntax errors? How do you discover logic errors?

★★ **R1.6** Write three versions of the HelloPrinter.java program that have different compile-time errors. Write a version that has a run-time error.

★★★ **R1.7** What do the following statements print? Don't guess; write programs to find out.

    a. System.out.println("3 + 4");

    b. System.out.println(3 + 4);

    c. System.out.println(3 + "4");

★★ **R1.8** Write an algorithm to settle the following question: A bank account starts out with $10,000. Interest is compounded monthly at 6 percent per year (0.5 percent per month). Every month, $500 is withdrawn to meet college expenses. After how many years is the account depleted?

★★★ **R1.9** Consider the question in Exercise R1.8. Suppose the numbers ($10,000, 6 percent, $500) were user selectable. Are there values for which the algorithm you developed would not terminate? If so, change the algorithm to make sure it always terminates.

★★★ **R1.10** In order to estimate the cost of painting a house, a painter needs to know the surface area of the exterior. Develop an algorithm for computing that value. Your inputs are the width, length, and height of the house, the number of windows and doors, and their dimensions. (Assume the windows and doors have a uniform size.)

★★ **R1.11** You want to decide whether you should drive your car to work or take the train. You know the one-way distance from your home to your place of work, and the fuel efficiency of your car (in miles per gallon). You also know the one-way price of a train ticket. You assume the cost of gas at $4 per gallon, and car maintenance at 5 cents per mile. Write an algorithm to decide which commute is cheaper.

★★ **R1.12** You want to find out which fraction of your car use is for commuting to work, and which is for personal use. You know the one-way distance from your home to your place of work. For a particular period, you recorded the beginning and ending mileage on the odometer and the number of work days. Write an algorithm to settle this question.

★ **R1.13** In the problem described in How To 1.1 on page 22, you made assumptions about the price of gas and the annual usage. Ideally, you would like to know which car is the better deal without making these assumptions. Why can't a computer program solve that problem?

Programming Exercises

★   **P1.1** Write a program `NamePrinter` that displays your name inside a box on the console
screen, like this:

```
+----+
|Dave|
+----+
```

Do your best to approximate lines with characters, such as |, -, and +.

★★★   **P1.2** Write a program that prints your name in large letters, such as

```
*    *    **    ****    ****    *    *
*    *   *  *   *   *   *   *   *   *
*****  *    *  ****    ****     * *
*    *  ******  *   *   *   *    *
*    *  *    *  *   *   *   *    *
```

★   **P1.3** Write a program `FacePrinter` that prints a face, using text characters, hopefully better
looking than this one:

```
  /////
 | o o |
(|  ^  |)
 | [_] |
  -----
```

Use *comments* to indicate the statements that print the hair, ears, mouth, and so on.

★★★   **P1.4** Write a program that prints an animal speaking a greeting, similar to (but different
from) the following

```
/\_/\      -----
( ' ' )  / Hello \
(  -  ) <  Junior |
 | | |   \ Coder!/
(_|_)      -----
```

★   **P1.5** Write a program `TicTacToeBoardPrinter` that prints a tic-tac-toe board:

```
+---+---+---+
|   |   |   |
+---+---+---+
|   |   |   |
+---+---+---+
|   |   |   |
+---+---+---+
```

★   **P1.6** Write a program `StaircasePrinter` that prints a staircase:

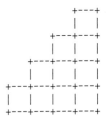

```
            +---+
            |   |
        +---+---+
        |   |   |
    +---+---+---+
    |   |   |   |
+---+---+---+---+
|   |   |   |   |
+---+---+---+---+
```

★   **P1.7** Write a program that prints three items, such as the names of your three best friends
or favorite movies, on three separate lines.

★★ **P1.8** Write a program that computes the sum of the first ten positive integers, $1 + 2 + \cdots + 10$. *Hint:* Write a program of the form

```java
public class Sum10
{
    public static void main(String[] args)
    {
        System.out.println(              );
    }
}
```

★★ **P1.9** Type in and run the following program:

```java
import javax.swing.JOptionPane;

public class DialogViewer
{
    public static void main(String[] args)
    {
        JOptionPane.showMessageDialog(null, "Hello, World!");
        System.exit(0);
    }
}
```

Then modify the program to show the message "Hello, *your name*!".

★★ **P1.10** Type in and run the following program:

```java
import javax.swing.JOptionPane;

public class DialogViewer
{
    public static void main(String[] args)
    {
        String name = JOptionPane.showInputDialog("What is your name?");
        System.out.println(name);
        System.exit(0);
    }
}
```

Then modify the program to print "Hello, *name*!", displaying the name that the user typed in.

★★ **P1.11** Run the following program:

```java
import java.net.URL;
import javax.swing.ImageIcon;
import javax.swing.JOptionPane;

public class Test
{
    public static void main(String[] args) throws Exception
    {
        URL imageLocation = new URL(
            "http://horstmann.com/bigjava/duke.gif");
        JOptionPane.showMessageDialog(null, "Hello", "Title",
            JOptionPane.PLAIN_MESSAGE, new ImageIcon(imageLocation));
        System.exit(0);
    }
}
```

Then modify it to show a different greeting and image.

Programming Projects

Project 1.1 This project builds on Exercises P1.9 and P1.10. Your program should read the user's name, then show a sequence of two dialog boxes:

- First, an input dialog box that asks: "What would you like me to do?"
- Then a message dialog box that says: "I'm sorry, *your name*. I'm afraid I can't do that."

Answers to Self-Check Questions

1. A program that reads the data on the CD and sends output to the speakers and the screen.
2. A CD player can do one thing—play music CDs. It cannot execute programs.
3. No—the program simply executes the instruction sequences that the programmers have prepared in advance.
4. In secondary storage, typically a hard disk.
5. The central processing unit.
6. 21 100
7. No—a compiler is intended for programmers, to translate high-level programming instructions into machine code.
8. Safety and portability.
9. No one person can learn the entire library—it is too large.
10. `System.out.println("Hello,"); System.out.println("World!");`
11. Yes—the line starting with `//` is a comment, intended for human readers. The compiler ignores comments.
12. The printout is `My lucky number is12`. It would be a good idea to add a space after the `is`.
13. Yes, but you must remember to save your file as "plain text."
14. A sequence of random characters, some funny-looking. Class files contain virtual machine instructions that are encoded as binary numbers.
15. A compile-time error. The compiler will not know what to do with the word `Display`.
16. It is a run-time error. After all, the program had been compiled in order for you to run it.
17. When a program has compiler errors, no class file is produced, and there is nothing to run.
18. 4 years:
    0 10,000
    1 12,000
    2 14,400
    3 17,280
    4 20,736

19. Is the number of minutes at most 300?

  a. If so, the answer is \$29.95 × 1.125 = \$33.70.

  b. If not,

  1. Compute the difference: (number of minutes) − 300.
  2. Multiply that difference by 0.45.
  3. Add \$29.95.
  4. Multiply the total by 1.125. That is the answer.

Chapter 2

An Introduction to Objects and Classes

CHAPTER GOALS

- To understand the concepts of classes, objects, and methods
- To learn about parameters and return values
- To understand the purpose and use of constructors
- To be able to browse the API documentation and write documentation comments
- To become familiar with the process of implementing classes
- T To implement test programs
- To understand how to access instance variables and local variables
- To understand the difference between objects and object references
- G To implement classes for drawing graphical shapes

Most useful programs don't just manipulate numbers and strings. Instead, they deal with data items that are more complex and that more closely represent entities in the real world. Examples of these data items include bank accounts, employee records, and graphical shapes.

The Java language is ideally suited for designing and manipulating such data items, or **objects**. In Java, you implement **classes** that describe the behavior of these objects. In this chapter, you will first learn how to manipulate objects that belong to classes that have already been implemented. Then you will learn how to implement your own classes.

CHAPTER CONTENTS

2.1 Objects, Classes, and Methods

Objects and classes are central concepts for Java programming. It will take you some time to master these concepts fully, but because every Java program uses at least a couple of objects and classes, it is a good idea to have a basic understanding of these concepts right away.

> Objects are entities in your program that you manipulate by calling methods.

An **object** is a value that you can manipulate by calling one or more of its **methods**. A method consists of a sequence of instructions that can access the internal data of an object. When you call the method, you do not know exactly what those instructions are, or even how the object is organized internally. However, the behavior of the method is well-defined, and that is what matters when we use it.

> A method is a sequence of instructions that accesses the data of an object.

For example, you saw in Chapter 1 that System.out refers to an object. You manipulate it by calling the println method. When the println method is called, some activities occur inside the object, and the ultimate effect is that text appears in the console window.

In Chapter 1, you encountered two objects:

- `System.out`
- `"Hello, World!"`

In Java, each object belongs to a **class**. The `System.out` object belongs to the class `PrintStream`. The `"Hello, World!"` object belongs to the class `String`. A class specifies the methods that you can apply to its objects.

> A class declares the methods that you can apply to its objects.

You can use the `println` method with any object that belongs to the `PrintStream` class. `System.out` is one such object. It is possible to obtain other objects of the `PrintStream` class. For example, you can construct a `PrintStream` object to send output to a file. However, we won't discuss files until Chapter 10.

Just as the `PrintStream` class provides methods such as `println` and `print` for its objects, the `String` class provides methods that you can apply to `String` objects. One of them is the `length` method. The `length` method counts the number of characters in a string. You can apply that method to any object of type `String`. For example, the expression

```
"Hello".length()
```

yields the number of characters in the `String` object `"Hello"`, that is, the number 5. (The quotation marks are not part of the string, and the `length` method does not count them.)

> The return value of a method is a result that the method has computed for use by the code that called it.

The value that is computed by a method is called the *return value*. We say, that the return value of the call `"Hello".length()` is the number 5.

To see this value, you can write a test program containing the statement

```
System.out.println("Hello".length());
```

> A parameter is an input to a method.

Many methods require inputs that give details about the work that the method needs to do. For example, the `println` method has an input: the item that should be printed. Computer scientists use the technical term **parameter** for method inputs. We say that the string `"Hello"` is a parameter of the method call

```
System.out.println("Hello");
```

> The implicit parameter of a method call is the object on which the method is invoked. All other parameters are explicit parameters.

Technically speaking, this parameter is an **explicit parameter** of the `println` method. The object on which you invoke the method is also considered a parameter of the method call; it is called the **implicit parameter**. For example, `System.out` is the implicit parameter of the method call

```
System.out.println("Hello");
```

Some methods require multiple explicit parameters, others don't require any explicit parameters at all. An example of the latter is the `length` method of the `String` class. All the information that the `length` method requires to do its job—namely, the character sequence of the string—is stored in the implicit parameter object.

Occasionally, a class declares two methods with the same name and different parameter types. For example, the `PrintStream` class declares a second method, also called `println`, as

```
public void println(int output)
```

That method is used to print an integer value. We say that the `println` name is **overloaded** because it refers to more than one method.

Finally, when you apply a method to an object, make sure that the method is declared in the appropriate class. For example, it is an error to call

```
System.out.length(); // This method call is an error
```

The `PrintStream` class (to which `System.out` belongs) has no `length` method.

SELF CHECK

1. How can you compute the length of the string `"Mississippi"`?
2. What are the implicit parameters, explicit parameters, and return values in the method call `"Hello".length()`?
3. Is it legal to call `"Hello".println()`? Why or why not?

2.2 Declaring Variables

> You use variables to store values that you want to use at a later time. A variable has a type, a name, and a value.

You often want to store values so that you can use them at a later time. To remember a value, you need to hold it in a **variable**. A variable is a storage location in the computer's memory that has a type, name, and contents. For example, here we declare three variables:

```
String greeting = "Hello";
PrintStream printer = System.out;
int lengthOfGreeting = greeting.length();
```

The first variable is called `greeting`. It can be used to store `String` values, and it is set to the value `"Hello"`. The second variable, `printer`, stores a `PrintStream` value, and the third stores an integer, namely the value returned by the call `greeting.length()`.

Variables can be used in place of the values that they store:

```
printer.println(greeting); // Same as System.out.println("Hello")
printer.println(lengthOfGreeting); // Same as System.out.println("Hello".length())
```

When you declare your own variables, you need to make two decisions.

- What name should you give the variable?
- What type should you use for the variable?

When deciding on a variable name, make a choice that describes the purpose of the variable. For example, the variable name `greeting` is a better choice than the name `g`.

> Identifiers for variables, methods, and classes are composed of letters, digits, and the underscore character.

An *identifier* is the name of a variable, method, or class. Java imposes the following rules for identifiers:

- Identifiers can be made up of letters, digits, and the underscore (_) character. They cannot start with a digit, though. A dollar sign ($) is also legal but reserved for variables that are machine-generated.
- You cannot use spaces or symbols such as ? or %.
- You cannot use **reserved words**, such as `public`, as names; these words are reserved exclusively for their special Java meanings. (See Appendix C for all reserved words in Java.)

> By convention, variable names should start with a lowercase letter.

Moreover, it is a convention that variable names should start with a lowercase letter. It is OK to use occasional uppercase letters, such as `lengthOfGreeting`. This mixture of lowercase and uppercase letters is sometimes called "camel case" because the uppercase letters stick out like the humps of a camel.

Syntax 2.1   Variable Declaration

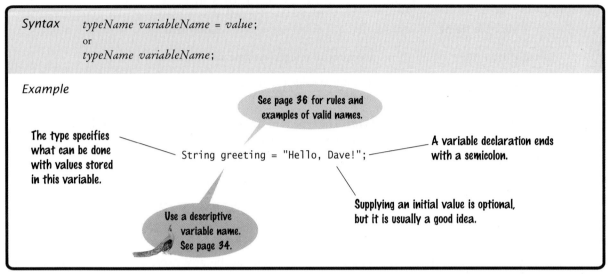

In Java, every variable has a **type**. If you want to store objects in the variable, the type is the name of the class. For example, in order to store strings, use the String type for your variable. However, in Java, numbers are not objects. Moreover, there are several number types to choose from. **Integers** are whole numbers; **floating-point numbers** can have fractional parts. For example, 13 is an integer and 1.3 is a floating-point number. (The name "floating-point" describes the representation of the number in the computer as a sequence of the significant digits and an indication of the position of the decimal point. For example, the numbers 13000.0, 1.3, 0.00013 all have the same decimal digits: 13. When a floating-point number is multiplied or divided by 10, only the position of the decimal point changes; it "floats".)

The int type denotes integers. The double type denotes floating-point numbers that can have fractional parts.

Use the int type for variables that can never have a fractional part (such as the length of a string). If you need to store numbers with a fractional part (such as a grade point average), use the type called double, which stands for "double precision floating-point number". Think of a number in double format as any number that can appear in the display panel of a calculator, such as 1.3, -0.333333333 or 6.0221415E23 (that is, 6.0221415×10^{23}.)

Use the assignment operator (=) to change the value of a variable.

You can change the value of a variable with the assignment operator (=). For example, consider the variable declaration

    int width = 10; ❶

If you want to change the value of the variable, simply assign the new value:

    width = 20; ❷

The assignment replaces the original value of the variable (see Figure 1).

❶   width =   10

Figure 1
Assigning a New
Value to a Variable

❷   width =   20

Table 1 Variable Declarations in Java

Variable Name	Comment
`int width = 10;`	Declares an integer variable and initializes it with 10.
`int area = width * height;`	The initial value can depend on other variables. (Of course, `width` and `height` must have been previously declared.)
🚫 `height = 5;`	**Error:** The type is missing. This statement is not a declaration but an assignment of a new value to an existing variable.
🚫 `int height = "5";`	**Error:** You cannot initialize a number with a string.
`int width, height;`	Declares two integer variables in a single statement. In this book, we will declare each variable in a separate statement.

Numbers and variables can be combined by arithmetic operators such as +, −, and *.

The right-hand side of the = symbol can be any *expression* that combines variables, numbers, operators, and method calls. For example,

```
width = height + 10;
```

This means "compute the value of `height + 10` and store that value in the variable `width`". Other commonly used operators are - (subtraction), * (multiplication), and / (division).

In the Java programming language, the = operator denotes an *action*, to replace the value of a variable. This usage differs from the mathematical usage of the = symbol, as a statement about equality. For example, in Java, the following statement is entirely legal:

```
width = width + 10;
```

Syntax 2.2 Assignment

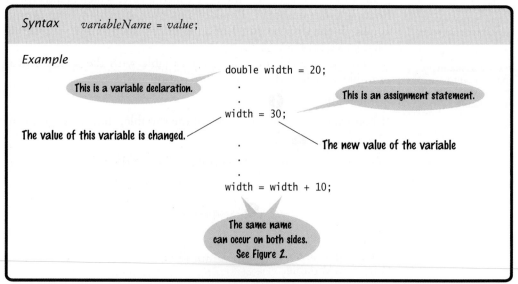

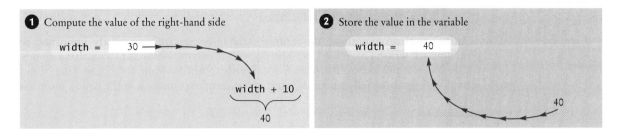

Figure 2 Executing the Statement `width = width + 10`

ANIMATION
Variable Initialization and Assignment

This means "compute the value of `width + 10` ❶ and store that value in the variable `width` ❷" (see Figure 2).

It is an error to use a variable that has never had a value assigned to it. For example, the following assignment statement has an error:

```
int height;
int area = width * height;   // ERROR—uninitialized variable height
```

The compiler will complain about an "uninitialized variable" when you use a variable that has never been assigned a value. (See Figure 3.)

Figure 3
An Uninitialized Variable

`height =` [   ]   No value has been assigned.

All variables must be initialized before you access them.

The remedy is to assign a value to the variable before you use it:

```
int height = 30;
int area = width * height; // OK
```

SELF CHECK

4. Which of the following are legal identifiers?

```
Greeting1
g
void
101dalmatians
Hello, World
<greeting>
```

5. Declare a variable to hold your name. Use camel case in the variable name.

6. How do you change the value of the `greeting` variable to `"Hello, Nina!"`?

Quality Tip 2.1

Choose Descriptive Names for Variables

In algebra, variable names are usually just one letter long, such as p or A, maybe with a subscript such as p_1. You might be tempted to save yourself a lot of typing by using short variable names in your Java programs:

```
int A = w * h;
```

Compare this with the following statement:

```
int area = width * height;
```

The advantage is obvious. Reading width is much easier than reading w and then figuring out that it must mean "width".

In practical programming, descriptive variable names are particularly important when programs are written by more than one person. It may be obvious to you that w stands for width, but is it obvious to the person who needs to update your code years later? For that matter, will you yourself remember what w means when you look at the code a month from now?

2.3 Constructing Objects

Most Java programs need to work on a variety of objects. In this section, you will see how to *construct* new objects. This allows you to go beyond String objects and the System.out object.

To learn about object construction, let us turn to another class: the Rectangle class in the Java class library. Objects of type Rectangle describe rectangular shapes—see Figure 4. These objects are useful for a variety of purposes. You can assemble rectangles into bar charts, and you can program simple games by moving rectangles inside a window.

Note that a Rectangle object isn't a rectangular shape—it's an object that contains a set of numbers. The numbers *describe* the rectangle (see Figure 5). Each rectangle is described by the x- and y-coordinates of its top-left corner, its width, and its height.

It is very important that you understand this distinction. In the computer, a Rectangle object is a block of memory that holds four numbers, for example $x = 5$, $y = 10$, *width* = 20, *height* = 30. In the imagination of the programmer who uses a Rectangle object, the object describes a geometric figure.

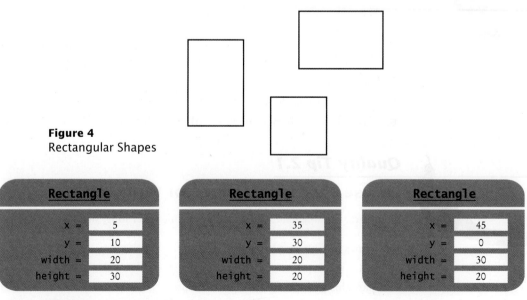

Figure 4
Rectangular Shapes

Figure 5 Rectangle Objects

Syntax 2.3   Object Construction

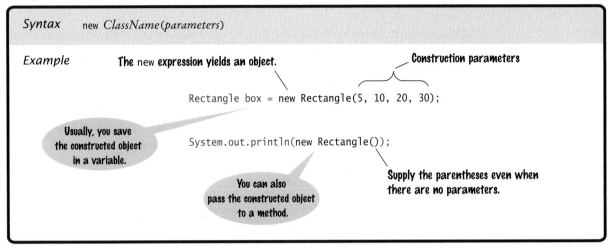

Syntax   new *ClassName*(*parameters*)

Example   **The** new **expression yields an object.**   **Construction parameters**

Rectangle box = new Rectangle(5, 10, 20, 30);

Usually, you save the constructed object in a variable.

System.out.println(new Rectangle());

You can also pass the constructed object to a method.

Supply the parentheses even when there are no parameters.

> Use the new operator, followed by a class name and parameters, to construct new objects.

To make a new rectangle, you need to specify the *x*, *y*, *width*, and *height* values. Then *invoke the* new *operator*, specifying the name of the class and the parameters that are required for constructing a new object. For example, you can make a new rectangle with its top-left corner at (5, 10), width 20, and height 30 as follows:

```
new Rectangle(5, 10, 20, 30)
```

Here is what happens in detail:

1. The new operator makes a Rectangle object.
2. It uses the parameters (in this case, 5, 10, 20, and 30) to initialize the data of the object.
3. It returns the object.

The process of creating a new object is called **construction**. The four values 5, 10, 20, and 30 are called the *construction parameters*.

The new expression yields an object, and you need to store the object if you want to use it later. Usually you assign the output of the new operator to a variable. For example,

```
Rectangle box = new Rectangle(5, 10, 20, 30);
```

Some classes let you construct objects in multiple ways. For example, you can also obtain a Rectangle object by supplying no construction parameters at all (but you must still supply the parentheses):

```
new Rectangle()
```

This expression constructs a (rather useless) rectangle with its top-left corner at the origin (0, 0), width 0, and height 0.

S E L F   C H E C K

7. How do you construct a square with center (100, 100) and side length 20?

8. The getWidth method returns the width of a Rectangle object. What does the following statement print?

```
System.out.println(new Rectangle().getWidth());
```

2.4 The API Documentation

The classes and methods of the Java library are listed in the **API documentation**. The API is the "application programming interface". A programmer who uses the Java classes to put together a computer program (or *application*) is an *application programmer*. That's you. In contrast, the programmers who designed and implemented the library classes such as PrintStream and Rectangle are *system programmers*.

> The API (Application Programming Interface) documentation lists the classes and methods of the Java library.

You can find the API documentation on the Web. Point your web browser to http://java.sun.com/javase/7/docs/api/index.html. Appendix D contains an abbreviated version of the API documentation that may be easier to use at first. It is fine if you rely on the abbreviated documentation for your first programs, but you should eventually move on to the real thing.

The API documentation documents all classes in the Java library—there are thousands of them (see Figure 6). Most of the classes are rather specialized, and only a few are of interest to the beginning programmer.

Locate the Rectangle link in the left pane, preferably by using the search function of your browser. Click on the link, and the right pane shows all the features of the Rectangle class (see Figure 7).

Figure 6 The API Documentation of the Standard Java Library

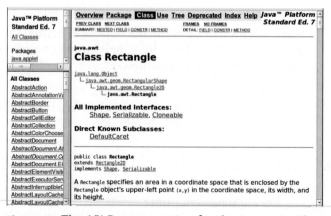

Figure 7 The API Documentation for the Rectangle Class

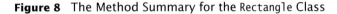

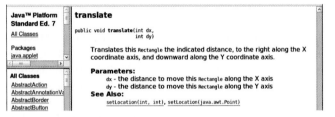

Figure 8 The Method Summary for the Rectangle Class

Figure 9 The API Documentation of the translate Method

The API documentation for each class starts out with a section that describes the purpose of the class. Then come summary tables for the constructors and methods (see Figure 8). Click on the link of a method to get a detailed description (see Figure 9).

The detailed description of a method shows

- The action that the method carries out.
- The parameters that the method receives.
- The value that it returns (or the reserved word void if the method doesn't return any value).

As you can see, the Rectangle class has quite a few methods. While occasionally intimidating for the beginning programmer, this is a strength of the standard library. If you ever need to do a computation involving rectangles, chances are that there is a method that does all the work for you.

For example, suppose you need to move a rectangle around, for example, to display an animation. If you browse through the API documentation, you will find a translate method with the description "Translates this Rectangle the indicated distance, to the right along the x-coordinate axis, and downward along the y-coordinate axis." (Mathematicians use the term "translation" for a rigid motion of the plane.) The method has two parameters, described as

- dx - the distance to move this Rectangle along the x-axis
- dy - the distance to move this Rectangle along the y-axis

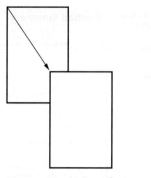

Figure 10 Using the translate
Method to Move a Rectangle

For example, the method call

```
box.translate(15, 25);
```

moves the rectangle by 15 units in the *x*-direction and 25 units in the *y*-direction (see Figure 10). Moving a rectangle doesn't change its width or height, but it changes the top-left corner. Afterward, the rectangle that had its top-left corner at (5, 10) now has it at (20, 35). In the next section, we will write a program that tests the translate method.

The API documentation contains another important piece of information about each class. The classes in the standard library are organized into **packages**. A package is a collection of classes with a related purpose. The Rectangle class belongs to the package java.awt (where awt is an abbreviation for "Abstract Windowing Toolkit"), which contains many classes for drawing windows and graphical shapes. You can see the package name java.awt in Figure 7, just above the class name.

To use the Rectangle class from the java.awt package, you must *import* the package. Simply place the following line at the top of your program:

> Java classes are grouped into packages. Use the import statement to use classes that are declared in other packages.

```
import java.awt.Rectangle;
```

Why don't you have to import the System and String classes? Because the System and String classes are in the java.lang package, and all classes from this package are automatically imported, so you never need to import them yourself.

Syntax 2.4   Importing a Class from a Package

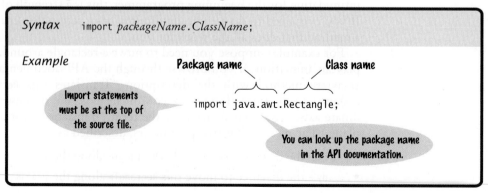

Syntax   import *packageName.ClassName*;

Example

Import statements must be at the top of the source file.

Package name   Class name

import java.awt.Rectangle;

You can look up the package name in the API documentation.

9. Look at the API documentation of the String class. Which method would you use to obtain the string "HELLO, WORLD!" from the string "Hello, World!"?

10. In the API documentation of the String class, look at the description of the trim method. What is the result of applying trim to the string " Hello, Space ! "? (Note the spaces in the string.)

11. The Random class is declared in the java.util package. What do you need to do in order to use that class in your program?

Productivity Hint 2.1

Don't Memorize—Use Online Help

The Java library has thousands of classes and methods. It is neither necessary nor useful trying to memorize them. Instead, you should become familiar with using the API documentation. Because you will need to use the API documentation all the time, it is best to download and install it onto your computer, particularly if your computer is not always connected to the Internet. You can download the documentation from http://java.sun.com/javase/downloads/index.html.

2.5 Implementing a Test Program

In this section, we discuss the steps that are necessary to implement a test program. The purpose of a test program is to verify that one or more methods have been implemented correctly. A test program calls methods and checks that they return the expected results. Writing test programs is a very important skill.

In this section, we will develop a simple program that tests a method in the Rectangle class. The program performs the following steps:

1. Provide a tester class.
2. Supply a main method.
3. Inside the main method, construct one or more objects.
4. Apply methods to the objects.
5. Display the results of the method calls.
6. Display the values that you expect to get.

> A test program verifies that methods behave as expected.

Our sample test program tests the behavior of the translate method. Here are the key steps (which have been placed inside the main method of the MoveTester class).

```
Rectangle box = new Rectangle(5, 10, 20, 30);

// Move the rectangle
box.translate(15, 25);

// Print information about the moved rectangle
System.out.print("x: ");
System.out.println(box.getX());
System.out.println("Expected: 20");
```

We print the value that is returned by the getX method, and then we print a message that describes the value we expect to see.

Determining the expected result in advance is an important part of testing.

This is a very important step. You want to spend some time thinking about the expected result before you run a test program. This thought process will help you understand how your program should behave, and it can help you track down errors at an early stage. Finding and fixing errors early is a very effective strategy that can save you a great deal of time.

In our case, the rectangle has been constructed with the top-left corner at (5, 10). The *x*-direction is moved by 15, so we expect an *x*-value of 5 + 15 = 20 after the move.

Here is a complete program that tests the moving of a rectangle.

ch02/rectangle/MoveTester.java

```java
 1  import java.awt.Rectangle;
 2
 3  public class MoveTester
 4  {
 5     public static void main(String[] args)
 6     {
 7        Rectangle box = new Rectangle(5, 10, 20, 30);
 8
 9        // Move the rectangle
10        box.translate(15, 25);
11
12        // Print information about the moved rectangle
13        System.out.print("x: ");
14        System.out.println(box.getX());
15        System.out.println("Expected: 20");
16
17        System.out.print("y: ");
18        System.out.println(box.getY());
19        System.out.println("Expected: 35");
20     }
21  }
```

Program Run

```
x: 20
Expected: 20
y: 35
Expected: 35
```

S E L F   C H E C K

12. Suppose we had called box.translate(25, 15) instead of box.translate(15, 25). What are the expected outputs?

13. Why doesn't the MoveTester program need to print the width and height of the rectangle?

Special Topic 2.1

Testing Classes in an Interactive Environment

Special Topic 2.1 describes how classes can be tested easily in the BlueJ environment, without having to write a separate tester class.

 **Worked Example 2.1**

How Many Days Have You Been Alive?

In this Worked Example, you explore the API of a class Day that represents a calendar day, and you write a program that computes how many days have elapsed since the day you were born.

 **Worked Example 2.2**

Working with Pictures

In this Worked Example, you use the API of a Picture class to edit photos.

2.6 Instance Variables

In the preceding sections, you learned how to use objects from existing classes. You will now start implementing your own classes. We begin with a very simple example that shows you how objects store their data, and how methods access the data of an object. You will then learn a systematic process for implementing classes.

Our first example is a class that models a *tally counter*, a mechanical device that is used to count people—for example, to find out how many people attend a concert or board a bus (see Figure 11).

Whenever the operator pushes a button, the counter value advances by one. We model this operation with a count method. A physical counter has a display to show the current value. In our simulation, we use a getValue method instead. For example,

```
Counter tally = new Counter();
tally.count();
tally.count();
int result = tally.getValue(); // Sets result to 2
```

When implementing the Counter class, we need to determine the data that each counter object contains. In this simple example, that is very straightforward. Each counter needs to store a variable that keeps track of how many times the counter has been advanced.

Figure 11 A Tally Counter

An object stores its data in **instance variables**. An *instance* of a class is an object of the class. Thus, an instance variable is a storage location that is present in each object of the class.

You specify instance variables in the class declaration:

```
public class Counter
{
    private int value;
    . . .
}
```

An instance variable declaration consists of the following parts:

- An **access specifier** (private)
- The **type** of the instance variable (such as int)
- The name of the instance variable (such as value)

Each object of a class has its own set of instance variables. For example, if concert-Counter and boardingCounter are two objects of the Counter class, then each object has its own value variable (see Figure 12). As you will see in Section 2.10, the instance variable value is set to 0 when a Counter object is constructed.

In order to gain a better understanding of how methods affect instance variables, we will have a quick look at the implementation of the methods of the Counter class. The count method advances the counter value by 1. We will cover the syntax of the method header in Section 2.7. For now, focus on the body of the method inside the braces:

```
public void count()
{
    value = value + 1;
}
```

Note how the count method accesses the instance variable value. *Which* instance variable? The one belonging to the object on which the method is invoked. For example, consider the call

```
concertCounter.count();
```

This call advances the value variable of the concertCounter object.

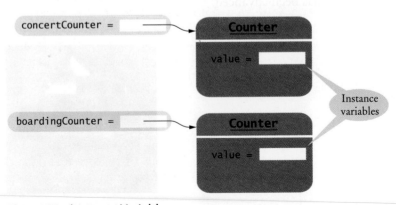

Figure 12 Instance Variables

Syntax 2.5   Instance Variable Declaration

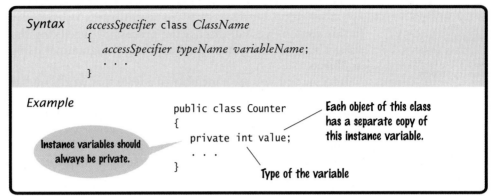

Syntax   *accessSpecifier* class *ClassName*
{
   accessSpecifier *typeName* *variableName*;
   . . .
}

Example   public class Counter
                                                   {
   Instance variables should   private int value;
   always be private.   . . .
                                                   }

Each object of this class
has a separate copy of
this instance variable.

Type of the variable

The getValue method returns the current value:

```
public int getValue()
{
   return value;
}
```

The return statement is a special statement that terminates the method call and returns a result to the method's caller.

Instance variables are generally declared with the access specifier private. That specifier means that they can be accessed only by the methods of the *same class*, not by any other method. For example, the value variable can be accessed by the count and getValue methods of the Counter class but not a method of another class. Those other methods need to use the Counter class methods if they want to manipulate a counter's value.

The process of hiding implementation details while providing a set of methods for working with objects is called **encapsulation**.

Why would you want to hide something from other programmers? If you design a class so that its users need not know about the internal structure, you simplify the life of the programmers using your class. You know this from your own experience. You are already able to use classes for string manipulation and console output, without worrying how these classes are implemented.

Encapsulation also helps with diagnosing errors. A large program may consist of hundreds of classes and thousands of methods, but if there is an error with the internal data of an object, you only need to look at the methods of one class. Finally, encapsulation makes it possible to change the implementation of a class without having to tell the programmers who use the class.

> Private instance variables can only be accessed by methods of the same class.

> Encapsulation is the process of hiding implementation details and providing methods for data access.

> Encapsulation allows a programmer to use a class without having to know its implementation.

SELF CHECK

14. Supply the body of a method public void reset() that resets the counter back to zero.

15. Suppose you use a class Clock with private instance variables hours and minutes. How can you access these variables in your program?

2.7 Specifying the Public Interface of a Class

The public interface of a class specifies what you can do with its objects.

In this section, we will discuss the process of specifying the **public interface** of a class. The public interface specifies what a programmer using the class can do with its objects.

Imagine that you are a member of a team that works on banking software. A fundamental concept in banking is a *bank account*. Your task is to understand the design of a BankAccount class so that you can implement it, which in turn allows other programmers on the team to use it.

In order to implement a class, you first need to know which methods are required.

You need to know exactly what features of a bank account need to be implemented. Some features are essential (such as deposits), whereas others are not important (such as the gift that a customer may receive for opening a bank account). Deciding which features are essential is not always an easy task. We will revisit that issue in Chapters 7 and 11. For now, we will assume that a competent designer has decided that the following are considered the essential operations of a bank account:

- Deposit money
- Withdraw money
- Get the current balance

In Java, operations are expressed as method calls. To figure out the exact specification of the method calls, imagine how a programmer would carry out the bank account operations. We'll assume that the variable harrysChecking contains a reference to an object of type BankAccount. We want to support method calls such as the following:

```
harrysChecking.deposit(2240.59);
harrysChecking.withdraw(500);
double currentBalance = harrysChecking.getBalance();
```

An accessor method does not change the internal data of its implicit parameter. A mutator method changes the data.

The first two methods are **mutator methods**. They modify the balance of the bank account and don't return a value. The third method is an **accessor method**. It returns a value that you store in a variable or pass to a method.

As you can see from the sample calls, the BankAccount class should declare three methods:

- `public void deposit(double amount)`
- `public void withdraw(double amount)`
- `public double getBalance()`

Recall that double denotes the double-precision floating-point type, and void indicates that a method does not return a value.

Here we only give the method *headers*. When you declare a method, you also need to provide the method *body*, consisting of statements that are executed when the method is called.

```
public void deposit(double amount)
{
    implementation—see Section 2.8
}
```

Syntax 2.6 Class Declaration

```
Syntax      accessSpecifier class ClassName
            {
                instance variables
                constructors
                methods
            }
```

```
Example           public class Counter
                  {
                      private int value;

                      public Counter(int initialValue) { value = initialValue; }

                      public void count() { value = value + 1; }
                      public int getValue() { return value; }
                  }
```

Public interface

Private implementation

> **In a method header, you specify the return type, method name, and the types and names of the parameters.**

Every method header contains the following parts:

- An **access specifier** (usually `public`), specifying which other methods can call this method. All methods in a program can call a `public` method, but `private` methods can only be called by other methods of the same class.
- The *return type* (the type of the value returned, such as `void` or `double`)
- The name of the method (such as `deposit`)
- A list of the **parameter variables** of the method (if any), enclosed in parentheses (such as `double amount`)

> **Constructors set the initial data for objects. The constructor name is always the same as the class name.**

Next, you need to supply constructors. A constructor initializes the instance variables of an object. In Java, a constructor is very similar to a method. However, constructors have no return type (not even void). The name of the constructor is always the same as the name of the class (e.g., `BankAccount`).

We want to construct bank accounts that initially have a zero balance, as well as accounts that have a given initial balance. For this purpose, we specify two constructors.

- `public BankAccount()`
- `public BankAccount(double initialBalance)`

They are used as follows:

```
BankAccount harrysChecking = new BankAccount();
BankAccount momsSavings = new BankAccount(5000);
```

Don't worry about the fact that there are two constructors with the same name—*all* constructors of a class have the same name, that is, the name of the class. The compiler can tell them apart because they take different parameters.

When declaring a class, you place all constructor and method declarations inside, like this:

```
public class BankAccount
{
    private instance variables—filled in later
```

```
    // Constructors
    public BankAccount()
    {
        implementation—filled in later
    }

    public BankAccount(double initialBalance)
    {
        implementation—filled in later
    }

    // Methods
    public void deposit(double amount)
    {
        implementation—filled in later
    }

    public void withdraw(double amount)
    {
        implementation—filled in later
    }

    public double getBalance()
    {
        implementation—filled in later
    }
}
```

The public constructors and methods of a class form the public interface of the class. These are the operations that any programmer can use to create and manipulate BankAccount objects.

You should always provide **documentation comments** to document the public interface. A documentation comment is placed before the class or method declaration that is being documented. It is enclosed in delimiters /** and */. First, you describe the method's *purpose*. Then, for each method parameter, supply a line that starts with @param, followed by the parameter name and a short explanation. Finally, if the method returns a value, supply a line that starts with @return, describing the return value. Here are two typical examples.

> Use documentation comments to describe the classes and public methods of your programs.

```
/**
    Withdraws money from the bank account.
    @param amount the amount to withdraw
*/
public void withdraw(double amount)

/**
    Gets the current balance of the bank account.
    @return the current balance
*/
public double getBalance()
```

Also supply a brief comment for each *class*, explaining its purpose:

```
/**
    A bank account has a balance that can be changed by
    deposits and withdrawals.
*/
public class BankAccount
{
```

. . .
```
   }
```

S E L F   C H E C K

16. How can you use the methods of the public interface to *empty* the harrysChecking bank account?

17. What is wrong with this sequence of statements?

```
BankAccount harrysChecking = new BankAccount(10000);
System.out.println(harrysChecking.withdraw(500));
```

18. Suppose you want a more powerful bank account abstraction that keeps track of an *account number* in addition to the balance. How would you change the public interface to accommodate this enhancement?

Common Error 2.1

Declaring a Constructor as void

Do not use the void reserved word when you declare a constructor:

```
public void BankAccount()  // Error—don't use void!
```

This would declare a method with return type void and *not* a constructor. Unfortunately, the Java compiler does not consider this a syntax error.

Productivity Hint 2.2

The javadoc Utility

If you insert documentation comments in your code, you can use the javadoc utility to produce documentation that you can view in a web browser. The first sentence of each method comment is used for a summary table of all methods of your class (see Figure 13). The @param

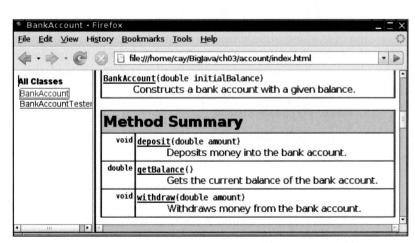

Figure 13 A Method Summary Generated by javadoc

Figure 14 Method Detail Generated by javadoc

and @return comments are neatly formatted in the detail description of each method (see Figure 14). This documentation format should look familiar. The programmers who implement the Java library use javadoc themselves. They too document every class, every method, every parameter, and every return value, and then use javadoc to extract the documentation in HTML format.

Most development environments can execute the javadoc utility for you. Alternatively, you can invoke the javadoc utility from a shell window, by issuing the command

```
javadoc MyClass.java
```

or, if you want to document multiple Java files,

```
javadoc *.java
```

2.8 Providing the Class Implementation

Now that you understand the specification of the public interface of the BankAccount class, let's provide the implementation.

> The private implementation of a class consists of instance variables, and the bodies of constructors and methods.

First, we need to determine the data that each bank account object contains. In the case of our simple bank account class, each object needs to store a single value, the current balance. (A more complex bank account class might store additional data—perhaps an account number, the interest rate paid, the date for mailing out the next statement, and so on.)

```
public class BankAccount
{
    private double balance;
    . . .
}
```

Now that we have determined the instance variables, let's complete the BankAccount class by supplying the bodies of the constructors and methods. Each body contains a sequence of statements. We'll start with the constructors because they are very straightforward. A constructor has a simple job: to initialize the instance variables of an object.

Recall that we designed the BankAccount class to have two constructors. The first constructor simply sets the balance to zero:

```
public BankAccount()
{
    balance = 0;
}
```

The second constructor sets the balance to the value supplied as the construction parameter:

```
public BankAccount(double initialBalance)
{
    balance = initialBalance;
}
```

To see how these constructors work, let us trace the statement

```
BankAccount harrysChecking = new BankAccount(1000);
```

one step at a time.

Here are the steps that are carried out when the statement executes.

- Create a new object of type BankAccount.
- Call the second constructor (because a parameter value is supplied in the constructor call).
- Set the parameter variable initialBalance to 1000.
- Set the balance instance variable of the newly created object to initialBalance.
- Return an object reference, that is, the memory location of the object, as the value of the new expression.
- Store that object reference in the harrysChecking variable.

Let's move on to implementing the BankAccount methods.

Syntax 2.7 Method Declaration

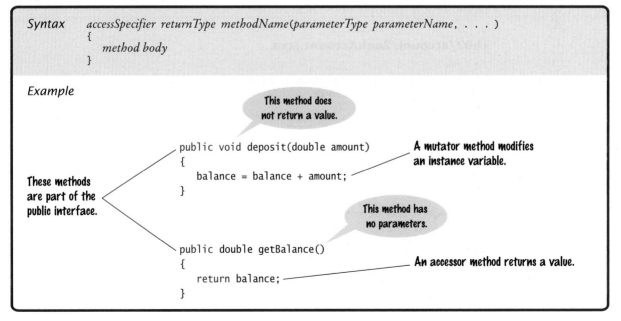

Syntax	*accessSpecifier returnType methodName(parameterType parameterName, . . .)*

```
{
    method body
}
```

Example

This method does not return a value.

These methods are part of the public interface.

```
public void deposit(double amount)
{
    balance = balance + amount;
}
```

A mutator method modifies an instance variable.

This method has no parameters.

```
public double getBalance()
{
    return balance;
}
```

An accessor method returns a value.

Here is the deposit method:

```
public void deposit(double amount)
{
    balance = balance + amount;
}
```

To understand exactly what the method does, consider this statement:

```
harrysChecking.deposit(500);
```

This statement carries out the following steps:

- Set the parameter variable amount to 500.
- Fetch the balance instance variable of the object whose location is stored in harrysChecking.
- Add the value of amount to balance.
- Store the sum in the balance instance variable, overwriting the old value.

The withdraw method is very similar to the deposit method:

```
public void withdraw(double amount)
{
    balance = balance - amount;
}
```

There is only one method left, getBalance. Unlike the deposit and withdraw methods, which modify the instance variable of the object on which they are invoked, the get-Balance method returns a value:

```
public double getBalance()
{
    return balance;
}
```

We have now completed the implementation of the BankAccount class—see the code listing below. There is only one step remaining: testing that the class works correctly. That is the topic of the next section.

ch02/account/BankAccount.java

```
 1  /**
 2      A bank account has a balance that can be changed by
 3      deposits and withdrawals.
 4  */
 5  public class BankAccount
 6  {
 7      private double balance;
 8
 9      /**
10          Constructs a bank account with a zero balance.
11      */
12      public BankAccount()
13      {
14          balance = 0;
15      }
16
```

```
17      /**
18          Constructs a bank account with a given balance.
19          @param initialBalance the initial balance
20      */
21      public BankAccount(double initialBalance)
22      {
23          balance = initialBalance;
24      }
25
26      /**
27          Deposits money into the bank account.
28          @param amount the amount to deposit
29      */
30      public void deposit(double amount)
31      {
32          balance = balance + amount;
33      }
34
35      /**
36          Withdraws money from the bank account.
37          @param amount the amount to withdraw
38      */
39      public void withdraw(double amount)
40      {
41          balance = balance - amount;
42      }
43
44      /**
45          Gets the current balance of the bank account.
46          @return the current balance
47      */
48      public double getBalance()
49      {
50          return balance;
51      }
52  }
```

SELF CHECK

19. Suppose we modify the BankAccount class so that each bank account has an account number. How does this change affect the instance variables?

20. Why does the following code not succeed in robbing mom's bank account?

```
public class BankRobber
{
    public static void main(String[] args)
    {
        BankAccount momsSavings = new BankAccount(1000);
        momsSavings.balance = 0;
    }
}
```

21. The Rectangle class has four instance variables: x, y, width, and height. Give a possible implementation of the getWidth method.

22. Give a possible implementation of the translate method of the Rectangle class.

How To 2.1

Implementing a Class

This "How To" section tells you how you implement a class from a given specification.

For example, a homework assignment might ask you to implement a class that models a cash register. Your class should allow a cashier to enter item prices and the amount of money that the customer paid. It should then calculate the change due.

Step 1 Find out which methods you are asked to supply.

In the cash register example, you won't have to provide every feature of a real cash register—there are too many. The assignment tells you, in plain English, *which aspects* of a cash register your class should simulate. Make a list of them:

- Ring up the sales price for a purchased item.
- Enter the amount of payment.
- Calculate the amount of change due to the customer.

Step 2 Specify the public interface.

Turn the list in Step 1 into a set of methods, with specific types for the parameters and the return values. Many programmers find this step simpler if they write out method calls that are applied to a sample object, like this:

```
CashRegister register = new CashRegister();
register.recordPurchase(29.95);
register.recordPurchase(9.95);
register.enterPayment(50);
double change = register.giveChange();
```

Now we have a specific list of methods.

- public void recordPurchase(double amount)
- public void enterPayment(double amount)
- public double giveChange()

To complete the public interface, you need to specify the constructors. Ask yourself what information you need in order to construct an object of your class. Sometimes you will want two constructors: one that sets all instance variables to a default and one that sets them to user-supplied values.

In the case of the cash register example, we can get by with a single constructor that creates an empty register. A more realistic cash register would start out with some coins and bills so that we can give exact change, but that is beyond the scope of our assignment.

Thus, we add a single constructor:

- public CashRegister()

Step 3 Document the public interface.

Here is the documentation, with comments, that describes the class and its methods:

```
/**
    A cash register totals up sales and computes change due.
*/
public class CashRegister
{
    /**
        Constructs a cash register with no money in it.
    */
    public CashRegister()
    {
    }
```

```
/**
    Records the sale of an item.
    @param amount the price of the item
*/
public void recordPurchase(double amount)
{
}

/**
    Enters the payment received from the customer.
    @param amount the amount of the payment
*/
public void enterPayment(double amount)
{
}

/**
    Computes the change due and resets the machine for the next customer.
    @return the change due to the customer
*/
public double giveChange()
{
}
}
```

Step 4 Determine instance variables.

Ask yourself what information an object needs to store to do its job. Remember, the methods can be called in any order! The object needs to have enough internal memory to be able to process every method using only its instance variables and the method parameters. Go through each method, perhaps starting with a simple one or an interesting one, and ask yourself what you need to carry out the method's task. Make instance variables to store the information that the method needs.

In the cash register example, you would want to keep track of the total purchase amount and the payment. You can compute the change due from these two amounts.

```
public class CashRegister
{
    private double purchase;
    private double payment;
    . . .
}
```

Step 5 Implement constructors and methods.

Implement the constructors and methods in your class, one at a time, starting with the easiest ones. For example, here is the implementation of the recordPurchase method:

```
public void recordPurchase(double amount)
{
    purchase = purchase + amount;
}
```

Here is the giveChange method. Note that this method is a bit more sophisticated—it computes the change due, and it also resets the cash register for the next sale.

```
public double giveChange()
{
    double change = payment - purchase;
    purchase = 0;
    payment = 0;
    return change;
}
```

If you find that you have trouble with the implementation, you may need to rethink your choice of instance variables. It is common for a beginner to start out with a set of instance variables that cannot accurately reflect the state of an object. Don't hesitate to go back and add or modify instance variables.

Once you have completed the implementation, compile your class and fix any compile-time errors.

You can find the complete implementation in the ch02/cashregister directory of your source code.

Step 6 Test your class.

Write a short tester program and execute it. The tester program can carry out the method calls that you found in Step 2.

```java
public class CashRegisterTester
{
    public static void main(String[] args)
    {
        CashRegister register = new CashRegister();

        register.recordPurchase(29.50);
        register.recordPurchase(9.25);
        register.enterPayment(50);

        double change = register.giveChange();

        System.out.println(change);
        System.out.println("Expected: 11.25");
    }
}
```

The output of this test program is:

```
11.25
Expected: 11.25
```

Alternatively, if you use a program that lets you test objects interactively, such as BlueJ, construct an object and apply the method calls.

⊕ *Worked Example 2.3*

Making a Simple Menu

Worked Example 2.3 shows how to implement a class that constructs simple menus.

2.9 Unit Testing

In the preceding section, we completed the implementation of the BankAccount class. What can you do with it? Of course, you can compile the file BankAccount.java. However, you can't *execute* the resulting BankAccount.class file. It doesn't contain a main method. That is normal—most classes don't contain a main method.

In the long run, your class may become a part of a larger program that interacts with users, stores data in files, and so on. However, before integrating a class into a

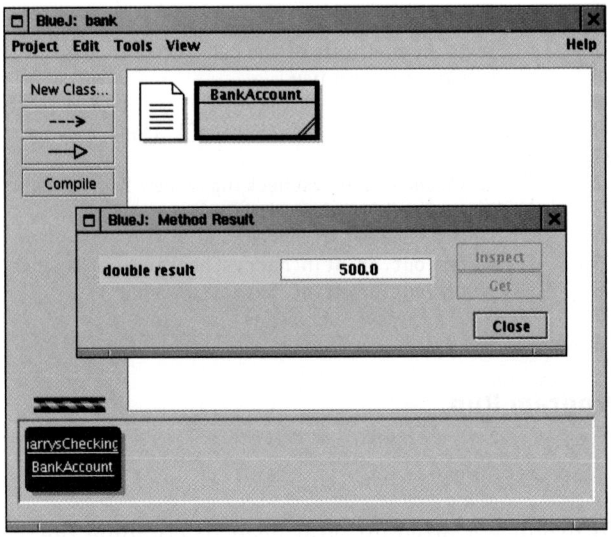

Figure 15
The Return Value of the
getBalance Method in BlueJ

program, it is always a good idea to test it in isolation. Testing in isolation, outside a complete program, is called **unit testing**.

A unit test verifies that a class works correctly in isolation, outside a complete program.

To test your class, you have two choices. Some interactive development environments have commands for constructing objects and invoking methods (see Special Topic 2.1 on page 44). Then you can test a class simply by constructing an object, calling methods, and verifying that you get the expected return values. Figure 15 shows the result of calling the getBalance method on a BankAccount object in BlueJ.

Alternatively, you can write a *tester class*. A tester class is a class with a main method that contains statements to run methods of another class. As discussed in Section 2.5, a tester class typically carries out the following steps:

1. Construct one or more objects of the class that is being tested.

2. Invoke one or more methods.

3. Print out one or more results.

4. Print the expected results.

The MoveTester class in Section 2.5 is a good example of a tester class. That class runs methods of the Rectangle class—a class in the Java library.

Here is a class to run methods of the BankAccount class. The main method constructs an object of type BankAccount, invokes the deposit and withdraw methods, and then displays the remaining balance on the console.

We also print the value that we expect to see. In our sample program, we deposit $2,000 and withdraw $500. We therefore expect a balance of $1,500.

ch02/account/BankAccountTester.java

```
1  /**
2      A class to test the BankAccount class.
3  */
4  public class BankAccountTester
5  {
```

```
6    /**
7        Tests the methods of the BankAccount class.
8        @param args  not used
9    */
10   public static void main(String[] args)
11   {
12       BankAccount harrysChecking = new BankAccount();
13       harrysChecking.deposit(2000);
14       harrysChecking.withdraw(500);
15       System.out.println(harrysChecking.getBalance());
16       System.out.println("Expected: 1500");
17   }
18 }
```

Program Run

```
1500
Expected: 1500
```

To produce a program, you need to combine the `BankAccount` and the `BankAccountTester` classes. The details for building the program depend on your compiler and development environment. In most environments, you need to carry out these steps:

1. Make a new subfolder for your program.
2. Make two files, one for each class.
3. Compile both files.
4. Run the test program.

Many students are surprised that such a simple program contains two classes. However, this is normal. The two classes have entirely different purposes. The `BankAccount` class describes objects that compute bank balances. The `BankAccountTester` class runs a test that puts a `BankAccount` object through its paces.

SELF CHECK

23. When you run the `BankAccountTester` program, how many objects of class `BankAccount` are constructed? How many objects of type `BankAccountTester`?

24. Why is the `BankAccountTester` class unnecessary in development environments that allow interactive testing, such as BlueJ?

2.10 Local Variables

Local variables are declared in the body of a method.

In this section, we discuss the behavior of *local* variables. A **local variable** is a variable that is declared in the body of a method. For example, the `giveChange` method in How To 2.1 on page 56 declares a local variable `change`:

```
public double giveChange()
{
    double change = payment - purchase;
    purchase = 0;
    payment = 0;
    return change;
}
```

When a method
exits, its local
variables are
removed.

Parameter variables are similar to local variables, but they are declared in method headers. For example, the following method declares a parameter variable amount:

```
public void enterPayment(double amount)
```

Local and parameter variables belong to methods. When a method runs, its local and parameter variables come to life. When the method exits, they are removed immediately. For example, if you call register.giveChange(), then a variable change is created. When the method exits, that variable is removed.

In contrast, instance variables belong to objects, not methods. When an object is constructed, its instance variables are created. The instance variables stay alive until no method uses the object any longer. (The Java virtual machine contains an agent called a **garbage collector** that periodically reclaims objects when they are no longer used.)

Lifetime of Variables

An important difference between instance variables and local variables is **initialization**. You must initialize all local variables. If you don't initialize a local variable, the compiler complains when you try to use it. (Note that parameter variables are initialized when the method is called.)

Instance variables are initialized with a default value before a constructor is invoked. Instance variables that are numbers are initialized to 0. Object references are set to a special value called null. If an object reference is null, then it refers to no object at all. We will discuss the null value in greater detail in Section 4.2.5.

Instance variables
are initialized to a
default value, but
you must initialize
local variables.

SELF CHECK

25. What do local variables and parameter variables have in common? In which essential aspect do they differ?

26. Why was it necessary to introduce the local variable change in the giveChange method? That is, why didn't the method simply end with the statement

```
return payment - purchase;
```

Common Error 2.2

Forgetting to Initialize Object References in a Constructor

Just as it is a common error to forget to initialize a local variable, it is easy to forget about instance variables. Every constructor needs to ensure that all instance variables are set to appropriate values.

If you do not initialize an instance variable, the Java compiler will initialize it for you. Numbers are initialized with 0, but object references—such as string variables—are set to the null reference.

Of course, 0 is often a convenient default for numbers. However, null is hardly ever a convenient default for objects. Consider this "lazy" constructor for a modified version of the BankAccount class:

```
public class BankAccount
{
    private double balance;
    private String owner;
    . . .
    public BankAccount(double initialBalance)
    {
        balance = initialBalance;
```

```
      }
    }
```

Then `balance` is initialized, but the `owner` variable is set to a `null` reference. This can be a problem—it is illegal to call methods on the `null` reference.

To avoid this problem, it is a good idea to initialize every instance variable:

```
public BankAccount(double initialBalance)
{
   balance = initialBalance;
   owner = "None";
}
```

2.11 Object References

In Java, a variable whose type is a class does not actually hold an object. It merely holds the memory *location* of an object. The object itself is stored elsewhere—see Figure 16.

There is a reason for this behavior. Objects can be very large. It is more efficient to store only the memory location instead of the entire object.

> An object reference describes the location of an object.

We use the technical term **object reference** to denote the memory location of an object. When a variable contains the memory location of an object, we say that it *refers* to an object. For example, after the statement

```
Rectangle box = new Rectangle(5, 10, 20, 30);
```

the variable `box` refers to the `Rectangle` object that the `new` operator constructed. Technically speaking, the `new` operator returned a reference to the new object, and that reference is stored in the `box` variable.

> Multiple object variables can contain references to the same object.

It is very important that you remember that the `box` variable *does not contain* the object. It *refers* to the object. Two object variables can refer to the same object:

```
Rectangle box2 = box;
```

Now you can access the same `Rectangle` object both as `box` and as `box2`, as shown in Figure 17.

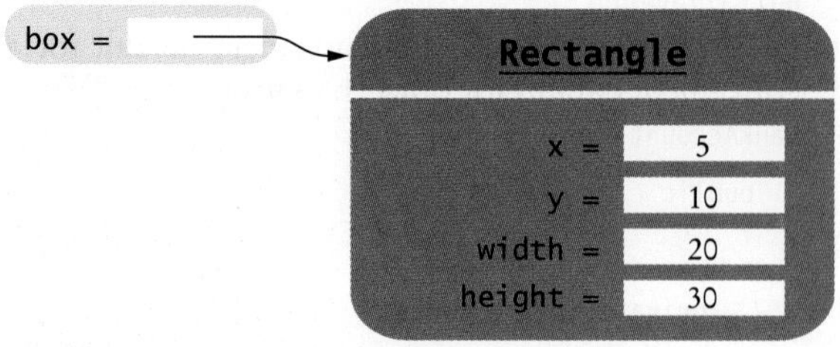

Figure 16
An Object Variable Containing an Object Reference

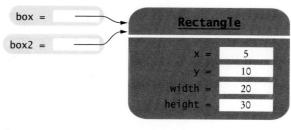

Figure 17
Two Object Variables Referring to the Same Object

However, number variables actually store numbers. When you declare

```
int luckyNumber = 13;
```

then the luckyNumber variable holds the number 13, not a reference to the number (see Figure 18). The reason is again efficiency. Because numbers require little storage, it is more efficient to store them directly in a variable.

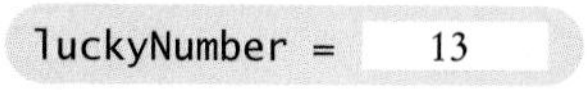

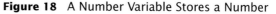

Figure 18 A Number Variable Stores a Number

Number variables store numbers. Object variables store references.

You can see the difference between number variables and object variables when you make a copy of a variable. When you copy a number, the original and the copy of the number are independent values. But when you copy an object reference, both the original and the copy are references to the same object.

Consider the following code, which copies a number and then changes the copy (see Figure 19):

```
int luckyNumber = 13;  ❶
int luckyNumber2 = luckyNumber;  ❷
luckyNumber2 = 12;  ❸
```

Now the variable luckyNumber contains the value 13, and luckyNumber2 contains 12.

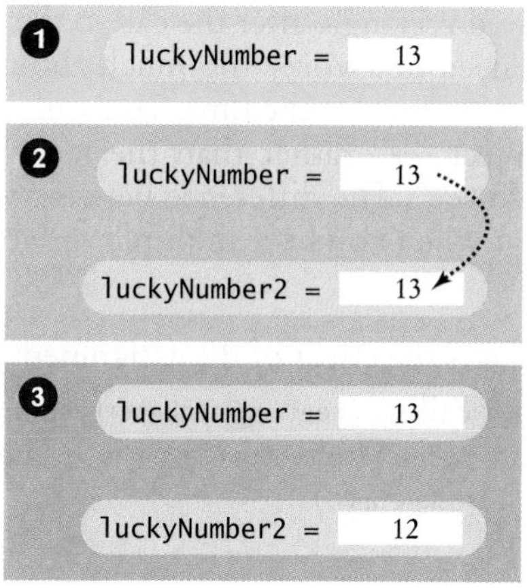

Figure 19
Copying Numbers

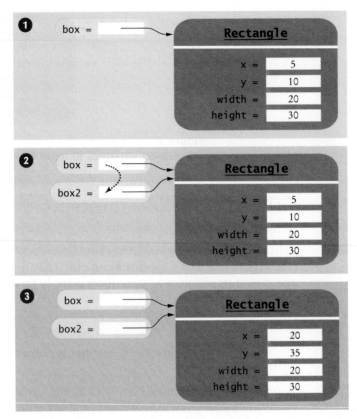

Figure 20 Copying Object References

Now consider the seemingly analogous code with Rectangle objects (see Figure 20).

ANIMATION
Object References

```
Rectangle box = new Rectangle(5, 10, 20, 30);  ❶
Rectangle box2 = box;  ❷
box2.translate(15, 25);  ❸
```

Since box and box2 refer to the same rectangle after step ❷, both variables refer to the moved rectangle after the call to the translate method.

You need not worry too much about the difference between objects and object references. Much of the time, you will have the correct intuition when you think of "the object box" rather than the technically more accurate "the object reference stored in box". The difference between objects and object references only becomes apparent when you have multiple variables that refer to the same object.

S E L F   C H E C K

27. What is the effect of the assignment String greeting2 = greeting?

28. After calling greeting2.toUpperCase(), what are the contents of greeting and greeting2? (The toUpperCase method is described in the API documentation of the String class.)

2.12 Implicit Parameters

In Section 2.1, you learned that a method has an **implicit parameter** (the object on which the method is invoked) in addition to the **explicit parameters**, which are enclosed in parentheses. In this section, we will examine implicit parameters in greater detail.

Have a look at a particular invocation of the deposit method:

```
momsSavings.deposit(500);
```

Here, the implicit parameter is momsSavings and the explicit parameter is 500.

Now look again at the code of the deposit method:

```
public void deposit(double amount)
{
   balance = balance + amount;
}
```

What does balance mean exactly? After all, our program may have multiple Bank-Account objects, and *each of them* has its own balance.

Of course, since we are depositing the money into momsSavings, balance must mean momsSavings.balance. In general, when you refer to an instance variable inside a method, it means the instance variable of the implicit parameter.

> Use of an instance variable name in a method denotes the instance variable of the implicit parameter.

If you need to, you can access the implicit parameter—the object on which the method is called—with the reserved word this. For example, in the preceding method invocation, this refers to the same object as momsSavings (see Figure 21).

The statement

```
balance = balance + amount;
```

actually means

> The this reference denotes the implicit parameter.

```
this.balance = this.balance + amount;
```

When you refer to an instance variable in a method, the compiler automatically applies it to the this reference. Some programmers actually prefer to manually insert the this reference before every instance variable because they find it makes the code clearer. Here is an example:

```
public BankAccount(double initialBalance)
{
   this.balance = initialBalance;
}
```

You may want to try it out and see if you like that style.

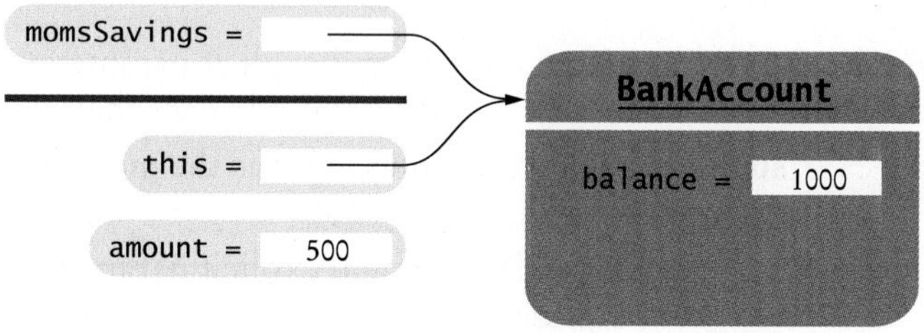

Figure 21 The Implicit Parameter of a Method Call

The `this` reference can also be used to distinguish between instance variables and local or parameter variables. Consider the constructor

```java
public BankAccount(double balance)
{
    this.balance = balance;
}
```

The expression `this.balance` clearly refers to the `balance` instance variable. However, the expression `balance` by itself seems ambiguous. It could denote either the parameter variable or the instance variable. In Java, local and parameter variables are considered first when looking up variable names. Therefore,

```java
this.balance = balance;
```

means: "Set the instance variable `balance` to the parameter variable `balance`".

There is another situation in which it is important to understand the implicit parameter. Consider the following modification to the `BankAccount` class. We add a method to apply the monthly account fee:

```java
public class BankAccount
{
    . . .
    public void monthlyFee()
    {
        withdraw(10); // Withdraw $10 from this account
    }
}
```

| A method call without an implicit parameter is applied to the same object. |

That means to withdraw from the *same* bank account object that is carrying out the `monthlyFee` operation. In other words, the implicit parameter of the `withdraw` method is the (invisible) implicit parameter of the `monthlyFee` method.

If you find it confusing to have an invisible parameter, you can use the `this` reference to make the method easier to read:

```java
public class BankAccount
{
    . . .
    public void monthlyFee()
    {
        this.withdraw(10); // Withdraw $10 from this account
    }
}
```

You have now seen how to use objects and implement classes, and you have learned some important technical details about variables and method parameters. The remainder of this chapter continues the optional graphics track. In the next chapter, you will learn more about the most fundamental data types of the Java language.

SELF CHECK

29. How many implicit and explicit parameters does the `withdraw` method of the BankAccount class have, and what are their names and types?

30. In the `deposit` method, what is the meaning of `this.amount`? Or, if the expression has no meaning, why not?

31. How many implicit and explicit parameters does the `main` method of the Bank-AccountTester class have, and what are they called?

Special Topic 2.2

Calling One Constructor from Another

Special Topic 2.2 describes how you can minimize common code in multiple constructors, by using the this reserved word for calling one constructor from another.

2.13 Graphical Applications and Frame Windows

This is the first of several optional sections that teach you how to write *graphical applications:* applications that display drawings inside a window. Graphical applications look more attractive than the console applications that show plain text in a console window.

> To show a frame, construct a JFrame object, set its size, and make it visible.

A graphical application shows information inside a **frame**: a window with a title bar, as shown in Figure 22. In this section, you will learn how to display a frame. In Section 2.16, you will learn how to create a drawing inside the frame.

To show a frame, carry out the following steps:

1. Construct an object of the JFrame class:

   ```
   JFrame frame = new JFrame();
   ```

2. Set the size of the frame:

   ```
   frame.setSize(300, 400);
   ```

   This frame will be 300 pixels wide and 400 pixels tall. If you omit this step the frame will be 0 by 0 pixels, and you won't be able to see it. (Pixels are the tiny dots from which digital images are composed.)

Figure 22
A Frame Window

3. If you'd like, set the title of the frame:

```
frame.setTitle("An Empty Frame");
```

If you omit this step, the title bar is simply left blank.

4. Set the "default close operation":

```
frame.setDefaultCloseOperation(JFrame.EXIT_ON_CLOSE);
```

When the user closes the frame, the program automatically exits. Don't omit this step. If you do, the program continues running even after the frame is closed.

5. Make the frame visible:

```
frame.setVisible(true);
```

The simple program below shows all of these steps. It produces the empty frame shown in Figure 22.

The JFrame class is a part of the javax.swing package. Swing is the nickname for the graphical user interface library in Java. The "x" in javax denotes the fact that Swing started out as a Java *extension* before it was added to the standard library.

We will go into much greater detail about Swing programming in Chapters 8, 9, and 17. For now, consider this program to be the essential plumbing that is required to show a frame.

ch02/emptyframe/EmptyFrameViewer.java

```java
 1  import javax.swing.JFrame;
 2
 3  public class EmptyFrameViewer
 4  {
 5     public static void main(String[] args)
 6     {
 7        JFrame frame = new JFrame();
 8
 9        frame.setSize(300, 400);
10        frame.setTitle("An Empty Frame");
11        frame.setDefaultCloseOperation(JFrame.EXIT_ON_CLOSE);
12
13        frame.setVisible(true);
14     }
15  }
```

S E L F   C H E C K

32. How do you display a square frame with a title bar that reads "Hello, World!"?

33. How can a program display two frames at once?

2.14 Drawing on a Component

In this section, you will learn how to make shapes appear inside a frame window. The first drawing will be exceedingly modest: just two rectangles (see Figure 23). You'll soon see how to produce more interesting drawings. The purpose of this example is to show you the basic outline of a program that creates a drawing. You cannot draw directly onto a frame. Whenever you want to show anything inside a frame, be it a button or a drawing, you have to construct a **component** object and

Figure 23
Drawing Rectangles

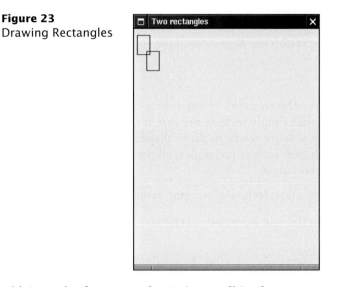

add it to the frame. In the Swing toolkit, the JComponent class represents a blank component.

Because we don't want to add a blank component, we have to modify the JComponent class and specify how the component should be painted. The solution is to declare a new class that extends the JComponent class. You will learn about the process of extending classes in Chapter 9. For now, simply use the following code as a template.

> In order to display a drawing in a frame, declare a class that extends the JComponent class.

```
public class RectangleComponent extends JComponent
{
    public void paintComponent(Graphics g)
    {
        Drawing instructions
    }
}
```

The extends reserved word indicates that our component class, RectangleComponent, can be used like a JComponent. However, the RectangleComponent class will be different from the plain JComponent class in one respect: Its paintComponent method will contain instructions to draw the rectangles.

> Place drawing instructions inside the paintComponent method. That method is called whenever the component needs to be repainted.

When the component is shown for the first time, the paintComponent method is called automatically. The method is also called when the window is resized, or when it is shown again after it was hidden.

The paintComponent method receives an object of type Graphics. The Graphics object stores the graphics state—the current color, font, and so on, that are used for drawing operations. However, the Graphics class is primitive. When programmers clamored for a more object-oriented approach for drawing graphics, the designers of Java created the Graphics2D class, which extends the Graphics class. Whenever the Swing toolkit calls the paintComponent method, it actually passes a parameter of type Graphics2D. Because we want to use the more sophisticated methods to draw two-dimensional graphics objects, we need to use the Graphics2D class. This is accomplished by using a **cast**:

> Use a cast to recover the Graphics2D object from the Graphics parameter of the paintComponent method.

```
public class RectangleComponent extends JComponent
{
    public void paintComponent(Graphics g)
```

```
    {
        // Recover Graphics2D
        Graphics2D g2 = (Graphics2D) g;
        . . .
    }
}
```

We cover the concepts of extending classes and of casting in Chapter 9. For now, you should simply include the cast at the top of your paintComponent methods.

Now you are ready to draw shapes. The draw method of the Graphics2D class can draw shapes, such as rectangles, ellipses, line segments, polygons, and arcs. Here we draw a rectangle:

```
public class RectangleComponent extends JComponent
{
    public void paintComponent(Graphics g)
    {
        . . .
        Rectangle box = new Rectangle(5, 10, 20, 30);
        g2.draw(box);
        . . .
    }
}
```

Following is the source code for the RectangleComponent class. Note that the paintComponent method of the RectangleComponent class draws two rectangles.

As you can see from the import statements, the Graphics and Graphics2D classes are part of the java.awt package.

ch02/rectangles/RectangleComponent.java

```
 1  import java.awt.Graphics;
 2  import java.awt.Graphics2D;
 3  import java.awt.Rectangle;
 4  import javax.swing.JComponent;
 5
 6  /*
 7      A component that draws two rectangles.
 8  */
 9  public class RectangleComponent extends JComponent
10  {
11      public void paintComponent(Graphics g)
12      {
13          // Recover Graphics2D
14          Graphics2D g2 = (Graphics2D) g;
15
16          // Construct a rectangle and draw it
17          Rectangle box = new Rectangle(5, 10, 20, 30);
18          g2.draw(box);
19
20          // Move rectangle 15 units to the right and 25 units down
21          box.translate(15, 25);
22
23          // Draw moved rectangle
24          g2.draw(box);
25      }
26  }
```

In order to see the drawing, one task remains. You need to display the frame into which you added a component object. Follow these steps:

1. Construct a frame as described in the preceding section.
2. Construct an object of your component class:

   ```
   RectangleComponent component = new RectangleComponent();
   ```
3. Add the component to the frame:

   ```
   frame.add(component);
   ```
4. Make the frame visible, as described in the preceding section.

The following listing shows the complete process.

ch02/rectangles/RectangleViewer.java

```
 1   import javax.swing.JFrame;
 2
 3   public class RectangleViewer
 4   {
 5      public static void main(String[] args)
 6      {
 7         JFrame frame = new JFrame();
 8
 9         frame.setSize(300, 400);
10         frame.setTitle("Two rectangles");
11         frame.setDefaultCloseOperation(JFrame.EXIT_ON_CLOSE);
12
13         RectangleComponent component = new RectangleComponent();
14         frame.add(component);
15
16         frame.setVisible(true);
17      }
18   }
```

Note that the rectangle drawing program consists of two classes:

- The RectangleComponent class, whose paintComponent method produces the drawing.
- The RectangleViewer class, whose main method constructs a frame and a RectangleComponent, adds the component to the frame, and makes the frame visible.

SELF CHECK   **34.** How do you modify the program to draw two squares?
  35. How do you modify the program to draw one rectangle and one square?
  36. What happens if you call g.draw(box) instead of g2.draw(box)?

Special Topic 2.3

Applets

Special Topic 2.3 shows how you can implement programs that show drawings as applets, programs that run inside a web browser.

2.15 Ellipses, Lines, Text, and Color

In Section 2.14 you learned how to write a program that draws rectangles. In this section you will learn how to draw other shapes: ellipses and lines. With these graphical elements, you can draw quite a few interesting pictures.

2.15.1 Ellipses and Circles

To draw an ellipse, you specify its bounding box (see Figure 24) in the same way that you would specify a rectangle, namely by the *x*- and *y*-coordinates of the top-left corner and the width and height of the box.

However, there is no simple `Ellipse` class that you can use. Instead, you must use one of the two classes `Ellipse2D.Float` and `Ellipse2D.Double`, depending on whether you want to store the ellipse coordinates as single- or double-precision floating-point values. Because the latter are more convenient to use in Java, we will always use the `Ellipse2D.Double` class. Here is how you construct an ellipse:

> The `Ellipse2D.Double` and `Line2D.Double` classes describe graphical shapes.

```
Ellipse2D.Double ellipse = new Ellipse2D.Double(x, y, width, height);
```

The class name `Ellipse2D.Double` looks different from the class names that you have encountered up to now. It consists of two class names `Ellipse2D` and `Double` separated by a period (.). This indicates that `Ellipse2D.Double` is a so-called **inner class** inside `Ellipse2D`. When constructing and using ellipses, you don't actually need to worry about the fact that `Ellipse2D.Double` is an inner class—just think of it as a class with a long name. However, in the `import` statement at the top of your program, you must be careful that you import only the outer class:

```
import java.awt.geom.Ellipse2D;
```

Drawing an ellipse is easy: Use exactly the same `draw` method of the `Graphics2D` class that you used for drawing rectangles.

```
g2.draw(ellipse);
```

To draw a circle, simply set the width and height to the same values:

```
Ellipse2D.Double circle = new Ellipse2D.Double(x, y, diameter, diameter);
g2.draw(circle);
```

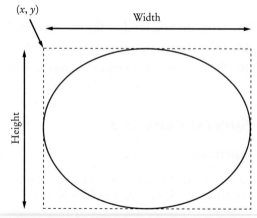

Figure 24 An Ellipse and Its Bounding Box

Notice that (x, y) is the top-left corner of the bounding box, not the center of the circle.

2.15.2 Lines

To draw a line, use an object of the `Line2D.Double` class. A line is constructed by specifying its two end points. You can do this in two ways. Simply give the *x*- and *y*-coordinates of both end points:

```
Line2D.Double segment = new Line2D.Double(x1, y1, x2, y2);
```

Or specify each end point as an object of the `Point2D.Double` class:

```
Point2D.Double from = new Point2D.Double(x1, y1);
Point2D.Double to = new Point2D.Double(x2, y2);

Line2D.Double segment = new Line2D.Double(from, to);
```

The second option is more object-oriented and is often more useful, particularly if the point objects can be reused elsewhere in the same drawing.

2.15.3 Drawing Text

The drawString method draws a string, starting at its basepoint.

You often want to put text inside a drawing, for example, to label some of the parts. Use the `drawString` method of the `Graphics2D` class to draw a string anywhere in a window. You must specify the string and the *x*- and *y*-coordinates of the basepoint of the first character in the string (see Figure 25). For example,

```
g2.drawString("Message", 50, 100);
```

Figure 25 Basepoint and Baseline

2.15.4 Colors

When you first start drawing, all shapes and strings are drawn with a black pen. To change the color, you need to supply an object of type `Color`. Java uses the RGB color model. That is, you specify a color by the amounts of the primary colors— red, green, and blue—that make up the color. The amounts are given as integers between 0 (primary color not present) and 255 (maximum amount present). For example,

```
Color magenta = new Color(255, 0, 255);
```

constructs a `Color` object with maximum red, no green, and maximum blue, yielding a bright purple color called magenta.

Table 2 Predefined Colors	
Color	RGB Value
Color.BLACK	0, 0, 0
Color.BLUE	0, 0, 255
Color.CYAN	0, 255, 255
Color.GRAY	128, 128, 128
Color.DARKGRAY	64, 64, 64
Color.LIGHTGRAY	192, 192, 192
Color.GREEN	0, 255, 0
Color.MAGENTA	255, 0, 255
Color.ORANGE	255, 200, 0
Color.PINK	255, 175, 175
Color.RED	255, 0, 0
Color.WHITE	255, 255, 255
Color.YELLOW	255, 255, 0

> When you set a new color in the graphics context, it is used for subsequent drawing operations.

For your convenience, a variety of colors have been declared in the Color class. Table 2 shows those colors and their RGB values. For example, Color.PINK has been declared to be the same color as new Color(255, 175, 175).

To draw a shape in a different color, first set the color of the Graphics2D object, then call the draw method:

```
g2.setColor(Color.RED);
g2.draw(circle); // Draws the shape in red
```

If you want to color the inside of the shape, use the fill method instead of the draw method. For example,

```
g2.fill(circle);
```

fills the inside of the circle with the current color.

The following program puts all these shapes to work, creating a simple drawing (see Figure 26).

Figure 26
An Alien Face

ch02/face/FaceComponent.java

```java
1  import java.awt.Color;
2  import java.awt.Graphics;
3  import java.awt.Graphics2D;
4  import java.awt.Rectangle;
5  import java.awt.geom.Ellipse2D;
6  import java.awt.geom.Line2D;
7  import javax.swing.JComponent;
8
9  /**
10     A component that draws an alien face.
11  */
12 public class FaceComponent extends JComponent
13 {
14    public void paintComponent(Graphics g)
15    {
16       // Recover Graphics2D
17       Graphics2D g2 = (Graphics2D) g;
18
19       // Draw the head
20       Ellipse2D.Double head = new Ellipse2D.Double(5, 10, 100, 150);
21       g2.draw(head);
22
23       // Draw the eyes
24       g2.setColor(Color.GREEN);
25       Rectangle eye = new Rectangle(25, 70, 15, 15);
26       g2.fill(eye);
27       eye.translate(50, 0);
28       g2.fill(eye);
29
30       // Draw the mouth
31       Line2D.Double mouth = new Line2D.Double(30, 110, 80, 110);
32       g2.setColor(Color.RED);
33       g2.draw(mouth);
34
35       // Draw the greeting
36       g2.setColor(Color.BLUE);
37       g2.drawString("Hello, World!", 5, 175);
38    }
39 }
```

ch02/face/FaceViewer.java

```java
1  import javax.swing.JFrame;
2
3  public class FaceViewer
4  {
5     public static void main(String[] args)
6     {
7        JFrame frame = new JFrame();
8        frame.setSize(150, 250);
9        frame.setTitle("An Alien Face");
10       frame.setDefaultCloseOperation(JFrame.EXIT_ON_CLOSE);
11
12       FaceComponent component = new FaceComponent();
13       frame.add(component);
14
15       frame.setVisible(true);
```

```
16    }
17  }
```

37. Give instructions to draw a circle with center (100, 100) and radius 25.

38. Give instructions to draw a letter "V" by drawing two line segments.

39. Give instructions to draw a string consisting of the letter "V".

40. What are the RGB color values of Color.BLUE?

41. How do you draw a yellow square on a red background?

2.16 Shape Classes

> It is a good idea to make a class for any part of a drawing that can occur more than once.

When you produce a drawing that is composed of complex parts, such as the one in Figure 27, it is a good idea to make a separate class for each part. Provide a draw method that draws the shape, and provide a constructor to set the position of the shape. For example, here is the outline of the Car class.

```java
public class Car
{
    public Car(int x, int y)
    {
        Remember position
        . . .
    }

    public void draw(Graphics2D g2)
    {
        Drawing instructions
        . . .
    }
}
```

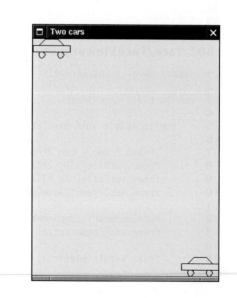

Figure 27
The Car Component
Draws Two Car Shapes

To figure out how to draw a complex shape, make a sketch on graph paper.

You will find the complete class declaration at the end of this section. The draw method contains a rather long sequence of instructions for drawing the body, roof, and tires. The coordinates of the car parts seem a bit arbitrary. To come up with suitable values, draw the image on graph paper and read off the coordinates (Figure 28).

The program that produces Figure 27 is composed of three classes.

- The Car class is responsible for drawing a single car. Two objects of this class are constructed, one for each car.
- The CarComponent class displays the drawing.
- The CarViewer class shows a frame that contains a CarComponent.

Let us look more closely at the CarComponent class. The paintComponent method draws two cars. We place one car in the top-left corner of the window, and the other car in the bottom right. To compute the bottom right position, we call the getWidth and getHeight methods of the JComponent class. These methods return the dimensions of the component. We subtract the dimensions of the car to determine the position of car2:

```
Car car1 = new Car(0, 0);
int x = getWidth() - 60;
int y = getHeight() - 30;
Car car2 = new Car(x, y);
```

Pay close attention to the call to getWidth inside the paintComponent method of CarComponent. The method call has no implicit parameter, which means that the method is applied to the same object that executes the paintComponent method. The component simply obtains *its own* width.

Run the program and resize the window. Note that the second car always ends up at the bottom-right corner of the window. Whenever the window is resized, the paintComponent method is called and the car position is recomputed, taking the current component dimensions into account.

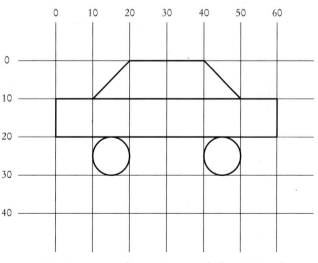

Figure 28   Using Graph Paper to Find Shape Coordinates

ch02/car/CarComponent.java

```java
1  import java.awt.Graphics;
2  import java.awt.Graphics2D;
3  import javax.swing.JComponent;
4
5  /**
6     This component draws two car shapes.
7  */
8  public class CarComponent extends JComponent
9  {
10    public void paintComponent(Graphics g)
11    {
12       Graphics2D g2 = (Graphics2D) g;
13
14       Car car1 = new Car(0, 0);
15
16       int x = getWidth() - 60;
17       int y = getHeight() - 30;
18
19       Car car2 = new Car(x, y);
20
21       car1.draw(g2);
22       car2.draw(g2);
23    }
24 }
```

ch02/car/Car.java

```java
1  import java.awt.Graphics2D;
2  import java.awt.Rectangle;
3  import java.awt.geom.Ellipse2D;
4  import java.awt.geom.Line2D;
5  import java.awt.geom.Point2D;
6
7  /**
8     A car shape that can be positioned anywhere on the screen.
9  */
10 public class Car
11 {
12    private int xLeft;
13    private int yTop;
14
15    /**
16       Constructs a car with a given top left corner.
17       @param x the x coordinate of the top left corner
18       @param y the y coordinate of the top left corner
19    */
20    public Car(int x, int y)
21    {
22       xLeft = x;
23       yTop = y;
24    }
25
26    /**
27       Draws the car.
28       @param g2 the graphics context
29    */
30    public void draw(Graphics2D g2)
31    {
```

```
32      Rectangle body
33          = new Rectangle(xLeft, yTop + 10, 60, 10);
34      Ellipse2D.Double frontTire
35          = new Ellipse2D.Double(xLeft + 10, yTop + 20, 10, 10);
36      Ellipse2D.Double rearTire
37          = new Ellipse2D.Double(xLeft + 40, yTop + 20, 10, 10);
38
39      // The bottom of the front windshield
40      Point2D.Double r1
41          = new Point2D.Double(xLeft + 10, yTop + 10);
42      // The front of the roof
43      Point2D.Double r2
44          = new Point2D.Double(xLeft + 20, yTop);
45      // The rear of the roof
46      Point2D.Double r3
47          = new Point2D.Double(xLeft + 40, yTop);
48      // The bottom of the rear windshield
49      Point2D.Double r4
50          = new Point2D.Double(xLeft + 50, yTop + 10);
51
52      Line2D.Double frontWindshield
53          = new Line2D.Double(r1, r2);
54      Line2D.Double roofTop
55          = new Line2D.Double(r2, r3);
56      Line2D.Double rearWindshield
57          = new Line2D.Double(r3, r4);
58
59      g2.draw(body);
60      g2.draw(frontTire);
61      g2.draw(rearTire);
62      g2.draw(frontWindshield);
63      g2.draw(roofTop);
64      g2.draw(rearWindshield);
65   }
66 }
```

ch02/car/CarViewer.java

```
1  import javax.swing.JFrame;
2
3  public class CarViewer
4  {
5     public static void main(String[] args)
6     {
7        JFrame frame = new JFrame();
8
9        frame.setSize(300, 400);
10       frame.setTitle("Two cars");
11       frame.setDefaultCloseOperation(JFrame.EXIT_ON_CLOSE);
12
13       CarComponent component = new CarComponent();
14       frame.add(component);
15
16       frame.setVisible(true);
17    }
18 }
```

42. Which class needs to be modified to have the two cars positioned next to each other?

43. Which class needs to be modified to have the car tires painted in black, and what modification do you need to make?

44. How do you make the cars twice as big?

How To 2.2

Drawing Graphical Shapes

You can write programs that display a wide variety of graphical shapes. These instructions give you a step-by-step procedure for decomposing a drawing into parts and implementing a program that produces the drawing. In this How To, we will create a program to draw a national flag.

Step 1   Determine the shapes that you need for the drawing.

You can use the following shapes:

• Squares and rectangles

• Circles and ellipses

• Lines

The outlines of these shapes can be drawn in any color, and you can fill the insides of these shapes with any color. You can also use text to label parts of your drawing.

Some national flag designs consist of three equally wide sections of different colors, side by side:

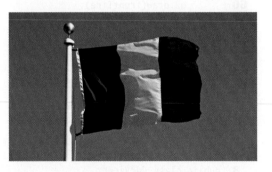

You could draw such a flag using three rectangles. But if the middle rectangle is white, as it is, for example, in the flag of Italy (green, white, red), it is easier and looks better to draw a line on the top and bottom of the middle portion:

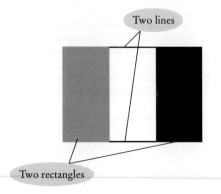

Two lines

Two rectangles

Step 2   Find the coordinates for the shapes.

You now need to find the exact positions for the geometric shapes.
- For rectangles, you need the *x*- and *y*-position of the top-left corner, the width, and the height.
- For ellipses, you need the top-left corner, width, and height of the bounding rectangle.
- For lines, you need the *x*- and *y*-positions of the starting point and the end point.
- For text, you need the *x*- and *y*-position of the basepoint.

A commonly-used size for a window is 300 by 300 pixels. You may not want the flag crammed all the way to the top, so perhaps the upper-left corner of the flag should be at point (100, 100).

Many flags, such as the flag of Italy, have a width : height ratio of 3 : 2. (You can often find exact proportions for a particular flag by doing a bit of Internet research on one of several Flags of the World sites.) For example, if you make the flag 90 pixels wide, then it should be 60 pixels tall. (Why not make it 100 pixels wide? Then the height would be $100 \cdot 2 / 3 \approx 67$, which seems more awkward.)

Now you can compute the coordinates of all the important points of the shape:

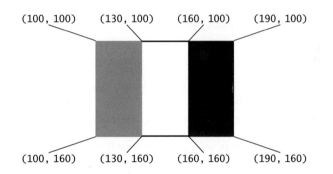

Step 3   Write Java statements to draw the shapes.

In our example, there are two rectangles and two lines:

```java
Rectangle leftRectangle
    = new Rectangle(100, 100, 30, 60);
Rectangle rightRectangle
    = new Rectangle(160, 100, 30, 60);
Line2D.Double topLine
    = new Line2D.Double(130, 100, 160, 100);
Line2D.Double bottomLine
    = new Line2D.Double(130, 160, 160, 160);
```

If you are more ambitious, then you can express the coordinates in terms of a few variables. In the case of the flag, we have arbitrarily chosen the top-left corner and the width. All other coordinates follow from those choices. If you decide to follow the ambitious approach, then the rectangles and lines are determined as follows:

```java
Rectangle leftRectangle = new Rectangle(
    xLeft, yTop,
    width / 3, width * 2 / 3);
Rectangle rightRectangle = new Rectangle(
    xLeft + 2 * width / 3, yTop,
    width / 3, width * 2 / 3);
Line2D.Double topLine = new Line2D.Double(
    xLeft + width / 3, yTop,
    xLeft + width * 2 / 3, yTop);
```

```
Line2D.Double bottomLine = new Line2D.Double(
        xLeft + width / 3, yTop + width * 2 / 3,
        xLeft + width * 2 / 3, yTop + width * 2 / 3);
```

Now you need to fill the rectangles and draw the lines. For the flag of Italy, the left rectangle is green and the right rectangle is red. Remember to switch colors before the filling and drawing operations:

```
g2.setColor(Color.GREEN);
g2.fill(leftRectangle);
g2.setColor(Color.RED);
g2.fill(rightRectangle);
g2.setColor(Color.BLACK);
g2.draw(topLine);
g2.draw(bottomLine);
```

Step 4 Combine the drawing statements with the component "plumbing".

```
public class MyComponent extends JComponent
{
    public void paintComponent(Graphics g)
    {
        Graphics2D g2 = (Graphics2D) g;
        Drawing instructions

        . . .
    }
}
```

In our example, you can simply add all shapes and drawing instructions inside the paint-Component method:

```
public class ItalianFlagComponent extends JComponent
{
    public void paintComponent(Graphics g)
    {
        Graphics2D g2 = (Graphics2D) g;
        Rectangle leftRectangle
            = new Rectangle(100, 100, 30, 60);
        . . .
        g2.setColor(Color.GREEN);
        g2.fill(leftRectangle);
        . . .
    }
}
```

That approach is acceptable for simple drawings, but it is not very object-oriented. After all, a flag is an object. It is better to make a separate class for the flag. Then you can draw different flags at different positions. Specify the sizes in a constructor and supply a draw method:

```
public class ItalianFlag
{
    private int xLeft;
    private int yTop;
    private int width;

    public ItalianFlag(int x, int y, int aWidth)
    {
        xLeft = x;
        yTop = y;
        width = aWidth;
    }
```

```
   public void draw(Graphics2D g2)
   {
      Rectangle leftRectangle = new Rectangle(
            xLeft, yTop,
            width / 3, width * 2 / 3);
      . . .
      g2.setColor(Color.GREEN);
      g2.fill(leftRectangle);
      . . .
   }
}
```

You still need a separate class for the component, but it is very simple:

```
public class ItalianFlagComponent extends JComponent
{
   public void paintComponent(Graphics g)
   {
      Graphics2D g2 = (Graphics2D) g;
      ItalianFlag flag = new ItalianFlag(100, 100, 90);
      flag.draw(g2);
   }
}
```

Step 5 Write the viewer class.

Provide a viewer class, with a main method in which you construct a frame, add your component, and make your frame visible. The viewer class is completely routine; you only need to change a single line to show a different component.

```
public class ItalianFlagViewer
{
   public static void main(String[] args)
   {
      JFrame frame = new JFrame();

      frame.setSize(300, 400);
      frame.setDefaultCloseOperation(JFrame.EXIT_ON_CLOSE);

      ItalianFlagComponent component = new ItalianFlagComponent();
      frame.add(component);

      frame.setVisible(true);
   }
}
```

Random Fact 2.1

Computer Graphics

Random Fact 2.1 discusses computer graphics, the technology of generating and manipulating visual images on a computer.

Summary of Learning Objectives

Declare objects, classes, and methods.

- Objects are entities in your program that you manipulate by calling methods.
- A method is a sequence of instructions that accesses the data of an object.
- A class declares the methods that you can apply to its objects.
- The return value of a method is a result that the method has computed for use by the code that called it.
- A parameter is an input to a method.
- The implicit parameter of a method call is the object on which the method is invoked. All other parameters are explicit parameters.

Write variable declarations in Java.

- You use variables to store values that you want to use at a later time. A variable has a type, a name, and a value.
- Identifiers for variables, methods, and classes are composed of letters, digits, and the underscore character.
- By convention, variable names should start with a lowercase letter.
- The int type denotes integers. The double type denotes floating-point numbers that can have fractional parts.
- Use the assignment operator (=) to change the value of a variable.
- Numbers and variables can be combined by arithmetic operators such as +, -, and *.
- All variables must be initialized before you access them.

Use constructors to construct new objects.

- Use the new operator, followed by a class name and parameters, to construct new objects.

Use the API documentation for finding method descriptions and packages.

- The API (Application Programming Interface) documentation lists the classes and methods of the Java library.
- Java classes are grouped into packages. Use the import statement to use classes that are declared in other packages.

Write programs that test behavior of methods.

- A test program verifies that methods behave as expected.
- Determining the expected result in advance is an important part of testing.

Understand instance variables and the methods that access them.

- An object's instance variables store the data required for executing its methods.
- Each object of a class has its own set of instance variables.
- Private instance variables can only be accessed by methods of the same class.
- Encapsulation is the process of hiding implementation details and providing methods for data access.
- Encapsulation allows a programmer to use a class without having to know its implementation.

Write method and constructor headers that describe the public interface of a class.

- The public interface of a class specifies what you can do with its objects.
- In order to implement a class, you first need to know which methods are required.
- An accessor method does not change the internal data of its implicit parameter. A mutator method changes the data.
- In a method header, you specify the return type, method name, and the types and names of the parameters.
- Constructors set the initial data for objects. The constructor name is always the same as the class name.
- Use documentation comments to describe the classes and public methods of your programs.

Provide the private implementation of a class.

- The private implementation of a class consists of instance variables, and the bodies of constructors and methods.

Write tests that verify that a class works correctly.

- A unit test verifies that a class works correctly in isolation, outside a complete program.

Compare lifetime and initialization of instance, local, and parameter variables.

- Local variables are declared in the body of a method.
- When a method exits, its local variables are removed.
- Instance variables are initialized to a default value, but you must initialize local variables.

Describe how multiple object references can refer to the same object.

- An object reference describes the location of an object.
- Multiple object variables can contain references to the same object.
- Number variables store numbers. Object variables store references.

Recognize the use of the implicit parameter in method declarations.

- Use of an instance variable name in a method denotes the instance variable of the implicit parameter.
- The this reference denotes the implicit parameter.
- A method call without an implicit parameter is applied to the same object.

Write programs that display drawings in frame windows.

- To show a frame, construct a JFrame object, set its size, and make it visible.
- In order to display a drawing in a frame, declare a class that extends the JComponent class.
- Place drawing instructions inside the paintComponent method. That method is called whenever the component needs to be repainted.
- Use a cast to recover the Graphics2D object from the Graphics parameter of the paintComponent method.

Use the Java API for drawing simple figures.

- The `Ellipse2D.Double` and `Line2D.Double` classes describe graphical shapes.
- The `drawString` method draws a string, starting at its basepoint.
- When you set a new color in the graphics context, it is used for subsequent drawing operations.

Implement classes that draw graphical shapes.

- It is a good idea to make a class for any part of a drawing that can occur more than once.
- To figure out how to draw a complex shape, make a sketch on graph paper.

Classes, Objects, and Methods Introduced in this Chapter

```
java.awt.Color                          java.lang.String
java.awt.Component                          length
    getHeight                               replace
    getWidth                                toLowerCase
    setSize                                 toUpperCase
    setVisible                          javax.swing.JComponent
java.awt.Frame                              paintComponent
    setTitle                            javax.swing.JFrame
java.awt.geom.Ellipse2D.Double              setDefaultCloseOperation
java.awt.geom.Line2D.Double
java.awt.geom.Point2D.Double
java.awt.Graphics
    setColor
java.awt.Graphics2D
    draw
    drawString
    fill
java.awt.Rectangle
    getX
    getY
    getHeight
    getWidth
    setSize
    translate
```

Media Resources

www.wiley.com/
go/global/
horstmann

- ***Worked Example*** How Many Days Have You Been Alive?
- ***Worked Example*** Working with Pictures
- ***Worked Example*** Making a Simple Menu
- Lab Exercises
- ➕ ***Animation*** Variable Initialization and Assignment
- ➕ ***Animation*** Lifetime of Variables
- ➕ ***Animation*** Object References
- ➕ Practice Quiz
- ➕ Code Completion Exercises

Review Exercises

★ **R2.1** Explain the difference between an object and an object reference.

★ **R2.2** Explain the difference between an object and an object variable.

★ **R2.3** Explain the difference between an object and a class.

★★ **R2.4** Give the Java code for constructing an *object* of class Rectangle, and for declaring an *object variable* of class Rectangle.

★★ **R2.5** Give Java code for objects with the following descriptions:
   a. A rectangle with center (100, 100) and all side lengths equal to 50
   b. A string with the contents "Hello, Dave"
   Create objects, not object variables.

★★ **R2.6** Repeat Exercise R2.5, but now declare object variables that are initialized with the required objects.

★★ **R2.7** Write a Java statement to initialize a variable square with a rectangle object whose top-left corner is (10, 20) and whose sides all have length 40. Then write a statement that replaces square with a rectangle of the same size and top left corner (20, 20).

★★ **R2.8** Write Java statements that initialize two variables square1 and square2 to refer to the same square with center (20, 20) and side length 40.

★★ **R2.9** Find the errors in the following statements:
   a. `Rectangle r = (5, 10, 15, 20);`
   b. `double width = Rectangle(5, 10, 15, 20).getWidth();`
   c. `Rectangle r;`
   `   r.translate(15, 25);`
   d. `r = new Rectangle();`
   `   r.translate("far, far away!");`

★ **R2.10** Name two accessor methods and two mutator methods of the Rectangle class.

★★ **R2.11** Look into the API documentation of the Rectangle class and locate the method

```
void add(int newx, int newy)
```

Read through the method documentation. Then determine the result of the following statements:

```
Rectangle box = new Rectangle(5, 10, 20, 30);
box.add(0, 0);
```

If you are not sure, write a small test program.

★ **R2.12** Consider a class Grade that represents a letter grade, such as A+ or B. Give two choices of instance variables that can be used for implementing the Grade class.

★★ **R2.13** Consider a class Time that represents a point in time, such as 9 A.M. or 3:30 P.M. Give two different sets of instance variables that can be used for implementing the Time class.

★ **R2.14** Suppose the implementor of the Time class of Exercise R2.13 changes from one implementation strategy to another, keeping the public interface unchanged. What do the programmers who use the Time class need to do?

★★ **R2.15** You can read the `value` instance variable of the `Counter` class with the `getValue` accessor method. Should there be a `setValue` mutator method to change it? Explain why or why not.

★★ **R2.16** Why does the `BankAccount` class not have a reset method?

★ **R2.17** What happens in our implementation of the `BankAccount` class when more money is withdrawn from the account than the current balance?

★★ **R2.18** What does the following method do? Give an example of how you can call the method.

```java
public class BankAccount
{
    public void mystery(BankAccount that, double amount)
    {
        this.balance = this.balance - amount;
        that.balance = that.balance + amount;
    }
    . . . // Other bank account methods
}
```

★★ **R2.19** Suppose you want to implement a class `TimeDepositAccount`. A time deposit account has a fixed interest rate that should be set in the constructor, together with the initial balance. Provide a method to get the current balance. Provide a method to add the earned interest to the account. This method should have no parameters because the interest rate is already known. It should have no return value because you already provided a method for obtaining the current balance. It is not possible to deposit additional funds into this account. Provide a `withdraw` method that removes the entire balance. Partial withdrawals are not allowed.

★ **R2.20** Consider the following implementation of a class `Square`:

```java
public class Square
{
    private int sideLength;
    private int area; // Not a good idea

    public Square(int length)
    {
        sideLength = length;
    }

    public int getArea()
    {
        area = sideLength * sideLength;
        return area;
    }
}
```

Why is it not a good idea to introduce an instance variable for the area? Rewrite the class so that area is a local variable.

★★ **R2.21** Consider the following implementation of a class `Square`:

```java
public class Square
{
```

```
        private int sideLength;
        private int area;

        public Square(int initialLength)
        {
            sideLength = initialLength;
            area = sideLength * sideLength;
        }

        public int getArea() { return area; }
        public void grow() { sideLength = 2 * sideLength(); }
    }
```

What error does this class have? How would you fix it?

★★T **R2.22** Provide a unit test class for the Counter class in Section 2.6.

★★T **R2.23** Read Exercise P2.17, but do not implement the Car class yet. Write a tester class that tests a scenario in which gas is added to the car, the car is driven, more gas is added, and the car is driven again. Print the actual and expected amount of gas in the tank.

★G **R2.24** What is the difference between a console application and a graphical application?

★★G **R2.25** Who calls the paintComponent method of a component? When does the call to the paintComponent method occur?

★★G **R2.26** Why does the parameter of the paintComponent method have type Graphics and not Graphics2D?

★★G **R2.27** Why are separate viewer and component classes used for graphical programs?

★★G **R2.28** Suppose you want to extend the car viewer program in Section 2.16 to show a sub-urban scene, with several cars and houses. Which classes do you need?

★★★G **R2.29** Explain why the calls to the getWidth and getHeight methods in the CarComponent class have no explicit parameter.

★★G **R2.30** How would you modify the Car class in order to show cars of varying sizes?

Programming Exercises

★T **P2.1** Write an AreaTester program that constructs a Rectangle object and then computes and prints its area. Use the getWidth and getHeight methods. Also print the expected answer.

★T **P2.2** Write a PerimeterTester program that constructs a Rectangle object and then computes and prints its perimeter. Use the getWidth and getHeight methods. Also print the expected answer.

★★ **P2.3** Write a program called FourRectanglePrinter that constructs a Rectangle object, prints its location by calling System.out.println(box), and then translates and prints it three more times, so that, if the rectangles were drawn, they would form one large rectangle:

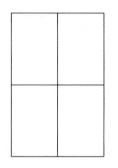

Your program will not produce a drawing. It will simply print the locations of the four rectangles.

★★ **P2.4** Write a `GrowSquarePrinter` program that constructs a `Rectangle` object `square` representing a square with top-left corner (100, 100) and side length 50, prints its location by calling `System.out.println(square)`, applies the `translate` and `grow` methods and calls `System.out.println(square)` again. The calls to `translate` and `grow` should modify the square so that it has twice the size and the same top-left corner as the original. If the squares were drawn, they would look like this:

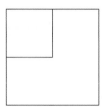

Your program will not produce a drawing. It will simply print the locations of square before and after calling the mutator methods.

Look up the description of the `grow` method in the API documentation.

★★★ **P2.5** The `intersection` method computes the *intersection* of two rectangles—that is, the rectangle that would be formed by two overlapping rectangles if they were drawn:

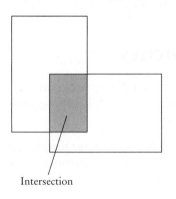

Intersection

You call this method as follows:

```
Rectangle r3 = r1.intersection(r2);
```

Write a program `IntersectionPrinter` that constructs two rectangle objects, prints them as described in Exercise P2.3, and then prints the rectangle object that describes the intersection. Then the program should print the result of the intersection method when the rectangles do not overlap. Add a comment to your program that explains how you can tell whether the resulting rectangle is empty.

★★★ **P2.6** In this exercise, you will explore a simple way of visualizing a Rectangle object. The setBounds method of the JFrame class moves a frame window to a given rectangle. Complete the following program to visually show the translate method of the Rectangle class:

```java
import java.awt.Rectangle;
import javax.swing.JFrame;
import javax.swing.JOptionPane;

public class TranslateDemo
{
    public static void main(String[] args)
    {
        // Construct a frame and show it
        JFrame frame = new JFrame();
        frame.setDefaultCloseOperation(JFrame.EXIT_ON_CLOSE);
        frame.setVisible(true);

        // Your work goes here:
        // Construct a rectangle and set the frame bounds

        JOptionPane.showMessageDialog(frame, "Click OK to continue");

        // Your work goes here:
        // Move the rectangle and set the frame bounds again
    }
}
```

★★ **P2.7** In the Java library, a color is specified by its red, green, and blue components between 0 and 255 (see Table 2 on page 74). Write a program BrighterDemo that constructs a Color object with red, green, and blue values of 50, 100, and 150. Then apply the brighter method and print the red, green, and blue values of the resulting color. (You won't actually see the color—see the next exercise on how to display the color.)

★★ **P2.8** Repeat Exercise P2.7, but place your code into the following class. Then the color will be displayed.

```java
import java.awt.Color;
import javax.swing.JFrame;

public class BrighterDemo
{
    public static void main(String[] args)
    {
        JFrame frame = new JFrame();
        frame.setSize(200, 200);
        Color myColor = ...;
        frame.getContentPane().setBackground(myColor);
        frame.setDefaultCloseOperation(JFrame.EXIT_ON_CLOSE);
        frame.setVisible(true);
    }
}
```

★★ **P2.9** Repeat Exercise P2.7, but apply the darker method twice to the object Color.RED. Call your class DarkerDemo.

★★ **P2.10** The Random class implements a *random number generator*, which produces sequences of numbers that appear to be random. To generate random integers, you construct an object of the Random class, and then apply the nextInt method. For example, the call generator.nextInt(6) gives you a random number between 0 and 5.

Write a program DieSimulator that uses the Random class to simulate the cast of a die, printing a random number between 1 and 6 every time that the program is run.

★T **P2.11** Write a BankAccountTester class whose main method constructs a bank account, deposits $1,000, withdraws $500, withdraws another $400, and then prints the remaining balance. Also print the expected result.

★ **P2.12** Add a method

```
public void addInterest(double rate)
```

to the BankAccount class that adds interest at the given rate. For example, after the statements

```
BankAccount momsSavings = new BankAccount(1000);
momsSavings.addInterest(10); // 10 percent interest
```

the balance in momsSavings is $1,100. Also supply a BankAccountTester class that prints the actual and expected balance.

★★ **P2.13** Write a class SavingsAccount that is similar to the BankAccount class, except that it has an added instance variable interest. Supply a constructor that sets both the initial balance and the interest rate. Supply a method addInterest (with no explicit parameter) that adds interest to the account. Write a SavingsAccountTester class that constructs a savings account with an initial balance of $1,000 and an interest rate of 10 percent. Then apply the addInterest method and print the resulting balance. Also compute the expected result by hand and print it.

★★★ **P2.14** Add a feature to the CashRegister class for computing sales tax. The tax rate should be supplied when constructing a CashRegister object. Add recordTaxablePurchase and getTotalTax methods. (Amounts added with recordPurchase are not taxable.) The giveChange method should correctly reflect the sales tax that is charged on taxable items.

★★ **P2.15** After closing time, the store manager would like to know how much business was transacted during the day. Modify the CashRegister class to enable this functionality. Supply methods getSalesTotal and getSalesCount to get the total amount of all sales and the number of sales. Supply a method reset that resets any counters and totals so that the next day's sales start from zero.

★★ **P2.16** Implement a class Employee. An employee has a name (a string) and a salary (a double). Provide a constructor with two parameters

```
public Employee(String employeeName, double currentSalary)
```

and methods

```
public String getName()
public double getSalary()
public void raiseSalary(double byPercent)
```

These methods return the name and salary, and raise the employee's salary by a certain percentage. Sample usage:

```
Employee harry = new Employee("Morgan, Harry", 50000);
harry.raiseSalary(10); // Harry gets a 10 percent raise
```

Supply an `EmployeeTester` class that tests all methods.

★★ **P2.17** Implement a class `Car` with the following properties. A car has a certain fuel efficiency (measured in miles/gallon or liters/km—pick one) and a certain amount of fuel in the gas tank. The efficiency is specified in the constructor, and the initial fuel level is 0. Supply a method `drive` that simulates driving the car for a certain distance, reducing the amount of gasoline in the fuel tank. Also supply methods `getGasInTank`, returning the current amount of gasoline in the fuel tank, and `addGas`, to add gasoline to the fuel tank. Sample usage:

```
Car myHybrid = new Car(50); // 50 miles per gallon
myHybrid.addGas(20); // Tank 20 gallons
myHybrid.drive(100); // Drive 100 miles
double gasLeft = myHybrid.getGasInTank(); // Get gas remaining in tank
```

You may assume that the `drive` method is never called with a distance that consumes more than the available gas. Supply a `CarTester` class that tests all methods.

★★ **P2.18** Implement a class `Student`. For the purpose of this exercise, a student has a name and a total quiz score. Supply an appropriate constructor and methods `getName()`, `addQuiz(int score)`, `getTotalScore()`, and `getAverageScore()`. To compute the latter, you also need to store the *number of quizzes* that the student took.

Supply a `StudentTester` class that tests all methods.

★ **P2.19** Implement a class `Product`. A product has a name and a price, for example `new Product("Toaster", 29.95)`. Supply methods `getName`, `getPrice`, and `reducePrice`. Supply a program `ProductPrinter` that makes two products, prints the name and price, reduces their prices by $5.00, and then prints the prices again.

★★ **P2.20** Write a class `Bug` that models a bug moving along a horizontal line. The bug moves either to the right or left. Initially, the bug moves to the right, but it can turn to change its direction. In each move, its position changes by one unit in the current direction. Provide a constructor

```
public Bug(int initialPosition)
```

and methods

```
public void turn()
public void move()
public int getPosition()
```

Sample usage:

```
Bug bugsy = new Bug(10);
bugsy.move(); // now the position is 11
bugsy.turn();
bugsy.move(); // now the position is 10
```

Your `BugTester` should construct a bug, make it move and turn a few times, and print the actual and expected position.

★★ **P2.21** Implement a class Moth that models a moth flying across a straight line. The moth has a position, the distance from a fixed origin. When the moth moves toward a point of light, its new position is halfway between its old position and the position of the light source. Supply a constructor

```
public Moth(double initialPosition)
```

and methods

```
public void moveToLight(double lightPosition)
public double getPosition()
```

Your MothTester should construct a moth, move it toward a couple of light sources, and check that the moth's position is as expected.

★★G **P2.22** Write a graphics program that draws your name in red, contained inside a blue rectangle. Provide a class NameViewer and a class NameComponent.

★★G **P2.23** Write a program to plot the following face.

Provide a class FaceViewer and a class FaceComponent.

★★G **P2.24** Draw a "bull's eye"—a set of concentric rings in alternating black and white colors. *Hint:* Fill a black circle, then fill a smaller white circle on top, and so on.

Your program should be composed of classes BullsEye, BullsEyeComponent, and BullsEyeViewer.

★★G **P2.25** Write a program that draws a picture of a house. It could be as simple as the accompanying figure, or if you like, make it more elaborate (3-D, skyscraper, marble columns in the entryway, whatever).

Implement a class House and supply a method draw(Graphics2D g2) that draws the house.

★★G **P2.26** Extend Exercise P2.25 by supplying a House constructor for specifying the position and size. Then populate your screen with a few houses of different sizes.

★★**G** **P2.27** Change the car viewer program in Section 2.16 to make the cars appear in different colors. Each `Car` object should store its own color. Supply modified `Car` and `Car-Component` classes.

★★**G** **P2.28** Change the `Car` class so that the size of a car can be specified in the constructor. Change the `CarComponent` class to make one of the cars appear twice the size of the original example.

★★**G** **P2.29** Write a program to plot the string "HELLO", using only lines and circles. Do not call `drawString`, and do not use `System.out`. Make classes `LetterH`, `LetterE`, `LetterL`, and `LetterO`.

★★**G** **P2.30** Write a program that displays the Olympic rings. Color the rings in the Olympic colors.

Provide a class `OlympicRingViewer` and a class `OlympicRingComponent`.

Programming Projects

Project 2.1 The `GregorianCalendar` class describes a point in time, as measured by the Gregorian calendar, the standard calendar that is commonly used throughout the world today. You construct a `GregorianCalendar` object from a year, month, and day of the month, like this:

```
GregorianCalendar cal = new GregorianCalendar(); // Today's date
GregorianCalendar eckertsBirthday = new GregorianCalendar(1919,
      Calendar.APRIL, 9);
```

Use the values `Calendar.JANUARY . . . Calendar.DECEMBER` to specify the month.

The `add` method can be used to add a number of days to a `GregorianCalendar` object:

```
cal.add(Calendar.DAY_OF_MONTH, 10); // Now cal is ten days from today
```

This is a mutator method—it changes the `cal` object.

The `get` method can be used to query a given `GregorianCalendar` object:

```
int dayOfMonth = cal.get(Calendar.DAY_OF_MONTH);
int month = cal.get(Calendar.MONTH);
int year = cal.get(Calendar.YEAR);
int weekday = cal.get(Calendar.DAY_OF_WEEK);
    // 1 is Sunday, 2 is Monday, . . . , 7 is Saturday
```

Your task is to write a program that prints the following information:

- The date and weekday that is 100 days from today
- The weekday of your birthday
- The date that is 10,000 days from your birthday

Use the birthday of a computer scientist if you don't want to reveal your own birthday.

Project 2.2 In this project, you will enhance the BankAccount class and see how abstraction and encapsulation enable evolutionary changes to software.

Begin with a simple enhancement: charging a fee for every deposit and withdrawal. Supply a mechanism for setting the fee and modify the deposit and withdraw methods so that the fee is levied. Test your resulting class and check that the fee is computed correctly.

Now make a more complex change. The bank will allow a fixed number of free transactions (deposits or withdrawals) every month, and charge for transactions exceeding the free allotment. The charge is not levied immediately but at the end of the month.

Supply a new method deductMonthlyCharge to the BankAccount class that deducts the monthly charge and resets the transaction count. (*Hint:* Use Math.max(actual transaction count, free transaction count) in your computation.)

Produce a test program that verifies that the fees are calculated correctly over several months.

Answers to Self-Check Questions

1. "Mississippi".length()
2. The implicit parameter is "Hello". There is no explicit parameter. The return value is 5.
3. It is not legal. The implicit parameter "Hello" has type String. The println method is not a method of the String class.
4. Only the first two are legal identifiers.
5. String myName = "John Q. Public";
6. greeting = "Hello, Nina!";
   Note that
   String greeting = "Hello, Nina!";
   is not the right answer—that statement declares a new variable.
7. new Rectangle(90, 90, 20, 20)
8. 0
9. toUpperCase
10. "Hello, Space !"—only the leading and trailing spaces are trimmed.
11. Add the statement import java.util.Random; at the top of your program.
12. x: 30, y: 25
13. Because the translate method doesn't modify the shape of the rectangle.
14. public void reset()
    {
        value = 0;
    }
15. You can only access them by invoking the methods of the Clock class.
16. harrysChecking.withdraw(harrysChecking.getBalance())
17. The withdraw method has return type void. It doesn't return a value. Use the getBalance method to obtain the balance after the withdrawal.

18. Add an `accountNumber` parameter to the constructors, and add a `getAccountNumber` method. There is no need for a `setAccountNumber` method—the account number never changes after construction.

19. An instance variable

```
private int accountNumber;
```

needs to be added to the class.

20. Because the `balance` instance variable is accessed from the `main` method of `BankRobber`. The compiler will report an error because `main` is not a method of the `BankAccount` class.

21.
```
public int getWidth()
{
    return width;
}
```

22. There is more than one correct answer. One possible implementation is as follows:
```
public void translate(int dx, int dy)
{
    int newx = x + dx;
    x = newx;
    int newy = y + dy;
    y = newy;
}
```

23. One `BankAccount` object, no `BankAccountTester` object. The purpose of the `BankAccount-Tester` class is merely to hold the `main` method.

24. In those environments, you can issue interactive commands to construct `BankAccount` objects, invoke methods, and display their return values.

25. Variables of both categories belong to methods—they come alive when the method is called, and they die when the method exits. They differ in their initialization. Parameter variables are initialized with the call values; local variables must be explicitly initialized.

26. After computing the change due, `payment` and `purchase` were set to zero. If the method returned `payment - purchase`, it would always return zero.

27. Now `greeting` and `greeting2` both refer to the same `String` object.

28. Both variables still refer to the same string, and the string has not been modified. Note that the `toUpperCase` method constructs a new string that contains uppercase characters, leaving the original string unchanged.

29. One implicit parameter, called `this`, of type `BankAccount`, and one explicit parameter, called `amount`, of type `double`.

30. It is not a legal expression. `this` is of type `BankAccount` and the `BankAccount` class has no instance variable named `amount`.

31. No implicit parameter—the `main` method is not invoked on any object—and one explicit parameter, called `args`.

32. Modify the `EmptyFrameViewer` program as follows:
```
frame.setSize(300, 300);
frame.setTitle("Hello, World!");
```

33. Construct two `JFrame` objects, set each of their sizes, and call `setVisible(true)` on each of them.

34. `Rectangle box = new Rectangle(5, 10, 20, 20);`

35. Replace the call to `box.translate(15, 25)` with

```
box = new Rectangle(20, 35, 20, 20);
```

36. The compiler complains that `g` doesn't have a `draw` method.

37. `g2.draw(new Ellipse2D.Double(75, 75, 50, 50));`

38.
```
Line2D.Double segment1 = new Line2D.Double(0, 0, 10, 30);
g2.draw(segment1);
Line2D.Double segment2 = new Line2D.Double(10, 30, 20, 0);
g2.draw(segment2);
```

39. `g2.drawString("V", 0, 30);`

40. `0, 0, 255`

41. First fill a big red square, then fill a small yellow square inside:

```
g2.setColor(Color.RED);
g2.fill(new Rectangle(0, 0, 200, 200));
g2.setColor(Color.YELLOW);
g2.fill(new Rectangle(50, 50, 100, 100));
```

42. `CarComponent`

43. In the `draw` method of the `Car` class, call

```
g2.fill(frontTire);
g2.fill(rearTire);
```

44. Double all measurements in the `draw` method of the `Car` class.

Chapter 3

Fundamental Data Types

CHAPTER GOALS

- To understand integer and floating-point numbers
- To recognize the limitations of the numeric types
- To become aware of causes for overflow and roundoff errors
- To understand the proper use of constants
- To write arithmetic expressions in Java
- To use the String type to manipulate character strings
- To learn how to read program input and produce formatted output

This chapter teaches how to manipulate numbers and character strings in Java. The goal of this chapter is to gain a firm understanding of these fundamental data types in Java.

You will learn about the properties and limitations of the number types in Java. You will see how to manipulate numbers and strings in your programs. Finally, we cover the important topic of input and output, which enables you to implement interactive programs.

CHAPTER CONTENTS

3.1 Number Types

Java has eight primitive types, including four integer types and two floating-point types.

In Java, every value is either a reference to an object, or it belongs to one of the eight **primitive types** shown in Table 1.

Six of the primitive types are number types; four of them for integers and two for floating-point numbers.

Each of the integer types has a different range—Special Topic 3.2 on page 102 explains why the range limits are related to powers of two. The largest number that can be represented in an int is denoted by Integer.MAX_VALUE. Its value is about 2.14 billion. Similarly, Integer.MIN_VALUE is the smallest integer, about –2.14 billion.

A numeric computation overflows if the result falls outside the range for the number type.

Generally, you will use the int type for integer quantities. However, occasionally, calculations involving integers can *overflow*. This happens if the result of a computation exceeds the range for the number type. For example:

```
int n = 1000000;
System.out.println(n * n);  // Prints –727379968, which is clearly wrong
```

The product n * n is 10^{12}, which is larger than the largest integer (about $2 \cdot 10^9$). The result is truncated to fit into an int, yielding a value that is completely wrong. Unfortunately, there is no warning when an integer overflow occurs.

If you run into this problem, the simplest remedy is to use the long type. Special Topic 3.1 on page 102 shows you how to use the BigInteger type in the unlikely event that even the long type overflows.

Overflow is not usually a problem for double-precision floating-point numbers. The double type has a range of about $\pm 10^{308}$ and about 15 significant digits. However, you want to avoid the float type—it has less than 7 significant digits. (Some programmers use float to save on memory if they need to store a huge set of numbers that do not require much precision.)

Type	Description	Size
int	The integer type, with range −2,147,483,648 (Integer.MIN_VALUE) . . . 2,147,483,647 (Integer.MAX_VALUE, about 2.14 billion)	4 bytes
byte	The type describing a single byte, with range −128 . . . 127	1 byte
short	The short integer type, with range −32,768 . . . 32,767	2 bytes
long	The long integer type, with range −9,223,372,036,854,775,808 . . . 9,223,372,036,854,775,807	8 bytes
double	The double-precision floating-point type, with a range of about $\pm 10^{308}$ and about 15 significant decimal digits	8 bytes
float	The single-precision floating-point type, with a range of about $\pm 10^{38}$ and about 7 significant decimal digits	4 bytes
char	The character type, representing code units in the Unicode encoding scheme (see Special Topic 3.5)	2 bytes
boolean	The type with the two truth values false and true (see Chapter 4)	1 bit

Table 1 Primitive Types

Rounding errors occur when an exact conversion between numbers is not possible.

Rounding errors are a more serious issue with floating-point values. Rounding errors can occur when you convert between binary and decimal numbers, or between integers and floating-point numbers. When a value cannot be converted exactly, it is rounded to the nearest match. Consider this example:

```
double f = 4.35;
System.out.println(100 * f); // Prints 434.99999999999994
```

This problem is caused because computers represent numbers in the binary number system. In the binary number system, there is no exact representation of the fraction 1/10, just as there is no exact representation of the fraction 1/3 = 0.33333 in the decimal number system. (See Special Topic 3.2 for more information.)

For this reason, the double type is not appropriate for financial calculations. In this book, we will continue to use double values for bank balances and other financial quantities so that we keep our programs as simple as possible. However, professional programs need to use the BigDecimal type for this purpose—see Special Topic 3.1.

In Java, it is legal to assign an integer value to a floating-point variable:

```
int dollars = 100;
double balance = dollars; // OK
```

But the opposite assignment is an error: You cannot assign a floating-point expression to an integer variable.

```
double balance = 13.75;
int dollars = balance; // Error
```

You will see in Section 3.3.5 how to convert a value of type double into an integer.

1. Which are the most commonly used number types in Java?
2. Suppose you want to write a program that works with population data from various countries. Which Java data type should you use?
3. Which of the following initializations are incorrect, and why?

   a. `int dollars = 100.0;`

   b. `double balance = 100;`

Special Topic 3.1

Big Numbers

Special Topic 3.1 shows you how to use the `BigInteger` and `BigDecimal` types to deal with really large numbers, or to better control roundoff errors.

Special Topic 3.2

Binary Numbers

Special Topic 3.2 discusses how numbers are encoded in the computer, using the binary number system.

Random Fact 3.1

The Pentium Floating-Point Bug

Random Fact 3.1 tells the story of the Intel Pentium floating-point bug, a flaw in a widely-sold processor that caused multiplication errors in rare circumstances. Discovered by a mathematics professor who used a computer in his research on prime numbers, it ultimately caused a recall of all affected chips.

3.2 Constants

In many programs, you need to use numerical **constants**—values that do not change and that have a special significance for a computation.

A typical example for the use of constants is a computation that involves coin values, such as the following:

```
payment = dollars + quarters * 0.25 + dimes * 0.1
       + nickels * 0.05 + pennies * 0.01;
```

Most of the code is self-documenting. However, the four numeric quantities, 0.25, 0.1, 0.05, and 0.01 are included in the arithmetic expression without any explanation. Of course, in this case, you know that the value of a nickel is five cents, which explains the 0.05, and so on. However, the next person who needs to maintain this code may live in another country and may not know that a nickel is worth five cents.

Syntax 3.1   Constant Declaration

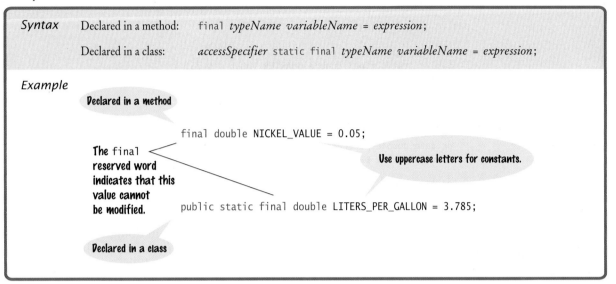

Syntax	Declared in a method:	`final` *typeName variableName* = *expression*;
	Declared in a class:	*accessSpecifier* `static final` *typeName variableName* = *expression*;

Example

Declared in a method

```
final double NICKEL_VALUE = 0.05;
```

The `final` reserved word indicates that this value cannot be modified.

Use uppercase letters for constants.

```
public static final double LITERS_PER_GALLON = 3.785;
```

Declared in a class

Thus, it is a good idea to use symbolic names for all values, even those that appear obvious. Here is a clearer version of the computation of the total:

```
double quarterValue = 0.25;
double dimeValue = 0.1;
double nickelValue = 0.05;
double pennyValue = 0.01;
payment = dollars + quarters * quarterValue + dimes * dimeValue
    + nickels * nickelValue + pennies * pennyValue;
```

There is another improvement we can make. There is a difference between the `nickels` and `nickelValue` variables. The `nickels` variable can truly vary over the life of the program, as we calculate different payments. But `nickelValue` is always 0.05.

In Java, constants are identified with the reserved word `final`. A variable tagged as `final` can never change after it has been set. If you try to change the value of a `final` variable, the compiler will report an error and your program will not compile.

> A final variable is a constant. Once its value has been set, it cannot be changed.

Many programmers use all-uppercase names for constants (`final` variables), such as `NICKEL_VALUE`. That way, it is easy to distinguish between variables (with mostly lowercase letters) and constants. We will follow this convention in this book. However, this rule is a matter of good style, not a requirement of the Java language. The compiler will not complain if you give a `final` variable a name with lowercase letters.

Here is an improved version of the code that computes the value of a payment.

> Use named constants to make your programs easier to read and maintain.

```
final double QUARTER_VALUE = 0.25;
final double DIME_VALUE = 0.1;
final double NICKEL_VALUE = 0.05;
final double PENNY_VALUE = 0.01;
payment = dollars + quarters * QUARTER_VALUE + dimes * DIME_VALUE
    + nickels * NICKEL_VALUE + pennies * PENNY_VALUE;
```

Frequently, constant values are needed in several methods. Then you should declare them together with the instance variables of a class and tag them as `static` and `final`. As before, `final` indicates that the value is a constant. The `static` reserved word means that the constant belongs to the class—this is explained in greater detail in Chapter 7.)

```java
public class CashRegister
{
    // Constants
    public static final double QUARTER_VALUE = 0.25;
    public static final double DIME_VALUE = 0.1;
    public static final double NICKEL_VALUE = 0.05;
    public static final double PENNY_VALUE = 0.01;

    // Instance variables
    private double purchase;
    private double payment;

    // Methods
    . . .
}
```

We declared the constants as `public`. There is no danger in doing this because constants cannot be modified. Methods of other classes can access a public constant by first specifying the name of the class in which it is declared, then a period, then the name of the constant, such as `CashRegister.NICKEL_VALUE`.

The `Math` class from the standard library declares a couple of useful constants:

```java
public class Math
{
    . . .
    public static final double E = 2.7182818284590452354;
    public static final double PI = 3.14159265358979323846;
}
```

You can refer to these constants as `Math.PI` and `Math.E` in any of your methods. For example,

```java
double circumference = Math.PI * diameter;
```

The sample program at the end of this section puts constants to work. The program shows a refinement of the `CashRegister` class of How To 2.1. The public interface of that class has been modified in order to solve a common business problem.

Busy cashiers sometimes make mistakes totaling up coin values. Our `CashRegister` class features a method whose inputs are the *coin counts.* For example, the call

```java
register.enterPayment(1, 2, 1, 1, 4);
```

enters a payment consisting of one dollar, two quarters, one dime, one nickel, and four pennies. The `enterPayment` method figures out the total value of the payment, $1.69. As you can see from the code listing, the method uses named constants for the coin values.

ch03/cashregister/CashRegister.java

```java
1  /**
2      A cash register totals up sales and computes change due.
3  */
4  public class CashRegister
5  {
6      public static final double QUARTER_VALUE = 0.25;
7      public static final double DIME_VALUE = 0.1;
```

```
 8      public static final double NICKEL_VALUE = 0.05;
 9      public static final double PENNY_VALUE = 0.01;
10
11      private double purchase;
12      private double payment;
13
14      /**
15          Constructs a cash register with no money in it.
16      */
17      public CashRegister()
18      {
19         purchase = 0;
20         payment = 0;
21      }
22
23      /**
24          Records the purchase price of an item.
25          @param amount the price of the purchased item
26      */
27      public void recordPurchase(double amount)
28      {
29         purchase = purchase + amount;
30      }
31
32      /**
33          Enters the payment received from the customer.
34          @param dollars the number of dollars in the payment
35          @param quarters the number of quarters in the payment
36          @param dimes the number of dimes in the payment
37          @param nickels the number of nickels in the payment
38          @param pennies the number of pennies in the payment
39      */
40      public void enterPayment(int dollars, int quarters,
41            int dimes, int nickels, int pennies)
42      {
43         payment = dollars + quarters * QUARTER_VALUE + dimes * DIME_VALUE
44            + nickels * NICKEL_VALUE + pennies * PENNY_VALUE;
45      }
46
47      /**
48          Computes the change due and resets the machine for the next customer.
49          @return the change due to the customer
50      */
51      public double giveChange()
52      {
53         double change = payment - purchase;
54         purchase = 0;
55         payment = 0;
56         return change;
57      }
58   }
```

ch03/cashregister/CashRegisterTester.java

```
1   /**
2       This class tests the CashRegister class.
3   */
4   public class CashRegisterTester
5   {
```

```
 6      public static void main(String[] args)
 7      {
 8         CashRegister register = new CashRegister();
 9
10         register.recordPurchase(0.75);
11         register.recordPurchase(1.50);
12         register.enterPayment(2, 0, 5, 0, 0);
13         System.out.print("Change: ");
14         System.out.println(register.giveChange());
15         System.out.println("Expected: 0.25");
16
17         register.recordPurchase(2.25);
18         register.recordPurchase(19.25);
19         register.enterPayment(23, 2, 0, 0, 0);
20         System.out.print("Change: ");
21         System.out.println(register.giveChange());
22         System.out.println("Expected: 2.0");
23      }
24   }
```

Program Run

```
Change: 0.25
Expected: 0.25
Change: 2.0
Expected: 2.0
```

SELF CHECK

4. What is the difference between the following two statements?

   ```
   final double CM_PER_INCH = 2.54;
   ```

   and

   ```
   public static final double CM_PER_INCH = 2.54;
   ```

5. What is wrong with the following statement sequence?

   ```
   double diameter = . . .;
   double circumference = 3.14 * diameter;
   ```

Quality Tip 3.1

Do Not Use Magic Numbers

A magic number is a numeric constant that appears in your code without explanation. For example, consider the following scary example that actually occurs in the Java library source:

```
h = 31 * h + ch;
```

Why 31? The number of days in January? One less than the number of bits in an integer? Actually, this code computes a "hash code" from a string—a number that is derived from the characters in such a way that different strings are likely to yield different hash codes. The value 31 turns out to scramble the character values nicely.

A better solution is to use a named constant:

```
final int HASH_MULTIPLIER = 31;
h = HASH_MULTIPLIER * h + ch;
```

You should never use magic numbers in your code. Any number that is not completely self-explanatory should be declared as a named constant. Even the most reasonable cosmic constant is going to change one day. You think there are 365 days in a year? Your customers on Mars are going to be pretty unhappy about your silly prejudice. Make a constant

```
final int DAYS_PER_YEAR = 365;
```

By the way, the device

```
final int THREE_HUNDRED_AND_SIXTY_FIVE = 365;
```

is counterproductive and frowned upon.

3.3 Arithmetic Operations and Mathematical Functions

In the following sections, you will learn how to carry out arithmetic calculations in Java.

3.3.1 Arithmetic Operators

Java supports the same four basic arithmetic operations as a calculator—addition, subtraction, multiplication, and division. As you have already seen, addition and subtraction use the familiar + and - operators, and the * operator denotes multiplication. Division is indicated with a /, not a fraction bar.
For example,

$$\frac{a + b}{2}$$

becomes

```
(a + b) / 2
```

Parentheses are used just as in algebra: to indicate in which order the subexpressions should be computed. For example, in the expression (a + b) / 2, the sum a + b is computed first, and then the sum is divided by 2. In contrast, in the expression

```
a + b / 2
```

only b is divided by 2, and then the sum of a and b / 2 is formed. Just as in regular algebraic notation, multiplication and division bind more strongly than addition and subtraction. For example, in the expression a + b / 2, the / is carried out first, even though the + operation occurs farther to the left.

3.3.2 Increment and Decrement

Incrementing a value by 1 is so common when writing programs that there is a special shorthand for it, namely

```
items++;
```

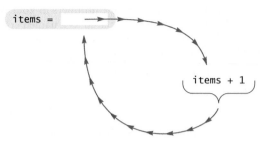

Figure 1 Incrementing a Variable

The ++ and --
operators increment
and decrement
a variable.

This statement adds 1 to items. It is easier to type and read than the equivalent assignment statement

```
items = items + 1;
```

As you might have guessed, there is also a decrement operator --. The statement

```
items--;
```

subtracts 1 from items.

3.3.3 Integer Division

If both arguments
of the / operator
are integers, the
result is an integer
and the remainder
is discarded.

Division works as you would expect, as long as at least one of the numbers involved is a floating-point number. That is,

```
7.0 / 4.0
7 / 4.0
7.0 / 4
```

all yield 1.75. However, if both numbers are integers, then the result of the division is always an integer, with the remainder discarded. That is,

```
7 / 4
```

evaluates to 1, because 7 divided by 4 is 1 with a remainder of 3 (which is discarded). Discarding the remainder is often useful, but it can also be a source of subtle programming errors—see Common Error 3.1 on page 112.

The % operator
computes the
remainder of
a division.

If you are interested only in the remainder of an integer division, use the % operator:

```
7 % 4
```

is 3, the remainder of the integer division of 7 by 4. The % symbol has no analog in algebra. It was chosen because it looks similar to /, and the remainder operation is related to division.

Here is a typical use for the integer / and % operations. Suppose you want to know how much change a cash register should give, using separate values for dollars and cents. You can compute the value as an integer, denominated in cents, and then compute the whole dollar amount and the remaining change:

```
final int PENNIES_PER_NICKEL = 5;
final int PENNIES_PER_DIME = 10;
final int PENNIES_PER_QUARTER = 25;
final int PENNIES_PER_DOLLAR = 100;
```

```
// Compute total value in pennies
int total = dollars * PENNIES_PER_DOLLAR + quarters * PENNIES_PER_QUARTER
        + nickels * PENNIES_PER_NICKEL + dimes * PENNIES_PER_DIME + pennies;

// Use integer division to convert to dollars, cents
int dollars = total / PENNIES_PER_DOLLAR;
int cents = total % PENNIES_PER_DOLLAR;
```

For example, if total is 243, then dollars is set to 2 and cents to 43.

3.3.4 Powers and Roots

The Math class contains methods sqrt and pow to compute square roots and powers.

To compute x^n, you write Math.pow(x, n). However, to compute x^2 it is significantly more efficient simply to compute x * x.

To take the square root of a number, you use the Math.sqrt method. For example, $\sqrt{x}$ is written as Math.sqrt(x).

In algebra, you use fractions, superscripts for exponents, and radical signs for roots to arrange expressions in a compact two-dimensional form. In Java, you have to write all expressions in a linear arrangement. For example, the subexpression

$$\frac{-b + \sqrt{b^2 - 4ac}}{2a}$$

of the quadratic formula becomes

```
(-b + Math.sqrt(b * b - 4 * a * c)) / (2 * a)
```

Figure 2 shows how to analyze such an expression. With complicated expressions like these, it is not always easy to keep the parentheses ( ) matched—see Common Error 3.2 on page 112.

Table 2 on page 110 shows additional methods of the Math class. Inputs and outputs are floating-point numbers.

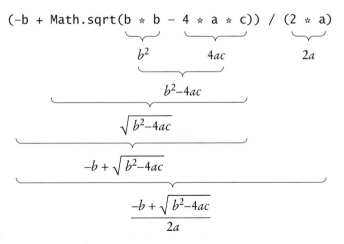

Figure 2 Analyzing an Expression

Table 2 Mathematical Methods	
Function	**Returns**
`Math.sqrt(x)`	Square root of x (≥ 0)
`Math.pow(x, y)`	x^y ($x > 0$, or $x = 0$ and $y > 0$, or $x < 0$ and y is an integer)
`Math.sin(x)`	Sine of x (x in radians)
`Math.cos(x)`	Cosine of x
`Math.tan(x)`	Tangent of x
`Math.asin(x)`	Arc sine ($\sin^{-1}x \in [-\pi/2, \pi/2]$, $x \in [-1, 1]$)
`Math.acos(x)`	Arc cosine ($\cos^{-1}x \in [0, \pi]$, $x \in [-1, 1]$)
`Math.atan(x)`	Arc tangent ($\tan^{-1}x \in [-\pi/2, \pi/2]$)
`Math.atan2(y, x)`	Arc tangent ($\tan^{-1}y/x \in [-\pi, \pi]$), x may be 0
`Math.toRadians(x)`	Convert x degrees to radians (i.e., returns $x \cdot \pi/180$)
`Math.toDegrees(x)`	Convert x radians to degrees (i.e., returns $x \cdot 180/\pi$)
`Math.exp(x)`	e^x
`Math.log(x)`	Natural log ($\ln(x)$, $x > 0$)
`Math.log10(x)`	Decimal log ($\log_{10}(x)$, $x > 0$)
`Math.round(x)`	Closest integer to x (as a `long`)
`Math.ceil(x)`	Smallest integer $\geq x$ (as a `double`)
`Math.floor(x)`	Largest integer $\leq x$ (as a `double`)
`Math.abs(x)`	Absolute value $|x|$
`Math.max(x, y)`	The larger of x and y
`Math.min(x, y)`	The smaller of x and y

3.3.5 Casting and Rounding

Occasionally, you have a value of type `double` that you need to convert to the type `int`. Use the *cast* operator `(int)` for this purpose. You write the cast operator before the expression that you want to convert:

```
double balance = total + tax;
int dollars = (int) balance;
```

You use a cast (*typeName*) to convert a value to a different type.

The cast `(int)` converts the floating-point value `balance` to an integer by discarding the fractional part. For example, if `balance` is 13.75, then `dollars` is set to 13.

The cast tells the compiler that you agree to *information loss,* in this case, to the loss of the fractional part. You can also cast to other types, such as `(float)` or `(byte)`.

Syntax 3.2 Cast

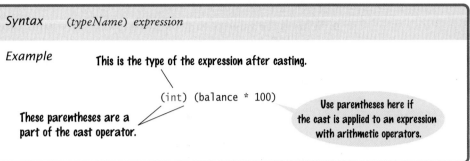

Use the Math.round method to round a floating-point number to the nearest integer.

If you want to round a floating-point number to the nearest whole number, use the Math.round method. This method returns a long integer, because large floating-point numbers cannot be stored in an int.

```
long rounded = Math.round(balance);
```

If balance is 13.75, then rounded is set to 14.

Table 3 Arithmetic Expressions

Mathematical Expression	Java Expression	Comments
$\dfrac{x+y}{2}$	(x + y) / 2	The parentheses are required; x + y / 2 computes $x + \dfrac{y}{2}$.
$\dfrac{xy}{2}$	x * y / 2	Parentheses are not required; operators with the same precedence are evaluated left to right.
$\left(1+\dfrac{r}{100}\right)^n$	Math.pow(1 + r / 100, n)	Complex formulas are "flattened" in Java.
$\sqrt{a^2+b^2}$	Math.sqrt(a * a + b * b)	a * a is simpler than Math.pow(a, 2).
$\dfrac{i+j+k}{3}$	(i + j + k) / 3.0	If i, j, and k are integers, using a denominator of 3.0 forces floating-point division.

SELF CHECK

6. What is the value of n after the following sequence of statements?
```
n--;
n++;
n--;
```

7. What is the value of 1729 / 100? Of 1729 % 100?

8. Why doesn't the following statement compute the average of s1, s2, and s3?

```
double average = s1 + s2 + s3 / 3; // Error
```

9. What is the value of `Math.sqrt(Math.pow(x, 2) + Math.pow(y, 2))` in mathematical notation?

10. When does the cast `(long)` x yield a different result from the call `Math.round(x)`?

11. How do you round the `double` value x to the nearest `int` value, assuming that you know that it is less than $2 \cdot 10^9$?

Common Error 3.1

Integer Division

It is unfortunate that Java uses the same symbol, namely /, for both integer and floating-point division. These are really quite different operations. It is a common error to use integer division by accident. Consider this program segment that computes the average of three integers.

```
int s1 = 5; // Score of test 1
int s2 = 6; // Score of test 2
int s3 = 3; // Score of test 3
double average = (s1 + s2 + s3) / 3;  // Error
System.out.print("Your average score is ");
System.out.println(average);
```

What could be wrong with that? Of course, the average of s1, s2, and s3 is

$$\frac{s_1 + s_2 + s_3}{3}$$

Here, however, the / does not mean division in the mathematical sense. It denotes integer division, because the values s1 + s2 + s3 and 3 are both integers. For example, if the scores add up to 14, the average is computed to be 4, the result of the integer division of 14 by 3. That integer 4 is then moved into the floating-point variable average. The remedy is to make either the numerator or denominator into a floating-point number:

```
double total = s1 + s2 + s3;
double average = total / 3;
```

or

```
double average = (s1 + s2 + s3) / 3.0;
```

Common Error 3.2

Unbalanced Parentheses

Consider the expression

```
1.5 * ((-(b - Math.sqrt(b * b - 4 * a * c)) / (2 * a))
```

What is wrong with it? Count the parentheses. There are five opening parentheses (and four closing parentheses). The parentheses are unbalanced. This kind of typing error is very common with complicated expressions. Now consider this expression.

```
1.5 * (Math.sqrt(b * b - 4 * a * c))) - ((b / (2 * a))
```

This expression has five opening parentheses (and five closing parentheses), but it is still not correct. In the middle of the expression,

```
1.5 * (Math.sqrt(b * b - 4 * a * c))) - ((b / (2 * a))
```

there are only two opening parentheses (but three closing parentheses), which is an error. In the middle of an expression, the count of opening parentheses must be greater than or equal to the count of closing parentheses, and at the end of the expression the two counts must be the same.

Here is a simple trick to make the counting easier without using pencil and paper. It is difficult for the brain to keep two counts simultaneously, so keep only one count when scanning the expression. Start with 1 at the first opening parenthesis; add 1 whenever you see an opening parenthesis; subtract 1 whenever you see a closing parenthesis. Say the numbers aloud as you scan the expression. If the count ever drops below zero, or if it is not zero at the end, the parentheses are unbalanced. For example, when scanning the previous expression, you would mutter

```
1.5 * (Math.sqrt(b * b - 4 * a * c) )   ) - ((b / (2 * a))
        1         2                 1 0 -1
```

and you would find the error.

Quality Tip 3.2

White Space

The compiler does not care whether you write your entire program onto a single line or place every symbol onto a separate line. The human reader, though, cares very much. You should use blank lines to group your code visually into sections. For example, you can signal to the reader that an output prompt and the corresponding input statement belong together by inserting a blank line before and after the group. You will find many examples in the source code listings in this book.

White space inside expressions is also important. It is easier to read

```
x1 = (-b + Math.sqrt(b * b - 4 * a * c)) / (2 * a);
```

than

```
x1=(-b+Math.sqrt(b*b-4*a*c))/(2*a);
```

Simply put spaces around all operators + - * / % =. However, don't put a space after a unary minus: a - used to negate a single quantity, as in -b. That way, it can be easily distinguished from a binary minus, as in a - b. Don't put spaces between a method name and the parentheses, but do put a space after every Java reserved word. That makes it easy to see that the sqrt in Math.sqrt(x) is a method name, whereas the if in if (x > 0) . . . is a reserved word.

Quality Tip 3.3

Factor Out Common Code

Suppose you want to find both solutions of the quadratic equation $ax^2 + bx + c = 0$. The quadratic formula tells us that the solutions are

$$x_{1,2} = \frac{-b \pm \sqrt{b^2 - 4ac}}{2a}$$

In Java, there is no analog to the ± operation, which indicates how to obtain two solutions simultaneously. Both solutions must be computed separately:

```
x1 = (-b + Math.sqrt(b * b - 4 * a * c)) / (2 * a);
x2 = (-b - Math.sqrt(b * b - 4 * a * c)) / (2 * a);
```

This approach has two problems. First, the computation of `Math.sqrt(b * b - 4 * a * c)` is carried out twice, which wastes time. Second, whenever the same code is replicated, the possibility of a typing error increases. The remedy is to factor out the common code:

```
double root = Math.sqrt(b * b - 4 * a * c);
x1 = (-b + root) / (2 * a);
x2 = (-b - root) / (2 * a);
```

You could go even further and factor out the computation of `2 * a`, but the gain from factoring out very simple computations is too small to warrant the effort.

Common Error 3.3

Roundoff Errors

Roundoff errors are a fact of life when calculating with floating-point numbers. You probably have encountered this phenomenon yourself with manual calculations. If you calculate 1/3 to two decimal places, you get 0.33. Multiplying again by 3, you obtain 0.99, not 1.00.

In the processor hardware, numbers are represented in the binary number system, not in decimal. You still get roundoff errors when binary digits are lost. They just may crop up at different places than you might expect. Here is an example:

```
double f = 4.35;
int n = (int) (100 * f);
System.out.println(n); // Prints 434!
```

Of course, one hundred times 4.35 is 435, but the program prints 434.

Computers represent numbers in the binary system (see Special Topic 3.2). In the binary system, there is no exact representation for 4.35, just as there is no exact representation for 1/3 in the decimal system. The representation used by the computer is just a little less than 4.35, so 100 times that value is just a little less than 435. When a floating-point value is converted to an integer, the entire fractional part is discarded, even if it is almost 1. As a result, the integer 434 is stored in n. Remedy: Use `Math.round` to convert floating-point numbers to integers. The round method returns the *closest* integer.

```
int n = (int) Math.round(100 * f);   // OK, n is 435
```

Special Topic 3.3

Combining Assignment and Arithmetic

Special Topic 3.3 covers special operators that combine assignment and arithmetic. For example, `balance += amount` is equivalent to `balance = balance + amount`.

3.4 Calling Static Methods

In the preceding section, you encountered the Math class, which contains a collection of helpful methods for carrying out mathematical computations. These methods have a special form: they are *static methods* that do not operate on an object.

That is, you don't call

```
double root = 100.sqrt(); // Error
```

In Java, numbers are not objects, so you can never invoke a method on a number. Instead, you pass a number as an explicit parameter to a method, enclosing the number in parentheses after the method name:

```
double root = Math.sqrt(100);
```

> A static method does not operate on an object.

This call makes it appear as if the sqrt method is applied to an object called Math. However, Math is a class, not an object. A method such as Math.sqrt that does not operate on any object is called a static method. (The term "static" is a historical holdover from the C and C++ programming languages. It has nothing to do with the usual meaning of the word.) In contrast, a method that is invoked on an object is class, is called an *instance method*:

```
harrysChecking.deposit(100); // deposit is an instance method
```

Static methods do not operate on objects, but they are still declared inside classes. When calling the method, you specify the class to which the sqrt method belongs—hence the call is Math.sqrt(100).

How can you tell that Math is a class and not an object? By convention, class names start with an uppercase letter (such as Math or BankAccount). Objects and methods start with a lowercase letter (such as harrysChecking and println). Therefore, harrysChecking.deposit(100) denotes a call of the deposit method on the harrysChecking object inside the System class. On the other hand, Math.sqrt(100) denotes a call to the sqrt method inside the Math class.

This use of upper- and lowercase letters is merely a convention, not a rule of the Java language. It is, however, a convention that the authors of the Java class libraries follow consistently. You should do the same in your programs so that you don't confuse your fellow programmers.

Syntax 3.3 Static Method Call

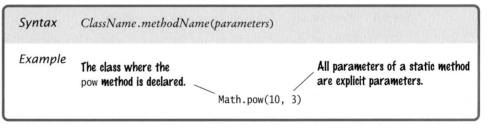

Syntax	*ClassName.methodName(parameters)*
Example	

The class where the pow **method is declared.**

All parameters of a static method are explicit parameters.

Math.pow(10, 3)

SELF CHECK

12. Why can't you call x.pow(y) to compute x^y?

13. Is the call System.out.println(4) a static method call?

How To 3.1

Carrying Out Computations

Many programming problems require that you use mathematical formulas to compute values. This How To shows how to turn a problem statement into a sequence of mathematical formulas and, ultimately, a class in the Java programming language.

Step 1 Understand the problem: What are the inputs? What are the desired outputs?

For example, suppose you are asked to simulate a postage stamp vending machine. A customer inserts money into the vending machine. Then the customer pushes a "First class stamps" button. The vending machine gives out as many first-class stamps as the customer paid for. (A first-class stamp cost 44 cents at the time this book was written.) Finally, the customer pushes a "Penny stamps" button. The machine gives the change in penny (1-cent) stamps.

In this problem, there is one input:

* The amount of money the customer inserts

There are two desired outputs:

* The number of first-class stamps the machine returns
* The number of penny stamps the machine returns

Step 2 Work out examples by hand.

This is a very important step. If you can't compute a couple of solutions by hand, it's unlikely that you'll be able to write a program that automates the computation.

Let's assume that a first-class stamp costs 44 cents and the customer inserts $1.00. That's enough for two stamps (88 cents) but not enough for three stamps ($1.32). Therefore, the machine returns two first-class stamps and 12 penny stamps.

Step 3 Design a class that carries out your computations.

How To 2.1 explains how to develop a class by finding methods and instance variables. In our case, the problem statement yields three methods:

* `public void insert(int dollars)`
* `public int giveFirstClassStamps()`
* `public int givePennyStamps()`

A bigger challenge is to determine instance variables that describe the state of the machine. In this example, an excellent choice is to keep a single variable, the customer balance. (See Exercise P3.12 for another choice.)

That balance is incremented by the `insert` method and decremented by the `giveFirstClassStamps` and `givePennyStamps` methods.

Step 4 Write pseudocode for implementing the methods.

Given an amount of money and the price of a first-class stamp, how can you compute how many first-class stamps can be purchased with the money? Clearly, the answer is related to the quotient

$$\frac{\text{amount of money}}{\text{price of first-class stamp}}$$

For example, suppose the customer paid $1.00. Use a pocket calculator to compute the quotient: $1.00/$0.44 ≈ 2.27.

How do you get "2 stamps" out of 2.27? It's the integer part. In Java, this is easy to compute if both arguments are integers. Therefore, let's switch our computation to pennies. Then we have

number of first-class stamps = 100 / 44 (integer division, without remainder)

What if the user inputs two dollars? Then the numerator becomes 200. What if the price of a stamp goes up? A more general equation is

input in pennies = 100 x dollars

number of first-class stamps = input in pennies / price of first-class stamps in pennies (without remainder)

How about the remaining balance after dispensing the first class stamps? Here is one way of computing it. When the customer gets the stamps, the remaining balance is the original balance, reduced by the value of the stamps purchased. In our example, the remainder is 12 cents — the difference between 100 and $2 \cdot 44$. Here is the general formula:

remaining balance = input in pennies – number of first-class stamps x price of first-class stamp in pennies

Step 5   Implement the class.

In Step 3, we decided that the state of the vending machine can be represented by the customer balance. In Step 4, it became clear that the balance is best represented in pennies.

It is a good idea to rewrite the pseudocode in terms of this newly found variable. We now use the instance variable balance for what was previously called **input in pennies**. When money is inserted, the balance increases:

```
balance = balance + 100 * dollars
```

When the first class stamps are requested, the balance decreases.

```
firstClassStamps = balance / FIRST_CLASS_STAMP_PRICE;
balance = balance - firstClassStamps * FIRST_CLASS_STAMP_PRICE;
```

What was previously called **remaining balance** is now simply the value of the balance instance variable.

Here is the implementation of the StampMachine class:

```java
public class StampMachine
{
    public static final double FIRST_CLASS_STAMP_PRICE = 44;
    private int balance;

    public StampMachine()
    {
        balance = 0;
    }

    public void insert(int dollars)
    {
        balance = balance + 100 * dollars;
    }

    public int giveFirstClassStamps()
    {
        int firstClassStamps = balance / FIRST_CLASS_STAMP_PRICE;
        balance = balance - firstClassStamps * FIRST_CLASS_STAMP_PRICE;
        return firstClassStamps;
    }

    public int givePennyStamps()
    {
        int pennyStamps = balance;
        balance = 0;
        return pennyStamps;
    }
}
```

Step 6 Test your class.

Run a test program (or use an integrated environment such as BlueJ) to verify that the values that your class computes are the same values that you computed by hand.

Here is a test program:

```java
public class StampMachineTester
{
   public static void main(String[] args)
   {
      StampMachine machine = new StampMachine();
      machine.insert(1);
      System.out.print("First class stamps: ");
      System.out.println(machine.giveFirstClassStamps());
      System.out.println("Expected: 2");
      System.out.print("Penny stamps: ");
      System.out.println(machine.givePennyStamps());
      System.out.println("Expected: 12");
   }
}
```

Program Run

```
First class stamps: 2
Expected: 2
Penny stamps: 12
Expected: 12
```

⊕ *Worked Example 3.1*

Computing the Volume and Surface Area of a Pyramid

This Worked Example shows how to design a class for computing the volume and surface area of a pyramid.

3.5 Strings

Many programs process text that consists of characters: letters, numbers, punctuation, spaces, and so on. A string is a sequence of characters, such as "Hello, World!". In the following sections, you will learn how to work with strings in Java.

3.5.1 The String Class

A string is a sequence of characters. Strings are objects of the String class.

In Java, strings are objects that belong to the class String. (You can tell that String is a class name because it starts with an uppercase letter. The primitive types int and double start with lowercase letters.)

You do not need to call a constructor to create a string object. You can obtain a string *literal* simply by enclosing a sequence of characters in double quotation marks. For example, the string literal "Harry" is an object of the String class.

The number of characters in a string is called the *length* of the string. As you have seen in Chapter 2, you can use the length method to obtain the length of a string. For example, `"Hello".length()` is 5, and the length of `"Hello, World!"` is 13. (The quotation marks are not part of the string and do not contribute to the length, but you must count spaces and punctuation marks.)

A string of length zero, containing no characters, is called the *empty string* and is written as `""`.

3.5.2 Concatenation

You can use the + operator to put strings together to form a longer string.

```
String name = "Dave";
String message = "Hello, " + name;
```

This process is called **concatenation**.

The + operator concatenates two strings, provided one of the expressions, either to the left or the right of a + operator, is a string. The other one is automatically forced to become a string as well, and both strings are concatenated.

For example, consider this code:

```
String a = "Agent";
int n = 7;
String bond = a + n;
```

Because a is a string, n is converted from the integer 7 to the string `"7"`. Then the two strings `"Agent"` and `"7"` are concatenated to form the string `"Agent7"`.

This concatenation is very useful to reduce the number of `System.out.print` instructions. For example, you can combine

```
System.out.print("The total is ");
System.out.println(total);
```

to the single call

```
System.out.println("The total is " + total);
```

The concatenation `"The total is "` + total computes a single string that consists of the string `"The total is "`, followed by the string equivalent of the number total.

3.5.3 Converting Strings to Numbers

Sometimes you have a string that contains a number, usually from user input. For example, suppose that the string variable input has the value `"19"`. To get the integer value 19, you use the static parseInt method of the Integer class.

```
int count = Integer.parseInt(input);
    // count is the integer 19
```

To convert a string containing floating-point digits to its floating-point value, use the static parseDouble method of the Double class. For example, suppose input is the string `"3.95"`.

```
double price = Double.parseDouble(input);
    // price is the floating-point number 3.95
```

However, if the string contains spaces or other characters that cannot occur inside numbers, an error occurs. For now, we will always assume that user input does not contain invalid characters.

Strings can be concatenated, that is, put end to end to yield a new longer string. String concatenation is denoted by the + operator.

Whenever one of the arguments of the + operator is a string, the other argument is converted to a string.

If a string contains the digits of a number, you use the Integer.parseInt or Double.parseDouble method to obtain the number value.

3.5.4 Substrings

Use the substring method to extract a part of a string.

The substring method computes substrings of a string. The call

```
s.substring(start, pastEnd)
```

returns a string that is made up of the characters in the string s, starting at position start, and containing all characters up to, but not including, the position pastEnd. Here is an example:

```
String greeting = "Hello, World!";
String sub = greeting.substring(0, 5); // sub is "Hello"
```

String positions are counted starting with 0.

The substring operation makes a string that consists of five characters taken from the string greeting. A curious aspect of the substring operation is the numbering of the starting and ending positions. The first string position is labeled 0, the second one 1, and so on. For example, Figure 3 shows the position numbers in the greeting string.

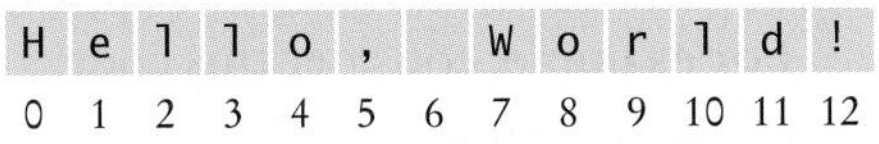
H e l l o ,   W o r l d !
0 1 2 3 4 5 6 7 8 9 10 11 12

Figure 3
String Positions

The position number of the last character (12 for the string "Hello, World!") is always 1 less than the length of the string.

Let us figure out how to extract the substring "World". Count characters starting at 0, not 1. You find that W, the eighth character, has position number 7. The first character that you don't want, !, is the character at position 12 (see Figure 4).

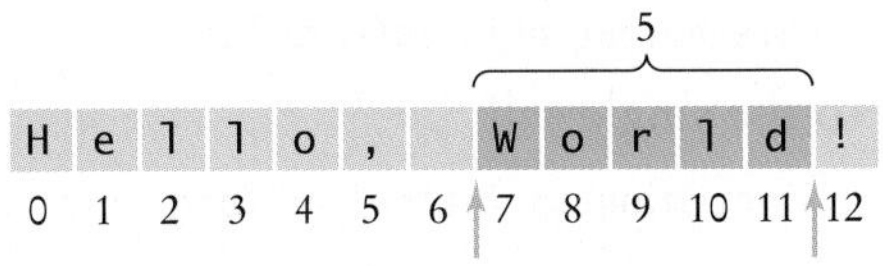
5
H e l l o ,   W o r l d !
0 1 2 3 4 5 6 7 8 9 10 11 12

Figure 4
Extracting a Substring

Therefore, the appropriate substring command is

```
String sub2 = greeting.substring(7, 12);
```

It is curious that you must specify the position of the first character that you do want and then the first character that you don't want. There is one advantage to this setup. You can easily compute the length of the substring: It is pastEnd - start. For example, the string "World" has length 12 – 7 = 5.

If you omit the second parameter of the substring method, then all characters from the starting position to the end of the string are copied. For example,

```
String tail = greeting.substring(7); // Copies all characters from position 7 on
```

sets tail to the string "World!".

If you supply an illegal string position (a negative number, or a value that is larger than the length of the string), then your program terminates with an error message.

In this section, we have made the assumption that each character in a string occupies a single position. Unfortunately, that assumption is not quite correct. If you process strings that contain characters from international alphabets or special symbols, some characters may occupy two positions—see Special Topic 3.5.

SELF CHECK

14. Assuming the String variable s holds the value "Agent", what is the effect of the assignment s = s + s.length()?

15. Assuming the String variable river holds the value "Mississippi", what is the value of river.substring(1, 2)? Of river.substring(2, river.length() - 3)?

Productivity Hint 3.1

Reading Exception Reports

You will often have programs that terminate and display an error message, such as

```
Exception in thread "main" java.lang.StringIndexOutOfBoundsException:
    String index out of range: -4
  at java.lang.String.substring(String.java:1444)
  at Homework1.main(Homework1.java:16)
```

An amazing number of students simply give up at that point, saying "it didn't work", or "my program died", without ever reading the error message. Admittedly, the format of the exception report is not very friendly. But it is actually easy to decipher it.

When you have a close look at the error message, you will notice two pieces of useful information:

1. The name of the exception, such as StringIndexOutOfBoundsException

2. The line number of the code that contained the statement that caused the exception, such as Homework1.java:16

The name of the exception is always in the first line of the report, and it ends in Exception. If you get a StringIndexOutOfBoundsException, then there was a problem with accessing an invalid position in a string. That is useful information.

The line number of the offending code is a little harder to determine. The exception report contains the entire stack trace—that is, the names of all methods that were pending when the exception hit. The first line of the stack trace is the method that actually generated the exception. The last line of the stack trace is a line in main. Often, the exception was thrown by a method that is in the standard library. Look for the first line in your code that appears in the exception report. For example, skip the line that refers to

```
java.lang.String.substring(String.java:1444)
```

The next line in our example mentions a line number in your code, Homework1.java. Once you have the line number in your code, open up the file, go to that line, and look at it! Also look at the name of the exception. In most cases, these two pieces of information will make it completely obvious what went wrong, and you can easily fix your error.

Special Topic 3.4

Escape Sequences

Special Topic 3.4 shows how you can embed special characters (such as quotation marks or line breaks) inside strings.

Special Topic 3.5

Strings and the char Type

Special Topic 3.5 discusses the char type. Strings are composed of code units of type char. For most programming tasks, you can simply use strings of length 1 instead of char values.

Random Fact 3.2

International Alphabets

Random Fact 3.2 explains how the Unicode character set provides an encoding for all characters that are in use around the world, including accented characters, scripts such as Hebrew or Thai, and tens of thousands of ideographs that are used in China, Japan, and Korea.

3.6 Reading Input

The Java programs that you have made so far have constructed objects, called methods, printed results, and exited. They were not interactive and took no user input. In this section, you will learn one method for reading user input.

Because output is sent to System.out, you might think that you use System.in for input. Unfortunately, it isn't quite that simple. When Java was first designed, not much attention was given to reading keyboard input. It was assumed that all programmers would produce graphical user interfaces with text fields and menus. System.in was given a minimal set of features—it can only read one byte at a time. Finally, in Java version 5, a Scanner class was added that lets you read keyboard input in a convenient manner.

> Use the Scanner class to read keyboard input in a console window.

To construct a Scanner object, simply pass the System.in object to the Scanner constructor:

```java
Scanner in = new Scanner(System.in);
```

You can create a scanner out of any input stream (such as a file), but you will usually want to use a scanner to read keyboard input from System.in.

Once you have a scanner, you use the nextInt or nextDouble methods to read the next integer or floating-point number.

```java
System.out.print("Enter quantity: ");
int quantity = in.nextInt();

System.out.print("Enter price: ");
double price = in.nextDouble();
```

When the nextInt or nextDouble method is called, the program waits until the user types a number and hits the Enter key. You should always provide instructions for the user (such as "Enter quantity:") before calling a Scanner method. Such an instruction is called a **prompt**.

If the user supplies an input that is not a number, then a run-time exception occurs. You will see in the next chapter how you can check whether the user supplied a numeric input.

The nextLine method returns the next line of input (until the user hits the Enter key) as a String object. The next method returns the next *word*, terminated by any **white space**, that is, a space, the end of a line, or a tab.

```java
System.out.print("Enter city: ");
String city = in.nextLine();

System.out.print("Enter state code: ");
String state = in.next();
```

Here, we use the nextLine method to read a city name that may consist of multiple words, such as San Francisco. We use the next method to read the state code (such as CA), which consists of a single word.

Here is an example of a program that takes user input. This program uses the CashRegister class and simulates a transaction in which a user purchases an item, pays for it, and receives change.

We call this class CashRegisterSimulator, not CashRegisterTester. We reserve the Tester suffix for classes whose sole purpose is to test other classes.

ch03/cashregister/CashRegisterSimulator.java

```java
1  import java.util.Scanner;
2
3  /**
4     This program simulates a transaction in which a user pays for an item
5     and receives change.
6  */
7  public class CashRegisterSimulator
8  {
9     public static void main(String[] args)
10    {
11       Scanner in = new Scanner(System.in);
12
13       CashRegister register = new CashRegister();
14
15       System.out.print("Enter price: ");
16       double price = in.nextDouble();
17       register.recordPurchase(price);
18
19       System.out.print("Enter dollars: ");
20       int dollars = in.nextInt();
21       System.out.print("Enter quarters: ");
22       int quarters = in.nextInt();
23       System.out.print("Enter dimes: ");
24       int dimes = in.nextInt();
25       System.out.print("Enter nickels: ");
26       int nickels = in.nextInt();
27       System.out.print("Enter pennies: ");
28       int pennies = in.nextInt();
29       register.enterPayment(dollars, quarters, dimes, nickels, pennies);
30
31       System.out.print("Your change: ");
32       System.out.println(register.giveChange());
33    }
34 }
```

Program Run

```
Enter price: 7.55
Enter dollars: 10
Enter quarters: 2
Enter dimes: 1
Enter nickels: 0
Enter pennies: 0
Your change: 3.05
```

SELF CHECK

16. Why can't input be read directly from System.in?
17. Suppose in is a Scanner object that reads from System.in, and your program calls
    ```
    String name = in.next();
    ```
    What is the value of name if the user enters John Q. Public?

 **Worked Example 3.2**

Extracting Initials

This Worked Example shows how to read names and print a set of corresponding initials.

Special Topic 3.6

Formatting Numbers

Special Topic 3.6 shows you how to control the number of digits after the decimal point when printing a number using the printf method. This is useful if you want to show a currency value rounded to two digits, such as 0.30 instead of 0.2975. Other options of the printf method are also discussed.

Special Topic 3.7

Using Dialog Boxes for Input and Output

Special Topic 3.7 shows how to use dialog boxes for reading input or displaying output.

Summary of Learning Objectives

Choose appropriate types for representing numeric data.

- Java has eight primitive types, including four integer types and two floating-point types.
- A numeric computation overflows if the result falls outside the range for the number type.
- Rounding errors occur when an exact conversion between numbers is not possible.

Write code that uses constants to document the purpose of numeric values.

- A final variable is a constant. Once its value has been set, it cannot be changed.
- Use named constants to make your programs easier to read and maintain.

Write arithmetic expressions in Java.

- The ++ and -- operators increment and decrement a variable.
- If both arguments of the / operator are integers, the result is an integer and the remainder is discarded.
- The % operator computes the remainder of a division.
- The Math class contains methods sqrt and pow to compute square roots and powers.
- You use a cast (*typeName*) to convert a value to a different type.
- Use the Math.round method to round a floating-point number to the nearest integer.

Distinguish between static methods and instance methods.

- A static method does not operate on an object.

Process strings in Java programs.

- A string is a sequence of characters. Strings are objects of the String class.
- Strings can be concatenated, that is, put end to end to yield a new longer string. String concatenation is denoted by the + operator.
- Whenever one of the arguments of the + operator is a string, the other argument is converted to a string.
- If a string contains the digits of a number, you use the Integer.parseInt or Double.parseDouble method to obtain the number value.
- Use the substring method to extract a part of a string.
- String positions are counted starting with 0.

Write programs that read user input.

- Use the Scanner class to read keyboard input in a console window.

Classes, Objects, and Methods Introduced in this Chapter

java.io.PrintStream	ceil	java.lang.String	java.util.Scanner
printf	cos	format	next
java.lang.Double	exp	substring	nextDouble
parseDouble	floor	java.lang.System	nextInt
java.lang.Integer	log	in	nextLine
MAX_VALUE	log10	java.math.BigDecimal	javax.swing.JOptionPane
MIN_VALUE	max	add	showInputDialog
parseInt	min	multiply	showMessageDialog
toString	pow	subtract	
java.lang.Math	round	java.math.BigInteger	
E	sin	add	
PI	sqrt	multiply	
abs	tan	subtract	
acos	toDegrees		
asin	toRadians		
atan			
atan2			

Media Resources

www.wiley.com/
go/global/
horstmann

- ***Worked Example*** Computing the Volume and Surface Area of a Pyramid
- ***Worked Example*** Extracting Initials
- Lab Exercises
- ➕ Practice Quiz
- ➕ Code Completion Exercises

Review Exercises

★★ **R3.1** Write the following mathematical expressions in Java.

$$s = s_0 + v_0 t + \frac{1}{2} g t^2$$

$$G = 4\pi^2 \frac{a^3}{P^2 (m_1 + m_2)}$$

$$FV = PV \cdot \left(1 + \frac{INT}{100}\right)^{YRS}$$

$$c = \sqrt{a^2 + b^2 - 2ab \cos \gamma}$$

★★ **R3.2** Write the following Java expressions in mathematical notation.

a. `dm = m * (Math.sqrt(1 + v / c) / (Math.sqrt(1 - v / c) - 1));`
b. `volume = Math.PI * r * r * h;`
c. `volume = 4 * Math.PI * Math.pow(r, 3) / 3;`
d. `p = Math.atan2(z, Math.sqrt(x * x + y * y));`

★★★ **R3.3** What is wrong with this version of the quadratic formula?

```
x1 = (-b - Math.sqrt(b * b - 4 * a * c)) / 2 * a;
x2 = (-b + Math.sqrt(b * b - 4 * a * c)) / 2 * a;
```

★★ **R3.4** Give an example of integer overflow. Would the same example work correctly if you used floating-point?

★★ **R3.5** Give an example of a floating-point roundoff error. Would the same example work correctly if you used integers and switched to a sufficiently small unit, such as cents instead of dollars, so that the values don't have a fractional part?

★★ **R3.6** Consider the following code:

```
CashRegister register = new CashRegister();
register.recordPurchase(19.93);
register.enterPayment(20, 0, 0, 0, 0);
System.out.print("Change: ");
System.out.println(register.giveChange());
```

The code segment prints the total as 0.07000000000000028. Explain why. Give a recommendation to improve the code so that users will not be confused.

★ **R3.7** Let n be an integer and x a floating-point number. Explain the difference between

```
n = (int) x;
```

and

```
n = (int) Math.round(x);
```

★★★ **R3.8** Let n be an integer and x a floating-point number. Explain the difference between

```
n = (int) (x + 0.5);
```

and

```
n = (int) Math.round(x);
```

For what values of x do they give the same result? For what values of x do they give different results?

★ **R3.9** Consider the vending machine implementation in How To 3.1 on page 116. What happens if the givePennyStamps method is invoked before the giveFirstClassStamps method?

★ **R3.10** Explain the differences between 2, 2.0, '2', "2", and "2.0".

★ **R3.11** Explain what each of the following two program segments computes:

```
int x = 2;
int y = x + x;
```

and

```
String s = "2";
String t = s + s;
```

★★ **R3.12** True or false? (x is an int and s is a String)

    a. Integer.parseInt("" + x) is the same as x

    b. "" + Integer.parseInt(s) is the same as s

    c. s.substring(0, s.length()) is the same as s

★★ **R3.13** How do you get the first character of a string? The last character? How do you remove the first character? The last character?

★★★ **R3.14** How do you get the last digit of an integer? The first digit? That is, if n is 23456, how do you find out that the first digit is 2 and the last digit is 6? Do not convert the number to a string. *Hint:* %, Math.log.

★★ **R3.15** This chapter contains several recommendations regarding variables and constants that make programs easier to read and maintain. Summarize these recommendations.

★★★ **R3.16** What is a final variable? Can you declare a final variable without supplying its value? (Try it out.)

★ **R3.17** What are the values of the following expressions? In each line, assume that

```
double x = 2.5;
double y = -1.5;
int m = 18;
int n = 4;
```

    a. x + n * y - (x + n) * y

    b. m / n + m % n

c. 5 * x - n / 5
d. Math.sqrt(Math.sqrt(n))
e. (int) Math.round(x)
f. (int) Math.round(x) + (int) Math.round(y)
g. 1 - (1 - (1 - (1 - (1 - n))))

★ **R3.18** What are the values of the following expressions? In each line, assume that

```
int n = 4;
String s = "Hello";
String t = "World";
```

a. s + t
b. s + n
c. n + t
d. s.substring(1, n)
e. s.length() + t.length()

Programming Exercises

★ **P3.1** Enhance the CashRegister class by adding separate methods enterDollars, enterQuarters, enterDimes, enterNickels, and enterPennies.

Use this tester class:

```java
public class CashRegisterTester
{
   public static void main (String[] args)
   {
      CashRegister register = new CashRegister();
      register.recordPurchase(20.37);
      register.enterDollars(20);
      register.enterQuarters(2);
      System.out.println("Change: " + register.giveChange());
      System.out.println("Expected: 0.13");
   }
}
```

★ **P3.2** Enhance the CashRegister class so that it keeps track of the total number of items in a sale. Count all recorded purchases and supply a method

```
int getItemCount()
```

that returns the number of items of the current purchase. Remember to reset the count at the end of the purchase.

★★ **P3.3** Implement a class IceCreamCone with methods getSurfaceArea() and getVolume(). In the constructor, supply the height and radius of the cone. Be careful when looking up the formula for the surface area—you should only include the outside area along the side of the cone since the cone has an opening on the top to hold the ice cream.

★★ **P3.4** Write a program that prompts the user for two numbers, then prints
- The sum
- The difference
- The product

- The average
- The distance (absolute value of the difference)
- The maximum (the larger of the two)
- The minimum (the smaller of the two)

To do so, implement a class

```java
public class Pair
{
    /**
        Constructs a pair.
        @param aFirst the first value of the pair
        @param aSecond the second value of the pair
    */
    public Pair(double aFirst, double aSecond) { . . . }

    /**
        Computes the sum of the values of this pair.
        @return the sum of the first and second values
    */
    public double getSum() { . . . }
    . . .
}
```

Then implement a class `PairTester` that constructs a `Pair` object, invokes its methods, and prints the results.

★ **P3.5** Declare a class `DataSet` that computes the sum and average of a sequence of integers. Supply methods

- `void addValue(int x)`
- `int getSum()`
- `double getAverage()`

Hint: Keep track of the sum and the count of the values.

Then write a test program `DataSetTester` that calls `addValue` four times and prints the expected and actual results.

★★ **P3.6** Write a class `DataSet` that computes the largest and smallest values in a sequence of numbers. Supply methods

- `void addValue(int x)`
- `int getLargest()`
- `int getSmallest()`

Keep track of the smallest and largest values that you've seen so far. Then use the `Math.min` and `Math.max` methods to update them in the `addValue` method. What should you use as initial values? *Hint:* `Integer.MIN_VALUE`, `Integer.MAX_VALUE`.

Write a test program `DataSetTester` that calls `addValue` four times and prints the expected and actual results.

★ **P3.7** Write a program that prompts the user for a measurement in meters and then converts it into miles, feet, and inches. Use a class

```java
public class Converter
{
```

```
/**
    Constructs a converter that can convert between two units.
    @param aConversionFactor the factor by which to multiply
    to convert to the target unit
*/
public Converter(double aConversionFactor) { . . . }

/**
    Converts from a source measurement to a target measurement.
    @param fromMeasurement the measurement
    @return the input value converted to the target unit
*/
public double convertTo(double fromMeasurement) { . . . }

/**
    Converts from a target measurement to a source measurement.
    @param toMeasurement the target measurement
    @return the value whose conversion is the target measurement
*/
public double convertFrom(double toMeasurement) { . . . }
}
```

In your `ConverterTester` class, construct and test the following `Converter` object:

```
final double MILE_TO_KM = 1.609;
Converter milesToMeters = new Converter(1000 * MILE_TO_KM);
```

★ **P3.8** Write a class `Square` whose constructor receives the length of the sides. Then supply methods to compute

- The area and perimeter of the square
- The length of the diagonal (use the Pythagorean theorem)

★★ **P3.9** Implement a class `SodaCan` whose constructor receives the height and diameter of the soda can. Supply methods `getVolume` and `getSurfaceArea`. Supply a `SodaCanTester` class that tests your class.

★★★ **P3.10** Implement a class `Balloon` that models a spherical balloon that is being filled with air. The constructor constructs an empty balloon. Supply these methods:

- `void addAir(double amount)` adds the given amount of air
- `double getVolume()` gets the current volume
- `double getSurfaceArea()` gets the current surface area
- `double getRadius()` gets the current radius

Supply a `BalloonTester` class that constructs a balloon, adds 100 cm^3 of air, tests the three accessor methods, adds another 100 cm^3 of air, and tests the accessor methods again.

★★ **P3.11** *Giving change.* Enhance the `CashRegister` class so that it directs a cashier how to give change. The cash register computes the amount to be returned to the customer, in pennies. Add the following methods to the `CashRegister` class:

- `int giveDollars()`
- `int giveQuarters()`
- `int giveDimes()`
- `int giveNickels()`
- `int givePennies()`

Each method computes the number of dollar bills or coins to return to the customer, and reduces the change due by the returned amount. You may assume that the methods are called in this order. Here is a test class:

```java
public class CashRegisterTester
{
    public static void main(String[] args)
    {
        CashRegister register = new CashRegister();

        register.recordPurchase(8.37);
        register.enterPayment(10, 0, 0, 0, 0);
        System.out.println("Dollars: " + register.giveDollars());
        System.out.println("Expected: 1");
        System.out.println("Quarters: " + register.giveQuarters());
        System.out.println("Expected: 2");
        System.out.println("Dimes: " + register.giveDimes());
        System.out.println("Expected: 1");
        System.out.println("Nickels: " + register.giveNickels());
        System.out.println("Expected: 0");
        System.out.println("Pennies: " + register.givePennies());
        System.out.println("Expected: 3");
    }
}
```

★★ **P3.12** In How To 3.1 on page 116, we represented the state of the vending machine by storing the balance in pennies. This is ingenious, but it is perhaps not the most obvious solution. Another possibility is to store the number of dollars that the customer inserted and the change that remains after giving out the first class stamps. Reimplement the vending machine in this way. Of course, the public interface should remain unchanged.

★★★ **P3.13** Write a program that reads in an integer and breaks it into a sequence of individual digits in reverse order. For example, the input 16384 is displayed as

```
4
8
3
6
1
```

You may assume that the input has no more than five digits and is not negative.

Declare a class DigitExtractor:

```java
public class DigitExtractor
{
    /**
        Constructs a digit extractor that gets the digits
        of an integer in reverse order.
        @param anInteger the integer to break up into digits
    */
    public DigitExtractor(int anInteger) { . . . }

    /**
        Returns the next digit to be extracted.
        @return the next digit
    */
    public int nextDigit() { . . . }
}
```

In your main class DigitPrinter, call System.out.println(myExtractor.nextDigit()) five times.

★★ **P3.14** Implement a class QuadraticEquation whose constructor receives the coefficients a, b, c of the quadratic equation $ax^2 + bx + c = 0$. Supply methods getSolution1 and getSolution2 that get the solutions, using the quadratic formula. Write a test class QuadraticEquationTester that constructs a QuadraticEquation object, and prints the two solutions.

★★★ **P3.15** Write a program that reads two times in military format (0900, 1730) and prints the number of hours and minutes between the two times. Here is a sample run. User input is in color.

```
Please enter the first time: 0900
Please enter the second time: 1730
8 hours 30 minutes
```

Extra credit if you can deal with the case where the first time is later than the second:

```
Please enter the first time: 1730
Please enter the second time: 0900
15 hours 30 minutes
```

Implement a class TimeInterval whose constructor takes two military times. The class should have two methods getHours and getMinutes.

★ **P3.16** *Writing large letters.* A large letter H can be produced like this:

```
*   *
*   *
*****
*   *
*   *
```

Use the class

```
public class LetterH
{
   public String toString()
   {
      return "*   *\n*   *\n*****\n*   *\n*   *\n";
   }
}
```

Declare similar classes for the letters E, L, and O. Then write the message

```
H
E
L
L
O
```

in large letters.

★★ **P3.17** Write a class ChristmasTree whose toString method yields a string depicting a Christmas tree:

Remember to use escape sequences.

★★ **P3.18** Your job is to transform numbers 1, 2, 3, . . ., 12 into the corresponding month names `January`, `February`, `March`, . . ., `December`. Implement a class `Month` whose constructor parameter is the month number and whose `getName` method returns the month name. *Hint:* Make a very long string `"January February March . . . "`, in which you add spaces such that each month name has the same length. Then use `substring` to extract the month you want.

★★ **P3.19** Write a class to compute the date of Easter Sunday. Easter Sunday is the first Sunday after the first full moon of spring. Use this algorithm, invented by the mathematician Carl Friedrich Gauss in 1800:

1. Let y be the year (such as 1800 or 2001).
2. Divide y by 19 and call the remainder a. Ignore the quotient.
3. Divide y by 100 to get a quotient b and a remainder c.
4. Divide b by 4 to get a quotient d and a remainder e.
5. Divide 8 * b + 13 by 25 to get a quotient g. Ignore the remainder.
6. Divide 19 * a + b - d - g + 15 by 30 to get a remainder h. Ignore the quotient.
7. Divide c by 4 to get a quotient j and a remainder k.
8. Divide a + 11 * h by 319 to get a quotient m. Ignore the remainder.
9. Divide 2 * e + 2 * j - k - h + m + 32 by 7 to get a remainder r. Ignore the quotient.
10. Divide h - m + r + 90 by 25 to get a quotient n. Ignore the remainder.
11. Divide h - m + r + n + 19 by 32 to get a remainder p. Ignore the quotient.

Then Easter falls on day p of month n. For example, if y is 2001:

```
a = 6           g = 6           r = 6
b = 20          h = 18          n = 4
c = 1           j = 0, k = 1    p = 15
d = 5, e = 0    m = 0
```

Therefore, in 2001, Easter Sunday fell on April 15. Write a class `Easter` with methods `getEasterSundayMonth` and `getEasterSundayDay`.

Programming Projects

Project 3.1 In this project, you will perform calculations with triangles. A triangle is defined by the *x*- and *y*-coordinates of its three corner points.

Your job is to compute the following properties of a given triangle:

- the lengths of all sides
- the angles at all corners
- the perimeter
- the area

Of course, you should implement a `Triangle` class with appropriate methods. Supply a program that prompts a user for the corner point coordinates and produces a nicely formatted table of the triangle properties.

This is a good team project for two students. Both students should agree on the `Triangle` interface. One student implements the `Triangle` class, the other simultaneously implements the user interaction and formatting.

Project 3.2 The CashRegister class has an unfortunate limitation: It is closely tied to the coin system in the United States and Canada. Research the system used in most of Europe. Your goal is to produce a cash register that works with euros and cents. Rather than designing another limited CashRegister implementation for the European market, you should design a separate Coin class and a cash register that can work with coins of all types.

Answers to Self-Check Questions

1. int and double.
2. The world's most populous country, China, has about 1.2×10^9 inhabitants. Therefore, individual population counts could be held in an int. However, the world population is over 6×10^9. If you compute totals or averages of multiple countries, you can exceed the largest int value. Therefore, double is a better choice. You could also use long, but there is no benefit because the exact population of a country is not known at any point in time.
3. The first initialization is incorrect. The right hand side is a value of type double, and it is not legal to initialize an int variable with a double value. The second initialization is correct—an int value can always be converted to a double.
4. The first declaration is used inside a method, the second inside a class.
5. (1) You should use a named constant, not the "magic number" 3.14.
   (2) 3.14 is not an accurate representation of π.
6. One less than it was before.
7. 17 and 29.
8. Only s3 is divided by 3. To get the correct result, use parentheses. Moreover, if s1, s2, and s3 are integers, you must divide by 3.0 to avoid integer division:

   `(s1 + s2 + s3) / 3.0`

9. $\sqrt{x^2 + y^2}$
10. When the fractional part of x is ≥ 0.5.
11. By using a cast: `(int) Math.round(x)`.
12. x is a number, not an object, and you cannot invoke methods on numbers.
13. No—the println method is called on the object System.out.
14. s is set to the string "Agent5".
15. The strings "i" and "ssissi".
16. The class only has a method to read a single byte. It would be very tedious to form characters, strings, and numbers from those bytes.
17. The value is "John". The next method reads the next *word*.

Chapter 4

Decisions

CHAPTER GOALS

- To be able to implement decisions using if statements
- To effectively group statements into blocks
- To learn how to compare integers, floating-point numbers, strings, and objects
- To correctly order decisions in multiple branches and nested branches
- To program conditions using Boolean operators and variables
- T To be able to design tests that cover all parts of a program

The programs we have seen so far were able to do fast computations and render graphs, but they were very inflexible. Except for variations in the input, they worked the same way with every program run. One of the essential features of nontrivial computer programs is their ability to make decisions and to carry out different actions, depending on the nature of the inputs. The goal of this chapter is to learn how to program simple and complex decisions.

CHAPTER CONTENTS

4.1 The if Statement

Computer programs often need to make *decisions*, taking different actions depending on a condition.

Consider the bank account class of Chapter 2. The withdraw method allows you to withdraw as much money from the account as you like. The balance just moves ever further into the negatives. That is not a realistic model for a bank account. Let's implement the withdraw method so that you cannot withdraw more money than you have in the account. That is, the withdraw method must make a *decision:* whether to allow the withdrawal or not.

The if statement is used to implement a decision. The if statement has two parts: a condition and a body. If the *condition* is true, the *body* of the statement is executed. The body of the if statement consists of a statement:

> The if statement lets a program carry out different actions depending on a condition.

```
if (amount <= balance)   // Condition
   balance = balance - amount;   // Body
```

The assignment statement is carried out only when the amount to be withdrawn is less than or equal to the balance (see Figure 1).

Let us make the withdraw method of the BankAccount class even more realistic. Most banks not only disallow withdrawals that exceed your account balance; they also charge you a penalty for every attempt to do so.

This operation can't be programmed simply by providing two complementary if statements, such as:

```
if (amount <= balance)
   balance = balance - amount;
if (amount > balance) // Use if/else instead
   balance = balance - OVERDRAFT_PENALTY;
```

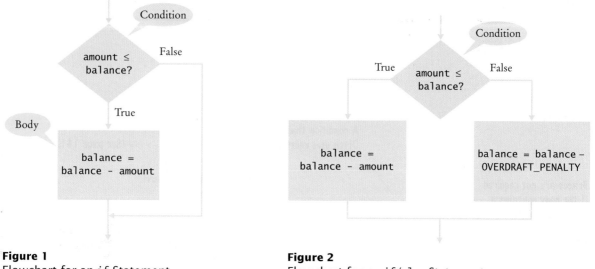

Figure 1
Flowchart for an if Statement

Figure 2
Flowchart for an if/else Statement

There are two problems with this approach. First, if you need to modify the condition amount <= balance for some reason, you must remember to update the condition amount > balance as well. If you do not, the logic of the program will no longer be correct. More importantly, if you modify the value of balance in the body of the first if statement (as in this example), then the second condition uses the new value.

To implement a choice between alternatives, use the if/else statement:

```
if (amount <= balance)
    balance = balance - amount;
else
    balance = balance - OVERDRAFT_PENALTY;
```

Now there is only one condition. If it is satisfied, the first statement is executed. Otherwise, the second is executed. The flowchart in Figure 2 gives a graphical representation of the branching behavior.

Quite often, however, the body of the if statement consists of multiple statements that must be executed in sequence whenever the condition is true. These statements must be grouped together to form a **block** statement by enclosing them in braces { }. Here is an example.

> A block statement groups several statements together.

```
if (amount <= balance)
{
    double newBalance = balance - amount;
    balance = newBalance;
}
```

In general, the body of an if statement must be a block statement, a *simple* statement, such as

```
balance = balance - amount;
```

or a *compound* statement (another if statement or a loop—see Chapter 5). The else alternative also must be a statement—that is, a simple statement, a compound statement, or a block statement.

Syntax 4.1 The if Statement

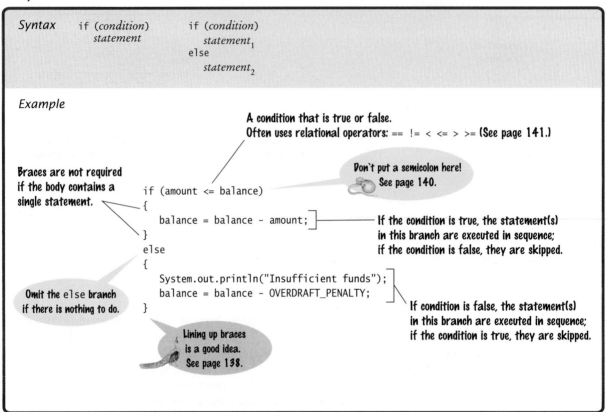

Syntax

```
if (condition)            if (condition)
    statement                 statement₁
                          else
                              statement₂
```

Example

A condition that is true or false.
Often uses relational operators: == != < <= > >= (See page 141.)

Braces are not required if the body contains a single statement.

Don't put a semicolon here! See page 140.

```
if (amount <= balance)
{
    balance = balance - amount;
}
else
{
    System.out.println("Insufficient funds");
    balance = balance - OVERDRAFT_PENALTY;
}
```

If the condition is true, the statement(s) in this branch are executed in sequence; if the condition is false, they are skipped.

Omit the else branch if there is nothing to do.

If condition is false, the statement(s) in this branch are executed in sequence; if the condition is true, they are skipped.

Lining up braces is a good idea. See page 138.

SELF CHECK

1. Why did we use the condition `amount <= balance` and not `amount < balance` in the example for the if/else statement?

2. What is logically wrong with the statement

   ```
   if (amount <= balance)
       newBalance = balance - amount; balance = newBalance;
   ```

   and how do you fix it?

Quality Tip 4.1

Brace Layout

The compiler doesn't care where you place braces, but we strongly recommend that you follow a simple rule: *Line up* { and }.

```
if (amount <= balance)
{
    double newBalance = balance - amount;
    balance = newBalance;
}
```

This scheme makes it easy to spot matching braces.

Some programmers put the opening brace on the same line as the if:

```
if (amount <= balance) {
   double newBalance = balance - amount;
   balance = newBalance;
}
```

This saves a line of code, but it makes it harder to match the braces.

It is important that you pick a layout scheme and stick with it. Which scheme you choose may depend on your personal preference or a coding style guide that you must follow.

Productivity Hint 4.1

Indentation and Tabs

When writing Java programs, use indentation to indicate nesting levels:

```
public class BankAccount
{
|  . . .
|  public void withdraw(double amount)
|  {
|  |  if (amount <= balance)
|  |  {
|  |  |  double newBalance = balance - amount;
|  |  |  balance = newBalance;
|  |  }
|  }
|  . . .
}
0  1  2  3
```
Indentation level

How many spaces should you use per indentation level? Some programmers use eight spaces per level, but that isn't a good choice:

```
public class BankAccount
{
        . . .
        public void withdraw(double amount)
        {
                if (amount <= balance)
                {
                        double newBalance =
                                balance - amount;
                        balance = newBalance;
                }
        }
        . . .
}
```

It crowds the code too much to the right side of the screen. As a consequence, long expressions frequently must be broken into separate lines. More common values are two, three, or four spaces per indentation level.

How do you move the cursor from the leftmost column to the appropriate indentation level? A perfectly reasonable strategy is to hit the space bar a sufficient number of times. However, many programmers use the Tab key instead. A tab moves the cursor to the next tab stop. By default, there are tab stops every eight columns, but most editors let you change that value; you should find out how to set your editor's tab stops to, say, every three columns.

Some editors help you out with an *autoindent* feature. They automatically insert as many tabs or spaces as the preceding line because the new line is quite likely to belong to the same logical indentation level. If it isn't, you must add or remove a tab, but that is still faster than tabbing all the way from the left margin.

While the Tab *key* is nice, some editors use *tab characters* for alignment, which is not so nice. Tab characters can lead to problems when you send your file to another person or a printer. There is no universal agreement on the width of a tab character, and some software will ignore tab characters altogether. It is therefore best to save your files with spaces instead of tabs. Most editors have settings to automatically convert all tabs to spaces. Look at your development environment's documentation to find out how to activate this useful setting.

Common Error 4.1

A Semicolon After the `if` Condition

The following code fragment has an unfortunate error:

```
if (input < 0) ; // ERROR
    System.out.println("Bad input);
```

There should be no semicolon after the `if` condition. The compiler interprets this statement as follows: If `input` is less than 0, execute the statement that is denoted by a single semicolon, that is, the do-nothing statement. The statement that follows the semicolon is no longer a part of the `if` statement. It is always executed—the error message appears for all inputs.

Special Topic 4.1

The Conditional Operator

Special Topic 4.1 discusses the `? :` conditional operator for conditions inside expressions.

4.2 Comparing Values

4.2.1 Relational Operators

Relational operators compare values. The `==` operator tests for equality.

A **relational operator** tests the relationship between two values. An example is the `<=` operator that we used in the test

```
if (amount <= balance)
```

Java has six relational operators, as shown in the table on page 141.

As you can see, only two relational operators (`>` and `<`) look as you would expect from the mathematical notation. Computer keyboards do not have keys for ≥, ≤, or ≠, but the `>=`, `<=`, and `!=` operators are easy to remember because they look similar.

Java	Math Notation	Description
>	>	Greater than
>=	≥	Greater than or equal
<	<	Less than
<=	≤	Less than or equal
==	=	Equal
!=	≠	Not equal

The == operator is initially confusing to most newcomers to Java. In Java, the = symbol already has a meaning, namely assignment. The == operator denotes equality testing:

```
a = 5; // Assign 5 to a
if (a == 5) . . . // Test whether a equals 5
```

You will have to remember to use == for equality testing, and to use = for assignment.

The relational operators have a lower precedence than the arithmetic operators. That means, you can write arithmetic expressions on either side of the relational operator without using parentheses. For example, in the expression

```
amount + fee <= balance
```

both sides (`amount + fee` and `balance`) of the < operator are evaluated, and the results are compared. Appendix B shows a table of the Java operators and their precedence.

4.2.2 Comparing Floating-Point Numbers

You have to be careful when comparing floating-point numbers, in order to cope with roundoff errors. For example, the following code multiplies the square root of 2 by itself and then subtracts 2.

```
double r = Math.sqrt(2);
double d = r * r - 2;
if (d == 0)
   System.out.println("sqrt(2) squared minus 2 is 0");
else
   System.out.println(
      "sqrt(2) squared minus 2 is not 0 but " + d);
```

Even though the laws of mathematics tell us that $\left(\sqrt{2}\right)^2 - 2$ equals 0, this program fragment prints

```
sqrt(2) squared minus 2 is not 0 but 4.440892098500626E-16
```

Unfortunately, such roundoff errors are unavoidable. It plainly does not make sense in most circumstances to compare floating-point numbers exactly. Instead, test whether they are *close enough*.

Syntax 4.2 Comparisons

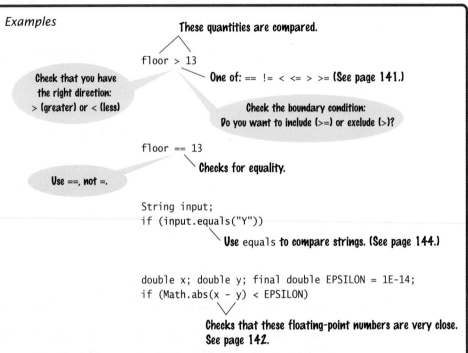

Examples

These quantities are compared.

floor > 13

Check that you have the right direction:
> (greater) or < (less)

One of: == != < <= > >= (See page 141.)

Check the boundary condition:
Do you want to include (>=) or exclude (>)?

floor == 13

Use ==, not =.

Checks for equality.

```
String input;
if (input.equals("Y"))
```

Use equals to compare strings. (See page 144.)

```
double x; double y; final double EPSILON = 1E-14;
if (Math.abs(x - y) < EPSILON)
```

Checks that these floating-point numbers are very close.
See page 142.

> **When comparing floating-point numbers, don't test for equality. Instead, check whether they are close enough.**

To test whether a number x is close to zero, you can test whether the absolute value $|x|$ (that is, the number with its sign removed) is less than a very small threshold number. That threshold value is often called ε (the Greek letter epsilon). It is common to set ε to 10^{-14} when testing double numbers.

Similarly, you can test whether two numbers are approximately equal by checking whether their difference is close to 0.

$$|x - y| \leq \varepsilon$$

In Java, we program the test as follows:

```
final double EPSILON = 1E-14;
if (Math.abs(x - y) <= EPSILON)
    // x is approximately equal to y
```

4.2.3 Comparing Strings

To test whether two strings are equal to each other, you must use the method called equals:

```
if (string1.equals(string2)) . . .
```

Do not use the == operator to compare strings. The expression

```
if (string1 == string2) // Not useful
```

> **Do not use the == operator to compare strings. Use the equals method instead.**

has an unrelated meaning. It tests whether the two string variables refer to the identical string object. You can have strings with identical contents stored in different objects, so this test never makes sense in actual programming; see Common Error 4.2 on page 144.

In Java, letter case matters. For example, `"Harry"` and `"HARRY"` are not the same string. To ignore the letter case, use the `equalsIgnoreCase` method:

```
if (string1.equalsIgnoreCase(string2)) . . .
```

> The `compareTo` method compares strings in dictionary order.

If two strings are not identical to each other, you still may want to know the relationship between them. The `compareTo` method compares strings in dictionary order. If

```
string1.compareTo(string2) < 0
```

then the string `string1` comes before the string `string2` in the dictionary. For example, this is the case if `string1` is `"Harry"`, and `string2` is `"Hello"`. If

```
string1.compareTo(string2) > 0
```

then `string1` comes after `string2` in dictionary order. Finally, if

```
string1.compareTo(string2) == 0
```

then `string1` and `string2` are equal.

	Table 1	**Relational Operator Examples**	
Expression		Value	Comment
`3 <= 4`		true	3 is less than 4; `<=` tests for "less than or equal".
🚫 `3 =< 4`		**Error**	The "less than or equal" operator is `<=`, not `=<`, with the "less than" symbol first.
`3 > 4`		false	`>` is the opposite of `<=`.
`4 < 4`		false	The left-hand side must be strictly smaller than the right-hand side.
`4 <= 4`		true	Both sides are equal; `<=` tests for "less than or equal".
`3 == 5 - 2`		true	`==` tests for equality.
`3 != 5 - 1`		true	`!=` tests for inequality. It is true that 3 is not 5 – 1.
🚫 `3 = 6 / 2`		**Error**	Use `==` to test for equality.
`1.0 / 3.0 == 0.333333333`		false	Although the values are very close to one another, they are not exactly equal. See Common Error 3.3.
🚫 `"10" > 5`		**Error**	You cannot compare a string to a number.
`"Tomato".substring(0, 3).equals("Tom")`		true	Always use the `equals` method to check whether two strings have the same contents.
`"Tomato".substring(0, 3) == ("Tom")`		false	Never use `==` to compare strings; it only checks whether the strings are stored in the same location. See Common Error 4.2 on page 144.
`"Tom".equalsIgnoreCase("TOM")`		true	Use the `equalsIgnoreCase` method if you don't want to distinguish between uppercase and lowercase letters.

Actually, the "dictionary" ordering used by Java is slightly different from that of a normal dictionary. Java is case sensitive and sorts characters by putting numbers first, then uppercase characters, then lowercase characters. For example, 1 comes before B, which comes before a. The space character comes before all other characters.

Let us investigate the comparison process closely. When Java compares two strings, corresponding letters are compared until one of the strings ends or the first difference is encountered. If one of the strings ends, the longer string is considered the later one. If a character mismatch is found, the characters are compared to determine which string comes later in the dictionary sequence. This process is called lexicographic comparison. For example, let's compare "car" with "cargo". The first three letters match, and we reach the end of the first string. Therefore "car" comes before "cargo" in the lexicographic ordering. Now compare "cathode" with "cargo". The first two letters match. In the third character position, t comes after r, so the string "cathode" comes after "cargo" in lexicographic ordering. (See Figure 3.)

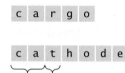

Figure 3
Lexicographic Comparison

Letters match r comes before t

Common Error 4.2

Using == to Compare Strings

It is an extremely common error in Java to write == when equals is intended. This is particularly true for strings. If you write

```
if (nickname == "Rob")
```

then the test succeeds only if the variable nickname refers to the exact same string object as the string constant "Rob". For efficiency, Java makes only one string object for every string constant. Therefore, the following test will pass:

```
String nickname = "Rob";
  . . .
if (nickname == "Rob") // Test is true
```

However, if the string with the letters R o b has been assembled in some other way, then the test will fail:

```
String name = "Robert";
String nickname = name.substring(0, 3);
  . . .
if (nickname == "Rob") // Test is false
```

This is a particularly distressing situation: The wrong code will sometimes do the right thing, sometimes the wrong thing. Because string objects are always constructed by the compiler, you never have an interest in whether two string objects are shared. You must remember never to use == to compare strings. Always use equals or compareTo to compare strings.

4.2.4 Comparing Objects

If you compare two object references with the == operator, you test whether the references refer to the same object. Here is an example:

```
Rectangle box1 = new Rectangle(5, 10, 20, 30);
Rectangle box2 = box1;
Rectangle box3 = new Rectangle(5, 10, 20, 30);
```

The comparison

```
box1 == box2
```

is true. Both object variables refer to the same object. But the comparison

```
box1 == box3
```

is false. The two object variables refer to different objects (see Figure 4). It does not matter that the objects have identical contents.

You can use the equals method to test whether two rectangles have the same contents, that is, whether they have the same upper-left corner and the same width and height. For example, the test

```
box1.equals(box3)
```

is true.

However, you must be careful when using the equals method. It works correctly only if the implementors of the class have supplied it. The Rectangle class has an equals method that is suitable for comparing rectangles.

For your own classes, you need to supply an appropriate equals method. You will learn how to do that in Chapter 9. Until that point, you should not use the equals method to compare objects of your own classes.

The == operator tests whether two object references are identical. To compare the contents of objects, you need to use the equals method.

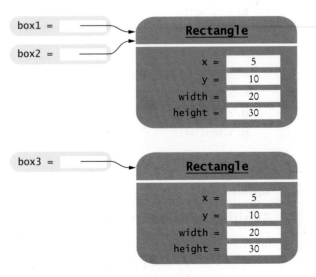

Figure 4 Comparing Object References

4.2.5 Testing for null

The null reference refers to no object.

An object reference can have the special value null if it refers to no object at all. It is common to use the null value to indicate that a value has never been set. For example,

```
String middleInitial = null; // Not set
if ( . . . )
   middleInitial = middleName.substring(0, 1);
```

You use the == operator (and not equals) to test whether an object reference is a null reference:

```
if (middleInitial == null)
   System.out.println(firstName + " " + lastName);
else
   System.out.println(firstName + " " + middleInitial + ". " + lastName);
```

Note that the null reference is not the same as the empty string "". The empty string is a valid string of length 0, whereas a null indicates that a string variable refers to no string at all.

SELF CHECK

3. What is the value of s.length() if s is

   a. the empty string ""?

   b. the string " " containing a space?

   c. null?

4. Which of the following comparisons are syntactically incorrect? Which of them are syntactically correct, but logically questionable?

```
String a = "1";
String b = "one";
double x = 1;
double y = 3 * (1.0 / 3);
```

   a. a == "1"

   b. a == null

   c. a.equals("")

   d. a == b

   e. a == x

   f. x == y

   g. x - y == null

   h. x.equals(y)

Quality Tip 4.2

Avoid Conditions with Side Effects

In Java, it is legal to nest assignments inside test conditions:

```
if ((d = b * b - 4 * a * c) >= 0) r = Math.sqrt(d);
```

It is legal to use the decrement operator inside other expressions:

```
if (n-- > 0) . . .
```

These are bad programming practices, because they mix a test with another activity. The other activity (setting the variable d, decrementing n) is called a **side effect** of the test.

As you will see in Special Topic 5.3, conditions with side effects can occasionally be helpful to simplify loops; for if statements they should always be avoided.

How To 4.1

Implementing an if Statement

This How To walks you through the process of implementing an if statement. We will illustrate the steps with the following example problem:

The university bookstore has a Kilobyte Day sale every October 24, giving an 8 percent discount on all computer accessory purchases if the price is less than $128, and a 16 percent discount if the price is at least $128. Write a program that asks the cashier for the original price and then prints the discounted price.

Step 1   In our sample problem, the obvious choice for the condition is:

original price < 128?

That is just fine, and we will use that condition in our solution.

But you could equally well come up with a correct solution if you choose the opposite condition: Is the original price at least $128? You might choose this condition if you put yourself into the position of a shopper who wants to know when the bigger discount applies.

Step 2   Give pseudocode for the work that needs to be done when the condition is fulfilled.

In this step, you list the action or actions that are taken in the "positive" branch. The details depend on your problem. You may want to print a message, compute values, or even exit the program.

In our example, we need to apply an 8 percent discount:

discounted price = 0.92 x original price

Step 3   Give pseudocode for the work (if any) that needs to be done when the condition is *not* fulfilled.

What do you want to do in the case that the condition of Step 1 is not fulfilled? Sometimes, you want to do nothing at all. In that case, use an if statement without an else branch.

In our example, the condition tested whether the price was less than $128. If that condition is *not* fulfilled, the price is at least $128, so the higher discount of 16 percent applies to the sale:

discounted price = 0.84 x original price

Step 4   Double-check relational operators.

First, be sure that the test goes in the right *direction*. It is a common error to confuse > and <. Next, consider whether you should use the < operator or its close cousin, the <= operator.

What should happen if the original price is exactly $128? Reading the problem carefully, we find that the lower discount applies if the original price is *less than* $128, and the higher discount applies when it is *at least* $128. A price of $128 should therefore *not* fulfill our condition, and we must use <, not <=.

Step 5   Remove duplication.

Check which actions are common to both branches, and move them outside. (See Quality Tip 3.3.)

In our example, we have two statements of the form

discounted price = ___ x original price

They only differ in the discount rate. It is best to just set the rate in the branches, and to do the computation afterwards:

```
If original price < 128
    discount rate = 0.92
Else
        discount rate = 0.84
discounted price = discount rate x original price
```

Step 6 Test both branches.

Formulate two test cases, one that fulfills the condition of the if statement, and one that does not. Ask yourself what should happen in each case. Then follow the pseudocode and act each of them out.

In our example, let us consider two scenarios for the original price: $100 and $200. We expect that the first price is discounted by $8, the second by $32.

When the original price is 100, then the condition 100 < 128 is true, and we get

```
discount rate = 0.92
discounted price = 0.92 x 100 = 92
```

When the original price is 200, then the condition 200 < 128 is false, and

```
discount rate = 0.84
discounted price = 0.84 x 200 = 168
```

In both cases, we get the expected answer.

Step 7 Assemble the if statement in Java.

Type the skeleton

```
if ()
{
}
else
{
}
```

and fill it in, as shown in Syntax 4.1 on page 138. Omit the else branch if it is not needed.

In our example, the completed statement is

```java
double HIGH_DISCOUNT_THRESHOLD = 128;
double HIGH_DISCOUNT = 0.92;
double LOW_DISCOUNT = 0.84;

if (originalPrice < HIGH_DISCOUNT_THRESHOLD)
{
    discountRate = HIGH_DISCOUNT;
}
else
{
    discountRate = LOW_DISCOUNT;
}
discountedPrice = discountRate * originalPrice;
```

Here we used named constants to make the program more maintainable (see Quality Tip 3.1).

⊕ *Worked Example 4.1*

Extracting the Middle

This Worked Example shows how to extract the middle character from a string, or the two middle characters if the length of the string is even.

c	r	a	t	e
0	1	2	3	4

4.3 Multiple Alternatives

4.3.1 Sequences of Comparisons

Multiple conditions can be combined to evaluate complex decisions. The correct arrangement depends on the logic of the problem to be solved.

Many computations require more than a single if/else decision. Sometimes, you need to make a series of related comparisons.

The following program asks for a value describing the magnitude of an earthquake on the Richter scale and prints a description of the likely impact of the quake. The Richter scale is a measurement for the strength of an earthquake. Every step in the scale, for example from 6.0 to 7.0, signifies a tenfold increase in the strength of the quake. The 1989 Loma Prieta earthquake that damaged the Bay Bridge in San Francisco and destroyed many buildings in several Bay area cities registered 7.1 on the Richter scale.

ch04/quake/Earthquake.java

```java
1  /**
2     A class that describes the effects of an earthquake.
3  */
4  public class Earthquake
5  {
6     private double richter;
7
8     /**
9        Constructs an Earthquake object.
10       @param magnitude the magnitude on the Richter scale
11    */
12    public Earthquake(double magnitude)
13    {
14       richter = magnitude;
15    }
16
17    /**
18       Gets a description of the effect of the earthquake.
19       @return the description of the effect
20    */
21    public String getDescription()
22    {
23       String r;
24       if (richter >= 8.0)
25          r = "Most structures fall";
26       else if (richter >= 7.0)
27          r = "Many buildings destroyed";
28       else if (richter >= 6.0)
29          r = "Many buildings considerably damaged, some collapse";
30       else if (richter >= 4.5)
31          r = "Damage to poorly constructed buildings";
32       else if (richter >= 3.5)
33          r = "Felt by many people, no destruction";
34       else if (richter >= 0)
35          r = "Generally not felt by people";
36       else
37          r = "Negative numbers are not valid";
38       return r;
39    }
40 }
```

ch04/quake/EarthquakeRunner.java

```java
1   import java.util.Scanner;
2
3   /**
4      This program prints a description of an earthquake of a given magnitude.
5   */
6   public class EarthquakeRunner
7   {
8      public static void main(String[] args)
9      {
10        Scanner in = new Scanner(System.in);
11
12        System.out.print("Enter a magnitude on the Richter scale: ");
13        double magnitude = in.nextDouble();
14        Earthquake quake = new Earthquake(magnitude);
15        System.out.println(quake.getDescription());
16     }
17  }
```

Program Run

```
Enter a magnitude on the Richter scale: 7.1
Many buildings destroyed
```

Here we must sort the conditions and test against the largest cutoff first. Suppose we reverse the order of tests:

```java
if (richter >= 0) // Tests in wrong order
   r = "Generally not felt by people";
else if (richter >= 3.5)
   r = "Felt by many people, no destruction";
else if (richter >= 4.5)
   r = "Damage to poorly constructed buildings";
else if (richter >= 6.0)
   r = "Many buildings considerably damaged, some collapse";
else if (richter >= 7.0)
   r = "Many buildings destroyed";
else if (richter >= 8.0)
   r = "Most structures fall";
```

This does not work. All nonnegative values of richter fall into the first case, and the other tests will never be attempted.

In this example, it is also important that we use an if/else if/else test, not just multiple independent if statements. Consider this sequence of independent tests:

```java
if (richter >= 8.0) // Didn't use else
   r = "Most structures fall";
if (richter >= 7.0)
   r = "Many buildings destroyed";
if (richter >= 6.0)
   r = "Many buildings considerably damaged, some collapse";
if (richter >= 4.5)
   r = "Damage to poorly constructed buildings";
if (richter >= 3.5)
   r = "Felt by many people, no destruction";
if (richter >= 0)
   r = "Generally not felt by people";
```

Now the alternatives are no longer exclusive. If richter is 6.0, then the last four tests all match, and r is set four times.

Special Topic 4.2

The switch **Statement**

Special Topic 4.2 discusses the switch statement, an alternative to the if/else if/else statement sequence in which all conditions test the same value against constants.

4.3.2 Nested Branches

Some computations have multiple *levels* of decision making. You first make one decision, and each of the outcomes leads to another decision. Here is a typical example.

In the United States, taxpayers pay federal income tax at different rates depending on their incomes and marital status. There are two main tax schedules: one for single taxpayers and one for married taxpayers "filing jointly", meaning that the married taxpayers add their incomes together and pay taxes on the total. Table 2 gives the tax rate computations for each of the filing categories, using a simplified version of the values for the 2008 federal tax return.

Table 2 Federal Tax Rate Schedule (2008, simplified)			
If your filing status is Single:		If your filing status is Married:	
Tax Bracket	Percentage	Tax Bracket	Percentage
$0 . . . $32,000	10%	$0 . . . $64,000	10%
Amount over $32,000	25%	Amount over $64,000	25%

Now let us compute the taxes due, given a filing status and an income figure. First, we must branch on the filing status. Then, for each filing status, we must have another branch on income level. (See Figure 5 for a flowchart.)

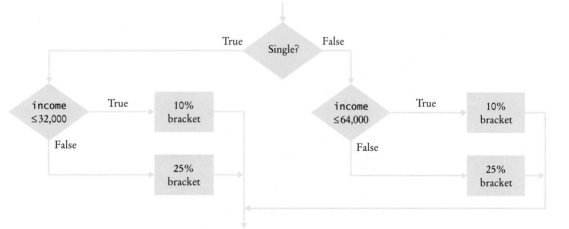

Figure 5   Income Tax Computation Using Simplified 2008 Schedule

The two-level decision process is reflected in two levels of if statements. We say that the income test is *nested* inside the test for filing status.

ch04/tax/TaxReturn.java

```java
1   /**
2       A tax return of a taxpayer in 2008.
3   */
4   public class TaxReturn
5   {
6       public static final int SINGLE = 1;
7       public static final int MARRIED = 2;
8
9       private static final double RATE1 = 0.10;
10      private static final double RATE2 = 0.25;
11      private static final double RATE1_SINGLE_LIMIT = 32000;
12      private static final double RATE1_MARRIED_LIMIT = 64000;
13
14      private double income;
15      private int status;
16
17      /**
18          Constructs a TaxReturn object for a given income and
19          marital status.
20          @param anIncome the taxpayer income
21          @param aStatus either SINGLE or MARRIED
22      */
23      public TaxReturn(double anIncome, int aStatus)
24      {
25          income = anIncome;
26          status = aStatus;
27      }
28
29      public double getTax()
30      {
31          double tax1 = 0;
32          double tax2 = 0;
33
34          if (status == SINGLE)
35          {
36              if (income <= RATE1_SINGLE_LIMIT)
37              {
38                  tax1 = RATE1 * income;
39              }
40              else
41              {
42                  tax1 = RATE1 * RATE1_SINGLE_LIMIT;
43                  tax2 = RATE2 * (income - RATE1_SINGLE_LIMIT);
44              }
45          }
46          else
47          {
48              if (income <= RATE1_MARRIED_LIMIT)
49              {
50                  tax1 = RATE1 * income;
51              }
52              else
53              {
```

```
54              tax1 = RATE1 * RATE1_MARRIED_LIMIT;
55              tax2 = RATE2 * (income - RATE1_MARRIED_LIMIT);
56          }
57      }
58
59      return tax1 + tax2;
60  }
61 }
```

ch04/tax/TaxCalculator.java

```
1  import java.util.Scanner;
2
3  /**
4     This program calculates a simple tax return.
5  */
6  public class TaxCalculator
7  {
8     public static void main(String[] args)
9     {
10        Scanner in = new Scanner(System.in);
11
12        System.out.print("Please enter your income: ");
13        double income = in.nextDouble();
14
15        System.out.print("Are you married? (Y/N) ");
16        String input = in.next();
17        int status;
18        if (input.equalsIgnoreCase("Y"))
19           status = TaxReturn.MARRIED;
20        else
21           status = TaxReturn.SINGLE;
22        TaxReturn aTaxReturn = new TaxReturn(income, status);
23
24        System.out.println("Tax: "
25              + aTaxReturn.getTax());
26     }
27 }
```

Program Run

```
Please enter your income: 80000
Are you married? (Y/N) Y
Tax: 10400.0
```

SELF CHECK

5. The if/else/else statement for the earthquake strength first tested for higher values, then descended to lower values. Can you reverse that order?

6. Some people object to higher tax rates for higher incomes, claiming that you might end up with *less* money after taxes when you get a raise for working hard. What is the flaw in this argument?

Common Error 4.3

The Dangling else Problem

When an if statement is nested inside another if statement, the following error may occur.

```java
if (richter >= 0)
   if (richter <= 4)
      System.out.println("The earthquake is harmless");
else // Pitfall!
   System.out.println("Negative value not allowed");
```

The indentation level seems to suggest that the else is grouped with the test richter >= 0. Unfortunately, that is not the case. The compiler ignores all indentation and follows the rule that an else always belongs to the closest if, like this:

```java
if (richter >= 0)
   if (richter <= 4)
      System.out.println("The earthquake is harmless");
   else // Pitfall!
      System.out.println("Negative value not allowed");
```

That isn't what we want. We want to group the else with the first if. For that, we must use braces.

```java
if (richter >= 0)
{
   if (richter <= 4)
      System.out.println("The earthquake is harmless");
}
else
   System.out.println("Negative value not allowed");
```

To avoid having to think about the pairing of the else, we recommend that you *always* use a set of braces when the body of an if contains another if. In the following example, the braces are not strictly necessary, but they help clarify the code:

```java
if (richter >= 0)
{
   if (richter <= 4)
      System.out.println("The earthquake is harmless");
   else
      System.out.println("Damage may occur");
}
```

The ambiguous else is called a *dangling* else, and it is enough of a syntactical blemish that some programming language designers developed an improved syntax that avoids it altogether. For example, Algol 68 uses the construction

if *condition* then *statement* else *statement* fi;

The else part is optional, but since the end of the if statement is clearly marked, the grouping is unambiguous if there are two ifs and only one else. Here are the two possible cases:

if c_1 then if c_2 then s_1 else s_2 fi fi;
if c_1 then if c_2 then s_1 fi else s_2 fi;

By the way, fi is just if backwards. Other languages use endif, which has the same purpose but is less fun.

Productivity Hint 4.2

Hand-Tracing

A very useful technique for understanding whether a program works correctly is called *hand-tracing*. You simulate the program's activity on a sheet of paper. You can use this method with pseudocode or Java code.

Get an index card, a cocktail napkin, or whatever sheet of paper is within reach. Make a column for each variable. Have the program code ready. Use a marker, such as a paper clip, to mark the current statement. In your mind, execute statements one at a time. Every time the value of a variable changes, cross out the old value and write the new value below the old one.

For example, let's trace the getTax method with the data from the program run on page 153.

When the TaxReturn object is constructed, the income instance variable is set to 80,000 and status is set to MARRIED. Then the getTax method is called. In lines 31 and 32 of TaxReturn.java, tax1 and tax2 are initialized to 0.

```
29 public double getTax()
30 {
31    double tax1 = 0;
32    double tax2 = 0;
33
```

income	status	tax1	tax2
80000	MARRIED	0	0

Because status is not SINGLE, we move to the else branch of the outer if statement (line 46).

```
34    if (status == SINGLE)
35    {
36       if (income <= RATE1_SINGLE_LIMIT)
37       {
38          tax1 = RATE1 * income;
39       }
40       else
41       {
42          tax1 = RATE1 * RATE1_SINGLE_LIMIT;
43          tax2 = RATE2 * (income - RATE1_SINGLE_LIMIT);
44       }
45    }
46    else
47    {
```

Since income is not <= 64000, we move to the else branch of the inner if statement (line 52).

```
48       if (income <= RATE1_MARRIED_LIMIT)
49       {
50          tax1 = RATE1 * income;
51       }
52       else
53       {
54          tax1 = RATE1 * RATE1_MARRIED_LIMIT;
55          tax2 = RATE2 * (income - RATE1_MARRIED_LIMIT);
56       }
```

The values of tax1 and tax2 are updated.

```
53       {
54          tax1 = RATE1 * RATE1_MARRIED_LIMIT;
55          tax2 = RATE2 * (income - RATE1_MARRIED_LIMIT);
56       }
57    }
```

income	status	tax1	tax2
80000	MARRIED	~~0~~	~~0~~
		6400	4000

Their sum is returned and the method ends.

```
58
59    return tax1 + tax2;
60 }
```

income	status	tax1	tax2	return value
80000	MARRIED	~~0~~	~~0~~	
		6400	4000	10400

Because the program trace shows the expected return value ($10,400), it successfully demonstrates that this test case works correctly.

Productivity Hint 4.3

Make a Schedule and Make Time for Unexpected Problems

Commercial software is notorious for being delivered later than promised. For example, Microsoft originally promised that its Windows Vista operating system would be available late in 2003, then in 2005, then in March 2006; it was finally released in January 2007. Some of the early promises might not have been realistic. It is in Microsoft's interest to let prospective customers expect the imminent availability of the product, so that they do not switch to a different product in the meantime. Undeniably, though, Microsoft had not anticipated the full complexity of the tasks it had set itself to solve.

Microsoft can delay the delivery of its product, but it is likely that you cannot. As a student or a programmer, you are expected to manage your time wisely and to finish your assignments on time. You can probably do simple programming exercises the night before the due date, but an assignment that looks twice as hard may well take four times as long, because more things can go wrong. You should therefore make a schedule whenever you start a programming project.

First, estimate realistically how much time it will take you to

- Design the program logic.
- Develop test cases.
- Type the program in and fix compile-time errors.
- Test and debug the program.

For example, for the income tax program I might estimate 30 minutes for the design, because it is mostly done; 30 minutes for developing test cases; one hour for data entry and fixing compile-time errors; and 2 hours for testing and debugging. That is a total of 4 hours. If I work 2 hours a day on this project, it will take me two days.

Then think of things that can go wrong. Your computer might break down. The lab might be crowded. You might be stumped by a problem with the computer system. (That is a particularly important concern for beginners. It is *very* common to lose a day over a trivial problem just because it takes time to track down a person who knows the "magic" command to overcome it.) As a rule of thumb, *double* the time of your estimate. That is, you should start four days, not two days, before the due date. If nothing goes wrong, great; you have the program done two days early. When the inevitable problem occurs, you have a cushion of time that protects you from embarrassment and failure.

Special Topic 4.3

Enumeration Types

Special Topic 4.3 introduces enumeration types—types that an hold one of a finite number of values. An example of an enumeration type is a type FilingStatus with values SINGLE and MARRIED. This is safer than using integer values, as we did in the TaxReturn class.

4.4 Using Boolean Expressions

4.4.1 The boolean Type

In Java, an expression such as amount < 1000 has a value, just as the expression amount + 1000 has a value. The value of a relational expression is either true or false. For example, if amount is 500, then the value of amount < 1000 is true. Try it out: The program fragment

```
double amount = 0;
System.out.println(amount < 1000);
```

The boolean type has two values: true and false.

prints true. The values true and false are not numbers, nor are they objects of a class. They belong to a separate type, called boolean. The **Boolean type** is named after the mathematician George Boole (1815–1864), a pioneer in the study of logic.

4.4.2 Predicate Methods

A **predicate method** is a method that returns a boolean value. Here is an example of a predicate method:

A predicate method returns a boolean value.

```
public class BankAccount
{
    public boolean isOverdrawn()
    {
        return balance < 0; // Returns true or false
    }
}
```

You can use the return value of the method as the condition of an if statement:

```
if (harrysChecking.isOverdrawn()) . . .
```

There are several useful static predicate methods in the Character class:

```
isDigit
isLetter
isUpperCase
isLowerCase
```

that let you test whether a character is a digit, a letter, an uppercase letter, or a lowercase letter:

```
if (Character.isUpperCase(ch)) . . .
```

It is a common convention to give the prefix "is" or "has" to the name of a predicate method.

The Scanner class has useful predicate methods for testing whether the next input will succeed. The hasNextInt method returns true if the next character sequence denotes an integer. It is a good idea to call that method before calling nextInt:

```
if (in.hasNextInt()) input = in.nextInt();
```

Similarly, the hasNextDouble method tests whether a call to nextDouble will succeed.

4.4.3 The Boolean Operators

Suppose you want to find whether amount is between 0 and 1000. Then two conditions have to be true: amount must be greater than 0, *and* it must be less than 1000. In Java you use the && operator to represent the *and* when combining test conditions. That is, you can write the test as follows:

```
if (0 < amount && amount < 1000) . . .
```

> You can form complex tests with the Boolean operators && (*and*), || (*or*), and ! (*not*).

The && (*and*) operator combines several tests into a new test that passes only when all conditions are true. An operator that combines Boolean values is called a **Boolean operator**.

The && operator has a lower precedence than the relational operators. For that reason, you can write relational expressions on either side of the && operator without using parentheses. For example, in the expression

```
0 < amount && amount < 1000
```

the expressions 0 < amount and amount < 1000 are evaluated first. Then the && operator combines the results. Appendix B shows a table of the Java operators and their precedence.

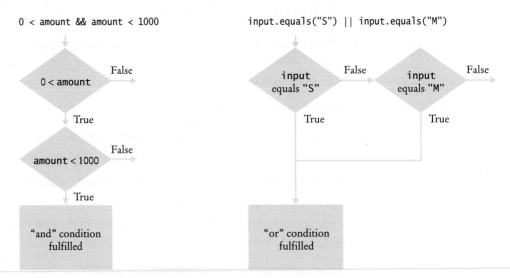

Figure 6 Flowcharts for && and || Combinations

The || (*or*) logical operator also combines two or more conditions. The resulting test succeeds if at least one of the conditions is true. For example, here is a test to check whether the string input is an "S" or "M":

```
if (input.equals("S") || input.equals("M")) . . .
```

Figure 6 shows flowcharts for these examples.

Sometimes you need to *invert* a condition with the ! (*not*) logical operator. For example, we may want to carry out a certain action only if two strings are *not* equal:

```
if (!input.equals("S")) . . .
```

The ! operator takes a single condition and evaluates to true if that condition is false and to false if the condition is true.

Here is a summary of the three logical operations:

A	B	A && B
true	true	true
true	false	false
false	*Any*	false

A	B	A || B
true	*Any*	true
false	true	true
false	false	false

A	!A
true	false
false	true

Table 3 Boolean Operators

Expression	Value	Comment
0 < 200 && 200 < 100	false	Only the first condition is true.
0 < 200 || 200 < 100	true	The first condition is true.
0 < 200 || 100 < 200	true	The || is not a test for "either-or". If both conditions are true, the result is true.
🚫 0 < 100 < 200	Syntax error	**Error:** The expression 0 < 100 is true, which cannot be compared against 200.
🚫 0 < x || x < 100	true	**Error:** This condition is always true. The programmer probably intended 0 < x && x < 100. (See Common Error 4.5).
0 < x && x < 100 || x == -1	(0 < x && x < 100) || x == -1	The && operator binds more strongly than the || operator. (See Appendix B.)
!(0 < 200)	false	0 < 200 is true, therefore its negation is false.
frozen == true	frozen	There is no need to compare a Boolean variable with true.
frozen == false	!frozen	It is clearer to use ! than to compare with false.

4.4.4 Using Boolean Variables

You can use a Boolean variable if you know that there are only two possible values. Have another look at the tax program in Section 4.3.2. The marital status is either single or married. Instead of using an integer, you can use a variable of type `boolean`:

```
private boolean married;
```

The advantage is that you can't accidentally store a third value in the variable.

Then you can use the Boolean variable in a test:

```
if (married)
   . . .
else
   . . .
```

> You can store the outcome of a condition in a Boolean variable.

Sometimes Boolean variables are called *flags* because they can have only two states: "up" and "down".

It pays to think carefully about the naming of Boolean variables. In our example, it would not be a good idea to give the name `maritalStatus` to the Boolean variable. What does it mean that the marital status is `true`? With a name like `married` there is no ambiguity; if `married` is `true`, the taxpayer is married.

By the way, it is considered gauche to write a test such as

```
if (married == true) . . . // Don't
```

Just use the simpler test

```
if (married) . . .
```

In Chapter 5 we will use Boolean variables to control complex loops.

SELF CHECK

7. When does the statement

   ```
   System.out.println(x > 0 || x < 0);
   ```

   print `false`?

8. Rewrite the following expression, avoiding the comparison with `false`:

   ```
   if (Character.isDigit(ch) == false) . . .
   ```

Common Error 4.4

Multiple Relational Operators

Consider the expression

```
if (0 < amount < 1000) . . . // Error
```

This looks just like the mathematical notation for "amount is between 0 and 1000". But in Java, it is a syntax error.

Let us dissect the condition. The first half, `0 < amount`, is a test with outcome `true` or `false`. The outcome of that test (`true` or `false`) is then compared against 1000. This seems to make no sense. Is `true` larger than 1000 or not? Can one compare truth values and numbers? In Java, you cannot. The Java compiler rejects this statement.

Instead, use && to combine two separate tests:

```
if (0 < amount && amount < 1000) . . .
```

Another common error, along the same lines, is to write

```
if (ch == 'S' || 'M') . . . // Error
```

to test whether ch is 'S' or 'M'. Again, the Java compiler flags this construct as an error. You cannot apply the || operator to characters. You need to write two Boolean expressions and join them with the || operator:

```
if (ch == 'S' || ch == 'M') . . .
```

Common Error 4.5

Confusing && and || Conditions

It is a surprisingly common error to confuse *and* and *or* conditions. A value lies between 0 and 100 if it is at least 0 *and* at most 100. It lies outside that range if it is less than 0 *or* greater than 100. There is no golden rule; you just have to think carefully.

Often the *and* or *or* is clearly stated, and then it isn't too hard to implement it. Sometimes, though, the wording isn't as explicit. It is quite common that the individual conditions are nicely set apart in a bulleted list, but with little indication of how they should be combined. The instructions for the 1992 tax return say that you can claim single filing status if any one of the following is true:

- You were never married.
- You were legally separated or divorced on December 31, 1992.
- You were widowed before January 1, 1992, and did not remarry in 1992.

Because the test passes if *any one* of the conditions is true, you must combine the conditions with *or*. Elsewhere, the same instructions state that you may use the more advantageous status of married filing jointly if all five of the following conditions are true:

- Your spouse died in 1990 or 1991 and you did not remarry in 1992.
- You have a child whom you can claim as dependent.
- That child lived in your home for all of 1992.
- You paid over half the cost of keeping up your home for this child.
- You filed (or could have filed) a joint return with your spouse the year he or she died.

Because *all* of the conditions must be true for the test to pass, you must combine them with an *and*.

Special Topic 4.4

Lazy Evaluation of Boolean Operators

Special Topic 4.4 explains lazy evaluation of Boolean operators: the fact that the right-hand side of && and || expressions is not evaluated if the left-hand side already determines the outcome.

Special Topic 4.5

De Morgan's Law

Special Topic 4.5 covers DeMorgan's law, a law of logic that is used to simplify conditions in which *not* operators are applied to *and/or* expressions.

Random Fact 4.1

Artificial Intelligence

Random Fact 4.1 discusses artificial intelligence computer processes that appear to simulate intelligent human reasoning.

4.5 Code Coverage

> Black-box testing describes a testing method that does not take the structure of the implementation into account.

Testing the functionality of a program without consideration of its internal structure is called **black-box testing**. This is an important part of testing, because, after all, the users of a program do not know its internal structure. If a program works perfectly on all inputs, then it surely does its job.

However, it is impossible to ensure absolutely that a program will work correctly on all inputs just by supplying a finite number of test cases. As the famous computer scientist Edsger Dijkstra pointed out, testing can show only the presence of bugs—not their absence. To gain more confidence in the correctness of a program, it is useful to consider its internal structure. Testing strategies that look inside a program are called **white-box testing**. Performing unit tests of each method is a part of white-box testing.

> White-box testing uses information about the structure of a program.

You want to make sure that each part of your program is exercised at least once by one of your test cases. This is called **code coverage**. If some code is never executed by any of your test cases, you have no way of knowing whether that code would perform correctly if it ever were executed by user input. That means that you need to look at every if/else branch to see that each of them is reached by some test case. Many conditional branches are in the code only to take care of strange and abnormal inputs, but they still do something. It is a common phenomenon that they end up doing something incorrectly, but those faults are never discovered during testing, because nobody supplied the strange and abnormal inputs. Of course, these flaws become immediately apparent when the program is released and the first user types in an unusual input and is incensed when the program misbehaves. The remedy is to ensure that each part of the code is covered by some test case.

> Code coverage is a measure of how many parts of a program have been tested.

For example, in testing the getTax method of the TaxReturn class, you want to make sure that every if statement is entered for at least one test case. You should test both single and married taxpayers, with incomes in each of the three tax brackets.

When you select test cases, you should make it a habit to include *boundary test cases:* legal values that lie at the boundary of the set of acceptable inputs.

> Boundary test cases are test cases that are at the boundary of acceptable inputs.

For example, what happens when you compute the taxes for an income of 0 or if a bank account has an interest rate of 0 percent? Boundary cases are still legitimate inputs, and you expect that the program will handle them correctly—often in some trivial way or through special cases. Testing boundary cases is important, because programmers often make mistakes dealing with boundary conditions. Division by zero, extracting characters from empty strings, and accessing null references are common symptoms of boundary errors.

9. How many test cases do you need to cover all branches of the getDescription method of the Earthquake class?
10. Give a boundary test case for the EarthquakeRunner program. What output do you expect?

Quality Tip 4.3

Calculate Sample Data Manually

It is usually difficult or impossible to prove that a given program functions correctly in all cases. For gaining confidence in the correctness of a program, or for understanding why it does not function as it should, manually calculated sample data are invaluable. If the program arrives at the same results as the manual calculation, our confidence in it is strengthened. If the manual results differ from the program results, we have a starting point for the debugging process.

Surprisingly, many programmers are reluctant to perform any manual calculations as soon as a program carries out the slightest bit of algebra. Their math phobia kicks in, and they irrationally hope that they can avoid the algebra and beat the program into submission by random tinkering, such as rearranging the + and - signs. Random tinkering is always a great time sink, but it rarely leads to useful results.

Let's have another look at the TaxReturn class. Suppose a single taxpayer earns $50,000. The rules in Table 2 on page 151 state that the first $32,000 are taxed at 10 percent. Compute $32,000 \times 0.10 = 3,200$. The amount above $32,000, is taxed at 25 percent. It is time to take out your calculator—real world numbers are usually nasty. That is $(50,000 - 32,000) \times 0.25 = 4,500$. The total tax is the sum, $3,200 + 4,500 = 7,700$. Now, that wasn't so hard.

Run the program and compare the results. Because the results match, we have an increased confidence in the correctness of the program.

It is even better to make manual calculations before writing the program. Doing so helps you understand the task at hand, and you will be able to implement your solution more quickly.

> You should calculate test cases by hand to double-check that your application computes the correct answer.

Quality Tip 4.4

Prepare Test Cases Ahead of Time

Let us consider how we can test the tax computation program. Of course, we cannot try out all possible inputs of filing status and income level. Even if we could, there would be no point in trying them all. If the program correctly computes one or two tax amounts in a given bracket, then we have a good reason to believe that all amounts within that bracket will be correct. We want to aim for complete *coverage* of all cases.

There are two possibilities for the filing status and three tax brackets for each status. That makes six test cases. Then we want to test *boundary conditions*, such as zero income or incomes that are at the boundary between two brackets. That makes six test cases. Compute manually the answers you expect (See Quality Tip 4.3). Write down the test cases before you start coding.

Test Case	Married	Expected Output	Comment
30,000	N	3,000	10% bracket
72,000	N	13,200	3,200 + 25% of 40,000
50,000	Y	5,000	10% bracket

Test Case	Married	Expected Output	Comment
104,000	Y	16,400	6,400 + 25% of 40,000
32,000	N	3,200	boundary case
0		0	boundary case

Should you really test six inputs for this simple program? You certainly should. Furthermore, if you find an error in the program that wasn't covered by one of the test cases, make another test case and add it to your collection. After you fix the known mistakes, *run all test cases again.* Experience has shown that the cases that you just tried to fix are probably working now, but that errors that you fixed two or three iterations ago have a good chance of coming back! If you find that an error keeps coming back, that is usually a reliable sign that you did not fully understand some subtle interaction between features of your program.

It is always a good idea to design test cases *before* starting to code. There are two reasons for this. Working through the test cases gives you a better understanding of the algorithm that you are about to program. Furthermore, it has been noted that programmers instinctively shy away from testing fragile parts of their code. That seems hard to believe, but you will often make that observation about your own work. Watch someone else test your program. There will be times when that person enters input that makes you very nervous because you are not sure that your program can handle it, and you never dared to test it yourself. This is a well-known phenomenon, and making the test plan before writing the code offers some protection.

Special Topic 4.6

Logging

Sometimes you run a program and you are not sure where it spends its time. To get a printout of the program flow, you can insert trace messages into the program, such as this one:

```java
public double getTax()
{
   . . .
   if (status == SINGLE)
   {
      System.out.println("status is SINGLE");
      . . .
   }
   . . .
}
```

However, there is a problem with using System.out.println for trace messages. When you are done testing the program, you need to remove all print statements that produce trace messages. If you find another error, however, you need to stick the print statements back in.

To overcome this problem, you should use the Logger class, which allows you to turn off the trace messages without removing them from the program.

Instead of printing directly to System.out, use the global logger object that is returned by the call Logger.getGlobal(). (Prior to Java 7, you obtained the global logger as Logger.getLogger("global").) Then call the info method:

```java
Logger.getGlobal().info("status is SINGLE");
```

Logging messages
can be deactivated
when testing
is complete.

By default, the message is printed. But if you call

```
Logger.getGlobal().setLevel(Level.OFF);
```

at the beginning of the main method of your program, all log message printing is suppressed. Set the level to Level.INFO to turn logging of info messages on again. Thus, you can turn off the log messages when your program works fine, and you can turn them back on if you find another error. In other words, using Logger.getGlobal().info is just like System.out.println, except that you can easily activate and deactivate the logging.

A common trick for tracing execution flow is to produce log messages when a method is called, and when it returns. At the beginning of a method, print out the parameters:

```
public TaxReturn(double anIncome, int aStatus)
{
   Logger.getGlobal().info("Parameters: anIncome = " + anIncome
         + " aStatus = " + aStatus);
   . . .
}
```

At the end of a method, print out the return value:

```
public double getTax()
{
   . . .
   Logger.getGlobal().info("Return value = " + tax);
   return tax;
}
```

The Logger class has many other options for industrial-strength logging. Check out the API documentation if you want to have more control over logging.

Summary of Learning Objectives

Use the if statement to implement a decision.

- The if statement lets a program carry out different actions depending on a condition.
- A block statement groups several statements together.

Implement comparisons of numbers and objects.

- Relational operators compare values. The == operator tests for equality.
- When comparing floating-point numbers, don't test for equality. Instead, check whether they are close enough.
- Do not use the == operator to compare strings. Use the equals method instead.
- The compareTo method compares strings in dictionary order.
- The == operator tests whether two object references are identical. To compare the contents of objects, you need to use the equals method.
- The null reference refers to no object.

Implement complex decisions that require multiple if statements.

- Multiple conditions can be combined to evaluate complex decisions. The correct arrangement depends on the logic of the problem to be solved.

Use the Boolean data type to store and combine conditions that can be true or false.
- The boolean type has two values: true and false.
- A predicate method returns a boolean value.
- You can form complex tests with the Boolean operators && (*and*), || (*or*), and ! (*not*).
- You can store the outcome of a condition in a Boolean variable.

Design test cases that cover all parts of a program.
- Black-box testing describes a testing method that does not take the structure of the implementation into account.
- White-box testing uses information about the structure of a program.
- Code coverage is a measure of how many parts of a program have been tested.
- Boundary test cases are test cases that are at the boundary of acceptable inputs.
- You should calculate test cases by hand to double-check that your application computes the correct answer.

Use the Java logging library for messages that can be easily turned on or off.
- Logging messages can be deactivated when testing is complete.

Classes, Objects, and Methods Introduced in this Chapter

java.lang.Character
    isDigit
    isLetter
    isLowerCase
    isUpperCase
java.lang.Object
    equals
java.lang.String
    equals
    equalsIgnoreCase
    compareTo
	java.util.Scanner
	    hasNextDouble
	    hasNextInt
	java.util.logging.Level
	    INFO
	    OFF
	java.util.logging.Logger
	    getGlobal
	    info
	    setLevel

Media Resources

www.wiley.com/
go/global/
horstmann

- ***Worked Example*** Extracting the Middle
- Lab Exercises
- ➕ Practice Quiz
- ➕ Code Completion Exercises

Review Exercises

★ **R4.1** What is the value of each variable after the if statement?

a. int n = 1; int k = 2; int r = n; if (k < n) r = k;

b. int n = 1; int k = 2; int r; if (n < k) r = k; else r = k + n;

c. int n = 1; int k = 2; int r = k; if (r < k) n = r; else k = n;

d. int n = 1; int k = 2; int r = 3; if (r < n + k) r = 2 * n; else k = 2 * r;

★★ **R4.2** Find the errors in the following if statements.

    a. if (1 + x > Math.pow(x, Math.sqrt(2)) y = y + x;
    b. if (x = 1) y++; else if (x = 2) y = y + 2;
    c. int x = Integer.parseInt(input);
       if (x != null) y = y + x;

★★ **R4.3** Find the error in the following if statement that is intended to select a language from a given country and state/province.

```
language = "English";
if (country.equals("Canada"))
    if (stateOrProvince.equals("Quebec")) language = "French";
else if (country.equals("China"))
    language = "Chinese";
```

★★ **R4.4** Find the errors in the following if statements.

    a. if (x && y == 0) { x = 1; y = 1; }
    b. if (1 <= x <= 10)
       System.out.println(x);
    c. if (!s.equals("nickels") || !s.equals("pennies")
         || !s.equals("dimes") || !s.equals("quarters"))
       System.out.print("Input error!");
    d. if (input.equalsIgnoreCase("N") || "NO")
       return;

★ **R4.5** Explain the following terms, and give an example for each construct:
    a. Expression
    b. Condition
    c. Statement
    d. Simple statement
    e. Compound statement
    f. Block

★ **R4.6** Explain the difference between an if statement with multiple else branches and nested if statements. Give an example for each.

★ **R4.7** Give an example for an if/else if/else statement where the order of the tests does not matter. Give an example where the order of the tests matters.

★ **R4.8** Of the following pairs of strings, which comes first in lexicographic order?
    a. "Tom", "Jerry"
    b. "Tom", "Tomato"
    c. "church", "Churchill"
    d. "car manufacturer", "carburetor"
    e. "Harry", "hairy"
    f. "C++", " Car"
    g. "Tom", "Tom"
    h. "Car", "Carl"
    i. "car", "bar"
    j. "101", "11"
    k. "1.01", "10.1"

★ **R4.9** Complete the following truth table by finding the truth values of the Boolean expressions for all combinations of the Boolean inputs p, q, and r.

p	q	r	(p && q) || !r	!(p && (q || !r))
false	false	false		
false	false	false		
false	false	false		
...	...	...		
5 more combinations				
...				

★★ **R4.10** Each square on a chess board can be described by a letter and number, such as g5 in this example:

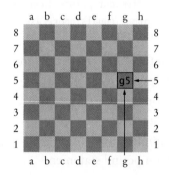

The following pseudocode describes an algorithm that determines whether a square with a given letter and number is dark (black) or light (white).

```
If the letter is an a, c, e, or g
    If the number is odd
        color = "black"
    Else
        color = "white"
Else
    If the number is even
        color = "black"
    Else
        color = "white"
```

Using the procedure in Productivity Hint 4.2 on page 155, trace this pseudocode with input g5.

★ **R4.11** Give a set of four test cases for the algorithm of Exercise R4.10 that covers all branches.

★★ **R4.12** In a scheduling program, we want to check whether two appointments overlap. For simplicity, appointments start at a full hour, and we use military time (with hours

0–24). The following pseudocode describes an algorithm that determines whether the appointment with start time **start1** and end time **end1** overlaps with the appointment with start time **start2** and end time **end2**.

```
If start1 > start2
    s = start1
Else
    s = start2
If end1 < end2
    e = end1
Else
    e = end2
If s < e
    The appointments overlap.
Else
    The appointments don't overlap.
```

Trace this algorithm with an appointment from 10–12 and one from 11–13, then with an appointment from 10–11 and one from 12–13.

★ **R4.13** Write pseudocode for a program that prompts the user for a month and day and prints out whether it is one of the following four holidays:

- New Year's Day (January 1)
- Independence Day (July 4)
- Veterans Day (November 11)
- Christmas Day (December 25)

★★★ **R4.14** True or false? A && B is the same as B && A for any Boolean conditions A and B.

★ **R4.15** Explain the difference between

```
s = 0;
if (x > 0) s++;
if (y > 0) s++;
```

and

```
s = 0;
if (x > 0) s++;
else if (y > 0) s++;
```

★★ **R4.16** Use de Morgan's law to simplify the following Boolean expressions.

a. !(x > 0 && y > 0)
b. !(x != 0 || y != 0)
c. !(country.equals("US") && !state.equals("HI")
        && !state.equals("AK"))
d. !(x % 4 != 0 || !(x % 100 == 0 && x % 400 == 0))

★★ **R4.17** Make up another Java code example that shows the dangling else problem, using the following statement: A student with a GPA of at least 1.5, but less than 2, is on probation; with less than 1.5, the student is failing.

★ **R4.18** Explain the difference between the == operator and the equals method when comparing strings.

★★ **R4.19** Explain the difference between the tests

```
r == s
```

and

```
r.equals(s)
```

where both r and s are of type Rectangle.

★★★ **R4.20** What is wrong with this test to see whether r is null? What happens when this code runs?

```
Rectangle r;
. . .
if (r.equals(null))
    r = new Rectangle(5, 10, 20, 30);
```

★ **R4.21** Explain how the lexicographic ordering of strings differs from the ordering of words in a dictionary or telephone book. *Hint:* Consider strings, such as IBM, wiley.com, Century 21, While-U-Wait, and 7-11.

★★★ **R4.22** Write Java code to test whether two objects of type Line2D.Double represent the same line when displayed on the graphics screen. *Do not* use a.equals(b).

```
Line2D.Double a;
Line2D.Double b;

if (your condition goes here)
    g2.drawString("They look the same!", x, y);
```

Hint: If p and q are points, then Line2D.Double(p, q) and Line2D.Double(q, p) look the same.

★ **R4.23** Explain why it is more difficult to compare floating-point numbers than integers. Write Java code to test whether an integer n equals 10 and whether a floating-point number x is approximately equal to 10.

★★ **R4.24** Consider the following test to see whether a point falls inside a rectangle.

```
Point2D.Double p = . . .
Rectangle r = . . .
boolean xInside = false;
if (r.getX() <= p.getX() && p.getX() <= r.getX() + r.getWidth())
    xInside = true;
boolean yInside = false;
if (r.getY() <= p.getY() && p.getY() <= r.getY() + r.getHeight())
    yInside = true;
if (xInside && yInside)
    g2.drawString("p is inside the rectangle.",
            p.getX(), p.getY());
```

Rewrite this code to eliminate the explicit true and false values, by setting xInside and yInside to the values of Boolean expressions.

★T **R4.25** Give a set of test cases for the earthquake program in Section 4.3.1. Ensure coverage of all branches.

★T **R4.26** Give an example of a boundary test case for the earthquake program in Section 4.3.1. What result do you expect?

Programming Exercises

★★   **P4.1** Write a program that prints all real solutions to the quadratic equation
$ax^2 + bx + c = 0$. Read in a, b, c and use the quadratic formula. If the *discriminant*
$b^2 - 4ac$ is negative, display a message stating that there are no real solutions.

Implement a class QuadraticEquation whose constructor receives the coefficients a, b,
c of the quadratic equation. Supply methods getSolution1 and getSolution2 that get
the solutions, using the quadratic formula, or 0 if no solution exists. The
getSolution1 method should return the smaller of the two solutions.

Supply a method

```
boolean hasSolutions()
```

that returns false if the discriminant is negative.

★★   **P4.2** Write a program that takes user input describing a playing card in the following
shorthand notation:

Notation	Meaning
A	Ace
2 ... 10	Card values
J	Jack
Q	Queen
K	King
D	Diamonds
H	Hearts
S	Spades
C	Clubs

Your program should print the full description of the card. For example,

```
Enter the card notation:
4S
Four of spades
```

Implement a class Card whose constructor takes the card notation string and whose
getDescription method returns a description of the card. If the notation string is not
in the correct format, the getDescription method should return the string "Unknown".

★★   **P4.3** Write a program that reads in three floating-point numbers and prints the three
inputs in sorted order. For example:

```
Please enter three numbers:
4
9
2.5
The inputs in sorted order are:
2.5
4
9
```

★ **P4.4** Write a program that translates a letter grade into a number grade. Letter grades are A B C D F, possibly followed by + or -. Their numeric values are 4, 3, 2, 1, and 0. There is no F+ or F-. A + increases the numeric value by 0.3, a - decreases it by 0.3. However, an A+ has the value 4.0. All other inputs have value −1.

```
Enter a letter grade:
B-
Numeric value: 2.7.
```

Use a class Grade with a method getNumericGrade.

★ **P4.5** Write a program that translates a number into the closest letter grade. For example, the number 2.8 (which might have been the average of several grades) would be converted to B-. Break ties in favor of the better grade; for example, 2.85 should be a B. Any value ≥ 4.15 should be an A+.

Use a class Grade with a method getLetterGrade.

★ **P4.6** Write a program that reads in three strings and prints them in lexicographically sorted order:

```
Please enter three strings:
Tom
Dick
Harry
The inputs in sorted order are:
Dick
Harry
Tom
```

★★ **P4.7** Change the implementation of the getTax method in the TaxReturn class, by setting a variable rate1_limit, depending on the marital status. Then have a single formula that computes the tax, depending on the income and the limit. Verify that your results are identical to that of the TaxReturn class in this chapter.

★★★ **P4.8** The original U.S. income tax of 1913 was quite simple. The tax was

- 1 percent on the first $50,000.
- 2 percent on the amount over $50,000 up to $75,000.
- 3 percent on the amount over $75,000 up to $100,000.
- 4 percent on the amount over $100,000 up to $250,000.
- 5 percent on the amount over $250,000 up to $500,000.
- 6 percent on the amount over $500,000.

There was no separate schedule for single or married taxpayers. Write a program that computes the income tax according to this schedule.

★★ **P4.9** Write a program that prompts for the day and month of the user's birthday and then prints a horoscope. Make up fortunes for programmers, like this:

```
Please enter your birthday (month and day): 6 16
Gemini are experts at figuring out the behavior of complicated programs.
You feel where bugs are coming from and then stay one step ahead. Tonight,
your style wins approval from a tough critic.
```

Each fortune should contain the name of the astrological sign. (You will find the names and date ranges of the signs at a distressingly large number of sites on the Internet.)

★ **P4.10** When two points in time are compared, each given as hours (in military time, ranging from 0 and 23) and minutes, the following pseudocode determines which comes first.

```
If hour1 < hour2
    time1 comes first.
Else if hour1 and hour2 are the same
    If minute1 < minute2
        time1 comes first.
    Else if minute1 and minute2 are the same
        time1 and time2 are the same.
    Else
        time2 comes first.
Else
    time2 comes first.
```

Write a program that prompts the user for two points in time and prints the time that comes first, then the other time.

★ **P4.11** The following algorithm yields the season (Spring, Summer, Fall, or Winter) for a given month and day.

```
If month is 1, 2, or 3, season = "Winter"
Else if month is 4, 5, or 6, season = "Spring"
Else if month is 7, 8, or 9, season = "Summer"
Else if month is 10, 11, or 12, season = "Fall"
If month is divisible by 3 and day >= 21
    If season is "Winter", season = "Spring"
    Else if season is "Spring", season = "Summer"
    Else if season is "Summer", season = "Fall"
    Else season = "Winter"
```

Write a program that prompts the user for a month and day and then prints the season, as determined by this algorithm.

★ **P4.12** A year with 366 days is called a *leap year*. A year is a leap year if it is divisible by 4 (for example, 1980). However, since the introduction of the Gregorian calendar on October 15, 1582, a year is not a leap year if it is divisible by 100 (for example, 1900); however, it is a leap year if it is divisible by 400 (for example, 2000). Write a program that asks the user for a year and computes whether that year is a leap year. Implement a class Year with a predicate method boolean isLeapYear().

★ **P4.13** Write a program that asks the user to enter a month (1 = January, 2 = February, and so on) and then prints the number of days of the month. For February, print "28 days".

```
Enter a month (1-12):
5
31 days
```

Implement a class Month with a method int getDays(). Do not use a separate if or else statement for each month. Use Boolean operators.

★★★ **P4.14** Write a program that reads in two floating-point numbers and tests (a) whether they are the same when rounded to two decimal places and (b) whether they differ by less than 0.01.

Here are two sample runs.

```
Enter two floating-point numbers:
2.0
1.99998
They are the same when rounded to two decimal places.
They differ by less than 0.01.

Enter two floating-point numbers:
0.999
0.991
They are different when rounded to two decimal places.
They differ by less than 0.01.
```

★ **P4.15** Enhance the BankAccount class of Chapter 2 by

- Rejecting negative amounts in the deposit and withdraw methods
- Rejecting withdrawals that would result in a negative balance

★ **P4.16** Write a program that reads in the hourly wage of an employee. Then ask how many hours the employee worked in the past week. Be sure to accept fractional hours. Compute the pay. Any overtime work (over 40 hours per week) is paid at 150 percent of the regular wage. Solve this problem by implementing a class Paycheck.

★★ **P4.17** Write a unit conversion program that asks users to identify the unit from which they want to convert and the unit to which they want to convert. Legal units are *in*, *ft*, *mi*, *mm*, *cm*, *m*, and *km*. Declare two objects of a class UnitConverter that convert between meters and a given unit.

```
Convert from:
in
Convert to:
mm
Value:
10
10 in = 254 mm
```

★★★ **P4.18** A line in the plane can be specified in various ways:

- by giving a point (x, y) and a slope m
- by giving two points (x_1, y_1), (x_2, y_2)
- as an equation in slope-intercept form $y = mx + b$
- as an equation $x = a$ if the line is vertical

Implement a class Line with four constructors, corresponding to the four cases above. Implement methods

```
boolean intersects(Line other)
boolean equals(Line other)
boolean isParallel(Line other)
```

★★G **P4.19** Write a program that draws a circle with radius 100 and center (200, 200). Ask the user to specify the *x*- and *y*-coordinates of a point. Draw the point as a small circle. If the point lies inside the circle, color the small circle green. Otherwise, color it red. In your exercise, declare a class Circle and a method boolean isInside(Point2D.Double p).

★★★G **P4.20** Write a graphics program that asks the user to specify the radii of two circles. The first circle has center (100, 200), and the second circle has center (200, 100). Draw the circles. If they intersect, then color both circles green. Otherwise, color them red. *Hint:* Compute the distance between the centers and compare it to the radii. Your program should draw nothing if the user enters a negative radius. In your exercise, declare a class Circle and a method boolean intersects(Circle other).

Programming Projects

Project 4.1 Implement a *combination lock* class. A combination lock has a dial with 26 positions labeled A . . . Z. The dial needs to be set three times. If it is set to the correct combination, the lock can be opened. When the lock is closed again, the combination can be entered again. If a user sets the dial more than three times, the last three settings determine whether the lock can be opened. An important part of this exercise is to implement a suitable interface for the CombinationLock class.

Project 4.2 Get the instructions for last year's form 1040 from http://www.irs.ustreas.gov. Find the tax brackets that were used last year for all categories of taxpayers (single, married filing jointly, married filing separately, and head of household). Write a program that computes taxes following that schedule. Ignore deductions, exemptions, and credits. Simply apply the tax rate to the income.

Answers to Self-Check Questions

1. If the withdrawal amount equals the balance, the result should be a zero balance and no penalty.
2. Only the first assignment statement is part of the if statement. Use braces to group both assignment statements into a block statement.
3. (a) 0; (b) 1; (c) An exception occurs.
4. Syntactically incorrect: e, g, h. Logically questionable: a, d, f
5. Yes, if you also reverse the comparisons:

```
if (richter < 3.5)
   r = "Generally not felt by people";
else if (richter < 4.5)
   r = "Felt by many people, no destruction";
else if (richter < 6.0)
   r = "Damage to poorly constructed buildings";
   . . .
```

6. The higher tax rate is only applied on the income in the higher bracket. Suppose you are single and make $31,900. Should you try to get a $200 raise? Absolutely: you get to keep 90 percent of the first $100 and 75 percent of the next $100.
7. When x is zero.
8. `if (!Character.isDigit(ch))` . . .
9. Seven
10. An input of 0 should yield an output of "Generally not felt by people". (If the output is "Negative numbers are not allowed", there is an error in the program.)

Chapter 5

Iteration

CHAPTER GOALS

- To be able to program loops with the while and for statements
- To avoid infinite loops and off-by-one errors
- To be able to use common loop algorithms
- To understand nested loops
- To implement simulations
- T To learn about the debugger

This chapter presents the various iteration constructs of the Java
language. These constructs execute one or more statements repeatedly until a goal is reached. You
will see how the techniques that you learn in this chapter can be applied to the processing of input
data and the programming of simulations.

CHAPTER CONTENTS

5.1 while Loops

In this chapter you will learn how to write programs that repeatedly execute one or more statements. We will illustrate these concepts by looking at typical investment situations. Consider a bank account with an initial balance of $10,000 that earns 5 percent interest. The interest is computed at the end of every year on the current balance and then deposited into the bank account. For example, after the first year, the account has earned $500 (5 percent of $10,000) of interest. The interest gets added to the bank account. Next year, the interest is $525 (5 percent of $10,500), and the balance is $11,025.

How many years does it take for the balance to reach $20,000? Of course, it won't take longer than 20 years, because at least $500 is added to the bank account each year. But it will take less than 20 years, because interest is computed on increasingly larger balances. To know the exact answer, we will write a program that repeatedly adds interest until the balance is reached.

In Java, the while statement implements such a repetition. The construct

> A while statement executes a block of code repeatedly. A condition controls how long the loop is executed.

```
while (condition)
    statement
```

keeps executing the statement while the condition is true.

Most commonly, the statement is a block statement, that is, a set of statements delimited by { }.

In our case, we want to know when the bank account has reached a particular balance. While the balance is less, we keep adding interest and incrementing the years counter:

```
while (balance < targetBalance)
{
   years++;
   double interest = balance * rate / 100;
   balance = balance + interest;
}
```

Figure 1 shows the flow of execution of this loop.

1 Check the loop condition   The condition is true

```
balance =   10000
                                  while (balance < targetBalance)
                                  {
   years =      0                    years++;
                                     double interest = balance * rate / 100;
                                     balance = balance + interest;
                                  }
```

2 Execute the statements in the loop

```
                                  while (balance < targetBalance)
balance =   10500                 {
                                     years++;
   years =      1                    double interest = balance * rate / 100;
                                     balance = balance + interest;
interest =     500                }
```

3 Check the loop condition again   The condition is still true

```
                                  while (balance < targetBalance)
balance =   10500                 {
                                     years++;
   years =      1                    double interest = balance * rate / 100;
                                     balance = balance + interest;
                                  }
```

                                            ⋮

4 After 15 iterations   The condition is
                                                                  no longer true
```
                                  while (balance < targetBalance)
balance =  20789.28               {
                                     years++;
   years =     15                    double interest = balance * rate / 100;
                                     balance = balance + interest;
                                  }
```

5 Execute the statement following the loop

```
                                  while (balance < targetBalance)
balance =  20789.28               {
                                     years++;
   years =     15                    double interest = balance * rate / 100;
                                     balance = balance + interest;
                                  }
                                  System.out.println(years);
```

Figure 1 Execution of a while Loop

For the full text of the sample program that solves our investment problem, see ch05/invest1/Investment.java in your source code, or view it in WileyPLUS.

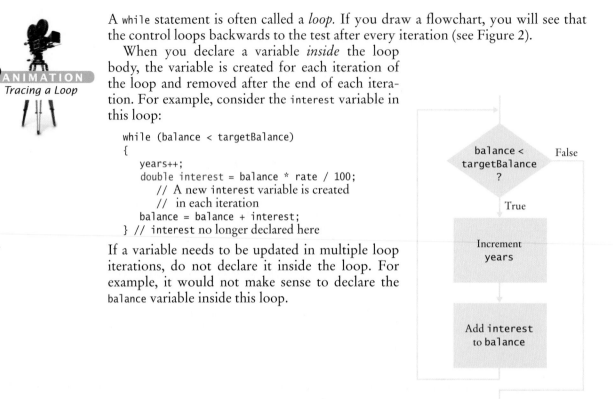

A `while` statement is often called a *loop*. If you draw a flowchart, you will see that the control loops backwards to the test after every iteration (see Figure 2).

When you declare a variable *inside* the loop body, the variable is created for each iteration of the loop and removed after the end of each iteration. For example, consider the `interest` variable in this loop:

```
while (balance < targetBalance)
{
   years++;
   double interest = balance * rate / 100;
      // A new interest variable is created
      // in each iteration
   balance = balance + interest;
} // interest no longer declared here
```

If a variable needs to be updated in multiple loop iterations, do not declare it inside the loop. For example, it would not make sense to declare the `balance` variable inside this loop.

Figure 2 Flowchart of a `while` Loop

Syntax 5.1 The `while` Statement

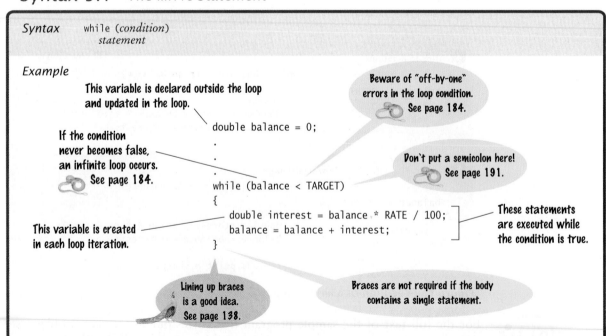

The following loop,

```
while (true)
    statement
```

executes the statement over and over, without terminating. Whoa! Why would you want that? The program would never stop. There are two reasons. Some programs indeed never stop; the software controlling an automated teller machine, a telephone switch, or a microwave oven doesn't ever stop (at least not until the device is turned off). Our programs aren't usually of that kind, but even if you can't terminate the loop, you can exit from the method that contains it. This can be helpful when the termination test naturally falls in the middle of the loop (see Special Topic 5.3 on page 202).

Table 1   while Loop Examples

Loop	Output	Explanation

```i = 0; sum = 0;```
```while (sum < 10)```
```{```
   ```i++; sum = sum + i;```
   Print i **and** sum;
```}```
	1 1
	2 3
	3 6
	4 10
		When sum is 10, the loop condition is false, and the loop ends.

```i = 0; sum = 0;```
```while (sum < 10)```
```{```
   ```i++; sum = sum - i;```
   Print i **and** sum;
```}```
	1 -1
	2 -3
	3 -6
	4 -10
	. . .
		Because sum never reaches 10, this is an "infinite loop" (see Common Error 5.1 on page 184).

```i = 0; sum = 0;```
```while (sum < 0)```
```{```
   ```i++; sum = sum - i;```
   Print i **and** sum;
```}```
	(No output)	The statement sum < 0 is false when the condition is first checked, and the loop is never executed.

```i = 0; sum = 0;```
```while (sum >= 10)```
```{```
   ```i++; sum = sum + i;```
   Print i **and** sum;
```}```
	(No output)	The programmer probably thought, "Stop when the sum is at least 10." However, the loop condition controls when the loop is executed, not when it ends.

```i = 0; sum = 0;```
```while (sum < 10) ;```
```{```
   ```i++; sum = sum + i;```
   Print i **and** sum;
```}```
	(No output, program does not terminate)	Note the semicolon before the {. This loop has an empty body. It runs forever, checking whether sum < 10 and doing nothing in the body (see Common Error 5.4 on page 191).

SELF CHECK

1. How many times is the following statement in the loop executed?

   `while (false)` *statement*;

2. What would happen if `RATE` was set to `0` in the `main` method of the `InvestmentRunner` program?

Productivity Hint 5.1

Hand-Tracing Loops

In Productivity Hint 4.2, you learned about the method of hand-tracing. This method is particularly effective for understanding how a loop works.

Consider this example loop. What value is displayed?

```
int n = 1729; ❶
int sum = 0;
while (n > 0) ❷
{
    int digit = n % 10; ❸ ❹ ❺ ❻
    sum = sum + digit;
    n = n / 10;
}
System.out.println(sum); ❼
```

1. There are three variables: `n`, `sum`, and `digit`. The first two variables are initialized with 1729 and 0 before the loop is entered.

n	sum	digit
1729	0	

2. Because `n` is positive, enter the loop.

3. The variable `digit` is set to 9 (the remainder of dividing 1729 by 10). The variable `sum` is set to 0 + 9 = 9. Finally, n becomes 172. (Recall that the remainder in the division 1729 / 10 is discarded because both arguments are integers.). Cross out the old values and write the new ones under the old ones.

n	sum	digit
~~1729~~	~~0~~	
172	9	9

4. Because n > 0, we repeat the loop. Now digit becomes 2, sum is set to 9 + 2 = 11, and n is set to 17.

n	sum	digit
~~1729~~	~~0~~	
~~172~~	~~9~~	~~9~~
17	11	2

5. Because n is still not zero, we repeat the loop, setting digit to 7, sum to 11 + 7 = 18, and n to 1.

n	sum	digit
~~1729~~	~~0~~	
~~172~~	~~9~~	~~9~~
~~17~~	~~11~~	~~2~~
1	18	7

6. We enter the loop one last time. Now digit is set to 1, sum to 19, and n becomes zero.

n	sum	digit
~~1729~~	~~0~~	
~~172~~	~~9~~	~~9~~
~~17~~	~~11~~	~~2~~
~~1~~	~~18~~	~~7~~
0	19	1

7. The condition n > 0 is now false, and we continue with the output statement after the loop. The value that is output is 19.

Of course, you can get the same answer simply by running the code. The hope is that by hand-tracing, you gain an *insight*. Consider again what happens in each iteration:

- We extract the last digit of n.
- We add that digit to sum.
- We strip the digit off n.

In other words, the loop forms the sum of the digits in n. You now know what the loop does for any value of n, not just the one in the example.

Why would anyone want to form the sum of the digits? Operations of this kind are useful for checking the validity of credit card numbers and other forms of ID number—see Exercise P5.2.

Common Error 5.1

Infinite Loops

One of the most annoying loop errors is an infinite loop: a loop that runs forever and can be stopped only by killing the program or restarting the computer. If there are output statements in the loop, then reams and reams of output flash by on the screen. Otherwise, the program just sits there and hangs, seeming to do nothing. On some systems you can kill a hanging program by hitting Ctrl+Break or Ctrl+C. On others, you can close the window in which the program runs.

A common reason for infinite loops is forgetting to advance the variable that controls the loop:

```
int years = 0;
while (years < 20)
{
   double interest = balance * rate / 100;
   balance = balance + interest;
}
```

Here the programmer forgot to add a statement for incrementing years in the loop. As a result, the value of years always stays 0, and the loop never comes to an end.

Another common reason for an infinite loop is accidentally incrementing a counter that should be decremented (or vice versa). Consider this example:

```
int years = 20;
while (years > 0)
{
   years++; // Oops, should have been years--
   double interest = balance * rate / 100;
   balance = balance + interest;
}
```

The years variable really should have been decremented, not incremented. This is a common error, because incrementing counters is so much more common than decrementing that your fingers may type the ++ on autopilot. As a consequence, years is always larger than 0, and the loop never terminates. (Actually, years eventually will exceed the largest representable positive integer and wrap around to a negative number. Then the loop exits—of course, that takes a long time, and the result is completely wrong.)

Common Error 5.2

Off-by-One Errors

Consider our computation of the number of years that are required to double an investment:

```
int years = 0;
while (balance < 2 * initialBalance)
{
   years++;
   double interest = balance * rate / 100;
   balance = balance + interest;
}
System.out.println("The investment reached the target after "
      + years + " years.");
```

Should years start at 0 or at 1? Should you test for balance < 2 * initialBalance or for balance <= 2 * initialBalance? It is easy to be *off by one* in these expressions.

Some people try to solve off-by-one errors by randomly inserting +1 or -1 until the program seems to work. That is, of course, a terrible strategy. It can take a long time to compile and test all the various possibilities. Expending a small amount of mental effort is a real time saver.

Fortunately, off-by-one errors are easy to avoid, simply by thinking through a couple of test cases and using the information from the test cases to come up with a rationale for the correct loop condition.

Should years start at 0 or at 1? Look at a scenario with simple values: an initial balance of $100 and an interest rate of 50 percent. After year 1, the balance is $150, and after year 2 it is $225, or over $200. So the investment doubled after 2 years. The loop executed two times, incrementing years each time. Hence years must start at 0, not at 1.

year	balance
0	$100
1	$150
2	$225

> An off-by-one error is a common error when programming loops. Think through simple test cases to avoid this type of error.

In other words, the `balance` variable denotes the balance *after* the end of the year. At the outset, the `balance` variable contains the balance after year 0 and not after year 1.

Next, should you use a `<` or `<=` comparison in the test? That is harder to figure out, because it is rare for the balance to be exactly twice the initial balance. Of course, there is one case when this happens, namely when the interest is 100 percent. The loop executes once. Now years is 1, and balance is exactly equal to `2 * initialBalance`. Has the investment doubled after one year? It has. Therefore, the loop should *not* execute again. If the test condition is `balance < 2 * initialBalance`, the loop stops, as it should. If the test condition had been `balance <= 2 * initialBalance`, the loop would have executed once more.

In other words, you keep adding interest while the balance *has not yet doubled*.

Special Topic 5.1

do **Loops**

Special Topic 5.1 discusses the do loop, an optional loop construct that tests the loop condition at the end of the loop body.

5.2 for Loops

One of the most common loop types has the form

```
i = start;
while (i <= end)
{
    . . .
    i++;
}
```

Because this loop is so common, there is a special form for it that emphasizes the pattern:

```
for (i = start; i <= end; i++)
{
    . . .
}
```

You can also declare the loop counter variable inside the `for` loop header. That convenient shorthand restricts the use of the variable to the body of the loop (as will be discussed further in Special Topic 5.2).

```
for (int i = start; i <= end; i++)
{
   . . .
}
```

A `for` loop can be used to find out the size of our $10,000 investment if 5 percent interest is compounded for 20 years. Of course, the balance will be larger than $20,000, because at least $500 is added every year. You may be surprised to find out just how much larger the balance is.

In our loop, we let `i` go from 1 to `numberOfYears`, the number of years for which we want to compound interest.

> You use a for loop when a variable runs from a starting to an ending value with a constant increment or decrement.

```
for (int i = 1; i <= numberOfYears; i++)
{
   double interest = balance * rate / 100;
   balance = balance + interest;
}
```

Figure 3 shows the corresponding flowchart. Figure 4 shows the flow of execution. The complete program is on page 189.

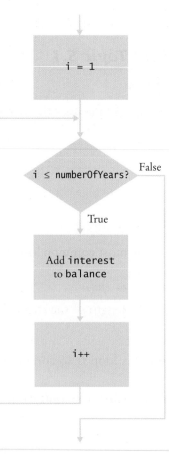

Figure 3
Flowchart of a for Loop

❶ Initialize counter

```
for (int i = 1; i <= numberOfYears; i++)
{
    double interest = balance * rate / 100;
    balance = balance + interest;
}
```

i = 1

❷ Check condition

```
for (int i = 1; i <= numberOfYears; i++)
{
    double interest = balance * rate / 100;
    balance = balance + interest;
}
```

i = 1

❸ Execute loop body

```
for (int i = 1; i <= numberOfYears; i++)
{
    double interest = balance * rate / 100;
    balance = balance + interest;
}
```

i = 1

❹ Update counter

```
for (int i = 1; i <= numberOfYears; i++)
{
    double interest = balance * rate / 100;
    balance = balance + interest;
}
```

i = 2

❺ Check condition again

```
for (int i = 1; i <= numberOfYears; i++)
{
    double interest = balance * rate / 100;
    balance = balance + interest;
}
```

i = 2

Figure 4 Execution of a for Loop

Another common use of the for loop is to traverse all characters of a string:

```
for (int i = 0; i < str.length(); i++)
{
    char ch = str.charAt(i);
    Process ch
}
```

Note that the counter variable i starts at 0, and the loop is terminated when i reaches the length of the string. For example, if str has length 5, i takes on the values 0, 1, 2, 3, and 4. These are the valid positions in the string.

Note too that the three slots in the for header can contain any three expressions. You can count down instead of up:

```
for (int i = 10; i > 0; i--)
```

The increment or decrement need not be in steps of 1:

```
for (int i = -10; i <= 10; i = i + 2) . . .
```

Syntax 5.2 The for Statement

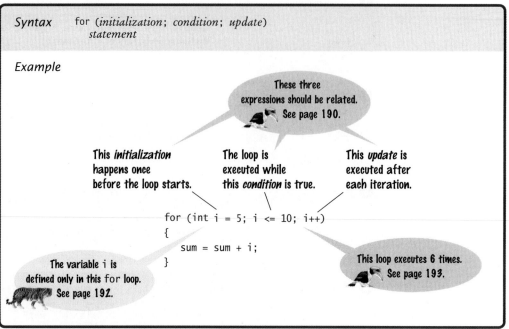

It is possible—but a sign of unbelievably bad taste—to put unrelated conditions into the loop header:

```
for (rate = 5; years-- > 0; System.out.println(balance))
    . . . // Bad taste
```

We won't even begin to decipher what that might mean. You should stick with `for` loops that initialize, test, and update a single variable.

Table 2 for Loop Examples		
Loop	Values of i	Comment
`for (i = 0; i <= 5; i++)`	0 1 2 3 4 5	Note that the loop is executed 6 times. (See Quality Tip 5.4 on page 193.)
`for (i = 5; i >= 0; i--)`	5 4 3 2 1 0	Use i-- for decreasing values.
`for (i = 0; i < 9; i = i + 2)`	0 2 4 6 8	Use i = i + 2 for a step size of 2.
`for (i = 0; i != 9; i = i + 2)`	0 2 4 6 8 10 12 14 ... (infinite loop)	You can use < or <= instead of != to avoid this problem.
`for (i = 1; i <= 20; i = i * 2)`	1 2 4 8 16	You can specify any rule for modifying i, such as doubling it in every step.
`for (i = 0; i < str.length(); i++)`	0 1 2 ... until the last valid index of the string str	In the loop body, use the expression str.charAt(i) to get the ith character.

ch05/invest2/Investment.java

```java
  1  /**
  2      A class to monitor the growth of an investment that
  3      accumulates interest at a fixed annual rate.
  4  */
  5  public class Investment
  6  {
  7     private double balance;
  8     private double rate;
  9     private int years;
 10
 11     /**
 12         Constructs an Investment object from a starting balance and
 13         interest rate.
 14         @param aBalance the starting balance
 15         @param aRate the interest rate in percent
 16     */
 17     public Investment(double aBalance, double aRate)
 18     {
 19        balance = aBalance;
 20        rate = aRate;
 21        years = 0;
 22     }
 23
 24     /**
 25         Keeps accumulating interest until a target balance has
 26         been reached.
 27         @param targetBalance the desired balance
 28     */
 29     public void waitForBalance(double targetBalance)
 30     {
 31        while (balance < targetBalance)
 32        {
 33           years++;
 34           double interest = balance * rate / 100;
 35           balance = balance + interest;
 36        }
 37     }
 38
 39     /**
 40         Keeps accumulating interest for a given number of years.
 41         @param numberOfYears the number of years to wait
 42     */
 43     public void waitYears(int numberOfYears)
 44     {
 45        for (int i = 1; i <= numberOfYears; i++)
 46        {
 47           double interest = balance * rate / 100;
 48           balance = balance + interest;
 49        }
 50        years = years + n;
 51     }
 52
 53     /**
 54         Gets the current investment balance.
 55         @return the current balance
 56     */
 57     public double getBalance()
 58     {
```

```
59        return balance;
60     }
61
62     /**
63        Gets the number of years this investment has accumulated
64        interest.
65        @return the number of years since the start of the investment
66     */
67     public int getYears()
68     {
69        return years;
70     }
71 }
```

ch05/invest2/InvestmentRunner.java

```
1  /**
2     This program computes how much an investment grows in
3     a given number of years.
4  */
5  public class InvestmentRunner
6  {
7     public static void main(String[] args)
8     {
9        final double INITIAL_BALANCE = 10000;
10       final double RATE = 5;
11       final int YEARS = 20;
12       Investment invest = new Investment(INITIAL_BALANCE, RATE);
13       invest.waitYears(YEARS);
14       double balance = invest.getBalance();
15       System.out.printf("The balance after %d years is %.2f\n",
16             YEARS, balance);
17     }
18 }
```

Program Run

```
The balance after 20 years is 26532.98
```

SELF CHECK

3. Rewrite the for loop in the waitYears method as a while loop.

4. How many times does the following for loop execute?

```
for (i = 0; i <= 10; i++)
   System.out.println(i * i);
```

Quality Tip 5.1

Use for Loops for Their Intended Purpose

A for loop is an *idiom* for a while loop of a particular form. A counter runs from the start to the end, with a constant increment:

```
for (Set counter to start; Test whether counter at end; Update counter by increment)
{  . . .
   // counter, start, end, increment not changed here
}
```

If your loop doesn't match this pattern, don't use the for construction. The compiler won't prevent you from writing idiotic for loops:

```java
// Bad style—unrelated header expressions
for (System.out.println("Inputs:");
      (x = in.nextDouble()) > 0;
      sum = sum + x)
   count++;

for (int i = 1; i <= years; i++)
{
   if (balance >= targetBalance)
      i = years;     // Bad style—modifies counter
   else
   {
      double interest = balance * rate / 100;
      balance = balance + interest;
   }
}
```

These loops will work, but they are plainly bad style. Use a while loop for iterations that do not fit the for pattern.

Common Error 5.3

Forgetting a Semicolon

Occasionally all the work of a loop is already done in the loop header. Suppose you ignored Quality Tip 5.1 on page 190; then you could write an investment doubling loop as follows:

```java
for (years = 1;
      (balance = balance + balance * rate / 100) < targetBalance;
      years++)
   ;
System.out.println(years);
```

The body of the for loop is completely empty, containing just one empty statement terminated by a semicolon.

If you do run into a loop without a body, it is important that you make sure the semicolon is not forgotten. If the semicolon is accidentally omitted, then the next line becomes part of the loop statement!

```java
for (years = 1;
      (balance = balance + balance * rate / 100) < targetBalance;
      years++)
   System.out.println(years);
```

You can avoid this error by using an empty block { } instead of an empty statement.

Common Error 5.4

A Semicolon Too Many

What does the following loop print?

```java
sum = 0;
for (i = 1; i <= 10; i++);
```

```
        sum = sum + i;
    System.out.println(sum);
```

Of course, this loop is supposed to compute $1 + 2 + \cdots + 10 = 55$. But actually, the print statement prints 11!

Why 11? Have another look. Did you spot the semicolon at the end of the for loop header? This loop is actually a loop with an empty body.

```
    for (i = 1; i <= 10; i++)
        ;
```

The loop does nothing 10 times, and when it is finished, sum is still 0 and i is 11. Then the statement

```
    sum = sum + i;
```

is executed, and sum is 11. The statement was indented, which fools the human reader. But the compiler pays no attention to indentation.

Of course, the semicolon at the end of the statement was a typing error. Someone's fingers were so used to typing a semicolon at the end of every line that a semicolon was added to the for loop by accident. The result was a loop with an empty body.

Quality Tip 5.2

Don't Use != to Test the End of a Range

Here is a loop with a hidden danger:

```
    for (i = 1; i != n; i++)
```

The test i != n is a poor idea. How does the loop behave if n happens to be zero or negative? The test i != n is never false, because i starts at 1 and increases with every step.

The remedy is simple. Use <= rather than != in the condition:

```
    for (i = 1; i <= n; i++)
```

Special Topic 5.2

Variables Declared in a for Loop Header

Special Topic 5.2 shows how to declare multiple variables in a for loop header, and it explains that such variables are not defined beyond the loop body.

Quality Tip 5.3

Symmetric and Asymmetric Bounds

It is easy to write a loop with i going from 1 to n:

```
    for (i = 1; i <= n; i++) . . .
```

The values for i are bounded by the relation $1 \leq i \leq n$. Because there are $\leq$ comparisons on both bounds, the bounds are called **symmetric**.

When traversing the characters in a string, the bounds are **asymmetric**.

```
for (i = 0; i < str.length(); i++) . . .
```

Make a choice between symmetric and asymmetric loop bounds.

The values for i are bounded by $0 \leq i < $ str.length(), with a $\leq$ comparison to the left and a $<$ comparison to the right. That is appropriate, because str.length() is not a valid position.

It is not a good idea to force symmetry artificially:

```
for (i = 0; i <= str.length() - 1; i++) . . .
```

That is more difficult to read and understand.

For every loop, consider which form is most natural for the problem, and use that.

Quality Tip 5.4

Count Iterations

Finding the correct lower and upper bounds for an iteration can be confusing. Should I start at 0? Should I use <= b or < b as a termination condition?

Counting the number of iterations is a very useful device for better understanding a loop. Counting is easier for loops with asymmetric bounds. The loop

```
for (i = a; i < b; i++) . . .
```

is executed b - a times. For example, the loop traversing the characters in a string,

```
for (i = 0; i < str.length(); i++) . . .
```

runs str.length() times. That makes perfect sense, because there are str.length() characters in a string.

The loop with symmetric bounds,

```
for (i = a; i <= b; i++)
```

is executed b - a + 1 times. That "+ 1" is the source of many programming errors. For example,

```
for (n = 0; n <= 10; n++)
```

runs 11 times. Maybe that is what you want; if not, start at 1 or use < 10.

Count the number of iterations to check that your for loop is correct.

One way to visualize this "+ 1" error is to think of the posts and sections of a fence. Suppose the fence has ten sections (=). How many posts (|) does it have?

```
|=|=|=|=|=|=|=|=|=|=|
```

A fence with ten sections has *eleven* posts. Each section has one post to the left, *and* there is one more post after the last section. Forgetting to count the last iteration of a "<=" loop is often called a "fence post error".

If the increment is a value c other than 1, and c divides b - a, then the counts are

$$(b - a) / c \qquad \text{for the asymmetric loop}$$

$$(b - a) / c + 1 \qquad \text{for the symmetric loop}$$

For example, the loop for (i = 10; i <= 40; i += 5) executes $(40 - 10)/5 + 1 = 7$ times.

5.3 Common Loop Algorithms

In the following sections, we discuss some of the most common algorithms that are implemented as loops. You can use them as starting points for your loop designs.

5.3.1 Computing a Total

Computing the sum of a number of inputs is a very common task. Keep a *running total:* a variable to which you add each input value. Of course, the total should be initialized with 0.

```java
double total = 0;
while (in.hasNextDouble())
{
   double input = in.nextDouble();
   total = total + input;
}
```

5.3.2 Counting Matches

You often want to know how many values fulfill a particular condition. For example, you may want to count how many uppercase letters are in a string. Keep a *counter*, a variable that is initialized with 0 and incremented whenever there is a match.

```java
int upperCaseLetters = 0;
for (int i = 0; i < str.length(); i++)
{
   char ch = str.charAt(i);
   if (Character.isUpperCase(ch))
   {
      upperCaseLetters++;
   }
}
```

For example, if str is the string "Hello, World!", upperCaseLetters is incremented twice (when i is 0 and 7).

5.3.3 Finding the First Match

When you count the values that fulfill a condition, you need to look at all values. However, if your task is to find a match, then you can stop as soon as the condition is fulfilled.

Here is a loop that finds the first lowercase letter in a string. Because we do not visit all elements in a string, a while loop is a better choice than a for loop:

```java
boolean found = false;
char ch = '?';
int position = 0;
```

```
while (!found && position < str.length())
{
    ch = str.charAt(position);
    if (Character.isLowerCase(ch)) { found = true; }
    else { position++; }
}
```

If a match was found, then found is true, ch is the first matching character, and its index is stored in the variable position. If the loop did not find a match, then found remains false and the loop continues until position reaches str.length().

Note that the variable ch is declared *outside* the while loop because you may want to use it after the loop has finished.

5.3.4 Prompting Until a Match is Found

In the preceding example, we searched a string for a character that matches a condition. You can apply the same process to user input. Suppose you are asking a user to enter a positive value < 100. Keep asking until the user provides a correct input:

```
boolean valid = false;
double input = 0;
while (!valid)
{
    System.out.print("Please enter a positive value < 100: ");
    input = in.nextDouble();
    if (0 < input && input < 100) { valid = true; }
    else { System.out.println("Invalid input."); }
}
```

As in the preceding example, the variable input is declared outside the while loop so that you can use it after the loop has finished.

5.3.5 Comparing Adjacent Values

When processing a sequence of values in a loop, you sometimes need to compare a value with the value that just preceded it. For example, suppose you want to check whether a sequence of inputs contains adjacent duplicates such as 1 7 2 9 9 4 9.

Now you face a challenge. Consider the typical loop for reading a value:

```
double input = 0;
while (in.hasNextDouble())
{
    input = in.nextDouble();
    . . .
}
```

How can you compare the current input with the preceding one? At any time, input contains the current input, overwriting the previous one.

The answer is to store the previous input, like this:

```
double input = 0;
while (in.hasNextDouble())
{
```

```
    double previous = input;
    input = in.nextDouble();
    if (input == previous) { System.out.println("Duplicate input"); }
}
```

One problem remains. When the loop is entered for the first time, there is no previous input value. You can solve this problem with an initial input operation outside the loop:

```
double input = in.nextDouble();
while (in.hasNextDouble())
{
    double previous = input;
    input = in.nextDouble();
    if (input == previous) { System.out.println("Duplicate input"); }
}
```

5.3.6 Processing Input with Sentinel Values

Suppose you want to process a set of values, for example a set of measurements. Your goal is to analyze the data and display properties of the data set, such as the average or the maximum value. You prompt the user for the first value, then the second value, then the third, and so on. When does the input end?

One common method for indicating the end of a data set is a **sentinel** value, a value that is not part of the data. Instead, the sentinel value indicates that the data has come to an end.

Some programmers choose numbers such as 0 or –1 as sentinel values. But that is not a good idea. These values may well be valid inputs. A better idea is to use an input that is not a number, such as the letter Q. Here is a typical program run:

```
Enter value, Q to quit: 1
Enter value, Q to quit: 2
Enter value, Q to quit: 3
Enter value, Q to quit: 4
Enter value, Q to quit: Q
Average = 2.5
Maximum = 4.0
```

Of course, we need to read each input as a string, not a number. Once we have tested that the input is not the letter Q, we convert the string into a number.

```
System.out.print("Enter value, Q to quit: ");
String input = in.next();
if (input.equalsIgnoreCase("Q"))
    We are done
else
{
    double x = Double.parseDouble(input);
    . . .
}
```

Now we have another problem. The test for loop termination occurs in the *middle* of the loop, not at the top or the bottom. You must first try to read input before you can test whether you have reached the end of input. In Java, there isn't a ready-made control structure for the pattern "do work, then test, then do more work". Therefore, we use a combination of a while loop and a boolean variable.

Sometimes, the termination condition of a loop can only be evaluated in the middle of a loop. You can introduce a Boolean variable to control such a loop.

```
boolean done = false;
while (!done)
{
    Print prompt
    String input = read input;
    if (end of input indicated)
        done = true;
    else
    {
        Process input
    }
}
```

This pattern is sometimes called "loop and a half". Some programmers find it clumsy to introduce a control variable for such a loop. Special Topic 5.3 shows several alternatives.

Here is a complete program that reads input and analyzes the data. We separate the input handling from the computation of the data set properties by using two classes, DataAnalyzer and DataSet. The DataAnalyzer class handles the input and adds values to a DataSet object with the add method. It then calls the getAverage method and the getMaximum method to obtain the average and maximum of all added data.

ch05/dataset/DataAnalyzer.java

```java
1   import java.util.Scanner;
2
3   /**
4      This program computes the average and maximum of a set
5      of input values.
6   */
7   public class DataAnalyzer
8   {
9      public static void main(String[] args)
10     {
11        Scanner in = new Scanner(System.in);
12        DataSet data = new DataSet();
13
14        boolean done = false;
15        while (!done)
16        {
17           System.out.print("Enter value, Q to quit: ");
18           String input = in.next();
19           if (input.equalsIgnoreCase("Q"))
20              done = true;
21           else
22           {
23              double x = Double.parseDouble(input);
24              data.add(x);
25           }
26        }
27
28        System.out.println("Average = " + data.getAverage());
29        System.out.println("Maximum = " + data.getMaximum());
30     }
31  }
```

ch05/dataset/DataSet.java

```
1   /**
2       Computes information about a set of data values.
3   */
4   public class DataSet
5   {
6      private double sum;
7      private double maximum;
8      private int count;
9
10     /**
11         Constructs an empty data set.
12     */
13     public DataSet()
14     {
15        sum = 0;
16        count = 0;
17        maximum = 0;
18     }
19
20     /**
21         Adds a data value to the data set.
22         @param x a data value
23     */
24     public void add(double x)
25     {
26        sum = sum + x;
27        if (count == 0 || maximum < x) maximum = x;
28        count++;
29     }
30
31     /**
32         Gets the average of the added data.
33         @return the average or 0 if no data has been added
34     */
35     public double getAverage()
36     {
37        if (count == 0) return 0;
38        else return sum / count;
39     }
40
41     /**
42         Gets the largest of the added data.
43         @return the maximum or 0 if no data has been added
44     */
45     public double getMaximum()
46     {
47        return maximum;
48     }
49  }
```

Program Run

```
Enter value, Q to quit: 10
Enter value, Q to quit: 0
Enter value, Q to quit: -1
Enter value, Q to quit: Q
Average = 3.0
Maximum = 10.0
```

SELF CHECK

5. How do you compute the total of all positive inputs?

6. What happens with the algorithm in Section 5.3.5 when no input is provided at all? How can you overcome that problem?

7. Why does the `DataAnalyzer` class call `in.next` and not `in.nextDouble`?

8. Would the `DataSet` class still compute the correct maximum if you simplified the update of the `maximum` variable in the `add` method to the following statement?

```
if (maximum < x) maximum = x;
```

How To 5.1

Writing a Loop

This How To walks you through the process of implementing a loop statement. We will illustrate the steps with the following example problem:

Read twelve temperature values (one for each month), and display the number of the month with the highest temperature. For example, according to `http://worldclimate.com`, the average maximum temperatures for Death Valley are (in order by month):

18.2 22.6 26.4 31.1 36.6 42.2
45.7 44.5 40.2 33.1 24.2 17.6

In this case, the month with the highest temperature (45.7 degrees Celsius) is July, and the program should display 7.

Step 1 Decide what work must be done *inside* the loop.

Every loop needs to do some kind of repetitive work, such as

- Reading another item.
- Updating a value (such as a bank balance or total).
- Incrementing a counter.

If you can't figure out what needs to go inside the loop, start by writing down the steps that you would take if you solved the problem by hand. For example, with the temperature reading problem, you might write

Read first value.
Read second value.
If second value is higher than the first, set highest temperature to that value, highest month to 2.
Read next value.
If value is higher than the first and second, set highest temperature to that value, highest month to 3.
Read next value.
If value is higher than the highest temperature seen so far, set highest temperature to that value,
   highest month to 4.
   . . .

Now look at these steps and reduce them to a set of *uniform* actions that can be placed into the loop body. The first action is easy:

Read next value.

The next action is trickier. In our description, we used tests "higher than the first", "higher than the first and second", "higher than the highest temperature seen so far". We need to settle on one test that works for all iterations. The last formulation is the most general.

Similarly, we must find a general way of setting the highest month. We need a variable that stores the current month, running from 1 to 12. Then we can formulate the second loop action:

If value is higher than the highest temperature, set highest temperature to that value,
   highest month to current month.

Altogether our loop is

Loop
> **Read next value.**
> **If value is higher than the highest temperature, set highest temperature to that value, highest month to current month.**
> **Increment current month.**

Step 2 Specify the loop condition.

What goal do you want to reach in your loop? Typical examples are

- Has a counter reached its final value?
- Have you read the last input value?
- Has a value reached a given threshold?

In our example, we simply want the current month to reach 12.

Step 3 Determine the loop type.

We distinguish between two major loop types. A *definite* or *count-controlled* loop is executed a definite number of times. In an *indefinite* or *event-controlled* loop, the number of iterations is not known in advance—the loop is executed until some event happens. A typical example of the latter is a loop that reads data until a sentinel is encountered.

Definite loops can be implemented as for statements. When you have an indefinite loop, consider the loop condition. Does it involve values that are only set inside the loop body? In that case, you should choose a do loop to ensure that the loop is executed at least once before the loop condition is be evaluated. Otherwise, use a while loop.

Sometimes, the condition for terminating a loop changes in the middle of the loop body. In that case, you can use a Boolean variable that specifies when you are ready to leave the loop. Follow this pattern:

```
boolean done = false;
while (!done)
{
    Do some work
    If all work has been completed
    {
        done = true;
    }
    else
    {
        Do more work
    }
}
```

Such a variable is called a *flag*.

In summary,

- If you know in advance how many times a loop is repeated, use a for loop.
- If the loop must be executed at least once, use a do loop.
- Otherwise, use a while loop.

In our example, we read 12 temperature values. Therefore, we choose a for loop.

Step 4 Set up variables for entering the loop for the first time.

List all variables that are used and updated in the loop, and determine how to initialize them. Commonly, counters are initialized with 0 or 1, totals with 0.

In our example, the variables are

```
current month
highest value
highest month
```

We need to be careful how we set up the highest temperature value. We can't simply set it to 0. After all, our program needs to work with temperature values from Antarctica, all of which may be negative.

A good option is to set the highest temperature value to the first input value. Of course, then we need to remember to only read in another 11 values, with the current month starting at 2.

We also need to initialize the highest month with 1. After all, in an Australian city, we may never find a month that is warmer than January.

Step 5 Process the result after the loop has finished.

In many cases, the desired result is simply a variable that was updated in the loop body. For example, in our temperature program, the result is the highest month. Sometimes, the loop computes values that contribute to the final result. For example, suppose you are asked to average the temperatures. Then the loop should compute the sum, not the average. After the loop has completed, you are ready compute the average: divide the sum by the number of inputs.

Here is our complete loop.

```
Read first value; store as highest value.
highest month = 1
for (current month = 2; current month <= 12; current month++)
    Read next value.
    If value is higher than the highest value, set highest value to that value,
        highest month to current month.
```

Step 6 Trace the loop with typical examples.

Hand trace your loop code, as described in Productivity Hint 5.1 on page 182. Choose example values that are not too complex—executing the loop 3–5 times is enough to check for the most common errors. Pay special attention when entering the loop for the first and last time.

Sometimes, you want to make a slight modification to make tracing feasible. For example, when hand tracing the investment doubling problem, use an interest rate of 20 percent rather than 5 percent. When hand tracing the temperature loop, use 4 data values, not 12.

Let's say the data are 22.6 36.6 44.5 24.2. Here is the walkthrough:

current month	current value	highest month	highest value
		~~1~~	~~22.6~~
~~2~~	36.6	~~2~~	~~36.6~~
~~3~~	44.5	3	44.5
4	24.2		

The trace demonstrates that **highest month** and **highest value** are properly set.

Step 7   Implement the loop in Java.

Here's the loop for our example. Exercise P5.1 asks you to complete the program.

```java
double highestValue = in.nextDouble();
int highestMonth = 1;
for (int currentMonth = 2; currentMonth <= 12; currentMonth++)
{
   double nextValue = in.nextDouble();
   if (nextValue > highestValue)
   {
      highestValue = nextValue;
      highestMonth = currentMonth;
   }
}
```

⊕ Worked Example 5.1

Credit Card Processing

This Worked Example uses a loop to remove spaces from a credit card number.

Special Topic 5.3

The "Loop and a Half" Problem

Special Topic 5.3 discusses two alternate strategies for implementing a loop whose termination condition is determined halfway into the loop body.

Special Topic 5.4

The break and continue Statements

Special Topic 5.4 discusses the optional break and continue statements. Neither statement is necessary for implementing loops, but they can occasionally make a complex loop more concise.

5.4 Nested Loops

Sometimes, the body of a loop is again a loop. We say that the inner loop is **nested** inside an outer loop. This happens often when you process two-dimensional structures, such as tables.

Let's look at an example that looks a bit more interesting than a table of numbers.

We want to generate the following triangular shape:

```
[]
[][]
[][][]
[][][][]
[][][][][]
[][][][][][]
[][][][][][][]
```

The basic idea is simple. We generate a sequence of rows:

```java
for (int i = 1; i <= width; i++)
{
    // Make triangle row
    . . .
}
```

How do you make a triangle row? Use another loop to concatenate the squares []
for that row. Then add a newline character at the end of the row. The ith row has i
symbols, so the loop counter goes from 1 to i.

```java
for (int j = 1; j <= i; j++)
    r = r + "[]";
r = r + "\n";
```

Putting both loops together yields two *nested loops:*

```java
String r = "";
for (int i = 1; i <= width; i++)
{
    // Make triangle row
    for (int j = 1; j <= i; j++)
        r = r + "[]";
    r = r + "\n";
}
return r;
```

For the full text of the program, see ch05/triangle1/ in your source code, or view it
in WileyPLUS.

Table 3 **Nested Loop Examples**		
Nested Loops	Output	Explanation

`for (i = 1; i <= 3; i++)`
`{`
`    for (j = 1; j <= 4; j++) { Print "*" }`
`    System.out.println();`
`}`
	****
	****
	****
		Prints 3 rows of 4 asterisks each.

`for (i = 1; i <= 4; i++)`
`{`
`    for (j = 1; j <= 3; j++) { Print "*" }`
`    System.out.println();`
`}`
	***
	***
	***
	***
		Prints 4 rows of 3 asterisks each.

Table 3 Nested Loop Examples, continued		
Nested Loops	Output	Explanation
``for (i = 1; i <= 4; i++)
{
for (j = 1; j <= i; j++) { Print "*" }
System.out.println();

}```	`*`
	`**`
	`***`
	`****`
		Prints 4 rows of lengths 1, 2, 3, and 4.

``for (i = 1; i <= 3; i++)
{
for (j = 1; j <= 5; j++)
{
if (j % 2 == 0) { Print "*" }
else { Print "-" }
}
System.out.println();
}```	`-*-*-` `-*-*-` `-*-*-`	Prints asterisks in even columns, dashes in odd columns.
``for (i = 1; i <= 3; i++)
{
for (j = 1; j <= 5; j++)
{
if ((i + j) % 2 == 0) { Print "*" }
else { Print " " }
}
System.out.println();

}```	`* * *`
	` * * `
	`* * *`
		Prints a checkerboard pattern.

SELF CHECK

9. How would you modify the nested loops so that you print a square instead of a triangle?

10. What is the value of n after the following nested loops?

```
int n = 0;
for (int i = 1; i <= 5; i++)
   for (int j = 0; j < i; j++)
      n = n + j;
```

⊕ **Worked Example 5.2**

Manipulating the Pixels in an Image

This Worked Example shows how to use nested loops for manipulating the pixels in an image. The outer loop traverses the rows of the image, and the inner loop accesses each pixel of a row.

5.5 Application: Random Numbers and Simulations

A *simulation program* uses the computer to simulate an activity in the real world (or an imaginary one). Simulations are commonly used for predicting climate change, analyzing traffic, picking stocks, and many other applications in science and business. In many simulations, one or more loops are used to modify the state of a system and observe the changes.

> In a simulation, you repeatedly generate random numbers and use them to simulate an activity.

Here is a typical problem that can be decided by running a simulation: the *Buffon needle experiment*, devised by Comte Georges-Louis Leclerc de Buffon (1707–1788), a French naturalist. On each *try*, a one-inch long needle is dropped onto paper that is ruled with lines 2 inches apart. If the needle drops onto a line, count it as a hit. (See Figure 5.) Buffon conjectured that the quotient *tries/hits* approximates π.

Now, how can you run this experiment in the computer? You don't actually want to build a robot that drops needles on paper. The Random class of the Java library implements a *random number generator*, which produces numbers that appear to be completely random. To generate random numbers, you construct an object of the Random class, and then apply one of the following methods:

Method	Returns
nextInt(n)	A random integer between the integers 0 (inclusive) and n (exclusive)
nextDouble()	A random floating-point number between 0 (inclusive) and 1 (exclusive)

For example, you can simulate the cast of a die as follows:

```
Random generator = new Random();
int d = 1 + generator.nextInt(6);
```

The call generator.nextInt(6) gives you a random number between 0 and 5 (inclusive). Add 1 to obtain a number between 1 and 6.

If you call nextInt ten times, you get a random sequence of numbers similar to the following:

```
6 5 6 3 2 6 3 4 4 1
```

Actually, the numbers are not completely random. They are drawn from very long sequences of numbers that don't repeat for a long time. These sequences are

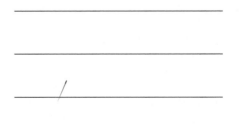

Figure 5 The Buffon Needle Experiment

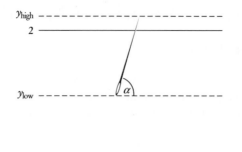

Figure 6 When Does the Needle Fall on a Line?

computed from fairly simple formulas; they just behave like random numbers. For that reason, they are often called **pseudorandom numbers**. Generating good sequences of numbers that behave like truly random sequences is an important and well-studied problem in computer science. We won't investigate this issue further, though; we'll just use the random numbers produced by the Random class.

To run the Buffon needle experiment, we have to work a little harder. When you throw a die, it has to come up with one of six faces. When throwing a needle, however, there are many possible outcomes. You must generate *two* random numbers: one to describe the starting position and one to describe the angle of the needle with the x-axis. Then you need to test whether the needle touches a grid line. Stop after 10,000 tries.

Let us agree to generate the *lower* point of the needle. Its x-coordinate is irrelevant, and you may assume its y-coordinate y_{low} to be any random number between 0 and 2. However, because it can be a random **floating-point number**, we use the nextDouble method of the Random class. It returns a random floating-point number between 0 and 1. Multiply by 2 to get a random number between 0 and 2.

The angle α between the needle and the x-axis can be any value between 0 degrees and 180 degrees. The upper end of the needle has y-coordinate

$$y_{high} = y_{low} + \sin(\alpha)$$

The needle is a hit if y_{high} is at least 2. See Figure 6.

For the program that carries out the simulation of the needle experiment, see ch05/ random2/ in your source code, or view it in WileyPLUS.

The point of this program is not to compute π—there are far more efficient ways to do that. Rather, the point is to show how a physical experiment can be simulated on the computer. Buffon had to physically drop the needle thousands of times and record the results, which must have been a rather dull activity. The computer can execute the experiment quickly and accurately.

Simulations are very common computer applications. Many simulations use essentially the same pattern as the code of this example: In a loop, a large number of sample values are generated, and the values of certain observations are recorded for each sample. When the simulation is completed, the averages, or other statistics of interest from the observed values are printed out.

A typical example of a simulation is the modeling of customer queues at a bank or a supermarket. Rather than observing real customers, one simulates their arrival and their transactions at the teller window or checkout stand in the computer. One can try different staffing or building layout patterns in the computer simply by making changes in the program. In the real world, making many such changes and measuring their effects would be impossible, or at least, very expensive.

SELF CHECK

11. How do you use a random number generator to simulate the toss of a coin?

12. Why is the NeedleSimulator program not an efficient method for computing π?

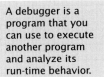

Special Topic 5.5

Loop Invariants

Special Topic 5.5 shows how you can use the technique of loop invariants to prove that a loop will always compute the correct result.

5.6 Using a Debugger

As you have undoubtedly realized by now, computer programs rarely run perfectly the first time. At times, it can be quite frustrating to find the bugs. Of course, you can insert print commands, run the program, and try to analyze the printout. If the printout does not clearly point to the problem, you may need to add and remove print commands and run the program again. That can be a time-consuming process.

> A debugger is a program that you can use to execute another program and analyze its run-time behavior.

Modern development environments contain special programs, called **debuggers**, that help you locate bugs by letting you follow the execution of a program. You can stop and restart your program and see the contents of variables whenever your program is temporarily stopped. At each stop, you have the choice of what variables to inspect and how many program steps to run until the next stop.

Some people feel that debuggers are just a tool to make programmers lazy. Admittedly some people write sloppy programs and then fix them up with a debugger, but the majority of programmers make an honest effort to write the best program they can before trying to run it through a debugger. These programmers realize that a debugger, while more convenient than print commands, is not cost-free. It does take time to set up and carry out an effective debugging session.

In actual practice, you cannot avoid using a debugger. The larger your programs get, the harder it is to debug them simply by inserting print commands. You will find that the time investment to learn about a debugger is amply repaid in your programming career.

Like compilers, debuggers vary widely from one system to another. On some systems they are quite primitive and require you to memorize a small set of arcane commands; on others they have an intuitive window interface. The screen shots in this chapter show the debugger in the Eclipse development environment, downloadable for free from the Eclipse Foundation web site (eclipse.org). Other integrated environments, such as BlueJ, also include debuggers. A free standalone debugger called JSwat is available from www.bluemarsh.com/java/jswat.

You will have to find out how to prepare a program for debugging and how to start a debugger on your system. If you use an integrated development environment, which contains an editor, compiler, and debugger, this step is usually very easy. You just build the program in the usual way and pick a menu command to start debugging. On some systems, you must manually build a debug version of your program and invoke the debugger.

> You can make effective use of a debugger by mastering just three concepts: breakpoints, single-stepping, and inspecting variables.

Once you have started the debugger, you can go a long way with just three debugging commands: "set breakpoint", "single step", and "inspect variable". The names and keystrokes or mouse clicks for these commands differ widely between debuggers, but all debuggers support these basic commands. You can find out how, either from the documentation or a lab manual, or by asking someone who has used the debugger before.

> When a debugger executes a program, the execution is suspended whenever a breakpoint is reached.

When you start the debugger, it runs at full speed until it reaches a **breakpoint**. Then execution stops, and the breakpoint that causes the stop is displayed (see Figure 7). You can now inspect variables and step through the program a line at a time, or continue running the program at full speed until it reaches the next breakpoint. When the program terminates, the debugger stops as well.

Breakpoints stay active until you remove them, so you should periodically clear the breakpoints that you no longer need.

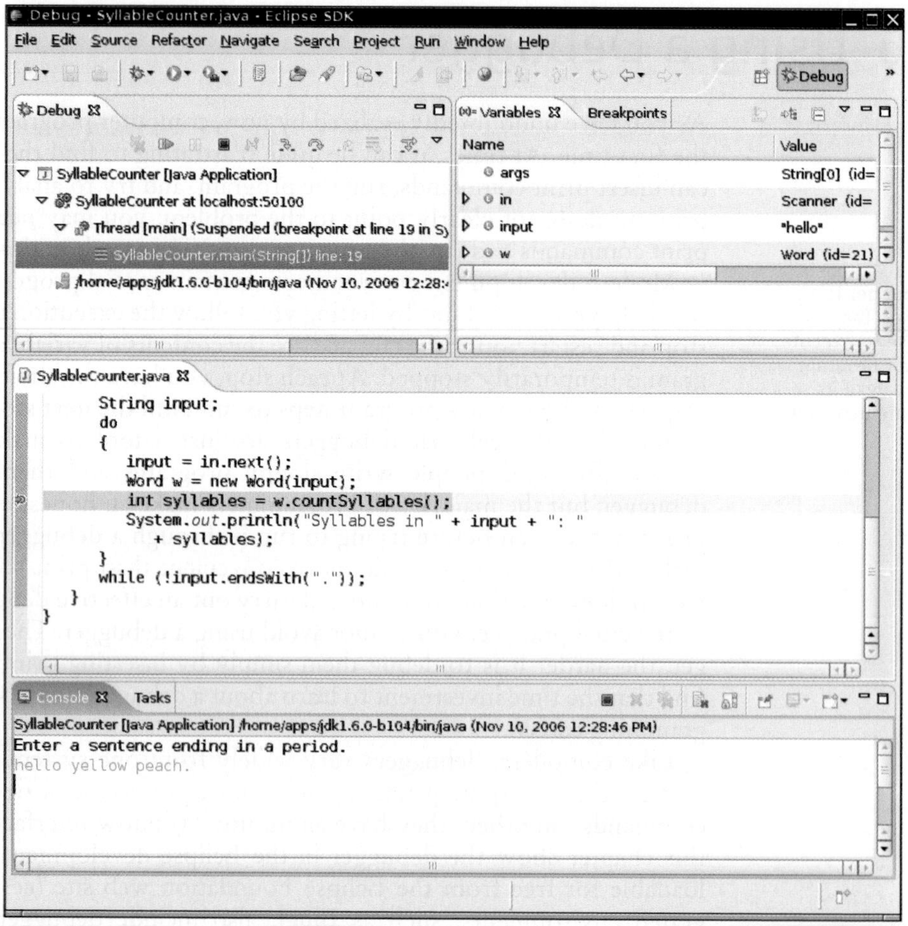

Figure 7 Stopping at a Breakpoint

Figure 8
Inspecting Variables

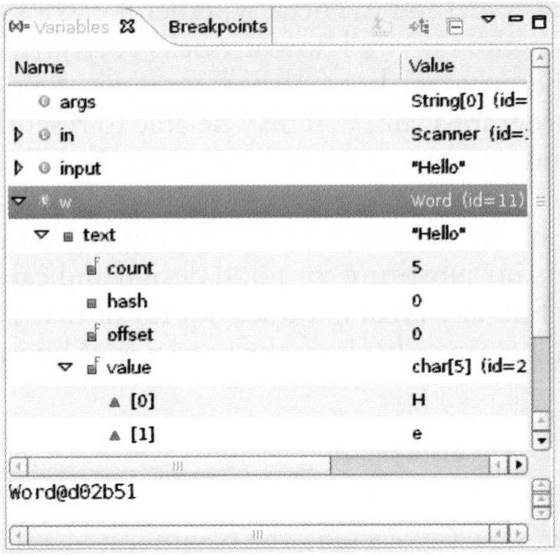

Once the program has stopped, you can look at the current values of variables. Again, the method for selecting the variables differs among debuggers. Some debuggers always show you a window with the current local variables. On other debuggers you issue a command such as "inspect variable" and type in or click on the variable. The debugger then displays the contents of the variable. If all variables contain what you expected, you can run the program until the next point where you want to stop.

When inspecting objects, you often need to give a command to "open up" the object, for example by clicking on a tree node. Once the object is opened up, you see its instance variables (see Figure 8).

The single-step command executes the program one line at a time.

Running to a breakpoint gets you there speedily, but you don't know how the program got there. You can also step through the program a line at a time. Then you know how the program flows, but it can take a long time to step through it. The *single-step command* executes the current line and stops at the next program line. Most debuggers have two single-step commands, one called *step into*, which steps inside method calls, and one called *step over*, which skips over method calls.

For example, suppose the current line is

```
String input = in.next();
Word w = new Word(input);
int syllables = w.countSyllables();
System.out.println("Syllables in " + input + ": " + syllables);
```

When you step over method calls, you get to the next line:

```
String input = in.next();
Word w = new Word(input);
int syllables = w.countSyllables();
System.out.println("Syllables in " + input + ": " + syllables);
```

However, if you step into method calls, you enter the first line of the countSyllables method.

```
public int countSyllables()
{
    int count = 0;
    int end = text.length() - 1;
    . . .
}
```

You should step *into* a method to check whether it carries out its job correctly. You should step *over* a method if you know it works correctly.

Finally, when the program has finished running, the debug session is also finished. To run the program again, you may be able to reset the debugger, or you may need to exit the debugging program and start over. Details depend on the particular debugger.

A debugger can be used only to analyze the presence of bugs, not to show that a program is bug-free.

A debugger can be an effective tool for finding and removing bugs in your program. However, it is no substitute for good design and careful programming. If the debugger does not find any errors, it does not mean that your program is bug-free. Testing and debugging can only show the presence of bugs, not their absence.

SELF CHECK

13. In the debugger, you are reaching a call to System.out.println. Should you step into the method or step over it?

14. In the debugger, you are reaching the beginning of a method with a couple of loops inside. You want to find out the return value that is computed at the end of the method. Should you set a breakpoint, or should you step through the method?

How To 5.2

Debugging

Now you know about the mechanics of debugging, but all that knowledge may still leave you helpless when you fire up a debugger to look at a sick program. There are a number of strategies that you can use to recognize bugs and their causes.

Step 1   Reproduce the error.

As you test your program, you notice that it sometimes does something wrong. It gives the wrong output, it seems to print something completely random, it goes in an infinite loop, or it crashes. Find out exactly how to reproduce that behavior. What numbers did you enter? Where did you click with the mouse?

Run the program again; type in exactly the same numbers, and click with the mouse on the same spots (or as close as you can get). Does the program exhibit the same behavior? If so, then it makes sense to fire up a debugger to study this particular problem. Debuggers are good for analyzing particular failures. They aren't terribly useful for studying a program in general.

Step 2   Simplify the error.

Before you fire up a debugger, it makes sense to spend a few minutes trying to come up with a simpler input that also produces an error. Can you use shorter words or simpler numbers and still have the program misbehave? If so, use those values during your debugging session.

Step 3   Divide and conquer.

Use the divide-and-conquer technique to locate the point of failure of a program.

Now that you have a particular failure, you want to get as close to the failure as possible. The key point of debugging is to locate the code that produces the failure. Just as with real insect pests, finding the bug can be hard, but once you find it, squashing it is usually the easy part. Suppose your program dies with a division by 0. Because there are many division operations in a typical program, it is often not feasible to set breakpoints to all of them. Instead, use a technique of divide and conquer. Step over the methods in main, but don't step inside them. Eventually, the failure will happen again. Now you know which method contains the bug: It is the last method that was called from main before the program died. Restart the debugger and go back to that line in main, then step inside that method. Repeat the process.

Eventually, you will have pinpointed the line that contains the bad division. Maybe it is completely obvious from the code why the denominator is not correct. If not, you need to find the location where it is computed. Unfortunately, you can't go back in the debugger. You need to restart the program and move to the point where the denominator computation happens.

Step 4   Know what your program should do.

> During debugging, compare the actual contents of variables against the values you know they should have.

A debugger shows you what the program does. You must know what the program *should* do, or you will not be able to find bugs. Before you trace through a loop, ask yourself how many iterations you expect the program to make. Before you inspect a variable, ask yourself what you expect to see. If you have no clue, set aside some time and think first. Have a calculator handy to make independent computations. When you know what the value should be, inspect the variable. This is the moment of truth. If the program is still on the right track, then that value is what you expected, and you must look further for the bug. If the value is different, you may be on to something. Double-check your computation. If you are sure your value is correct, find out why your program comes up with a different value.

In many cases, program bugs are the result of simple errors such as loop termination conditions that are off by one. Quite often, however, programs make computational errors. Maybe they are supposed to add two numbers, but by accident the code was written to subtract them. Unlike your calculus instructor, programs don't make a special effort to ensure that everything is a simple integer (and neither do real-world problems). You will need to make some calculations with large integers or nasty floating-point numbers. Sometimes these calculations can be avoided if you just ask yourself, "Should this quantity be positive? Should it be larger than that value?" Then inspect variables to verify those theories.

Step 5   Look at all details.

When you debug a program, you often have a theory about what the problem is. Nevertheless, keep an open mind and look around at all details. What strange messages are displayed? Why does the program take another unexpected action? These details count. When you run a debugging session, you really are a detective who needs to look at every clue available.

If you notice another failure on the way to the problem that you are about to pin down, don't just say, "I'll come back to it later". That very failure may be the original cause for your current problem. It is better to make a note of the current problem, fix what you just found, and then return to the original mission.

Step 6   Make sure you understand each bug before you fix it.

Once you find that a loop makes too many iterations, it is very tempting to apply a "Band-Aid" solution and subtract 1 from a variable so that the particular problem doesn't appear again. Such a quick fix has an overwhelming probability of creating trouble elsewhere. You really need to have a thorough understanding of how the program should be written before you apply a fix.

It does occasionally happen that you find bug after bug and apply fix after fix, and the problem just moves around. That usually is a symptom of a larger problem with the program logic. There is little you can do with the debugger. You must rethink the program design and reorganize it.

➕ **Worked Example 5.3**

A Sample Debugging Session

This Worked Example shows how to find bugs in an algorithm for counting the syllables of a word.

Random Fact 5.1

The First Bug

According to legend, the first bug was one found in 1947 in the Mark II, a huge electro-mechanical computer at Harvard University. It really was caused by a bug—a moth was trapped in a relay switch. Actually, from the note that the operator left in the log book next to the moth (see the figure), it appears as if the term "bug" had already been in active use at the time.

The First Bug

The pioneering computer scientist Maurice Wilkes wrote: "Somehow, at the Moore School and afterwards, one had always assumed there would be no particular difficulty in getting programs right. I can remember the exact instant in time at which it dawned on me that a great part of my future life would be spent finding mistakes in my own programs."

Summary of Learning Objectives

Explain the flow of execution in a loop.

- A while statement executes a block of code repeatedly. A condition controls for how long the loop is executed.
- An off-by-one error is a common error when programming loops. Think through simple test cases to avoid this type of error.

Use for loops to implement counting loops.

- You use a for loop when a variable runs from a starting to an ending value with a constant increment or decrement.
- Make a choice between symmetric and asymmetric loop bounds.
- Count the number of iterations to check that your for loop is correct.

Implement loops that process a data set until a sentinel value is encountered.

- Sometimes, the termination condition of a loop can only be evaluated in the middle of a loop. You can introduce a Boolean variable to control such a loop.

Use nested loops to implement multiple levels of iterations.

- When the body of a loop contains another loop, the loops are nested. A typical use of nested loops is printing a table with rows and columns.

Apply loops to the implementation of simulations that involve random values.

- In a simulation, you repeatedly generate random numbers and use them to simulate an activity.

Use a debugger to locate errors in a running program.

- A debugger is a program that you can use to execute another program and analyze its run-time behavior.
- You can make effective use of a debugger by mastering just three concepts: breakpoints, single-stepping, and inspecting variables.
- When a debugger executes a program, the execution is suspended when-ever a breakpoint is reached.
- The single-step command executes the program one line at a time.
- A debugger can be used only to analyze the presence of bugs, not to show that a program is bug-free.
- Use the divide-and-conquer technique to locate the point of failure of a program.
- During debugging, compare the actual contents of variables against the values you know they should have.

Classes, Objects, and Methods Introduced in this Chapter

```
java.util.Random
    nextDouble
    nextInt
```

Media Resources

- **_Worked Example_** Credit Card Processing
- **_Worked Example_** Manipulating the Pixels in an Image
- **_Worked Example_** A Sample Debugging Session
- Lab Exercises
- ⊕ **_Animation_** Tracing a Loop
- ⊕ **_Animation_** The for Loop
- ⊕ Practice Quiz
- ⊕ Code Completion Exercises

Review Exercises

★★ **R5.1** Which loop statements does Java support? Give simple rules when to use each loop type.

★★ **R5.2** What does the following code print?

```
for (int i = 0; i < 10; i++)
{
```

```
            for (int j = 0; j < 10; j++)
                System.out.print(i * j % 10);
            System.out.println();
        }
```

★★ **R5.3** How many iterations do the following loops carry out? Assume that i is an integer variable that is not changed in the loop body.

    a. for (i = 1; i <= 10; i++) . . .
    b. for (i = 0; i < 10; i++) . . .
    c. for (i = 10; i > 0; i--) . . .
    d. for (i = -10; i <= 10; i++) . . .
    e. for (i = 10; i >= 0; i++) . . .
    f. for (i = -10; i <= 10; i = i + 2) . . .
    g. for (i = -10; i <= 10; i = i + 3) . . .

★ **R5.4** Rewrite the following for loop into a while loop.

```
int s = 0;
for (int i = 1; i <= 10; i++) s = s + i;
```

★★ **R5.5** Rewrite the following do loop into a while loop.

```
int n = 1;
double x = 0;
double s;
do
{
    s = 1.0 / (n * n);
    x = x + s;
    n++;
}
while (s > 0.01);
```

★ **R5.6** What is an infinite loop? On your computer, how can you terminate a program that executes an infinite loop?

★★★ **R5.7** Give three strategies for implementing the following "loop and a half":

Loop
    Read name of bridge.
    If not OK, exit loop.
    Read length of bridge in feet.
    If not OK, exit loop.
    Convert length to meters.
    Print bridge data.

Use a Boolean variable, a break statement, and a method with multiple return statements. Which of these three approaches do you find clearest?

★ **R5.8** Implement a loop that prompts a user to enter a number between 1 and 10, giving three tries to get it right.

★ **R5.9** Sometimes students write programs with instructions such as "Enter data, 0 to quit" and that exit the data entry loop when the user enters the number 0. Explain why that is usually a poor idea.

★ **R5.10** How would you use a random number generator to simulate the drawing of a playing card?

★ **R5.11** What is an "off-by-one error"? Give an example from your own programming experience.

★★ **R5.12** Give an example of a for loop in which symmetric bounds are more natural. Give an example of a for loop in which asymmetric bounds are more natural.

★ **R5.13** What are nested loops? Give an example where a nested loop is typically used.

★T **R5.14** Explain the differences between these debugger operations:
- Stepping into a method
- Stepping over a method

★★T **R5.15** Explain in detail how to inspect the string stored in a String object in your debugger.

★★T **R5.16** Explain in detail how to inspect the information stored in a Rectangle object in your debugger.

★★T **R5.17** Explain in detail how to use your debugger to inspect the balance stored in a Bank-Account object.

★★T **R5.18** Explain the divide-and-conquer strategy to get close to a bug in a debugger.

Programming Exercises

★ **P5.1** Complete the program in How To 5.1 on page 199. Your program should read twelve temperature values and print the month with the highest temperature.

★★★ **P5.2** *Credit Card Number Check.* The last digit of a credit card number is the *check digit*, which protects against transcription errors such as an error in a single digit or switching two digits. The following method is used to verify actual credit card numbers but, for simplicity, we will describe it for numbers with 8 digits instead of 16:
- Starting from the rightmost digit, form the sum of every other digit. For example, if the credit card number is 4358 9795, then you form the sum 5 + 7 + 8 + 3 = 23.
- Double each of the digits that were not included in the preceding step. Add all digits of the resulting numbers. For example, with the number given above, doubling the digits, starting with the next-to-last one, yields 18 18 10 8. Adding all digits in these values yields 1 + 8 + 1 + 8 + 1 + 0 + 8 = 27.
- Add the sums of the two preceding steps. If the last digit of the result is 0, the number is valid. In our case, 23 + 27 = 50, so the number is valid.

Write a program that implements this algorithm. The user should supply an 8-digit number, and you should print out whether the number is valid or not. If it is not valid, you should print out the value of the check digit that would make the number valid.

★ **P5.3** *Currency conversion.* Write a program CurrencyConverter that asks the user to enter today's price of one dollar in euro. Then the program reads U.S. dollar values and converts each to euro values. Stop when the user enters Q.

★★★   **P5.4** *Projectile flight.* Suppose a cannonball is propelled vertically into the air with a starting velocity v_0. Any calculus book will tell us that the position of the ball after t seconds is $s(t) = -0.5 \cdot g \cdot t^2 + v_0 \cdot t$, where $g = 9.81$ m/sec^2 is the gravitational force of the earth. No calculus book ever mentions why someone would want to carry out such an obviously dangerous experiment, so we will do it in the safety of the computer.

In fact, we will confirm the theorem from calculus by a simulation. In our simulation, we will consider how the ball moves in very short time intervals Δt. In a short time interval the velocity v is nearly constant, and we can compute the distance the ball moves as $\Delta s = v \cdot \Delta t$. In our program, we will simply set

```
double deltaT = 0.01;
```

and update the position by

```
s = s + v * deltaT;
```

The velocity changes constantly—in fact, it is reduced by the gravitational force of the earth. In a short time interval, v decreases by $g \cdot \Delta t$, and we must keep the velocity updated as

```
v = v - g * deltaT;
```

In the next iteration the new velocity is used to update the distance.

Now run the simulation until the cannonball falls back to the earth. Get the initial velocity as an input (100 m/sec is a good value). Update the position and velocity 100 times per second, but only print out the position every full second. Also print out the values from the exact formula $s(t) = -0.5 \cdot g \cdot t^2 + v_0 \cdot t$ for comparison. Use a class `Cannonball`.

What is the benefit of this kind of simulation when an exact formula is available? Well, the formula from the calculus book is *not* exact. Actually, the gravitational force diminishes the farther the cannonball is away from the surface of the earth. This complicates the algebra sufficiently that it is not possible to give an exact formula for the actual motion, but the computer simulation can simply be extended to apply a variable gravitational force. For cannonballs, the calculus-book formula is actually good enough, but computers are necessary to compute accurate trajectories for higher-flying objects such as ballistic missiles.

★★   **P5.5** Write a program that prints the powers of ten

```
1.0
10.0
100.0
1000.0
10000.0
100000.0
1000000.0
1.0E7
1.0E8
1.0E9
1.0E10
1.0E11
```

Implement a class

```
public class PowerGenerator
{
```

```
/**
    Constructs a power generator.
    @param aFactor  the number that will be multiplied by itself
*/
public PowerGenerator(double aFactor) { . . . }

/**
    Computes the next power.
*/
public double nextPower() { . . . }
    . . .
}
```

Then supply a test class PowerGeneratorRunner that calls System.out.println(
myGenerator.nextPower()) twelve times.

★★   **P5.6**   The *Fibonacci sequence* is defined by the following rule. The first two values in the
sequence are 1 and 1. Every subsequent value is the sum of the two values preceding
it. For example, the third value is $1 + 1 = 2$, the fourth value is $1 + 2 = 3$, and the fifth
is $2 + 3 = 5$. If f_n denotes the nth value in the Fibonacci sequence, then

$$f_1 = 1$$
$$f_2 = 1$$
$$f_n = f_{n-1} + f_{n-2} \quad \text{if } n > 2$$

Write a program that prompts the user for n and prints the first n values in the
Fibonacci sequence. Use a class FibonacciGenerator with a method nextNumber.

Hint: There is no need to store all values for f_n. You only need the last two values to
compute the next one in the series:

```
fold1 = 1;
fold2 = 1;
fnew = fold1 + fold2;
```

After that, discard fold2, which is no longer needed, and set fold2 to fold1 and fold1
to fnew.

Your generator class will be tested with this runner program:

```
public class FibonacciRunner
{
    public static void main(String[] args)
    {
        Scanner in = new Scanner(System.in);

        System.out.println("Enter n:");
        int n = in.nextInt();

        FibonacciGenerator fg = new FibonacciGenerator();

        for (int i = 1; i <= n; i++)
            System.out.println(fg.nextNumber());
    }
}
```

★★ **P5.7** *Mean and standard deviation.* Write a program that reads a set of floating-point data values from the input. When the user indicates the end of input, print out the count of the values, the average, and the standard deviation. The average of a data set $x_1, \ldots, x_n$ is

$$\bar{x} = \frac{\sum x_i}{n}$$

where $\sum x_i = x_1 + \cdots + x_n$ is the sum of the input values. The standard deviation is

$$s = \sqrt{\frac{\sum (x_i - \bar{x})^2}{n - 1}}$$

However, that formula is not suitable for our task. By the time you have computed the mean, the individual x_i are long gone. Until you know how to save these values, use the numerically less stable formula

$$s = \sqrt{\frac{\sum x_i^2 - \frac{1}{n}\left(\sum x_i\right)^2}{n - 1}}$$

You can compute this quantity by keeping track of the count, the sum, and the sum of squares in the DataSet class as you process the input values.

★★ **P5.8** *Factoring of integers.* Write a program that asks the user for an integer and then prints out all its factors in increasing order. For example, when the user enters 150, the program should print

```
2
3
5
5
```

Use a class FactorGenerator with a constructor FactorGenerator(int numberToFactor) and methods nextFactor and hasMoreFactors. Supply a class FactorPrinter whose main method reads a user input, constructs a FactorGenerator object, and prints the factors.

★★ **P5.9** *Prime numbers.* Write a program that prompts the user for an integer and then prints out all prime numbers up to that integer. For example, when the user enters 20, the program should print

```
2
3
5
7
11
13
17
19
```

Recall that a number is a prime number if it is not divisible by any number except 1 and itself.

Supply a class PrimeGenerator with a method nextPrime.

★★ **P5.10** The *Heron method* is a method for computing square roots that was known to the ancient Greeks. If x is a guess for the value $\sqrt{a}$, then the average of x and a/x is a better guess.

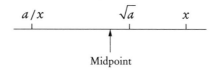

Implement a class `RootApproximator` that starts with an initial guess of 1 and whose
`nextGuess` method produces a sequence of increasingly better guesses. Supply a
method `hasMoreGuesses` that returns `false` if two successive guesses are sufficiently
close to each other (that is, they differ by no more than a small value ε). Then test
your class like this:

```
RootApproximator approx = new RootApproximator(a, EPSILON);
while (approx.hasMoreGuesses())
    System.out.println(approx.nextGuess());
```

★★ **P5.11** The best known iterative method for computing the roots of a function f (that is,
the x-values for which $f(x)$ is 0) is Newton–Raphson approximation. To find the
zero of a function whose derivative is also known, compute

$$x_{\text{new}} = x_{\text{old}} - f\left(x_{\text{old}}\right)/f'\left(x_{\text{old}}\right).$$

For this exercise, write a program to compute nth roots of floating-point
numbers. Prompt the user for a and n, then obtain $\sqrt[n]{a}$ by computing a zero of
the function $f(x) = x^n - a$. Follow the approach of Exercise P5.10.

★★ **P5.12** The value of e^x can be computed as the power series

$$e^x = \sum_{n=0}^{\infty} \frac{x^n}{n!}$$

where $n! = 1 \cdot 2 \cdot 3 \cdot \ldots \cdot n$.

Write a program that computes e^x using this formula. Of course, you can't compute
an infinite sum. Just keep adding values until an individual summand (term) is less
than a certain threshold. At each step, you need to compute the new term and add it
to the total. Update these terms as follows:

```
term = term * x / n;
```

Follow the approach of the preceding two exercises, by implementing a class
`ExpApproximator`. Its first guess should be 1.

★ **P5.13** Write a program `RandomDataAnalyzer` that generates 100 random numbers between 0
and 1000 and adds them to a `DataSet`. Print out the average and the maximum.

★★ **P5.14** Program the following simulation: Darts are thrown at random points onto the
square with corners (1,1) and (−1,−1). If the dart lands inside the unit circle (that is,
the circle with center (0,0) and radius 1), it is a hit. Otherwise it is a miss. Run this
simulation and use it to determine an approximate value for π. Extra credit if you
explain why this is a better method for estimating π than the Buffon needle
program.

★★★G **P5.15** *Random walk.* Simulate the wandering of an intoxicated person in a square street
grid. Draw a grid of 20 streets horizontally and 20 streets vertically. Represent the
simulated drunkard by a dot, placed in the middle of the grid to start. For 100 times,
have the simulated drunkard randomly pick a direction (east, west, north, south),

move one block in the chosen direction, and draw the dot. (One might expect that on average the person might not get anywhere because the moves to different directions cancel one another out in the long run, but in fact it can be shown with probability 1 that the person eventually moves outside any finite region. Use classes for the grid and the drunkard.

★★★G **P5.16** This exercise is a continuation of Exercise P5.4. Most cannonballs are not shot upright but at an angle. If the starting velocity has magnitude v and the starting angle is α, then the velocity is a vector with components $v_x = v \cdot \cos(\alpha)$, $v_y = v \cdot \sin(\alpha)$. In the x-direction the velocity does not change. In the y-direction the gravitational force takes its toll. Repeat the simulation from the previous exercise, but update the x and y components of the location and the velocity separately. In every iteration, plot the location of the cannonball on the graphics display as a tiny circle. Repeat until the cannonball has reached the earth again.

This kind of problem is of historical interest. The first computers were designed to carry out just such ballistic calculations, taking into account the diminishing gravity for high-flying projectiles and wind speeds.

★G **P5.17** Write a graphical application that displays a checkerboard with 64 squares, alternating white and black.

★★G **P5.18** Write a graphical application that prompts a user to enter a number n and that draws n circles with random diameter and random location. The circles should be completely contained inside the window.

★★★G **P5.19** Write a graphical application that draws a spiral, such as the following:

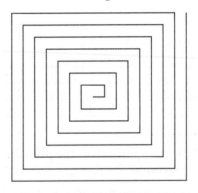

★★G **P5.20** It is easy and fun to draw graphs of curves with the Java graphics library. Simply draw 100 line segments joining the points $(x, f(x))$ and $(x + d, f(x + d))$, where x ranges from x_{min} to x_{max} and $d = (x_{max} - x_{min})/100$.

Draw the curve $f(x) = 0.00005x^3 - 0.03x^2 + 4x + 200$, where x ranges from 0 to 400 in this fashion.

★★★G **P5.21** Draw a picture of the "four-leaved rose" whose equation in polar coordinates is $r = \cos(2\theta)$. Let θ go from 0 to 2π in 100 steps. Each time, compute r and then compute the (x,y) coordinates from the polar coordinates by using the formula

$$x = r \cdot \cos(\theta), y = r \cdot \sin(\theta)$$

Programming Projects

Project 5.1 *Flesch Readability Index.* The following index was invented by Rudolf Flesch as a tool to gauge the legibility of a document without linguistic analysis.

- Count all words in the file. A *word* is any sequence of characters delimited by white space, whether or not it is an actual English word.

- Count all syllables in each word. To make this simple, use the following rules: Each *group* of adjacent vowels (a, e, i, o, u, y) counts as one syllable (for example, the "ea" in "real" contributes one syllable, but the "e . . . a" in "regal" count as two syllables). However, an "e" at the end of a word doesn't count as a syllable. Also, each word has at least one syllable, even if the previous rules give a count of 0.

- Count all sentences. A sentence is ended by a period, colon, semicolon, question mark, or exclamation mark.

- The index is computed by

$$\text{Index} = 206.835$$
$$- 84.6 \times \left(\text{Number of syllables/Number of words}\right)$$
$$- 1.015 \times \left(\text{Number of words/Number of sentences}\right)$$

rounded to the nearest integer.

The purpose of the index is to force authors to rewrite their text until the index is high enough. This is achieved by reducing the length of sentences and by removing long words. For example, the sentence

> The following index was invented by Flesch as a simple tool to estimate the legibility of a document without linguistic analysis.

can be rewritten as

> Flesch invented an index to check whether a text is easy to read. To compute the index, you need not look at the meaning of the words.

This index is a number, usually between 0 and 100, indicating how difficult the text is to read. Some example indices for random material from various publications are:

Comics	95
Consumer ads	82
Sports Illustrated	65
Time	57
New York Times	39
Auto insurance policy	10
Internal Revenue Code	−6

Translated into educational levels, the indices are:

91–100	5th grader
81–90	6th grader
71–80	7th grader
66–70	8th grader
61–65	9th grader
51–60	High school student
31–50	College student
0–30	College graduate
Less than 0	Law school graduate

Your program should read a text file in, compute the legibility index, and print out the equivalent educational level. Use classes Word and Document.

Project 5.2 *The game of Nim.* This is a well-known game with a number of variants. We will consider the following variant, which has an interesting winning strategy. Two players alternately take marbles from a pile. In each move, a player chooses how many marbles to take. The player must take at least one but at most half of the marbles. Then the other player takes a turn. The player who takes the last marble loses.

Write a program in which the computer plays against a human opponent. Generate a random integer between 10 and 100 to denote the initial size of the pile. Generate a random integer between 0 and 1 to decide whether the computer or the human takes the first turn. Generate a random integer between 0 and 1 to decide whether the computer plays *smart* or *stupid*. In stupid mode, the computer simply takes a random legal value (between 1 and $n/2$) from the pile whenever it has a turn. In smart mode the computer takes off enough marbles to make the size of the pile a power of 2 minus 1—that is, 3, 7, 15, 31, or 63. That is always a legal move, except if the size of the pile is currently one less than a power of 2. In that case, the computer makes a random legal move.

Note that the computer cannot be beaten in smart mode when it has the first move, unless the pile size happens to be 15, 31, or 63. Of course, a human player who has the first turn and knows the winning strategy can win against the computer.

When you implement this program, be sure to use classes Pile, Player, and Game. A player can be either stupid, smart, or human. (Human Player objects prompt for input.)

Answers to Self-Check Questions

1. Never.
2. The waitForBalance method would never return due to an infinite loop.
3. ```
   int i = 1;
   while (i <= numberOfYears)
   {
      double interest = balance * rate / 100;
      balance = balance + interest;
      i++;
   }
   ```
4. 11 times.
5. ```
   double total = 0;
   while (in.hasNextDouble())
   {
      double input = in.nextDouble();
      if (value > 0) total = total + input;
   }
   ```
6. The initial call to in.nextDouble() fails, terminating the program. One solution is to do all input in the loop and introduce a Boolean variable that checks whether the loop is entered for the first time.
   ```
   double input = 0;
   boolean first = true;
   while (in.hasNextDouble())
   {
      double previous = input;
      input = in.nextDouble();
      if (first) { first = false; }
      else if (input == previous) { System.out.println("Duplicate input"); }
   }
   ```
7. Because we don't know whether the next input is a number or the letter Q.
8. No. If *all* input values are negative, the maximum is also negative. However, the maximum variable is initialized with 0. With this simplification, the maximum would be falsely computed as 0.
9. Change the inner loop to for (int j = 1; j <= width; j++).
10. 20.
11. int n = generator.nextInt(2); // 0 = heads, 1 = tails
12. The program repeatedly calls Math.toRadians(angle). You could simply call Math.toRadians(180) to compute π.
13. You should step over it because you are not interested in debugging the internals of the println method.
14. You should set a breakpoint. Stepping through loops can be tedious.

Arrays and Array Lists

CHAPTER GOALS

- To become familiar with using arrays and array lists
- To learn about wrapper classes, auto-boxing, and the enhanced for loop
- To study common array algorithms
- To learn how to use two-dimensional arrays
- To understand when to choose array lists and arrays in your programs
- To implement partially filled arrays
- T To understand the concept of regression testing

In order to process large quantities of data, you need to have a mechanism for collecting values. In Java, arrays and array lists serve this purpose. In this chapter, you will learn how to construct arrays and array lists, fill them with values, and access the stored values. We introduce the enhanced for loop, a convenient statement for processing all elements of a collection. You will see how to use the enhanced for loop, as well as ordinary loops, to implement common array algorithms. The chapter concludes with a discussion of two-dimensional arrays, which are useful for handling rows and columns of data.

CHAPTER CONTENTS

6.1 Arrays

In many programs, you need to manipulate collections of related values. It would be impractical to use a sequence of variables such as value1, value2, value3, . . . , and so on. The array construct provides a better way of storing a collection of values.

> An array is a
> sequence of values
> of the same type.

An **array** is a sequence of values of the same type. The values that are stored in an array are called its "elements". For example, here is how you construct an array of 10 floating-point numbers:

```
new double[10]
```

The number of elements (here, 10) is called the length of the array.

The new operator merely constructs the array. You will want to store a reference to the array in a variable so that you can access it later.

The type of an array variable is the element type, followed by []. In this example, the type is double[], because the element type is double. Here is the declaration of an array variable:

```
double[] values = new double[10];
```

That is, values is a reference to an array of floating-point numbers. It is initialized with an array of 10 numbers (see Figure 1).

You can also form arrays of objects, for example

```
BankAccount[] accounts = new BankAccount[10];
```

When an array is first created, all elements are initialized with 0 (for an array of numbers such as int[] or double[]), false (for a boolean[] array), or null (for an array of object references).

Figure 1
An Array Reference
and an Array

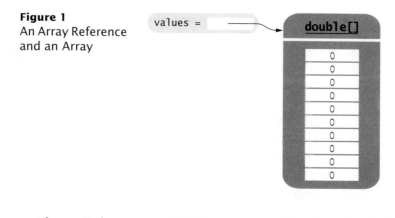

Alternatively, you can initialize an array with other values. List all elements that you want to include in the array, enclosed in braces and separated by commas:

```
int[] primes = { 2, 3, 5, 7, 11 };
```

The Java compiler counts how many elements you want to place in the array, allocates an array of the correct size, and fills it with the elements that you specify.

Each element in the array is specified by an integer index that is placed inside square brackets ([]). For example, the expression

```
values[4]
```

denotes the element of the values array with index 4.

You can store a value at a location with an assignment statement, such as the following.

```
values[2] = 29.95;
```

Now the position with index 2 of values is filled with 29.95 (see Figure 2).

To read the element at index 2, simply use the expression values[2] as you would any variable of type double:

```
System.out.println("The element at index 2 is " + values[2]);
```

If you look closely at Figure 2, you will notice that the index values start at 0. That is,

values[0] is the first element

values[1] is the second element

values[2] is the third element

> You access an array element with an integer index, using the [] operator.

Figure 2
Modifying an
Array Element

Index values of an array range from 0 to length - 1.

Accessing a nonexistent element results in a bounds error.

The expression *array*.length yields the number of elements in an array.

and so on. This convention can be a source of grief for the newcomer, so you should pay close attention to the index values. In particular, the *last* element in the array has an index *one less than* the array length. For example, values refers to an array with length 10. The last element is values[9].

If you try to access an element that does not exist, then an "array index out of bounds" exception occurs. For example, the statement

```
values[10] = 29.95; // ERROR
```

is a **bounds error**.

To avoid bounds errors, you will want to know how many elements are in an array. The expression

```
values.length
```

is the length of the values array. Note that there are no parentheses following length—it is an instance variable of the array object, not a method. However, you cannot modify this instance variable. In other words, length is a final public instance variable. This is quite an anomaly. Normally, Java programmers use a method to inquire about the properties of an object. You just have to remember to omit the parentheses in this case.

The following code ensures that you only access the array when the index variable i is within the legal bounds:

```
if (0 <= i && i < values.length) values[i] = value;
```

Arrays suffer from a significant limitation: *their length is fixed*. If you start out with an array of 10 elements and later decide that you need to add additional elements, then you need to make a new array and copy all elements of the existing array into the new array. We will discuss this process in detail in Section 6.6.

Table 1 Declaring Arrays

`int[] numbers = new int[10];`	An array of ten integers. All elements are initialized with zero.
`final int NUMBERS_LENGTH = 10;` `int[] numbers = new int[NUMBERS_LENGTH];`	It is a good idea to use a named constant instead of a "magic number".
`int valuesLength = in.nextInt();` `double[] values = new double[valuesLength];`	The length need not be a constant.
`int[] squares = { 0, 1, 4, 9, 16 };`	An array of five integers, with initial values.
`String[] names = new String[3];`	An array of three string references, all initially null.
`String[] friends = { "Emily", "Bob", "Cindy" };`	Another array of three strings.
`double[] values = new int[10]`	**Error:** You cannot initialize a double[] variable with an array of type int[].

Syntax 6.1 Arrays

Syntax   To construct an array: new *typeName*[*length*]

To access an element: *arrayReference*[*index*]

Example

Type of array variable

Name of array variable

Element type

Length

Initialized with zero

```
double[] values = new double[10];
```

```
double[] moreValues = { 32, 54, 67.5, 29, 35 };
```

Initialized with these elements

Use brackets to access an element.

```
values[i] = 29.95;
```

The index must be ≥ 0 and < the length of the array.
See page 229.

SELF CHECK

1. What elements does the values array contain after the following statements?

   ```
   double[] values = new double[10];
   for (int i = 0; i < values.length; i++) values[i] = i * i;
   ```

2. What do the following program segments print? Or, if there is an error, describe the error and specify whether it is detected at compile-time or at run-time.

   a. ```
   double[] a = new double[10];
   System.out.println(a[0]);
   ```

   **b.** ```
   double[] b = new double[10];
   System.out.println(b[10]);
   ```

   c. ```
   double[] c;
   System.out.println(c[0]);
   ```

## *Common Error 6.1*

### Bounds Errors

A very common array error is attempting to access a nonexistent position.

```
double[] data = new double[10];
data[10] = 29.95;   // Error—only have elements with index values 0 . . . 9
```

When the program runs, an out-of-bounds index generates an exception and terminates the program.

This is a great improvement over languages such as C and C++. With those languages there is no error message; instead, the program will quietly (or not so quietly) corrupt the memory location that is 10 elements away from the start of the array. Sometimes that corruption goes unnoticed, but at other times, the program will act flaky or die a horrible death many instructions later. These are serious problems that make C and C++ programs difficult to debug. Bounds errors in C and C++ programs are a major cause of security vulnerabilities—see Random Fact 6.1 on page 232.
```

Common Error 6.2

Uninitialized and Unfilled Arrays

A common error is to allocate an array reference, but not an actual array.

```
double[] values;
values[0] = 29.95; // Error—values not initialized
```

Array variables work exactly like object variables—they are only references to the actual array. To construct the actual array, you must use the new operator:

```
double[] values = new double[10];
```

Another common error is to allocate an array of objects and expect it to be filled with objects.

```
BankAccount[] accounts = new BankAccount[10]; // Contains ten null references
```

This array contains null references, not default bank accounts. You need to remember to fill the array, for example:

```
for (int i = 0; i < 10; i++)
{
    accounts[i] = new BankAccount();
}
```

Quality Tip 6.1

Use Arrays for Sequences of Related Values

Arrays are intended for storing sequences of values with the same meaning. For example, an array of test scores makes perfect sense:

```
int[] scores = new int[NUMBER_OF_SCORES];
```

But it is a bad design to use an array

```
double[] personalData = new double[3];
```

that holds a person's age, bank balance, and shoe size as personalData[0], personalData[1], and personalData[2]. It would be tedious for the programmer to remember which of these data items is stored in which array location. In this situation, it is far better to use three variables

```
int age;
double bankBalance;
double shoeSize;
```

Quality Tip 6.2

Make Parallel Arrays into Arrays of Objects

Programmers who are familiar with arrays, but unfamiliar with object-oriented programming, sometimes distribute information across separate arrays. Here is a typical example. A program needs to manage bank data, consisting of account numbers and balances. Don't store the account numbers and balances in separate arrays.

```
// Don't do this
int[] accountNumbers;
double[] balances;
```

Arrays such as these are called parallel arrays (see Figure 3). The ith slice (accountNumbers[i] and balances[i]) contains data that need to be processed together.

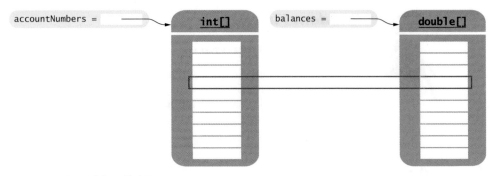

Figure 3 Avoid Parallel Arrays

If you find yourself using two arrays that have the same length, ask yourself whether you couldn't replace them with a single array of a class type. Look at a slice and find the concept that it represents. Then make the concept into a class. In our example each slice contains an account number and a balance, describing a bank account. Therefore, it is an easy matter to use a single array of objects

```
BankAccount[] accounts;
```

(See Figure 4.)

Why is this beneficial? Think ahead. Maybe your program will change and you will need to store the owner of the bank account as well. It is a simple matter to update the BankAccount class. It may well be quite complicated to add a new array and make sure that all methods that accessed the original two arrays now also correctly access the third one.

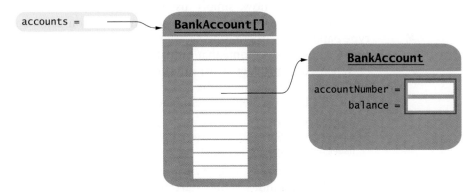

Figure 4 Reorganizing Parallel Arrays into an Array of Objects

Special Topic 6.1

Methods with a Variable Number of Parameters

Special Topic 6.1 shows how to implement a method that takes a variable number of parameters, and how to retrieve the parameter values from an array.

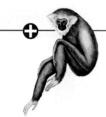

Random Fact 6.1

An Early Internet Worm

Random Fact 6.1 tells the story of the first serious Internet virus, launched by a graduate student at Cornell University. The virus exploited an array overrun vulnerability that is present in the C programming language but not in Java.

6.2 Array Lists

The ArrayList class
manages a sequence
of objects whose
size can change.

The array construct is rather primitive. In this section, we introduce the ArrayList class. It lets you collect objects, just like an array does, but array lists offer two significant benefits:

- Array lists can grow and shrink as needed.
- The ArrayList class supplies methods for many common tasks, such as inserting and removing elements.

You declare an array list of strings as follows:

```
ArrayList<String> names = new ArrayList<String>();
```

The ArrayList class
is a generic class:
ArrayList<*TypeName*>
collects objects of
the given type.

The type ArrayList<String> denotes an array list of strings. The angle brackets around the String type tell you that String is a **type parameter**. You can replace String with any other class and get a different array list type. For that reason, ArrayList is called a **generic class**. You will learn more about generic classes in Chapter 16. For now, simply use an ArrayList<T> whenever you want to collect objects of type T. However, keep in mind that you cannot use primitive types as type parameters—there is no ArrayList<int> or ArrayList<double>. You will see in Section 6.3 how to overcome that limitation.

When you construct an ArrayList object, it has size 0. You use the add method to add an object to the end of the array list. The size increases after each call to add (see Figure 5). The size method yields the current size of the array list.

```
names.add("Emily"); // Now names has size 1 and element "Emily"
names.add("Bob"); // Now names has size 2 and elements "Emily", "Bob"
names.add("Cindy"); // names has size 3 and elements "Emily", "Bob", and "Cindy"
```

To obtain the value of an array list element, use the get method, not the [] operator. As with arrays, index values start at 0. For example, names.get(2) retrieves the element with index 2, the third element in the array list:

```
String name = names.get(2);
```

As with arrays, it is an error to access a nonexistent element. A very common bounds error is to use the following:

```
int i = names.size();
name = names.get(i);  // Error
```

The last valid index is names.size() - 1.

To set an array list element to a new value, use the set method.

```
names.set(2, "Carolyn");
```

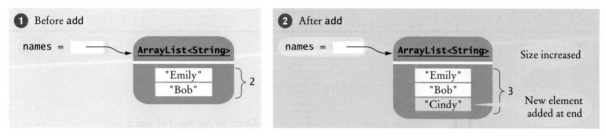

Figure 5 Adding an Element with add

This call sets position 2 of the names array list to "Carolyn", overwriting whatever value was there before.

The set method can only overwrite existing values. It is different from the add method, which adds a new object to the end of the array list.

You can also insert an object in the middle of an array list. The call names.add(1, "Ann") moves all elements with index 1 or larger by one position and adds the string "Ann" at index 1 (see Figure 6). After each call to the add method, the size of the array list increases by 1.

Conversely, the remove method removes the element at a given index, moves all elements after the removed element to the next lower index, and reduces the size of the array list by 1. Part 3 of Figure 6 illustrates the call names.remove(1).

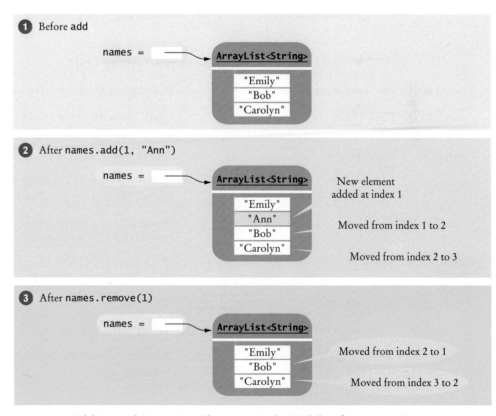

Figure 6 Adding and Removing Elements in the Middle of an Array List

Syntax 6.2 Array Lists

Syntax   To construct an array list: new ArrayList<*typeName*>()

To access an element: *arraylistReference*.get(index)
arraylistReference.set(index, value)

Example

Variable type   **Variable name**   **An array list object of size 0**

ArrayList<String> friends = new ArrayList<String>();

friends.add("Cindy");
String name = friends.get(i);
friends.set(i, "Harry");

The add method appends an element to the array list, increasing its size.

Use the get **and** set **methods to access an element.**

The index must be ≥ 0 **and** < friends.size(). See page 229.

The following program demonstrates how to use ArrayList class for collecting BankAccount objects. The BankAccount class has been enhanced from the version in Chapter 2. Each bank account has an account number. Note that you import the generic class java.util.ArrayList, without the type parameter.

Table 2 Working with Array Lists

`ArrayList<String> names = new ArrayList<String>();`	Constructs an empty array list that can hold strings.
`names.add("Ann");` `names.add("Cindy");`	Adds elements to the end.
`System.out.println(names);`	Prints [Ann, Cindy].
`names.add(1, "Bob");`	Inserts an element at index 1. names is now [Ann, Bob, Cindy].
`names.remove(0);`	Removes the element at index 0. names is now [Bob, Cindy].
`names.set(0, "Bill");`	Replaces an element with a different value. names is now [Bill, Cindy].
`String name = names.get(i);`	Gets an element.
`String last = names.get(names.size() - 1);`	Gets the last element.

`ArrayList<Integer> squares = new ArrayList<Integer>();`
`for (int i = 0; i < 10; i++)`
`{`
`   squares.add(i * i);`
`}`
	Constructs an array list holding the first ten squares.

ch06/arraylist/ArrayListTester.java

```java
1   import java.util.ArrayList;
2
3   /**
4      This program tests the ArrayList class.
5   */
6   public class ArrayListTester
7   {
8      public static void main(String[] args)
9      {
10        ArrayList<BankAccount> accounts = new ArrayList<BankAccount>();
11        accounts.add(new BankAccount(1001));
12        accounts.add(new BankAccount(1015));
13        accounts.add(new BankAccount(1729));
14        accounts.add(1, new BankAccount(1008));
15        accounts.remove(0);
16
17        System.out.println("Size: " + accounts.size());
18        System.out.println("Expected: 3");
19        BankAccount first = accounts.get(0);
20        System.out.println("First account number: "
21              + first.getAccountNumber());
22        System.out.println("Expected: 1008");
23        BankAccount last = accounts.get(accounts.size() - 1);
24        System.out.println("Last account number: "
25              + last.getAccountNumber());
26        System.out.println("Expected: 1729");
27     }
28  }
```

ch06/arraylist/BankAccount.java

```java
1   /**
2      A bank account has a balance that can be changed by
3      deposits and withdrawals.
4   */
5   public class BankAccount
6   {
7      private int accountNumber;
8      private double balance;
9
10     /**
11        Constructs a bank account with a zero balance.
12        @param anAccountNumber  the account number for this account
13     */
14     public BankAccount(int anAccountNumber)
15     {
16        accountNumber = anAccountNumber;
17        balance = 0;
18     }
19
20     /**
21        Constructs a bank account with a given balance.
22        @param anAccountNumber  the account number for this account
23        @param initialBalance  the initial balance
24     */
25     public BankAccount(int anAccountNumber, double initialBalance)
26     {
27        accountNumber = anAccountNumber;
```

```
28        balance = initialBalance;
29     }
30
31     /**
32        Gets the account number of this bank account.
33        @return the account number
34     */
35     public int getAccountNumber()
36     {
37        return accountNumber;
38     }
39
40     /**
41        Deposits money into the bank account.
42        @param amount the amount to deposit
43     */
44     public void deposit(double amount)
45     {
46        double newBalance = balance + amount;
47        balance = newBalance;
48     }
49
50     /**
51        Withdraws money from the bank account.
52        @param amount the amount to withdraw
53     */
54     public void withdraw(double amount)
55     {
56        double newBalance = balance - amount;
57        balance = newBalance;
58     }
59
60     /**
61        Gets the current balance of the bank account.
62        @return the current balance
63     */
64     public double getBalance()
65     {
66        return balance;
67     }
68  }
```

Program Run

```
Size: 3
Expected: 3
First account number: 1008
Expected: 1008
Last account number: 1729
Expected: 1729
```

SELF CHECK

3. How do you construct an array of 10 strings? An array list of strings?

4. What is the content of names after the following statements?

```
ArrayList<String> names = new ArrayList<String>();
names.add("A");
names.add(0, "B");
names.add("C");
names.remove(1);
```

Common Error 6.3

Length and Size

Unfortunately, the Java syntax for determining the number of elements in an array, an array list, and a string is not at all consistent. It is a common error to confuse these. You just have to remember the correct syntax for every data type.

Data Type	Number of Elements
Array	`a.length`
Array list	`a.size()`
String	`a.length()`

Special Topic 6.2

ArrayList Syntax Enhancements in Java 7

Java 7 introduces several convenient syntax enhancements for array lists.

When you declare and construct an array list, you need not repeat the type parameter in the constructor. That is, you can write

```
ArrayList<String> names = new ArrayList<>();
```

instead of

```
ArrayList<String> names = new ArrayList<String>();
```

This shortcut is called the "diamond syntax" because the empty brackets <> look like a diamond shape.

You can supply initial values as follows:

```
ArrayList<String> names = new ArrayList<>(["Ann", "Cindy", "Bob"]);
```

In Java 7, you can access array list elements with the [] operator instead of the get and put methods. That is, the compiler translates

```
String name = names[i];
```

into

```
String name = names.get(i);
```

and

```
names[i] = "Fred";
```

into

```
names.set(i, "Fred");
```

6.3 Wrappers and Auto-boxing

> To treat primitive type values as objects, you must use wrapper classes.

Because numbers are not objects in Java, you cannot directly insert them into array lists. For example, you cannot form an `ArrayList<double>`. To store sequences of numbers in an array list, you must turn them into objects by using **wrapper classes**. There are wrapper classes for all eight primitive types:

Primitive Type	Wrapper Class
byte	Byte
boolean	Boolean
char	Character
double	Double
float	Float
int	Integer
long	Long
short	Short

Note that the wrapper class names start with uppercase letters, and that two of them differ from the names of the corresponding primitive type: `Integer` and `Character`.

Each wrapper class object contains a value of the corresponding primitive type. For example, an object of the class `Double` contains a value of type `double` (see Figure 7).

Wrapper objects can be used anywhere that objects are required instead of primitive type values. For example, you can collect a sequence of floating-point numbers in an `ArrayList<Double>`.

Conversion between primitive types and the corresponding wrapper classes is automatic. This process is called **auto-boxing** (even though *auto-wrapping* would have been more consistent).

For example, if you assign a number to a `Double` object, the number is automatically "put into a box", namely a wrapper object.

```java
Double d = 29.95; // Auto-boxing; same as Double d = new Double(29.95);
```

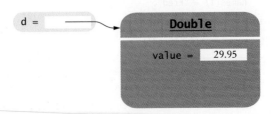

Figure 7 An Object of a Wrapper Class

Conversely, wrapper objects are automatically "unboxed" to primitive types.

```
double x = d; // Auto-unboxing; same as double x = d.doubleValue();
```

Auto-boxing even works inside arithmetic expressions. For example, the statement

```
d = d + 1;
```

is perfectly legal. It means:

- Auto-unbox `d` into a `double`
- Add 1
- Auto-box the result into a new `Double`
- Store a reference to the newly created wrapper object in `d`

In order to collect numbers in an array list, simply remember to use the wrapper type as the type parameter, and then rely on auto-boxing.

```
ArrayList<Double> values = new ArrayList<Double>();
values.add(29.95);
double x = values.get(0);
```

Keep in mind that storing wrapped numbers is quite inefficient. The use of wrappers is acceptable if you only collect a few numbers, but you should use arrays for long sequences of numbers or characters.

SELF CHECK

5. What is the difference between the types `double` and `Double`?
6. Suppose `values` is an `ArrayList<Double>` of size > 0. How do you increment the element with index 0?

6.4 The Enhanced for Loop

Java version 5.0 introduces a very convenient shortcut for a common loop type. Often, you need to iterate through a sequence of elements—such as the elements of an array or array list. The enhanced `for` loop makes this process particularly easy to program.

> The enhanced for loop traverses all elements of a collection.

Suppose you want to total up all elements in an array `values`. Here is how you use the enhanced `for` loop to carry out that task.

```
double[] values = . . .;
double sum = 0;
for (double element : values)
{
    sum = sum + element;
}
```

The loop body is executed for each element in the array `values`. At the beginning of each loop iteration, the next element is assigned to the variable `element`. Then the loop body is executed. You should read this loop as "for each `element` in `values`".

You may wonder why Java doesn't let you write "for each (element in values)". Unquestionably, this would have been neater, and the Java language designers seriously considered this. However, the "for each" construct was added to Java several

Syntax 6.3 The "for each" Loop

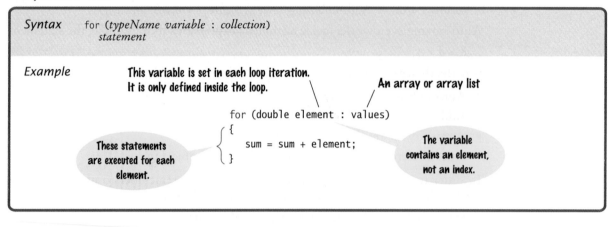

Syntax   for (*typeName variable* : *collection*)
            statement

Example   This variable is set in each loop iteration.
             It is only defined inside the loop.

             An array or array list

             for (double element : values)
             {
                 sum = sum + element;
             }

             These statements
             are executed for each
             element.

             The variable
             contains an element,
             not an index.

years after its initial release. Had new reserved words each and in been added to the language, then older programs that happened to use those identifiers as variable or method names (such as System.in) would no longer have compiled correctly.

You don't have to use the "for each" construct to loop through all elements in an array. You can implement the same loop with a straightforward for loop and an explicit index variable:

```
double[] values = . . .;
double sum = 0;
for (int i = 0; i < values.length; i++)
{
   double element = values[i];
   sum = sum + element;
}
```

In an enhanced for loop, the loop variable contains an element, not an index.

Note an important difference between the "for each" loop and the ordinary for loop. In the "for each" loop, the loop variable e is assigned *elements:* values[0], values[1], and so on. In the ordinary for loop, the loop variable i is assigned *index values:* 0, 1, and so on.

You can also use the enhanced for loop to visit all elements of an array list. For example, the following loop computes the total of the balances of all accounts:

```
ArrayList<BankAccount> accounts = . . . ;
double sum = 0;
for (BankAccount account : accounts)
{
   sum = sum + account.getBalance();
}
```

This loop is equivalent to the following ordinary for loop:

```
double sum = 0;
for (int i = 0; i < accounts.size(); i++)
{
   BankAccount account = accounts.get(i);
   sum = sum + account.getBalance();
}
```

Keep in mind that the "for each" loop has a very specific purpose: getting the elements of a collection, from the beginning to the end. It is not suitable for all array algorithms. In particular, the "for each" loop does not allow you to modify the contents of an array. The following loop does *not* fill an array with zeroes:

```
for (double element : values)
{
    element = 0; // ERROR—this assignment does not modify array elements
}
```

When the loop is executed, the variable `element` is first set to `values[0]`. Then `element` is set to 0, then to `values[1]`, then to 0, and so on. The `values` array is not modified. The remedy is simple: Use an ordinary `for` loop

```
for (int i = 0; i < values.length; i++)
{
    values[i] = 0; // OK
}
```

SELF CHECK

7. Write a "for each" loop that prints all elements in the array `values`.
8. What does this "for each" loop do?

```
int counter = 0;
for (BankAccount a : accounts)
{
    if (a.getBalance() == 0) { counter++; }
}
```

6.5 Partially Filled Arrays

Suppose you write a program that reads a sequence of numbers into an array. How many numbers will the user enter? You can't very well ask the user to count the items before entering them—that is just the kind of work that the user expects the computer to do. Unfortunately, you now run into a problem. You need to set the size of the array before you know how many elements you need. Once the array size is set, it cannot be changed.

To solve this problem, make an array that is guaranteed to be larger than the largest possible number of entries, and partially fill it. For example, you can decide that the user will never provide more than 100 input values. Then allocate an array of size 100:

```
final int VALUES_LENGTH = 100;
double[] values = new double[VALUES_LENGTH];
```

> With a partially filled array, keep a companion variable to track how many elements are used.

Then keep a companion variable that tells how many elements in the array are actually used. It is an excellent idea always to name this companion variable by adding the suffix `Size` to the name of the array.

```
int valuesSize = 0;
```

Now `values.length` is the capacity of the array `values`, and `valuesSize` is the current size of the array (see Figure 8). Keep adding elements into the array, incrementing the `valuesSize` variable each time.

```
values[valuesSize] = x;
valuesSize++;
```

This way, `valuesSize` always contains the correct element count.

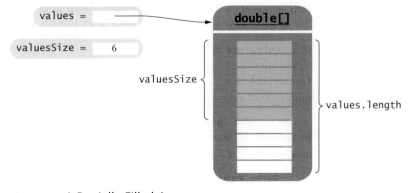

Figure 8 A Partially Filled Array

The following code segment shows how to read numbers into a partially filled array.

```
int valuesSize = 0;
Scanner in = new Scanner(System.in);
while (in.hasNextDouble())
{
    if (valuesSize < values.length)
    {
        values[valuesSize] = in.nextDouble();
        valuesSize++;
    }
}
```

At the end of this loop, valuesSize contains the actual number of elements in the array. Note that you have to stop accepting inputs if the valuesSize companion variable reaches the array length. Section 6.6 shows how you can overcome that limitation by growing the array.

To process the gathered array elements, you again use the companion variable, not the array length. This loop prints the partially filled array:

```
for (int i = 0; i < valuesSize; i++)
{
    System.out.println(values[i]);
}
```

Array lists use this technique behind the scenes. An array list contains an array of objects. When the array runs out of space, the array list allocates a larger array and copies the elements. However, all of this happens inside the array list methods, so you never need to think about it.

SELF CHECK

9. Write a loop to print the elements of the partially filled array values in reverse order, starting with the last element.

10. How do you remove the last element of the partially filled array values?

11. Why would a programmer use a partially filled array of numbers instead of an array list?

Common Error 6.4

Underestimating the Size of a Data Set

Programmers frequently underestimate the amount of input data that a user will pour into an unsuspecting program. A common problem results from the use of fixed-sized arrays. Suppose you write a program to search for text in a file. You store each line in a string, and keep an array of strings. How big do you make the array? Surely nobody is going to challenge your program with an input that is more than 100 lines. Really? It is easy to feed in the entire text of *Alice in Wonderland* or *War and Peace* (which are available on the Internet). All of a sudden, your program has to deal with tens or hundreds of thousands of lines. What will it do? Will it handle the input? Will it politely reject the excess input? Will it crash and burn?

A famous article (Barton P. Miller, Louis Fericksen, and Bryan So, "An Empirical Study of the Reliability of Unix Utilities", *Communications of the ACM*, vol. 33, no. 12, pp. 32–44) analyzed how several UNIX programs reacted when they were fed large or random data sets. Sadly, about a quarter didn't do well at all, crashing or hanging without a reasonable error message. For example, in some older versions of UNIX the tape backup program tar was not able to handle file names longer than 100 characters, which is a pretty unreasonable limitation. Many of these shortcomings are caused by features of the C language that, unlike Java, make it difficult to store strings and collections of arbitrary size.

6.6 Common Array Algorithms

In the following sections, we discuss some of the most common algorithms for working with arrays and array lists.

In the examples, we show a mixture of arrays and array lists so that you become familiar with the syntax for both constructs.

6.6.1 Filling

This loop fills an array with zeroes:

```
for (int i = 0; i < values.length; i++)
{
   values[i] = 0;
}
```

Here, we fill an array list with squares (0, 1, 4, 9, 16, ...). Note that the element with index 0 contains 0^2, the element with index 1 contains 1^2, and so on.

```
for (int i = 0; i < values.size(); i++)
{
   values.set(i, i * i);
}
```

6.6.2 Computing Sum and Average Values

To compute the sum of all elements, simply keep a running total.

```
double total = 0;
for (double element : values)
{
```

```
        total = total + element;
    }
```

To obtain the average, divide by the number of elements:

```
double average = total / values.size(); // For an array list
```

Be sure to check that the size is not zero.

6.6.3 Counting Matches

To count values, check all elements and count the matches until you reach the end.

Suppose you want to find how many accounts of a certain type you have. Then you must go through the entire collection and increment a counter each time you find a match. Here we count the number of accounts whose balance is at least as much as a given threshold:

```java
public class Bank
{
    private ArrayList<BankAccount> accounts;

    public int count(double atLeast)
    {
        int matches = 0;
        for (BankAccount account : accounts)
        {
            if (account.getBalance() >= atLeast) matches++; // Found a match
        }
        return matches;
    }
    . . .
}
```

6.6.4 Finding the Maximum or Minimum

To compute the maximum or minimum value, initialize a candidate with the starting element. Then compare the candidate with the remaining elements and update it if you find a larger or smaller value.

Suppose you want to find the account with the largest balance in the bank. Keep a candidate for the maximum. If you find an element with a larger value, then replace the candidate with that value. When you have reached the end of the sequence, you have found the maximum.

There is just one problem. When you visit the starting element, you don't yet have a candidate for the maximum. One way to overcome that is to set the candidate to the starting element and make the first comparison with the next element.

```java
BankAccount largestYet = accounts.get(0);
for (int i = 1; i < accounts.size(); i++)
{
    BankAccount a = accounts.get(i);
    if (a.getBalance() > largestYet.getBalance())
        largestYet = a;
}
return largestYet;
```

Here we use an explicit for loop because the loop no longer visits all elements—it skips the starting element.

Of course, this approach works only if there is at least one element. It doesn't make a lot of sense to ask for the largest element of an empty collection. We can return null in that case:

```
if (accounts.size() == 0) return null;
BankAccount largestYet = accounts.get(0);
. . .
```

See Exercises R6.5 and R6.6 for slight modifications to this algorithm.

To compute the minimum of a data set, keep a candidate for the minimum and replace it whenever you encounter a *smaller* value. At the end of the sequence, you have found the minimum.

6.6.5 Searching for a Value

To find a value, check all elements until you have found a match.

Suppose you want to know whether there is a bank account with a particular account number in your bank. Simply inspect each element until you find a match or reach the end of the sequence. Note that the loop might fail to find an answer, namely if none of the accounts match. This search process is called a **linear search**.

```
public class Bank
{
   . . .
   public BankAccount find(int accountNumber)
   {
      for (BankAccount account : accounts)
      {
         if (account.getAccountNumber() == accountNumber) // Found a match
            return account;
      }
      return null; // No match in the entire array list
   }
   . . .
}
```

Note that the method returns null if no match is found.

6.6.6 Locating the Position of an Element

You often need to locate the position of an element so that you can replace or remove it. Use a variation of the linear search algorithm, but remember the position instead of the matching element. Here we locate the position of the first element that is larger than 100.

```
int pos = 0;
boolean found = false;
while (pos < values.size() && !found)
{
   if (values.get(pos) > 100)
   {
      found = true;
   }
   else
   {
      pos++;
   }
}
if (found) { System.out.println("Position: " + pos); }
else { System.out.println("Not found"); }
```

6.6.7 Removing an Element

Removing an element from an array list is very easy—simply use the remove method. With an array, you have to work harder.

Suppose you want to remove the element with index pos from the array values. First off, you need to keep a companion variable for tracking the number of elements in the array, as explained in Section 6.5.

If the elements in the array are not in any particular order, simply overwrite the element to be removed with the *last* element of the array, then decrement the variable tracking the size of the array. (See Figure 9.)

```
values[pos] = values[valuesSize - 1];
valuesSize--;
```

ANIMATION
Removing from an Array

The situation is more complex if the order of the elements matters. Then you must move all elements following the element to be removed to a lower index, and then decrement the variable holding the size of the array. (See Figure 10.)

```
for (int i = pos; i < valuesSize - 1; i++)
{
    values[i] = values[i + 1];
}
valuesSize--;
```

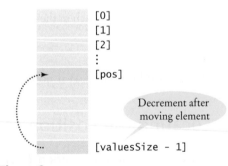

Figure 9
Removing an Element in an Unordered Array

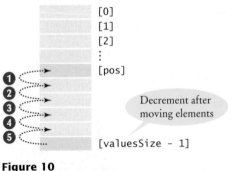

Figure 10
Removing an Element in an Ordered Array

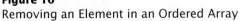

6.6.8 Inserting an Element

To insert an element into an array list, simply use the add method.

In this section, you will see how to insert an element into an array. Note that you need a companion variable for tracking the array size, as explained in Section 6.5. If the order of the elements does not matter, you can simply insert new elements at the end, incrementing the variable tracking the size.

```
if (valuesSize < values.length)
{
    values[valuesSize] = newElement;
    valuesSize++;
}
```

ANIMATION
Inserting into an Array

It is more work to insert an element at a particular position in the middle of an array. First, move all elements above the insertion location to a higher index. Then insert the new element.

Note the order of the movement: When you remove an element, you first move the next element down to a lower index, then the one after that, until you finally get to the end of the array. When you insert an element, you start at the end of the array, move that element to a higher index, then move the one before that, and so on until you finally get to the insertion location (see Figure 12).

```
if (valuesSize < values.length)
{
    for (int i = valuesSize; i > pos; i--)
    {
        values[i] = values[i - 1];
    }
    values[pos] = newElement;
    valuesSize++;
}
```

Figure 11
Inserting an Element in
an Unordered Array

Figure 12
Inserting an Element in
an Ordered Array

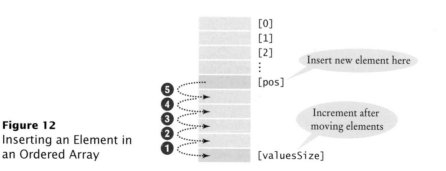

6.6.9 Copying and Growing Arrays

An array variable stores a reference to the array. Copying the variable yields a second reference to the same array.

Array variables work just like object variables—they hold a reference to the actual array. If you copy the reference, you get another reference to the same array (see Figure 13):

```
double[] values = new double[6];
. . . // Fill array
double[] prices = values; ❶
```

If you want to make a true copy of an array, call the Arrays.copyOf method.

Use the Arrays.copyOf method to copy the elements of an array.

```
double[] prices = Arrays.copyOf(values, values.length); ❷
```

Another use for Arrays.copyOf is to grow an array that has run out of space. The following statement has the effect of doubling the length of an array:

```
values = Arrays.copyOf(values, 2 * values.length);
```

See Figure 14.

For example, here is how you can read an arbitrarily long sequence numbers into an array, without running out of space:

```
int valuesSize = 0;
while (in.hasNextDouble())
{
   if (valuesSize == values.length)
      values = Arrays.copyOf(values, 2 * values.length);
   values[valuesSize] = in.nextDouble();
   valuesSize++;
}
```

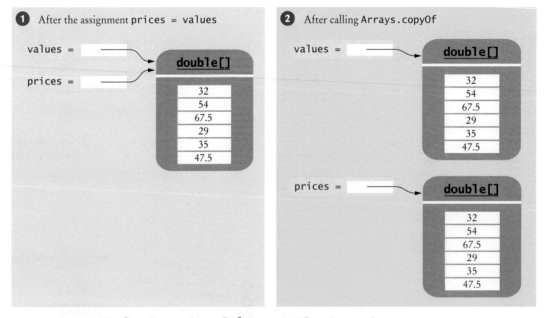

Figure 13 Copying an Array Reference vs. Copying an Array

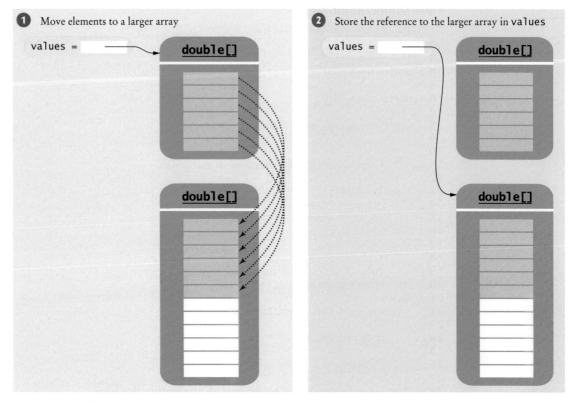

Figure 14 Growing an Array

6.6.10 Printing Element Separators

When you display the elements of an array or array list, you usually want to separate them, often with commas or vertical lines, like this:

```
Ann | Bob | Cindy
```

Note that there is one fewer separator than there are elements. Print the separator before each element *except the initial one* (with index 0):

```java
for (int i = 0; i < names.size(); i++)
{
   if (i > 0)
   {
      System.out.print(" | ");
   }
   System.out.print(names.get(i));
}
```

The following sample program implements a Bank class that stores an array list of bank accounts. The methods of the Bank class use some of the algorithms that we have discussed in this section.

ch06/bank/Bank.java

```java
 1  import java.util.ArrayList;
 2
 3  /**
 4     This bank contains a collection of bank accounts.
 5  */
 6  public class Bank
 7  {
 8     private ArrayList<BankAccount> accounts;
 9
10     /**
11        Constructs a bank with no bank accounts.
12     */
13     public Bank()
14     {
15        accounts = new ArrayList<BankAccount>();
16     }
17
18     /**
19        Adds an account to this bank.
20        @param a the account to add
21     */
22     public void addAccount(BankAccount a)
23     {
24        accounts.add(a);
25     }
26
27     /**
28        Gets the sum of the balances of all accounts in this bank.
29        @return the sum of the balances
30     */
31     public double getTotalBalance()
32     {
33        double total = 0;
34        for (BankAccount a : accounts)
35        {
36           total = total + a.getBalance();
37        }
38        return total;
39     }
40
41     /**
42        Counts the number of bank accounts whose balance is at
43        least a given value.
44        @param atLeast the balance required to count an account
45        @return the number of accounts having at least the given balance
46     */
47     public int countBalancesAtLeast(double atLeast)
48     {
49        int matches = 0;
50        for (BankAccount a : accounts)
51        {
52           if (a.getBalance() >= atLeast) matches++; // Found a match
53        }
54        return matches;
55     }
56
```

```
57    /**
58        Finds a bank account with a given number.
59        @param accountNumber the number to find
60        @return the account with the given number, or null if there
61        is no such account
62    */
63    public BankAccount find(int accountNumber)
64    {
65        for (BankAccount a : accounts)
66        {
67            if (a.getAccountNumber() == accountNumber) // Found a match
68                return a;
69        }
70        return null; // No match in the entire array list
71    }
72
73    /**
74        Gets the bank account with the largest balance.
75        @return the account with the largest balance, or null if the
76        bank has no accounts
77    */
78    public BankAccount getMaximum()
79    {
80        if (accounts.size() == 0) return null;
81        BankAccount largestYet = accounts.get(0);
82        for (int i = 1; i < accounts.size(); i++)
83        {
84            BankAccount a = accounts.get(i);
85            if (a.getBalance() > largestYet.getBalance())
86                largestYet = a;
87        }
88        return largestYet;
89    }
90 }
```

ch06/bank/BankTester.java

```
1    /**
2        This program tests the Bank class.
3    */
4    public class BankTester
5    {
6        public static void main(String[] args)
7        {
8            Bank firstBankOfJava = new Bank();
9            firstBankOfJava.addAccount(new BankAccount(1001, 20000));
10           firstBankOfJava.addAccount(new BankAccount(1015, 10000));
11           firstBankOfJava.addAccount(new BankAccount(1729, 15000));
12
13           double threshold = 15000;
14           int count = firstBankOfJava.countBalancesAtLeast(threshold);
15           System.out.println("Count: " + count);
16           System.out.println("Expected: 2");
17
18           int accountNumber = 1015;
19           BankAccount account = firstBankOfJava.find(accountNumber);
20           if (account == null)
21               System.out.println("No matching account");
```

```
22        else
23           System.out.println("Balance of matching account: "
24              + account.getBalance());
25        System.out.println("Expected: 10000");
26
27        BankAccount max = firstBankOfJava.getMaximum();
28        System.out.println("Account with largest balance: "
29           + max.getAccountNumber());
30        System.out.println("Expected: 1001");
31     }
32  }
```

Program Run

```
Count: 2
Expected: 2
Balance of matching account: 10000.0
Expected: 10000
Account with largest balance: 1001
Expected: 1001
```

SELF CHECK

12. What does the find method do if there are two bank accounts with a matching account number?

13. Would it be possible to use a "for each" loop in the getMaximum method?

14. When printing separators, we skipped the separator before the initial element. Rewrite the loop so that the separator is printed *after* each element, except for the last element.

15. The following replacement has been suggested for the algorithm in Section 6.6.10.

```
System.out.print(names.get(0));
for (int i = 1; i < names.size(); i++) System.out.print(" | " + names.get(i));
```

What is problematic about this suggestion?

Productivity Hint 6.1

Easy Printing of Arrays and Array Lists

If values is an array, the expression

```
Arrays.toString(values)
```

returns a string describing the elements, using a format that looks like this:

```
[32, 54, 67.5, 29, 35, 47.5]
```

The elements are surrounded by a pair of brackets and separated by commas. This can be convenient for debugging:

```
System.out.println("values=" + Arrays.toString(values));
```

With an array list, it is even easier to get a quick printout. Simply pass the array list to the println method:

```
System.out.println(names); // Prints [Ann, Bob, Cindy]
```

How To 6.1

Working with Arrays and Array Lists

When you process a sequence of values, you usually need to use array lists or arrays. (In some very simple situations, you can process data as you read them in, without storing them.) This How To walks you through the necessary steps.

Consider this example problem: You are given the quiz scores of a student. You are to compute the final quiz score, which is the sum of all scores after dropping the lowest one. For example, if the scores are

8 7 8.5 9.5 7 5 10

then the final score is 50.

However, if there is only one score, it would seem cruel to remove it. In that case, that score will be the final score. If there is no score, the final score should be 0.

Step 1   Decompose your task into steps.

You will usually want to break down your task into multiple steps, such as

- Reading the data into an array list or array.
- Processing the data in one or more steps.
- Displaying the results.

When deciding how to process the data, you should be familiar with the array algorithms in Section 6.6. Most processing tasks can be solved by using one or more of these algorithms.

In our sample problem, we will want to read the data. Then we will remove the minimum and compute the total. For example, if the input is 8 7 8.5 9.5 7 5 10, we will remove the minimum of 5, yielding 8 7 8.5 9.5 7 10. The sum of those values is the final score of 50.

Thus, we have identified three steps:

Read inputs.
Remove the minimum.
Calculate the sum.

Step 2   Choose between array lists and arrays.

Generally, array lists are more convenient than arrays. You would choose arrays if one of the following applies:

- You know in advance how many elements you will collect, and the size will not change.
- You collect a large sequence of numbers.

None of these cases applies here, so we will store the scores in an array list. An alternate solution using arrays is included with the companion code for the book (ch06/scores2 directory).

Step 3   Determine which algorithm(s) you need.

Sometimes, a step corresponds to exactly one of the basic array algorithms. That is the case with calculating the sum. At other times, you need to combine several algorithms. To remove the minimum value, you can find the minimum value (Section 6.6.4), find its position (Section 6.6.6), and remove the element at that position (Section 6.6.7).

We have now refined our plan as follows:

Read inputs.
Find the minimum.
Find its position.
Remove the minimum.
Calculate the sum.

This plan will work, but it is possible to do a bit better. It is easier to compute the sum and subtract the minimum. Then we don't have to find its position. The revised plan is

Read inputs.
Find the minimum.
Calculate the sum.
Subtract the minimum.

Step 4 Use classes and methods to structure the program.

Even though it may be possible to put all steps into the main method, this is rarely a good idea. It is better to carry out each processing step in a separate method. It is also a good idea to come up with a class that is responsible for collecting and processing the data, such as the DataSet class in Chapter 5 or the Bank class in the preceding section.

In our example, let's collect the scores in a GradeBook class.

```java
public class GradeBook
{
   private ArrayList<Double> scores;
   . . .
   public void addScore(double score) { . . . }
   public double finalScore() { . . . }
}
```

A second class, ScoreAnalyzer, is responsible for reading the user input and displaying the result. Its main method simply calls the GradeBook methods:

```java
GradeBook book = new GradeBook();
System.out.println("Please enter values, Q to quit:");
while (in.hasNextDouble())
{
   book.addScore(in.nextDouble());
}
System.out.println("Final score: " + book.finalScore());
```

Now the finalScore method must do the heavy lifting. It too should not have to do all the work. Instead, we will supply helper methods

```java
public double sum()
public double minimum()
```

These methods simply implement the algorithms in Section 6.6.2 and Section 6.6.4. Then the finalScore method becomes

```java
public double finalScore()
{
   if (scores.size() == 0)
      return 0;
   else if (scores.size() == 1)
      return scores.get(0);
   else
      return sum() - minimum();
}
```

Step 5 Assemble and test the program.

Implement your classes and test them, as described in How To 2.1. Review your code and check that you handle both normal and exceptional situations. What happens with an empty array or array list? One that contains a single element? When no match is found? When there are multiple matches? Consider these boundary conditions and make sure that your program works correctly.

In our example, it is impossible to compute the minimum if the array list is empty. In that case, we should determine the special score of 0 *before* attempting to call the `minimum` method.

What if the minimum value occurs more than once? That means that a student had more than one test with the same low score. We subtract only one of the occurrences of that low score, and that is the desired behavior.

The following table shows test cases and their expected output:

Test Case	Expected Output	Comment
8 7 8.5 9.5 7 5 10	50	See Step 1.
8 7 7 9	24	Only one instance of the low score should be removed.
8	8	Don't remove the lowest score if there is only one.
(no inputs)	0	An empty grade book has score 0.

The complete program is in the `ch06/scores` directory of the book's companion code.

⊕ **Worked Example 6.1**

Rolling the Dice

This Worked Example shows how to analyze a set of die tosses to see whether the die is "fair".

6.7 Regression Testing

It is a common and useful practice to make a new test whenever you find a program bug. You can use that test to verify that your bug fix really works. Don't throw the test away; feed it to the next version after that and all subsequent versions. Such a collection of test cases is called a **test suite**.

You will be surprised how often a bug that you fixed will reappear in a future version. This is a phenomenon known as *cycling*. Sometimes you don't quite understand the reason for a bug and apply a quick fix that appears to work. Later, you apply a different quick fix that solves a second problem but makes the first problem appear again. Of course, it is always best to think through what really causes a bug and fix the root cause instead of doing a sequence of "Band-Aid" solutions. If you don't succeed in doing that, however, you at least want to have an honest appraisal of how well the program works. By keeping all old test cases around and testing them against every new version, you get that feedback. The process of checking each version of a program against a test suite is called **regression testing**.

How do you organize a suite of tests? An easy technique is to produce multiple tester classes, such as BankTester1, BankTester2, and so on.

Another useful approach is to provide a generic tester, and feed it inputs from multiple files. Consider this tester for the Bank class of Section 6.6:

ch06/regression/BankTester.java

```java
 1  import java.util.Scanner;
 2
 3  /**
 4      This program tests the Bank class.
 5  */
 6  public class BankTester
 7  {
 8     public static void main(String[] args)
 9     {
10        Bank firstBankOfJava = new Bank();
11        firstBankOfJava.addAccount(new BankAccount(1001, 20000));
12        firstBankOfJava.addAccount(new BankAccount(1015, 10000));
13        firstBankOfJava.addAccount(new BankAccount(1729, 15000));
14
15        Scanner in = new Scanner(System.in);
16
17        double threshold = in.nextDouble();
18        int c = firstBankOfJava.count(threshold);
19        System.out.println("Count: " + c);
20        int expectedCount = in.nextInt();
21        System.out.println("Expected: " + expectedCount);
22
23        int accountNumber = in.nextInt();
24        BankAccount a = firstBankOfJava.find(accountNumber);
25        if (a == null)
26           System.out.println("No matching account");
27        else
28        {
29           System.out.println("Balance of matching account: " + a.getBalance());
30           int matchingBalance = in.nextInt();
31           System.out.println("Expected: " + matchingBalance);
32        }
33     }
34  }
```

Rather than using fixed values for the threshold and the account number to be found, the program reads these values, and the expected responses. By running the program with different inputs, we can test different scenarios, such as the ones for diagnosing off-by-one errors discussed in Common Error 5.2.

Of course, it would be tedious to type in the input values by hand every time the test is executed. It is much better to save the inputs in a file, such as the following:

ch06/regression/input1.txt

```
15000
2
1015
10000
```

The command line interfaces of most operating systems provide a way to link a file to the input of a program, as if all the characters in the file had actually been typed by a user. Type the following command into a shell window:

```
java BankTester < input1.txt
```

The program is executed, but it no longer reads input from the keyboard. Instead, the System.in object (and the Scanner that reads from System.in) gets the input from the file input1.txt. This process is called *input redirection*.

The output is still displayed in the console window:

Program Run

```
Count: 2
Expected: 2
Balance of matching account: 10000
Expected: 10000
```

You can also redirect output. To capture the output of a program in a file, use the command

```
java BankTester < input1.txt > output1.txt
```

This is useful for archiving test cases.

SELF CHECK

16. Suppose you modified the code for a method. Why do you want to repeat tests that already passed with the previous version of the code?

17. Suppose a customer of your program finds an error. What action should you take beyond fixing the error?

18. Why doesn't the BankTester program contain prompts for the inputs?

Productivity Hint 6.2

Batch Files and Shell Scripts

Productivity Hint 6.2 shows how you can automate repetitive tasks by writing batch files or shell scripts.

Random Fact 6.2

The Therac-25 Incidents

Random Fact 6.2 tells the story of the Therac-25, a computerized device to deliver radiation treatment to cancer patients. Due to poor design and insufficient testing, the machine delivered serious overdoses, killing some patients and seriously maiming others.

6.8 Two-Dimensional Arrays

Arrays and array lists can store linear sequences. Occasionally you want to store collections that have a two-dimensional layout. The traditional example is the tic-tac-toe board (see Figure 15).

Figure 15
A Tic-Tac-Toe Board

> Two-dimensional arrays form a tabular, two-dimensional arrangement. You access elements with an index pair a[i][j].

Such an arrangement, consisting of rows and columns of values, is called a **two-dimensional array** or matrix. When constructing a two-dimensional array, you specify how many rows and columns you need. In this case, ask for 3 rows and 3 columns:

```
final int ROWS = 3;
final int COLUMNS = 3;
String[][] board = new String[ROWS][COLUMNS];
```

This yields a two-dimensional array with 9 elements

```
board[0][0]   board[0][1]   board[0][2]
board[1][0]   board[1][1]   board[1][2]
board[2][0]   board[2][1]   board[2][2]
```

To access a particular element, specify two index values in separate brackets. For example:

```
board[1][1] = "x";
board[2][1] = "o";
```

When filling or searching a two-dimensional array, it is common to use two nested loops. For example, this pair of loops sets all elements in the array to spaces.

```
for (int i = 0; i < ROWS; i++)
   for (int j = 0; j < COLUMNS; j++)
      board[i][j] = " ";
```

In this loop, we used constants for the number of rows and columns. You can also recover the array dimensions from the array variable:

- `board.length` is the number of rows.
- `board[0].length` is the number of columns. (See Special Topic 6.3 on page 261 for an explanation of this expression.)

You can rewrite the loop for filling the tic-tac-toe board as

```
for (int i = 0; i < board.length; i++)
   for (int j = 0; j < board[0].length; j++)
      board[i][j] = " ";
```

Here is a class and a test program for playing tic-tac-toe. This class does not check whether a player has won the game. That is left as an exercise—see Exercise P6.13.

ch06/twodim/TicTacToe.java

```java
1   /**
2      A 3 x 3 tic-tac-toe board.
3   */
4   public class TicTacToe
5   {
6      private String[][] board;
7      private static final int ROWS = 3;
8      private static final int COLUMNS = 3;
9
10     /**
11        Constructs an empty board.
12     */
13     public TicTacToe()
14     {
15        board = new String[ROWS][COLUMNS];
16        // Fill with spaces
17        for (int i = 0; i < ROWS; i++)
18           for (int j = 0; j < COLUMNS; j++)
19              board[i][j] = " ";
20     }
21
22     /**
23        Sets a field in the board. The field must be unoccupied.
24        @param i the row index
25        @param j the column index
26        @param player the player ("x" or "o")
27     */
28     public void set(int i, int j, String player)
29     {
30        if (board[i][j].equals(" "))
31           board[i][j] = player;
32     }
33
34     /**
35        Creates a string representation of the board, such as
36        |x o|
37        | x |
38        | o|.
39        @return the string representation
40     */
41     public String toString()
42     {
43        String r = "";
44        for (int i = 0; i < ROWS; i++)
45        {
46           r = r + "|";
47           for (int j = 0; j < COLUMNS; j++)
48              r = r + board[i][j];
49           r = r + "|\n";
50        }
51        return r;
52     }
53  }
```

ch06/twodim/TicTacToeRunner.java

```java
1   import java.util.Scanner;
2
3   /**
4      This program runs a TicTacToe game. It prompts the
5      user to set positions on the board and prints out the
6      result.
7   */
8   public class TicTacToeRunner
9   {
10     public static void main(String[] args)
11     {
12        Scanner in = new Scanner(System.in);
13        String player = "x";
14        TicTacToe game = new TicTacToe();
15        boolean done = false;
16        while (!done)
17        {
18           System.out.print(game.toString());
19           System.out.print(
20              "Row for " + player + " (-1 to exit): ");
21           int row = in.nextInt();
22           if (row < 0) done = true;
23           else
24           {
25              System.out.print("Column for " + player + ": ");
26              int column = in.nextInt();
27              game.set(row, column, player);
28              if (player.equals("x"))
29                 player = "o";
30              else
31                 player = "x";
32           }
33        }
34     }
35  }
```

Program Run

```
|   |   |
|   |   |
|   |   |
Row for x (-1 to exit): 1
Column for x: 2
|   |   |
|   | x|
|   |   |
Row for o (-1 to exit): 0
Column for o: 0
|o  |   |
|   | x|
|   |   |
Row for x (-1 to exit): -1
```

SELF CHECK

19. How do you declare and initialize a 4-by-4 array of integers?

20. How do you count the number of spaces in the tic-tac-toe board?

 ***Worked
Example 6.2***

A World Population Table

This Worked Example shows how to print world population data in a table with row and column headers, and totals for each of the data columns.

 *Special Topic 6.3*

Two-Dimensional Arrays with Variable Row Lengths

Special Topic 6.3 discusses two-dimensional arrays in which rows have different lengths.

 *Special Topic 6.4*

Multidimensional Arrays

Special Topic 6.4 discusses arrays of three or more dimensions.

Summary of Learning Objectives

Use arrays for collecting values.
- An array is a sequence of values of the same type.
- You access an array element with an integer index, using the [] operator.
- Index values of an array range from 0 to length - 1.
- Accessing a nonexistent element results in a bounds error.
- The expression *array*.length yields the number of elements in an array.
- Avoid parallel arrays by changing them into arrays of objects.

Use array lists for managing collections whose size can change.
- The ArrayList class manages a sequence of objects whose size can change.
- The ArrayList class is a generic class: ArrayList<*TypeName*> collects objects of the given type.

Use wrapper classes when working with array lists of numbers.
- To treat primitive type values as objects, you must use wrapper classes.

Use the enhanced for loop to visit all elements of a collection.
- The enhanced for loop traverses all elements of a collection.
- In an enhanced for loop, the loop variable contains an element, not an index.

Work with arrays that are partially filled.
- With a partially filled array, keep a companion variable to track how many elements are used.

Be able to use common array algorithms.

- To count values, check all elements and count the matches until you reach the end.
- To compute the maximum or minimum value, initialize a candidate with the starting element. Then compare the candidate with the remaining elements and update it if you find a larger or smaller value.
- To find a value, check all elements until you have found a match.
- An array variable stores a reference to the array. Copying the variable yields a second reference to the same array.
- Use the `Arrays.copyOf` method to copy the elements of an array.

Describe the process of regression testing.

- A test suite is a set of tests for repeated testing.
- Regression testing involves repeating previously run tests to ensure that known failures of prior versions do not appear in new versions of the software.

Use two-dimensional arrays for data that is arranged in rows and columns.

- Two-dimensional arrays form a tabular, two-dimensional arrangement. You access elements with an index pair `a[i][j]`.

Classes, Objects, and Methods Introduced in this Chapter

```
java.lang.Boolean
    booleanValue
java.lang.Double
    doubleValue
java.lang.Integer
    intValue
java.util.Arrays
    copyOf
    toString
```

```
java.util.ArrayList<E>
    add
    get
    remove
    set
    size
```

Media Resources

www.wiley.com/
go/global/
horstmann

- ***Worked Example*** Rolling the Dice
- ***Worked Example*** A World Population Table
- Lab Exercises
- ➕ ***Animation*** Removing from an Array
- ➕ ***Animation*** Inserting into an Array
- ➕ Practice Quiz
- ➕ Code Completion Exercises

Review Exercises

★ **R6.1** What is an index? What are the bounds of an array or array list? What is a bounds error?

★   **R6.2** Write a program that contains a bounds error. Run the program. What happens on your computer? How does the error message help you locate the error?

★★   **R6.3** Write Java code for a loop that simultaneously computes the maximum and minimum values of an array list. Use an array list of accounts as an example.

★   **R6.4** Write a loop that reads 10 strings and inserts them into an array list. Write a second loop that prints out the strings in the opposite order from which they were entered.

★★   **R6.5** Consider the algorithm that we used for determining the maximum value in an array list. We set largestYet to the starting element, which meant that we were no longer able to use the "for each" loop. An alternate approach is to initialize largestYet with null, then loop through all elements. Of course, inside the loop you need to test whether largestYet is still null. Modify the loop that finds the bank account with the largest balance, using this technique. Is this approach more or less efficient than the one used in the text?

★★★   **R6.6** Consider another variation of the algorithm for determining the maximum value. Here, we compute the maximum value of an array of numbers.

```
double max = 0; // Contains an error!
for (double element : values)
{
    if (element > max) max = element;
}
```

However, this approach contains a subtle error. What is the error, and how can you fix it?

★   **R6.7** For each of the following sets of values, write code that fills an array a with the values.

a. 1 2 3 4 5 6 7 8 9 10

b. 0 2 4 6 8 10 12 14 16 18 20

c. 1 4 9 16 25 36 49 64 81 100

d. 0 0 0 0 0 0 0 0 0 0

e. 1 4 9 16 9 7 4 9 11

Use a loop when appropriate.

★★   **R6.8** Write a loop that fills an array a with 10 random numbers between 1 and 100. Write code (using one or more loops) to fill a with 10 different random numbers between 1 and 100.

★   **R6.9** What is wrong with the following loop?

```
double[] values = new double[10];
for (int i = 1; i <= 10; i++) values[i] = i * i;
```

Explain two ways of fixing the error.

★★★T **R6.10** Write a program that constructs an array of 20 integers and fills the first ten elements with the numbers 1, 4, 9, . . . , 100. Compile it and launch the debugger. After the array has been filled with three numbers, inspect it. What are the contents of the elements in the array beyond those that you filled?

★★ **R6.11** Rewrite the following loops without using the "for each" construct. Here, `values` has type `double`.

    a. `for (double element : values) sum = sum + element;`

    b. `for (double element : values) if (element == target) return true;`

    c. `int i = 0;`
      `for (double element : values) { values[i] = 2 * element; i++; }`

★★ **R6.12** Rewrite the following loops, using the "for each" construct. Here, `values` has type `double`.

    a. `for (int i = 0; i < values.length; i++) sum = sum + values[i];`

    b. `for (int i = 1; i < values.length; i++) sum = sum + values[i];`

    c. `for (int i = 0; i < values.length; i++)`
        `if (values[i] == target) return i;`

★★ **R6.13** What is wrong with these statements for printing an array list with separators?

```
System.out.print(values.get(0));
for (int i = 1; i < values.size(); i++)
{
    System.out.print(", " + values.get(i));
}
```

★★ **R6.14** When finding the position of a match in Section 6.6.6, we used a `while` loop, not a `for` loop. What is wrong with using this loop instead?

```
for (pos = 0; pos < values.size() && !found; pos++)
{
    if (values.get(pos) > 100)
    {
        found = true;
    }
}
```

★★ **R6.15** When inserting an element into an array in Section 6.6.8, we moved the elements with larger index values, starting at the end of the array. Why is it wrong to start at the insertion location, like this?

```
for (int i = pos; i < size - 1; i++)
{
    values[i + 1] = values[i];
}
```

★★ **R6.16** In Section 6.6.9, we doubled the length of the array when growing it. Why didn't we just increase the size by one element?

★ **R6.17** What are parallel arrays? Why are parallel arrays indications of poor programming? How can they be avoided?

★ **R6.18** True or false?

    a. All elements of an array are of the same type.

    b. An array index must be an integer.

    c. Arrays cannot contain string references as elements.

    d. Arrays cannot contain `null` references as elements.

    e. Parallel arrays must have equal length.

    f. Two-dimensional arrays always have the same numbers of rows and columns.

g. Two parallel arrays can be replaced by a two-dimensional array.

h. Elements of different columns in a two-dimensional array can have different types.

★T **R6.19** Define the terms *regression testing* and *test suite*.

★T **R6.20** What is the debugging phenomenon known as *cycling*? What can you do to avoid it?

Programming Exercises

★ **P6.1** Implement a class Purse. A purse contains a collection of coins. For simplicity, we will only store the coin names in an ArrayList<String>. (We will discuss a better representation in Chapter 7.) Supply a method

```
void addCoin(String coinName)
```

Add a method toString to the Purse class that prints the coins in the purse in the format

```
Purse[Quarter,Dime,Nickel,Dime]
```

★ **P6.2** Write a method reverse that reverses the sequence of coins in a purse. Use the toString method of the preceding assignment to test your code. For example, if reverse is called with a purse

```
Purse[Quarter,Dime,Nickel,Dime]
```

then the purse is changed to

```
Purse[Dime,Nickel,Dime,Quarter]
```

★ **P6.3** Add a method to the Purse class

```
public void transfer(Purse other)
```

that transfers the contents of one purse to another. For example, if a is

```
Purse[Quarter,Dime,Nickel,Dime]
```

and b is

```
Purse[Dime,Nickel]
```

then after the call a.transfer(b), a is

```
Purse[Quarter,Dime,Nickel,Dime,Dime,Nickel]
```

and b is empty.

★ **P6.4** Write a method for the Purse class

```
public boolean sameContents(Purse other)
```

that checks whether the other purse has the same coins in the same order.

★★ **P6.5** Write a method for the Purse class

```
public boolean sameCoins(Purse other)
```

that checks whether the other purse has the same coins, perhaps in a different order. For example, the purses

```
Purse[Quarter,Dime,Nickel,Dime]    and    Purse[Nickel,Dime,Dime,Quarter]
```

should be considered equal.

You will probably need one or more helper methods.

★★ **P6.6** A `Polygon` is a closed curve made up from line segments that join the polygon's corner points. Implement a class `Polygon` with methods

```
public double perimeter()
```

and

```
public double area()
```

that compute the circumference and area of a polygon. To compute the perimeter, compute the distance between adjacent points, and total up the distances. The area of a polygon with corners $(x_0, y_0), \ldots, (x_{n-1}, y_{n-1})$ is

$$\frac{1}{2}\left(x_0 y_1 + x_1 y_2 + \cdots + x_{n-1} y_0 - y_0 x_1 - y_1 x_2 - \cdots - y_{n-1} x_0\right)$$

As test cases, compute the perimeter and area of a rectangle and of a regular hexagon. *Note:* You need not draw the polygon — that is done in Exercise P6.18.

★ **P6.7** Write a program that reads a sequence of integers into an array and that computes the alternating sum of all elements in the array. For example, if the program is executed with the input data

$$1 \quad 4 \quad 9 \quad 16 \quad 9 \quad 7 \quad 4 \quad 9 \quad 11$$

then it computes

$$1 - 4 + 9 - 16 + 9 - 7 + 4 - 9 + 11 = -2$$

★★ **P6.8** Write a program that produces random permutations of the numbers 1 to 10. To generate a random permutation, you need to fill an array with the numbers 1 to 10 so that no two entries of the array have the same contents. You could do it by brute force, by calling `Random.nextInt` until it produces a value that is not yet in the array. Instead, you should implement a smart method. Make a second array and fill it with the numbers 1 to 10. Then pick one of those at random, remove it, and append it to the permutation array. Repeat 10 times. Implement a class `PermutationGenerator` with a method

```
int[] nextPermutation
```

★★ **P6.9** A *run* is a sequence of adjacent repeated values. Write a program that generates a sequence of 20 random die tosses and that prints the die values, marking the runs by including them in parentheses, like this:

```
1 2 (5 5) 3 1 2 4 3 (2 2 2 2) 3 6 (5 5) 6 3 1
```

Use the following pseudocode:

```
Set a boolean variable inRun to false.
For each valid index i in the array list
    If inRun
        If values[i] is different from the preceding value
            Print )
            inRun = false
    Else
        If values[i] is the same as the following value
            Print (
            inRun = true
    Print values[i]
If inRun, print )
```

★★★ **P6.10** Write a program that generates a sequence of 20 random die tosses and that prints the die values, marking only the longest run, like this:

1 2 5 5 3 1 2 4 3 (2 2 2 2) 3 6 5 5 6 3 1

If there is more than one run of maximum length, mark the first one.

★★ **P6.11** It is a well-researched fact that men in a restroom generally prefer to maximize their distance from already occupied stalls, by occupying the middle of the longest sequence of unoccupied places.

For example, consider the situation where ten stalls are empty.

_ _ _ _ _ _ _ _ _ _

The first visitor will occupy a middle position:

_ _ _ _ _ X _ _ _ _

The next visitor will be in the middle of the empty area at the left.

_ _ X _ _ X _ _ _ _

Write a program that reads the number of stalls and then prints out diagrams in the format given above when the stalls become filled, one at a time. *Hint:* Use an array of boolean values to indicate whether a stall is occupied.

★★★ **P6.12** In this assignment, you will model the game of *Bulgarian Solitaire*. The game starts with 45 cards. (They need not be playing cards. Unmarked index cards work just as well.) Randomly divide them into some number of piles of random size. For example, you might start with piles of size 20, 5, 1, 9, and 10. In each round, you take one card from each pile, forming a new pile with these cards. For example, the sample starting configuration would be transformed into piles of size 19, 4, 8, 10, and 5. The solitaire is over when the piles have size 1, 2, 3, 4, 5, 6, 7, 8, and 9, in some order. (It can be shown that you always end up with such a configuration.)

In your program, produce a random starting configuration and print it. Then keep applying the solitaire step and print the result. Stop when the solitaire final configuration is reached.

★★ **P6.13** Add a method getWinner to the TicTacToe class of Section 6.8. It should return "x" or "o" to indicate a winner, or " " if there is no winner yet. Recall that a winning position has three matching marks in a row, column, or diagonal.

★★★ **P6.14** Write an application that plays tic-tac-toe. Your program should draw the game board, change players after every successful move, and pronounce the winner.

★★ **P6.15** *Magic squares.* An $n \times n$ matrix that is filled with the numbers $1, 2, 3, \ldots, n^2$ is a magic square if the sum of the elements in each row, in each column, and in the two diagonals is the same value. For example,

16	3	2	13
5	10	11	8
9	6	7	12
4	15	14	1

Write a program that reads in n^2 values from the keyboard and tests whether they form a magic square when arranged as a square matrix.

You need to test three features:

- Did the user enter n^2 numbers for some n?
- Do each of the numbers $1, 2, \ldots, n^2$ occur exactly once in the user input?
- When the numbers are put into a square, are the sums of the rows, columns, and diagonals equal to each other?

If the size of the input is a square, test whether all numbers between 1 and n^2 are present. Then compute the row, column, and diagonal sums. Implement a class Square with methods

```
public void add(int i)
public boolean isMagic()
```

★★ **P6.16** Implement the following algorithm to construct magic n-by-n^2 squares; it works only if n is odd. Place a 1 in the middle of the bottom row. After k has been placed in the (i, j) square, place $k + 1$ into the square to the right and down, wrapping around the borders. However, if the square to the right and down has already been filled, or if you are in the lower-right corner, then you must move to the square straight up instead. Here is the 5×5 square that you get if you follow this method:

Write a program whose input is the number n and whose output is the magic square of order n if n is odd. Implement a class MagicSquare with a constructor that constructs the square and a toString method that returns a representation of the square.

★G **P6.17** Implement a class Cloud that contains an array list of Point2D.Double objects. Support methods

```
public void add(Point2D.Double aPoint)
public void draw(Graphics2D g2)
```

Draw each point as a tiny circle.

Write a graphical application that draws a cloud of 100 random points.

★★G **P6.18** Implement a class Polygon that contains an array list of Point2D.Double objects. Support methods

```
public void add(Point2D.Double aPoint)
public void draw(Graphics2D g2)
```

Draw the polygon by joining adjacent points with a line, and then closing it up by joining the end and start points.

Write a graphical application that draws a square and a pentagon using two Polygon objects.

★G **P6.19** Write a class Chart with methods

```
public void add(int value)
public void draw(Graphics2D g2)
```

that displays a stick chart of the added values, like this:

You may assume that the values are pixel positions.

★★**G** **P6.20** Write a class BarChart with methods

```
public void add(double value)
public void draw(Graphics2D g2)
```

that displays a chart of the added values. You may assume that all added values are positive. Stretch the bars so that they fill the entire area of the screen. You must figure out the maximum of the values, and then scale each bar.

★★★**G** **P6.21** Improve the BarChart class of Exercise P6.20 to work correctly when the data contains negative values.

★★**G** **P6.22** Write a class PieChart with methods

```
public void add(double value)
public void draw(Graphics2D g2)
```

that displays a pie chart of the added values. You may assume that all data values are positive.

Programming Projects

Project 6.1 *Poker Simulator.* In this assignment, you will implement a simulation of a popular casino game usually called video poker. The card deck contains 52 cards, 13 of each suit. At the beginning of the game, the deck is shuffled. You need to devise a fair method for shuffling. (It does not have to be efficient.) Then the top five cards of the deck are presented to the player. The player can reject none, some, or all of the cards. The rejected cards are replaced from the top of the deck. Now the hand is scored. Your program should pronounce it to be one of the following:

- No pair—The lowest hand, containing five separate cards that do not match up to create any of the hands below.

- One pair—Two cards of the same value, for example two queens.

- Two pairs—Two pairs, for example two queens and two 5's.

- Three of a kind—Three cards of the same value, for example three queens.

- Straight—Five cards with consecutive values, not necessarily of the same suit, such as 4, 5, 6, 7, and 8. The ace can either precede a 2 or follow a king.

- Flush—Five cards, not necessarily in order, of the same suit.

- Full House—Three of a kind and a pair, for example three queens and two 5's

- Four of a Kind—Four cards of the same value, such as four queens.

- Straight Flush—A straight and a flush: Five cards with consecutive values of the same suit.

- Royal Flush—The best possible hand in poker. A 10, jack, queen, king, and ace, all of the same suit.

If you are so inclined, you can implement a wager. The player pays a JavaDollar for each game, and wins according to the following payout chart:

Hand	Payout	Hand	Payout
Royal Flush	250	Straight	4
Straight Flush	50	Three of a Kind	3
Four of a Kind	25	Two Pair	2
Full House	6	Pair of Jacks or Better	1
Flush	5		

Project 6.2 *The Game of Life* is a well-known mathematical game that gives rise to amazingly complex behavior, although it can be specified by a few simple rules. (It is not actually a game in the traditional sense, with players competing for a win.) Here are the rules. The game is played on a rectangular board. Each square can be either empty or occupied. At the beginning, you can specify empty and occupied cells in some way; then the game runs automatically. In each *generation*, the next generation is computed. A new cell is born on an empty square if it is surrounded by exactly three occupied neighbor cells. A cell dies of overcrowding if it is surrounded by four or more neighbors, and it dies of loneliness if it is surrounded by zero or one neighbor. A neighbor is an occupant of an adjacent square to the left, right, top, or bottom or in a diagonal direction. Figure 16 shows a cell and its neighbor cells.

Many configurations show interesting behavior when subjected to these rules. Figure 17 shows a *glider*, observed over five generations. Note how it moves. After four generations, it is transformed into the identical shape, but located one square to the right and below.

One of the more amazing configurations is the glider gun: a complex collection of cells that, after 30 moves, turns back into itself and a glider (see Figure 18).

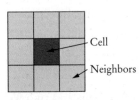

Cell

Neighbors

Figure 16
Neighborhood of a Cell

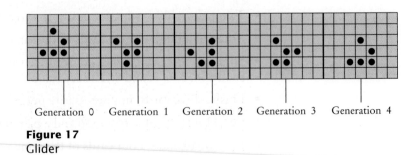

Generation 0   Generation 1   Generation 2   Generation 3   Generation 4

Figure 17
Glider

Program the game to eliminate the drudgery of computing successive generations by hand. Use a two-dimensional array to store the rectangular configuration. Write a program that shows successive generations of the game. You may get extra credit if you implement a graphical application that allows the user to add or remove cells by clicking with the mouse.

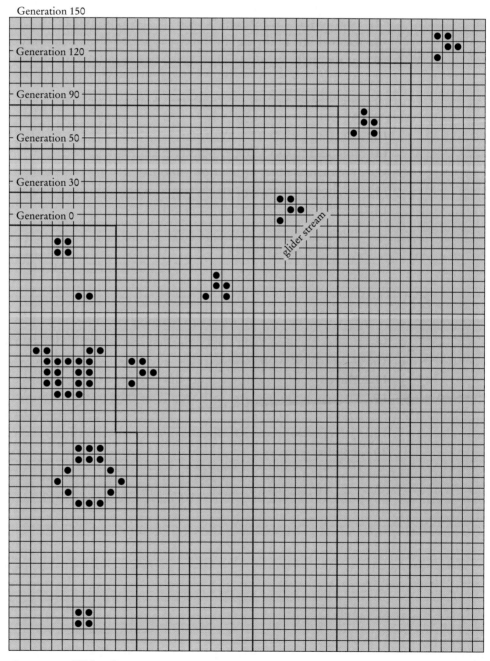

Figure 18 Glider Gun

Answers to Self-Check Questions

1. 0, 1, 4, 9, 16, 25, 36, 49, 64, 81, but *not* 100.
2. (a) 0; (b) a run-time error: array index out of bounds; (c) a compile-time error: c is not initialized.
3. ```
   new String[10];
   new ArrayList<String>();
   ```
4. `names` contains the strings "B" and "C" at positions 0 and 1.
5. `double` is one of the eight primitive types. `Double` is a class type.
6. `values.set(0, values.get(0) + 1);`
7. `for (double element : values) System.out.println(element);`
8. It counts how many accounts have a zero balance.
9. `for (int i = valuesSize - 1; i >= 0; i--) System.out.println(values[i]);`
10. `valuesSize--;`
11. You need to use wrapper objects in an `ArrayList<Double>`, which is less efficient.
12. It returns the first match that it finds.
13. Yes, but the first comparison would always fail.
14. ```
    for (int i = 0; i < values.size(); i++)
    {
        System.out.print(values.get(i));
        if (i < values.size() - 1)
        {
            System.out.print(" | ");
        }
    }
    ```
    Now you know why we set up the loop the other way.
15. If `names` happens to be empty, the first line causes a bounds error.
16. It is possible to introduce errors when modifying code.
17. Add a test case to the test suite that verifies that the error is fixed.
18. There is no human user who would see the prompts because input is provided from a file.
19. `int[][] array = new int[4][4];`
20. ```
    int count = 0;
    for (int i = 0; i < ROWS; i++)
        for (int j = 0; j < COLUMNS; j++)
            if (board[i][j].equals(" ")) count++;
    ```
    ```

Chapter **7**

Designing Classes

CHAPTER GOALS

- To learn how to choose appropriate classes for a given problem
- To understand the concepts of cohesion and coupling
- To minimize the use of side effects
- To document the responsibilities of methods and their callers with preconditions and postconditions
- To understand static methods and variables
- To understand the scope rules for local variables and instance variables
- To learn about packages
- T To learn about unit testing frameworks

In this chapter you will learn more about designing classes. First, we will discuss the process of discovering classes and declaring methods. Next, we will discuss how the concepts of pre- and postconditions enable you to specify, implement, and invoke methods correctly. You will also learn about several more technical issues, such as static methods and variables. Finally, you will see how to use packages to organize your classes.

CHAPTER CONTENTS

7.1 Discovering Classes

You have used a good number of classes in the preceding chapters and probably designed a few classes yourself as part of your programming assignments. Designing a class can be a challenge—it is not always easy to tell how to start or whether the result is of good quality.

What makes a good class? Most importantly, a class should *represent a single concept* from a problem domain. Some of the classes that you have seen represent concepts from mathematics:

A class should represent a single concept from a problem domain, such as business, science, or mathematics.

- Point
- Rectangle
- Ellipse

Other classes are abstractions of real-life entities:

- BankAccount
- CashRegister

For these classes, the properties of a typical object are easy to understand. A Rectangle object has a width and height. Given a BankAccount object, you can deposit and withdraw money. Generally, concepts from the part of the universe that a program concerns, such as science, business, or a game, make good classes. The name for such a class should be a noun that describes the concept. In fact, a simple rule of thumb for getting started with class design is to look for nouns in the problem description.

One useful category of classes can be described as *actors*. Objects of an actor class carry out certain tasks for you. Examples of actors are the Scanner class of

Chapter 3 and the Random class in Chapter 5. A Scanner object scans a stream for numbers and strings. A Random object generates random numbers. It is a good idea to choose class names for actors that end in "-er" or "-or". (A better name for the Random class might be RandomNumberGenerator.)

Very occasionally, a class has no objects, but it contains a collection of related static methods and constants. The Math class is a typical example. Such a class is called a *utility class*.

Finally, you have seen classes with only a main method. Their sole purpose is to start a program. From a design perspective, these are somewhat degenerate examples of classes.

What might not be a good class? If you can't tell from the class name what an object of the class is supposed to do, then you are probably not on the right track. For example, your homework assignment might ask you to write a program that prints paychecks. Suppose you start by trying to design a class PaycheckProgram. What would an object of this class do? An object of this class would have to do everything that the homework needs to do. That doesn't simplify anything. A better class would be Paycheck. Then your program can manipulate one or more Paycheck objects.

Another common mistake is to turn a single operation into a class. For example, if your homework assignment is to compute a paycheck, you may consider writing a class ComputePaycheck. But can you visualize a "ComputePaycheck" object? The fact that "ComputePaycheck" isn't a noun tips you off that you are on the wrong track. On the other hand, a Paycheck class makes intuitive sense. The word "paycheck" is a noun. You can visualize a paycheck object. You can then think about useful methods of the Paycheck class, such as computeTaxes, that help you solve the assignment.

SELF CHECK

1. What is a simple rule of thumb for finding classes?
2. Your job is to write a program that plays chess. Might ChessBoard be an appropriate class? How about MovePiece?

7.2 Cohesion and Coupling

In this section you will learn two useful criteria for analyzing the quality of a class—qualities of its public interface.

The public interface of a class is cohesive if all of its features are related to the concept that the class represents.

A class should represent a single concept. The public methods and constants that the public interface exposes should be *cohesive*. That is, all interface features should be closely related to the single concept that the class represents.

If you find that the public interface of a class refers to multiple concepts, then that is a good sign that it may be time to use separate classes instead. Consider, for example, the public interface of the CashRegister class in Chapter 3:

```
public class CashRegister
{
    public static final double NICKEL_VALUE = 0.05;
    public static final double DIME_VALUE = 0.1;
    public static final double QUARTER_VALUE = 0.25;
    . . .
```

```
      public void enterPayment(int dollars, int quarters,
            int dimes, int nickels, int pennies)
      . . .
   }
```

There are really two concepts here: a cash register that holds coins and computes their total, and the values of individual coins. (For simplicity, we assume that the cash register only holds coins, not bills. Exercise P7.1 discusses a more general solution.)

It makes sense to have a separate Coin class and have coins responsible for knowing their values.

```
   public class Coin
   {
      . . .
      public Coin(double aValue, String aName) { . . . }
      public double getValue() { . . . }
      . . .
   }
```

Then the CashRegister class can be simplified:

```
   public class CashRegister
   {
      . . .
      public void enterPayment(int coinCount, Coin coinType) { . . . }
      . . .
   }
```

Now the CashRegister class no longer needs to know anything about coin values. The same class can equally well handle euros or zorkmids!

This is clearly a better solution, because it separates the responsibilities of the cash register and the coins. The only reason we didn't follow this approach in Chapter 3 was to keep the CashRegister example simple.

Many classes need other classes in order to do their jobs. For example, the restructured CashRegister class now depends on the Coin class to determine the value of the payment.

To visualize relationships, such as dependence between classes, programmers draw class diagrams. In this book, we use the UML ("Unified Modeling Language") notation for objects and classes. UML is a notation for object-oriented analysis and design invented by Grady Booch, Ivar Jacobson, and James Rumbaugh, three leading researchers in object-oriented software development. The

> A class depends on another class if it uses objects of that class.

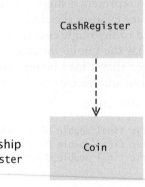

Figure 1
Dependency Relationship Between the CashRegister and Coin Classes

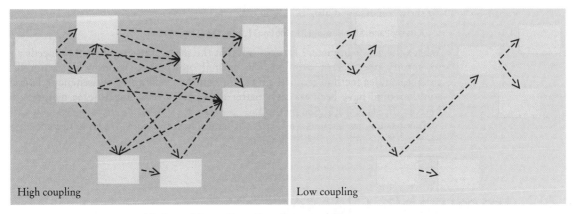

Figure 2 High and Low Coupling Between Classes

UML notation distinguishes between *object diagrams* and class diagrams. In an object diagram the class names are underlined; in a class diagram the class names are not underlined. In a class diagram, you denote dependency by a dashed line with a ⤏-shaped open arrow tip that points to the dependent class. Figure 1 shows a class diagram indicating that the CashRegister class depends on the Coin class.

Note that the Coin class does *not* depend on the CashRegister class. Coins have no idea that they are being collected in cash registers, and they can carry out their work without ever calling any method in the CashRegister class.

If many classes of a program depend on each other, then we say that the **coupling** between classes is high. Conversely, if there are few dependencies between classes, then we say that the coupling is low (see Figure 2).

Why does coupling matter? If the Coin class changes in the next release of the program, all the classes that depend on it may be affected. If the change is drastic, the coupled classes must all be updated. Furthermore, if we would like to use a class in another program, we have to take with it all the classes on which it depends. Thus, we want to remove unnecessary coupling between classes.

> It is a good practice to minimize the coupling (i.e., dependency) between classes.

S E L F   C H E C K

3. Why is the CashRegister class from Chapter 3 not cohesive?
4. Why does the Coin class not depend on the CashRegister class?
5. Why should coupling be minimized between classes?

Quality Tip 7.1

Consistency

In this section you learned of two criteria for analyzing the quality of the public interface of a class. You should maximize cohesion and remove unnecessary coupling. There is another criterion that we would like you to pay attention to—*consistency*. When you have a set of methods, follow a consistent scheme for their names and parameters. This is simply a sign of good craftsmanship.

Sadly, you can find any number of inconsistencies in the standard library. Here is an example. To show an input dialog box, you call

```
JOptionPane.showInputDialog(promptString)
```

To show a message dialog box, you call

```
JOptionPane.showMessageDialog(null, messageString)
```

What's the null parameter? It turns out that the showMessageDialog method needs a parameter to specify the parent window, or null if no parent window is required. But the showInputDialog method requires no parent window. Why the inconsistency? There is no reason. It would have been an easy matter to supply a showMessageDialog method that exactly mirrors the showInputDialog method.

Inconsistencies such as these are not fatal flaws, but they are an annoyance, particularly because they can be so easily avoided.

7.3 Immutable Classes

When analyzing a program that consists of many classes, it is not only important to understand which parts of the program use a given class. We also want to understand who *modifies* objects of a class. The following sections are concerned with this aspect of class design.

Recall that a **mutator method** modifies the object on which it is invoked, whereas an **accessor method** merely accesses information without making any modifications. For example, in the BankAccount class, the deposit and withdraw methods are mutator methods. Calling

```
account.deposit(1000);
```

modifies the state of the account object, but calling

```
double balance = account.getBalance();
```

does not modify the state of account.

> An immutable class has no mutator methods.

You can call an accessor method as many times as you like—you always get the same answer, and the method does not change the state of your object. That is clearly a desirable property, because it makes the behavior of such a method very predictable.

Some classes have been designed to have only accessor methods and no mutator methods at all. Such classes are called **immutable**. An example is the String class. Once a string has been constructed, its content never changes. No method in the String class can modify the contents of a string. For example, the toUpperCase method does not change characters from the original string. Instead, it constructs a *new* string that contains the uppercase characters:

```
String name = "John Q. Public";
String uppercased = name.toUpperCase(); // name is not changed
```

> References to objects of an immutable class can be safely shared.

An immutable class has a major advantage: It is safe to give out references to its objects freely. If no method can change the object's value, then no code can modify the object at an unexpected time. In contrast, if you give out a BankAccount reference to any other method, you have to be aware that the state of your object may change—the other method can call the deposit and withdraw methods on the reference that you gave it.

SELF CHECK

6. Is the substring method of the String class an accessor or a mutator?
7. Is the Rectangle class immutable?

7.4 Side Effects

A side effect of a
method is any
externally
observable data
modification.

A **side effect** of a method is any kind of modification of data that is observable outside the method. Mutator methods have a side effect, namely the modification of the implicit parameter. For example, when you call

```
harrysChecking.deposit(1000);
```

you can tell that something changed by calling `harrysChecking.getBalance()`.

Now consider the explicit parameter of a method, such as `studentNames` here:

```
public class GradeBook
{
   . . .
   /**
      Adds student names to this grade book.
      @param studentNames  a list of student names
   */
   public void addStudents(ArrayList<String> studentNames)
   {
      while (studentNames.size() > 0)
      {
         String name = studentNames.remove(0); // Not recommended
         Add name to gradebook
      }
   }
}
```

This method *removes* all names from the `studentNames` parameter as it adds them to the grade book. That too is a side effect. After a call

```
book.addStudents(listOfNames);
```

the call `listOfNames.size()` returns 0. Such a side effect would not be what most programmers expect. It is better if the method reads the names from the list without modifying it.

Now consider the following method:

```
public class BankAccount
{
   . . .
   /**
      Transfers money from this account to another account.
      @param amount  the amount of money to transfer
      @param other  the account into which to transfer the money
   */
   public void transfer(double amount, BankAccount other)
   {
      balance = balance - amount;
      other.deposit(amount);
   }
}
```

This method modifies both the implicit parameter and the explicit parameter `other`. Neither side effect is surprising for a `transfer` method, and there is no reason to avoid them.

Another example of a side effect is output. Consider how we have always printed a bank balance:

```
System.out.println("The balance is now $" + momsSavings.getBalance());
```

Why don't we simply have a printBalance method?

```java
public void printBalance() // Not recommended
{
    System.out.println("The balance is now $" + balance);
}
```

That would be more convenient when you actually want to print the value. But, of course, there are cases when you want the value for some other purpose. Thus, you can't simply drop the getBalance method in favor of printBalance.

More importantly, the printBalance method forces strong assumptions on the BankAccount class.

- The message is in English—you assume that the user of your software reads English. The majority of people on the planet don't.
- You rely on System.out. A method that relies on System.out won't work in an embedded system, such as the computer inside an automatic teller machine.

In other words, this design violates the rule of minimizing the coupling of the classes. The printBalance method couples the BankAccount class with the System and PrintStream classes. It is best to decouple input/output from the actual work of your classes.

S E L F C H E C K

8. If a refers to a bank account, then the call a.deposit(100) modifies the bank account object. Is that a side effect?

9. Consider the DataSet class of Chapter 5. Suppose we add a method

```java
void read(Scanner in)
{
    while (in.hasNextDouble())
        add(in.nextDouble());
}
```

Does this method have a side effect other than mutating the data set?

Common Error 7.1

Trying to Modify Primitive Type Parameters

Methods can't update parameters of primitive type (numbers, char, and boolean). To illustrate this point, let's try to write a method that updates a number parameter:

```java
public class BankAccount
{
    . . .
    /**
        Transfers money from this account and tries to add it to a balance.
        @param amount  the amount of money to transfer
        @param otherBalance  balance to add the amount to
    */
    void transfer(double amount, double otherBalance)  ❷
    {
        balance = balance - amount;
        otherBalance = otherBalance + amount;
            // Won't work
    }  ❸
}
```

ANIMATION
*A Method Cannot
Modify a Numeric
Parameter*

This doesn't work. Let's consider a method call.

```
double savingsBalance = 1000;
harrysChecking.transfer(500, savingsBalance);  ❶
System.out.println(savingsBalance);  ❹
```

As the method starts, the parameter variable otherBalance is set to the same value as savingsBalance (see Figure 3). Then the value of the otherBalance value is modified, but that modification has no effect on savingsBalance, because otherBalance is a separate variable. When the method terminates, the otherBalance variable dies, and savingsBalance isn't increased.

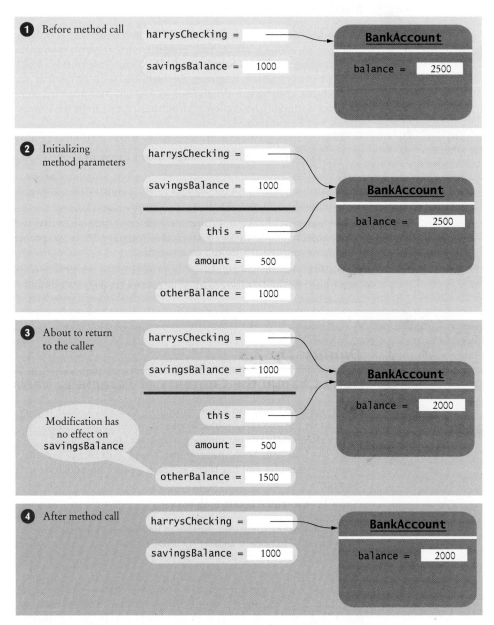

Figure 3 Modifying a Numeric Parameter Has No Effect on Caller

In Java, a method can never change parameters of primitive type.

Why did the example at the beginning of Section 7.4 work, where the second explicit parameter was a BankAccount reference? Then the parameter variable contained a *copy* of the object reference. Through that reference, the method is able to modify the object.

You already saw this difference between objects and primitive types in Chapter 2. As a consequence, a Java method can *never* modify numbers that are passed to it.

Quality Tip 7.2

Minimize Side Effects

In an ideal world, all methods would be accessors that simply return an answer without changing any value at all. (In fact, programs that are written in so-called *functional* programming languages, such as Scheme and ML, come close to this ideal.) Of course, in an object-oriented programming language, we use objects to remember state changes. Therefore, a method that just changes the state of its implicit parameter is certainly acceptable. Although side effects cannot be completely eliminated, they can be the cause of surprises and problems and should be minimized.

When designing methods, minimize side effects.

When analyzing side effects, we can categorize methods as follows:

* Accessor methods with no changes to any explicit parameters—no side effects. Example: getBalance.

* Mutator methods with no changes to any explicit parameters—an acceptable side effect. Example: BankAccount.withdraw is acceptable.

* Methods that change an explicit parameter—a side effect that should be avoided when possible. Example: BankAccount.transfer on page 279 is acceptable, but GradeBook.add-Students on page 279 should be changed.

* Methods that change another object (such as System.out)—a side effect that should be avoided. Example: BankAccount.printBalance on page 280 should not be implemented.

Quality Tip 7.3

Don't Change the Contents of Parameter Variables

As explained in Common Error 7.1 on page 280 and Special Topic 7.1 on page 283, a method can treat its parameter variables like local variables and change their contents. However, that change affects only the parameter variable within the method itself—not any values supplied in the method call. Some programmers take "advantage" of the temporary nature of the parameter variables and use them as "convenient" holders for intermediate results, as in this example:

```java
public void deposit(double amount)
{
    // Using the parameter variable to hold an intermediate value
    amount = balance + amount; // Poor style
    . . .
}
```

That code would produce errors if another statement in the method referred to amount expecting it to be the value of the parameter, and it will confuse later programmers maintaining this method. You should always treat the parameter variables as if they were constants. Don't assign new values to them. Instead, introduce a new local variable.

```
public void deposit(double amount)
{
    double newBalance = balance + amount;
    . . .
}
```

Special Topic 7.1

Call by Value and Call by Reference

Special Topic 7.1 explains the theoretical concepts of "call by value" and "call by reference" and demonstrates that the Java programming language always uses "call by value".

7.5 Preconditions and Postconditions

A precondition is a requirement that the caller of a method must meet.

A **precondition** is a requirement that the caller of a method must obey. For example, the deposit method of the BankAccount class has a precondition that the amount to be deposited should not be negative. It is the responsibility of the caller never to call a method if one of its preconditions is violated. If the method is called anyway, it is not responsible for producing a correct result.

Therefore, a precondition is an important part of the method, and you must document it. Here we document the precondition that the amount parameter must not be negative.

```
/**
    Deposits money into this account.
    @param amount  the amount of money to deposit
    (Precondition: amount >= 0)
*/
```

Some javadoc extensions support a @precondition or @requires tag, but it is not a part of the standard javadoc program. Because the standard javadoc tool skips all unknown tags, we simply add the precondition to the method explanation or the appropriate @param tag.

Preconditions are typically provided for one of two reasons:

1. To restrict the parameters of a method
2. To require that a method is only called when it is in the appropriate *state*

For example, once a Scanner has run out of input, it is no longer legal to call the next method. Thus, a precondition for the next method is that the hasNext method returns true.

If a method is called in violation of a precondition, the method is not responsible for computing the correct result.

A method is responsible for operating correctly only when its caller has fulfilled all preconditions. The method is free to do *anything* if a precondition is not fulfilled. What should a method actually do when it is called with inappropriate inputs? For example, what should account.deposit(-1000) do? There are two choices.

1. A method can check for the violation and **throw an exception**. Then the method does not return to its caller; instead, control is transferred to an

exception handler. If no handler is present, then the program terminates. We will discuss exceptions in Chapter 10.

2. A method can skip the check and work under the assumption that the preconditions are fulfilled. If they aren't, then any data corruption (such as a negative balance) or other failures are the caller's fault.

The first approach can be inefficient, particularly if the same check is carried out many times by several methods. The second approach can be dangerous. The *assertion mechanism* was invented to give you the best of both approaches.

An **assertion** is a condition that you believe to be true at all times in a particular program location. An assertion check tests whether an assertion is true. Here is a typical assertion check that tests a precondition:

An assertion is a logical condition in a program that you believe to be true.

```java
public double deposit (double amount)
{
    assert amount >= 0;
    balance = balance + amount;
}
```

In this method, the programmer expects that the quantity amount can never be negative. When the assertion is correct, no harm is done, and the program works in the normal way. If, for some reason, the assertion fails, *and assertion checking is enabled*, then the program terminates with an AssertionError.

However, if assertion checking is disabled, then the assertion is never checked, and the program runs at full speed. By default, assertion checking is disabled when you execute a program. To execute a program with assertion checking turned on, use this command:

```
java -enableassertions MainClass
```

You can also use the shortcut -ea instead of -enableassertions. You definitely want to turn assertion checking on during program development and testing.

You don't have to use assertions for checking preconditions—throwing an exception is another reasonable option. But assertions have one advantage: You can turn them off after you have tested your program, so that it runs at maximum speed. That way, you never have to feel bad about putting lots of assertions into your code. You can also use assertions for checking conditions other than preconditions.

Many beginning programmers think that it isn't "nice" to abort the program when a precondition is violated. Why not simply return to the caller instead?

```java
public void deposit(double amount)
{
    if (amount < 0)
        return; // Not recommended
    balance = balance + amount;
}
```

That is legal—after all, a method can do anything if its preconditions are violated. But it is not as good as an assertion check. If the program calling the deposit method has a few bugs that cause it to pass a negative amount as an input value, then the version that generates an assertion failure will make the bugs very obvious during testing—it is hard to ignore when the program aborts. The quiet version, on the other hand, will not alert you, and you may not notice that it performs some wrong calculations as a consequence. Think of assertions as the "tough love" approach to precondition checking.

Syntax 7.1   Assertion

Syntax   assert *condition*;

Example

assert amount >= 0;

If the condition is false and assertion checking is enabled, an exception occurs.

Condition that is claimed to be true.

When a method is called in accordance with its preconditions, then the method promises to do its job correctly. A different kind of promise that the method makes is called a **postcondition**. There are two kinds of postconditions:

> If a method has been called in accordance with its preconditions, then it must ensure that its postconditions are valid.

1. The return value is computed correctly.
2. The object is in a certain state after the method call is completed.

Here is a postcondition that makes a statement about the object state after the deposit method is called.

```
/**
   Deposits money into this account.
   (Postcondition: getBalance() >= 0)
   @param amount the amount of money to deposit
   (Precondition: amount >= 0)
*/
```

As long as the precondition is fulfilled, this method guarantees that the balance after the deposit is not negative.

Some javadoc extensions support a @postcondition or @ensures tag. However, just as with preconditions, we simply add postconditions to the method explanation or the @return tag, because the standard javadoc program skips all tags that it doesn't know.

Some programmers feel that they must specify a postcondition for every method. When you use javadoc, however, you already specify a part of the postcondition in the @return tag, and you shouldn't repeat it in a postcondition.

```
// This postcondition statement is overly repetitive.
/**
   Returns the current balance of this account.
   @return the account balance
   (Postcondition: The return value equals the account balance.)
*/
```

Note that we formulate pre- and postconditions only in terms of the *interface* of the class. Thus, we state the precondition of the withdraw method as amount <= getBalance(), not amount <= balance. After all, the caller, which needs to check the precondition, has access only to the public interface, not the private implementation.

Preconditions and postconditions are often compared to *contracts*. In real life, contracts spell out the obligations of the contracting parties. For example, a car dealer may promise you a car in good working order, and you promise in turn to pay a certain amount of money. If either party breaks the promise, then the other is not bound by the terms of the contract. In the same fashion, pre- and postconditions are contractual terms between a method and its caller. The method promises to fulfill the postcondition for all inputs that fulfill the precondition. The caller promises never to call the method with illegal inputs. If the caller fulfills its promise and gets a wrong answer, it can take the method to "programmer's court". If the caller doesn't fulfill its promise and something terrible happens as a consequence, it has no recourse.

S E L F   C H E C K

10. Why might you want to add a precondition to a method that you provide for other programmers?

11. When you implement a method with a precondition and you notice that the caller did not fulfill the precondition, do you have to notify the caller?

Special Topic 7.2

Class Invariants

Special Topic 7.2 introduces the topic of class invariants, logical statements that are true after every constructor and method call. Class invariants can be used for correctness proofs.

7.6 Static Methods

> A static method is not invoked on an object.

Sometimes you need a method that is not invoked on an object. Such a method is called a **static method** or a *class method.* In contrast, the methods that you have written up to now are often called **instance methods** because they operate on a particular instance of an object.

A typical example of a static method is the sqrt method in the Math class. When you call Math.sqrt(x), you don't supply any implicit parameter. (Recall that Math is the name of a class, not an object.)

Why would you want to write a method that does not operate on an object? The most common reason is that you want to encapsulate some computation that involves only numbers. Because numbers aren't objects, you can't invoke methods on them. For example, the call x.sqrt() can never be legal in Java.

Here is a typical example of a static method that carries out some simple algebra: to compute p percent of the amount a. Because the parameters are numbers, the method doesn't operate on any objects at all, so we make it into a static method:

```
/**
    Computes a percentage of an amount.
    @param p the percentage to apply
    @param a the amount to which the percentage is applied
    @return p percent of a
*/
public static double percentOf(double p, double a)
{
    return (p / 100) * a;
}
```

You need to find a home for this method. Let us come up with a new class (similar to the Math class of the standard Java library). Because the percentOf method has to

When you design a static method, you must find a class into which it should be placed.

do with financial calculations, we'll design a class `Financial` to hold it. Here is the class:

```java
public class Financial
{
    public static double percentOf(double p, double a)
    {
        return (p / 100) * a;
    }
    // More financial methods can be added here.
}
```

When calling a static method, you supply the name of the class containing the method so that the compiler can find it. For example,

```java
double tax = Financial.percentOf(taxRate, total);
```

Note that you do not supply an object of type `Financial` when you call the method.

There is another reason why static methods are sometimes necessary. If a method manipulates a class that you do not own, you cannot add it to that class. Consider a method that computes the area of a rectangle. The `Rectangle` class in the standard library has no such feature, and we cannot modify that class. A static method solves this problem:

```java
public class Geometry
{
    public static double area(Rectangle rect)
    {
        return rect.getWidth() * rect.getHeight();
    }
    // More geometry methods can be added here.
}
```

Now we can tell you why the `main` method is static. When the program starts, there aren't any objects. Therefore, the *first* method in the program must be a static method.

You may well wonder why these methods are called static. The normal meaning of the word *static* ("staying fixed at one place") does not seem to have anything to do with what static methods do. Indeed, it's used by accident. Java uses the `static` reserved word because C++ uses it in the same context. C++ uses `static` to denote class methods because the inventors of C++ did not want to invent another reserved word. Someone noted that there was a relatively rarely used reserved word, `static`, that denotes certain variables that stay in a fixed location for multiple method calls. (Java does not have this feature, nor does it need it.) It turned out that the reserved word could be reused to denote class methods without confusing the compiler. The fact that it can confuse humans was apparently not a big concern. You'll just have to live with the fact that "static method" means "class method": a method that has only explicit parameters.

SELF CHECK

12. Suppose that Java had no static methods. How would you use the `Math.sqrt` method for computing the square root of a number *x*?

13. The following method computes the average of an array list of numbers:
    ```java
    public static double average(ArrayList<Double> values)
    ```
    Why must it be a static method?

Quality Tip 7.4

Minimize the Use of Static Methods

It is possible to solve programming problems by using classes with only static methods. In fact, before object-oriented programming was invented, that approach was quite common. However, it usually leads to a design that is not object-oriented and makes it hard to evolve a program.

Consider the task of How To 6.1. A program reads scores for a student and prints the final score, which is obtained by dropping the lowest one. We solved the problem by implementing a GradeBook class that stores student scores. Of course, we could have simply written a program with a few static methods:

```
public class ScoreAnalyzer
{
   public static double[] readInputs() { . . . }
   public static double sum(double[] values) { . . . }
   public static double minimum(double[] values) { . . . }
   public static double finalScore(double[] values)
   {
      if (values.length == 0) return 0;
      else if (values.length == 1) return 1;
      else return sum(values) - minimum(values);
   }

   public static void main(String[] args)
   {
      System.out.println(finalScore(readInputs()));
   }
}
```

That solution is fine if one's sole objective is to solve a simple homework problem. But suppose you need to modify the program so that it deals with multiple students. An object-oriented program can evolve the GradeBook class to store grades for many students. In contrast, adding more functionality to static methods gets messy quickly (see Exercise P7.7).

7.7 Static Variables

Sometimes, a value properly belongs to a class, not to any object of the class. You use a **static variable** for this purpose. Here is a typical example. We want to assign bank account numbers sequentially. That is, we want the bank account constructor to construct the first account with number 1001, the next with number 1002, and so on. Therefore, we must store the last assigned account number somewhere.

Of course, it makes no sense to make this value into an instance variable:

```
public class BankAccount
{
   private double balance;
   private int accountNumber;
   private int lastAssignedNumber = 1000; // NO—won't work
   . . .
}
```

In that case each *instance* of the BankAccount class would have its own value of last-AssignedNumber.

Instead, we need to have a single value of lastAssignedNumber that is the same for the entire *class*. Such a variable is called a static variable, because you declare it using the static reserved word.

```
public class BankAccount
{
    private double balance;
    private int accountNumber;
    private static int lastAssignedNumber = 1000;
    . . .
}
```

Every BankAccount object has its own balance and accountNumber instance variables, but there is only a single copy of the lastAssignedNumber variable (see Figure 4). That variable is stored in a separate location, outside any BankAccount objects.

A static variable is sometimes called a *class variable* because there is a single variable for the entire class.

Every method of a class can access its static variables. Here is the constructor of the BankAccount class, which increments the last assigned number and then uses it to initialize the account number of the object to be constructed:

```
public class BankAccount
{
    . . .
    public BankAccount()
    {
        lastAssignedNumber++; // Updates the static variable
        accountNumber = lastAssignedNumber; // Sets the instance variable
    }
}
```

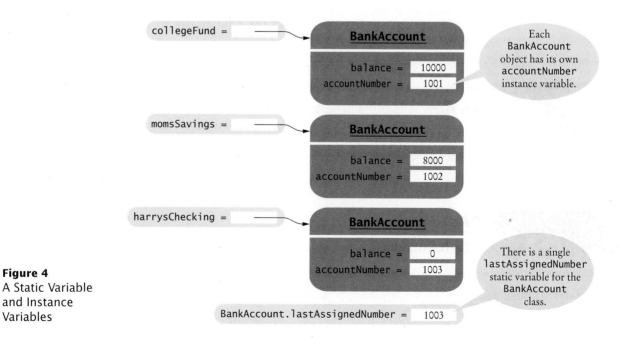

Figure 4
A Static Variable and Instance Variables

There are three ways to initialize a static variable:

1. Do nothing. The static variable is then initialized with 0 (for numbers), false (for boolean values), or null (for objects).

2. Use an explicit initializer, such as

```
public class BankAccount
{
    private static int lastAssignedNumber = 1000;
    . . .
}
```

3. Use a static initialization block (see Special Topic 7.4).

Like instance variables, static variables should always be declared as private to ensure that methods of other classes do not change their values. The exception to this rule are static *constants*, which may be either private or public. For example, the BankAccount class may want to declare a public constant value, such as

```
public class BankAccount
{
    public static final double OVERDRAFT_FEE = 29.95;
    . . .
}
```

Methods from any class can refer to such a constant as BankAccount.OVERDRAFT_FEE.

It makes sense to declare constants as static—you wouldn't want every object of the BankAccount class to have its own set of variables with these constant values. It is sufficient to have one set of them for the class.

Why are class variables called static? As with static methods, the static reserved word itself is just a meaningless holdover from C++. But static variables and static methods have much in common: They apply to the entire *class*, not to specific instances of the class.

In general, you want to minimize the use of static methods and variables. If you find yourself using lots of static methods that access static variables, then that's an indication that you have not found the right classes to solve your problem in an object-oriented way.

SELF CHECK

14. Name two static variables of the System class.

15. Harry tells you that he has found a great way to avoid those pesky objects: Put all code into a single class and declare all methods and variables static. Then main can call the other static methods, and all of them can access the static variables. Will Harry's plan work? Is it a good idea?

Special Topic 7.3

Static Imports

Special Topic 7.3 introduces the "static import" syntax for importing static constants so that they can be used without a class prefix.

Special Topic 7.4

Alternative Forms of Instance and Static Variable Initialization

Special Topic 7.4 covers two less common mechanisms for instance variable initialization: specifying initial values for instance variables, and using initialization blocks.

7.8 Scope

> The scope of a variable is the region of a program in which the variable can be accessed.

The **scope** of a variable is the part of the program in which the variable can be accessed. It is considered good design to minimize the scope of a variable. This reduces the possibility of accidental modification and name conflicts.

In the following sections, you will learn how to determine the scopes of local and instance variables, and how to resolve name conflicts if the scopes overlap.

7.8.1 Scope of Variables

The scope of a local variable extends from the point of its declaration to the end of the block or for loop that encloses it. The scope of a parameter variable is the entire method.

```
public static void process(double[] values) // values is a parameter variable
{
    for (int i = 0; i < 10; i++) // i is a local variable declared in a for loop
    {
        if (values[i] == 0)
        {
            double r = Math.random(); // r is a local variable declared in a block
            values[i] = r;
        } // Scope of r ends here
    } // Scope of i ends here
} // Scope of values ends here
```

> The scope of a local variable cannot contain the declaration of another local variable with the same name.

In Java, the scope of a local variable can never contain the declaration of another local variable with the same name. For example, the following is an error:

```
public static void main(String[] args)
{
    double r = Math.random();
    if (r > 0.5)
    {
        Rectangle r = new Rectangle(5, 10, 20, 30);
        // Error—can't declare another variable called r here
        . . .
    }
}
```

However, you can have local variables with identical names if their scopes do not overlap, such as

```
if (Math.random() > 0.5)
{
```

```
        Rectangle r = new Rectangle(5, 10, 20, 30);
        . . .
} // Scope of r ends here
else
{
        int r = 5;
        // OK—it is legal to declare another r here
        . . .
}
```

These variables are independent from each other, or, in other words, their scopes are disjoint. You can have local variables with the same name r in different methods, just as you can have different motels with the same name "Bates Motel" in different cities.

In contrast, the scope of instance variables and static variables consists of the entire class in which they are declared.

7.8.2 Overlapping Scope

Problems arise if you have two identical variable names with overlapping scope. This can never occur with local variables, but the scopes of identically named local variables and instance variables can overlap. Here is a purposefully bad example.

```
public class Coin
{
    private String name;
    private double value; // Instance variable
    . . .
    public double getExchangeValue(double exchangeRate)
    {
        double value; // Local variable with the same name
        . . .
        return value;
    }
}
```

Inside the getExchangeValue method, the variable name value could potentially have two meanings: the **local variable** or the **instance variable**. The Java language specifies that in this situation the *local* variable wins out. It *shadows* the instance variable. This sounds pretty arbitrary, but there is actually a good reason: You can still refer to the instance variable as this.value.

> A local variable can shadow an instance variable with the same name. You can access the shadowed variable name through the this reference.

```
value = this.value * exchangeRate;
```

Of course, it is not a good idea to write code like this. You can easily change the name of the local variable to something else, such as result.

However, there is one situation where overlapping scope is acceptable. When implementing constructors or setter methods, it can be awkward to come up with different names for instance variables and parameters. Here is how you can use the same name for both:

```
public Coin(double value, String name)
{
    this.value = value;
    this.name = name;
}
```

The expression this.value refers to the instance variable, and value is the parameter.

SELF CHECK

16. Consider the following program that uses two variables named r. Is this legal?

```java
public class RectangleTester
{
   public static double area(Rectangle rect)
   {
      double r = rect.getWidth() * rect.getHeight();
      return r;
   }

   public static void main(String[] args)
   {
      Rectangle r = new Rectangle(5, 10, 20, 30);
      double a = area(r);
      System.out.println(r);
   }
}
```

17. What is the scope of the `balance` variable of the `BankAccount` class?

Common Error 7.2

Shadowing

Accidentally using the same name for a local variable and an instance variable is a surprisingly common error. As you saw in the preceding section, the local variable then *shadows* the instance variable. Even though you may have meant to access the instance variable, the local variable is quietly accessed. Look at this example of an incorrect constructor:

```java
public class Coin
{
   private double value;
   private String name;
   . . .
   public Coin(double aValue, String aName)
   {
      value = aValue;
      String name = aName; // Oops . . .
   }
}
```

The programmer declared a local variable `name` in the constructor. In all likelihood, that was just a typo—the programmer's fingers were on autopilot and typed the reserved word `String`, even though the programmer all the time intended to access the instance variable. Unfortunately, the compiler gives no warning in this situation and quietly sets the local variable to the value of `aName`. The instance variable of the object that is being constructed is never touched, and remains `null`.

Some programmers give all instance variable names a special prefix to distinguish them from other variables. A common convention is to prefix all instance variable names with the prefix `my`, such as `myValue` or `myName`.

Another way of avoiding this problem is to use the `this` parameter when accessing an instance variable:

```java
this.name = aName;
```

Quality Tip 7.5

Minimize Variable Scope

You should give each variable the smallest scope that it needs.

When you make the scope of a variable as small as possible, it becomes less likely that the variable is accidentally corrupted. It also becomes easier to modify or eliminate the variable as you reorganize your code.

As already mentioned, don't make an instance variable public. (The Java library has a few classes with public instance variables, but their creators later regretted their decision when they were unable to make optimizations later.)

When you have a constant, ask yourself who needs it. Everybody (`public static final`)? Only the class (`private static final`)? Only a single method (a `final` local variable)? Choose the smallest scope.

Beware of unnecessary instance variables. For example, consider the `Pyramid` class in Worked Example 3.1. You would not want an instance variable for the volume:

```java
public class Pyramid
{
   private double height;
   private double baseLength;
   private double volume; // Not a good idea to use class scope for this variable
   . . .
}
```

Instead, compute the volume when it is needed in the `getVolume` method. That way, no other method can accidentally modify the `volume` variable, or forget to modify it when changing the height or base length.

Finally, with local variables, declare them only when you need them.

7.9 Packages

A package is a set of related classes.

A Java program consists of a collection of classes. So far, most of your programs have consisted of a small number of classes. As programs get larger, however, simply distributing the classes over multiple files isn't enough. An additional structuring mechanism is needed.

In Java, packages provide this structuring mechanism. A Java **package** is a set of related classes. For example, the Java library consists of several hundred packages, some of which are listed in Table 1.

Syntax 7.2   Package Specification

> *Syntax*   package *packageName*;
>
> *Example*
>   package com.horstmann.bigjava;
>
> The classes in this file belong to this package.
>
> A good choice for a package name is a domain name in reverse.

Table 1 Important Packages in the Java Library		
Package	Purpose	Sample Class
java.lang	Language support	Math
java.util	Utilities	Random
java.io	Input and output	PrintStream
java.awt	Abstract Windowing Toolkit	Color
java.applet	Applets	Applet
java.net	Networking	Socket
java.sql	Database access through Structured Query Language	ResultSet
javax.swing	Swing user interface	JButton
omg.w3c.dom	Document Object Model for XML documents	Document

7.9.1 Organizing Related Classes into Packages

To put one of your classes in a package, you must place a line

```
package packageName;
```

as the first instruction in the source file containing the class. A package name consists of one or more identifiers separated by periods. (See Section 7.9.3 for tips on constructing package names.)

For example, let's put the Financial class introduced in this chapter into a package named com.horstmann.bigjava. The Financial.java file must start as follows:

```
package com.horstmann.bigjava;
public class Financial
{
   . . .
}
```

In addition to the named packages (such as java.util or com.horstmann.bigjava), there is a special package, called the *default package*, which has no name. If you did not include any package statement at the top of your source file, its classes are placed in the default package.

7.9.2 Importing Packages

If you want to use a class from a package, you can refer to it by its full name (package name plus class name). For example, java.util.Scanner refers to the Scanner class in the java.util package:

```
java.util.Scanner in = new java.util.Scanner(System.in);
```

The import directive lets you refer to a class of a package by its class name, without the package prefix.

Naturally, that is somewhat inconvenient. You can instead *import* a name with an `import` statement:

```
import java.util.Scanner;
```

Then you can refer to the class as `Scanner` without the package prefix.

You can import *all classes* of a package with an `import` statement that ends in `.*`. For example, you can use the statement

```
import java.util.*;
```

to import all classes from the `java.util` package. That statement lets you refer to classes like `Scanner` or `Random` without a `java.util` prefix.

However, you never need to import the classes in the `java.lang` package explicitly. That is the package containing the most basic Java classes, such as `Math` and `Object`. These classes are always available to you. In effect, an automatic `import java.lang.*;` statement has been placed into every source file.

Finally, you don't need to import other classes in the same package. For example, when you implement the class `homework1.Tester`, you don't need to import the class `homework1.Bank`. The compiler will find the `Bank` class without an `import` statement because it is located in the same package, `homework1`.

7.9.3 Package Names

Placing related classes into a package is clearly a convenient mechanism to organize classes. However, there is a more important reason for packages: to avoid **name clashes**. In a large project, it is inevitable that two people will come up with the same name for the same concept. This even happens in the standard Java class library (which has now grown to thousands of classes). There is a class `Timer` in the `java.util` package and another class called `Timer` in the `javax.swing` package. You can still tell the Java compiler exactly which `Timer` class you need, simply by referring to them as `java.util.Timer` and `javax.swing.Timer`.

Of course, for the package-naming convention to work, there must be some way to ensure that package names are unique. It wouldn't be good if the car maker BMW placed all its Java code into the package `bmw`, and some other programmer (perhaps Britney M. Walters) had the same bright idea. To avoid this problem, the inventors of Java recommend that you use a package-naming scheme that takes advantage of the uniqueness of Internet domain names.

Use a domain name in reverse to construct an unambiguous package name.

For example, I have a domain name `horstmann.com`, and there is nobody else on the planet with the same domain name. (I was lucky that the domain name `horstmann.com` had not been taken by anyone else when I applied. If your name is Walters, you will sadly find that someone else beat you to `walters.com`.) To get a package name, turn the domain name around to produce a package name prefix, such as `com.horstmann`.

If you don't have your own domain name, you can still create a package name that has a high probability of being unique by writing your e-mail address backwards. For example, if Britney Walters has an e-mail address `walters@cs.sjsu.edu`, then she can use a package name `edu.sjsu.cs.walters` for her own classes.

Some instructors will want you to place each of your assignments into a separate package, such as `homework1`, `homework2`, and so on. The reason is again to avoid name collision. You can have two classes, `homework1.Bank` and `homework2.Bank`, with slightly different properties.

7.9.4 Packages and Source Files

> The path of a class file must match its package name.

A source file must be located in a subdirectory that matches the package name. The parts of the name between periods represent successively nested directories. For example, the source files for classes in the package `com.horstmann.bigjava` would be placed in a subdirectory `com/horstmann/bigjava`. You place the subdirectory inside the *base directory* holding your program's files. For example, if you do your homework assignment in a directory `/home/britney/hw8/problem1`, then you can place the class files for the `com.horstmann.bigjava` package into the directory `/home/britney/hw8/problem1/com/horstmann/bigjava`, as shown in Figure 5. (Here, we are using UNIX-style file names. Under Windows, you might use `c:\Users\Britney\hw8\problem1\com\horstmann\bigjava`.)

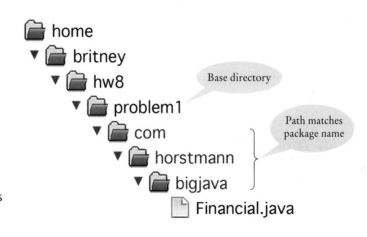

Figure 5
Base Directories and Subdirectories for Packages

SELF CHECK

18. Which of the following are packages?

    a. `java`

    b. `java.lang`

    c. `java.util`

    d. `java.lang.Math`

19. Is a Java program without `import` statements limited to using the default and `java.lang` packages?

20. Suppose your homework assignments are located in the directory `/home/me/cs101` (`c:\Users\Me\cs101` on Windows). Your instructor tells you to place your homework into packages. In which directory do you place the class `hw1.problem1.TicTacToeTester`?

Common Error 7.3

Confusing Dots

In Java, the dot symbol (.) is used as a separator in the following situations:

- Between package names (`java.util`)
- Between package and class names (`homework1.Bank`)
- Between class and inner class names (`Ellipse2D.Double`)
- Between class and instance variable names (`Math.PI`)
- Between objects and methods (`account.getBalance()`)

When you see a long chain of dot-separated names, it can be a challenge to find out which part is the package name, which part is the class name, which part is an instance variable name, and which part is a method name. Consider

```
java.lang.System.out.println(x);
```

Because `println` is followed by an opening parenthesis, it must be a method name. Therefore, `out` must be either an object or a class with a static `println` method. (Of course, we know that `out` is an object reference of type `PrintStream`.) Again, it is not at all clear, without context, whether `System` is another object, with a public variable `out`, or a class with a `static` variable. Judging from the number of pages that the Java language specification devotes to this issue, even the compiler has trouble interpreting these dot-separated sequences of strings.

To avoid problems, it is helpful to adopt a strict coding style. If class names always start with an uppercase letter, and variable, method, and package names always start with a lowercase letter, then confusion can be avoided.

Special Topic 7.5

Package Access

If a class, field, or method has no `public` or `private` modifier, then all methods of classes in the same package can access the feature. For example, if a class is declared as `public`, then all other classes in all packages can use it. But if a class is declared without an access modifier, then only the other classes in the *same* package can use it. Package access is a reasonable default for classes, but it is extremely unfortunate for instance variables.

It is a common error to *forget* the reserved word `private`, thereby opening up a potential security hole. For example, at the time of this writing, the `Window` class in the `java.awt` package contained the following declaration:

> A field or method that is not declared as public or private can be accessed by all classes in the same package, which is usually not desirable.

```
public class Window extends Container
{
   String warningString;
   . . .
}
```

There actually was no good reason to grant package access to the `warningString` instance variable—no other class accesses it.

Package access for instance variables is rarely useful and always a potential security risk. Most instance variables are given package access by accident because the programmer simply forgot the `private` reserved word. It is a good idea to get into the habit of scanning your instance variable declarations for missing `private` modifiers.

How To 7.1

Programming with Packages

This How To explains in detail how to place your programs into packages. For example, your instructor may ask you to place each homework assignment into a separate package. That way, you can have classes with the same name but different implementations in separate packages (such as homework1.problem1.Bank and homework1.problem2.Bank).

Step 1   Come up with a package name.

Your instructor may give you a package name to use, such as homework1.problem2. Or, perhaps you want to use a package name that is unique to you. Start with your e-mail address, written backwards. For example, walters@cs.sjsu.edu becomes edu.sjsu.cs.walters. Then add a subpackage that describes your project, such as edu.sjsu.cs.walters.cs1project.

Step 2   Pick a *base directory*.

The base directory is the directory that contains the directories for your various packages, for example, /home/britney or c:\Users\Britney.

Step 3   Make a subdirectory from the base directory that matches your package name.

The subdirectory must be contained in your base directory. Each segment must match a segment of the package name. For example,

```
mkdir -p /home/britney/homework1/problem2 (in UNIX)
```
or
```
mkdir /s c:\Users\Britney\homework1\problem2 (in Windows)
```

Step 4   Place your source files into the package subdirectory.

For example, if your homework consists of the files Tester.java and Bank.java, then you place them into

```
/home/britney/homework1/problem2/Tester.java
/home/britney/homework1/problem2/Bank.java
```
or
```
c:\Users\Britney\homework1\problem2\Tester.java
c:\Users\Britney\homework1\problem2\Bank.java
```

Step 5   Use the package statement in each source file.

The first noncomment line of each file must be a package statement that lists the name of the package, such as

```
package homework1.problem2;
```

Step 6   Compile your source files from the *base directory*.

Change to the base directory (from Step 2) to compile your files. For example,

```
cd /home/britney
javac homework1/problem2/Tester.java
```
or
```
c:
cd \Users\Britney
javac homework1\problem2\Tester.java
```

Note that the Java compiler needs the *source file name and not the class name. That is, you need to supply file separators* (/ on UNIX, \ on Windows) and a file extension (.java).

Step 7 Run your program from the *base directory*.

Unlike the Java compiler, the Java interpreter needs the *class name (and not a file name) of the class containing the* main *method*. That is, use periods as package separators, and don't use a file extension. For example,

```
cd /home/britney
java homework1.problem2.Tester
```

or

```
c:
cd \Users\Britney
java homework1.problem2.Tester
```

Random Fact 7.1

The Explosive Growth of Personal Computers

Random Fact 7.1 traces the history of the personal computer, from the advent of the first microprocessor to the first Macintosh.

7.10 Unit Test Frameworks

Up to now, we have used a very simple approach to testing. We provided tester classes whose main method computes values and prints actual and expected values. However, that approach has limitations. The main method gets messy if it contains many tests. And if an exception occurs during one of the tests, the remaining tests are not executed.

Unit testing frameworks were designed to quickly execute and evaluate test suites, and to make it easy to incrementally add test cases. One of the most popular testing frameworks is JUnit. It is freely available at http://junit.org, and it is also built into a number of development environments, including BlueJ and Eclipse. Here we describe JUnit 4, the most current version of the library as this book is written.

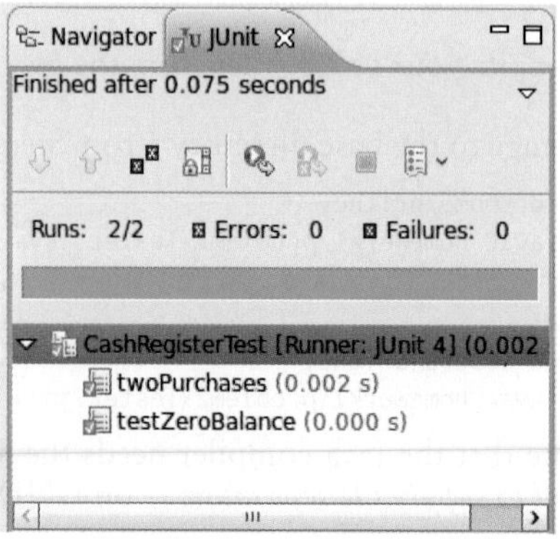

> Unit test frameworks simplify the task of writing classes that contain many test cases.

Figure 6
Unit Testing with JUnit

When you use JUnit, you design a companion test class for each class that you develop. You provide a method for each test case that you want to have executed. You use "annotations" to mark the test methods. An annotation is an advanced Java feature that places a marker into the code that is interpreted by another tool. In the case of JUnit, the @Test annotation is used to mark test methods.

In each test case, you make some computations and then compute some condition that you believe to be true. You then pass the result to a method that communicates a test result to the framework, most commonly the assertEquals method. The assertEquals method takes as parameters the expected and actual values and, for floating-point numbers, a tolerance value.

It is also customary (but not required) that the name of the test class ends in Test, such as CashRegisterTest. Here is a typical example:

```java
import org.junit.Test;
import org.junit.Assert;

public class CashRegisterTest
{
   @Test public void twoPurchases()
   {
      CashRegister register = new CashRegister();
      register.recordPurchase(0.75);
      register.recordPurchase(1.50);
      register.enterPayment(2, 0, 5, 0, 0);
      double expected = 0.25;
      Assert.assertEquals(expected, register.giveChange(), EPSILON);
   }
   // More test cases
   . . .
}
```

If all test cases pass, the JUnit tool shows a green bar (see Figure 6). If any of the test cases fail, the JUnit tool shows a red bar and an error message.

Your test class can also have other methods (whose names should not be annotated with @Test). These methods typically carry out steps that you want to share among test methods.

The JUnit philosophy is simple. Whenever you implement a class, also make a companion test class. You design the tests as you design the program, one test method at a time. The test cases just keep accumulating in the test class. Whenever you have detected an actual failure, add a test case that flushes it out, so that you can be sure that you won't introduce that particular bug again. Whenever you modify your class, simply run the tests again.

If all tests pass, the user interface shows a green bar and you can relax. Otherwise, there is a red bar, but that's also good. It is much easier to fix a bug in isolation than inside a complex program.

> The JUnit philosophy is to run all tests whenever you change your code.

SELF CHECK

21. Provide a JUnit test class with one test case for the Earthquake class in Chapter 4.

22. What is the significance of the EPSILON parameter in the assertEquals method?

Summary of Learning Objectives

Find classes that are appropriate for solving a programming problem.

- A class should represent a single concept from a problem domain, such as business, science, or mathematics.

Analyze cohesiveness and coupling of classes.

- The public interface of a class is cohesive if all of its features are related to the concept that the class represents.
- A class depends on another class if it uses objects of that class.
- It is a good practice to minimize the coupling (i.e., dependency) between classes.

Recognize immutable classes and their benefits.

- An immutable class has no mutator methods.
- References to objects of an immutable class can be safely shared.

Recognize side effects and the need to minimize them.

- A side effect of a method is any externally observable data modification.
- In Java, a method can never change parameters of primitive type.
- When designing methods, minimize side effects.

Document preconditions and postconditions of methods.

- A precondition is a requirement that the caller of a method must meet.
- If a method is called in violation of a precondition, the method is not responsible for computing the correct result.
- An assertion is a logical condition in a program that you believe to be true.
- If a method has been called in accordance with its preconditions, then it must ensure that its postconditions are valid.

Implement static methods that do not operate on objects.

- A static method is not invoked on an object.
- When you design a static method, you must find a class into which it should be placed.

Use static variables to describe properties of a class.

- A static variable belongs to the class, not to any object of the class.

Determine the scopes of local variables and instance variables.

- The scope of a variable is the region of a program in which the variable can be accessed.
- The scope of a local variable cannot contain the declaration of another local variable with the same name.
- A local variable can shadow an instance variable with the same name. You can access the shadowed variable name through the this reference.
- You should give each variable the smallest scope that it needs.

Use packages to organize sets of related classes.

- A package is a set of related classes.
- The import directive lets you refer to a class of a package by its class name, without the package prefix.
- Use a domain name in reverse to construct an unambiguous package name.
- The path of a class file must match its package name.
- A field or method that is not declared as public or private can be accessed by all classes in the same package, which is usually not desirable.

Use JUnit for writing unit tests.

- Unit test frameworks simplify the task of writing classes that contain many test cases.
- The JUnit philosophy is to run all tests whenever you change your code.

Media Resources

www.wiley.com/
go/global/
horstmann

- Lab Exercises
- ➕ **_Animation_** A Method Cannot Modify a Numeric Parameter
- ➕ Practice Quiz
- ➕ Code Completion Exercises

Review Exercises

★★ **R7.1** Consider the following problem description:

Users place coins in a vending machine and select a product by pushing a button. If the inserted coins are sufficient to cover the purchase price of the product, the product is dispensed and change is given. Otherwise, the inserted coins are returned to the user.

What classes should you use to implement it?

★★ **R7.2** Consider the following problem description:

Employees receive their biweekly paychecks. They are paid their hourly rates for each hour worked; however, if they worked more than 40 hours per week, they are paid at 150 percent of their regular wage for those overtime hours.

What classes should you use to implement it?

★★★ **R7.3** Consider the following problem description:

Customers order products from a store. Invoices are generated to list the items and quantities ordered, payments received, and amounts still due. Products are shipped to the shipping address of the customer, and invoices are sent to the billing address.

What classes should you use to implement it?

★★★ **R7.4** Look at the public interface of the java.lang.System class and discuss whether or not it is cohesive.

★★ **R7.5** Suppose an `Invoice` object contains descriptions of the products ordered, and the billing and shipping addresses of the customer. Draw a UML diagram showing the dependencies between the classes `Invoice`, `Address`, `Customer`, and `Product`.

★★ **R7.6** Suppose a vending machine contains products, and users insert coins into the vending machine to purchase products. Draw a UML diagram showing the dependencies between the classes `VendingMachine`, `Coin`, and `Product`.

★★ **R7.7** On which classes does the class `Integer` in the standard library depend?

★★ **R7.8** On which classes does the class `Rectangle` in the standard library depend?

★ **R7.9** Classify the methods of the class `Scanner` that are used in this book as accessors and mutators.

★ **R7.10** Classify the methods of the class `Rectangle` as accessors and mutators.

★ **R7.11** Which of the following classes are immutable?

    a. `Rectangle`
    b. `String`
    c. `Random`

★ **R7.12** Which of the following classes are immutable?

    a. `PrintStream`
    b. `Date`
    c. `Integer`

★★ **R7.13** What side effect, if any, do the following three methods have:

```java
public class Coin
{
    . . .
    public void print()
    {
        System.out.println(name + " " + value);
    }

    public void print(PrintStream stream)
    {
        stream.println(name + " " + value);
    }

    public String toString()
    {
        return name + " " + value;
    }
}
```

★★★ **R7.14** Ideally, a method should have no side effects. Can you write a program in which no method has a side effect? Would such a program be useful?

★★ **R7.15** Write preconditions for the following methods. Do not implement the methods.

    a. `public static double sqrt(double x)`
    b. `public static String romanNumeral(int n)`
    c. `public static double slope(Line2D.Double a)`
    d. `public static String weekday(int day)`

★★ **R7.16** What preconditions do the following methods from the standard Java library have?

   a. `Math.sqrt`
   b. `Math.tan`
   c. `Math.log`
   d. `Math.pow`
   e. `Math.abs`

★★ **R7.17** What preconditions do the following methods from the standard Java library have?

   a. `Integer.parseInt(String s)`
   b. `StringTokenizer.nextToken()`
   c. `Random.nextInt(int n)`
   d. `String.substring(int m, int n)`

★★★ **R7.18** When a method is called with parameters that violate its precondition(s), it can terminate (by throwing an exception or an assertion error), or it can return to its caller. Give two examples of library methods (standard or the library methods used in this book) that return some result to their callers when called with invalid parameters, and give two examples of library methods that terminate.

★★ **R7.19** Consider a `CashRegister` class with methods

   • `public void enterPayment(int coinCount, Coin coinType)`
   • `public double getTotalPayment()`

   Give a reasonable postcondition of the `enterPayment` method. What preconditions would you need so that the `CashRegister` class can ensure that postcondition?

★★ **R7.20** Consider the following method that is intended to swap the values of two floating-point numbers:

```
public static void falseSwap(double a, double b)
{
   double temp = a;
   a = b;
   b = temp;
}

public static void main(String[] args)
{
   double x = 3;
   double y = 4;
   falseSwap(x, y);
   System.out.println(x + " " + y);
}
```

Why doesn't the method swap the contents of x and y?

★★★ **R7.21** How can you write a method that swaps two floating-point numbers?
Hint: `Point2D.Double`.

★★ **R7.22** Draw a memory diagram that shows why the following method can't swap two
`BankAccount` objects:

```
public static void falseSwap(BankAccount a, BankAccount b)
{
   BankAccount temp = a;
   a = b;
   b = temp;
}
```

★ **R7.23** Consider an enhancement of the Die class of Chapter 5 with a static variable

```java
public class Die
{
   private int sides;
   private static Random generator = new Random();
   public Die(int s) { . . . }
   public int cast() { . . . }
}
```

Draw a memory diagram that shows three dice:

```java
Die d4 = new Die(4);
Die d6 = new Die(6);
Die d8 = new Die(8);
```

Be sure to indicate the values of the sides and generator variables.

★ **R7.24** Try compiling the following program. Explain the error message that you get.

```java
public class Print13
{
   public void print(int x)
   {
      System.out.println(x);
   }

   public static void main(String[] args)
   {
      int n = 13;
      print(n);
   }
}
```

★ **R7.25** Look at the methods in the Integer class. Which are static? Why?

★★ **R7.26** Look at the methods in the String class (but ignore the ones that take a parameter of type char[]). Which are static? Why?

★★ **R7.27** The in and out variables of the System class are public static variables of the System class. Is that good design? If not, how could you improve on it?

★★ **R7.28** In the following class, the variable n occurs in multiple scopes. Which declarations of n are legal and which are illegal?

```java
public class X
{
   private int n;

   public int f()
   {
      int n = 1;
      return n;
   }

   public int g(int k)
   {
      int a;
      for (int n = 1; n <= k; n++)
         a = a + n;
      return a;
   }
}
```

```java
public int h(int n)
{
   int b;
   for (int n = 1; n <= 10; n++)
      b = b + n;
   return b + n;
}

public int k(int n)
{
   if (n < 0)
   {
      int k = -n;
      int n = (int) (Math.sqrt(k));
      return n;
   }
   else return n;
}

public int m(int k)
{
   int a;
   for (int n = 1; n <= k; n++)
      a = a + n;
   for (int n = k; n >= 1; n++)
      a = a + n;
   return a;
}
}
```

★★   R7.29 Every Java program can be rewritten to avoid import statements. Explain how, and rewrite RectangleComponent.java from Chapter 2 to avoid import statements.

★   R7.30 What is the default package? Have you used it before this chapter in your programming?

★★T   R7.31 What does JUnit do when a test method throws an exception? Try it out and report your findings.

Programming Exercises

★★   P7.1 Implement the Coin class described in Section 7.2. Modify the CashRegister class so that coins can be added to the cash register, by supplying a method

```java
void enterPayment(int coinCount, Coin coinType)
```

The caller needs to invoke this method multiple times, once for each type of coin that is present in the payment.

★★   P7.2 Modify the giveChange method of the CashRegister class so that it returns the number of coins of a particular type to return:

```java
int giveChange(Coin coinType)
```

The caller needs to invoke this method for each coin type, in decreasing value.

★   P7.3 Real cash registers can handle both bills and coins. Design a single class that expresses the commonality of these concepts. Redesign the CashRegister class and provide a method for entering payments that are described by your class. Your primary challenge is to come up with a good name for this class.

★ **P7.4** Enhance the BankAccount class by adding preconditions for the constructor and the deposit method that require the amount parameter to be at least zero, and a precondition for the withdraw method that requires amount to be a value between 0 and the current balance. Use assertions to test the preconditions.

★★ **P7.5** Write static methods

- `public static double sphereVolume(double r)`
- `public static double sphereSurface(double r)`
- `public static double cylinderVolume(double r, double h)`
- `public static double cylinderSurface(double r, double h)`
- `public static double coneVolume(double r, double h)`
- `public static double coneSurface(double r, double h)`

that compute the volume and surface area of a sphere with radius r, a cylinder with circular base with radius r and height h, and a cone with circular base with radius r and height h. Place them into a class Geometry. Then write a program that prompts the user for the values of r and h, calls the six methods, and prints the results.

★★ **P7.6** Solve Exercise P7.5 by implementing classes Sphere, Cylinder, and Cone. Which approach is more object-oriented?

★★ **P7.7** Modify the grade book application of How To 6.1 so that it can deal with multiple students. First, ask the user for all student names. Then read in the scores for all quizzes, prompting for the score of each student. Finally, print the names of all students and their final scores. Use a single class and only static methods.

★★★ **P7.8** Repeat Exercise P7.7, using multiple classes. Modify the GradeBook class so that it collects objects of type Student. Each such object should have a list of scores.

★★★ **P7.9** Write methods

```
public static double perimeter(Ellipse2D.Double e);
public static double area(Ellipse2D.Double e);
```

that compute the area and the perimeter of the ellipse e. Add these methods to a class Geometry. The challenging part of this assignment is to find and implement an accurate formula for the perimeter. Why does it make sense to use a static method in this case?

★★ **P7.10** Write methods

```
public static double angle(Point2D.Double p, Point2D.Double q)
public static double slope(Point2D.Double p, Point2D.Double q)
```

that compute the angle between the x-axis and the line joining two points, measured in degrees, and the slope of that line. Add the methods to the class Geometry. Supply suitable preconditions. Why does it make sense to use a static method in this case?

★★★ **P7.11** Write methods

```
public static boolean isInside(Point2D.Double p, Ellipse2D.Double e)
public static boolean isOnBoundary(Point2D.Double p, Ellipse2D.Double e)
```

that test whether a point is inside or on the boundary of an ellipse. Add the methods to the class Geometry.

★ **P7.12** Write a method

```
public static int readInt(
        Scanner in, String prompt, String error, int min, int max)
```

that displays the prompt string, reads an integer, and tests whether it is between the minimum and maximum. If not, print an error message and repeat reading the input. Add the method to a class Input.

★★ **P7.13** Consider the following algorithm for computing x^n for an integer n. If $n < 0$, x^n is $1/x^{-n}$. If n is positive and even, then $x^n = (x^{n/2})^2$. If n is positive and odd, then $x^n = x^{n-1} \cdot x$. Implement a static method double intPower(double x, int n) that uses this algorithm. Add it to a class called Numeric.

★★ **P7.14** Improve the Needle class of Chapter 5. Turn the generator variable into a static variable so that all needles share a single random number generator.

★★ **P7.15** Implement a Coin and CashRegister class as described in Exercise P7.1. Place the classes into a package called money. Keep the CashRegisterTester class in the default package.

★ **P7.16** Place a BankAccount class in a package whose name is derived from your e-mail address, as described in Section 7.9. Keep the BankAccountTester class in the default package.

★★T **P7.17** Provide a JUnit test class BankTest with three test methods, each of which tests a different method of the Bank class in Chapter 6.

★★T **P7.18** Provide JUnit test class TaxReturnTest with three test methods that test different tax situations for the TaxReturn class in Chapter 4.

★G **P7.19** Write methods

- public static void drawH(Graphics2D g2, Point2D.Double p);
- public static void drawE(Graphics2D g2, Point2D.Double p);
- public static void drawL(Graphics2D g2, Point2D.Double p);
- public static void drawO(Graphics2D g2, Point2D.Double p);

that show the letters H, E, L, O on the graphics window, where the point p is the top-left corner of the letter. Then call the methods to draw the words "HELLO" and "HOLE" on the graphics display. Draw lines and ellipses. Do not use the drawString method. Do not use System.out.

★★G **P7.20** Repeat Exercise P7.17 by designing classes LetterH, LetterE, LetterL, and LetterO, each with a constructor that takes a Point2D.Double parameter (the top-left corner) and a method draw(Graphics2D g2). Which solution is more object-oriented?

Programming Projects

Project 7.1 Implement a program that prints paychecks for a group of student assistants. Deduct federal and Social Security taxes. (You may want to use the tax computation used in Chapter 4. Find out about Social Security taxes on the Internet.) Your program should prompt for the names, hourly wages, and hours worked of each student.

Project 7.2 For faster sorting of letters, the United States Postal Service encourages companies that send large volumes of mail to use a bar code denoting the ZIP code (see Figure 7).

The encoding scheme for a five-digit ZIP code is shown in Figure 8. There are full-height frame bars on each side. The five encoded digits are followed by a check digit, which is computed as follows: Add up all digits, and choose the check digit to make the sum a multiple of 10. For example, the sum of the digits in the ZIP code 95014 is 19, so the check digit is 1 to make the sum equal to 20.

Each digit of the ZIP code, and the check digit, is encoded according to the table at right, where 0 denotes a half bar and 1 a full bar. Note that they represent all combinations of two full and three half bars. The digit can be computed easily from the bar code using the column weights 7, 4, 2, 1, 0. For example, 01100 is

$$0 \cdot 7 + 1 \cdot 4 + 1 \cdot 2 + 0 \cdot 1 + 0 \cdot 0 = 6$$

The only exception is 0, which would yield 11 according to the weight formula.

Write a program that asks the user for a ZIP code and prints the bar code. Use : for half bars, | for full bars. For example, 95014 becomes

||:|:::|:|:|||:::::||:|::|:::|||

(Alternatively, write a graphical application that draws real bars.)

	7	4	2	1	0
1	0	0	0	1	1
2	0	0	1	0	1
3	0	0	1	1	1
4	0	1	0	0	0
5	0	1	0	1	1
6	0	1	1	0	0
7	1	0	0	0	0
8	1	0	0	1	1
9	1	0	1	0	0
0	1	1	0	0	0

Your program should also be able to carry out the opposite conversion: Translate bars into their ZIP code, reporting any errors in the input format or a mismatch of the digits.

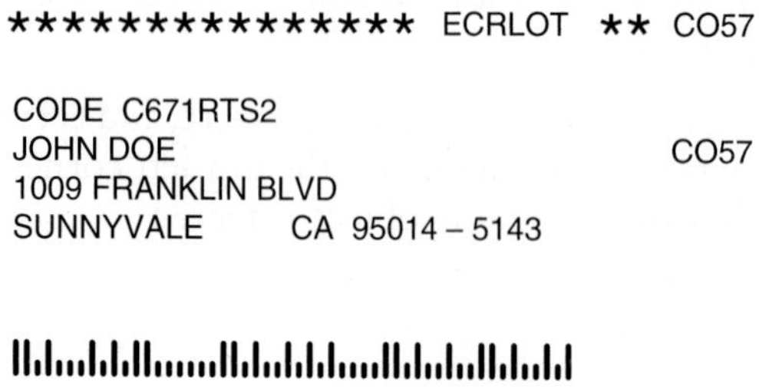

✦✦✦✦✦✦✦✦✦✦✦✦✦✦ ECRLOT ✦✦ CO57

CODE C671RTS2
JOHN DOE   CO57
1009 FRANKLIN BLVD
SUNNYVALE   CA 95014 – 5143

||||..|.|.||.....||.|..|.|.|....||.|..|..||.|..|.|

Figure 7 A Postal Bar Code

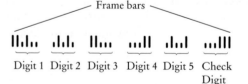

Digit 1 Digit 2 Digit 3 Digit 4 Digit 5 Check
                                                Digit

Figure 8 Encoding for Five-Digit Bar Codes

Answers to Self-Check Questions

1. Look for nouns in the problem description.
2. Yes (`ChessBoard`) and no (`MovePiece`).
3. Some of its features deal with payments, others with coin values.
4. None of the coin operations require the `CashRegister` class.
5. If a class doesn't depend on another, it is not affected by interface changes in the other class.
6. It is an accessor—calling `substring` doesn't modify the string on which the method is invoked. In fact, all methods of the `String` class are accessors.
7. No—`translate` is a mutator.
8. It is a side effect; this kind of side effect is common in object-oriented programming.
9. Yes—the method affects the state of the `Scanner` parameter.
10. Then you don't have to worry about checking for invalid values—it becomes the caller's responsibility.
11. No—you can take any action that is convenient for you.
12. `Math m = new Math(); y = m.sqrt(x);`
13. You cannot add a method to the `ArrayList` class—it is a class in the standard Java library that you cannot modify.
14. `System.in` and `System.out`.
15. Yes, it works. Static methods can access static variables of the same class. But it is a terrible idea. As your programming tasks get more complex, you will want to use objects and classes to organize your programs.
16. Yes. The scopes are disjoint.
17. It starts at the beginning of the class and ends at the end of the class.
18. (a) No; (b) Yes; (c) Yes; (d) No
19. No—you simply use fully qualified names for all other classes, such as `java.util.Random` and `java.awt.Rectangle`.
20. `/home/me/cs101/hw1/problem1` or, on Windows, `c:\Users\Me\cs101\hw1\problem1`.
21. Here is one possible answer.

```
public class EarthquakeTest
{
   @Test public void testLevel4()
   {
      Earthquake quake = new Earthquake(4);
      Assert.assertEquals("Felt by many people, no destruction",
            quake.getDescription());
   }
}
```

22. It is a tolerance threshold for comparing floating-point numbers. We want the equality test to pass if there is a small roundoff error.

Interfaces and Polymorphism

CHAPTER GOALS

- To be able to declare and use interface types
- To understand the concept of polymorphism
- To appreciate how interfaces can be used to decouple classes
- To learn how to implement helper classes as inner classes
- **G** To implement event listeners in graphical applications

In order to increase programming productivity, we want to be able to *reuse* software components in multiple projects. However, some adaptations are often required to make reuse possible. In this chapter, you will learn an important strategy for separating the reusable part of a computation from the parts that vary in each reuse scenario. The reusable part invokes methods of an *interface*. It is combined with a class that implements the interface methods. To produce a different application, you simply plug in another class that implements the same interface. The program's behavior varies according to the implementation that is plugged in—this phenomenon is called *polymorphism*.

CHAPTER CONTENTS

8.1 Using Interfaces for Algorithm Reuse

It is often possible to make a service available to a wider set of inputs by focusing on the essential operations that the service requires. *Interface types* are used to express these common operations.

Consider the DataSet class of Chapter 5. That class provides a service, namely computing the average and maximum of a set of input values. Unfortunately, the class is suitable only for computing the average of a set of *numbers*. If we wanted to process bank accounts to find the bank account with the highest balance, we could not use the class in its current form. We could modify the class, like this:

```
public class DataSet // Modified for BankAccount objects
{
    private double sum;
    private BankAccount maximum;
    private int count;
    . . .
    public void add(BankAccount x)
    {
        sum = sum + x.getBalance();
        if (count == 0 || maximum.getBalance() < x.getBalance())
            maximum = x;
        count++;
    }
```

```
    public BankAccount getMaximum()
    {
        return maximum;
    }
}
```

Or suppose we wanted to find the coin with the highest value among a set of coins. We would need to modify the DataSet class again.

```
public class DataSet // Modified for Coin objects
{
    private double sum;
    private Coin maximum;
    private int count;
    . . .
    public void add(Coin x)
    {
        sum = sum + x.getValue();
        if (count == 0 || maximum.getValue() < x.getValue())
            maximum = x;
        count++;
    }

    public Coin getMaximum()
    {
        return maximum;
    }
}
```

Clearly, the algorithm for the data analysis service is the same in all cases, but the details of measurement differ. We would like to provide a *single* class that provides this service to any objects that can be measured.

Suppose that the various classes agree on a method getMeasure that obtains the measure to be used in the data analysis. For bank accounts, getMeasure returns the balance. For coins, getMeasure returns the coin value, and so on. Then we can implement a DataSet class whose add method looks like this:

```
sum = sum + x.getMeasure();
if (count == 0 || maximum.getMeasure() < x.getMeasure())
    maximum = x;
count++;
```

What is the type of the variable x? Ideally, x should refer to any class that has a getMeasure method.

In Java, an **interface type** is used to specify required operations. We will declare an interface type that we call Measurable:

A Java interface type declares methods but does not provide their implementations.

```
public interface Measurable
{
    double getMeasure();
}
```

The interface declaration lists all methods that the interface type requires. The Measurable interface type requires a single method, but in general, an interface type can require multiple methods.

Note that the Measurable type is not a type in the standard library—it is a type that was created specifically for this book, in order to make the DataSet class more reusable.

Syntax 8.1 Declaring an Interface

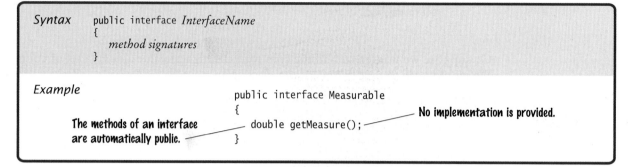

An interface type is similar to a class, but there are several important differences:

> Unlike a class, an interface type provides no implementation.

- All methods in an interface type are *abstract*; that is, they have a name, parameters, and a return type, but they don't have an implementation.
- All methods in an interface type are automatically public.
- An interface type does not have instance variables.

Now we can use the interface type Measurable to declare the variables x and maximum.

```
public class DataSet
{
    private double sum;
    private Measurable maximum;
    private int count;
    . . .
    public void add(Measurable x)
    {
        sum = sum + x.getMeasure();
        if (count == 0 || maximum.getMeasure() < x.getMeasure())
            maximum = x;
        count++;
    }

    public Measurable getMaximum()
    {
        return maximum;
    }
}
```

> Use the implements reserved word to indicate that a class implements an interface type.

This DataSet class is usable for analyzing objects of any class that implements the Measurable interface. A class **implements an interface** type if it declares the interface in an implements clause. It should then implement the method or methods that the interface requires.

```
public class BankAccount implements Measurable
{
    . . .
    public double getMeasure()
    {
        return balance;
    }
}
```

Figure 1
Attachments Conform to the
Mixer's Interface

Note that the class must declare the method as `public`, whereas the interface need not—all methods in an interface are public.

Similarly, it is an easy matter to modify the `Coin` class to implement the `Measurable` interface.

```
public class Coin implements Measurable
{
   public double getMeasure()
   {
      return value;
   }
   . . .
}
```

In summary, the `Measurable` interface expresses what all measurable objects have in common. This commonality makes the flexibility of the improved `DataSet` class possible. A data set can analyze objects of *any* class that implements the `Measurable` interface.

Use interface types to make code more reusable.

This is a typical usage for interface types. A service provider—in this case, the `DataSet`—specifies an interface for participating in the service. Any class that conforms to that interface can then be used with the service. This is similar to the way a mixer will provide rotation to any attachment that fits its interface (see Figure 1).

Syntax 8.2   Implementing an Interface

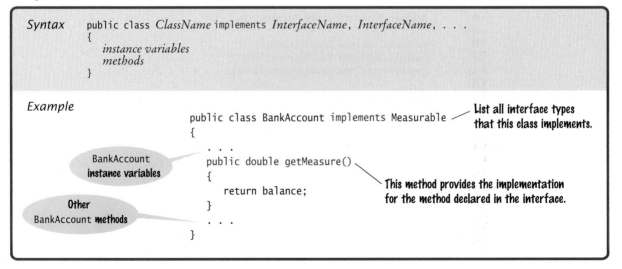

Syntax   public class *ClassName* implements *InterfaceName*, *InterfaceName*, . . .
            {
               instance variables
               methods
            }

Example

```
public class BankAccount implements Measurable
{
   . . .
   public double getMeasure()
   {
      return balance;
   }
   . . .
}
```

List all interface types that this class implements.

BankAccount instance variables

Other BankAccount methods

This method provides the implementation for the method declared in the interface.

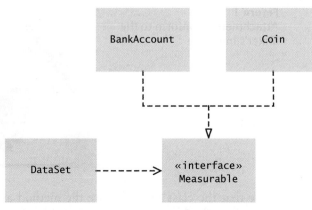

Figure 2 UML Diagram of the DataSet Class and the Classes that Implement the Measurable Interface

Figure 2 shows the relationships between the DataSet class, the Measurable interface, and the classes that implement the interface. Note that the DataSet class depends only on the Measurable interface. It is decoupled from the BankAccount and Coin classes.

In the UML notation, interfaces are tagged with an indicator «interface». A dotted arrow with a triangular tip denotes the "*is-a*" relationship between a class and an interface. You have to look carefully at the arrow tips—a dotted line with an open arrow tip (➤) denotes the "*uses*" relationship or dependency.

ch08/measure1/DataSetTester.java

```
1   /**
2       This program tests the DataSet class.
3   */
4   public class DataSetTester
5   {
6      public static void main(String[] args)
7      {
8         DataSet bankData = new DataSet();
9
10        bankData.add(new BankAccount(0));
11        bankData.add(new BankAccount(10000));
12        bankData.add(new BankAccount(2000));
13
14        System.out.println("Average balance: " + bankData.getAverage());
15        System.out.println("Expected: 4000");
16        Measurable max = bankData.getMaximum();
17        System.out.println("Highest balance: " + max.getMeasure());
18        System.out.println("Expected: 10000");
19
20        DataSet coinData = new DataSet();
21
22        coinData.add(new Coin(0.25, "quarter"));
23        coinData.add(new Coin(0.1, "dime"));
24        coinData.add(new Coin(0.05, "nickel"));
25
```

```
26        System.out.println("Average coin value: " + coinData.getAverage());
27        System.out.println("Expected: 0.133");
28        max = coinData.getMaximum();
29        System.out.println("Highest coin value: " + max.getMeasure());
30        System.out.println("Expected: 0.25");
31    }
32 }
```

Program Run

```
Average balance: 4000.0
Expected: 4000
Highest balance: 10000.0
Expected: 10000
Average coin value: 0.13333333333333333
Expected: 0.133
Highest coin value: 0.25
Expected: 0.25
```

SELF CHECK

1. Suppose you want to use the DataSet class to find the Country object with the largest population. What condition must the Country class fulfill?
2. Why can't the add method of the DataSet class have a parameter of type Object?

Common Error 8.1

Forgetting to Declare Implementing Methods as Public

The methods in an interface are not declared as public, because they are public by default. However, the methods in a class are not public by default—their default access level is "package" access, which we discuss in Chapter 7. It is a common error to forget the public reserved word when declaring a method from an interface:

```
public class BankAccount implements Measurable
{
    . . .
    double getMeasure() // Oops—should be public
    {
        return balance;
    }
}
```

Then the compiler complains that the method has a weaker access level, namely package access instead of public access. The remedy is to declare the method as public.

Special Topic 8.1

Constants in Interfaces

Interfaces cannot have instance variables, but it is legal to specify *constants*. For example, the SwingConstants interface declares various constants, such as SwingConstants.NORTH, SwingConstants.EAST, and so on.

When declaring a constant in an interface, you can (and should) omit the reserved words public static final, because all variables in an interface are automatically public static final.

For example,

```
public interface SwingConstants
{
    int NORTH = 1;
    int NORTHEAST = 2;
    int EAST = 3;
    . . .
}
```

8.2 Converting Between Class and Interface Types

Interfaces are used to express the commonality between classes. In this section, we discuss when it is legal to convert between class and interface types.

Have a close look at the call

```
bankData.add(new BankAccount(1000));
```

from the test program of the preceding section. Here we pass an object of type BankAccount to the add method of the DataSet class. However, that method has a parameter of type Measurable:

```
public void add(Measurable x)
```

It it legal to convert from the BankAccount type to the Measurable type. In general, you can convert from a class type to the type of any interface that the class implements. For example,

> You can convert from a class type to an interface type, provided the class implements the interface.

```
BankAccount account = new BankAccount(1000);
Measurable meas = account; // OK
```

Alternatively, a Measurable variable can refer to an object of the Coin class of the preceding section because that class also implements the Measurable interface.

```
Coin dime = new Coin(0.1, "dime");
Measurable meas = dime; // Also OK
```

However, the Rectangle class from the standard library doesn't implement the Measurable interface. Therefore, the following assignment is an error:

```
Measurable meas = new Rectangle(5, 10, 20, 30); // Error
```

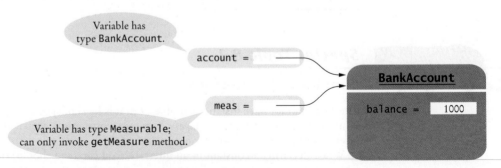

Figure 3 Variables of Class and Interface Types

Occasionally, it happens that you store an object in an interface reference and you need to convert its type back. This happens in the getMaximum method of the DataSet class. The DataSet stores the object with the largest measure, *as a* Measurable *reference*.

```
DataSet coinData = new DataSet();
coinData.add(new Coin(0.25, "quarter"));
coinData.add(new Coin(0.1, "dime"));
coinData.add(new Coin(0.05, "nickel"));
Measurable max = coinData.getMaximum();
```

Now what can you do with the max reference? *You* know it refers to a Coin object, but the compiler doesn't. For example, you cannot call the getName method:

```
String coinName = max.getName(); // Error
```

That call is an error, because the Measurable type has no getName method.

However, as long as you are absolutely sure that max refers to a Coin object, you can use the **cast** notation to convert its type back:

You need a cast to convert from an interface type to a class type.

```
Coin maxCoin = (Coin) max;
String name = maxCoin.getName();
```

If you are wrong, and the object doesn't actually refer to a coin, a run-time exception will occur.

This cast notation is the same notation that you saw in Chapter 3 to convert between number types. For example, if x is a floating-point number, then (int) x is the integer part of the number. The intent is similar—to convert from one type to another. However, there is one big difference between casting of number types and casting of class types. When casting number types, you may *lose information*, and you use the cast to tell the compiler that you agree to the potential information loss. When casting object types, on the other hand, you *take a risk* of causing an exception, and you tell the compiler that you agree to that risk.

S E L F   C H E C K

3. Can you use a cast (BankAccount) meas to convert a Measurable variable meas to a BankAccount reference?

4. If both BankAccount and Coin implement the Measurable interface, can a Coin reference be converted to a BankAccount reference?

Common Error 8.2

Trying to Instantiate an Interface

You can declare variables whose type is an interface, for example:

```
Measurable meas;
```

However, you can *never* construct an object of an interface type:

```
Measurable meas = new Measurable(); // Error
```

Interfaces aren't classes. There are no objects whose types are interfaces. If an interface variable refers to an object, then the object must belong to some class—a class that implements the interface:

```
Measurable meas = new BankAccount(); // OK
```

8.3 Polymorphism

When multiple classes implement the same interface, each class can implement the methods of the interface in different ways. How is the correct method executed when the interface method is invoked? We will answer that question in this section.

It is worth emphasizing once again that it is perfectly legal—and in fact very common—to have variables whose type is an interface, such as

```
Measurable meas;
```

Just remember that the object to which meas refers doesn't have type Measurable. In fact, *no object* has type Measurable. Instead, the type of the object is some class that implements the Measurable interface. This might be an object of the BankAccount or Coin class, or some other class with a getMeasure method.

ANIMATION
Polymorphism

```
meas = new BankAccount(1000); // OK
meas = new Coin(0.1, "dime"); // OK
```

What can you do with an interface variable, given that you don't know the class of the object that it references? You can invoke the methods of the interface:

```
double m = meas.getMeasure();
```

The DataSet class took advantage of this capability by computing the measure of the added object, without knowing exactly what kind of object was added.

Now let's think through the call to the getMeasure method more carefully. *Which* getMeasure method? The BankAccount and Coin classes provide two *different* implementations of that method. How did the correct method get called if the caller didn't even know the exact class to which meas belongs?

The Java virtual machine locates the correct method by first looking at the class of the actual object, and then calling the method with the given name in that class. That is, if meas refers to a BankAccount object, then the BankAccount.getMeasure method is called. If meas refers to a Coin object, then the Coin.getMeasure method is called. This means that one method call

> When the virtual machine calls an instance method, it locates the method of the implicit parameter's class. This is called dynamic method lookup.

```
double m = meas.getMeasure();
```

can invoke different methods depending on the momentary contents of meas. This mechanism for locating the appropriate method is called *dynamic method lookup*.

Dynamic method lookup enables a programming technique called **polymorphism**. The term "polymorphism" comes from the Greek words for "many shapes". The same computation works for objects of many shapes, and adapts itself to the nature of the objects.

> Polymorphism denotes the ability to treat objects with differences in behavior in a uniform way.

Figure 4 An Interface Reference Can Refer to an Object of Any Class that Implements the Interface

SELF CHECK

5. Why is it impossible to construct a Measurable object?

6. Why can you nevertheless declare a variable whose type is Measurable?

7. What does this code fragment print? Why is this an example of polymorphism?

```
DataSet data = new DataSet();
data.add(new BankAccount(1000));
data.add(new Coin(0.1, "dime"));
System.out.println(data.getAverage());
```

⊕ **Worked Example 8.1**

Investigating Number Sequences

Worked Example 8.1 uses a Sequence interface to investigate properties of arbitrary number sequences.

8.4 Using Interfaces for Callbacks

In this section, we introduce the notion of a callback, show how it leads to a more flexible DataSet class, and study how a callback can be implemented in Java by using interface types.

To understand why a further improvement to the DataSet class is desirable, consider these limitations of the Measurable interface:

- You can add the Measurable interface only to classes under your control. If you want to process a set of Rectangle objects, you cannot make the Rectangle class implement another interface—it is a system class, which you cannot change.

- You can measure an object in only one way. If you want to analyze a set of savings accounts both by bank balance and by interest rate, you are stuck.

Therefore, let's rethink the DataSet class. The data set needs to measure the objects that are added. When the objects are required to be of type Measurable, the responsibility of measuring lies with the added objects themselves, which is the cause of the limitations that we noted.

It would be better if we could give a method for measuring objects to a data set. When collecting rectangles, we might give it a method for computing the area of a rectangle. When collecting savings accounts, we might give it a method for getting the account's interest rate.

Such a method is called a **callback**. A callback is a mechanism for bundling up a block of code so that it can be invoked at a later time.

In some programming languages, it is possible to specify callbacks directly, as blocks of code or names of methods. But Java is an object-oriented language. Therefore, you turn callbacks into objects. This process starts by declaring an interface for the callback:

A callback is a mechanism for specifying code that is executed at a later time.

```
public interface Measurer
{
    double measure(Object anObject);
}
```

The measure method measures an object and returns its measurement. Here we use the fact that all objects can be converted to the type Object, the "lowest common denominator" of all classes in Java. We will discuss the Object type in greater detail in Chapter 9.

The code that makes the call to the callback receives an object of a class that implements this interface. In our case, the improved DataSet class is constructed with a Measurer object (that is, an object of some class that implements the Measurer interface). That object is saved in a measurer instance variable.

```java
public DataSet(Measurer aMeasurer)
{
    sum = 0;
    count = 0;
    maximum = null;
    measurer = aMeasurer;
}
```

The measurer variable is used to carry out the measurements, like this:

```java
public void add(Object x)
{
    sum = sum + measurer.measure(x);
    if (count == 0 || measurer.measure(maximum) < measurer.measure(x))
        maximum = x;
    count++;
}
```

The DataSet class simply makes a callback to the measure method whenever it needs to measure any object.

Finally, a specific callback is obtained by implementing the Measurer interface. For example, here is how you can measure rectangles by area. Provide a class

```java
public class RectangleMeasurer implements Measurer
{
    public double measure(Object anObject)
    {
        Rectangle aRectangle = (Rectangle) anObject;
        double area = aRectangle.getWidth() * aRectangle.getHeight();
        return area;
    }
}
```

Note that the measure method must accept a parameter of type Object, even though this particular measurer just wants to measure rectangles. The method parameter types must match those of the measure method in the Measurer interface. Therefore, the Object parameter is cast to the Rectangle type:

```java
Rectangle aRectangle = (Rectangle) anObject;
```

What can you do with a RectangleMeasurer? You need it for a DataSet that compares rectangles by area. Construct an object of the RectangleMeasurer class and pass it to the DataSet constructor.

```java
Measurer m = new RectangleMeasurer();
DataSet data = new DataSet(m);
```

Next, add rectangles to the data set.

```java
data.add(new Rectangle(5, 10, 20, 30));
data.add(new Rectangle(10, 20, 30, 40));
. . .
```

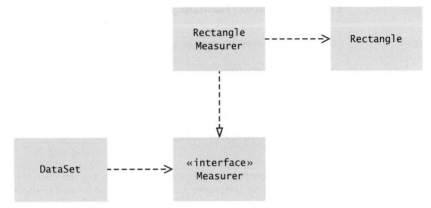

Figure 5 UML Diagram of the DataSet Class and the Measurer Interface

The data set will ask the RectangleMeasurer object to measure the rectangles. In other words, the data set uses the RectangleMeasurer object to carry out callbacks.

Figure 5 shows the UML diagram of the classes and interfaces of this solution. As in Figure 2, the DataSet class is decoupled from the Rectangle class whose objects it processes. However, unlike in Figure 2, the Rectangle class is no longer coupled with another class. Instead, to process rectangles, you provide a small "helper" class RectangleMeasurer. This helper class has only one purpose: to tell the DataSet how to measure its objects.

ch08/measure2/Measurer.java

```
1   /**
2       Describes any class whose objects can measure other objects.
3   */
4   public interface Measurer
5   {
6       /**
7           Computes the measure of an object.
8           @param anObject  the object to be measured
9           @return  the measure
10      */
11      double measure(Object anObject);
12  }
```

ch08/measure2/RectangleMeasurer.java

```
1   import java.awt.Rectangle;
2
3   /**
4       Objects of this class measure rectangles by area.
5   */
6   public class RectangleMeasurer implements Measurer
7   {
8       public double measure(Object anObject)
9       {
10          Rectangle aRectangle = (Rectangle) anObject;
11          double area = aRectangle.getWidth() * aRectangle.getHeight();
12          return area;
13      }
14  }
```

ch08/measure2/DataSet.java

```
1   /**
2       Computes the average of a set of data values.
3   */
4   public class DataSet
5   {
6       private double sum;
7       private Object maximum;
8       private int count;
9       private Measurer measurer;
10
11      /**
12          Constructs an empty data set with a given measurer.
13          @param aMeasurer the measurer that is used to measure data values
14      */
15      public DataSet(Measurer aMeasurer)
16      {
17          sum = 0;
18          count = 0;
19          maximum = null;
20          measurer = aMeasurer;
21      }
22
23      /**
24          Adds a data value to the data set.
25          @param x a data value
26      */
27      public void add(Object x)
28      {
29          sum = sum + measurer.measure(x);
30          if (count == 0 || measurer.measure(maximum) < measurer.measure(x))
31              maximum = x;
32          count++;
33      }
34
35      /**
36          Gets the average of the added data.
37          @return the average or 0 if no data has been added
38      */
39      public double getAverage()
40      {
41          if (count == 0) return 0;
42          else return sum / count;
43      }
44
45      /**
46          Gets the largest of the added data.
47          @return the maximum or 0 if no data has been added
48      */
49      public Object getMaximum()
50      {
51          return maximum;
52      }
53  }
```

ch08/measure2/DataSetTester2.java

```
1   import java.awt.Rectangle;
2
```

```
 3   /**
 4       This program demonstrates the use of a Measurer.
 5   */
 6   public class DataSetTester2
 7   {
 8      public static void main(String[] args)
 9      {
10         Measurer m = new RectangleMeasurer();
11
12         DataSet data = new DataSet(m);
13
14         data.add(new Rectangle(5, 10, 20, 30));
15         data.add(new Rectangle(10, 20, 30, 40));
16         data.add(new Rectangle(20, 30, 5, 15));
17
18         System.out.println("Average area: " + data.getAverage());
19         System.out.println("Expected: 625");
20
21         Rectangle max = (Rectangle) data.getMaximum();
22         System.out.println("Maximum area rectangle: " + max);
23         System.out.println("Expected: "
24             + "java.awt.Rectangle[x=10,y=20,width=30,height=40]");
25      }
26   }
```

Program Run

```
Average area: 625
Expected: 625
Maximum area rectangle: java.awt.Rectangle[x=10,y=20,width=30,height=40]
Expected: java.awt.Rectangle[x=10,y=20,width=30,height=40]
```

SELF CHECK

8. Suppose you want to use the DataSet class of Section 8.1 to find the longest String from a set of inputs. Why can't this work?

9. How can you use the DataSet class of this section to find the longest String from a set of inputs?

10. Why does the measure method of the Measurer interface have one more parameter than the getMeasure method of the Measurable interface?

8.5 Inner Classes

The RectangleMeasurer class is a very trivial class. We need this class only because the DataSet class needs an object of some class that implements the Measurer interface. When you have a class that serves a very limited purpose, such as this one, you can declare the class inside the method that needs it:

```
public class DataSetTester3
{
   public static void main(String[] args)
   {
      class RectangleMeasurer implements Measurer
      {
         . . .
```

```
            }

            Measurer m = new RectangleMeasurer();
            DataSet data = new DataSet(m);
            . . .
        }
    }
```

A class that is declared inside another class, such as the RectangleMeasurer class in this example, is called an **inner class**. This arrangement signals to the reader of your program that the RectangleMeasurer class is not interesting beyond the scope of this method. Since an inner class inside a method is not a publicly accessible feature, you don't need to document it as thoroughly.

You can also declare an inner class inside an enclosing class, but outside of its methods. Then the inner class is available to all methods of the enclosing class.

```
public class DataSetTester3
{
    class RectangleMeasurer implements Measurer
    {
        . . .
    }

    public static void main(String[] args)
    {

        Measurer m = new RectangleMeasurer();
        DataSet data = new DataSet(m);
        . . .
    }
}
```

When you compile the source files for a program that uses inner classes, have a look at the class files in your program directory—you will find that the inner classes are stored in files with curious names, such as DataSetTester3$1RectangleMeasurer.class. The exact names aren't important. The point is that the compiler turns an inner class into a regular class file.

ch08/measure3/DataSetTester3.java

```
 1  import java.awt.Rectangle;
 2
 3  /**
 4      This program demonstrates the use of an inner class.
 5  */
 6  public class DataSetTester3
 7  {
 8      public static void main(String[] args)
 9      {
10          class RectangleMeasurer implements Measurer
11          {
12              public double measure(Object anObject)
13              {
14                  Rectangle aRectangle = (Rectangle) anObject;
15                  double area
16                      = aRectangle.getWidth() * aRectangle.getHeight();
17                  return area;
18              }
19          }
20
```

```
21          Measurer m = new RectangleMeasurer();
22
23          DataSet data = new DataSet(m);
24
25          data.add(new Rectangle(5, 10, 20, 30));
26          data.add(new Rectangle(10, 20, 30, 40));
27          data.add(new Rectangle(20, 30, 5, 15));
28
29          System.out.println("Average area: " + data.getAverage());
30          System.out.println("Expected: 625");
31
32          Rectangle max = (Rectangle) data.getMaximum();
33          System.out.println("Maximum area rectangle: " + max);
34          System.out.println("Expected: "
35              + "java.awt.Rectangle[x=10,y=20,width=30,height=40]");
36      }
37  }
```

SELF CHECK

11. Why would you use an inner class instead of a regular class?
12. How many class files are produced when you compile the DataSetTester3 program?

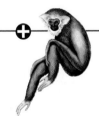

Special Topic 8.2

Anonymous Classes

Special Topic 8.2 shows how you can simplify the declaration of inner classes with the "anonymous class" syntax.

Random Fact 8.1

Operating Systems

Random Fact 8.1 discusses operating systems, the software that provides common services to all programs that execute on a computer.

8.6 Mock Objects

When you work on a program that consists of multiple classes, you often want to test some of the classes before the entire program has been completed. A very effective technique for this purpose is the use of **mock objects**. A mock object provides the same services as another object, but in a simplified manner.

Consider a grade book application that manages quiz scores for students. This calls for a class GradeBook with methods such as

A mock object provides the same services as another object, but in a simplified manner.

```
public void addScore(int studentId, double score)
public double getAverageScore(int studentId)
public void save(String filename)
```

Now consider the class GradingProgram that manipulates a GradeBook object. That class calls the methods of the GradeBook class. We would like to test the GradingProgram class without having a fully functional GradeBook class.

To make this work, declare an interface type with the same methods that the GradeBook class provides. A common convention is to use the letter I as the prefix for such an interface:

```
public interface IGradeBook
{
    void addScore(int studentId, double score);
    double getAverageScore(int studentId);
    void save(String filename);
    . . .
}
```

The GradingProgram class should *only* use this interface, never the GradeBook class. Of course, the GradeBook class implements this interface, but as already mentioned, it may not be ready for some time.

> Both the mock class and the actual class implement the same interface.

In the meantime, provide a mock implementation that makes some simplifying assumptions. Saving is not actually necessary for testing the user interface. We can temporarily restrict to the case of a single student.

```
public class MockGradeBook implements IGradeBook
{
    private ArrayList<Double> scores;

    public void addScore(int studentId, double score)
    {
        // Ignore studentId
        scores.add(score);
    }
    double getAverageScore(int studentId)
    {
        double total = 0;
        for (double x : scores) { total = total + x; }
        return total / scores.size();
    }
    void save(String filename)
    {
        // Do nothing
    }
    . . .
}
```

Now construct an instance of MockGradeBook and use it in the GradingProgram class. You can immediately test the GradingProgram class. When you are ready to test the actual class, simply use a GradeBook instance instead. Don't erase the mock class—it will still come in handy for regression testing.

SELF CHECK

13. Why is it necessary that the real class and the mock class implement the same interface type?

14. Why is the technique of mock objects particularly effective when the GradeBook and GradingProgram class are developed by two programmers?

8.7 Events, Event Sources, and Event Listeners

This and the following sections continue the book's graphics track. You will learn how interfaces are used when programming graphical user interfaces.

In the applications that you have written so far, user input was under control of the *program*. The program asked the user for input in a specific order. For example, a program might ask the user to supply first a name, then a dollar amount. But the programs that you use every day on your computer don't work like that. In a program with a graphical user interface, the *user* is in control. The user can use both the mouse and the keyboard and can manipulate many parts of the user interface in any desired order. For example, the user can enter information into text fields, pull down menus, click buttons, and drag scroll bars in any order. The program must react to the user commands, in whatever order they arrive. Having to deal with many possible inputs in random order is quite a bit harder than simply forcing the user to supply input in a fixed order.

> User-interface events include key presses, mouse moves, button clicks, menu selections, and so on.

In the following sections, you will learn how to write Java programs that can react to user-interface events, such as menu selections and mouse clicks. The Java windowing toolkit has a very sophisticated mechanism that allows a program to specify the events in which it is interested and which objects to notify when one of these events occurs.

Whenever the user of a graphical program types characters or uses the mouse anywhere inside one of the windows of the program, the Java windowing toolkit sends a notification to the program that an **event** has occurred. The windowing toolkit generates huge numbers of events. For example, whenever the mouse moves a tiny interval over a window, a "mouse move" event is generated. Whenever the mouse button is clicked, a "mouse pressed" and a "mouse released" event are generated. In addition, higher level events are generated when a user selects a menu item or button.

> An event listener belongs to a class that is provided by the application programmer. Its methods describe the actions to be taken when an event occurs.

Most programs don't want to be flooded by boring events. For example, consider what happens when selecting a menu item with the mouse. The mouse moves over the menu item, then the mouse button is pressed, and finally the mouse button is released. Rather than receiving lots of irrelevant mouse events, a program can indicate that it only cares about menu selections, not about the underlying mouse events. However, if the mouse input is used for drawing shapes on a virtual canvas, it is necessary to closely track mouse events.

Every program must indicate which events it needs to receive. It does that by installing **event listener** objects. An event listener object belongs to a class that you provide. The methods of your event listener classes contain the instructions that you want to have executed when the events occur.

> Event sources report on events. When an event occurs, the event source notifies all event listeners.

To install a listener, you need to know the **event source**. The event source is the user-interface component that generates a particular event. You add an event listener object to the appropriate event sources. Whenever the event occurs, the event source calls the appropriate methods of all attached event listeners.

This sounds somewhat abstract, so let's run through an extremely simple program that prints a message whenever a button is clicked (see Figure 6).

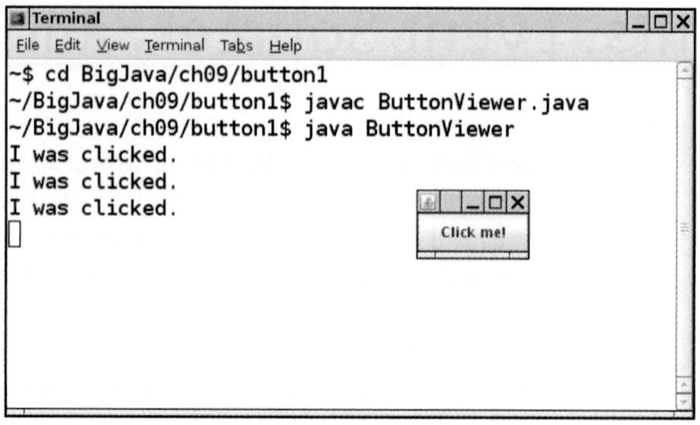

Figure 6 Implementing an Action Listener

Use `JButton` components for buttons. Attach an `ActionListener` to each button.

Button listeners must belong to a class that implements the `ActionListener` interface:

```
public interface ActionListener
{
   void actionPerformed(ActionEvent event);
}
```

This particular interface has a single method, `actionPerformed`. It is your job to supply a class whose `actionPerformed` method contains the instructions that you want executed whenever the button is clicked. Here is a very simple example of such a listener class:

ch08/button1/ClickListener.java

```
import java.awt.event.ActionEvent;
import java.awt.event.ActionListener;

/**
   An action listener that prints a message.
*/
public class ClickListener implements ActionListener
{
   public void actionPerformed(ActionEvent event)
   {
      System.out.println("I was clicked.");
   }
}
```

We ignore the `event` parameter of the `actionPerformed` method—it contains additional details about the event, such as the time at which it occurred.

Once the listener class has been declared, we need to construct an object of the class and add it to the button:

```
ActionListener listener = new ClickListener();
button.addActionListener(listener);
```

Whenever the button is clicked, it calls

```
listener.actionPerformed(event);
```

As a result, the message is printed.

You can think of the `actionPerformed` method as another example of a callback, similar to the `measure` method of the `Measurer` class. The windowing toolkit calls the actionPerformed method whenever the button is pressed, whereas the DataSet calls the measure method whenever it needs to measure an object.

The ButtonViewer class, whose source code is provided at the end of this section, constructs a frame with a button and adds a ClickListener to the button. You can test this program out by opening a console window, starting the ButtonViewer program from that console window, clicking the button, and watching the messages in the console window.

ch08/button1/ButtonViewer.java

```java
1   import java.awt.event.ActionListener;
2   import javax.swing.JButton;
3   import javax.swing.JFrame;
4
5   /**
6      This program demonstrates how to install an action listener.
7   */
8   public class ButtonViewer
9   {
10     private static final int FRAME_WIDTH = 100;
11     private static final int FRAME_HEIGHT = 60;
12
13     public static void main(String[] args)
14     {
15        JFrame frame = new JFrame();
16        JButton button = new JButton("Click me!");
17        frame.add(button);
18
19        ActionListener listener = new ClickListener();
20        button.addActionListener(listener);
21
22        frame.setSize(FRAME_WIDTH, FRAME_HEIGHT);
23        frame.setDefaultCloseOperation(JFrame.EXIT_ON_CLOSE);
24        frame.setVisible(true);
25     }
26  }
```

SELF CHECK

15. Which objects are the event source and the event listener in the ButtonViewer program?

16. Why is it legal to assign a ClickListener object to a variable of type ActionListener?

Common Error 8.3

Modifying Parameter Types in the Implementing Method

When you implement an interface, you must declare each method *exactly* as it is specified in the interface. Accidentally making small changes to the parameter types is a common error. Here is the classic example,

```java
class MyListener implements ActionListener
{
   public void actionPerformed()
   // Oops . . . forgot ActionEvent parameter
   {
      . . .
```

334 Chapter 8 Interfaces and Polymorphism

Graphics Track

```
      }
   }
```

As far as the compiler is concerned, this class fails to provide the method

```
public void actionPerformed(ActionEvent event)
```

You have to read the error message carefully and pay attention to the parameter and return types to find your error.

8.8 Using Inner Classes for Listeners

In the preceding section, you saw how the code that is executed when a button is clicked is placed into a listener class. It is common to implement listener classes as inner classes like this:

```
JButton button = new JButton(". . .");

// This inner class is declared in the same method as the button variable
class MyListener implements ActionListener
{
   . . .
};

ActionListener listener = new MyListener();
button.addActionListener(listener);
```

There are two reasons for this arrangement. The trivial listener class is located exactly where it is needed, without cluttering up the remainder of the project. Moreover, inner classes have a very attractive feature: Their methods can access variables that are declared in surrounding blocks. In this regard, method declarations of inner classes behave similarly to nested blocks.

Recall that a block is a statement group enclosed by braces. If a block is nested inside another, the inner block has access to all variables from the surrounding block:

```
{  // Surrounding block
   BankAccount account = new BankAccount();
   if (. . .)
   {  // Inner block

      . . .
      // OK to access variable from surrounding block
      account.deposit(interest);
   . . .
   }  // End of inner block
   . . .
}  // End of surrounding block
```

> Methods of an inner class can access local and instance variables from the surrounding scope.

The same nesting works for inner classes. Except for some technical restrictions, which we will examine later in this section, the methods of an inner class can access the variables from the enclosing scope. This feature is very useful when implementing event handlers. It allows the inner class to access variables without having to pass them as constructor or method parameters.

Let's look at an example. Suppose we want to add interest to a bank account whenever a button is clicked.

```
JButton button = new JButton("Add Interest");
final BankAccount account = new BankAccount(INITIAL_BALANCE);

// This inner class is declared in the same method as the account and button variables.
class AddInterestListener implements ActionListener
{
    public void actionPerformed(ActionEvent event)
    {
        // The listener method accesses the account variable
        // from the surrounding block
        double interest = account.getBalance() * INTEREST_RATE / 100;
        account.deposit(interest);
    }
};

ActionListener listener = new AddInterestListener();
button.addActionListener(listener);
```

Local variables that are accessed by an inner class method must be declared as final.

There is a technical wrinkle. An inner class can access surrounding *local* variables only if they are declared as final. That sounds like a restriction, but it is usually not an issue in practice. Keep in mind that an object variable is final when the variable always refers to the same object. The state of the object can change, but the variable can't refer to a different object. For example, in our program, we never intended to have the account variable refer to multiple bank accounts, so there was no harm in declaring it as final.

An inner class can also access *instance* variables of the surrounding class, again with a restriction. The instance variable must belong to the object that constructed the inner class object. If the inner class object was created inside a static method, it can only access static variables.

Here is the source code for the program.

ch08/button2/InvestmentViewer1.java

```
 1  import java.awt.event.ActionEvent;
 2  import java.awt.event.ActionListener;
 3  import javax.swing.JButton;
 4  import javax.swing.JFrame;
 5
 6  /**
 7      This program demonstrates how an action listener can access
 8      a variable from a surrounding block.
 9  */
10  public class InvestmentViewer1
11  {
12      private static final int FRAME_WIDTH = 120;
13      private static final int FRAME_HEIGHT = 60;
14
15      private static final double INTEREST_RATE = 10;
16      private static final double INITIAL_BALANCE = 1000;
17
18      public static void main(String[] args)
19      {
20          JFrame frame = new JFrame();
21
22          // The button to trigger the calculation
23          JButton button = new JButton("Add Interest");
24          frame.add(button);
25
```

```
26        // The application adds interest to this bank account
27        final BankAccount account = new BankAccount(INITIAL_BALANCE);
28
29        class AddInterestListener implements ActionListener
30        {
31           public void actionPerformed(ActionEvent event)
32           {
33              // The listener method accesses the account variable
34              // from the surrounding block
35              double interest = account.getBalance() * INTEREST_RATE / 100;
36              account.deposit(interest);
37              System.out.println("balance: " + account.getBalance());
38           }
39        }
40
41        ActionListener listener = new AddInterestListener();
42        button.addActionListener(listener);
43
44        frame.setSize(FRAME_WIDTH, FRAME_HEIGHT);
45        frame.setDefaultCloseOperation(JFrame.EXIT_ON_CLOSE);
46        frame.setVisible(true);
47     }
48  }
```

Program Run

```
balance: 1100.0
balance: 1210.0
balance: 1331.0
balance: 1464.1
```

SELF CHECK

17. Why would an inner class method want to access a variable from a surrounding scope?

18. If an inner class accesses a local variable from a surrounding scope, what special rule applies?

8.9 Building Applications with Buttons

In this section, you will learn how to structure a graphical application that contains buttons. We will put a button to work in our simple investment viewer program. Whenever the button is clicked, interest is added to a bank account, and the new balance is displayed (see Figure 7).

First, we construct an object of the JButton class. Pass the button label to the constructor:

```
JButton button = new JButton("Add Interest");
```

We also need a user-interface component that displays a message, namely the current bank balance. Such a component is called a *label*. You pass the initial message string to the JLabel constructor, like this:

```
JLabel label = new JLabel("balance: " + account.getBalance());
```

Use a JPanel container to group multiple user-interface components together.

The frame of our application contains both the button and the label. However, we cannot simply add both components directly to the frame—they would be placed

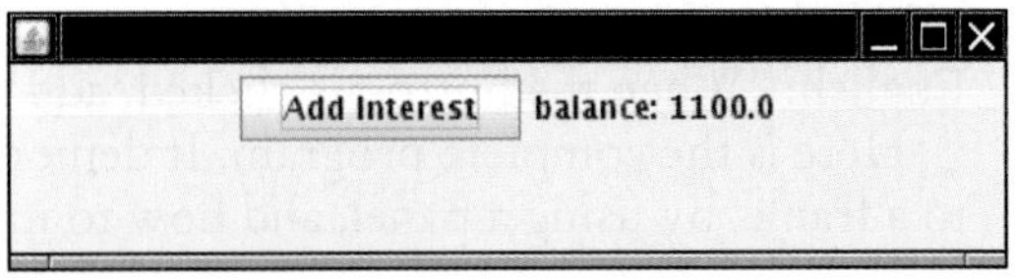

Figure 7 An Application with a Button

on top of each other. The solution is to put them into a **panel**, a container for other user-interface components, and then add the panel to the frame:

```
JPanel panel = new JPanel();
panel.add(button);
panel.add(label);
frame.add(panel);
```

You specify button click actions through classes that implement the ActionListener interface.

Now we are ready for the hard part—the event listener that handles button clicks. As in the preceding section, it is necessary to provide a class that implements the ActionListener interface, and to place the button action into the actionPerformed method. Our listener class adds interest and displays the new balance:

```
class AddInterestListener implements ActionListener
{
   public void actionPerformed(ActionEvent event)
   {
      double interest = account.getBalance() * INTEREST_RATE / 100;
      account.deposit(interest);
      label.setText("balance: " + account.getBalance());
   }
}
```

There is just a minor technicality. The actionPerformed method manipulates the account and label variables. These are local variables of the main method of the investment viewer program, not instance variables of the AddInterestListener class. We therefore need to declare the account and label variables as final so that the action-Performed method can access them.

Let's put the pieces together.

```
public static void main(String[] args)
{
   . . .
   JButton button = new JButton("Add Interest");
   final BankAccount account = new BankAccount(INITIAL_BALANCE);
   final JLabel label = new JLabel("balance: " + account.getBalance());

   class AddInterestListener implements ActionListener
   {
      public void actionPerformed(ActionEvent event)
      {
         double interest = account.getBalance() * INTEREST_RATE / 100;
         account.deposit(interest);
         label.setText("balance: " + account.getBalance());
      }
   }

   ActionListener listener = new AddInterestListener();
   button.addActionListener(listener);
   . . .
}
```

With a bit of practice, you will learn to glance at this code and translate it into plain English: "When the button is clicked, add interest and set the label text."

Here is the complete program. It demonstrates how to add multiple components to a frame, by using a panel, and how to implement listeners as inner classes.

ch08/button3/InvestmentViewer2.java

```java
1   import java.awt.event.ActionEvent;
2   import java.awt.event.ActionListener;
3   import javax.swing.JButton;
4   import javax.swing.JFrame;
5   import javax.swing.JLabel;
6   import javax.swing.JPanel;
7   import javax.swing.JTextField;
8
9   /**
10     This program displays the growth of an investment.
11  */
12  public class InvestmentViewer2
13  {
14     private static final int FRAME_WIDTH = 400;
15     private static final int FRAME_HEIGHT = 100;
16
17     private static final double INTEREST_RATE = 10;
18     private static final double INITIAL_BALANCE = 1000;
19
20     public static void main(String[] args)
21     {
22        JFrame frame = new JFrame();
23
24        // The button to trigger the calculation
25        JButton button = new JButton("Add Interest");
26
27        // The application adds interest to this bank account
28        final BankAccount account = new BankAccount(INITIAL_BALANCE);
29
30        // The label for displaying the results
31        final JLabel label = new JLabel("balance: " + account.getBalance());
32
33        // The panel that holds the user-interface components
34        JPanel panel = new JPanel();
35        panel.add(button);
36        panel.add(label);
37        frame.add(panel);
38
39        class AddInterestListener implements ActionListener
40        {
41           public void actionPerformed(ActionEvent event)
42           {
43              double interest = account.getBalance() * INTEREST_RATE / 100;
44              account.deposit(interest);
45              label.setText("balance: " + account.getBalance());
46           }
47        }
48
49        ActionListener listener = new AddInterestListener();
50        button.addActionListener(listener);
51
```

```
52        frame.setSize(FRAME_WIDTH, FRAME_HEIGHT);
53        frame.setDefaultCloseOperation(JFrame.EXIT_ON_CLOSE);
54        frame.setVisible(true);
55     }
56 }
```

S E L F   C H E C K

19. How do you place the "balance: . . ." message to the left of the "Add Interest" button?

20. Why was it not necessary to declare the button variable as final?

Common Error 8.4

Forgetting to Attach a Listener

If you run your program and find that your buttons seem to be dead, double-check that you attached the button listener. The same holds for other user-interface components. It is a surprisingly common error to program the listener class and the event handler action without actually attaching the listener to the event source.

Productivity Hint 8.1

Don't Use a Container as a Listener

In this book, we use inner classes for event listeners. That approach works for many different event types. Once you master the technique, you don't have to think about it anymore. Many development environments automatically generate code with inner classes, so it is a good idea to be familiar with them.

However, some programmers bypass the event listener classes and instead turn a container (such as a panel or frame) into a listener. Here is a typical example. The actionPerformed method is added to the viewer class. That is, the viewer implements the ActionListener interface.

```
public class InvestmentViewer
      implements ActionListener // This approach is not recommended
{
   public InvestmentViewer()
   {
      JButton button = new JButton("Add Interest");
      button.addActionListener(this);
      . . .
   }

   public void actionPerformed(ActionEvent event)
   {
      . . .
   }
   . . .
}
```

Now the actionPerformed method is a part of the InvestmentViewer class rather than part of a separate listener class. The listener is installed as this.

This technique has two major flaws. First, it separates the button declaration from the button action. Also, it doesn't *scale* well. If the viewer class contains two buttons that each generate action events, then the `actionPerformed` method must investigate the event source, which leads to code that is tedious and error-prone.

Common Error 8.5

By Default, Components Have Zero Width and Height

You must be careful when you add a painted component to a panel, such as a component displaying a car. You add the component in the same way as a button or label:

```
panel.add(button);
panel.add(label);
panel.add(carComponent);
```

However, the default size for a component is 0 by 0 pixels, and the car component will not be visible. The remedy is to call the `setPreferredSize` method, like this:

```
carComponent.setPreferredSize(new Dimension(CAR_COMPONENT_WIDTH, CAR_COMPONENT_HEIGHT));
```

Sections 8.10 and 8.11, available in WileyPLUS or on the companion web site, show how you can process timer and mouse events.

Common Error 8.6

Forgetting to Repaint

You have to be careful when your event handlers change the data in a painted component. When you make a change to the data, the component is not automatically painted with the new data. You must call the `repaint` method of the component, either in the event handler or in the component's mutator methods. Your component's `paintComponent` method will then be invoked with an appropriate `Graphics` object. Note that you should not call the `paintComponent` method directly.

This is a concern only for your own painted components. When you make a change to a standard Swing component such as a `JLabel`, the component is automatically repainted.

Special Topic 8.3

Event Adapters

Special Topic 8.3 shows how to use event adapter classes to simplify listener classes.

Random Fact 8.2

Programming Languages

Random Fact 8.2 traces the history of several common programming languages.

Summary of Learning Objectives

Use interfaces for making a service available to multiple classes.

- A Java interface type declares methods but does not provide their implementations.
- Unlike a class, an interface type provides no implementation.
- Use the implements reserved word to indicate that a class implements an interface type.
- Use interface types to make code more reusable.

Describe how to convert between class and interface types.

- You can convert from a class type to an interface type, provided the class implements the interface.
- You need a cast to convert from an interface type to a class type.

Describe dynamic method lookup and polymorphism.

- When the virtual machine calls an instance method, it locates the method of the implicit parameter's class. This is called dynamic method lookup.
- Polymorphism denotes the ability to treat objects with differences in behavior in a uniform way.

Describe how to use interface types for providing callbacks.

- A callback is a mechanism for specifying code that is executed at a later time.

Use inner classes to limit the scope of a utility class.

- An inner class is declared inside another class.
- Inner classes are commonly used for utility classes that should not be visible elsewhere in a program.

Use mock objects for supplying test versions of classes.

- A mock object provides the same services as another object, but in a simplified manner.
- Both the mock class and the actual class implement the same interface.

Recognize the use of events and event listeners in user-interface programming.

- User-interface events include key presses, mouse moves, button clicks, menu selections, and so on.
- An event listener belongs to a class that is provided by the application programmer. Its methods describe the actions to be taken when an event occurs.
- Event sources report on events. When an event occurs, the event source notifies all event listeners.
- Use JButton components for buttons. Attach an ActionListener to each button.

Implement event listeners as inner classes.

- Methods of an inner class can access local and instance variables from the surrounding scope.
- Local variables that are accessed by an inner class method must be declared as final.

Build graphical applications that use buttons.

- Use a JPanel container to group multiple user-interface components together.
- You specify button click actions through classes that implement the ActionListener interface.

Classes, Objects, and Methods Introduced in this Chapter

java.awt.Component	java.awt.event.MouseListener
addMouseListener	mouseClicked
repaint	mouseEntered
setPreferredSize	mouseExited
java.awt.Container	mousePressed
add	mouseReleased
java.awt.Dimension	javax.swing.AbstractButton
java.awt.Rectangle	addActionListener
setLocation	javax.swing.JButton
java.awt.event.ActionListener	javax.swing.JLabel
actionPerformed	javax.swing.JPanel
java.awt.event.MouseEvent	javax.swing.Timer
getX	start
getY	stop

Media Resources

www.wiley.com/
go/global/
horstmann

- **Worked Example** Investigating Number Sequences
- Lab Exercises
- ⊕ **Animation** Polymorphism
- ⊕ Practice Quiz
- ⊕ Code Completion Exercises

Review Exercises

★ **R8.1** Suppose C is a class that implements the interfaces I and J. Which of the following assignments require a cast?

```
C c = . . .;
I i = . . .;
J j = . . .;
```

a. c = i;

b. j = c;

c. i = j;

★ **R8.2** Suppose C is a class that implements the interfaces I and J, and suppose i is declared as

```
I i = new C();
```

Which of the following statements will throw an exception?

a. C c = (C) i;

b. J j = (J) i;

c. i = (I) null;

R8.3 Suppose the class Sandwich implements the Edible interface, and you are given the variable declarations

```
Sandwich sub = new Sandwich();
Rectangle cerealBox = new Rectangle(5, 10, 20, 30);
Edible e = null;
```

Which of the following assignment statements are legal?

a. e = sub;
b. sub = e;
c. sub = (Sandwich) e;
d. sub = (Sandwich) cerealBox;
e. e = cerealBox;
f. e = (Edible) cerealBox;
g. e = (Rectangle) cerealBox;
h. e = (Rectangle) null;

R8.4 How does a cast such as (BankAccount) x differ from a cast of number values such as (int) x?

R8.5 The classes Rectangle2D.Double, Ellipse2D.Double, and Line2D.Double implement the Shape interface. The Graphics2D class depends on the Shape interface but not on the rectangle, ellipse, and line classes. Draw a UML diagram denoting these facts.

R8.6 Suppose r contains a reference to a new Rectangle(5, 10, 20, 30). Which of the following assignments is legal? (Look inside the API documentation to check which interfaces the Rectangle class implements.)

a. Rectangle a = r;
b. Shape b = r;
c. String c = r;
d. ActionListener d = r;
e. Measurable e = r;
f. Serializable f = r;
g. Object g = r;

R8.7 Classes such as Rectangle2D.Double, Ellipse2D.Double and Line2D.Double implement the Shape interface. The Shape interface has a method

```
Rectangle getBounds()
```

that returns a rectangle completely enclosing the shape. Consider the method call:

```
Shape s = . . .;
Rectangle r = s.getBounds();
```

Explain why this is an example of polymorphism.

R8.8 In Java, a method call such as x.f() uses dynamic method lookup—the exact method to be called depends on the type of the object to which x refers. Give two kinds of method calls that do not use dynamic method lookup in Java.

R8.9 Suppose you need to process an array of employees to find the average and the highest salaries. Discuss what you need to do to use the implementation of the DataSet class in Section 8.1 (which processes Measurable objects). What do you need to do to use the second implementation (in Section 8.4)? Which is easier?

★★★ **R8.10** What happens if you add a String object to the implementation of the DataSet class in Section 8.1? What happens if you add a String object to a DataSet object of the implementation in Section 8.4 that uses a RectangleMeasurer class?

★ **R8.11** How would you reorganize the DataSetTester3 program if you needed to make RectangleMeasurer into a top-level class (that is, not an inner class)?

★★ **R8.12** What is a callback? Can you think of another use for a callback for the DataSet class? (*Hint:* Exercise P8.12.)

★★ **R8.13** Consider this top-level and inner class. Which variables can the f method access?

```java
public class T
{
   private int t;

   public void m(final int x, int y)
   {
      int a;
      final int b;

      class C implements I
      {
         public void f()
         {
            . . .
         }
      }

      final int c;
      . . .
   }
}
```

★★ **R8.14** What happens when an inner class tries to access a non-final local variable? Try it out and explain your findings.

★★★G **R8.15** How would you reorganize the InvestmentViewer1 program if you needed to make AddInterestListener into a top-level class (that is, not an inner class)?

★G **R8.16** What is an event object? An event source? An event listener?

★G **R8.17** From a programmer's perspective, what is the most important difference between the user interfaces of a console application and a graphical application?

★G **R8.18** What is the difference between an ActionEvent and a MouseEvent?

★★G **R8.19** Why does the ActionListener interface have only one method, whereas the MouseListener has five methods?

★★G **R8.20** Can a class be an event source for multiple event types? If so, give an example.

★★G **R8.21** What information does an action event object carry? What additional information does a mouse event object carry?

★★★G **R8.22** Why are we using inner classes for event listeners? If Java did not have inner classes, could we still implement event listeners? How?

★★G **R8.23** What is the difference between the paintComponent and repaint methods?

★G **R8.24** What is the difference between a frame and a panel?

Programming Exercises

★ **P8.1** Have the Die class of Chapter 5 implement the Measurable interface. Generate dice, cast them, and add them to the implementation of the DataSet class in Section 8.1. Display the average.

★ **P8.2** Implement a class Quiz that implements the Measurable interface. A quiz has a score and a letter grade (such as B+). Use the implementation of the DataSet class in Section 8.1 to process a collection of quizzes. Display the average score and the quiz with the highest score (both letter grade and score).

★ **P8.3** A person has a name and a height in centimeters. Use the implementation of the DataSet class in Section 8.4 to process a collection of Person objects. Display the average height and the name of the tallest person.

★ **P8.4** Modify the implementation of the DataSet class in Section 8.1 (the one processing Measurable objects) to also compute the minimum data element.

★ **P8.5** Modify the implementation of the DataSet class in Section 8.4 (the one using a Measurer object) to also compute the minimum data element.

★ **P8.6** Using a different Measurer object, process a set of Rectangle objects to find the rectangle with the largest perimeter.

★★★ **P8.7** Enhance the DataSet class so that it can either be used with a Measurer object or for processing Measurable objects. *Hint:* Supply a constructor with no parameters that implements a Measurer that processes Measurable objects.

★ **P8.8** Modify the display method of the LastDigitDistribution class of Worked Example 8.1 so that it produces a histogram, like this:

```
0: *************
1: ******************
2: *************
```

Scale the bars so that widest one has length 40.

★★ **P8.9** Write a class PrimeSequence that implements the Sequence interface of Worked Example 8.1, producing the sequence of prime numbers.

★ **P8.10** Add a method hasNext to the Sequence interface of Worked Example 8.1 that returns false if the sequence has no more values. Implement a class MySequence producing a sequence of real data of your choice, such as populations of cities or countries, temperatures, or stock prices. Obtain the data from the Internet and reformat the values so that they are placed into an array. Return one value at a time in the next method, until you reach the end of the data. Your SequenceTester class should display all data in the sequence and check whether the last digits are randomly distributed.

★ **P8.11** Provide a class FirstDigitDistribution that works just like the LastDigitDistribution class of Worked Example 8.1, except that it counts the distribution of the first digit of each value. (It is a well-known fact that the first digits of random values are *not* uniformly distributed. This fact has been used to detect accounting fraud, when sequences of transaction amounts had an unnatural distribution of their first digits.)

★★ **P8.12** Declare an interface `Filter` as follows:

```java
public interface Filter
{
    boolean accept(Object x);
}
```

Modify the implementation of the `DataSet` class in Section 8.4 to use both a `Measurer` and a `Filter` object. Only objects that the filter accepts should be processed. Demonstrate your modification by having a data set process a collection of bank accounts, filtering out all accounts with balances less than $1,000.

★★ **P8.13** The standard Java library provides a `Comparable` interface:

```java
public interface Comparable
{
    /**
        Compares this object with another.
        @param other the object to be compared
        @return a negative integer, zero, or a positive integer if this object
        is less than, equal to, or greater than, other
    */
    public int compareTo(Object other);
}
```

Modify the `DataSet` class of Section 8.1 to accept `Comparable` objects. With this interface, it is no longer meaningful to compute the average. The `DataSet` class should record the minimum and maximum data values. Test your modified `DataSet` class by adding a number of `String` objects. (The `String` class implements the `Comparable` interface.)

★ **P8.14** Modify the `Coin` class to have it implement the `Comparable` interface described in Exercise P8.13.

★★ **P8.15** The `System.out.printf` method has predefined formats for printing integers, floating-point numbers, and other data types. But it is also extensible. If you use the `s` format, you can print any class that implements the `Formattable` interface. That interface has a single method:

```java
void formatTo(Formatter formatter, int flags, int width, int precision)
```

In this exercise, you should make the `BankAccount` class implement the `Formattable` interface. Ignore the flags and precision and simply format the bank balance, using the given width. In order to achieve this task, you need to get an `Appendable` reference like this:

```java
Appendable a = formatter.out();
```

`Appendable` is another interface with a method

```java
void append(CharSequence sequence)
```

`CharSequence` is yet another interface that is implemented by (among others) the `String` class. Construct a string by first converting the bank balance into a string and then padding it with spaces so that it has the desired width. Pass that string to the append method.

★★★ **P8.16** Enhance the `formatTo` method of Exercise P8.15 by taking into account the precision.

★T **P8.17** Consider the task of writing a program that plays TicTacToe against a human opponent. A user interface `TicTacToeUI` reads the user's moves and displays the computer's moves and the board. A class `TicTacToeStrategy` determines the next move that the computer makes. A class `TicTacToeBoard` represents the current state of the board. Complete all classes except for the strategy class. Instead, use a mock class that simply picks the first available empty square.

★★T **P8.18** Consider the task of translating a plain text book from Project Gutenberg (http://gutenberg.org) to HTML. For example, here is the start of the first chapter of Tolstoy's Anna Karenina:

```
Chapter 1

Happy families are all alike; every unhappy family is unhappy in
its own way.

Everything was in confusion in the Oblonskys' house. The wife
had discovered that the husband was carrying on an intrigue with
a French girl, who had been a governess in their family, and she
had announced to her husband that she could not go on living in
the same house with him ...
```

The equivalent HTML is:

```
<h1>Chapter 1</h1>
<p>Happy families are all alike; every unhappy family is unhappy in
its own way.</p>
<p>Everything was in confusion in the Oblonskys&rsquo; house. The wife
had discovered that the husband was carrying on an intrigue with
a French girl, who had been a governess in their family, and she
had announced to her husband that she could not go on living in
the same house with him ...</p>
```

The HTML conversion can be carried out in two steps. First, the plain text is assembled into *segments*, blocks of text of the same kind (heading, paragraph, and so on). Then each segment is converted, by surrounding it with the HTML tags and converting special characters.

Plain Text	HTML
" "	“ (left) *or* ” (right)
' '	‘ (left) *or* ’ (right)
—	&emdash;
<	&lt;
>	&gt;
&	&amp;

Fetching the text from the Internet and breaking it into segments is a challenging task. Provide an interface and a mock implementation. Combine it with a class that uses the mock implementation to finish the formatting task.

★★★G **P8.19** Write a method `randomShape` that randomly generates objects implementing the `Shape` interface: some mixture of rectangles, ellipses, and lines, with random positions. Call it 10 times and draw all of them.

★G **P8.20** Enhance the ButtonViewer program so that it prints a message "I was clicked *n* times!" whenever the button is clicked. The value *n* should be incremented with each click.

★★G **P8.21** Enhance the ButtonViewer program so that it has two buttons, each of which prints a message "I was clicked *n* times!" whenever the button is clicked. Each button should have a separate click count.

★★G **P8.22** Enhance the ButtonViewer program so that it has two buttons labeled A and B, each of which prints a message "Button *x* was clicked!", where *x* is A or B.

★★G **P8.23** Implement a ButtonViewer program as in Exercise P8.22, using only a single listener class.

★G **P8.24** Enhance the ButtonViewer program so that it prints the time at which the button was clicked.

★★★G **P8.25** Implement the AddInterestListener in the InvestmentViewer1 program as a regular class (that is, not an inner class). *Hint:* Store a reference to the bank account. Add a constructor to the listener class that sets the reference.

★★★G **P8.26** Implement the AddInterestListener in the InvestmentViewer2 program as a regular class (that is, not an inner class). *Hint:* Store references to the bank account and the label in the listener. Add a constructor to the listener class that sets the references.

★★G **P8.27** Write a program that demonstrates the growth of a roach population. Start with two roaches and double the number of roaches with each button click.

★★G **P8.28** Write a program that uses a timer to print the current time once a second. *Hint:* The following code prints the current time:

```
Date now = new Date();
System.out.println(now);
```

The Date class is in the java.util package.

★★★G **P8.29** Change the RectangleComponent for the animation program in Section 8.10 so that the rectangle bounces off the edges of the component rather than simply moving outside. (See ch08/timer/ in your source code.)

★★G **P8.30** Write a program that animates a car so that it moves across a frame.

★★★G **P8.31** Write a program that animates two cars moving across a frame in opposite directions (but at different heights so that they don't collide.)

★G **P8.32** Change the RectangleComponent for the mouse listener program in Section 8.11 so that a new rectangle is added to the component whenever the mouse is clicked. *Hint:* Keep an ArrayList<Rectangle> and draw all rectangles in the paintComponent method. (See ch08/mouse/ in your source code.)

★G **P8.33** Write a program that prompts the user to enter the *x*- and *y*-positions of the center and a radius, using JOptionPane dialogs. When the user clicks a "Draw" button, draw a circle with that center and radius in a component.

★★G **P8.34** Write a program that allows the user to specify a circle by typing the radius in a JOptionPane and then clicking on the center. Note that you don't need a "Draw" button.

★★★G **P8.35** Write a program that allows the user to specify a circle with two mouse presses, the first one on the center and the second on a point on the periphery. *Hint:* In the mouse press handler, you must keep track of whether you already received the center point in a previous mouse press.

Programming Projects

Project 8.1   Design an interface `MoveableShape` that can be used as a generic mechanism for animating a shape. A moveable shape must have two methods: `move` and `draw`. Write a generic `AnimationPanel` that paints and moves any `MoveableShape` (or array list of `MoveableShape` objects if you covered Chapter 6). Supply moveable rectangle and car shapes.

Project 8.2   Your task is to design a general program for managing board games with two players. Your program should be flexible enough to handle games such as tic-tac-toe, chess, or the Game of Nim of Project 5.2.

Design an interface `Game` that describes a board game. Think about what your program needs to do. It asks the first player to input a move—a string in a game-specific format, such as `Be3` in chess. Your program knows nothing about specific games, so the `Game` interface must have a method such as

```
boolean isValidMove(String move)
```

Once the move is found to be valid, it needs to be executed—the interface needs another method `executeMove`. Next, your program needs to check whether the game is over. If not, the other player's move is processed. You should also provide some mechanism for displaying the current state of the board.

Design the `Game` interface and provide two implementations of your choice—such as `Nim` and `Chess` (or `TicTacToe` if you are less ambitious). Your `GamePlayer` class should manage a `Game` reference without knowing which game is played, and process the moves from both players. Supply two programs that differ only in the initialization of the `Game` reference.

Answers to Self-Check Questions

1. It must implement the `Measurable` interface, and its `getMeasure` method must return the population.
2. The `Object` class doesn't have a `getMeasure` method, and the `add` method invokes the `getMeasure` method.
3. Only if x actually refers to a `BankAccount` object.
4. No—a `Coin` reference can be converted to a `Measurable` reference, but if you attempt to cast that reference to a `BankAccount`, an exception occurs.
5. `Measurable` is an interface. Interfaces have no instance variables and no method implementations.
6. That variable never refers to a `Measurable` object. It refers to an object of some class—a class that implements the `Measurable` interface.
7. The code fragment prints 500.05. Each call to add results in a call x.getMeasure(). In the first call, x is a `BankAccount`. In the second call, x is a `Coin`. A different getMeasure

method is called in each case. The first call returns the account balance, the second one the coin value.

8. The `String` class doesn't implement the `Measurable` interface.

9. Implement a class `StringMeasurer` that implements the `Measurer` interface.

10. A measurer measures an object, whereas `getMeasure` measures "itself", that is, the implicit parameter.

11. Inner classes are convenient for insignificant classes. Also, their methods can access local and instance variables from the surrounding scope.

12. Four: one for the outer class, one for the inner class, and two for the `DataSet` and `Measurer` classes.

13. You want to implement the `GradingProgram` class in terms of that interface so that it doesn't have to change when you switch between the mock class and the actual class.

14. Because the developer of `GradingProgram` doesn't have to wait for the `GradeBook` class to be complete.

15. The `button` object is the event source. The `listener` object is the event listener.

16. The `ClickListener` class implements the `ActionListener` interface.

17. Direct access is simpler than the alternative—passing the variable as a parameter to a constructor or method.

18. The local variable must be declared as `final`.

19. First add `label` to the `panel`, then add `button`.

20. The `actionPerformed` method does not access that variable.

21. The timer needs to call some method whenever the time interval expires. It calls the `actionPerformed` method of the listener object.

Inheritance

CHAPTER GOALS

- To learn about inheritance
- To understand how to inherit and override superclass methods
- To be able to invoke superclass constructors
- To learn about protected and package access control
- To understand the common superclass Object and how to override its toString and equals methods
- **G** To use inheritance for customizing user interfaces

In this chapter, we discuss the important concept of inheritance. Specialized classes can be created that inherit behavior from more general classes. You will learn how to implement inheritance in Java, and how to make use of the Object class—the most general class in the inheritance hierarchy.

CHAPTER CONTENTS

9.1 Inheritance Hierarchies

In the real world, you often categorize concepts into *hierarchies*. Hierarchies are frequently represented as trees, with the most general concepts at the root of the hierarchy and more specialized ones towards the branches. Figure 1 shows a typical example.

In Java it is equally common to group classes in *inheritance hierarchies*. The classes representing the most general concepts are near the root, more specialized classes towards the branches. For example, Figure 2 shows part of the hierarchy of Swing user-interface components in Java.

> Sets of classes can form complex inheritance hierarchies.

We must introduce some more terminology for expressing the relationship between the classes in an inheritance hierarchy. The more general class is called the **superclass**. The more specialized class that inherits from the superclass is called the **subclass**. In our example, JPanel is a subclass of JComponent.

Figure 2 uses the UML notation for inheritance. In a class diagram, you denote inheritance by a solid arrow with a "hollow triangle" tip that points to the superclass.

When designing a hierarchy of classes, you ask yourself which features and behaviors are common to all the classes that you are designing. Those common properties are placed in a superclass. For example, all user-interface components have a width and height, and the getWidth and getHeight methods of the JComponent

352

Figure 1
A Hierarchy of Vehicle Types

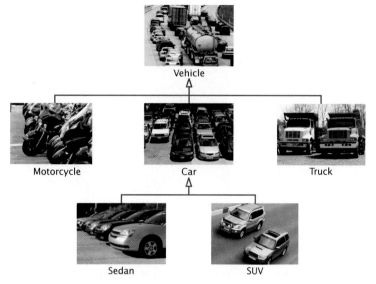

class return the component's dimensions. More specialized properties can be found in subclasses. For example, buttons can have text and icon labels. The class Abstract-Button, but not the superclass JComponent, has methods to set and get the button text and icon, and instance variables to store them. The individual button classes (such

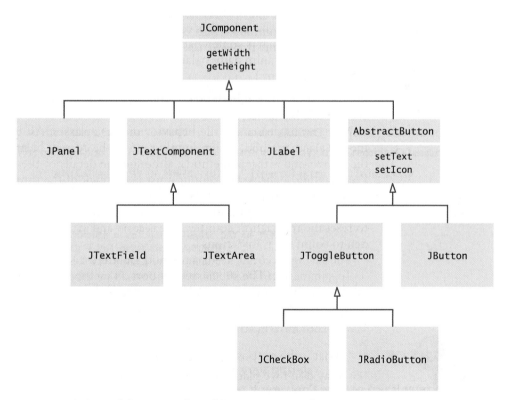

Figure 2   A Part of the Hierarchy of Swing User-Interface Components

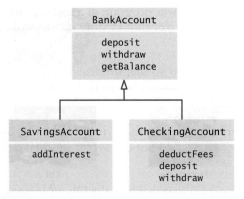

Figure 3 Inheritance Hierarchy for Bank Account Classes

as JButton, JRadioButton, and JCheckBox) inherit these properties. In fact, the Abstract-Button class was created to express the commonality among these buttons.

We will use a simpler example of a hierarchy in our study of inheritance concepts. Consider a bank that offers its customers the following account types:

1. The checking account has no interest, gives you a small number of free transactions per month, and charges a transaction fee for each additional transaction.

2. The savings account earns interest that compounds monthly. (In our implementation, the interest is compounded using the balance of the last day of the month, which is somewhat unrealistic. Typically, banks use either the average or the minimum daily balance. Exercise P9.1 asks you to implement this enhancement.)

Figure 3 shows the inheritance hierarchy. Exercise P9.2 asks you to add another class to this hierarchy.

Next, let us determine the behavior of these classes. All bank accounts support the getBalance method, which simply reports the current balance. They also support the deposit and withdraw methods, although the details of the implementation differ. For example, a checking account must keep track of the number of transactions to account for the transaction fees.

The checking account needs a method deductFees to deduct the monthly fees and to reset the transaction counter. The deposit and withdraw methods must be overridden to count the transactions.

The savings account needs a method addInterest to add interest.

To summarize: The subclasses support all methods from the superclass, but their implementations may be modified to match the specialized purposes of the subclasses. In addition, subclasses are free to introduce additional methods.

SELF CHECK

1. What is the purpose of the JTextComponent class in Figure 2?
2. Why don't we place the addInterest method in the BankAccount class?

9.2 Implementing Subclasses

Inheritance is a mechanism for extending existing classes by adding instance variables and methods.

In this section, we begin building the inheritance hierarchy of bank account classes. You will learn how to form a subclass from a given superclass. Let's start with the SavingsAccount class. Here is the syntax for the class declaration:

```
public class SavingsAccount extends BankAccount
{
    added instance variables
    new methods
}
```

A subclass inherits the methods of its superclass.

In the SavingsAccount class declaration you specify only new methods and instance variables. The SavingsAccount class *automatically inherits* the methods of the BankAccount class. For example, the deposit method automatically applies to savings accounts:

```
SavingsAccount collegeFund = new SavingsAccount(10);
    // Savings account with 10% interest
collegeFund.deposit(500);
    // OK to use BankAccount method with SavingsAccount object
```

Let's see how savings account objects are different from BankAccount objects. We will set an interest rate in the constructor, and we need a method to apply that interest periodically. That is, in addition to the three methods that can be applied to every account, there is an additional method addInterest. The new method and instance variable must be declared in the subclass.

```
public class SavingsAccount extends BankAccount
{
    private double interestRate;

    public SavingsAccount(double rate)
    {
        Constructor implementation
    }

    public void addInterest()
    {
        Method implementation
    }
}
```

The instance variables declared in the superclass are present in subclass objects.

A subclass object automatically has the instance variables declared in the superclass. For example, a SavingsAccount object has an instance variable balance that was declared in the BankAccount class.

Any new instance variables that you declare in the subclass are present only in subclass objects. For example, every SavingsAccount object has an instance variable interestRate. Figure 4 shows the layout of a SavingsAccount object.

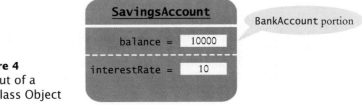

Figure 4
Layout of a
Subclass Object

Syntax 9.1 Inheritance

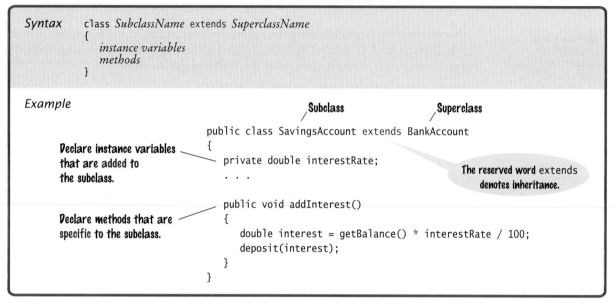

Syntax
```
class SubclassName extends SuperclassName
{
    instance variables
    methods
}
```

Example

Subclass   Superclass

```
public class SavingsAccount extends BankAccount
{
    private double interestRate;
    . . .

    public void addInterest()
    {
        double interest = getBalance() * interestRate / 100;
        deposit(interest);
    }
}
```

Declare instance variables that are added to the subclass.

The reserved word extends denotes inheritance.

Declare methods that are specific to the subclass.

Next, you need to implement the new addInterest method. The method computes the interest due on the current balance and deposits that interest to the account.

```
public class SavingsAccount extends BankAccount
{
    private double interestRate;

    public SavingsAccount(double rate)
    {
        interestRate = rate;
    }

    public void addInterest()
    {
        double interest = getBalance() * interestRate / 100;
        deposit(interest);
    }
}
```

A subclass has no access to private instance variables of its superclass.

The addInterest method calls the getBalance and deposit methods rather than directly updating the balance variable of the superclass. This is a consequence of **encapsulation**. The balance variable was declared as private in the BankAccount class. The addInterest method is declared in the SavingsAccount class. It does not have the right to access a private instance variable of another class.

Note how the addInterest method calls the inherited getBalance and deposit methods without specifying an implicit parameter. This means that the calls apply to the implicit parameter of the addInterest method.

In other words, the statements in the addInterest method are a shorthand for the following statements:

```
double interest = this.getBalance() * this.interestRate / 100;
this.deposit(interest);
```

This completes the implementation of the SavingsAccount class. You will find the complete source code below.

> Inheriting from a class differs from implementing an interface: The subclass inherits behavior from the superclass.

You may wonder at this point in what way inheritance differs from implementing an interface. An interface is not a class. It has *no behavior*. It merely tells you which methods you should implement. A superclass has specific behavior that the subclasses inherit.

ch09/accounts/SavingsAccount.java

```java
1  /**
2     An account that earns interest at a fixed rate.
3  */
4  public class SavingsAccount extends BankAccount
5  {
6     private double interestRate;
7
8     /**
9        Constructs a bank account with a given interest rate.
10       @param rate the interest rate
11    */
12    public SavingsAccount(double rate)
13    {
14       interestRate = rate;
15    }
16
17    /**
18       Adds the earned interest to the account balance.
19    */
20    public void addInterest()
21    {
22       double interest = getBalance() * interestRate / 100;
23       deposit(interest);
24    }
25 }
```

SELF CHECK

3. Which instance variables does an object of class SavingsAccount have?
4. Name four methods that you can apply to SavingsAccount objects.
5. If the class Manager extends the class Employee, which class is the superclass and which is the subclass?

Common Error 9.1

Confusing Super- and Subclasses

If you compare an object of type SavingsAccount with an object of type BankAccount, then you find that

- The reserved word extends suggests that the SavingsAccount object is an extended version of a BankAccount.
- The SavingsAccount object is larger; it has an added instance variable interestRate.
- The SavingsAccount object is more capable; it has an addInterest method.

It seems a superior object in every way. So why is SavingsAccount called the *subclass* and BankAccount the *superclass*?

The *super/sub* terminology comes from set theory. Look at the set of all bank accounts. Not all of them are SavingsAccount objects; some of them are other kinds of bank accounts. Therefore, the set of SavingsAccount objects is a *subset* of the set of all BankAccount objects, and the set of BankAccount objects is a *superset* of the set of SavingsAccount objects. The more specialized objects in the subset have a richer state and more capabilities.

Common Error 9.2

Shadowing Instance Variables

A subclass has no access to the private instance variables of the superclass. For example, the methods of the SavingsAccount class cannot access the balance instance variable:

```
public class SavingsAccount extends BankAccount
{
   public void addInterest()
   {
      double interest = getBalance() * interestRate / 100;
      balance = balance + interest; // Error
   }
   . . .
}
```

It is a common beginner's error to "solve" this problem by adding *another* instance variable with the same name.

```
public class SavingsAccount extends BankAccount
{
   private double balance; // Don't
   . . .
   public void addInterest()
   {
      double interest = getBalance() * interestRate / 100;
      balance = balance + interest; // Compiles but doesn't update the correct balance
   }
}
```

Sure, now the addInterest method compiles, but it doesn't update the correct balance! Such a SavingsAccount object has two instance variables, both named balance (see Figure 5). The getBalance method of the superclass retrieves one of them, and the addInterest method of the subclass updates the other.

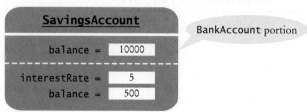

Figure 5 Shadowing Instance Variables

9.3 Overriding Methods

A subclass can inherit a superclass method or override it by providing another implementation.

A subclass method **overrides** a superclass method if it has the same name and parameter types as a superclass method. When such a method is applied to a subclass object, the overriding method, and not the original method, is executed.

We turn to the CheckingAccount class for an example of overriding methods. Recall that the BankAccount class has three methods:

```java
public class BankAccount
{
   . . .
   public void deposit(double amount) { . . . }
   public void withdraw(double amount) { . . . }
   public double getBalance() { . . . }
}
```

The CheckingAccount class declares these methods:

```java
public class CheckingAccount extends BankAccount
{
   . . .
   public void deposit(double amount) { . . . }
   public void withdraw(double amount) { . . . }
   public void deductFees() { . . . }
}
```

These methods override BankAccount **methods.**

The deposit and withdraw methods of the CheckingAccount class override the deposit and withdraw methods of the BankAccount class to handle transaction fees. However, the deductFees method does not override another method, and the getBalance method is not overridden.

Let's implement the deposit method of the CheckingAccount class. It increments the transaction count and deposits the money:

```java
public class CheckingAccount extends BankAccount
{
   . . .
   public void deposit(double amount)
   {
      transactionCount++;
      // Now add amount to balance
      . . .
   }
}
```

Now we have a problem. We can't simply add amount to balance:

```java
public class CheckingAccount extends BankAccount
{
   . . .
   public void deposit(double amount)
   {
      transactionCount++;
      // Now add amount to balance
      balance = balance + amount; // Error
   }
}
```

Although every CheckingAccount object has a balance instance variable, that instance variable is *private* to the superclass BankAccount. Subclass methods have no more

Syntax 9.2   Calling a Superclass Method

Syntax   super.*methodName*(*parameters*);

Example

```
public void deposit(double amount)
{
    transactionCount++;
    super.deposit(amount);
}
```

Calls the method of the superclass instead of the method of the current class.

If you omit super, this method calls itself. See page 362.

access rights to the private data of the superclass than any other methods. If you want to modify a private superclass instance variable, you must use a public method of the superclass.

How can we add the deposit amount to the balance, using the public interface of the BankAccount class? There is a perfectly good method for that purpose—namely, the deposit method of the BankAccount class. So we must invoke the deposit method on some object. On which object? The checking account into which the money is deposited—that is, the implicit parameter of the deposit method of the Checking-Account class. To invoke another method on the implicit parameter, you don't specify the parameter but simply write the method name, like this:

```
public class CheckingAccount extends BankAccount
{
    public void deposit(double amount)
    {
        transactionCount++;
        // Now add amount to balance
        deposit(amount); // Not complete
    }
    . . .
}
```

But this won't quite work. The compiler interprets

```
deposit(amount);
```

as

```
this.deposit(amount);
```

The this parameter is of type CheckingAccount. There is a method called deposit in the CheckingAccount class. Therefore, that method will be called—but that is just the method we are currently writing! The method will call itself over and over, and the program will die in an infinite recursion (discussed in Chapter 12).

Instead, we must be specific that we want to invoke only the *superclass's* deposit method. There is a special reserved word super for this purpose:

Use the super reserved word to call a method of the superclass.

```
public class CheckingAccount extends BankAccount
{
    public void deposit(double amount)
    {
```

```
        transactionCount++;
        // Now add amount to balance
        super.deposit(amount);
    }
    . . .
}
```

This version of the deposit method is correct. To deposit money into a checking account, update the transaction count and call the deposit method of the superclass.

The remaining methods of the CheckingAccount class also invoke a superclass method.

```java
public class CheckingAccount extends BankAccount
{
    private static final int FREE_TRANSACTIONS = 3;
    private static final double TRANSACTION_FEE = 2.0;

    private int transactionCount;
    . . .
    public void withdraw(double amount)
    {
        transactionCount++;
        // Now subtract amount from balance
        super.withdraw(amount);
    }

    public void deductFees()
    {
        if (transactionCount > FREE_TRANSACTIONS)
        {
            double fees = TRANSACTION_FEE * (transactionCount - FREE_TRANSACTIONS);
            super.withdraw(fees);
        }
        transactionCount = 0;
    }
    . . .
}
```

SELF CHECK

6. Categorize the methods of the SavingsAccount class as inherited, new, and overridden.

7. Why does the withdraw method of the CheckingAccount class call super.withdraw?

8. Why does the deductFees method set the transaction count to zero?

Common Error 9.3

Accidental Overloading

Recall from Section 2.1 that two methods can have the same name, provided they have *different* method parameters. For example, the PrintStream class has methods called println with headers

```java
void println(int x)
```

and

```java
void println(String x)
```

These are different methods, each with its own implementation. The Java compiler considers them to be completely unrelated. We say that the println name is **overloaded**. This is different from overriding, where a subclass method provides an implementation of a method with the *same* method parameters.

If you mean to override a method but supply a different parameter type, then you accidentally introduce an overloaded method. For example,

```
public class CheckingAccount extends BankAccount
{
   . . .
   public void deposit(int amount) // Error: should be double
   {
      . . .
   }
}
```

The compiler will not complain. It thinks that you want to provide a deposit method just for int parameters, while inheriting another deposit method for double parameters.

When overriding a method, be sure to check that the parameter types match exactly.

Common Error 9.4

Failing to Invoke the Superclass Method

A common error in extending the functionality of a superclass method is to forget the super qualifier. For example, to withdraw money from a checking account, update the transaction count and then withdraw the amount:

```
public void withdraw(double amount)
{
   transactionCount++;
   withdraw(amount);
   // Error—should be super.withdraw(amount)
}
```

Here withdraw(amount) refers to the withdraw method applied to the implicit parameter of the method. The implicit parameter is of type CheckingAccount, and the CheckingAccount class has a withdraw method, so that method is called. Of course, that calls the current method all over again, which will call itself yet again, over and over, until the program runs out of memory. Instead, you must precisely identify which withdraw method you want to call.

Another common error is to forget to call the superclass method altogether. Then the functionality of the superclass mysteriously vanishes.

9.4 Subclass Construction

In this section, we discuss the implementation of constructors in subclasses. As an example, let's declare a constructor to set the initial balance of a checking account.

We want to invoke the BankAccount constructor to set the balance to the initial balance. There is a special instruction to call the superclass constructor from a subclass constructor. You use the reserved word super, followed by the construction parameters in parentheses:

```
public class CheckingAccount extends BankAccount
{
    public CheckingAccount(double initialBalance)
    {
        // Construct superclass
        super(initialBalance);
        // Initialize transaction count
        transactionCount = 0;
    }
    . . .
}
```

> To call the superclass constructor, you use the super reserved word in the first statement of the subclass constructor.

When the reserved word super is immediately followed by a parenthesis, it indicates a call to the superclass constructor. When used in this way, the constructor call must be *the first statement of the subclass constructor*. If super is followed by a period and a method name, on the other hand, it indicates a call to a superclass method, as you saw in the preceding section. Such a call can be made anywhere in any subclass method.

The dual use of the super reserved word is analogous to the dual use of the this reserved word (see Special Topic 2.2).

If a subclass constructor does not call the superclass constructor, the superclass must have a constructor without parameters. That constructor is used to initialize the superclass data. However, if all constructors of the superclass require parameters, then the compiler reports an error.

For example, you can implement the CheckingAccount constructor without calling the superclass constructor. Then the BankAccount class is constructed with its BankAccount() constructor, which sets the balance to zero. Of course, then the CheckingAccount constructor must explicitly deposit the initial balance.

Most commonly, however, subclass constructors have some parameters that they pass on to the superclass and others that they use to initialize subclass instance variables.

Syntax 9.3   Calling a Superclass Constructor

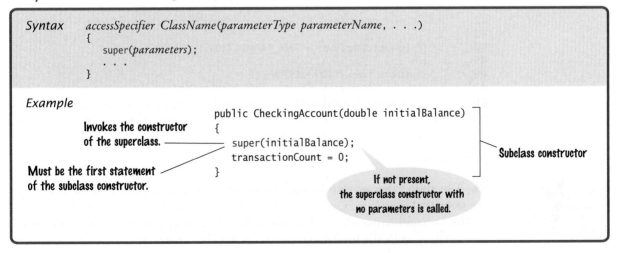

ch09/accounts/CheckingAccount.java

```java
1   /**
2       A checking account that charges transaction fees.
3   */
4   public class CheckingAccount extends BankAccount
5   {
6      private static final int FREE_TRANSACTIONS = 3;
7      private static final double TRANSACTION_FEE = 2.0;
8
9      private int transactionCount;
10
11     /**
12         Constructs a checking account with a given balance.
13         @param initialBalance the initial balance
14     */
15     public CheckingAccount(double initialBalance)
16     {
17        // Construct superclass
18        super(initialBalance);
19
20        // Initialize transaction count
21        transactionCount = 0;
22     }
23
24     public void deposit(double amount)
25     {
26        transactionCount++;
27        // Now add amount to balance
28        super.deposit(amount);
29     }
30
31     public void withdraw(double amount)
32     {
33        transactionCount++;
34        // Now subtract amount from balance
35        super.withdraw(amount);
36     }
37
38     /**
39         Deducts the accumulated fees and resets the
40         transaction count.
41     */
42     public void deductFees()
43     {
44        if (transactionCount > FREE_TRANSACTIONS)
45        {
46           double fees = TRANSACTION_FEE *
47                 (transactionCount - FREE_TRANSACTIONS);
48           super.withdraw(fees);
49        }
50        transactionCount = 0;
51     }
52  }
```

SELF CHECK

9. Why didn't the SavingsAccount constructor in Section 9.2 call its superclass constructor?

10. When you invoke a superclass method with the super reserved word, does the call have to be the first statement of the subclass method?

9.5 Converting Between Subclass and Superclass Types

It is often necessary to convert a subclass type to a superclass type. Occasionally, you need to carry out the conversion in the opposite direction. This section discusses the conversion rules.

The class `SavingsAccount` extends the class `BankAccount`. In other words, a `SavingsAccount` object is a special case of a `BankAccount` object. Therefore, a reference to a `SavingsAccount` object can be converted to a `BankAccount` reference.

```
SavingsAccount collegeFund = new SavingsAccount(10);
BankAccount anAccount = collegeFund; // OK
```

Furthermore, all references can be converted to the type `Object`.

```
Object anObject = collegeFund; // OK
```

Now the three object references stored in `collegeFund`, `anAccount`, and `anObject` all refer to the same object of type `SavingsAccount` (see Figure 6).

However, the variables `anAccount` and `anObject` know less than the full story about the object references that they store. Because `anAccount` is a variable of type `BankAccount`, you can invoke the `deposit` and `withdraw` methods. You cannot use the `addInterest` method, though—it is not a method of the `BankAccount` class:

```
anAccount.deposit(1000); // OK
anAccount.addInterest(); // No—not a method of the type of the anAccount variable
```

And, of course, the variable `anObject` knows even less. You can't even invoke the `deposit` method on it—`deposit` is not a method of the `Object` class.

Why would anyone *want* to know less about an object reference and use a variable whose type is a superclass? This can happen if you want to *reuse code* that knows about the superclass but not the subclass. Here is a typical example. Consider a `transfer` method that transfers money from one account to another:

```
public void transfer(double amount, BankAccount other)
{
   withdraw(amount);
   other.deposit(amount);
}
```

You can use this method to transfer money from one bank account to another:

```
BankAccount momsAccount = . . . ;
BankAccount harrysAccount = . . . ;
momsAccount.transfer(1000, harrysAccount);
```

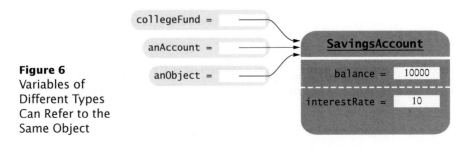

Figure 6
Variables of Different Types Can Refer to the Same Object

You can *also* use the method to transfer money into a CheckingAccount:

```
CheckingAccount harrysChecking = . . . ;
momsAccount.transfer(1000, harrysChecking);
    // OK to pass a CheckingAccount reference to a method expecting a BankAccount
```

The transfer method expects a reference to a BankAccount, and it gets a reference to a CheckingAccount object. That is perfectly legal. The transfer method doesn't actually know that, in this case, the parameter variable other contains a reference to a CheckingAccount object. All it cares about is that the object can carry out the deposit method. This is assured because the other variable has the type BankAccount.

Very occasionally, you need to carry out the opposite conversion, from a superclass type to a subclass type. For example, you may have a variable of type Object, and you know that it actually holds a BankAccount reference. In that case, you can use a cast to convert the type:

```
BankAccount anAccount = (BankAccount) anObject;
```

However, this cast is somewhat dangerous. If you are wrong, and anObject actually refers to an object of an unrelated type, then an exception is thrown.

To protect against bad casts, you can use the instanceof operator. It tests whether an object belongs to a particular type. For example,

> The instanceof operator tests whether an object belongs to a particular type.

```
anObject instanceof BankAccount
```

returns true if the type of anObject is convertible to BankAccount. This happens if anObject refers to an actual BankAccount or a subclass such as SavingsAccount. Using the instanceof operator, a safe cast can be programmed as follows:

```
if (anObject instanceof BankAccount)
{
    BankAccount anAccount = (BankAccount) anObject;
    . . .
}
```

Syntax 9.4 The instanceof Operator

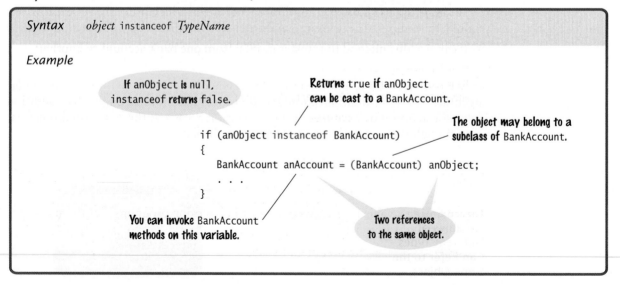

SELF CHECK

11. Why did the second parameter of the transfer method have to be of type BankAccount and not, for example, SavingsAccount?

12. Why can't we change the second parameter of the transfer method to the type Object?

9.6 Polymorphism and Inheritance

In Java, the type of a variable does not determine the type of the object to which it refers. For example, a variable of type BankAccount can hold a reference to a BankAccount object or to a subclass object such as SavingsAccount. You already encountered this phenomenon in Chapter 8 with variables whose type was an interface. A variable whose type is Measurable holds a reference to an object of a class that implements the Measurable interface, perhaps a Coin object or an object of an entirely different class.

What happens when you invoke a method on a variable of type BankAccount? For example,

```
BankAccount anAccount = new CheckingAccount();
anAccount.deposit(1000);
```

Which deposit method is called? The anAccount variable has type BankAccount, so it would appear as if BankAccount.deposit is called. On the other hand, the CheckingAccount class provides its own deposit method that updates the transaction count. The reference stored in the anAccount variable actually refers to an object of the subclass CheckingAccount, so it would be appropriate if the CheckingAccount.deposit method were called instead.

> When the virtual machine calls an instance method, it locates the method of the implicit parameter's class. This is called dynamic method lookup.

Java uses *dynamic method lookup* to determine which method to invoke. The method to be called is always determined by the type of the actual object, not the type of the variable. That is, if the actual object has the type CheckingAccount, then the CheckingAccount.deposit method is called. It does not matter that the object reference is stored in a variable of type BankAccount.

Have another look at the transfer method:

```
public void transfer(double amount, BankAccount other)
{
    withdraw(amount);
    other.deposit(amount);
}
```

Suppose you call

```
anAccount.transfer(1000, anotherAccount);
```

Two method calls are the result:

```
anAccount.withdraw(1000);
anotherAccount.deposit(1000);
```

Depending on the actual types of the objects whose references are stored in anAccount and anotherAccount, different versions of the withdraw and deposit methods are called. This is an example of *polymorphism*. As we discussed in Chapter 8, polymorphism is the ability to treat objects with differences in behavior in a uniform way.

If you look into the implementation of the transfer method, it may not be immediately obvious that the first method call

```
withdraw(amount);
```

depends on the type of an object. However, that call is a shortcut for

```
this.withdraw(amount);
```

The this parameter holds a reference to the implicit parameter, which can refer to a BankAccount or a subclass object.

The following program calls the polymorphic withdraw and deposit methods. You should manually calculate what the program should print for each account balance, and confirm that the correct methods have in fact been called.

ch09/accounts/AccountTester.java

```java
1  /**
2      This program tests the BankAccount class and
3      its subclasses.
4  */
5  public class AccountTester
6  {
7      public static void main(String[] args)
8      {
9          SavingsAccount momsSavings = new SavingsAccount(0.5);
10
11         CheckingAccount harrysChecking = new CheckingAccount(100);
12
13         momsSavings.deposit(10000);
14
15         momsSavings.transfer(2000, harrysChecking);
16         harrysChecking.withdraw(1500);
17         harrysChecking.withdraw(80);
18
19         momsSavings.transfer(1000, harrysChecking);
20         harrysChecking.withdraw(400);
21
22         // Simulate end of month
23         momsSavings.addInterest();
24         harrysChecking.deductFees();
25
26         System.out.println("Mom's savings balance: "
27             + momsSavings.getBalance());
28         System.out.println("Expected: 7035");
29
30         System.out.println("Harry's checking balance: "
31             + harrysChecking.getBalance());
32         System.out.println("Expected: 1116");
33     }
34 }
```

Program Run

```
Mom's savings balance: 7035.0
Expected: 7035
Harry's checking balance: 1116.0
Expected: 1116
```

SELF CHECK

13. If a is a variable of type BankAccount that holds a non-null reference, what do you know about the object to which a refers?

14. If a refers to a checking account, what is the effect of calling a.transfer(1000, a)?

Special Topic 9.1

Abstract Classes

Special Topic 9.1 introduces the concept of abstract classes and methods. An abstract method has no implementation. (All methods of an interface are automatically abstract.) You cannot construct objects of abstract classes, typically because the class has one or more abstract methods. However, abstract classes differ from interfaces in an important way—they can have instance variables, and they can have concrete methods and constructors.

Special Topic 9.2

Final Methods and Classes

Special Topic 9.2 discusses final methods and classes. A final method cannot be overridden in a subclass. A final class cannot be subclassed.

Common Error 9.5

Overriding Methods to Be Less Accessible

If a superclass declares a method to be publicly accessible, you cannot override it to be more private. For example,

```
public class BankAccount
{
   public void withdraw(double amount) { . . . }
   . . .
}

public class CheckingAccount extends BankAccount
{
   private void withdraw(double amount) { . . . }
      // Error—subclass method cannot be more private
   . . .
}
```

The compiler does not allow this, because the increased privacy would conflict with polymorphism. Suppose the AccountTester class has this method call:

```
BankAccount account = new CheckingAccount();
account.withdraw(100000); // Should CheckingAccount.withdraw be called?
```

Polymorphism dictates that CheckingAccount.withdraw should be called, but that is a private method that should not be accessible in AccountTester.

Therefore, the compiler reports an error if you override a public method and make it private or give it package access. The latter is a common oversight. If you forget the public modifier, your subclass method has package access, which is more restrictive. Simply restore the public modifier, and the error will go away.

Special Topic 9.3
Protected Access

Special Topic 9.3 covers the protected access specifier. A protected instance variable or method can be accessed by all subclasses and by all classes in the same package.

How To 9.1

Developing an Inheritance Hierarchy

When you work with a set of classes, some of which are more general and others more specialized, you want to organize them into an inheritance hierarchy. This enables you to process objects of different classes in a uniform way.

To illustrate the design process, consider an application that presents a quiz and grades the user's responses. A quiz consists of questions, and there are different kinds of questions:

- Fill-in-the-blank
- Choice (single or multiple)
- Numeric (where an approximate answer is ok; e.g., 1.33 when the actual answer is 4/3)
- Free response

Step 1 List the classes that are part of the hierarchy.

From the problem description, we can find these classes:

FillInQuestion (fill in the blank)
ChoiceQuestion (offers answer choices to the user)
MultiChoiceQuestion (offers answer choices to the user; user can pick more than one)
NumericQuestion
FreeResponseQuestion

In addition, we introduce a common superclass Question to model the commonality among these classes.

Step 2 Organize the classes into an inheritance hierarchy.

Draw a UML diagram that shows super- and subclasses. Here is the diagram for our example.

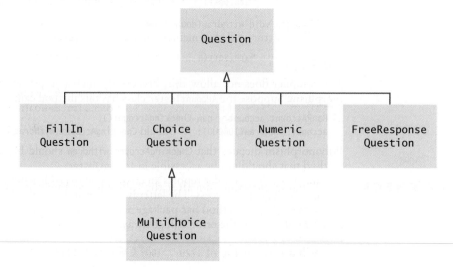

Step 3 Determine the common responsibilities.

In Step 2, you will have identified a class at the root of the hierarchy. That class needs to have sufficient responsibilities to carry out the tasks at hand.

To find out what those tasks are, write pseudocode for processing the objects.

> **For each question**
>   **Display the question to the user.**
>   **Get the user response.**
>   **Check whether the response is correct.**

From the pseudocode, we obtain the following list of common responsibilities that every question must carry out:

> **Display the question.**
> **Check the response.**

Step 4 Decide which methods are overridden in subclasses.

For each subclass and each of the common responsibilities, decide whether the inherited behavior is appropriate or whether it needs to be overridden. Be sure to declare any methods that are inherited or overridden in the root of the hierarchy.

We place the responsibilities common to all questions into the Question superclass.

```
public class Question
{
    . . .
    /**
        Displays this question.
    */
    public void display() { . . . }

    /**
        Checks a given response for correctness.
        @param response the response to check
        @return true if the response was correct, false otherwise
    */
    public boolean checkAnswer(String response) { . . . }
}
```

The ChoiceQuestion class will need to override the display method to display all the choices. The NumericQuestion class will need to override the checkAnswer method, converting the response to a number and checking that it is approximately the same as the expected answer.

From now on, we will only consider the ChoiceQuestion in detail. For the other question types, see the programming exercises at the end of this chapter.

Step 5 Define the public interface of each subclass.

Typically, subclasses have responsibilities other than those of the superclass. List those, as well as the methods that need to be overridden. You also need to specify how the objects of the subclasses should be constructed.

With the ChoiceQuestion, we need a way of adding choices, like this:

```
ChoiceQuestion question = new ChoiceQuestion(
    "In which country was the inventor of Java born?");
question.addChoice("Australia", false);
question.addChoice("Canada", true);
question.addChoice("Denmark", false);
question.addChoice("United States", false);
```

We then override the `display` method to display those choices in the form

```
1: Australia
2: Canada
3: Denmark
4: United States
```

Here are the methods that we just discovered for the `ChoiceQuestion` class:

```java
public class ChoiceQuestion extends Question
{
    . . .
    /**
        Adds an answer choice to this question.
        @param choice  the choice to add
        @param correct  true if this is the correct choice, false otherwise
    */
    public void addChoice(String choice, boolean correct)

    public void display() { . . . } // Overrides superclass method
}
```

Step 6   Identify instance variables.

List the instance variables for each class. If you find a instance variable that is common to all classes, be sure to place it in the base of the hierarchy.

All questions have a question text and an answer. We store those values in the `Question` superclass.

```java
public class Question
{
    private String text;
    private String answer;
    . . .
}
```

The `ChoiceQuestion` class needs to store the list of choices.

```java
public class ChoiceQuestion extends Question
{
    private ArrayList<String> choices;
    . . .
}
```

We need to spend some thought on how question objects are constructed. We can supply the question text in the constructor. However, the answer for a choice question is only known when the correct choice is added, so we need a setter method for it:

```java
public class Question
{
    . . .
    /**
        Constructs a question with a given text and an empty answer.
        @param questionText  the text of this question
    */
    public Question(String questionText) { . . . }

    /**
        Sets the answer for this question.
        @param correctResponse  the answer
    */
    public void setAnswer(String correctResponse) { . . . }
}
```

Step 7 Implement constructors and methods.

The methods of the Question class are very straightforward:

```java
public class Question
{
   . . .
   public Question(String questionText)
   {
      text = questionText;
      answer = "";
   }

   public void setAnswer(String correctResponse)
   {
      answer = correctResponse;
   }

   public boolean checkAnswer(String response)
   {
      return response.equals(answer);
   }

   public void display()
   {
      System.out.println(text);
   }
}
```

The ChoiceQuestion constructor must call the superclass constructor to set the question text:

```java
public ChoiceQuestion(String questionText)
{
   super(questionText);
   choices = new ArrayList<String>();
}
```

The addChoice method sets the answer when the correct choice is added.

```java
public void addChoice(String choice, boolean correct)
{
   choices.add(choice);
   if (correct)
   {
      // Convert choices.size() to string
      String choiceString = "" + choices.size();
      setAnswer(choiceString);
   }
}
```

Finally, the display method of the ChoiceQuestion class displays the question text, then the choices. Note the call to the superclass method.

```java
public void display()
{
   super.display();
   for (int i = 0; i < choices.size(); i++)
   {
      int choiceNumber = i + 1;
      System.out.println(choiceNumber + ": " + choices.get(i));
   }
}
```

Step 8   Construct objects of different subclasses and process them.

In our sample program, we construct two questions and present them to the user.

```java
public class QuestionDemo
{
    public static void main(String[] args)
    {
        Question[] quiz = new Question[2];

        quiz[0] = new Question("Who was the inventor of Java?");
        quiz[0].setAnswer("James Gosling");

        ChoiceQuestion question = new ChoiceQuestion(
            "In which country was the inventor of Java born?");
        question.addChoice("Australia", false);
        question.addChoice("Canada", true);
        question.addChoice("Denmark", false);
        question.addChoice("United States", false);
        quiz[1] = question;

        Scanner in = new Scanner(System.in);
        for (Question q : quiz)
        {
            q.display();
            System.out.print("Your answer: ");
            String response = in.nextLine();
            System.out.println(q.checkAnswer(response));
        }
    }
}
```

Program Run

```
Who was the inventor of Java?
Your answer: James Gosling
true
In which country was the inventor of Java born?
1: Australia
2: Canada
3: Denmark
4: United States
Your answer: 4
false
```

The complete program is contained in the ch09/questions directory of your source code.

 **Worked Example 9.1**

Implementing an Employee Hierarchy for Payroll Processing

This Worked Example shows how to implement payroll processing that works for different kinds of employees.

9.7 Object: The Cosmic Superclass

Every class extends the Object class either directly or indirectly.

In Java, every class that is declared without an explicit extends clause automatically extends the class Object. That is, the class Object is the direct or indirect superclass of *every* class in Java (see Figure 7).

Of course, the methods of the Object class are very general. Here are the most useful ones:

Method	Purpose
String toString()	Returns a string representation of the object
boolean equals(Object otherObject)	Tests whether the object equals another object
Object clone()	Makes a full copy of an object

It is a good idea for you to override these methods in your classes.

9.7.1 Overriding the toString Method

In your classes, provide toString methods that describe each object's state.

The toString method returns a string representation for each object. It is useful for debugging. For example,

```
Rectangle box = new Rectangle(5, 10, 20, 30);
String s = box.toString();
   // Sets s to "java.awt.Rectangle[x=5,y=10,width=20,height=30]"
```

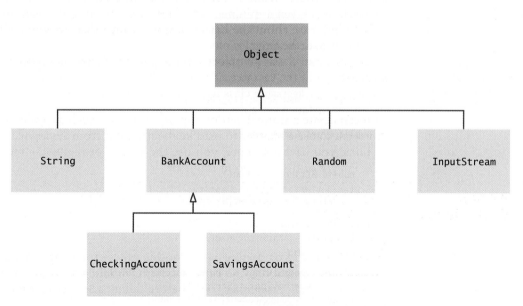

Figure 7 The Object Class Is the Superclass of Every Java Class

In fact, this toString method is called whenever you concatenate a string with an object. Consider the concatenation

```
"box=" + box;
```

On one side of the + concatenation operator is a string, but on the other side is an object reference. The Java compiler automatically invokes the toString method to turn the object into a string. Then both strings are concatenated. In this case, the result is the string

```
"box=java.awt.Rectangle[x=5,y=10,width=20,height=30]"
```

The compiler can invoke the toString method, because it knows that *every* object has a toString method: Every class extends the Object class, and that class provides a toString method.

As you know, numbers are also converted to strings when they are concatenated with other strings. For example,

```
int age = 18;
String s = "Harry's age is " + age;
   // Sets s to "Harry's age is 18"
```

In this case, the toString method is not involved. Numbers are not objects, and there is no toString method for them. There is only a small set of primitive types, however, and the compiler knows how to convert them to strings.

Let's try the toString method for the BankAccount class:

```
BankAccount momsSavings = new BankAccount(5000);
String s = momsSavings.toString();
   // Sets s to something like "BankAccount@d24606bf"
```

That's disappointing—all that's printed is the name of the class, followed by the **hash code**, a seemingly random code. The hash code can be used to tell objects apart—different objects are likely to have different hash codes. (See Chapter 15 for the details.)

We don't care about the hash code. We want to know what is inside the object. But, of course, the toString method of the Object class does not know what is inside the BankAccount class. Therefore, we have to override the method and supply our own version in the BankAccount class. We'll follow the same format that the toString method of the Rectangle class uses: first print the name of the class, and then the values of the instance variables inside brackets.

```
public class BankAccount
{
   . . .
   public String toString()
   {
      return "BankAccount[balance=" + balance + "]";
   }
}
```

This works better:

```
BankAccount momsSavings = new BankAccount(5000);
String s = momsSavings.toString();
   // Sets s to "BankAccount[balance=5000]"
```

9.7.2 Overriding the equals Method

The `equals` method is called whenever you want to compare whether two objects have the same contents:

```
if (coin1.equals(coin2)) . . .
    // Contents are the same—see Figure 8
```

This is different from the test with the `==` operator, which tests whether the two references are to the *same object:*

```
if (coin1 == coin2) . . .
    // Objects are the same—see Figure 9
```

Let us implement the `equals` method for the `Coin` class. You need to override the `equals` method of the `Object` class:

```
public class Coin
{
   . . .
   public boolean equals(Object otherObject)
   {
      . . .
   }
   . . .
}
```

Now you have a slight problem. The `Object` class knows nothing about coins, so it declares the `otherObject` parameter of the `equals` method to have the type `Object`. When overriding the method, you are not allowed to change the parameter type. To overcome this problem, cast the parameter to the class `Coin`:

```
Coin other = (Coin) otherObject;
```

Then you can compare the two coins.

```
public boolean equals(Object otherObject)
{
   Coin other = (Coin) otherObject;
   return name.equals(other.name) && value == other.value;
}
```

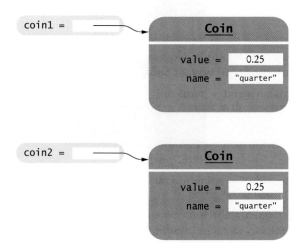

Figure 8 Two References to Equal Objects

Figure 9 Two References to the Same Object

Note that you must use `equals` to compare object references, but use `==` to compare numbers.

When you override the `equals` method, you should also override the `hashCode` method so that equal objects have the same hash code—see Chapter 15 for details.

9.7.3 The `clone` Method

You know that copying an object reference simply gives you two references to the same object:

```
BankAccount account = new BankAccount(1000);
BankAccount account2 = account;
account2.deposit(500);
    // Now both account and account2 refer to a bank account with a balance of 1500
```

The `clone` method makes a new object with the same state as an existing object.

What can you do if you actually want to make a copy of an object? That is the purpose of the `clone` method. The `clone` method must return a *new* object that has an identical state to the existing object (see Figure 10).

Implementing the `clone` method is quite a bit more difficult than implementing the `toString` or `equals` methods—see Special Topic 9.6 for details.

Let us suppose that someone has implemented the `clone` method for the BankAccount class. Here is how to call it:

```
BankAccount clonedAccount = (BankAccount) account.clone();
```

The return type of the `clone` method is the class `Object`. When you call the method, you must use a cast to convince the compiler that `account.clone()` really has the same type as `clonedAccount`.

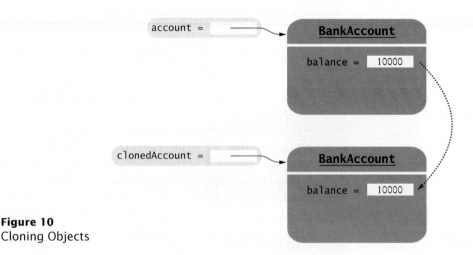

Figure 10
Cloning Objects

SELF CHECK

15. Should the call `x.equals(x)` always return `true`?

16. Can you implement `equals` in terms of `toString`? Should you?

Quality Tip 9.1

Supply toString in All Classes

If you have a class whose toString() method returns a string that describes the object state, then you can simply call System.out.println(x) whenever you need to inspect the current state of an object x. This works because the println method of the PrintStream class invokes x.toString() when it needs to print an object, which is extremely helpful if there is an error in your program and the objects don't behave the way you think they should. You can simply insert a few print statements and peek inside the object state during the program run. Some debuggers can even invoke the toString method on objects that you inspect.

Sure, it is a bit more trouble to write a toString method when you aren't sure your program ever needs one—after all, it might work correctly on the first try. Then again, many programs don't work on the first try. As soon as you find out that yours doesn't, consider adding those toString methods to help you debug the program.

Special Topic 9.4

Inheritance and the toString Method

Special Topic 9.4 gives a recipe for implementing the toString method so that it can be easily extended in subclasses.

Common Error 9.6

Declaring the equals Method with the Wrong Parameter Type

Consider the following, seemingly simpler, version of the equals method for the Coin class:

```
public boolean equals(Coin other) // Don't do this!
{
    return name.equals(other.name) && value == other.value;
}
```

Here, the parameter of the equals method has the type Coin, not Object.

Unfortunately, this method *does not override* the equals method in the Object class. Instead, the Coin class now has two different equals methods:

```
boolean equals(Coin other) // Declared in the Coin class
boolean equals(Object otherObject) // Inherited from the Object class
```

This is error-prone because the wrong equals method can be called. For example, consider these variable declarations:

```
Coin aCoin = new Coin(0.25, "quarter");
Object anObject = new Coin(0.25, "quarter");
```

The call aCoin.equals(anObject) calls the second equals method, which returns false.

The remedy is to ensure that you use the Object type for the explicit parameter of the equals method.

Special Topic 9.5

Inheritance and the equals Method

Special Topic 9.5 analyzes the subtle problems that arise when the equals method is overridden in a subclass, and it gives you a recipe for minimizing these problems.

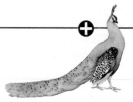

Quality Tip 9.2

Clone Mutable Instance Variables in Accessor Methods

Quality Tip 9.2 suggests that your accessor methods should not give out references to mutable instance variables, but that the instance variable values should first be cloned.

Special Topic 9.6

Implementing the clone Method

Special Topic 9.6 explains how to implement the clone method for your own classes.

Special Topic 9.7

Enumeration Types Revisited

Special Topic 9.7 revisits enumeration types and explains that they are all subclasses of the class Enum. The Enum class has suitable implementations of the toString, equals, and clone methods that are inherited by all enumeration types.

Random Fact 9.1

Scripting Languages

Random Fact 9.1 discusses scripting languages that are designed for rapid development, having a simple structure and fewer syntax rules, and often supporting a particular application (such as office software or a web browser).

9.8 Using Inheritance to Customize Frames

Provide a JFrame
subclass for a
complex frame.
As you add more user-interface components to a frame, the frame can get quite
complex. Your programs will become easier to understand when you use inheritance for complex frames.

To do so, design a subclass of JFrame. Store the components as instance variables.
Initialize them in the constructor of your subclass. If the initialization code gets
complex, simply add some helper methods.

Here, we carry out this process for the investment viewer program in Chapter 8.

```java
public class InvestmentFrame extends JFrame
{
    private JButton button;
    private JLabel label;
    private JPanel panel;
    private BankAccount account;

    public InvestmentFrame()
    {
        account = new BankAccount(INITIAL_BALANCE);

        // Use instance variables for components
        label = new JLabel("balance: " + account.getBalance());

        // Use helper methods
        createButton();
        createPanel();

        setSize(FRAME_WIDTH, FRAME_HEIGHT);
    }

    private void createButton()
    {
        button = new JButton("Add Interest");
        ActionListener listener = new AddInterestListener();
        button.addActionListener(listener);
    }

    private void createPanel()
    {
        panel = new JPanel();
        panel.add(button);
        panel.add(label);
        add(panel);
    }
    . . .
}
```

This approach differs from the programs in Chapter 8. In those programs, we simply configured the frame in the main method of a viewer class.

It is a bit more work to provide a separate class for the frame. However, the
frame class makes it easier to organize the code that constructs the user-interface
elements.

Of course, we still need a class with a main method:

```java
public class InvestmentViewer2
{
```

```
public static void main(String[] args)
{
    JFrame frame = new InvestmentFrame();
    frame.setDefaultCloseOperation(JFrame.EXIT_ON_CLOSE);
    frame.setVisible(true);
}
}
```

SELF CHECK

17. How many Java source files are required by the investment viewer application when we use inheritance to declare the frame class?

18. Why does the InvestmentFrame constructor call setSize(FRAME_WIDTH, FRAME_HEIGHT), whereas the main method of the investment viewer class in Chapter 8 called frame.setSize(FRAME_WIDTH, FRAME_HEIGHT)?

Special Topic 9.8

Adding the main Method to the Frame Class

Have another look at the InvestmentFrame and InvestmentViewer2 classes. Some programmers prefer to combine these two classes, by adding the main method to the frame class:

```
public class InvestmentFrame extends JFrame
{
    public static void main(String[] args)
    {
        JFrame frame = new InvestmentFrame();
        frame.setDefaultCloseOperation(JFrame.EXIT_ON_CLOSE);
        frame.setVisible(true);
    }

    public InvestmentFrame()
    {
        account = new BankAccount(INITIAL_BALANCE);

        // Use instance variables for components
        label = new JLabel("balance: " + account.getBalance());

        // Use helper methods
        createButton();
        createPanel();

        setSize(FRAME_WIDTH, FRAME_HEIGHT);
    }
    . . .
}
```

This is a convenient shortcut that you will find in many programs, but it does muddle the responsibilities between the frame class and the program. Therefore, we do not use this approach in this book.

Summary of Learning Objectives

Explain the notions of inheritance, superclasses, and subclasses.

- Sets of classes can form complex inheritance hierarchies.

Implement subclasses in Java.

- Inheritance is a mechanism for extending existing classes by adding instance variables and methods.
- A subclass inherits the methods of its superclass.
- The instance variables declared in the superclass are present in subclass objects.
- A subclass has no access to private instance variables of its superclass.
- The more general class is called a superclass. The more specialized class that inherits from the superclass is called the subclass.
- Inheriting from a class differs from implementing an interface: The subclass inherits behavior from the superclass.

Describe how a subclass can override methods from its superclass.

- A subclass can inherit a superclass method or override it by providing another implementation.
- Use the super reserved word to call a method of the superclass.

Describe how a subclass can construct its superclass.

- To call the superclass constructor, you use the super reserved word in the first statement of the subclass constructor.

Describe how to convert between class and superclass types.

- Subclass references can be converted to superclass references.
- The instanceof operator tests whether an object belongs to a particular type.

Describe dynamic method lookup and polymorphism.

- When the virtual machine calls an instance method, it locates the method of the implicit parameter's class. This is called dynamic method lookup.

Provide appropriate overrides of the methods of the Object superclass.

- Every class extends the Object class either directly or indirectly.
- In your classes, provide toString methods that describe each object's state.
- When implementing the equals method, test whether two objects have equal state.
- The clone method makes a new object with the same state as an existing object.

Use inheritance to customize frames.

- Provide a JFrame subclass for a complex frame.

Classes, Objects, and Methods Introduced in this Chapter

```
java.lang.Cloneable
java.lang.CloneNotSupportedException
```

```
java.lang.Object
  clone
  toString
```

Media Resources

www.wiley.com/
go/global/
horstmann

- **Worked Example** Implementing an Employee Hierarchy for Payroll Processing
- Lab Exercises
- ✚ **Animation** Inheritance
- ✚ Practice Quiz
- ✚ Code Completion Exercises

Review Exercises

★ **R9.1** What is the balance of b after the following operations?

```
SavingsAccount b = new SavingsAccount(10);
b.deposit(5000);
b.withdraw(b.getBalance() / 2);
b.addInterest();
```

★ **R9.2** Describe all constructors of the SavingsAccount class. List all methods that are inherited from the BankAccount class. List all methods that are added to the SavingsAccount class.

★★ **R9.3** Can you convert a superclass reference into a subclass reference? A subclass reference into a superclass reference? If so, give examples. If not, explain why not.

★★ **R9.4** Identify the superclass and the subclass in each of the following pairs of classes.

- **a.** Employee, Manager
- **b.** Polygon, Triangle
- **c.** GraduateStudent, Student
- **d.** Person, Student
- **e.** Employee, GraduateStudent
- **f.** BankAccount, CheckingAccount
- **g.** Vehicle, Car
- **h.** Vehicle, Minivan
- **i.** Car, Minivan
- **j.** Truck, Vehicle

★ **R9.5** Suppose the class Sub extends the class Sandwich. Which of the following assignments are legal?

```
Sandwich x = new Sandwich();
Sub y = new Sub();
```

- **a.** x = y;
- **b.** y = x;
- **c.** y = new Sandwich();
- **d.** x = new Sub();

★ **R9.6** Draw an inheritance diagram that shows the inheritance relationships between the classes:

- Person
- Employee
- Student
- Instructor
- Classroom
- Object

★★ **R9.7** In an object-oriented traffic simulation system, we have the following classes:

- Vehicle
- Car
- Truck
- Sedan
- Coupe
- PickupTruck
- SportUtilityVehicle
- Minivan
- Bicycle
- Motorcycle

Draw an inheritance diagram that shows the relationships between these classes.

★★ **R9.8** What inheritance relationships would you establish among the following classes?

- Student
- Professor
- TeachingAssistant
- Employee
- Secretary
- DepartmentChair
- Janitor
- SeminarSpeaker
- Person
- Course
- Seminar
- Lecture
- ComputerLab

★★★ **R9.9** Which of these conditions returns true? Check the Java documentation for the inheritance patterns.

```
Rectangle r = new Rectangle(5, 10, 20, 30);
```

a. if (r instanceof Rectangle) . . .

b. if (r instanceof Point) . . .

c. if (r instanceof Rectangle2D.Double) . . .

d. if (r instanceof RectangularShape) . . .

e. if (r instanceof Object) . . .

f. if (r instanceof Shape) . . .

★★ **R9.10** Explain the two meanings of the super reserved word. Explain the two meanings of the this reserved word. How are they related?

★★★ **R9.11** (Tricky.) Consider the two calls

```java
public class D extends B
{
    public void f()
    {
        this.g(); // 1
    }
    public void g()
    {
        super.g(); // 2
    }
    . . .
}
```

Which of them is an example of polymorphism?

★★★ **R9.12** Consider this program:

```java
public class AccountPrinter
{
```

```
        public static void main(String[] args)
        {
            SavingsAccount momsSavings
                = new SavingsAccount(0.5);

            CheckingAccount harrysChecking
                = new CheckingAccount(0);

            . . .
            endOfMonth(momsSavings);
            endOfMonth(harrysChecking);
            printBalance(momsSavings);
            printBalance(harrysChecking);
        }

        public static void endOfMonth(SavingsAccount savings)
        {
            savings.addInterest();
        }

        public static void endOfMonth(CheckingAccount checking)
        {
            checking.deductFees();
        }

        public static void printBalance(BankAccount account)
        {
            System.out.println("The balance is $"
                + account.getBalance());
        }
    }
```

Do the calls to the endOfMonth methods use dynamic method invocation? Inside the printBalance method, does the call to getBalance use dynamic method invocation?

★ **R9.13** Explain the terms *shallow copy* and *deep copy*.

★ **R9.14** What access attribute should instance variables have? What access attribute should static variables have? How about static final variables?

★ **R9.15** What access attribute should instance methods have? Does the same hold for static methods?

★★ **R9.16** The static variables System.in and System.out are public. Is it possible to overwrite them? If so, how?

★★ **R9.17** Why are public instance variables dangerous? Are public static variables more dangerous than public instance variables?

Programming Exercises

★ **P9.1** Enhance the addInterest method of the SavingsAccount class to compute the interest on the *minimum* balance since the last call to addInterest. *Hint:* You need to modify the withdraw method as well, and you need to add an instance variable to remember the minimum balance.

★★ **P9.2** Add a `TimeDepositAccount` class to the bank account hierarchy. The time deposit account is just like a savings account, but you promise to leave the money in the account for a particular number of months, and there is a $20 penalty for early withdrawal. Construct the account with the interest rate and the number of months to maturity. In the `addInterest` method, decrement the count of months. If the count is positive during a withdrawal, charge the withdrawal penalty.

★ **P9.3** Add a class `NumericQuestion` to the question hierarchy of How To 9.1. If the response and the expected answer differ by no more than 0.01, then accept it as correct.

★★ **P9.4** Add a class `FillInQuestion` to the question hierarchy of How To 9.1. An object of this class is constructed with a string that contains the answer, surrounded by _ _, for example, `"The inventor of Java was _James Gosling_"`. The question should be displayed as

```
The inventor of Java was _____
```

★ **P9.5** Modify the `checkAnswer` method of the `Question` class of How To 9.1 so that it does not take into account different spaces or upper/lowercase characters. For example, the response `" JAMES gosling"` should match an answer of `"James Gosling"`.

★ **P9.6** Add a class `MultiChoiceQuestion` to the question hierarchy of How To 9.1 that allows multiple correct choices. The respondent should provide all correct choices, separated by spaces. Provide instructions in the question text.

★ **P9.7** Add a class `AnyCorrectChoiceQuestion` to the question hierarchy of How To 9.1 that allows multiple correct choices. The respondent should provide any one of the correct choices. The answer string should contain all of the correct choices, separated by spaces.

★ **P9.8** Add a method `addText` to the `Question` class of How To 9.1 and provide a different implementation of `ChoiceQuestion` that calls `addText` rather than storing an array list of choices.

★★ **P9.9** Provide `toString` and `equals` methods for the `Question` and `ChoiceQuestion` classes of How To 9.1.

★ **P9.10** Implement a subclass `Square` that extends the `Rectangle` class. In the constructor, accept the *x*- and *y*-positions of the *center* and the side length of the square. Call the `setLocation` and `setSize` methods of the `Rectangle` class. Look up these methods in the documentation for the `Rectangle` class. Also supply a method `getArea` that computes and returns the area of the square. Write a sample program that asks for the center and side length, then prints out the square (using the `toString` method that you inherit from `Rectangle`) and the area of the square.

★ **P9.11** Implement a superclass `Person`. Make two classes, `Student` and `Instructor`, that inherit from `Person`. A person has a name and a year of birth. A student has a major, and an instructor has a salary. Write the class declarations, the constructors, and the methods `toString` for all classes. Supply a test program that tests these classes and methods.

★★ **P9.12** Make a class `Employee` with a name and salary. Make a class `Manager` inherit from `Employee`. Add an instance variable, named `department`, of type `String`. Supply a method `toString` that prints the manager's name, department, and salary. Make a class Executive inherit from Manager. Supply appropriate toString methods for all classes. Supply a test program that tests these classes and methods.

★★★ **P9.13** Reorganize the bank account classes as follows. In the BankAccount class, introduce an abstract method endOfMonth with no implementation. Rename the addInterest and deductFees methods into endOfMonth in the subclasses. Which classes are now abstract and which are concrete? Write a static method void test(BankAccount account) that makes five transactions and then calls endOfMonth. Test it with instances of all concrete account classes.

★★★G **P9.14** Implement an abstract class Vehicle and concrete subclasses Car and Truck. A vehicle has a position on the screen. Write methods draw that draw cars and trucks as follows:

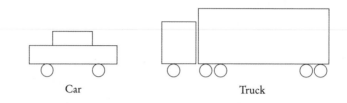

Then write a method randomVehicle that randomly generates Vehicle references, with an equal probability for constructing cars and trucks, with random positions. Call it 10 times and draw all of them.

★★G **P9.15** Write a program that prompts the user for an integer, using a JOptionPane, and then draws as many rectangles at random positions in a component as the user requested. Use inheritance for your frame class.

★★G **P9.16** Write a program that asks the user to enter an integer n into a JOptionPane, and then draws an *n*-by-*n* grid. Use inheritance for the frame class.

Programming Projects

Project 9.1 Your task is to program robots with varying behaviors. The robots try to escape a maze, such as the following:

```
*  *******
*     *  *
* ***** *
* * *   *
* * *** *
*   *   *
*** * * *
*     * *
******* *
```

A robot has a position and a method void move(Maze m) that modifies the position. Provide a common superclass Robot whose move method does nothing. Provide subclasses RandomRobot, RightHandRuleRobot, and MemoryRobot. Each of these robots has a different strategy for escaping. The RandomRobot simply makes random moves. The RightHandRuleRobot moves around the maze so that it's right hand always touches a wall. The MemoryRobot remembers all positions that it has previously occupied and never goes back to a position that it knows to be a dead end.

Project 9.2   Implement the toString, equals, and clone methods for all subclasses of the BankAccount class, as well as the Bank class of Chapter 6. Write unit tests that verify that your methods work correctly. Be sure to test a Bank that holds objects from a mixture of account classes.

Answers to Self-Check Questions

1. To express the common behavior of text fields and text components.
2. Not all bank accounts earn interest.
3. Two instance variables: balance and interestRate.
4. deposit, withdraw, getBalance, and addInterest.
5. Manager is the subclass; Employee is the superclass.
6. The SavingsAccount class inherits the deposit, withdraw, and getBalance methods. The addInterest method is new. No methods override superclass methods.
7. It needs to reduce the balance, and it cannot access the balance instance variable directly.
8. So that the count can reflect the number of transactions for the following month.
9. It was content to use the superclass constructor without parameters, which sets the balance to zero.
10. No—this is a requirement only for constructors. For example, the CheckingAccount.deposit method first increments the transaction count, then calls the superclass method.
11. We want to use the method for all kinds of bank accounts. Had we used a parameter of type SavingsAccount, we couldn't have called the method with a CheckingAccount object.
12. We cannot invoke the deposit method on a variable of type Object.
13. The object is an instance of BankAccount or one of its subclasses.
14. The balance of a is unchanged (you withdraw from and deposit to the same account), and the transaction count is incremented twice.
15. It certainly should—unless, of course, x is null.
16. If toString returns a string that describes all instance variables, you can simply call toString on the implicit and explicit parameters, and compare the results. However, comparing the instance variables is more efficient than converting them into strings.
17. Three: InvestmentFrameViewer, InvestmentFrame, and BankAccount.
18. The InvestmentFrame constructor adds the panel to *itself*.

Input/Output and Exception Handling

CHAPTER GOALS

- To be able to read and write text files
- To learn how to throw and catch exceptions
- To be able to design your own exception classes
- To understand the difference between checked and unchecked exceptions
- To know when and where to catch an exception

This chapter starts with a discussion of file input and output.

Whenever you read or write data, potential errors are to be expected. A file may have been corrupted or deleted, or it may be stored on another computer that was just disconnected from the network. In order to deal with these issues, you need to know about exception handling. This chapter tells you how your programs can report exceptional conditions, and how they can recover when an exceptional condition has occurred.

CHAPTER CONTENTS

10.1 Reading and Writing Text Files

We begin this chapter by discussing the common task of reading and writing files that contain text. Examples are files that are created with a simple text editor, such as Windows Notepad, as well as Java source code and HTML files.

The simplest mechanism for reading text is to use the Scanner class. You already know how to use a Scanner for reading console input. To read input from a disk file, the Scanner class relies on another class, File, which describes disk files and directories. (The File class has many methods that we do not discuss in this book; for example, methods that delete or rename a file.) First construct a File object with the name of the input file, then use the File to construct a Scanner object:

```
File inFile = new File("input.txt");
Scanner in = new Scanner(inFile);
```

When reading text files, use the Scanner class.

This Scanner object reads text from the file input.txt. You can use the Scanner methods (such as next, nextLine, nextInt, and nextDouble) to read data from the input file.

To write output to a file, you construct a PrintWriter object with the given file name, for example

```
PrintWriter out = new PrintWriter("output.txt");
```

When writing text files, use the PrintWriter class.

If the output file already exists, it is emptied before the new data are written into it. If the file doesn't exist, an empty file is created. You can also construct a PrintWriter object from a File object. This is useful if you use a file chooser (see Special Topic 10.1 on page 395).

The PrintWriter class is an enhancement of the PrintStream class that you already know—System.out is a PrintStream object. You can use the familiar print, println, and printf methods with any PrintWriter object:

```
out.print(29.95);
out.println(new Rectangle(5, 10, 15, 25));
out.printf("%10.2f", price);
```

When you are done writing to a file, be sure to *close* the PrintWriter:

```
out.close();
```

If your program exits without closing the PrintWriter, the disk file may not contain all of the output.

You must close a print stream when you are done writing output.

The following program puts these concepts to work. It reads all lines of an input file and sends them to the output file, preceded by *line numbers*. If the input file is

```
Mary had a little lamb
Whose fleece was white as snow.
And everywhere that Mary went,
The lamb was sure to go!
```

then the program produces the output file

```
/* 1 */ Mary had a little lamb
/* 2 */ Whose fleece was white as snow.
/* 3 */ And everywhere that Mary went,
/* 4 */ The lamb was sure to go!
```

The line numbers are enclosed in /* */ delimiters so that the program can be used for numbering Java source files.

There is one additional issue that we need to tackle. When the input or output file doesn't exist, a FileNotFoundException can occur. The compiler insists that we tell it what the program should do when that happens. (In this regard, the FileNotFoundException is different from the exceptions that you have already encountered. We will discuss this difference in detail in Section 10.4.) In our sample program, we take the easy way out and acknowledge that the main method should simply be terminated if the exception occurs. We label the main method like this:

```
public static void main(String[] args) throws FileNotFoundException
```

You will see in the following sections how to deal with exceptions in a more professional way.

ch10/lines/LineNumberer.java

```java
1  import java.io.File;
2  import java.io.FileNotFoundException;
3  import java.io.PrintWriter;
4  import java.util.Scanner;
5
6  /**
7     This program applies line numbers to a file.
8  */
9  public class LineNumberer
10 {
11    public static void main(String[] args) throws FileNotFoundException
12    {
13       // Prompt for the input and output file names
14
15       Scanner console = new Scanner(System.in);
16       System.out.print("Input file: ");
17       String inputFileName = console.next();
18       System.out.print("Output file: ");
19       String outputFileName = console.next();
20
```

```
21       // Construct the Scanner and PrintWriter objects for reading and writing
22
23       File inputFile = new File(inputFileName);
24       Scanner in = new Scanner(inputFile);
25       PrintWriter out = new PrintWriter(outputFileName);
26       int lineNumber = 1;
27
28       // Read the input and write the output
29
30       while (in.hasNextLine())
31       {
32          String line = in.nextLine();
33          out.println("/* " + lineNumber + " */ " + line);
34          lineNumber++;
35       }
36
37       in.close();
38       out.close();
39    }
40 }
```

SELF CHECK

1. What happens when you supply the same name for the input and output files to the `LineNumberer` program?
2. What happens when you supply the name of a nonexistent input file to the `LineNumberer` program?

Common Error 10.1

Backslashes in File Names

When you specify a file name as a string literal, and the name contains backslash characters (as in a Windows file name), you must supply each backslash twice:

```
inFile = new File("c:\\homework\\input.dat");
```

Recall that a single backslash inside quoted strings is an **escape character** that is combined with another character to form a special meaning, such as \n for a newline character. The \\ combination denotes a single backslash.

When a user supplies a file name to a program, however, the user should not type the backslash twice.

Common Error 10.2

Constructing a Scanner with a String

When you construct a `PrintWriter` with a string, it writes to a file:

```
PrintWriter out = new PrintWriter("output.txt");
```

However, this does *not* work for a `Scanner`. The statement

```
Scanner in = new Scanner("input.txt"); // ERROR?
```

does *not* open a file. Instead, it simply reads through the string: `in.nextLine()` returns the string "input.txt". This feature can be useful—see Section 10.2.3 for an example.

You must simply remember to use `File` objects in the `Scanner` constructor:

```
Scanner in = new Scanner(new File("input.txt")); // OK
```

Special Topic 10.1

File Dialog Boxes

Special Topic 10.1 shows you how you can present a file chooser dialog box to users of your programs.

Special Topic 10.2

Reading Web Pages

You can read the contents of a web page with this sequence of commands:

```
String address = "http://java.sun.com/index.html";
URL locator = new URL(address);
Scanner in = new Scanner(locator.openStream());
```

Now simply read the contents of the web page with the `Scanner` in the usual way. The `URL` constructor and the `openStream` method can throw an `IOException`. You need to tag the `main` method with `throws IOException`. (See Section 10.3 for more information on the `throws` clause.)

Special Topic 10.3

Command Line Arguments

Special Topic 10.3 shows you how you can process *command line arguments*, strings that are supplied after the name of a program that is launched from a command shell. The command line arguments are passed to the `args` parameter of the `main` method.

10.2 Reading Text Input

In the following sections, you will learn how to process complex text input that you often encounter in real life situations.

10.2.1 Reading Words

In the preceding example program, we read input a line at a time. Sometimes, it is useful to read words rather than lines. For example, consider the loop

```
while (in.hasNext())
{
   String input = in.next();
   System.out.println(input);
```

```
    }
```

With our sample input, this loop would print a word on every line:

```
Mary
had
a
little
lamb
```

In Java, a *word* is not the same as in English. It is any sequence of characters that is not white space. White space includes spaces, tab characters, and the newline characters that separate lines. For example, the following are considered words:

```
snow.
1729
C++
```

(Note the period after snow—it is considered a part of the word because it is not white space.)

Here is precisely what happens when the next method is executed. Input characters that are *white space* are *consumed*—that is, removed from the input. However, they do not become part of the word. The first character that is not white space becomes the first character of the word. More characters are added until either another white space character occurs, or the end of the input has been reached.

Sometimes, you want to read just the words and discard anything that isn't a letter. You achieve this task by calling the useDelimiter method on your Scanner object:

```
Scanner in = new Scanner(. . .);
in.useDelimiter("[^A-Za-z]+");
```

Here, we set the character pattern that separates words to "any sequence of characters other than letters". (The notation used for describing the character pattern is called a *regular expression*. See Productivity Hint 10.1 on page 399 if you are interested in more details.) With this setting, punctuation and numbers are stripped off from the words returned by the next method.

10.2.2 Processing Lines

When each line of a file is a data record, it is often best to read entire lines with the nextLine method:

```
String line = in.nextLine();
```

The nextLine method consumes the next input line (including the newline character) and returns the line without the newline character. You can then take the line apart for further processing.

Here is a typical example of processing lines in a file. A file with population data from the CIA Fact Book site (http://www.cia.gov/library/publications/the-world-factbook/) contains lines such as the following:

```
China   1330044605
India   1147995898
United States 303824646
. . .
```

Because some country names have more than one word, it would be tedious to read this file using the next method. For example, after reading United, how would your program know that it still needs to read another word before reading the population count?

Instead, read each input line into a string. Then use the `isDigit` and `isWhitespace` methods to find out where the name ends and the number starts.

Locate the first digit:

```
int i = 0;
while (!Character.isDigit(line.charAt(i))) { i++; }
```

Then extract the country name and population:

```
String countryName = line.substring(0, i);
String population = line.substring(i);
```

However, the country name contains one or more spaces at the end. Use the `trim` method to remove them:

```
countryName = countryName.trim();
```

The `trim` method returns the string with all white space at the beginning and end removed.

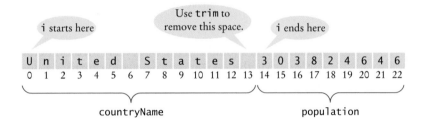

There is another problem. The population is stored in a string, not a number. Use the `Integer.parseInt` method to convert it:

```
int populationValue = Integer.parseInt(population);
```

You need to be careful when calling the `Integer.parseInt` method. Its parameter value must be a string containing the digits of an integer or a `NumberFormatException` occurs. The parameter value may not contain any additional characters. Not even spaces are allowed! In our situation, we happen to know that there won't be any spaces at the beginning of the string, but there might be some at the end. Therefore, we use the `trim` method:

```
int populationValue = Integer.parseInt(population.trim());
```

Here you saw how to break a string into parts by looking at individual characters. Another approach is occasionally easier. Construct a new `Scanner` object to read the characters from a string:

```
Scanner lineScanner = new Scanner(line);
```

Then you can use `lineScanner` like any other `Scanner` object, reading words and numbers:

```
String countryName = lineScanner.next();
while (!lineScanner.hasNextInt())
{
    countryName = countryName + " " + lineScanner.next();
}
int populationValue = lineScanner.nextInt();
```

10.2.3 Reading Numbers

The nextInt and nextDouble methods consume white space and the next number.

You have used the nextInt and nextDouble methods of the Scanner class many times, but here we will have a look at their behavior in detail. Suppose you call

```
double value = in.nextDouble();
```

The nextDouble method recognizes floating-point numbers such as 3.14159, -21, or 1E12 (a billion in scientific notation). However, if there is *no number* in the input, then a NoSuchElementException occurs.

Consider an input containing the characters

```
2 1 s t   c e n t u r y
```

White space is consumed and the word 21st is read. However, this word is not a properly formatted number. In this situation, an "input mismatch exception" occurs.

To avoid exceptions, use the hasNextDouble method to screen the input. For example,

```
if (in.hasNextDouble())
{
    double value = in.nextDouble();
    . . .
}
```

Similarly, you should call the hasNextInt method before calling nextInt.

Note that the nextInt and nextDouble methods *do not* consume the white space that follows a number. This can be a problem if you alternate between calling nextInt/nextDouble and nextLine. Suppose a file contains student IDs and names in this format:

```
1729
Harry Morgan
1730
Diana Lin
. . .
```

Now suppose you read the file with these instructions:

```
while (in.hasNextInt())
{
    int studentID = in.nextInt();
    String name = in.nextLine();
    Process the student ID and name
}
```

Initially, the input contains

```
1 7 2 9 \n H a r r y
```

After the first call to nextInt, the input contains

```
\n H a r r y
```

The call to nextLine reads an empty string! The remedy is to add a call to nextLine after reading the ID:

```
int studentID = in.nextInt();
in.nextLine(); // Consume the newline
String name = in.nextLine();
```

10.2.4 Reading Characters

To read one character at a time, set the delimiter pattern to the empty string.

Sometimes, you want to read a file one character at a time. You achieve this task by calling the useDelimiter method on your Scanner object with an empty string:

```
Scanner in = new Scanner(. . .);
in.useDelimiter("");
```

Now each call to next returns a string consisting of a single character. Here is how you can process the characters:

```
while (in.hasNext())
{
   char ch = in.next().charAt(0);
   Process ch
}
```

SELF CHECK

3. Suppose the input contains the characters 6,995.0. What is the value of number and input after these statements?

```
int number = in.nextInt();
String input = in.next();
```

4. Suppose the input contains the characters 6,995.00 12. What is the value of price and quantity after these statements?

```
double price = in.nextDouble();
int quantity = in.nextInt();
```

5. Your input file contains a sequence of numbers, but sometimes a value is not available and marked as N/A. How can you read the numbers and skip over the markers?

Productivity Hint 10.1

Regular Expressions

Regular expressions describe character patterns. For example, numbers have a simple form. They contain one or more digits. The regular expression describing numbers is [0-9]+. The set [0-9] denotes any digit between 0 and 9, and the + means "one or more".

The search commands of professional programming editors understand regular expressions. Moreover, several utility programs use regular expressions to locate matching text. A commonly used program that uses regular expressions is *grep* (which stands for "global regular expression print"). You can run grep from a command line or from inside some compilation environments. Grep is part of the UNIX operating system, and versions are available for Windows. It needs a regular expression and one or more files to search. When grep runs, it displays a set of lines that match the regular expression.

Suppose you want to look for all magic numbers (see Quality Tip 3.1) in a file. The command

```
grep [0-9]+ Homework.java
```

lists all lines in the file Homework.java that contain sequences of digits. That isn't terribly useful; lines with variable names x1 will be listed. OK, you want sequences of digits that do *not* immediately follow letters:

```
grep [^A-Za-z][0-9]+ Homework.java
```

The set [^A-Za-z] denotes any characters that are *not* in the ranges A to Z and a to z. This works much better, and it shows only lines that contain actual numbers.

The useDelimiter method of the Scanner class accepts a regular expression to describe delimiters—the blocks of text that separate words. As already mentioned, if you set the delimiter pattern to [^A-Za-z]+, a delimiter is a sequence of one or more characters that are not letters.

For more information on regular expressions, consult one of the many tutorials on the Internet by pointing your search engine to "regular expression tutorial".

How To 10.1   Processing Text Files

Processing text files that contain real data can be surprisingly challenging. This How To gives you step-by-step guidance.

As an example, we will consider this task: Read two country data files, worldpop.txt and worldarea.txt (supplied with your book code). Both files contain data for the same countries in the same order. Write a file world_pop_density.txt that contains country names and population densities (people per square km), with the country names aligned left and the numbers aligned right:

```
Afghanistan                              50.56
Akrotiri                                127.64
Albania                                 125.91
Algeria                                  14.18
American Samoa                          288.92
. . .
```

Step 1   Understand the processing task.

As always, you need to have a clear understanding of the task before designing a solution. Can you carry out the task by hand (perhaps with smaller input files)? If not, get more information about the problem.

One important aspect that you need to consider is whether you can process the data as it becomes available, or whether you need to store it first. For example, if you are asked to write out sorted data, you need to first collect all input, perhaps by placing it in an array list. However, it is often possible to process the data "on the go", without storing it.

In our example, we can read each file a line at a time and compute the density for each line because our input files store the population and area data in the same order.

The following pseudocode describes our processing task.

> **While there are more lines to be read**
>   **Read a line from each file.**
>   **Extract the country name.**
>   **population = number following the country name in the line from the first file**
>   **area = number following the country name in the line from the second file**
>   **If area != 0**
>   **density = population / area**
>   **Print country name and density.**

Step 2   Determine which files you need to read and write.

This should be clear from the problem. In our example, there are two input files, the population data and the area data, and one output file.

Step 3 Choose a mechanism for obtaining the file names.

There are four options:

- Hard-coding the file names (such as `"worldpop.txt"`)
- Asking the user:

```
Scanner in = new Scanner(System.in);
System.out.print("Enter filename: ");
String inFile = in.nextLine();
```

- Using command line arguments for the file names (see Special Topic 10.3)
- Using a file dialog box (see Special Topic 10.1)

In our example, we use hard-coded file names for simplicity.

Step 4 Choose between line, word, and character-based input.

As a rule of thumb, read lines if the input data is grouped by lines. That is the case with tabular data, such as in our example, or when you need to report line numbers.

When gathering data that can be distributed over several lines, then it makes more sense to read words. Keep in mind that you lose all white space when you read words.

Reading characters is mostly useful for tasks that require access to individual characters. Examples include analyzing character frequencies, changing tabs to spaces, or encryption.

Step 5 With line-oriented input, extract the required data.

It is simple to read a line of input with the `nextLine` method. Then you need to get the data out of that line. You can extract substrings, as described in Section 10.2.2.

Typically, you will use methods such as `Character.isWhitespace` and `Character.isDigit` to find the boundaries of substrings.

If you need any of the substrings as numbers, you must convert them, using `Integer.parseInt` or `Double.parseDouble`.

Step 6 Use classes and methods to factor out common tasks.

Processing input files usually has repetitive tasks, such as skipping over white space or extracting numbers from strings. It really pays off to isolate these tedious operations from the remainder of the code.

In our example, we have a task that occurs twice: splitting an input line into the country name and the value that follows. We implement a simple `CountryValue` class for this purpose, using the technique described in Section 10.2.2.

Here is the complete source code.

ch10/population/CountryValue.java

```
1   /**
2        Describes a value that is associated with a country.
3   */
4   public class CountryValue
5   {
6       private String country;
7       private double value;
8
9       /**
10          Constructs a CountryValue from an input line.
11          @param line a line containing a country name, followed by a value
12      */
13      public CountryValue(String line)
14      {
15          int i = 0; // Locate the start of the first digit
16          while (!Character.isDigit(line.charAt(i))) { i++; }
```

```java
17          int j = i - 1; // Locate the end of the preceding word
18          while (Character.isWhitespace(line.charAt(j))) { j--; }
19          country = line.substring(0, j + 1); // Extract the country name
20          value = Double.parseDouble(line.substring(i).trim()); // Extract the value
21       }
22
23       /**
24          Gets the country name.
25          @return the country name
26       */
27       public String getCountry() { return country; }
28
29       /**
30          Gets the associated value.
31          @return the value associated with the country
32       */
33       public double getValue() { return value; }
34    }
```

ch10/population/PopulationDensity.java

```java
 1   import java.io.File;
 2   import java.io.FileNotFoundException;
 3   import java.io.PrintWriter;
 4   import java.util.Scanner;
 5
 6   public class PopulationDensity
 7   {
 8      public static void main(String[] args) throws FileNotFoundException
 9      {
10         // Open input files
11         Scanner in1 = new Scanner(new File("worldpop.txt"));
12         Scanner in2 = new Scanner(new File("worldarea.txt"));
13
14         // Open output file
15         PrintWriter out = new PrintWriter("world_pop_density.txt");
16
17         // Read lines from each file
18         while (in1.hasNextLine() && in2.hasNextLine())
19         {
20            CountryValue population = new CountryValue(in1.nextLine());
21            CountryValue area = new CountryValue(in2.nextLine());
22
23            // Compute and print the population density
24            double density = 0;
25            if (area.getValue() != 0) // Protect against division by zero
26            {
27               density = population.getValue() / area.getValue();
28            }
29            out.printf("%-40s%15.2f\n", population.getCountry(), density);
30         }
31
32         in1.close();
33         in2.close();
34         out.close();
35      }
36   }
```

Worked Example 10.1

Analyzing Baby Names

In this Worked Example, you will use data from the Social Security Administration to analyze the most popular baby names.

10.3 Throwing Exceptions

There are two main aspects to exception handling: *reporting* and *recovery*. A major challenge of error handling is that the point of reporting is usually far apart from the point of recovery. For example, the get method of the ArrayList class may detect that a nonexistent element is being accessed, but it does not have enough information to decide what to do about this failure. Should the user be asked to try a different operation? Should the program be aborted after saving the user's work? These decisions must be made in a different part of the program.

In Java, *exception handling* provides a flexible mechanism for passing control from the point of error reporting to a competent recovery handler. In the remainder of this chapter, we will look into the details of this mechanism.

> To signal an exceptional condition, use the throw statement to throw an exception object.

When you detect an error condition, your job is really easy. You just throw an appropriate exception object, and you are done. For example, suppose someone tries to withdraw too much money from a bank account.

```java
public class BankAccount
{
   . . .
   public void withdraw(double amount)
   {
      if (amount > balance)
         // Now what?
      . . .
   }
}
```

Syntax 10.1   Throwing an Exception

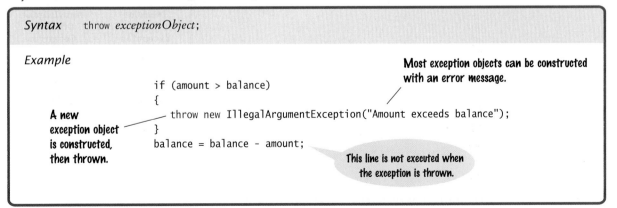

Syntax   throw *exceptionObject*;

Example

Most exception objects can be constructed with an error message.

```java
if (amount > balance)
{
   throw new IllegalArgumentException("Amount exceeds balance");
}
balance = balance - amount;
```

A new exception object is constructed, then thrown.

This line is not executed when the exception is thrown.

First look for an appropriate exception class. The Java library provides many classes to signal all sorts of exceptional conditions. Figure 1 shows the most useful ones.

Look around for an exception type that might describe your situation. How about the IllegalStateException? Is the bank account in an illegal state for the

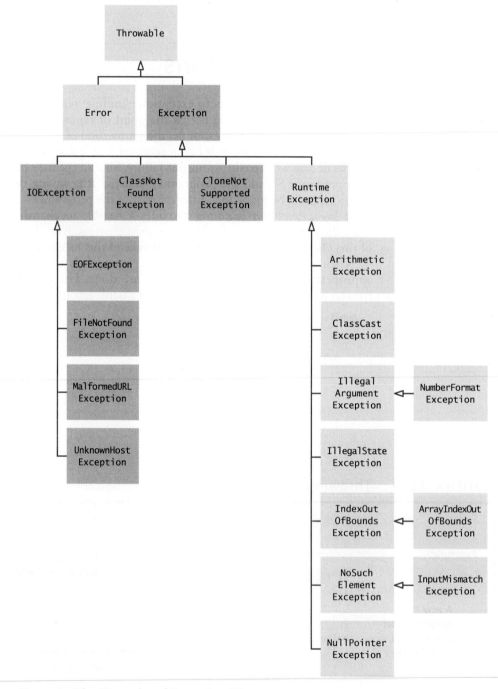

Figure 1 The Hierarchy of Exception Classes

withdraw operation? Not really—some withdraw operations could succeed. Is the parameter value illegal? Indeed it is. It is just too large. Therefore, let's throw an IllegalArgumentException. (The term **argument** is an alternative term for a parameter value.)

```java
public class BankAccount
{
    public void withdraw(double amount)
    {
        if (amount > balance)
        {
            throw new IllegalArgumentException("Amount exceeds balance");
        }
        balance = balance - amount;
    }
    . . .
}
```

The statement

```java
throw new IllegalArgumentException("Amount exceeds balance");
```

> When you throw an exception, the current method terminates immediately.

constructs an object of type IllegalArgumentException and throws that object.

When you throw an exception, execution does not continue with the next statement but with an **exception handler**. For now, we won't worry about the handling of the exception. That is the topic of Section 10.5.

SELF CHECK

6. How should you modify the deposit method to ensure that the balance is never negative?

7. Suppose you construct a new bank account object with a zero balance and then call withdraw(10). What is the value of balance afterwards?

10.4 Checked and Unchecked Exceptions

> There are two kinds of exceptions: *checked* and *unchecked*. Unchecked exceptions extend the class RuntimeException or Error.

Java exceptions fall into two categories, called *checked* and *unchecked* exceptions. When you call a method that throws a **checked exception**, the compiler checks that you don't ignore it. You must tell the compiler what you are going to do about the exception if it is ever thrown. For example, all subclasses of IOException are checked exceptions. On the other hand, the compiler does not require you to keep track of **unchecked exceptions**. Exceptions such as NumberFormatException, IllegalArgument-Exception, and NullPointerException are unchecked exceptions. More generally, all exceptions that belong to subclasses of RuntimeException are unchecked, and all other subclasses of the class Exception are checked. (In Figure 1, the checked exceptions are shaded in a darker color.) There is a second category of internal errors that are reported by throwing objects of type Error. One example is the OutOfMemoryError, which is thrown when all available memory has been used up. These are fatal errors that happen rarely and are beyond your control. They too are unchecked.

Why have two kinds of exceptions? A checked exception describes a problem that is likely to occur at times, no matter how careful you are. The unchecked exceptions, on the other hand, are your fault. For example, an unexpected end of file can be caused by forces beyond your control, such as a disk error or a broken

Checked exceptions are due to external circumstances that the programmer cannot prevent. The compiler checks that your program handles these exceptions.

network connection. But you are to blame for a `NullPointerException`, because your code was wrong when it tried to use a `null` reference.

The compiler doesn't check whether you handle a `NullPointerException`, because you should test your references for `null` before using them rather than install a handler for that exception. The compiler does insist that your program be able to handle error conditions that you cannot prevent.

Actually, those categories aren't perfect. For example, the `Scanner.nextInt` method throws an unchecked `InputMismatchException` if the input does not contain a valid integer. A checked exception would have been more appropriate because the programmer cannot prevent users from entering incorrect input. (The designers of the `Scanner` class made this choice to make it easy to use for beginning programmers.)

As you can see from Figure 1, the majority of checked exceptions occur when you deal with input and output. That is a fertile ground for external failures beyond your control—a file might have been corrupted or removed, a network connection might be overloaded, a server might have crashed, and so on. Therefore, you will need to deal with checked exceptions principally when programming with files and streams.

You have seen how to use the `Scanner` class to read data from a file, by passing a `File` object to the `Scanner` constructor:

```
String filename = . . .;
File inFile = new File(filename);
Scanner in = new Scanner(inFile);
```

However, the `Scanner` constructor can throw a `FileNotFoundException`. The `FileNotFoundException` is a checked exception, so you need to tell the compiler what you are going to do about it. You have two choices. You can handle the exception, using the techniques that you will see in Section 10.5. Or you can simply tell the compiler that you are aware of this exception and that you want your method to be terminated when it occurs. The method that reads input does not usually know what to do about an unexpected error, so that is usually the better option.

To declare that a method should be terminated when a checked exception occurs within it, tag the method with a `throws` clause.

```
public void read(String filename) throws FileNotFoundException
{
    File inFile = new File(filename);
    Scanner in = new Scanner(inFile);
    . . .
}
```

Add a throws clause to a method that can throw a checked exception.

The `throws` clause in turn signals the caller of your method that it may encounter a `FileNotFoundException`. Then the caller needs to make the same decision—handle the exception, or tell its caller that the exception may be thrown.

If your method can throw exceptions of different types, you separate the exception class names by commas:

```
public void read(String filename)
        throws FileNotFoundException, NoSuchElementException
```

Always keep in mind that exception classes form an inheritance hierarchy. For example, `FileNotFoundException` is a subclass of `IOException`. Thus, if a method can throw both an `IOException` and a `FileNotFoundException`, you only tag it as `throws IOException`.

Syntax 10.2 The throws Clause

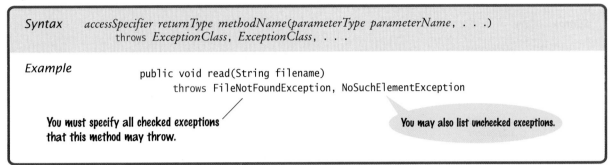

Syntax   accessSpecifier returnType methodName(parameterType parameterName, . . .)
            throws ExceptionClass, ExceptionClass, . . .

Example
```
public void read(String filename)
        throws FileNotFoundException, NoSuchElementException
```

You must specify all checked exceptions that this method may throw.

You may also list unchecked exceptions.

It sounds somehow irresponsible not to handle an exception when you know that it happened. Actually, though, it is usually best not to catch an exception if you don't know how to remedy the situation. After all, what can you do in a low-level read method? Can you tell the user? How? By sending a message to System.out? You don't know whether this method is called in a graphical program or an embedded system (such as a vending machine), where the user may never see System.out. And even if your users can see your error message, how do you know that they can understand English? Your class may be used to build an application for users in another country. If you can't tell the user, can you patch up the data and keep going? How? If you set a variable to zero, null, or an empty string, that may just cause the program to break later, with much greater mystery.

Of course, some methods in the program know how to communicate with the user or take other remedial action. By allowing the exception to reach those methods, you make it possible for the exception to be processed by a competent handler.

SELF CHECK

8. Suppose a method calls the Scanner constructor, which can throw a FileNot-FoundException, and the nextInt method of the Scanner class, which can cause a NoSuchElementException or InputMismatchException. Which exceptions should be included in the throws clause?

9. Why is a NullPointerException not a checked exception?

10.5 Catching Exceptions

In a method that is ready to handle a particular exception type, place the statements that can cause the exception inside a try block, and the handler inside a catch clause.

Every exception should be handled somewhere in your program. If an exception has no handler, an error message is printed, and your program terminates. That may be fine for a student program. But you would not want a professionally written program to die just because some method detected an unexpected error. Therefore, you should install exception handlers for all exceptions that your program might throw.

You install an exception handler with the try/catch statement. Each try block contains one or more statements that may cause an exception. Each catch clause contains the handler for an exception type.

Syntax 10.3 Catching Exceptions

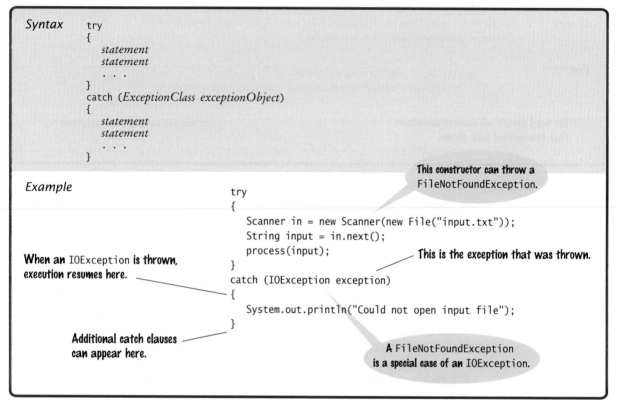

Here is an example:

```
try
{
    String filename = . . .;
    File inFile = new File(filename);
    Scanner in = new Scanner(inFile);
    String input = in.next();
    int value = Integer.parseInt(input);
    . . .
}
catch (IOException exception)
{
    exception.printStackTrace();
}
catch (NumberFormatException exception)
{
    System.out.println("Input was not a number");
}
```

Three exceptions may be thrown in this try block: The Scanner constructor can throw a FileNotFoundException, Scanner.next can throw a NoSuchElementException, and Integer.parseInt can throw a NumberFormatException.

If any of these exceptions is actually thrown, then the rest of the instructions in the try block are skipped. Here is what happens for the various exception types:

- If a `FileNotFoundException` is thrown, then the catch clause for the `IOException` is executed. (Recall that `FileNotFoundException` is a subclass of `IOException`.)
- If a `NumberFormatException` occurs, then the second catch clause is executed.
- A `NoSuchElementException` is *not caught* by any of the catch clauses. The exception remains thrown until it is caught by another try block or the main method terminates.

When the `catch (IOException exception)` block is executed, then some method in the try block has failed with an `IOException`. The variable exception contains a reference to the exception object that was thrown. The catch clause can analyze that object to find out more details about the failure. For example, you can get a printout of the chain of method calls that lead to the exception, by calling

```
exception.printStackTrace()
```

In these sample catch clauses, we merely inform the user of the source of the problem. A better way of dealing with the exception would be to give the user another chance to provide a correct input—see Section 10.8 for a solution.

It is important to remember that you should place catch clauses only in methods in which you can competently handle the particular exception type.

SELF CHECK

10. Suppose the file with the given file name exists and has no contents. Trace the flow of execution in the try block in this section.
11. Is there a difference between catching checked and unchecked exceptions?

Quality Tip 10.1

Throw Early, Catch Late

When a method detects a problem that it cannot solve, it is better to throw an exception rather than to try to come up with an imperfect fix. For example, suppose a method expects to read a number from a file, and the file doesn't contain a number. Simply using a zero value would be a poor choice because it hides the actual problem and perhaps causes a different problem elsewhere.

Throw an exception as soon as a problem is detected. Catch it only when the problem can be handled.

Conversely, a method should only catch an exception if it can really remedy the situation. Otherwise, the best remedy is simply to have the exception propagate to its caller, allowing it to be caught by a competent handler.

These principles can be summarized with the slogan "throw early, catch late".

Quality Tip 10.2

Do Not Squelch Exceptions

When you call a method that throws a checked exception and you haven't specified a handler, the compiler complains. In your eagerness to continue your work, it is an understandable impulse to shut the compiler up by squelching the exception:

```
try
{
```

```
        File inFile = new File(filename);
        Scanner in = new Scanner(inFile);
        // Compiler complained about FileNotFoundException
        . . .
    }
    catch (Exception e) {} // So there!
```

The do-nothing exception handler fools the compiler into thinking that the exception has been handled. In the long run, this is clearly a bad idea. Exceptions were designed to transmit problem reports to a competent handler. Installing an incompetent handler simply hides an error condition that could be serious.

10.6 The finally Clause

Occasionally, you need to take some action whether or not an exception is thrown. The finally construct is used to handle this situation. Here is a typical situation.

It is important to close a PrintWriter to ensure that all output is written to the file. In the following code segment, we open a stream, call one or more methods, and then close the stream:

```
PrintWriter out = new PrintWriter(filename);
writeData(out);
out.close(); // May never get here
```

Now suppose that one of the methods before the last line throws an exception. Then the call to close is never executed! Solve this problem by placing the call to close inside a finally clause:

```
PrintWriter out = new PrintWriter(filename);
try
{
    writeData(out);
}
finally
{
    out.close();
}
```

Once a try block is entered, the statements in a finally clause are guaranteed to be executed, whether or not an exception is thrown.

In a normal case, there will be no problem. When the try block is completed, the finally clause is executed, and the writer is closed. However, if an exception occurs, the finally clause is also executed before the exception is passed to its handler.

Use the finally clause whenever you need to do some clean up, such as closing a file, to ensure that the clean up happens no matter how the method exits.

It is also possible to have a finally clause following one or more catch clauses. Then the code in the finally clause is executed whenever the try block is exited in any of three ways:

1. After completing the last statement of the try block
2. After completing the last statement of a catch clause, if this try block caught an exception
3. When an exception was thrown in the try block and not caught

However, we recommend that you don't mix catch and finally clauses in the same try block—see Quality Tip 10.3 on page 411.

Syntax 10.4 The finally Clause

Syntax
```
try
{
    statement
    statement
    . . .
}
finally
{
    statement
    statement
    . . .
}
```

Example

This variable **must** be declared outside the `try` block so that the `finally` clause can access it.

```
PrintWriter out = new PrintWriter(filename);
try
{
    writeData(out);
}
finally
{
    out.close();
}
```

This code may throw exceptions.

This code is always executed, even if an exception occurs.

SELF CHECK

12. Why was the out variable declared outside the try block?
13. Suppose the file with the given name does not exist. Trace the flow of execution of the code segment in this section.

Quality Tip 10.3

Do Not Use catch **and** finally **in the Same** try **Statement**

It is tempting to combine catch and finally clauses, but the resulting code can be hard to understand. Instead, you should use a try/finally statement to close resources and a separate try/catch statement to handle errors. For example,

```
try
{
    PrintWriter out = new PrintWriter(filename);
    try
    {
        Write output to out
    }
    finally
    {
        out.close();
```

```
        }
    }
    catch (IOException exception)
    {
        Handle exception
    }
```

Note that the nested statements work correctly if the `PrintWriter` constructor throws an exception—see Exercise R10.18.

Special Topic 10.4

Automatic Resource Management in Java 7

In Java 7, you can use a new form of the try block that automatically closes an object that implements the `Closeable` interface, such as a `PrintWriter` or `Scanner`. Here is the syntax:

```
try (PrintWriter out = new PrintWriter(filename))
{
    Write output to out
}
```

The `close` method is automatically invoked on the out object when the try block ends, whether or not an exception has occurred. A `finally` statement is not required.

10.7 Designing Your Own Exception Types

Sometimes none of the standard exception types describe your particular error condition well enough. In that case, you can design your own exception class. Consider a bank account. Let's report an `InsufficientFundsException` when an attempt is made to withdraw an amount from a bank account that exceeds the current balance.

```
if (amount > balance)
{
    throw new InsufficientFundsException(
        "withdrawal of " + amount + " exceeds balance of " + balance);
}
```

> To describe an error condition, provide a subclass of an existing exception class.

Now you need to provide the `InsufficientFundsException` class. Should it be a checked or an unchecked exception? Is it the fault of some external event, or is it the fault of the programmer? We take the position that the programmer could have prevented the exceptional condition—after all, it would have been an easy matter to check whether `amount <= account.getBalance()` before calling the `withdraw` method. Therefore, the exception should be an unchecked exception and extend the `RuntimeException` class or one of its subclasses.

It is a good idea to extend an appropriate class in the exception hierarchy. For example, we can consider an `InsufficientFundsException` a special case of an `IllegalArgumentException`. This enables other programmers to catch the exception as an `IllegalArgumentException` if they are not interested in the exact nature of the problem.

It is customary to provide two constructors for an exception class: a constructor with no parameters and a constructor that accepts a message string describing the reason for the exception. Here is the declaration of the exception class.

```
public class InsufficientFundsException extends IllegalArgumentException
{
    public InsufficientFundsException() {}

    public InsufficientFundsException(String message)
    {
        super(message);
    }
}
```

When the exception is caught, its message string can be retrieved using the get-Message method of the Throwable class.

SELF CHECK

14. What is the purpose of the call super(message) in the second InsufficientFunds-Exception constructor?

15. Suppose you read bank account data from a file. Contrary to your expectation, the next input value is not of type double. You decide to implement a BadData-Exception. Which exception class should you extend?

Quality Tip 10.4

Do Throw Specific Exceptions

When throwing an exception, you should choose an exception class that describes the situation as closely as possible. For example, it would be a bad idea to simply throw a Runtime-Exception object when a bank account has insufficient funds. This would make it far too difficult to catch the exception. After all, if you caught all exceptions of type Runtime-Exception, your catch clause would also be activated by exceptions of the type NullPointer-Exception, ArrayIndexOutOfBoundsException, and so on. You would then need to carefully examine the exception object and attempt to deduce whether the exception was caused by insufficient funds.

If the standard library does not have an exception class that describes your particular error situation, simply provide a new exception class.

10.8 Case Study: A Complete Example

This section walks through a complete example of a program with exception handling. The program asks a user for the name of a file. The file is expected to contain data values. The first line of the file contains the total number of values, and the remaining lines contain the data. A typical input file looks like this:

```
3
1.45
-2.1
0.05
```

What can go wrong? There are two principal risks.

- The file might not exist.
- The file might have data in the wrong format.

Who can detect these faults? The Scanner constructor will throw an exception when the file does not exist. The methods that process the input values need to throw an exception when they find an error in the data format.

What exceptions can be thrown? The Scanner constructor throws a FileNot-FoundException when the file does not exist, which is appropriate in our situation. Finally, when the file data is in the wrong format, we will throw a BadDataException, a custom checked exception class. We use a checked exception because corruption of a data file is beyond the control of the programmer.

Who can remedy the faults that the exceptions report? Only the main method of the DataAnalyzer program interacts with the user. It catches the exceptions, prints appropriate error messages, and gives the user another chance to enter a correct file.

ch10/data/DataAnalyzer.java

```
1   import java.io.FileNotFoundException;
2   import java.io.IOException;
3   import java.util.Scanner;
4
5   /**
6      This program reads a file containing numbers and analyzes its contents.
7      If the file doesn't exist or contains strings that are not numbers, an
8      error message is displayed.
9   */
10  public class DataAnalyzer
11  {
12     public static void main(String[] args)
13     {
14        Scanner in = new Scanner(System.in);
15        DataSetReader reader = new DataSetReader();
16
17        boolean done = false;
18        while (!done)
19        {
20           try
21           {
22              System.out.println("Please enter the file name: ");
23              String filename = in.next();
24
25              double[] data = reader.readFile(filename);
26              double sum = 0;
27              for (double d : data) sum = sum + d;
28              System.out.println("The sum is " + sum);
29              done = true;
30           }
31           catch (FileNotFoundException exception)
32           {
33              System.out.println("File not found.");
34           }
35           catch (BadDataException exception)
36           {
37              System.out.println("Bad data: " + exception.getMessage());
38           }
```

```
39              catch (IOException exception)
40              {
41                  exception.printStackTrace();
42              }
43          }
44      }
45  }
```

The catch clauses in the main method give a human-readable error report if the file was not found or bad data was encountered.

The following readFile method of the DataSetReader class constructs the Scanner object and calls the readData method. It is completely unconcerned with any exceptions. If there is a problem with the input file, it simply passes the exception to its caller.

```java
public double[] readFile(String filename) throws IOException
{
   File inFile = new File(filename);
   Scanner in = new Scanner(inFile);
   try
   {
      readData(in);
      return data;
   }
   finally
   {
      in.close();
   }
}
```

The method throws an IOException, the common superclass of FileNotFoundException (thrown by the Scanner constructor) and BadDataException (thrown by the readData method).

Next, here is the readData method of the DataSetReader class. It reads the number of values, constructs an array, and calls readValue for each data value.

```java
private void readData(Scanner in) throws BadDataException
{
   if (!in.hasNextInt())
      throw new BadDataException("Length expected");
   int numberOfValues = in.nextInt();
   data = new double[numberOfValues];

   for (int i = 0; i < numberOfValues; i++)
      readValue(in, i);

   if (in.hasNext())
      throw new BadDataException("End of file expected");
}
```

This method checks for two potential errors. The file might not start with an integer, or it might have additional data after reading all values.

However, this method makes no attempt to catch any exceptions. Plus, if the readValue method throws an exception—which it will if there aren't enough values in the file—the exception is simply passed on to the caller.

Here is the readValue method:

```
private void readValue(Scanner in, int i) throws BadDataException
{
    if (!in.hasNextDouble())
        throw new BadDataException("Data value expected");
    data[i] = in.nextDouble();
}
```

ANIMATION
Exception Handling

To see the exception handling at work, look at a specific error scenario.

1. DataAnalyzer.main calls DataSetReader.readFile.

2. readFile calls readData.

3. readData calls readValue.

4. readValue doesn't find the expected value and throws a BadDataException.

5. readValue has no handler for the exception and terminates immediately.

6. readData has no handler for the exception and terminates immediately.

7. readFile has no handler for the exception and terminates immediately after executing the finally clause and closing the Scanner object.

8. DataAnalyzer.main has a handler for a BadDataException. That handler prints a message to the user. Afterwards, the user is given another chance to enter a file name. Note that the statements computing the sum of the values have been skipped.

This example shows the separation between error detection (in the DataSetReader.readValue method) and error handling (in the DataAnalyzer.main method). In between the two are the readData and readFile methods, which just pass exceptions along.

ch10/data/DataSetReader.java

```
 1  import java.io.File;
 2  import java.io.IOException;
 3  import java.util.Scanner;
 4
 5  /**
 6      Reads a data set from a file. The file must have the format
 7      numberOfValues
 8      value1
 9      value2
10      . . .
11  */
12  public class DataSetReader
13  {
14      private double[] data;
15
16      /**
17          Reads a data set.
18          @param filename the name of the file holding the data
19          @return the data in the file
20      */
21      public double[] readFile(String filename) throws IOException
22      {
23          File inFile = new File(filename);
24          Scanner in = new Scanner(inFile);
25
```

```
26          try
27          {
28              readData(in);
29              return data;
30          }
31          finally
32          {
33              in.close();
34          }
35      }
36
37      /**
38          Reads all data.
39          @param in the scanner that scans the data
40      */
41      private void readData(Scanner in) throws BadDataException
42      {
43          if (!in.hasNextInt())
44              throw new BadDataException("Length expected");
45          int numberOfValues = in.nextInt();
46          data = new double[numberOfValues];
47
48          for (int i = 0; i < numberOfValues; i++)
49              readValue(in, i);
50
51          if (in.hasNext())
52              throw new BadDataException("End of file expected");
53      }
54
55      /**
56          Reads one data value.
57          @param in the scanner that scans the data
58          @param i the position of the value to read
59      */
60      private void readValue(Scanner in, int i) throws BadDataException
61      {
62          if (!in.hasNextDouble())
63              throw new BadDataException("Data value expected");
64          data[i] = in.nextDouble();
65      }
66  }
```

ch10/data/BadDataException.java

```
1   import java.io.IOException;
2
3   /**
4       This class reports bad input data.
5   */
6   public class BadDataException extends IOException
7   {
8       public BadDataException() {}
9       public BadDataException(String message)
10      {
11          super(message);
12      }
13  }
```

SELF CHECK

16. Why doesn't the `DataSetReader.readFile` method catch any exceptions?

17. Suppose the user specifies a file that exists and is empty. Trace the flow of execution.

Random Fact 10.1

The Ariane Rocket Incident

Random Fact 10.1 tells the story of the Ariane 5 rocket that blew itself up due to an unhandled exception.

Summary of Learning Objectives

Read and write text that is stored in files.
- When reading text files, use the `Scanner` class.
- When writing text files, use the `PrintWriter` class.
- You must close a print stream when you are done writing output.

Choose an appropriate mechanism for processing input.
- The `next` method reads a word at a time. Call `Scanner.useDelimiter` to specify a pattern for word boundaries.
- The `nextLine` method reads a line of input and consumes the newline character at the end of the line.
- The `nextInt` and `nextDouble` methods consume white space and the next number.
- To read one character at a time, set the delimiter pattern to the empty string.

Understand when and how to throw an exception.
- To signal an exceptional condition, use the `throw` statement to throw an exception object.
- When you throw an exception, the current method terminates immediately.

Choose between checked and unchecked exceptions.
- There are two kinds of exceptions: *checked* and *unchecked*. Unchecked exceptions extend the class `RuntimeException` or `Error`.
- Checked exceptions are due to external circumstances that the programmer cannot prevent. The compiler checks that your program handles these exceptions.
- Add a `throws` clause to a method that can throw a checked exception.

Use exception handlers to decouple error detection and error reporting.
- In a method that is ready to handle a particular exception type, place the statements that can cause the exception inside a `try` block, and the handler inside a `catch` clause.
- Throw an exception as soon as a problem is detected. Catch it only when the problem can be handled.

Use the `finally` clause to ensure that resources are released when an exception is thrown.

- Once a `try` block is entered, the statements in a `finally` clause are guaranteed to be executed, whether or not an exception is thrown.

Design exception types to describe error conditions.

- To describe an error condition, provide a subclass of an existing exception class.

Classes, Objects, and Methods Introduced in this Chapter

```
java.io.EOFException                java.lang.RuntimeException
java.io.File                        java.lang.Throwable
java.io.FileNotFoundException           getMessage
java.io.IOException                     printStackTrace
java.io.PrintWriter                 java.util.NoSuchElementException
   close                            java.util.Scanner
java.lang.Error                         close
java.lang.IllegalArgumentException  javax.swing.JFileChooser
java.lang.IllegalStateException         getSelectedFile
java.lang.NullPointerException          showOpenDialog
java.lang.NumberFormatException         showSaveDialog
```

Media Resources

www.wiley.com/
go/global/
horstmann

- ***Worked Example*** Analyzing Baby Names
- Lab Exercises
- ✚ ***Animation*** Exception Handling
- ✚ Practice Quiz
- ✚ Code Completion Exercises

Review Exercises

★★ **R10.1** What happens if you try to open a file for reading that doesn't exist? What happens if you try to open a file for writing that doesn't exist?

★★★ **R10.2** What happens if you try to open a file for writing, but the file or device is write-protected (sometimes called read-only)? Try it out with a short test program.

★   **R10.3** How do you open a file whose name contains a backslash, like `c:\temp\output.dat`?

★★★ **R10.4** What is a command line? How can a program read its command line arguments?

★★ **R10.5** Give two examples of programs on your computer that read arguments from the command line.

★★ **R10.6** If a program Woozle is started with the command

```
java Woozle -Dname=piglet -I\eeyore -v heff.txt a.txt lump.txt
```

what are the values of `args[0]`, `args[1]`, and so on?

★★   **R10.7** What is the difference between throwing an exception and catching an exception?

★★   **R10.8** What is a checked exception? What is an unchecked exception? Is a `NullPointer-Exception` checked or unchecked? Which exceptions do you need to declare with the `throws` reserved word?

★   **R10.9** Why don't you need to declare that your method might throw a `NullPointer-Exception`?

★★ **R10.10** When your program executes a `throw` statement, which statement is executed next?

★ **R10.11** What happens if an exception does not have a matching `catch` clause?

★ **R10.12** What can your program do with the exception object that a `catch` clause receives?

★ **R10.13** Is the type of the exception object always the same as the type declared in the `catch` clause that catches it?

★ **R10.14** What kind of values can you throw? Can you throw a string? An integer?

★★ **R10.15** What is the purpose of the `finally` clause? Give an example of how it can be used.

★★★ **R10.16** What happens when an exception is thrown, the code of a `finally` clause executes, and that code throws an exception of a different kind than the original one? Which one is caught by a surrounding `catch` clause? Write a sample program to try it out.

★★ **R10.17** Which exceptions can the `next` and `nextInt` methods of the `Scanner` class throw? Are they checked exceptions or unchecked exceptions?

★★★ **R10.18** Suppose the code in Quality Tip 10.3 on page 411 had been condensed to a single try/catch/finally statement:

```
PrintWriter out = new PrintWriter(filename);
try
{
    Write output
}
catch (IOException exception)
{
    Handle exception
}
finally
{
    out.close();
}
```

What is the disadvantage of this version? (*Hint:* What happens when the `PrintWriter` constructor throws an exception?) Why can't you solve the problem by moving the declaration of the out variable inside the `try` block?

★★ **R10.19** Suppose the program in Section 10.8 reads a file containing the following values:

```
0
1
2
3
```

What is the outcome? How could the program be improved to give a more accurate error report?

★★ **R10.20** Can the `readFile` method in Section 10.8 throw a `NullPointerException`? If so, how?

Programming Exercises

★★ **P10.1** Write a program that asks a user for a file name and prints the number of characters, words, and lines in that file.

★★ **P10.2** Write a program that asks the user for a file name and counts the number of characters, words, and lines in that file. Then the program asks for the name of the next file. When the user enters a file that doesn't exist, the program prints the total counts of characters, words, and lines in all processed files and exits.

★★ **P10.3** Write a program CopyFile that copies one file to another. The file names are specified on the command line. For example,

```
java CopyFile report.txt report.sav
```

★★ **P10.4** Write a program that *concatenates* the contents of several files into one file. For example,

```
java CatFiles chapter1.txt chapter2.txt chapter3.txt book.txt
```

makes a long file, book.txt, that contains the contents of the files chapter1.txt, chapter2.txt, and chapter3.txt. The output file is always the last file specified on the command line.

★★ **P10.5** Write a program Find that searches all files specified on the command line and prints out all lines containing a reserved word. For example, if you call

```
java Find ring report.txt address.txt Homework.java
```

then the program might print

```
report.txt: has broken up an international ring of DVD bootleggers that
address.txt: Kris Kringle, North Pole
address.txt: Homer Simpson, Springfield
Homework.java: String filename;
```

The reserved word is always the first command line argument.

★★ **P10.6** Write a program that checks the spelling of all words in a file. It should read each word of a file and check whether it is contained in a word list. A word list is available on most UNIX systems in the file /usr/dict/words. (If you don't have access to a UNIX system, your instructor should be able to get you a copy.) The program should print out all words that it cannot find in the word list.

★★ **P10.7** Write a program that replaces each line of a file with its reverse. For example, if you run

```
java Reverse HelloPrinter.java
```

then the contents of HelloPrinter.java are changed to

```
retnirPolleH ssalc cilbup
{
)sgra ][gnirtS(niam diov citats cilbup
{
wodniw elosnoc eht ni gniteerg a yalpsiD //

;)"!dlroW ,olleH"(nltnirp.tuo.metsyS
}
}
```

Of course, if you run Reverse twice on the same file, you get back the original file.

★ **P10.8** Get the data for names in prior decades from the Social Security Administration. Paste the table data in files named `babynames80s.txt`, etc. Modify the `BabyNames.java` program so that it prompts the user for a file name. The numbers in the files have comma separators, so modify the program to handle them. Can you spot a trend in the frequencies?

★ **P10.9** Write a program that reads in `babynames.txt` and produces two files `boynames.txt` and `girlnames.txt`, separating the data for the boys and girls.

★★ **P10.10** Write a program that reads a file in the same format as `babynames.txt` and prints all names that are both boy and girl names (such as Alexis or Morgan).

★★★ **P10.11** Write a program that replaces all tab characters `'\t'` in a file with the *appropriate* number of spaces. By default, the distance between tab columns should be 3 (the value we use in this book for Java programs) but it can be changed by the user. Expand tabs to the number of spaces necessary to move to the next tab column. That may be *less* than three spaces. For example, consider the line containing `"\t|\t||\t|"`. The first tab is changed to three spaces, the second to two spaces, and the third to one space. Your program should be executed as

```
java TabExpander filename
```

or

```
java TabExpander -t tabwidth filename
```

★ **P10.12** Modify the `BankAccount` class to throw an `IllegalArgumentException` when the account is constructed with a negative balance, when a negative amount is deposited, or when an amount that is not between 0 and the current balance is withdrawn. Write a test program that causes all three exceptions to occur and that catches them all.

★★ **P10.13** Repeat Exercise P10.12, but throw exceptions of three exception types that you provide.

★★ **P10.14** Write a program that asks the user to input a set of floating-point values. When the user enters a value that is not a number, give the user a second chance to enter the value. After two chances, quit reading input. Add all correctly specified values and print the sum when the user is done entering data. Use exception handling to detect improper inputs.

★★ **P10.15** Repeat Exercise P10.14, but give the user as many chances as necessary to enter a correct value. Quit the program only when the user enters a blank input.

★ **P10.16** Modify the `DataSetReader` class so that you do not call `hasNextInt` or `hasNextDouble`. Simply have `nextInt` and `nextDouble` throw a `NoSuchElementException` and catch it in the `main` method.

★★ **P10.17** Write a program that reads in a set of coin descriptions from a file. The input file has the format

```
coinName1 coinValue1
coinName2 coinValue2
. . .
```

Add a method

```
void read(Scanner in) throws FileNotFoundException
```

to the `Coin` class. Throw an exception if the current line is not properly formatted. Then implement a method

```
static ArrayList<Coin> readFile(String filename)
    throws FileNotFoundException
```

In the `main` method, call `readFile`. If an exception is thrown, give the user a chance to select another file. If you read all coins successfully, print the total value.

★★★ **P10.18** Design a class `Bank` that contains a number of bank accounts. Each account has an account number and a current balance. Add an `accountNumber` field to the `BankAccount` class. Store the bank accounts in an array list. Write a `readFile` method of the `Bank` class for reading a file with the format

```
accountNumber1  balance1
accountNumber2  balance2
. . .
```

Implement `read` methods for the `Bank` and `BankAccount` classes. Write a sample program to read in a file with bank accounts, then print the account with the highest balance. If the file is not properly formatted, give the user a chance to select another file.

Programming Projects

Project 10.1 You can read the contents of a web page with this sequence of commands.

```
String address = "http://java.sun.com/index.html";
URL u = new URL(address);
Scanner in = new Scanner(u.openStream());
. . .
```

Some of these methods may throw exceptions—check out the API documentation. Design a class `LinkFinder` that finds all hyperlinks of the form

```
<a href="link">link text</a>
```

Throw an exception if you find a malformed hyperlink. Extra credit if your program can follow the links that it finds and find links in those web pages as well. (This is the method that search engines such as Google use to find web sites.)

Answers to Self-Check Questions

1. When the `PrintWriter` object is created, the output file is emptied. Sadly, that is the same file as the input file. The input file is now empty and the `while` loop exits immediately.
2. The `Scanner` constructor throws a `FileNotFoundException`, and the program terminates.
3. `number` is 6, `input` is `",995.0"`
4. `price` is set to 6 because the comma is not considered a part of a floating-point number in Java. Then the call to `nextInt` causes an exception, and `quantity` is not set.

5. Read them as strings, and convert those strings to numbers that are not equal to N/A:

```
String input = in.next();
if (!input.equals("N/A"))
{
    double value = Double.parseDouble(input);
    Process value
}
```

6. Throw an exception if the amount being deposited is less than zero.

7. The balance is still zero because the last statement of the withdraw method was never executed.

8. You must include the FileNotFoundException and you may include the NoSuchElementException if you consider it important for documentation purposes. InputMismatchException is a subclass of NoSuchElementException. It is your choice whether to include it.

9. Because programmers should simply check for null pointers instead of trying to handle a NullPointerException.

10. The Scanner constructor succeeds, and in is constructed. Then the call in.next() throws a NoSuchElementException, and the try block is aborted. None of the catch clauses match, so none are executed. If none of the enclosing method calls catch the exception, the program terminates.

11. No—you catch both exception types in the same way, as you can see from the code example on page 408. Recall that IOException is a checked exception and NumberFormatException is an unchecked exception.

12. If it had been declared inside the try block, its scope would only have extended to the end of the try block, and the finally clause could not have closed it.

13. The PrintWriter constructor throws an exception. The assignment to out and the try block are skipped. The finally clause is not executed. This is the correct behavior because out has not been initialized.

14. To pass the exception message string to the RuntimeException superclass.

15. Because file corruption is beyond the control of the programmer, this should be a checked exception, so it would be wrong to extend RuntimeException or IllegalArgumentException. Because the error is related to input, IOException would be a good choice.

16. It would not be able to do much with them. The DataSetReader class is a reusable class that may be used for systems with different languages and different user interfaces. Thus, it cannot engage in a dialog with the program user.

17. DataAnalyzer.main calls DataSetReader.readFile, which calls readData. The call in.hasNextInt() returns false, and readData throws a BadDataException. The readFile method doesn't catch it, so it propagates back to main, where it is caught.

Object-Oriented Design

CHAPTER GOALS

- To learn about the software life cycle
- To learn how to discover new classes and methods
- To understand the use of CRC cards for class discovery
- To be able to identify inheritance, aggregation, and dependency relationships between classes
- To master the use of UML class diagrams to describe class relationships
- To learn how to use object-oriented design to build complex programs

To implement a software system successfully, be it as simple as your next homework project or as complex as the next air traffic monitoring system, some amount of planning, design, and testing is required. In fact, for larger projects, the amount of time spent on planning is much higher than the amount of time spent on programming and testing.

If you find that most of your homework time is spent in front of the computer, keying in code and fixing bugs, you are probably spending more time on your homework than you should. You could cut down your total time by spending more on the planning and design phase. This chapter tells you how to approach these tasks in a systematic manner, using the object-oriented design methodology.

CHAPTER CONTENTS

11.1 The Software Life Cycle

> The software life cycle encompasses all activities from initial analysis until obsolescence.

In this section we will discuss the **software life cycle**: the activities that take place between the time a software program is first conceived and the time it is finally retired.

A software project usually starts because a customer has a problem and is willing to pay money to have it solved. The Department of Defense, the customer of many programming projects, was an early proponent of a *formal process* for software development. A formal process identifies and describes different phases and gives guidelines for carrying out the phases and when to move from one phase to the next.

> A formal process for software development describes phases of the development process and gives guidelines for how to carry out the phases.

Many software engineers break the development process down into the following five phases:

- Analysis
- Design
- Implementation
- Testing
- Deployment

In the *analysis* phase, you decide *what* the project is supposed to accomplish; you do not think about *how* the program will accomplish its tasks. The output of the analysis phase is a *requirements document*, which describes in complete detail what the program will be able to do once it is completed. Part of this requirements document can be a user manual that tells how the user will operate the program to derive the promised benefits. Another part sets performance criteria—how many inputs the program must be able to handle in what time, or what its maximum memory and disk storage requirements are.

In the *design* phase, you develop a plan for how you will implement the system. You discover the structures that underlie the problem to be solved. When you use object-oriented design, you decide what classes you need and what their most important methods are. The output of this phase is a description of the classes and methods, with diagrams that show the relationships among the classes.

In the *implementation* phase, you write and compile program code to implement the classes and methods that were discovered in the design phase. The output of this phase is the completed program.

In the *testing* phase, you run tests to verify that the program works correctly. The output of this phase is a report describing the tests that you carried out and their results.

In the *deployment* phase, the users of the program install it and use it for its intended purpose.

When formal development processes were first established in the early 1970s, software engineers had a very simple visual model of these phases. They postulated that one phase would run to completion, its output would spill over to the next phase, and the next phase would begin. This model is called the **waterfall model** of software development (see Figure 1).

In an ideal world the waterfall model has a lot of appeal: You figure out what to do; then you figure out how to do it; then you do it; then you verify that you did it right; then you hand the product to the customer. When rigidly applied, though, the waterfall model simply did not work. It was very difficult to come up with a perfect requirement specification. It was quite common to discover in the design phase that the requirements were inconsistent or that a small change in the requirements would lead to a system that was both easier to design and more useful for the customer, but the analysis phase was over, so the designers had no choice—they had to take the existing requirements, errors and all. This problem would repeat itself during implementation. The designers may have thought they knew how to solve the problem as efficiently as possible, but when the design was actually implemented, it turned out that the resulting program was not as fast as the designers had thought. The next transition is one with which you are surely familiar. When the program was handed to the quality assurance department for testing, many bugs were found that would best be fixed by reimplementing, or maybe even redesigning, the program, but the waterfall model did not allow for this. Finally, when the customers received the finished product, they were often not at all happy with it. Even though the customers typically were very involved in the analysis phase, often they

The waterfall model of software development describes a sequential process of analysis, design, implementation, testing, and deployment.

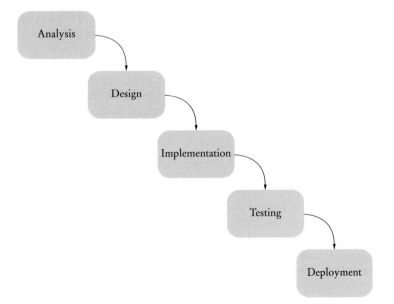

Figure 1 The Waterfall Model

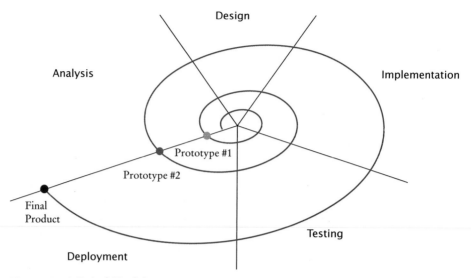

Figure 2 A Spiral Model

themselves were not sure exactly what they needed. After all, it can be very difficult to describe how you want to use a product that you have never seen before. But when the customers started using the program, they began to realize what they would have liked. Of course, then it was too late, and they had to live with what they got.

Having some level of iteration is clearly necessary. There simply must be a mechanism to deal with errors from the preceding phase. A **spiral model**, originally proposed by Barry Boehm in 1988, breaks the development process down into multiple phases (see Figure 2). Early phases focus on the construction of *prototypes*. A prototype is a small system that shows some aspects of the final system. Because prototypes model only a part of a system and do not need to withstand customer abuse, they can be implemented quickly. It is common to build a *user interface prototype* that shows the user interface in action. This gives customers an early chance to become more familiar with the system and to suggest improvements before the analysis is complete. Other prototypes can be built to validate interfaces with external systems, to test performance, and so on. Lessons learned from the development of one prototype can be applied to the next iteration of the spiral.

By building in repeated trials and feedback, a development process that follows the spiral model has a greater chance of delivering a satisfactory system. However, there is also a danger. If engineers believe that they don't have to do a good job because they can always do another iteration, then there will be many iterations, and the process will take a very long time to complete.

Figure 3 shows activity levels in the "Rational Unified Process", a development process methodology by the inventors of UML (see Grady Booch, James Rumbaugh, and Ivar Jacobson, *The Unified Modeling Language User Guide*, Addison-Wesley, 1999). The details are not important, but as you can see, this is a complex process involving multiple iterations.

Even complex development processes with many iterations have not always met with success. In 1999, Kent Beck published an influential book on **Extreme Programming**, a development methodology that strives for simplicity by cutting out

> The spiral model of software development describes an iterative process in which design and implementation are repeated.

> Extreme Programming is a development methodology that strives for simplicity by removing formal structure and focusing on best practices.

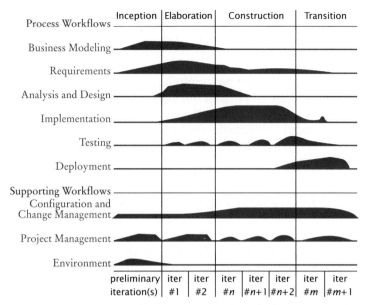

Figure 3 Activity Levels in the Rational Unified Process Methodology

most of the formal trappings of a traditional development methodology and instead focusing on a set of *practices:*

- *Realistic planning:* Customers are to make business decisions, programmers are to make technical decisions. Update the plan when it conflicts with reality.
- *Small releases:* Release a useful system quickly, then release updates on a very short cycle.
- *Metaphor:* All programmers should have a simple shared story that explains the system under development.
- *Simplicity:* Design everything to be as simple as possible instead of preparing for future complexity.
- *Testing:* Both programmers and customers are to write test cases. The system is continuously tested.
- *Refactoring:* Programmers are to restructure the system continuously to improve the code and eliminate duplication.
- *Pair programming:* Put programmers together in pairs, and require each pair to write code on a single computer.
- *Collective ownership:* All programmers have permission to change all code as it becomes necessary.
- *Continuous integration:* Whenever a task is completed, build the entire system and test it.
- *40-hour week:* Don't cover up unrealistic schedules with bursts of heroic effort.
- *On-site customer:* An actual customer of the system is to be accessible to team members at all times.
- *Coding standards:* Programmers are to follow standards that emphasize self-documenting code.

Many of these practices are common sense. Others, such as the pair programming requirement, are surprising. Beck claims that the value of the Extreme Programming approach lies in the synergy of these practices—the sum is bigger than the parts.

In your first programming course, you will not develop systems that are so complex that you need a full-fledged methodology to solve your homework problems. This introduction to the development process should, however, show you that successful software development involves more than just coding. In the remainder of this chapter we will have a closer look at the *design phase* of the software development process.

SELF CHECK

1. Suppose you sign a contract, promising that you will, for an agreed-upon price, design, implement, and test a software package exactly as it has been specified in a requirements document. What is the primary risk you and your customer are facing with this business arrangement?
2. Does Extreme Programming follow a waterfall or a spiral model?
3. What is the purpose of the "on-site customer" in Extreme Programming?

Random Fact 11.1

Programmer Productivity

Random Fact 11.1 presents information about the productivity of individual programmers and teams.

11.2 Discovering Classes

In the design phase of software development, your task is to discover structures that make it possible to implement a set of tasks on a computer. When you use the object-oriented design process, you carry out the following tasks:

> In object-oriented design, you discover classes, determine the responsibilities of classes, and describe the relationships between classes.

1. Discover classes.
2. Determine the responsibilities of each class.
3. Describe the relationships between the classes.

A class represents some useful concept. You have seen classes for concrete entities, such as bank accounts, ellipses, and products. Other classes represent abstract concepts, such as streams and windows.

> Make a list of candidates for classes, starting with nouns in the task description.

A simple rule for finding classes is to look for *nouns* in the task description. For example, suppose your job is to print an invoice such as the one in Figure 4. Obvious classes that come to mind are Invoice, LineItem, and Customer. It is a good idea to keep a list of *candidate classes* on a whiteboard or a sheet of paper. As you brainstorm, simply put all ideas for classes onto the list. You can always cross out the ones that weren't useful after all.

When finding classes, keep the following points in mind:

- A class represents a set of objects with the same behavior. Entities with multiple occurrences in your problem description, such as customers or products, are good candidates for objects. Find out what they have in common, and design classes to capture those commonalities.

- Some entities should be represented as objects, others as primitive types. For example, should an address be an object of an Address class, or should it simply be a string? There is no perfect answer—it depends on the task that you want to solve. If your software needs to analyze addresses (for example, to determine shipping costs), then an Address class is an appropriate design. However, if your software will never need such a capability, you should not waste time on an overly complex design. It is your job to find a balanced design; one that is not too limiting or excessively general.

- Not all classes can be discovered in the analysis phase. Most complex programs need classes for tactical purposes, such as file or database access, user interfaces, control mechanisms, and so on.

- Some of the classes that you need may already exist, either in the standard library or in a program that you developed previously. You also may be able to use inheritance to extend existing classes into classes that match your needs.

Once a set of classes has been identified, you need to define the behavior for each class. That is, you need to find out what methods each object needs to do to solve the programming problem. A simple rule for finding these methods is to look for *verbs* in the task description, then match the verbs to the appropriate objects. For example, in the invoice program, a class needs to compute the amount due. Now you need to figure out *which class* is responsible for this method. Do customers

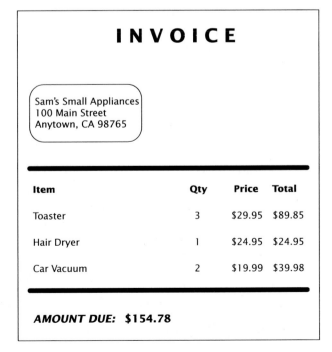

Figure 4
An Invoice

compute what they owe? Do invoices total up the amount due? Do the items total themselves up? The best choice is to make "compute amount due" the responsibility of the Invoice class.

An excellent way to carry out this task is the "**CRC card** method." *CRC* stands for "classes", "responsibilities", "collaborators", and in its simplest form, the method works as follows. Use an index card for each *class* (see Figure 5). As you think about verbs in the task description that indicate methods, you pick the card of the class that you think should be responsible, and write that *responsibility* on the card.

For each responsibility, you record which other classes are needed to fulfill it. Those classes are the **collaborators**.

For example, suppose you decide that an invoice should compute the amount due. Then you write "compute amount due" on the left-hand side of an index card with the title Invoice.

If a class can carry out that responsibility by itself, do nothing further. But if the class needs the help of other classes, write the names of these collaborators on the right-hand side of the card.

To compute the total, the invoice needs to ask each line item about its total price. Therefore, the LineItem class is a collaborator.

This is a good time to look up the index card for the LineItem class. Does it have a "get total price" method? If not, add one.

How do you know that you are on the right track? For each responsibility, ask yourself how it can actually be done, using the responsibilities written on the various cards. Many people find it helpful to group the cards on a table so that the collaborators are close to each other, and to simulate tasks by moving a token (such as a coin) from one card to the next to indicate which object is currently active.

Keep in mind that the responsibilities that you list on the CRC card are on a *high level*. Sometimes a single responsibility may need two or more Java methods for carrying it out. Some researchers say that a CRC card should have no more than three distinct responsibilities.

The CRC card method is informal on purpose, so that you can be creative and discover classes and their properties. Once you find that you have settled on a good set of classes, you will want to know how they are related to each other. Can you find

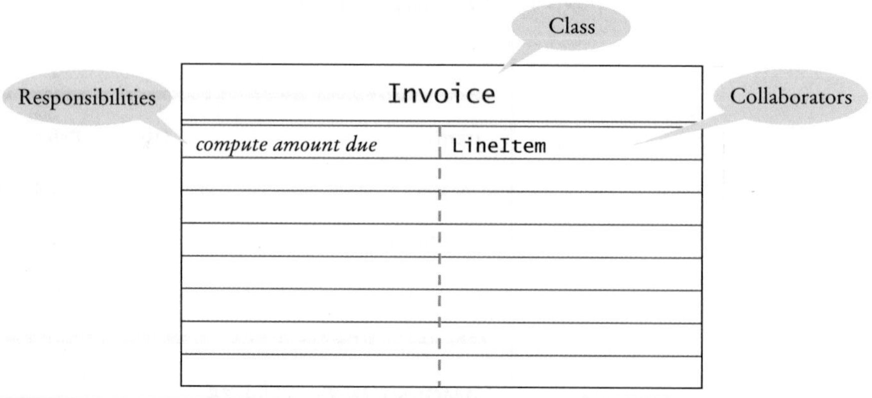

> A CRC card describes a class, its responsibilities, and its collaborating classes.

Figure 5 A CRC Card

classes with common properties, so that some responsibilities can be taken care of by a common superclass? Can you organize classes into clusters that are independent of each other? Finding class relationships and documenting them with diagrams is the topic of the next section.

SELF CHECK

4. Suppose the invoice is to be saved to a file. Name a likely collaborator.
5. Looking at the invoice in Figure 4, what is a likely responsibility of the Customer class?
6. What do you do if a CRC card has ten responsibilities?

11.3 Relationships Between Classes

When designing a program, it is useful to document the relationships between classes. This helps you in a number of ways. For example, if you find classes with common behavior, you can save effort by placing the common behavior into a superclass. If you know that some classes are *not* related to each other, you can assign different programmers to implement each of them, without worrying that one of them has to wait for the other.

You have seen the inheritance relationship between classes many times in this book. Inheritance is a very important relationship, but, as it turns out, it is not the only useful relationship, and it can be overused.

Inheritance is a relationship between a more general class (the superclass) and a more specialized class (the subclass). This relationship is often described as the *is-a* relationship. Every truck is a vehicle. Every savings account is a bank account. Every circle is an ellipse (with equal width and height).

> Inheritance (the *is-a* relationship) is sometimes inappropriately used when the *has-a* relationship would be more appropriate.

Inheritance is sometimes abused, however. For example, consider a Tire class that describes a car tire. Should the class Tire be a subclass of a class Circle? It sounds convenient. There are quite a few useful methods in the Circle class—for example, the Tire class may inherit methods that compute the radius, perimeter, and center point, which should come in handy when drawing tire shapes. Though it may be convenient for the programmer, this arrangement makes no sense conceptually. It isn't true that every tire is a circle. Tires are car parts, whereas circles are geometric objects. There is a relationship between tires and circles, though. A tire *has a* circle as its boundary. Java lets us model that *has-a* relationship, too. Use an instance variable:

```java
public class Tire
{
    private String rating;
    private Circle boundary;
    . . .
}
```

The technical term for this relationship is **aggregation**. Each Tire aggregates a Circle object. In general, a class aggregates another class if its objects have objects of the other class.

Aggregation (the *has-a* relationship) denotes that objects of one class contain references to objects of another class.

Here is another example. Every car *is a* vehicle. Every car *has a* tire (in fact, it has typically four or, if you count the spare, five). Thus, you would use inheritance from Vehicle and use aggregation of Tire objects:

```
public class Car extends Vehicle
{
    private Tire[] tires;
    . . .
}
```

In this book, we use the UML notation for class diagrams. You have already seen many examples of the UML notation for inheritance—an arrow with an open triangle pointing to the superclass. In the UML notation, aggregation is denoted by a solid line with a diamond-shaped symbol next to the aggregating class. Figure 6 shows a class diagram with an inheritance and an aggregation relationship.

Dependency is another name for the *uses* relationship.

The aggregation relationship is related to the **dependency** relationship, which you saw in Chapter 7. Recall that a class depends on another if one of its methods *uses* an object of the other class in some way.

For example, many of our applications depend on the Scanner class, because they use a Scanner object to read input.

You need to be able to distinguish the UML notations for inheritance, interface implementation, aggregation, and dependency.

Aggregation is a stronger form of dependency. If a class has objects of another class, it certainly uses the other class. However, the converse is not true. For example, a class may use the Scanner class without ever declaring an instance variable of class Scanner. The class may simply construct a local variable of type Scanner, or its methods may receive Scanner objects as parameters. This use is not aggregation because the objects of the class don't contain Scanner objects—they just create or receive them for the duration of a single method.

Generally, you need aggregation when an object needs to remember another object *between method calls.*

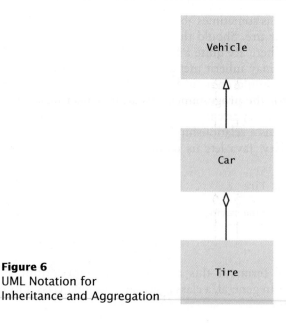

Figure 6
UML Notation for
Inheritance and Aggregation

As you saw in Chapter 7, the UML notation for dependency is a dashed line with an open arrow that points to the dependent class.

The arrows in the UML notation can get confusing. Table 1 shows a summary of the four UML relationship symbols that we use in this book.

Table 1	UML Relationship Symbols		
Relationship	Symbol	Line Style	Arrow Tip
Inheritance	——————▷	Solid	Triangle
Interface Implementation	--------▷	Dotted	Triangle
Aggregation	◇———————	Solid	Diamond
Dependency	-------→	Dotted	Open

SELF CHECK

7. Consider the Bank and BankAccount classes of Chapter 6. How are they related?

8. Consider the BankAccount and SavingsAccount objects of Chapter 9. How are they related?

9. Consider the BankAccountTester class of Chapter 2. Which classes does it depend on?

How To 11.1

CRC Cards and UML Diagrams

Before writing code for a complex problem, you need to design a solution. The methodology introduced in this chapter suggests that you follow a design process that is composed of the following tasks:

- Discover classes.
- Determine the responsibilities of each class.
- Describe the relationships between the classes.

CRC cards and UML diagrams help you discover and record this information.

Step 1 Discover classes.

Highlight the nouns in the problem description. Make a list of the nouns. Cross out those that don't seem to be reasonable candidates for classes.

Step 2 Discover responsibilities.

Make a list of the major tasks that your system needs to fulfill. From those tasks, pick one that is not trivial and that is intuitive to you. Find a class that is responsible for carrying out that task. Make an index card and write the name and the task on it. Now ask yourself how an object of the class can carry out the task. It probably needs help from other objects. Then make CRC cards for the classes to which those objects belong and write the responsibilities on them.

Don't be afraid to cross out, move, split, or merge responsibilities. Rip up cards if they become too messy. This is an informal process.

You are done when you have walked through all major tasks and are satisfied that they can all be solved with the classes and responsibilities that you discovered.

Step 3 Describe relationships.

Make a class diagram that shows the relationships between all the classes that you discovered.

Start with inheritance—the *is-a* relationship between classes. Is any class a specialization of another? If so, draw inheritance arrows. Keep in mind that many designs, especially for simple programs, don't use inheritance extensively.

The "collaborators" column of the CRC cards tell you which classes use others. Draw usage arrows for the collaborators on the CRC cards.

Some dependency relationships give rise to aggregations. For each of the dependency relationships, ask yourself: How does the object locate its collaborator? Does it navigate to it directly because it stores a reference? In that case, draw an aggregation arrow. Or is the collaborator a method parameter or return value? Then simply draw a dependency arrow.

Special Topic 11.1 – 11.3

UML Notation

Special Topics 11.1–11.3 discuss advanced features of the UML notation: attributes and methods in class diagrams, multiplicities, and the association relationship.

11.4 Case Study: Printing an Invoice

In this chapter, we discuss a five-part development process that is particularly well suited for beginning programmers:

1. Gather requirements.
2. Use CRC cards to find classes, responsibilities, and collaborators.
3. Use UML diagrams to record class relationships.
4. Use javadoc to document method behavior.
5. Implement your program.

There isn't a lot of notation to learn. The class diagrams are simple to draw. The deliverables of the design phase are obviously useful for the implementation phase—you simply take the source files and start adding the method code. Of course, as your projects get more complex, you will want to learn more about formal design methods. There are many techniques to describe object scenarios, call sequencing, the large-scale structure of programs, and so on, that are very beneficial even for relatively simple projects. *The Unified Modeling Language User Guide* gives a good overview of these techniques.

In this section, we will walk through the object-oriented design technique with a very simple example. In this case, the methodology may feel overblown, but it is a good introduction to the mechanics of each step. You will then be better prepared for the more complex example that follows.

11.4.1 Requirements

Start the
development process
by gathering and
documenting
program
requirements.

Before you begin designing a solution, you should gather all requirements for your program in plain English. Write down what your program should do. It is helpful to include typical scenarios in addition to a general description.

The task of our sample program is to print out an invoice. An invoice describes the charges for a set of products in certain quantities. (We omit complexities such as dates, taxes, and invoice and customer numbers.) The program simply prints the billing address, all line items, and the amount due. Each line item contains the description and unit price of a product, the quantity ordered, and the total price.

```
               I N V O I C E

    Sam's Small Appliances
    100 Main Street
    Anytown, CA 98765

    Description          Price  Qty  Total
    Toaster              29.95   3   89.85
    Hair dryer           24.95   1   24.95
    Car vacuum           19.99   2   39.98

    AMOUNT DUE: $154.78
```

Also, in the interest of simplicity, we do not provide a user interface. We just supply a test program that adds line items to the invoice and then prints it.

11.4.2 CRC Cards

Use CRC cards to
find classes,
responsibilities,
and collaborators.

When designing an object-oriented program, you need to discover classes. Classes correspond to nouns in the requirements description. In this problem, it is pretty obvious what the nouns are:

Invoice	Address
LineItem	Product
Description	Price
Quantity	Total
Amount due	

(Of course, Toaster doesn't count—it is the description of a LineItem object and therefore a data value, not the name of a class.)

Description and price are attributes of the Product class. What about the quantity? The quantity is not an attribute of a Product. Just as in the printed invoice, let's have a class LineItem that records the product and the quantity (such as "3 toasters").

The total and amount due are computed—not stored anywhere. Thus, they don't lead to classes.

After this process of elimination, we are left with four candidates for classes:

Invoice
Address
LineItem
Product

Each of them represents a useful concept, so let's make them all into classes.

The purpose of the program is to print an invoice. However, the Invoice class won't necessarily know whether to display the output in System.out, in a text area, or in a file. Therefore, let's relax the task slightly and make the invoice responsible for *formatting* the invoice. The result is a string (containing multiple lines) that can be printed out or displayed. Record that responsibility on a CRC card:

Invoice	
format the invoice	

How does an invoice format itself? It must format the billing address, format all line items, and then add the amount due. How can the invoice format an address? It can't—that really is the responsibility of the Address class. This leads to a second CRC card:

Address	
format the address	

Similarly, formatting of a line item is the responsibility of the LineItem class.

The format method of the Invoice class calls the format methods of the Address and LineItem classes. Whenever a method uses another class, you list that other class as a collaborator. In other words, Address and LineItem are collaborators of Invoice:

Invoice	
format the invoice	Address
	LineItem

When formatting the invoice, the invoice also needs to compute the total amount due. To obtain that amount, it must ask each line item about the total price of the item.

How does a line item obtain that total? It must ask the product for the unit price, and then multiply it by the quantity. That is, the Product class must reveal the unit price, and it is a collaborator of the LineItem class.

Finally, the invoice must be populated with products and quantities, so that it makes sense to format the result. That too is a responsibility of the Invoice class.

We now have a set of CRC cards that completes the CRC card process.

Product	
get description	
get unit price	

LineItem	
format the item	Product
get total price	

Invoice	
format the invoice	Address
add a product and quantity	LineItem
	Product

11.4.3 UML Diagrams

Use UML diagrams to record class relationships.

After you have discovered classes and their relationships with CRC cards, you should record your findings in UML diagrams. The dependency relationships come from the collaboration column on the CRC cards. Each class depends on the classes with which it collaborates. In our example, the Invoice class collaborates with the Address, LineItem, and Product classes. The LineItem class collaborates with the Product class.

Now ask yourself which of these dependencies are actually aggregations. How does an invoice know about the address, line item, and product objects with which it collaborates? An invoice object must hold references to the address and the line items when it formats the invoice. But an invoice object need not hold a reference to a product object when adding a product. The product is turned into a line item, and then it is the item's responsibility to hold a reference to it.

Therefore, the `Invoice` class aggregates the `Address` and `LineItem` classes. The `LineItem` class aggregates the `Product` class. However, there is no *has-a* relationship between an invoice and a product. An invoice doesn't store products directly—they are stored in the `LineItem` objects.

There is no inheritance in this example.

Figure 7 shows the class relationships that we discovered.

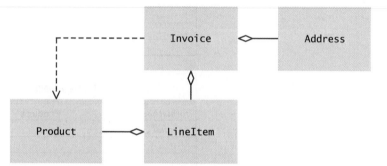

Figure 7 The Relationships Between the Invoice Classes

11.4.4 Method Documentation

> Use javadoc comments (with the method bodies left blank) to record the behavior of classes.

The final step of the design phase is to write the documentation of the discovered classes and methods. Simply write a Java source file for each class, write the method comments for those methods that you have discovered, and leave the bodies of the methods blank.

```
/**
    Describes an invoice for a set of purchased products.
*/
public class Invoice
{
    /**
        Adds a charge for a product to this invoice.
        @param aProduct  the product that the customer ordered
        @param quantity  the quantity of the product
    */
    public void add(Product aProduct, int quantity)
    {
    }

    /**
        Formats the invoice.
        @return  the formatted invoice
    */
    public String format()
    {
```

```java
    }
}

/**
    Describes a quantity of an article to purchase.
*/
public class LineItem
{
    /**
        Computes the total cost of this line item.
        @return the total price
    */
    public double getTotalPrice()
    {
    }

    /**
        Formats this item.
        @return a formatted string of this item
    */
    public String format()
    {
    }
}

/**
    Describes a product with a description and a price.
*/
public class Product
{
    /**
        Gets the product description.
        @return the description
    */
    public String getDescription()
    {
    }

    /**
        Gets the product price.
        @return the unit price
    */
    public double getPrice()
    {
    }
}

/**
    Describes a mailing address.
*/
public class Address
{
    /**
        Formats the address.
        @return the address as a string with three lines
    */
    public String format()
    {
    }
}
```

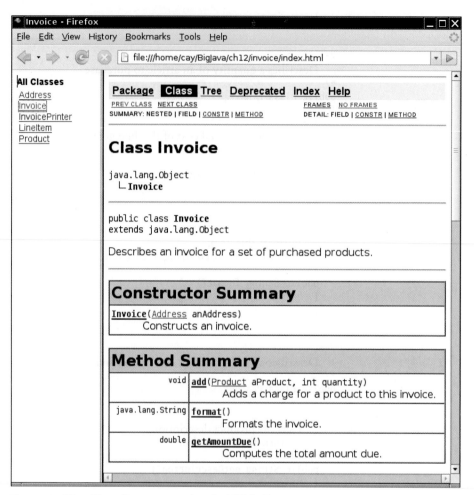

Figure 8 The Class Documentation in HTML Format

Then run the javadoc program to obtain a prettily formatted version of your documentation in HTML format (see Figure 8).

This approach for documenting your classes has a number of advantages. You can share the HTML documentation with others if you work in a team. You use a format that is immediately useful—Java source files that you can carry into the implementation phase. And, most importantly, you supply the comments of the key methods—a task that less prepared programmers leave for later, and then often neglect for lack of time.

11.4.5 Implementation

After completing the design, implement your classes.

After you have completed the object-oriented design, you are ready to implement the classes.

You already have the method parameters and comments from the previous step. Now look at the UML diagram to add instance variables. Aggregated classes yield instance variables. Start with the Invoice class. An invoice aggregates Address and

LineItem. Every invoice has one billing address, but it can have many line items. To store multiple LineItem objects, you can use an array list. Now you have the instance variables of the Invoice class:

```java
public class Invoice
{
   private Address billingAddress;
   private ArrayList<LineItem> items;
   . . .
}
```

A line item needs to store a Product object and the product quantity. That leads to the following instance variables:

```java
public class LineItem
{
   private int quantity;
   private Product theProduct;
   . . .
}
```

The methods themselves are now easy to implement. Here is a typical example. You already know what the getTotalPrice method of the LineItem class needs to do—get the unit price of the product and multiply it with the quantity.

```java
/**
   Computes the total cost of this line item.
   @return the total price
*/
public double getTotalPrice()
{
   return theProduct.getPrice() * quantity;
}
```

We will not discuss the other methods in detail—they are equally straightforward.

Finally, you need to supply constructors, another routine task.

Here is the entire program. It is a good practice to go through it in detail and match up the classes and methods against the CRC cards and UML diagram.

ch11/invoice/InvoicePrinter.java

```java
1   /**
2      This program demonstrates the invoice classes by
3      printing a sample invoice.
4   */
5   public class InvoicePrinter
6   {
7      public static void main(String[] args)
8      {
9         Address samsAddress
10           = new Address("Sam's Small Appliances",
11           "100 Main Street", "Anytown", "CA", "98765");
12
13        Invoice samsInvoice = new Invoice(samsAddress);
14        samsInvoice.add(new Product("Toaster", 29.95), 3);
15        samsInvoice.add(new Product("Hair dryer", 24.95), 1);
16        samsInvoice.add(new Product("Car vacuum", 19.99), 2);
17
18        System.out.println(samsInvoice.format());
19     }
20  }
```

ch11/invoice/Invoice.java

```java
1   import java.util.ArrayList;
2
3   /**
4       Describes an invoice for a set of purchased products.
5   */
6   public class Invoice
7   {
8       private Address billingAddress;
9       private ArrayList<LineItem> items;
10
11      /**
12          Constructs an invoice.
13          @param anAddress the billing address
14      */
15      public Invoice(Address anAddress)
16      {
17          items = new ArrayList<LineItem>();
18          billingAddress = anAddress;
19      }
20
21      /**
22          Adds a charge for a product to this invoice.
23          @param aProduct the product that the customer ordered
24          @param quantity the quantity of the product
25      */
26      public void add(Product aProduct, int quantity)
27      {
28          LineItem anItem = new LineItem(aProduct, quantity);
29          items.add(anItem);
30      }
31
32      /**
33          Formats the invoice.
34          @return the formatted invoice
35      */
36      public String format()
37      {
38          String r = "                       I N V O I C E\n\n"
39              + billingAddress.format()
40              + String.format("\n\n%-30s%8s%5s%8s\n",
41              "Description", "Price", "Qty", "Total");
42
43          for (LineItem item : items)
44          {
45              r = r + item.format() + "\n";
46          }
47
48          r = r + String.format("\nAMOUNT DUE: $%8.2f", getAmountDue());
49
50          return r;
51      }
52
```

```
53      /**
54          Computes the total amount due.
55          @return the amount due
56      */
57      public double getAmountDue()
58      {
59          double amountDue = 0;
60          for (LineItem item : items)
61          {
62              amountDue = amountDue + item.getTotalPrice();
63          }
64          return amountDue;
65      }
66  }
```

ch11/invoice/LineItem.java

```
1   /**
2       Describes a quantity of an article to purchase.
3   */
4   public class LineItem
5   {
6       private int quantity;
7       private Product theProduct;
8
9       /**
10          Constructs an item from the product and quantity.
11          @param aProduct the product
12          @param aQuantity the item quantity
13      */
14      public LineItem(Product aProduct, int aQuantity)
15      {
16          theProduct = aProduct;
17          quantity = aQuantity;
18      }
19
20      /**
21          Computes the total cost of this line item.
22          @return the total price
23      */
24      public double getTotalPrice()
25      {
26          return theProduct.getPrice() * quantity;
27      }
28
29      /**
30          Formats this item.
31          @return a formatted string of this line item
32      */
33      public String format()
34      {
35          return String.format("%-30s%8.2f%5d%8.2f",
36              theProduct.getDescription(), theProduct.getPrice(),
37              quantity, getTotalPrice());
38      }
39  }
```

ch11/invoice/Product.java

```java
1   /**
2       Describes a product with a description and a price.
3   */
4   public class Product
5   {
6       private String description;
7       private double price;
8
9       /**
10          Constructs a product from a description and a price.
11          @param aDescription the product description
12          @param aPrice the product price
13      */
14      public Product(String aDescription, double aPrice)
15      {
16          description = aDescription;
17          price = aPrice;
18      }
19
20      /**
21          Gets the product description.
22          @return the description
23      */
24      public String getDescription()
25      {
26          return description;
27      }
28
29      /**
30          Gets the product price.
31          @return the unit price
32      */
33      public double getPrice()
34      {
35          return price;
36      }
37  }
```

ch11/invoice/Address.java

```java
1   /**
2       Describes a mailing address.
3   */
4   public class Address
5   {
6       private String name;
7       private String street;
8       private String city;
9       private String state;
10      private String zip;
11
12      /**
13          Constructs a mailing address.
14          @param aName the recipient name
15          @param aStreet the street
16          @param aCity the city
```

```
17        @param aState  the two-letter state code
18        @param aZip  the ZIP postal code
19     */
20     public Address(String aName, String aStreet,
21           String aCity, String aState, String aZip)
22     {
23        name = aName;
24        street = aStreet;
25        city = aCity;
26        state = aState;
27        zip = aZip;
28     }
29
30     /**
31        Formats the address.
32        @return  the address as a string with three lines
33     */
34     public String format()
35     {
36        return name + "\n" + street + "\n"
37              + city + ", " + state + " " + zip;
38     }
39  }
```

SELF CHECK

10. Which class is responsible for computing the amount due? What are its collaborators for this task?

11. Why do the format methods return String objects instead of directly printing to System.out?

11.5 Case Study: An Automatic Teller Machine

11.5.1 Requirements

The purpose of this project is to design a simulation of an automatic teller machine (ATM). The ATM is used by the customers of a bank. Each customer has two accounts: a checking account and a savings account. Each customer also has a customer number and a personal identification number (PIN); both are required to gain access to the accounts. (In a real ATM, the customer number would be recorded on the magnetic strip of the ATM card. In this simulation, the customer will need to type it in.) With the ATM, customers can select an account (checking or savings). The balance of the selected account is displayed. Then the customer can deposit and withdraw money. This process is repeated until the customer chooses to exit.

The details of the user interaction depend on the user interface that we choose for the simulation. We will develop two separate interfaces: a graphical interface that closely mimics an actual ATM (see Figure 9), and a text-based interface that allows you to test the ATM and bank classes without being distracted by GUI programming.

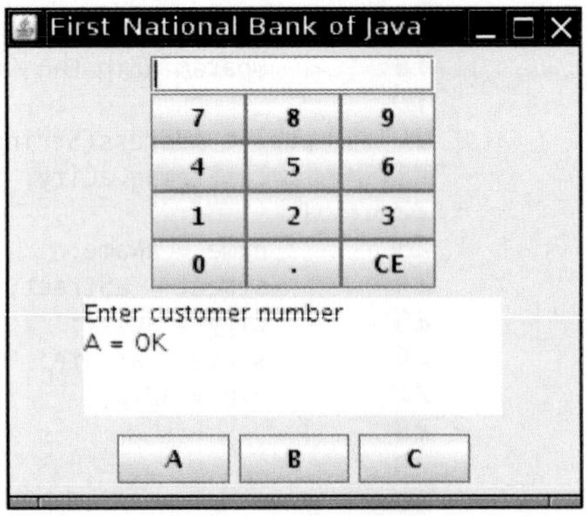

Figure 9
Graphical User Interface
for the Automatic Teller Machine

In the GUI interface, the ATM has a keypad to enter numbers, a display to show messages, and a set of buttons, labeled A, B, and C, whose function depends on the state of the machine.

Specifically, the user interaction is as follows. When the ATM starts up, it expects a user to enter a customer number. The display shows the following message:

```
Enter customer number
A = OK
```

The user enters the customer number on the keypad and presses the A button. The display message changes to

```
Enter PIN
A = OK
```

Next, the user enters the PIN and presses the A button again. If the customer number and ID match those of one of the customers in the bank, then the customer can proceed. If not, the user is again prompted to enter the customer number.

If the customer has been authorized to use the system, then the display message changes to

```
Select Account
A = Checking
B = Savings
C = Exit
```

If the user presses the C button, the ATM reverts to its original state and asks the next user to enter a customer number.

If the user presses the A or B buttons, the ATM remembers the selected account, and the display message changes to

```
Balance = balance of selected account
Enter amount and select transaction
A = Withdraw
B = Deposit
C = Cancel
```

If the user presses the A or B buttons, the value entered in the keypad is withdrawn from or deposited into the selected account. (This is just a simulation, so no money is dispensed and no deposit is accepted.) Afterwards, the ATM reverts to the preceding state, allowing the user to select another account or to exit.

If the user presses the C button, the ATM reverts to the preceding state without executing any transaction.

In the text-based interaction, we read input from System.in instead of the buttons. Here is a typical dialog:

```
Enter account number: 1
Enter PIN: 1234
A=Checking, B=Savings, C=Quit: A
Balance=0.0
A=Deposit, B=Withdrawal, C=Cancel: A
Amount: 1000
A=Checking, B=Savings, C=Quit: C
```

In our solution, only the user interface classes are affected by the choice of user interface. The remainder of the classes can be used for both solutions—they are decoupled from the user interface.

Because this is a simulation, the ATM does not actually communicate with a bank. It simply loads a set of customer numbers and PINs from a file. All accounts are initialized with a zero balance.

11.5.2 CRC Cards

We will again follow the recipe of Section 11.2 and show how to discover classes, responsibilities, and relationships and how to obtain a detailed design for the ATM program.

Recall that the first rule for finding classes is "Look for nouns in the problem description". Here is a list of the nouns:

```
ATM
User
Keypad
Display
Display message
Button
State
Bank account
Checking account
Savings account
Customer
Customer number
PIN
Bank
```

Of course, not all of these nouns will become names of classes, and we may yet discover the need for classes that aren't in this list, but it is a good start.

Users and customers represent the same concept in this program. Let's use a class Customer. A customer has two bank accounts, and we will require that a Customer object should be able to locate these accounts. (Another possible design would make the Bank class responsible for locating the accounts of a given customer—see Exercise P11.9.)

A customer also has a customer number and a PIN. We can, of course, require that a customer object give us the customer number and the PIN. But perhaps that isn't so secure. Instead, simply require that a customer object, when given a customer number and a PIN, will tell us whether it matches its own information or not.

Customer
get accounts
match number and PIN

A bank contains a collection of customers. When a user walks up to the ATM and enters a customer number and PIN, it is the job of the bank to find the matching customer. How can the bank do this? It needs to check for each customer whether its customer number and PIN match. Thus, it needs to call the *match number and PIN* method of the Customer class that we just discovered. Because the *find customer* method calls a Customer method, it collaborates with the Customer class. We record that fact in the right-hand column of the CRC card.

When the simulation starts up, the bank must also be able to read account information from a file.

Bank	
find customer	Customer
read customers	

The BankAccount class is our familiar class with methods to get the balance and to deposit and withdraw money.

In this program there is nothing that distinguishes checking accounts from savings accounts. The ATM does not add interest or deduct fees. Therefore, we decide not to implement separate subclasses for checking and savings accounts.

Finally, we are left with the ATM class itself. An important notion of the ATM is the **state**. The current machine state determines the text of the prompts and the function of the buttons. For example, when you first log in, you use the A and B buttons to select an account. Next, you use the same buttons to choose between deposit and withdrawal. The ATM must remember the current state so that it can correctly interpret the buttons.

There are four states:

1. START: Enter customer ID

2. PIN: Enter PIN

3. ACCOUNT: Select account

4. TRANSACT: Select transaction

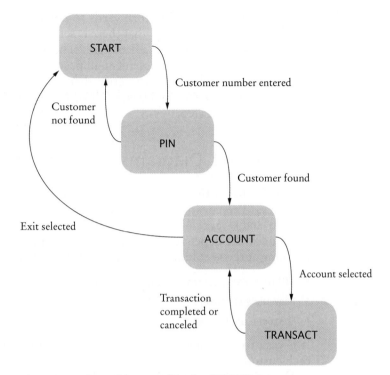

Figure 10 State Diagram for the ATM Class

To understand how to move from one state to the next, it is useful to draw a **state diagram** (Figure 10). The UML notation has standardized shapes for state diagrams. Draw states as rectangles with rounded corners. Draw state changes as arrows, with labels that indicate the reason for the change.

The user must type a valid customer number and PIN. Then the ATM can ask the bank to find the customer. This calls for a *select customer* method. It collaborates with the bank, asking the bank for the customer that matches the customer number and PIN. Next, there must be a *select account* method that asks the current customer for the checking or savings account. Finally, the ATM must carry out the selected transaction on the current account.

ATM	
manage state	Customer
select customer	Bank
select account	BankAccount
execute transaction	

Of course, discovering these classes and methods was not as neat and orderly as it appears from this discussion. When I designed these classes for this book, it took me several trials and many torn cards to come up with a satisfactory design. It is also important to remember that there is seldom one best design.

This design has several advantages. The classes describe clear concepts. The methods are sufficient to implement all necessary tasks. (I mentally walked through every ATM usage scenario to verify that.) There are not too many collaboration dependencies between the classes. Thus, I was satisfied with this design and proceeded to the next step.

11.5.3 UML Diagrams

Figure 11 shows the relationships between these classes, using the graphical user interface. (The console user interface uses a single class ATMSimulator instead of the ATMFrame and Keypad classes.)

To draw the dependencies, use the "collaborator" columns from the CRC cards. Looking at those columns, you find that the dependencies are as follows:

- ATM uses Bank, Customer, and BankAccount.
- Bank uses Customer.
- Customer uses BankAccount.

It is easy to see some of the aggregation relationships. A bank has customers, and each customer has two bank accounts.

Does the ATM class aggregate Bank? To answer this question, ask yourself whether an ATM object needs to store a reference to a bank object. Does it need to locate the same bank object across multiple method calls? Indeed it does. Therefore, aggregation is the appropriate relationship.

Does an ATM aggregate customers? Clearly, the ATM is not responsible for storing all of the bank's customers. That's the bank's job. But in our design, the ATM remembers the *current* customer. If a customer has logged in, subsequent commands refer to the same customer. The ATM needs to either store a reference to the customer, or ask the bank to look up the object whenever it needs the current

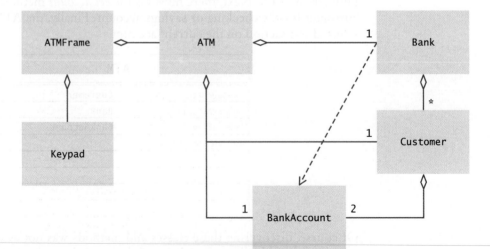

Figure 11 Relationships Between the ATM Classes

customer. It is a design decision: either store the object, or look it up when needed. We will decide to store the current customer object. That is, we will use aggregation. Note that the choice of aggregation is not an automatic consequence of the problem description—it is a design decision.

Similarly, we will decide to store the current bank account (checking or savings) that the user selects. Therefore, we have an aggregation relationship between ATM and BankAccount.

The class diagram is a good tool to visualize dependencies. Look at the GUI classes. They are completely independent from the rest of the ATM system. You can replace the GUI with a console interface, and you can take out the Keypad class and use it in another application. Also, the Bank, BankAccount, and Customer classes, although dependent on each other, don't know anything about the ATM class. That makes sense—you can have banks without ATMs. As you can see, when you analyze relationships, you look for both the absence and presence of relationships.

11.5.4 Method Documentation

Now you are ready for the final step of the design phase: documenting the classes and methods that you discovered. Here is a part of the documentation for the ATM class:

```java
/**
    An ATM that accesses a bank.
*/
public class ATM
{
   . . .
   /**
      Constructs an ATM for a given bank.
      @param aBank  the bank to which this ATM connects
   */
   public ATM(Bank aBank) { }

   /**
      Sets the current customer number
      and sets state to PIN.
      (Precondition: state is START)
      @param number  the customer number
   */
   public void setCustomerNumber(int number) { }

   /**
      Finds customer in bank.
      If found sets state to ACCOUNT, else to START.
      (Precondition: state is PIN)
      @param pin  the PIN of the current customer
   */
   public void selectCustomer(int pin) { }

   /**
      Sets current account to checking or savings. Sets
      state to TRANSACT.
      (Precondition: state is ACCOUNT or TRANSACT)
      @param account  one of CHECKING or SAVINGS
   */
   public void selectAccount(int account) { }
```

```
/**
    Withdraws amount from current account.
    (Precondition: state is TRANSACT)
    @param value the amount to withdraw
*/
public void withdraw(double value) { }
}
```

Then run the `javadoc` utility to turn this documentation into HTML format.

For conciseness, we omit the documentation of the other classes.

11.5.5 Implementation

Finally, the time has come to implement the ATM simulator. The implementation phase is very straightforward and should take *much less time than the design phase.*

A good strategy for implementing the classes is to go "bottom-up". Start with the classes that don't depend on others, such as `Keypad` and `BankAccount`. Then implement a class such as `Customer` that depends only on the `BankAccount` class. This "bottom-up" approach allows you to test your classes individually. You will find the implementations of these classes at the end of this section.

The most complex class is the `ATM` class. In order to implement the methods, you need to declare the necessary instance variables. From the class diagram, you can tell that the ATM has a bank object. It becomes an instance variable of the class:

```
public class ATM
{
    private Bank theBank;
    . . .
}
```

From the description of the ATM states, it is clear that we require additional instance variables to store the current state, customer, and bank account.

```
public class ATM
{
    private int state;
    private Customer currentCustomer;
    private BankAccount currentAccount;
    . . .
}
```

Most methods are very straightforward to implement. Consider the `selectCustomer` method. From the design documentation, we have the description

```
/**
    Finds customer in bank.
    If found sets state to ACCOUNT, else to START.
    (Precondition: state is PIN)
    @param pin the PIN of the current customer
*/
```

This description can be almost literally translated to Java instructions:

```
public void selectCustomer(int pin)
{
    assert state == PIN;
    currentCustomer = theBank.findCustomer(customerNumber, pin);
```

```
      if (currentCustomer == null)
         state = START;
      else
         state = ACCOUNT;
   }
```

We won't go through a method-by-method description of the ATM program. You should take some time and compare the actual implementation against the CRC cards and the UML diagram.

ch11/atm/ATM.java

```
1   /**
2       An ATM that accesses a bank.
3   */
4   public class ATM
5   {
6      public static final int CHECKING = 1;
7      public static final int SAVINGS = 2;
8
9      private int state;
10     private int customerNumber;
11     private Customer currentCustomer;
12     private BankAccount currentAccount;
13     private Bank theBank;
14
15     public static final int START = 1;
16     public static final int PIN = 2;
17     public static final int ACCOUNT = 3;
18     public static final int TRANSACT = 4;
19
20     /**
21         Constructs an ATM for a given bank.
22         @param aBank  the bank to which this ATM connects
23     */
24     public ATM(Bank aBank)
25     {
26        theBank = aBank;
27        reset();
28     }
29
30     /**
31         Resets the ATM to the initial state.
32     */
33     public void reset()
34     {
35        customerNumber = -1;
36        currentAccount = null;
37        state = START;
38     }
39
40     /**
41         Sets the current customer number
42         and sets state to PIN.
43         (Precondition: state is START)
44         @param number  the customer number
45     */
46     public void setCustomerNumber(int number)
47     {
```

```
48        assert state == START;
49        customerNumber = number;
50        state = PIN;
51     }
52
53     /**
54        Finds customer in bank.
55        If found, sets state to ACCOUNT, else to START.
56        (Precondition: state is PIN)
57        @param pin the PIN of the current customer
58     */
59     public void selectCustomer(int pin)
60     {
61        assert state == PIN;
62        currentCustomer = theBank.findCustomer(customerNumber, pin);
63        if (currentCustomer == null)
64           state = START;
65        else
66           state = ACCOUNT;
67     }
68
69     /**
70        Sets current account to checking or savings. Sets
71        state to TRANSACT.
72        (Precondition: state is ACCOUNT or TRANSACT)
73        @param account one of CHECKING or SAVINGS
74     */
75     public void selectAccount(int account)
76     {
77        assert state == ACCOUNT || state == TRANSACT;
78        if (account == CHECKING)
79           currentAccount = currentCustomer.getCheckingAccount();
80        else
81           currentAccount = currentCustomer.getSavingsAccount();
82        state = TRANSACT;
83     }
84
85     /**
86        Withdraws amount from current account.
87        (Precondition: state is TRANSACT)
88        @param value the amount to withdraw
89     */
90     public void withdraw(double value)
91     {
92        assert state == TRANSACT;
93        currentAccount.withdraw(value);
94     }
95
96     /**
97        Deposits amount to current account.
98        (Precondition: state is TRANSACT)
99        @param value the amount to deposit
100    */
101    public void deposit(double value)
102    {
103       assert state == TRANSACT;
104       currentAccount.deposit(value);
105    }
106
```

```
107    /**
108       Gets the balance of the current account.
109       (Precondition: state is TRANSACT)
110       @return the balance
111    */
112    public double getBalance()
113    {
114       assert state == TRANSACT;
115       return currentAccount.getBalance();
116    }
117
118    /**
119       Moves back to the previous state.
120    */
121    public void back()
122    {
123       if (state == TRANSACT)
124          state = ACCOUNT;
125       else if (state == ACCOUNT)
126          state = PIN;
127       else if (state == PIN)
128          state = START;
129    }
130
131    /**
132       Gets the current state of this ATM.
133       @return the current state
134    */
135    public int getState()
136    {
137       return state;
138    }
139 }
```

ch11/atm/Bank.java

```
1   import java.io.File;
2   import java.io.IOException;
3   import java.util.ArrayList;
4   import java.util.Scanner;
5
6   /**
7      A bank contains customers with bank accounts.
8   */
9   public class Bank
10  {
11     private ArrayList<Customer> customers;
12
13     /**
14        Constructs a bank with no customers.
15     */
16     public Bank()
17     {
18        customers = new ArrayList<Customer>();
19     }
20
```

```
21    /**
22        Reads the customer numbers and pins
23        and initializes the bank accounts.
24        @param filename the name of the customer file
25    */
26    public void readCustomers(String filename)
27          throws IOException
28    {
29        Scanner in = new Scanner(new File(filename));
30        while (in.hasNext())
31        {
32           int number = in.nextInt();
33           int pin = in.nextInt();
34           Customer c = new Customer(number, pin);
35           addCustomer(c);
36        }
37        in.close();
38    }
39
40    /**
41        Adds a customer to the bank.
42        @param c the customer to add
43    */
44    public void addCustomer(Customer c)
45    {
46        customers.add(c);
47    }
48
49    /**
50        Finds a customer in the bank.
51        @param aNumber a customer number
52        @param aPin a personal identification number
53        @return the matching customer, or null if no customer
54        matches
55    */
56    public Customer findCustomer(int aNumber, int aPin)
57    {
58        for (Customer c : customers)
59        {
60           if (c.match(aNumber, aPin))
61              return c;
62        }
63        return null;
64    }
65 }
```

ch11/atm/Customer.java

```
1    /**
2        A bank customer with a checking and a savings account.
3    */
4    public class Customer
5    {
6        private int customerNumber;
7        private int pin;
8        private BankAccount checkingAccount;
9        private BankAccount savingsAccount;
10
```

```
11      /**
12          Constructs a customer with a given number and PIN.
13          @param aNumber the customer number
14          @param aPin the personal identification number
15      */
16      public Customer(int aNumber, int aPin)
17      {
18          customerNumber = aNumber;
19          pin = aPin;
20          checkingAccount = new BankAccount();
21          savingsAccount = new BankAccount();
22      }
23
24      /**
25          Tests if this customer matches a customer number
26          and PIN.
27          @param aNumber a customer number
28          @param aPin a personal identification number
29          @return true if the customer number and PIN match
30      */
31      public boolean match(int aNumber, int aPin)
32      {
33          return customerNumber == aNumber && pin == aPin;
34      }
35
36      /**
37          Gets the checking account of this customer.
38          @return the checking account
39      */
40      public BankAccount getCheckingAccount()
41      {
42          return checkingAccount;
43      }
44
45      /**
46          Gets the savings account of this customer.
47          @return the checking account
48      */
49      public BankAccount getSavingsAccount()
50      {
51          return savingsAccount;
52      }
53 }
```

The following class implements a console user interface for the ATM.

ch11/atm/ATMSimulator.java

```
1   import java.io.IOException;
2   import java.util.Scanner;
3
4   /**
5       A text-based simulation of an automatic teller machine.
6   */
7   public class ATMSimulator
8   {
9       public static void main(String[] args)
10      {
11          ATM theATM;
```

```
12     try
13     {
14        Bank theBank = new Bank();
15        theBank.readCustomers("customers.txt");
16        theATM = new ATM(theBank);
17     }
18     catch(IOException e)
19     {
20        System.out.println("Error opening accounts file.");
21        return;
22     }
23
24     Scanner in = new Scanner(System.in);
25
26     while (true)
27     {
28        int state = theATM.getState();
29        if (state == ATM.START)
30        {
31           System.out.print("Enter customer number: ");
32           int number = in.nextInt();
33           theATM.setCustomerNumber(number);
34        }
35        else if (state == ATM.PIN)
36        {
37           System.out.print("Enter PIN: ");
38           int pin = in.nextInt();
39           theATM.selectCustomer(pin);
40        }
41        else if (state == ATM.ACCOUNT)
42        {
43           System.out.print("A=Checking, B=Savings, C=Quit: ");
44           String command = in.next();
45           if (command.equalsIgnoreCase("A"))
46              theATM.selectAccount(ATM.CHECKING);
47           else if (command.equalsIgnoreCase("B"))
48              theATM.selectAccount(ATM.SAVINGS);
49           else if (command.equalsIgnoreCase("C"))
50              theATM.reset();
51           else
52                 System.out.println("Illegal input!");
53        }
54        else if (state == ATM.TRANSACT)
55        {
56           System.out.println("Balance=" + theATM.getBalance());
57           System.out.print("A=Deposit, B=Withdrawal, C=Cancel: ");
58           String command = in.next();
59           if (command.equalsIgnoreCase("A"))
60           {
61              System.out.print("Amount: ");
62              double amount = in.nextDouble();
63              theATM.deposit(amount);
64              theATM.back();
65           }
66           else if (command.equalsIgnoreCase("B"))
67           {
68              System.out.print("Amount: ");
69              double amount = in.nextDouble();
```

```
70                    theATM.withdraw(amount);
71                    theATM.back();
72                 }
73                 else if (command.equalsIgnoreCase("C"))
74                    theATM.back();
75                 else
76                    System.out.println("Illegal input!");
77              }
78           }
79        }
80 }
```

Program Run

```
Enter account number: 1
Enter PIN: 1234
A=Checking, B=Savings, C=Quit: A
Balance=0.0
A=Deposit, B=Withdrawal, C=Cancel: A
Amount: 1000
A=Checking, B=Savings, C=Quit: C
. . .
```

Here are the user interface classes for the GUI version of the user interface.

ch11/atm/ATMViewer.java

```java
 1  import java.io.IOException;
 2  import javax.swing.JFrame;
 3  import javax.swing.JOptionPane;
 4
 5  /**
 6     A graphical simulation of an automatic teller machine.
 7  */
 8  public class ATMViewer
 9  {
10     public static void main(String[] args)
11     {
12        ATM theATM;
13
14        try
15        {
16           Bank theBank = new Bank();
17           theBank.readCustomers("customers.txt");
18           theATM = new ATM(theBank);
19        }
20        catch(IOException e)
21        {
22           JOptionPane.showMessageDialog(null, "Error opening accounts file.");
23           return;
24        }
25
26        JFrame frame = new ATMFrame(theATM);
27        frame.setTitle("First National Bank of Java");
28        frame.setDefaultCloseOperation(JFrame.EXIT_ON_CLOSE);
29        frame.setVisible(true);
30     }
31  }
```

ch11/atm/ATMFrame.java

```java
1    import java.awt.FlowLayout;
2    import java.awt.GridLayout;
3    import java.awt.event.ActionEvent;
4    import java.awt.event.ActionListener;
5    import javax.swing.JButton;
6    import javax.swing.JFrame;
7    import javax.swing.JPanel;
8    import javax.swing.JTextArea;
9
10   /**
11      A frame displaying the components of an ATM.
12   */
13   public class ATMFrame extends JFrame
14   {
15      private static final int FRAME_WIDTH = 300;
16      private static final int FRAME_HEIGHT = 300;
17
18      private JButton aButton;
19      private JButton bButton;
20      private JButton cButton;
21
22      private KeyPad pad;
23      private JTextArea display;
24
25      private ATM theATM;
26
27      /**
28         Constructs the user interface of the ATM frame.
29      */
30      public ATMFrame(ATM anATM)
31      {
32         theATM = anATM;
33
34         // Construct components
35         pad = new KeyPad();
36
37         display = new JTextArea(4, 20);
38
39         aButton = new JButton(" A ");
40         aButton.addActionListener(new AButtonListener());
41
42         bButton = new JButton(" B ");
43         bButton.addActionListener(new BButtonListener());
44
45         cButton = new JButton(" C ");
46         cButton.addActionListener(new CButtonListener());
47
48         // Add components
49
50         JPanel buttonPanel = new JPanel();
51         buttonPanel.add(aButton);
52         buttonPanel.add(bButton);
53         buttonPanel.add(cButton);
54
55         setLayout(new FlowLayout());
56         add(pad);
57         add(display);
```

```java
58        add(buttonPanel);
59        showState();
60
61        setSize(FRAME_WIDTH, FRAME_HEIGHT);
62     }
63
64     /**
65        Updates display message.
66     */
67     public void showState()
68     {
69        int state = theATM.getState();
70        pad.clear();
71        if (state == ATM.START)
72           display.setText("Enter customer number\nA = OK");
73        else if (state == ATM.PIN)
74           display.setText("Enter PIN\nA = OK");
75        else if (state == ATM.ACCOUNT)
76           display.setText("Select Account\n"
77              + "A = Checking\nB = Savings\nC = Exit");
78        else if (state == ATM.TRANSACT)
79           display.setText("Balance = "
80              + theATM.getBalance()
81              + "\nEnter amount and select transaction\n"
82              + "A = Withdraw\nB = Deposit\nC = Cancel");
83     }
84
85     class AButtonListener implements ActionListener
86     {
87        public void actionPerformed(ActionEvent event)
88        {
89           int state = theATM.getState();
90           if (state == ATM.START)
91              theATM.setCustomerNumber((int) pad.getValue());
92           else if (state == ATM.PIN)
93              theATM.selectCustomer((int) pad.getValue());
94           else if (state == ATM.ACCOUNT)
95              theATM.selectAccount(ATM.CHECKING);
96           else if (state == ATM.TRANSACT)
97           {
98              theATM.withdraw(pad.getValue());
99              theATM.back();
100          }
101          showState();
102       }
103    }
104
105    class BButtonListener implements ActionListener
106    {
107       public void actionPerformed(ActionEvent event)
108       {
109          int state = theATM.getState();
110          if (state == ATM.ACCOUNT)
111             theATM.selectAccount(ATM.SAVINGS);
112          else if (state == ATM.TRANSACT)
113          {
114             theATM.deposit(pad.getValue());
115             theATM.back();
```

```
116          }
117          showState();
118        }
119    }
120
121    class CButtonListener implements ActionListener
122    {
123        public void actionPerformed(ActionEvent event)
124        {
125            int state = theATM.getState();
126            if (state == ATM.ACCOUNT)
127                theATM.reset();
128            else if (state == ATM.TRANSACT)
129                theATM.back();
130            showState();
131        }
132    }
133 }
```

This class uses layout managers to arrange the text field and the keypad buttons. See Chapter 17 for more information about layout managers.

ch11/atm/KeyPad.java

```java
1    import java.awt.BorderLayout;
2    import java.awt.GridLayout;
3    import java.awt.event.ActionEvent;
4    import java.awt.event.ActionListener;
5    import javax.swing.JButton;
6    import javax.swing.JPanel;
7    import javax.swing.JTextField;
8
9    /**
10       A component that lets the user enter a number, using
11       a keypad labeled with digits.
12    */
13    public class KeyPad extends JPanel
14    {
15        private JPanel buttonPanel;
16        private JButton clearButton;
17        private JTextField display;
18
19        /**
20           Constructs the keypad panel.
21        */
22        public KeyPad()
23        {
24            setLayout(new BorderLayout());
25
26            // Add display field
27
28            display = new JTextField();
29            add(display, "North");
30
31            // Make button panel
32
33            buttonPanel = new JPanel();
34            buttonPanel.setLayout(new GridLayout(4, 3));
```

```java
35
36        // Add digit buttons
37
38        addButton("7");
39        addButton("8");
40        addButton("9");
41        addButton("4");
42        addButton("5");
43        addButton("6");
44        addButton("1");
45        addButton("2");
46        addButton("3");
47        addButton("0");
48        addButton(".");
49
50        // Add clear entry button
51
52        clearButton = new JButton("CE");
53        buttonPanel.add(clearButton);
54
55        class ClearButtonListener implements ActionListener
56        {
57           public void actionPerformed(ActionEvent event)
58           {
59              display.setText("");
60           }
61        }
62        ActionListener listener = new ClearButtonListener();
63
64        clearButton.addActionListener(new
65              ClearButtonListener());
66
67        add(buttonPanel, "Center");
68     }
69
70     /**
71        Adds a button to the button panel.
72        @param label the button label
73     */
74     private void addButton(final String label)
75     {
76        class DigitButtonListener implements ActionListener
77        {
78           public void actionPerformed(ActionEvent event)
79           {
80
81              // Don't add two decimal points
82              if (label.equals(".")
83                    && display.getText().indexOf(".") != -1)
84                 return;
85
86              // Append label text to button
87              display.setText(display.getText() + label);
88           }
89        }
90
91        JButton button = new JButton(label);
92        buttonPanel.add(button);
```

```
93        ActionListener listener = new DigitButtonListener();
94        button.addActionListener(listener);
95     }
96
97     /**
98        Gets the value that the user entered.
99        @return the value in the text field of the keypad
100    */
101    public double getValue()
102    {
103       return Double.parseDouble(display.getText());
104    }
105
106    /**
107       Clears the display.
108    */
109    public void clear()
110    {
111       display.setText("");
112    }
113 }
```

In this chapter, you learned a systematic approach for building a relatively complex program. However, object-oriented design is definitely not a spectator sport. To really learn how to design and implement programs, you have to gain experience by repeating this process with your own projects. It is quite possible that you don't immediately home in on a good solution and that you need to go back and reorganize your classes and responsibilities. That is normal and only to be expected. The purpose of the object-oriented design process is to spot these problems in the design phase, when they are still easy to rectify, instead of in the implementation phase, when massive reorganization is more difficult and time consuming.

SELF CHECK

12. Why does the Bank class in this example not store an array list of bank accounts?

13. Suppose the requirements change—you need to save the current account balances to a file after every transaction and reload them when the program starts. What is the impact of this change on the design?

Random Fact 11.2

Software Development—Art or Science?

Random Fact 11.2 discusses whether software developers are best characterized as artists, craftspeople, scientists, or engineers.

Summary of Learning Objectives

Describe the software life cycle alternatives for the software development process.

- The software life cycle encompasses all activities from initial analysis until obsolescence.
- A formal process for software development describes phases of the development process and gives guidelines for how to carry out the phases.
- The waterfall model of software development describes a sequential process of analysis, design, implementation, testing, and deployment.
- The spiral model of software development describes an iterative process in which design and implementation are repeated.
- Extreme Programming is a development methodology that strives for simplicity by removing formal structure and focusing on best practices.

Recognize how to discover classes and their responsibilities.

- In object-oriented design, you discover classes, determine the responsibilities of classes, and describe the relationships between classes.
- Make a list of candidates for classes, starting with nouns in the task description.
- A CRC card describes a class, its responsibilities, and its collaborating classes.

Categorize relationships between classes and produce UML diagrams that describe them.

- Inheritance (the *is-a* relationship) is sometimes inappropriately used when the *has-a* relationship would be more appropriate.
- Aggregation (the *has-a* relationship) denotes that objects of one class contain references to objects of another class.
- Dependency is another name for the *uses* relationship.
- You need to be able to distinguish the UML notations for inheritance, interface implementation, aggregation, and dependency.

Apply an object-oriented development process to designing a program.

- Start the development process by gathering and documenting program requirements.
- Use CRC cards to find classes, responsibilities, and collaborators.
- Use UML diagrams to record class relationships.
- Use javadoc comments (with the method bodies left blank) to record the behavior of classes.
- After completing the design, implement your classes.

Media Resources

www.wiley.com/ go/global/ horstmann

- Lab Exercises
- ✚ Practice Quiz
- ✚ Code Completion Exercises

Review Exercises

★ **R11.1** What is the software life cycle?

★★ **R11.2** List the steps in the process of object-oriented design that this chapter recommends for student use.

★ **R11.3** Give a rule of thumb for how to find classes when designing a program.

★ **R11.4** Give a rule of thumb for how to find methods when designing a program.

★★ **R11.5** After discovering a method, why is it important to identify the object that is *responsible* for carrying out the action?

★ **R11.6** What relationship is appropriate between the following classes: aggregation, inheritance, or neither?

    a. University–Student
    b. Student–TeachingAssistant
    c. Student–Freshman
    d. Student–Professor
    e. Car–Door
    f. Truck–Vehicle
    g. Traffic–TrafficSign
    h. TrafficSign–Color

★★ **R11.7** Every BMW is a vehicle. Should a class BMW inherit from the class Vehicle? BMW is a vehicle manufacturer. Does that mean that the class BMW should inherit from the class VehicleManufacturer?

★★ **R11.8** Some books on object-oriented programming recommend using inheritance so that the class Circle extends the class Point. Then the Circle class inherits the setLocation method from the Point superclass. Explain why the setLocation method need not be overridden in the subclass. Why is it nevertheless not a good idea to have Circle inherit from Point? Conversely, would inheriting Point from Circle fulfill the *is-a* rule? Would it be a good idea?

★ **R11.9** Write CRC cards for the Coin and CashRegister classes described in Section 7.2.

★ **R11.10** Write CRC cards for the Bank and BankAccount classes in Section 6.2.

★★ **R11.11** Draw a UML diagram for the Coin and CashRegister classes described in Section 7.2.

★★★ **R11.12** A file contains a set of records describing countries. Each record consists of the name of the country, its population, and its area. Suppose your task is to write a program that reads in such a file and prints

    • The country with the largest area
    • The country with the largest population
    • The country with the largest population density (people per square kilometer)

Think through the problems that you need to solve. What classes and methods will you need? Produce a set of CRC cards, a UML diagram, and a set of javadoc comments.

★★★ **R11.13** Discover classes and methods for generating a student report card that lists all classes, grades, and the grade point average for a semester. Produce a set of CRC cards, a UML diagram, and a set of javadoc comments.

★★★ **R11.14** Consider a quiz grading system that grades student responses to quizzes. A quiz consists of questions. There are different types of questions, including essay questions and multiple-choice questions. Students turn in submissions for quizzes, and the grading system grades them. Draw a UML diagram for classes Quiz, Question, EssayQuestion, MultipleChoiceQuestion, Student, and Submission.

Programming Exercises

★★ **P11.1** Enhance the invoice-printing program by providing for two kinds of line items: One kind describes products that are purchased in certain numerical quantities (such as "3 toasters"), another describes a fixed charge (such as "shipping: $5.00"). *Hint:* Use inheritance. Produce a UML diagram of your modified implementation.

★★ **P11.2** The invoice-printing program is somewhat unrealistic because the formatting of the LineItem objects won't lead to good visual results when the prices and quantities have varying numbers of digits. Enhance the format method in two ways: Accept an int[] array of column widths as a parameter. Use the NumberFormat class to format the currency values.

★★ **P11.3** The invoice-printing program has an unfortunate flaw—it mixes "application logic", the computation of total charges, and "presentation", the visual appearance of the invoice. To appreciate this flaw, imagine the changes that would be necessary to draw the invoice in HTML for presentation on the Web. Reimplement the program, using a separate InvoiceFormatter class to format the invoice. That is, the Invoice and LineItem methods are no longer responsible for formatting. However, they will acquire other responsibilities, because the InvoiceFormatter class needs to query them for the values that it requires.

★★★ **P11.4** Write a program that teaches arithmetic to a young child. The program tests addition and subtraction. In level 1 it tests only addition of numbers less than 10 whose sum is less than 10. In level 2 it tests addition of arbitrary one-digit numbers. In level 3 it tests subtraction of one-digit numbers with a nonnegative difference. Generate random problems and get the player input. The player gets up to two tries per problem. Advance from one level to the next when the player has achieved a score of five points.

★★★ **P11.5** Design a simple e-mail messaging system. A message has a recipient, a sender, and a message text. A mailbox can store messages. Supply a number of mailboxes for different users and a user interface for users to log in, send messages to other users, read their own messages, and log out. Follow the design process that was described in this chapter.

★★ **P11.6** Write a program that simulates a vending machine. Products can be purchased by inserting coins with a value at least equal to the cost of the product. A user selects a product from a list of available products, adds coins, and either gets the product or gets the coins returned if insufficient money was supplied or if the product is sold out. The machine does not give change if too much money was added. Products can be restocked and money removed by an operator. Follow the design process that was described in this chapter. Your solution should include a class VendingMachine that is not coupled with the Scanner or PrintStream classes.

★★★ **P11.7** Write a program to design an appointment calendar. An appointment includes the date, starting time, ending time, and a description; for example,

```
Dentist 2007/10/1 17:30 18:30
CS1 class 2007/10/2 08:30 10:00
```

Supply a user interface to add appointments, remove canceled appointments, and print out a list of appointments for a particular day. Follow the design process that was described in this chapter. Your solution should include a class Appointment-Calendar that is not coupled with the Scanner or PrintStream classes.

★★★ **P11.8** *Airline seating.* Write a program that assigns seats on an airplane. Assume the airplane has 20 seats in first class (5 rows of 4 seats each, separated by an aisle) and 90 seats in economy class (15 rows of 6 seats each, separated by an aisle). Your program should take three commands: add passengers, show seating, and quit. When passengers are added, ask for the class (first or economy), the number of passengers traveling together (1 or 2 in first class; 1 to 3 in economy), and the seating preference (aisle or window in first class; aisle, center, or window in economy). Then try to find a match and assign the seats. If no match exists, print a message. Your solution should include a class Airplane that is not coupled with the Scanner or PrintStream classes. Follow the design process that was described in this chapter.

★★ **P11.9** Modify the implementations of the classes in the ATM example so that the bank manages a collection of bank accounts and a separate collection of customers. Allow joint accounts in which some accounts can have more than one customer.

★★★ **P11.10** Write a program that administers and grades quizzes. A quiz consists of questions. There are four types of questions: text questions, number questions, choice questions with a single answer, and choice questions with multiple answers. When grading a text question, ignore leading or trailing spaces and letter case. When grading a numeric question, accept a response that is approximately the same as the answer.

A quiz is specified in a text file. Each question starts with a letter indicating the question type (T, N, S, M), followed by a line containing the question text. The next line of a non-choice question contains the answer. Choice questions have a list of choices that is terminated by a blank line. Each choice starts with + (correct) or - (incorrect). Here is a sample file:

```
T
Which Java reserved word is used to declare a subclass?
extends
S
What is the original name of the Java language?
- *7
- C--
+ Oak
- Gosling

M
Which of the following types are supertypes of Rectangle?
- PrintStream
+ Shape
```

```
+ RectangularShape
+ Object
- String

N
What is the square root of 2?
1.41421356
```

Your program should read in a quiz file, prompt the user for responses to all questions, and grade the responses. Follow the design process that was described in this chapter.

★★★G **P11.11** Implement a program to teach a young child to read the clock. In the game, present an analog clock, such as the one in Figure 12. Generate random times and display the clock. Accept guesses from the player. Reward the player for correct guesses. After two incorrect guesses, display the correct answer and make a new random time. Implement several levels of play. In level 1, only show full hours. In level 2, show quarter hours. In level 3, show five-minute multiples, and in level 4, show any number of minutes. After a player has achieved five correct guesses at one level, advance to the next level.

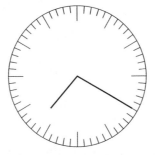

Figure 12   An Analog Clock

★★★G **P11.12** Write a program that can be used to design a suburban scene, with houses, streets, and cars. Users can add houses and cars of various colors to a street. Write more specific requirements that include a detailed description of the user interface. Then, discover classes and methods, provide UML diagrams, and implement your program.

★★★G **P11.13** Write a simple graphics editor that allows users to add a mixture of shapes (ellipses, rectangles, and lines in different colors) to a panel. Supply commands to load and save the picture. Discover classes, supply a UML diagram, and implement your program.

Programming Projects

Project 11.1 Produce a requirements document for a program that allows a company to send out personalized mailings, either by e-mail or through the postal service. Template files contain the message text, together with variable fields (such as Dear [Title] [Last Name] . . .). A database (stored as a text file) contains the field values for each recipient. Use HTML as the output file format. Then design and implement the program.

Project 11.2 Write a tic-tac-toe game that allows a human player to play against the computer. Your program will play many turns against a human opponent, and it will learn. When it is the computer's turn, the computer randomly selects an empty field, except that it won't ever choose a losing combination. For that purpose, your program must keep an array of losing combinations. Whenever the human wins, the immediately preceding combination is stored as losing. For example, suppose that X = computer and 0 = human. Suppose the current combination is

Now it is the human's turn, who will of course choose

The computer should then remember the preceding combination

as a losing combination. As a result, the computer will never again choose that combination from

or

Discover classes and supply a UML diagram before you begin to program.

Answers to Self-Check Questions

1. It is unlikely that the customer did a perfect job with the requirements document. If you don't accommodate changes, your customer may not like the outcome. If you charge for the changes, your customer may not like the cost.
2. An "extreme" spiral model, with lots of iterations.
3. To give frequent feedback as to whether the current iteration of the product fits customer needs.
4. `PrintStream`
5. To produce the shipping address of the customer.
6. Reword the responsibilities so that they are at a higher level, or come up with more classes to handle the responsibilities.
7. Through aggregation. The bank manages bank account objects.
8. Through inheritance.
9. The `BankAccount`, `System`, and `PrintStream` classes.
10. The `Invoice` class is responsible for computing the amount due. It collaborates with the `LineItem` class.
11. This design decision reduces coupling. It enables us to reuse the classes when we want to show the invoice in a dialog box or on a web page.
12. The bank needs to store the list of customers so that customers can log in. We need to locate all bank accounts of a customer, and we chose to simply store them in the customer class. In this program, there is no further need to access bank accounts.
13. The `Bank` class needs to have an additional responsibility: to load and save the accounts. The bank can carry out this responsibility because it has access to the customer objects and, through them, to the bank accounts.

Recursion

CHAPTER GOALS

- To learn about the technique of recursion
- To understand the relationship between recursion and iteration
- To analyze problems that are much easier to solve by recursion than by iteration
- To learn to "think recursively"
- To be able to use recursive helper methods
- To understand when the use of recursion affects the efficiency of an algorithm

Recursion is a powerful technique for reducing complex computational problems to simpler ones. The term "recursion" refers to the fact that the same computation recurs, or occurs repeatedly, as the problem is solved. Recursion is often the most natural way of thinking about a problem, and there are some computations that are very difficult to perform without recursion. This chapter shows you simple and complex examples of recursion and teaches you how to "think recursively".

CHAPTER CONTENTS

12.1 Triangle Numbers

We begin this chapter with a very simple example that demonstrates the power of thinking recursively. In this example, we will look at triangle shapes such as this one:

```
[]
[][]
[][][]
```

We'd like to compute the area of a triangle of width n, assuming that each [] square has area 1. This value is sometimes called the nth *triangle number*. For example, as you can tell from looking at the triangle above, the third triangle number is 6.

You may know that there is a very simple formula to compute these numbers, but you should pretend for now that you don't know about it. The ultimate purpose of this section is not to compute triangle numbers, but to learn about the concept of **recursion** by working through a simple example.

Here is the outline of the class that we will develop:

```java
public class Triangle
{
    private int width;

    public Triangle(int aWidth)
    {
        width = aWidth;
    }

    public int getArea()
    {
        . . .
    }
}
```

If the width of the triangle is 1, then the triangle consists of a single square, and its area is 1. Let's take care of this case first.

```java
public int getArea()
{
    if (width == 1) { return 1; }
    . . .
}
```

To deal with the general case, consider this picture.

```
[]
[][]
[][][]
[][][][]
```

Suppose we knew the area of the smaller, colored triangle. Then we could easily compute the area of the larger triangle as

```
smallerArea + width
```

How can we get the smaller area? Let's make a smaller triangle and ask it!

```
Triangle smallerTriangle = new Triangle(width - 1);
int smallerArea = smallerTriangle.getArea();
```

Now we can complete the getArea method:

```
public int getArea()
{
    if (width == 1) { return 1; }
    Triangle smallerTriangle = new Triangle(width - 1);
    int smallerArea = smallerTriangle.getArea();
    return smallerArea + width;
}
```

A recursive computation solves a problem by using the solution of the same problem with simpler values.

Here is an illustration of what happens when we compute the area of a triangle of width 4.

- The getArea method makes a smaller triangle of width 3.
- It calls getArea on that triangle.
  - That method makes a smaller triangle of width 2.
  - It calls getArea on that triangle.
    - That method makes a smaller triangle of width 1.
    - It calls getArea on that triangle.
      - That method returns 1.
    - The method returns smallerArea + width = 1 + 2 = 3.
  - The method returns smallerArea + width = 3 + 3 = 6.
- The method returns smallerArea + width = 6 + 4 = 10.

This solution has one remarkable aspect. To solve the area problem for a triangle of a given width, we use the fact that we can solve the same problem for a lesser width. This is called a *recursive* solution.

The call pattern of a **recursive method** looks complicated, and the key to the successful design of a recursive method is *not to think about it*. Instead, look at the getArea method one more time and notice how utterly reasonable it is. If the width is 1, then, of course, the area is 1. The next part is just as reasonable. Compute the area of the smaller triangle *and don't think about why that works*. Then the area of the larger triangle is clearly the sum of the smaller area and the width.

There are two key requirements to make sure that the recursion is successful:

- Every recursive call must simplify the computation in some way.
- There must be special cases to handle the simplest computations directly.

For a recursion to terminate, there must be special cases for the simplest values.

The getArea method calls itself again with smaller and smaller width values. Eventually the width must reach 1, and there is a special case for computing the area of a triangle with width 1. Thus, the getArea method always succeeds.

Actually, you have to be careful. What happens when you call the area of a triangle with width –1? It computes the area of a triangle with width –2, which computes the area of a triangle with width –3, and so on. To avoid this, the getArea method should return 0 if the width is ≤ 0.

Recursion is not really necessary to compute the triangle numbers. The area of a triangle equals the sum

```
1 + 2 + 3 + . . . + width
```

Of course, we can program a simple loop:

```
double area = 0;
for (int i = 1; i <= width; i++)
{
    area = area + i;
}
```

Many simple recursions can be computed as loops. However, loop equivalents for more complex recursions—such as the one in our next example—can be complex.

Actually, in this case, you don't even need a loop to compute the answer. The sum of the first n integers can be computed as

$$1 + 2 + \cdots + n = n \times (n + 1)/2$$

Thus, the area equals

```
width * (width + 1) / 2
```

Therefore, neither recursion nor a loop is required to solve this problem. The recursive solution is intended as a "warm-up" to introduce you to the concept of recursion.

ANIMATION
Tracing a Recursion

ch12/triangle/Triangle.java

```
1   /**
2      A triangular shape composed of stacked unit squares like this:
3      []
4      [][]
5      [][][]
6      . . .
7   */
8   public class Triangle
9   {
10      private int width;
11
12      /**
13         Constructs a triangular shape.
14         @param aWidth the width (and height) of the triangle
15      */
16      public Triangle(int aWidth)
17      {
18         width = aWidth;
19      }
20
```

```
21    /**
22       Computes the area of the triangle.
23       @return the area
24    */
25    public int getArea()
26    {
27       if (width <= 0) { return 0; }
28       if (width == 1) { return 1; }
29       Triangle smallerTriangle = new Triangle(width - 1);
30       int smallerArea = smallerTriangle.getArea();
31       return smallerArea + width;
32    }
33 }
```

ch12/triangle/TriangleTester.java

```
 1  public class TriangleTester
 2  {
 3     public static void main(String[] args)
 4     {
 5        Triangle t = new Triangle(10);
 6        int area = t.getArea();
 7        System.out.println("Area: " + area);
 8        System.out.println("Expected: 55");
 9     }
10 }
```

Program Run

```
Enter width: 10
Area: 55
Expected: 55
```

SELF CHECK

1. Why is the statement if (width == 1) { return 1; } in the getArea method unnecessary?

2. How would you modify the program to recursively compute the area of a square?

Common Error 12.1

Infinite Recursion

A common programming error is an infinite recursion: a method calling itself over and over with no end in sight. The computer needs some amount of memory for bookkeeping for each call. After some number of calls, all memory that is available for this purpose is exhausted. Your program shuts down and reports a "stack overflow".

Infinite recursion happens either because the parameter values don't get simpler or because a special terminating case is missing. For example, suppose the getArea method was allowed to compute the area of a triangle with width 0. If it weren't for the special test, the method would construct triangles with width –1, –2, –3, and so on.

Common Error 12.2

Tracing Through Recursive Methods

Debugging a recursive method can be somewhat challenging. When you set a **breakpoint** in a recursive method, the program stops as soon as that program line is encountered in *any call to the recursive method.* Suppose you want to debug the recursive getArea method of the Triangle class. Debug the TriangleTester program and run until the beginning of the getArea method. Inspect the width instance variable. It is 10.

Remove the breakpoint and now run until the statement return smallerArea + width; (see Figure 1). When you inspect width again, its value is 2! That makes no sense. There was no instruction that changed the value of width. Is that a bug with the debugger?

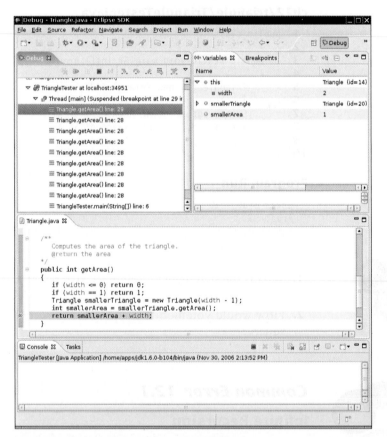

Figure 1 Debugging a Recursive Method

No. The program stopped in the first recursive call to getArea that reached the return statement. If you are confused, look at the **call stack** (top left in the figure). You will see that nine calls to getArea are pending.

You can debug recursive methods with the debugger. You just need to be particularly careful, and watch the call stack to understand which nested call you currently are in.

How To 12.1

Thinking Recursively

To solve a problem recursively requires a different mindset than to solve it by programming a loop. In fact, it helps if you pretend to be a bit lazy, asking others to do most of the work for you. If you need to solve a complex problem, pretend that "someone else" will do most of the heavy lifting and solve the problem for simpler inputs. Then you only need to figure out how you can turn the solutions with simpler inputs into a solution for the whole problem.

To illustrate the technique of recursion, let us consider the following problem. We want to test whether a sentence is a *palindrome*—a string that is equal to itself when you reverse all characters. Typical examples of palindromes are

- A man, a plan, a canal—Panama!
- Go hang a salami, I'm a lasagna hog

and, of course, the oldest palindrome of all:

- Madam, I'm Adam

When testing for a palindrome, we match upper- and lowercase letters, and ignore all spaces and punctuation marks.

We want to implement the isPalindrome method in the following class:

```java
public class Sentence
{
    private String text;

    /**
        Constructs a sentence.
        @param aText a string containing all characters of the sentence
    */
    public Sentence(String aText)
    {
        text = aText;
    }

    /**
        Tests whether this sentence is a palindrome.
        @return true if this sentence is a palindrome, false otherwise
    */
    public boolean isPalindrome()
    {
        . . .
    }
}
```

Step 1   Consider various ways to simplify inputs.

In your mind, fix a particular input or set of inputs for the problem that you want to solve.

Think how you can simplify the inputs in such a way that the same problem can be applied to the simpler input.

When you consider simpler inputs, you may want to remove just a little bit from the original input—maybe remove one or two characters from a string, or remove a small portion of a geometric shape. But sometimes it is more useful to cut the input in half and then see what it means to solve the problem for both halves.

In the palindrome test problem, the input is the string that we need to test. How can you simplify the input? Here are several possibilities:

- Remove the first character.
- Remove the last character.
- Remove both the first and last characters.

- Remove a character from the middle.
- Cut the string into two halves.

These simpler inputs are all potential inputs for the palindrome test.

Step 2 Combine solutions with simpler inputs into a solution of the original problem.

In your mind, consider the solutions of your problem for the simpler inputs that you discovered in Step 1. Don't worry *how* those solutions are obtained. Simply have faith that the solutions are readily available. Just say to yourself: These are simpler inputs, so someone else will solve the problem for me.

Now think how you can turn the solution for the simpler inputs into a solution for the input that you are currently thinking about. Maybe you need to add a small quantity, related to the quantity that you lopped off to arrive at the simpler input. Maybe you cut the original input in half and have solutions for each half. Then you may need to add both solutions to arrive at a solution for the whole.

Consider the methods for simplifying the inputs for the palindrome test. Cutting the string in half doesn't seem a good idea. If you cut

```
"Madam, I'm Adam"
```

in half, you get two strings:

```
"Madam, I"
```

and

```
"'m Adam"
```

Neither of them is a palindrome. Cutting the input in half and testing whether the halves are palindromes seems a dead end.

The most promising simplification is to remove the first *and* last characters. Removing the M at the front and the m at the back yields

```
"adam, I'm Ada"
```

Suppose you can verify that the shorter string is a palindrome. Then *of course* the original string is a palindrome—we put the same letter in the front and the back. That's extremely promising. A word is a palindrome if

- The first and last letters match (ignoring letter case)

and

- The word obtained by removing the first and last letters is a palindrome.

Again, don't worry how the test works for the shorter string. It just works.

There is one other case to consider. What if the first or last letter of the word is not a letter? For example, the string

```
"A man, a plan, a canal, Panama!"
```

ends in a ! character, which does not match the A in the front. But we should ignore nonletters when testing for palindromes. Thus, when the last character is not a letter but the first character is a letter, it doesn't make sense to remove both the first and the last characters. That's not a problem. Remove only the last character. If the shorter string is a palindrome, then it stays a palindrome when you attach a nonletter.

The same argument applies if the first character is not a letter. Now we have a complete set of cases.

- If the first and last characters are both letters, then check whether they match. If so, remove both and test the shorter string.
- Otherwise, if the last character isn't a letter, remove it and test the shorter string.
- Otherwise, the first character isn't a letter. Remove it and test the shorter string.

In all three cases, you can use the solution to the simpler problem to arrive at a solution to your problem.

Step 3 Find solutions to the simplest inputs.

A recursive computation keeps simplifying its inputs. Eventually it arrives at very simple inputs. To make sure that the recursion comes to a stop, you must deal with the simplest inputs separately. Come up with special solutions for them, which is usually very easy.

However, sometimes you get into philosophical questions dealing with *degenerate* inputs: empty strings, shapes with no area, and so on. Then you may want to investigate a slightly larger input that gets reduced to such a trivial input and see what value you should attach to the degenerate inputs so that the simpler value, when used according to the rules you discovered in Step 2, yields the correct answer.

Let's look at the simplest strings for the palindrome test:

- Strings with two characters
- Strings with a single character
- The empty string

We don't have to come up with a special solution for strings with two characters. Step 2 still applies to those strings—either or both of the characters are removed. But we do need to worry about strings of length 0 and 1. In those cases, Step 2 can't apply. There aren't two characters to remove.

The empty string is a palindrome—it's the same string when you read it backwards. If you find that too artificial, consider a string "mm". According to the rule discovered in Step 2, this string is a palindrome if the first and last characters of that string match and the remainder—that is, the empty string—is also a palindrome. Therefore, it makes sense to consider the empty string a palindrome.

A string with a single letter, such as "I", is a palindrome. How about the case in which the character is not a letter, such as "!"? Removing the ! yields the empty string, which is a palindrome. Thus, we conclude that all strings of length 0 or 1 are palindromes.

Step 4 Implement the solution by combining the simple cases and the reduction step.

Now you are ready to implement the solution. Make separate cases for the simple inputs that you considered in Step 3. If the input isn't one of the simplest cases, then implement the logic you discovered in Step 2.

Here is the isPalindrome method.

```java
public boolean isPalindrome()
{
   int length = text.length();

   // Separate case for shortest strings.
   if (length <= 1) { return true; }

   // Get first and last characters, converted to lowercase.
   char first = Character.toLowerCase(text.charAt(0));
   char last = Character.toLowerCase(text.charAt(length - 1));

   if (Character.isLetter(first) && Character.isLetter(last))
   {
      // Both are letters.
      if (first == last)
      {
         // Remove both first and last character.
         Sentence shorter = new Sentence(text.substring(1, length - 1));
         return shorter.isPalindrome();
      }
      else
      {
         return false;
```

```
            }
        }
        else if (!Character.isLetter(last))
        {
            // Remove last character.
            Sentence shorter = new Sentence(text.substring(0, length - 1));
            return shorter.isPalindrome();
        }
        else
        {
            // Remove first character.
            Sentence shorter = new Sentence(text.substring(1));
            return shorter.isPalindrome();
        }
    }
```

Worked Example 12.1

Finding Files

In this Worked Example, we find all files with a given extension in a directory tree.

bigjava
▾ ch01
  ▾ hello
    HelloPrinter.java

12.2 Recursive Helper Methods

Sometimes it is easier to find a recursive solution if you make a slight change to the original problem.

Sometimes it is easier to find a recursive solution if you change the original problem slightly. Then the original problem can be solved by calling a recursive helper method.

Here is a typical example. Consider the palindrome test of How To 12.1. It is a bit inefficient to construct new Sentence objects in every step. Now consider the following change in the problem. Rather than testing whether the entire sentence is a palindrome, let's check whether a substring is a palindrome:

```
/**
    Tests whether a substring of the sentence is a palindrome.
    @param start the index of the first character of the substring
    @param end the index of the last character of the substring
    @return true if the substring is a palindrome
*/
public boolean isPalindrome(int start, int end)
```

This method turns out to be even easier to implement than the original test. In the recursive calls, simply adjust the start and end parameters to skip over matching letter pairs and characters that are not letters. There is no need to construct new Sentence objects to represent the shorter strings.

```
public boolean isPalindrome(int start, int end)
{
    // Separate case for substrings of length 0 and 1.
    if (start >= end) { return true; }
```

```
// Get first and last characters, converted to lowercase.
char first = Character.toLowerCase(text.charAt(start));
char last = Character.toLowerCase(text.charAt(end));

if (Character.isLetter(first) && Character.isLetter(last))
{
    if (first == last)
    {
        // Test substring that doesn't contain the matching letters.
        return isPalindrome(start + 1, end - 1);
    }
    else
    {
        return false;
    }
}
else if (!Character.isLetter(last))
{
    // Test substring that doesn't contain the last character.
    return isPalindrome(start, end - 1);
}
else
{
    // Test substring that doesn't contain the first character.
    return isPalindrome(start + 1, end);
}
}
```

You should still supply a method to solve the whole problem—the user of your method shouldn't have to know about the trick with the substring positions. Simply call the helper method with positions that test the entire string:

```
public boolean isPalindrome()
{
    return isPalindrome(0, text.length() - 1);
}
```

Note that this call is *not* a recursive method. The isPalindrome() method calls the helper method isPalindrome(int, int). In this example, we use overloading to declare two methods with the same name. The isPalindrome method without parameters is the method that we expect the public to use. The second method, with two int parameters, is the recursive helper method. If you prefer, you can avoid overloaded methods by choosing a different name for the helper method, such as substringIsPalindrome.

Use the technique of recursive helper methods whenever it is easier to solve a recursive problem that is equivalent to the original problem—but more amenable to a recursive solution.

SELF CHECK

3. Do we have to give the same name to both isPalindrome methods?
4. When does the recursive isPalindrome method stop calling itself?

12.3 The Efficiency of Recursion

As you have seen in this chapter, recursion can be a powerful tool to implement complex algorithms. On the other hand, recursion can lead to algorithms that perform poorly. In this section, we will analyze the question of when recursion is beneficial and when it is inefficient.

Consider the Fibonacci sequence: a sequence of numbers defined by the equation

$$f_1 = 1$$
$$f_2 = 1$$
$$f_n = f_{n-1} + f_{n-2}$$

That is, each value of the sequence is the sum of the two preceding values. The first ten terms of the sequence are

$$1, 1, 2, 3, 5, 8, 13, 21, 34, 55$$

It is easy to extend this sequence indefinitely. Just keep appending the sum of the last two values of the sequence. For example, the next entry is $34 + 55 = 89$.

We would like to write a function that computes f_n for any value of n. Let us translate the definition directly into a recursive method:

ch12/fib/RecursiveFib.java

```java
1   import java.util.Scanner;
2
3   /**
4      This program computes Fibonacci numbers using a recursive method.
5   */
6   public class RecursiveFib
7   {
8      public static void main(String[] args)
9      {
10        Scanner in = new Scanner(System.in);
11        System.out.print("Enter n: ");
12        int n = in.nextInt();
13
14        for (int i = 1; i <= n; i++)
15        {
16           long f = fib(i);
17           System.out.println("fib(" + i + ") = " + f);
18        }
19     }
20
21     /**
22        Computes a Fibonacci number.
23        @param n an integer
24        @return the nth Fibonacci number
25     */
26     public static long fib(int n)
27     {
28        if (n <= 2) { return 1; }
29        else return fib(n - 1) + fib(n - 2);
30     }
31   }
```

Program Run

```
Enter n: 50
fib(1) = 1
fib(2) = 1
fib(3) = 2
fib(4) = 3
fib(5) = 5
fib(6) = 8
fib(7) = 13
. . .
fib(50) = 12586269025
```

That is certainly simple, and the method will work correctly. But watch the output closely as you run the test program. The first few calls to the fib method are fast. For larger values, though, the program pauses an amazingly long time between outputs.

That makes no sense. Armed with pencil, paper, and a pocket calculator you could calculate these numbers pretty quickly, so it shouldn't take the computer anywhere near that long.

To find out the problem, let us insert **trace messages** into the method:

ch12/fib/RecursiveFibTracer.java

```java
1   import java.util.Scanner;
2
3   /**
4      This program prints trace messages that show how often the
5      recursive method for computing Fibonacci numbers calls itself.
6   */
7   public class RecursiveFibTracer
8   {
9      public static void main(String[] args)
10     {
11        Scanner in = new Scanner(System.in);
12        System.out.print("Enter n: ");
13        int n = in.nextInt();
14
15        long f = fib(n);
16
17        System.out.println("fib(" + n + ") = " + f);
18     }
19
20     /**
21        Computes a Fibonacci number.
22        @param n an integer
23        @return the nth Fibonacci number
24     */
25     public static long fib(int n)
26     {
27        System.out.println("Entering fib: n = " + n);
28        long f;
29        if (n <= 2) { f = 1; }
30        else { f = fib(n - 1) + fib(n - 2); }
31        System.out.println("Exiting fib: n = " + n
32              + " return value = " + f);
33        return f;
34     }
35  }
```

Program Run

```
Enter n: 6
Entering fib: n = 6
Entering fib: n = 5
Entering fib: n = 4
Entering fib: n = 3
Entering fib: n = 2
Exiting fib: n = 2 return value = 1
Entering fib: n = 1
Exiting fib: n = 1 return value = 1
Exiting fib: n = 3 return value = 2
Entering fib: n = 2
Exiting fib: n = 2 return value = 1
Exiting fib: n = 4 return value = 3
Entering fib: n = 3
Entering fib: n = 2
Exiting fib: n = 2 return value = 1
Entering fib: n = 1
Exiting fib: n = 1 return value = 1
Exiting fib: n = 3 return value = 2
Exiting fib: n = 5 return value = 5
Entering fib: n = 4
Entering fib: n = 3
Entering fib: n = 2
Exiting fib: n = 2 return value = 1
Entering fib: n = 1
Exiting fib: n = 1 return value = 1
Exiting fib: n = 3 return value = 2
Entering fib: n = 2
Exiting fib: n = 2 return value = 1
Exiting fib: n = 4 return value = 3
Exiting fib: n = 6 return value = 8
fib(6) = 8
```

Figure 2 shows the call tree for computing fib(6). Now it is becoming apparent why the method takes so long. It is computing the same values over and over. For example, the computation of fib(6) calls fib(4) twice and fib(3) three times. That is very different from the computation we would do with pencil and paper. There we would just write down the values as they were computed and add up the last two to

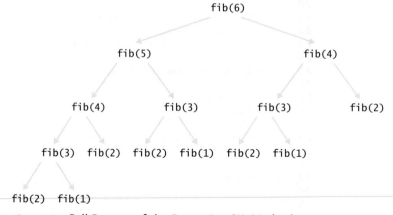

Figure 2 Call Pattern of the Recursive fib Method

get the next one until we reached the desired entry; no sequence value would ever be computed twice.

If we imitate the pencil-and-paper process, then we get the following program.

ch12/fib/LoopFib.java

```java
1   import java.util.Scanner;
2
3   /**
4       This program computes Fibonacci numbers using an iterative method.
5   */
6   public class LoopFib
7   {
8       public static void main(String[] args)
9       {
10          Scanner in = new Scanner(System.in);
11          System.out.print("Enter n: ");
12          int n = in.nextInt();
13
14          for (int i = 1; i <= n; i++)
15          {
16              long f = fib(i);
17              System.out.println("fib(" + i + ") = " + f);
18          }
19      }
20
21      /**
22          Computes a Fibonacci number.
23          @param n an integer
24          @return the nth Fibonacci number
25      */
26      public static long fib(int n)
27      {
28          if (n <= 2) { return 1; }
29          long olderValue = 1;
30          long oldValue = 1;
31          long newValue = 1;
32          for (int i = 3; i <= n; i++)
33          {
34              newValue = oldValue + olderValue;
35              olderValue = oldValue;
36              oldValue = newValue;
37          }
38          return newValue;
39      }
40  }
```

Program Run

```
Enter n: 50
fib(1) = 1
fib(2) = 1
fib(3) = 2
fib(4) = 3
fib(5) = 5
fib(6) = 8
fib(7) = 13
. . .
fib(50) = 12586269025
```

This method runs *much* faster than the recursive version.

In this example of the fib method, the recursive solution was easy to program because it exactly followed the mathematical definition, but it ran far more slowly than the iterative solution, because it computed many intermediate results multiple times.

Can you always speed up a recursive solution by changing it into a loop? Frequently, the iterative and recursive solution have essentially the same performance. For example, here is an iterative solution for the palindrome test.

```java
public boolean isPalindrome()
{
    int start = 0;
    int end = text.length() - 1;
    while (start < end)
    {
        char first = Character.toLowerCase(text.charAt(start));
        char last = Character.toLowerCase(text.charAt(end);

        if (Character.isLetter(first) && Character.isLetter(last))
        {
            // Both are letters.
            if (first == last)
            {
                start++;
                end--;
            }
            else
            {
                return false;
            }
        }
        if (!Character.isLetter(last)) { end--; }
        if (!Character.isLetter(first)) { start++; }
    }
    return true;
}
```

This solution keeps two index variables: start and end. The first index starts at the beginning of the string and is advanced whenever a letter has been matched or a nonletter has been ignored. The second index starts at the end of the string and moves toward the beginning. When the two index variables meet, the iteration stops.

Both the iteration and the recursion run at about the same speed. If a palindrome has n characters, the iteration executes the loop between $n/2$ and n times, depending on how many of the characters are letters, since one or both index variables are moved in each step. Similarly, the recursive solution calls itself between $n/2$ and n times, because one or two characters are removed in each step.

In such a situation, the iterative solution tends to be a bit faster, because each recursive method call takes a certain amount of processor time. In principle, it is possible for a smart compiler to avoid recursive method calls if they follow simple patterns, but most compilers don't do that. From that point of view, an iterative solution is preferable.

However, many problems have recursive solutions that are easier to understand and implement correctly than their iterative counterparts. Sometimes there is no obvious iterative solution at all—see the example in the next section. There is a certain elegance and economy of thought to recursive solutions that makes them more appealing. As the computer scientist (and creator of the GhostScript interpreter for the PostScript graphics description language) L. Peter Deutsch put it: "To iterate is human, to recurse divine."

SELF CHECK

5. Is it faster to compute the triangle numbers recursively, as shown in Section 12.1, or is it faster to use a loop that computes $1 + 2 + 3 + \ldots + \text{width}$?

6. You can compute the factorial function either with a loop, using the definition that $n! = 1 \times 2 \times \ldots \times n$, or recursively, using the definition that $0! = 1$ and $n! = (n - 1)! \times n$. Is the recursive approach inefficient in this case?

12.4 Permutations

> The permutations of a string can be obtained more naturally through recursion than with a loop.

In this section, we will study a more complex example of recursion that would be difficult to program with a simple loop. (As Exercise P12.11 shows, it is possible to avoid the recursion, but the resulting solution is quite complex, and no faster).

We will design a class that lists all permutations of a string. A permutation is simply a rearrangement of the letters in the string. For example, the string "eat" has six permutations (including the original string itself):

```
"eat"
"eta"
"aet"
"ate"
"tea"
"tae"
```

As in the preceding section, we will declare a class that is in charge of computing the answer. In this case, the answer is not a single number but a collection of permuted strings. Here is our generator class:

```
public class PermutationGenerator
{
    public PermutationGenerator(String aWord) { . . . }
    ArrayList<String> getPermutations() { . . . }
}
```

And here is the program that prints out all permutations of the string "eat":

ch12/permute/PermutationGeneratorDemo.java

```
 1  import java.util.ArrayList;
 2
 3  /**
 4      This program demonstrates the permutation generator.
 5  */
 6  public class PermutationGeneratorDemo
 7  {
 8      public static void main(String[] args)
 9      {
10          PermutationGenerator generator = new PermutationGenerator("eat");
11          ArrayList<String> permutations = generator.getPermutations();
12          for (String s : permutations)
13          {
```

```
14          System.out.println(s);
15      }
16   }
17 }
```

Program Run

```
eat
eta
aet
ate
tea
tae
```

Now we need a way to generate the permutations recursively. Consider the string "eat". Let's simplify the problem. First, we'll generate all permutations that start with the letter 'e', then those that start with 'a', and finally those that start with 't'. How do we generate the permutations that start with 'e'? We need to know the permutations of the substring "at". But that's the same problem—to generate all permutations—with a simpler input, namely the shorter string "at". Thus, we can use recursion. Generate the permutations of the substring "at". They are

```
"at"
"ta"
```

For each permutation of that substring, prepend the letter 'e' to get the permutations of "eat" that start with 'e', namely

```
"eat"
"eta"
```

Now let's turn our attention to the permutations of "eat" that start with 'a'. We need to produce the permutations of the remaining letters, "et". They are:

```
"et"
"te"
```

We add the letter 'a' to the front of the strings and obtain

```
"aet"
"ate"
```

We generate the permutations that start with 't' in the same way.

That's the idea. The implementation is fairly straightforward. In the getPermutations method, we loop through all positions in the word to be permuted. For each of them, we compute the shorter word that is obtained by removing the ith letter:

```
String shorterWord = word.substring(0, i) + word.substring(i + 1);
```

We construct a permutation generator to get the permutations of the shorter word, and ask it to give us all permutations of the shorter word.

```
PermutationGenerator shorterPermutationGenerator
      = new PermutationGenerator(shorterWord);
ArrayList<String> shorterWordPermutations
      = shorterPermutationGenerator.getPermutations();
```

Finally, we add the removed letter to the front of all permutations of the shorter word.

```
for (String s : shorterWordPermutations)
{
```

```
        permutations.add(word.charAt(i) + s);
    }
```

As always, we have to provide a special case for the simplest strings. The simplest possible string is the empty string, which has a single permutation—itself.

Here is the complete PermutationGenerator class.

ch12/permute/PermutationGenerator.java

```java
 1  import java.util.ArrayList;
 2
 3  /**
 4     This class generates permutations of a word.
 5  */
 6  public class PermutationGenerator
 7  {
 8     private String word;
 9
10     /**
11        Constructs a permutation generator.
12        @param aWord the word to permute
13     */
14     public PermutationGenerator(String aWord)
15     {
16        word = aWord;
17     }
18
19     /**
20        Gets all permutations of a given word.
21     */
22     public ArrayList<String> getPermutations()
23     {
24        ArrayList<String> permutations = new ArrayList<String>();
25
26        // The empty string has a single permutation: itself
27        if (word.length() == 0)
28        {
29           permutations.add(word);
30           return permutations;
31        }
32
33        // Loop through all character positions
34        for (int i = 0; i < word.length(); i++)
35        {
36           // Form a simpler word by removing the ith character
37           String shorterWord = word.substring(0, i)
38              + word.substring(i + 1);
39
40           // Generate all permutations of the simpler word
41           PermutationGenerator shorterPermutationGenerator
42              = new PermutationGenerator(shorterWord);
43           ArrayList<String> shorterWordPermutations
44              = shorterPermutationGenerator.getPermutations();
45
46           // Add the removed character to the front of
47           // each permutation of the simpler word
48           for (String s : shorterWordPermutations)
49           {
50              permutations.add(word.charAt(i) + s);
```

```
51          }
52        }
53        // Return all permutations
54        return permutations;
55      }
56  }
```

Compare the `PermutationGenerator` and `Triangle` classes. Both of them work on the same principle. When they work on a more complex input, they first solve the problem for a simpler input. Then they combine the result for the simpler input with additional work to deliver the results for the more complex input. There really is no particular complexity behind that process as long as you think about the solution on that level only. However, behind the scenes, the simpler input creates even simpler input, which creates yet another simplification, and so on, until one input is so simple that the result can be obtained without further help. It is interesting to think about this process, but it can also be confusing. What's important is that you can focus on the one level that matters—putting a solution together from the slightly simpler problem, ignoring the fact that the simpler problem also uses recursion to get its results.

SELF CHECK

7. What are all permutations of the four-letter word beat?

8. Our recursion for the permutation generator stops at the empty string. What simple modification would make the recursion stop at strings of length 0 or 1?

9. Why isn't it easy to develop an iterative solution for the permutation generator?

Random Fact 12.1

The Limits of Computation

Random Fact 12.1 discusses problems that are intrinsically beyond the capabilities of any computer. For example, theoretical computer scientists have proven that it is impossible to write a program that can grade your programming homework by comparing your program against the instructor's solution and telling with certainty whether these two programs always produce the same results when given the same inputs.

12.5 Mutual Recursions

In a mutual recursion, a set of cooperating methods calls each other repeatedly.

In the preceding examples, a method called itself to solve a simpler problem. Sometimes, a set of cooperating methods calls each other in a recursive fashion. In this section, we will explore a typical situation of such a mutual recursion. This technique is significantly more advanced than the simple recursion that we discussed in the preceding sections.

We will develop a program that can compute the values of arithmetic expressions such as

```
3+4*5
(3+4)*5
1-(2-(3-(4-5)))
```

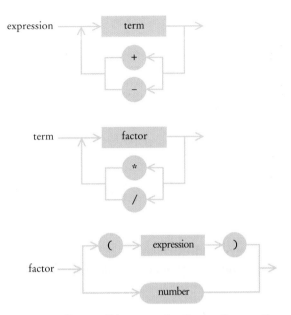

Figure 3 Syntax Diagrams for Evaluating an Expression

Computing such an expression is complicated by the fact that * and / bind more strongly than + and -, and that parentheses can be used to group subexpressions.

Figure 3 shows a set of **syntax diagrams** that describes the syntax of these expressions. To see how the syntax diagrams work, consider the expression 3+4*5. When you enter the *expression* syntax diagram, the arrow points directly to *term*, giving you no alternative but to enter the *term* syntax diagram. The arrow points to *factor*, again giving you no choice. You enter the *factor* diagram, and now you have two choices: to follow the top branch or the bottom branch. Because the first input token is the number 3 and not a (, you must follow the bottom branch. You accept the input token because it matches the *number*. Follow the arrow out of *number* to the end of *factor*. Just like in a method call, you now back up, returning to the end of the *factor* element of the *term* diagram. Now you have another choice—to loop back in the *term* diagram, or to exit. The next input token is a +, and it matches neither the * or the / that would be required to loop back. So you exit, returning to *expression*. Again, you have a choice, to loop back or to exit. Now the + matches one of the choices in the loop. Accept the + in the input and move back to the *term* element.

In this fashion, an expression is broken down into a sequence of terms, separated by + or -, each term is broken down into a sequence of factors, each separated by * or /, and each factor is either a parenthesized expression or a number. You can draw this breakdown as a tree. Figure 4 shows how the expressions 3+4*5 and (3+4)*5 are derived from the syntax diagram.

Why do the syntax diagrams help us compute the value of the tree? If you look at the syntax trees, you will see that they accurately represent which operations should be carried out first. In the first tree, 4 and 5 should be multiplied, and then the result should be added to 3. In the second tree, 3 and 4 should be added, and the result should be multiplied by 5.

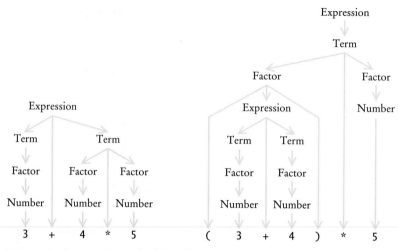

Figure 4 Syntax Trees for Two Expressions

At the end of this section, you will find the implementation of the Evaluator class, which evaluates these expressions. The Evaluator makes use of an Expression-Tokenizer class, which breaks up an input string into tokens—numbers, operators, and parentheses. (For simplicity, we only accept positive integers as numbers, and we don't allow spaces in the input.)

When you call nextToken, the next input token is returned as a string. We also supply another method, peekToken, which allows you to see the next token without consuming it. To see why the peekToken method is necessary, consider the syntax diagram of the factor type. If the next token is a "*" or "/", you want to continue adding and subtracting terms. But if the next token is another character, such as a "+" or "-", you want to stop without actually consuming it, so that the token can be considered later.

To compute the value of an expression, we implement three methods: get-ExpressionValue, getTermValue, and getFactorValue. The getExpressionValue method first calls getTermValue to get the value of the first term of the expression. Then it checks whether the next input token is one of + or -. If so, it calls getTermValue again and adds or subtracts it.

```
public int getExpressionValue()
{
   int value = getTermValue();
   boolean done = false;
   while (!done)
   {
      String next = tokenizer.peekToken();
      if ("+".equals(next) || "-".equals(next))
      {
         tokenizer.nextToken(); // Discard "+" or "-"
         int value2 = getTermValue();
         if ("+".equals(next)) value = value + value2;
         else value = value - value2;
```

```
      }
      else
      {
         done = true;
      }
   }
   return value;
}
```

The `getTermValue` method calls `getFactorValue` in the same way, multiplying or dividing the factor values.

Finally, the `getFactorValue` method checks whether the next input is a number, or whether it begins with a (token. In the first case, the value is simply the value of the number. However, in the second case, the `getFactorValue` method makes a recursive call to `getExpressionValue`. Thus, the three methods are mutually recursive.

```
public int getFactorValue()
{
   int value;
   String next = tokenizer.peekToken();
   if ("(".equals(next))
   {
      tokenizer.nextToken(); // Discard "("
      value = getExpressionValue();
      tokenizer.nextToken(); // Discard ")"
   }
   else
   {
      value = Integer.parseInt(tokenizer.nextToken());
   }
   return value;
}
```

To see the mutual recursion clearly, trace through the expression (3+4)*5:

- `getExpressionValue` calls `getTermValue`
  - `getTermValue` calls `getFactorValue`
    - `getFactorValue` consumes the (input
    - `getFactorValue` calls `getExpressionValue`
      - `getExpressionValue` returns eventually with the value of 7, having consumed 3 + 4. This is the recursive call.
    - `getFactorValue` consumes the) input
    - `getFactorValue` returns 7
  - `getTermValue` consumes the inputs * and 5 and returns 35
- `getExpressionValue` returns 35

As always with a recursive solution, you need to ensure that the recursion terminates. In this situation, that is easy to see when you consider the situation in which `getExpressionValue` calls itself. The second call works on a shorter subexpression than the original expression. At each recursive call, at least some of the tokens of the input string are consumed, so eventually the recursion must come to an end.

ch12/expr/Evaluator.java

```
 1  /**
 2      A class that can compute the value of an arithmetic expression.
 3  */
 4  public class Evaluator
 5  {
 6      private ExpressionTokenizer tokenizer;
 7
 8      /**
 9          Constructs an evaluator.
10          @param anExpression a string containing the expression
11          to be evaluated
12      */
13      public Evaluator(String anExpression)
14      {
15          tokenizer = new ExpressionTokenizer(anExpression);
16      }
17
18      /**
19          Evaluates the expression.
20          @return the value of the expression
21      */
22      public int getExpressionValue()
23      {
24          int value = getTermValue();
25          boolean done = false;
26          while (!done)
27          {
28              String next = tokenizer.peekToken();
29              if ("+".equals(next) || "-".equals(next))
30              {
31                  tokenizer.nextToken(); // Discard "+" or "-"
32                  int value2 = getTermValue();
33                  if ("+".equals(next)) { value = value + value2; }
34                  else { value = value - value2; }
35              }
36              else
37              {
38                  done = true;
39              }
40          }
41          return value;
42      }
43
44      /**
45          Evaluates the next term found in the expression.
46          @return the value of the term
47      */
48      public int getTermValue()
49      {
50          int value = getFactorValue();
51          boolean done = false;
52          while (!done)
53          {
54              String next = tokenizer.peekToken();
55              if ("*".equals(next) || "/".equals(next))
56              {
```

```
57              tokenizer.nextToken();
58              int value2 = getFactorValue();
59              if ("*".equals(next)) { value = value * value2; }
60              else { value = value / value2; }
61           }
62           else
63           {
64              done = true;
65           }
66        }
67        return value;
68     }
69
70     /**
71        Evaluates the next factor found in the expression.
72        @return the value of the factor
73     */
74     public int getFactorValue()
75     {
76        int value;
77        String next = tokenizer.peekToken();
78        if ("(".equals(next))
79        {
80           tokenizer.nextToken(); // Discard "("
81           value = getExpressionValue();
82           tokenizer.nextToken(); // Discard ")"
83        }
84        else
85        {
86           value = Integer.parseInt(tokenizer.nextToken());
87        }
88        return value;
89     }
90 }
```

ch12/expr/ExpressionTokenizer.java

```
1  /**
2     This class breaks up a string describing an expression
3     into tokens: numbers, parentheses, and operators.
4  */
5  public class ExpressionTokenizer
6  {
7     private String input;
8     private int start; // The start of the current token
9     private int end; // The position after the end of the current token
10
11    /**
12       Constructs a tokenizer.
13       @param anInput the string to tokenize
14    */
15    public ExpressionTokenizer(String anInput)
16    {
17       input = anInput;
18       start = 0;
19       end = 0;
20       nextToken(); // Find the first token
21    }
```

```
22
23    /**
24        Peeks at the next token without consuming it.
25        @return the next token or null if there are no more tokens
26    */
27    public String peekToken()
28    {
29        if (start >= input.length()) { return null; }
30        else { return input.substring(start, end); }
31    }
32
33    /**
34        Gets the next token and moves the tokenizer to the following token.
35        @return the next token or null if there are no more tokens
36    */
37    public String nextToken()
38    {
39        String r = peekToken();
40        start = end;
41        if (start >= input.length()) { return r; }
42        if (Character.isDigit(input.charAt(start)))
43        {
44            end = start + 1;
45            while (end < input.length()
46                    && Character.isDigit(input.charAt(end)))
47            {
48                end++;
49            }
50        }
51        else
52        {
53            end = start + 1;
54        }
55        return r;
56    }
57 }
```

ch12/expr/ExpressionCalculator.java

```
1  import java.util.Scanner;
2
3  /**
4      This program calculates the value of an expression
5      consisting of numbers, arithmetic operators, and parentheses.
6  */
7  public class ExpressionCalculator
8  {
9      public static void main(String[] args)
10     {
11         Scanner in = new Scanner(System.in);
12         System.out.print("Enter an expression: ");
13         String input = in.nextLine();
14         Evaluator e = new Evaluator(input);
15         int value = e.getExpressionValue();
16         System.out.println(input + "=" + value);
17     }
18 }
```

Program Run

```
Enter an expression: 3+4*5
3+4*5=23
```

SELF CHECK

10. What is the difference between a term and a factor? Why do we need both concepts?
11. Why does the expression parser use mutual recursion?
12. What happens if you try to parse the illegal expression 3+4*)5? Specifically, which method throws an exception?

Summary of Learning Objectives

Understand the control flow in a recursive computation.

- A recursive computation solves a problem by using the solution of the same problem with simpler values.
- For a recursion to terminate, there must be special cases for the simplest values.

Identify recursive helper methods for solving a problem.

- Sometimes it is easier to find a recursive solution if you make a slight change to the original problem.

Contrast the efficiency of recursive and non-recursive algorithms.

- Occasionally, a recursive solution runs much slower than its iterative counterpart. However, in most cases, the recursive solution is only slightly slower.
- In many cases, a recursive solution is easier to understand and implement correctly than an iterative solution.

Review a complex recursion example that cannot be solved with a simple loop.

- The permutations of a string can be obtained more naturally through recursion than with a loop.

Recognize the phenomenon of mutual recursion in a parsing application.

- In a mutual recursion, a set of cooperating methods calls each other repeatedly.

Media Resources

www.wiley.com/ go/global/ horstmann

- ***Worked Example*** Finding Files
- Lab Exercises
- ⊕ ***Animation*** Tracing a Recursion
- ⊕ Practice Quiz
- ⊕ Code Completion Exercises

Review Exercises

★ **R12.1** Define the terms
   a. Recursion
   b. Iteration
   c. Infinite recursion
   d. Recursive helper method

★★ **R12.2** Outline, but do not implement, a recursive solution for finding the smallest value in an array.

★★ **R12.3** Outline, but do not implement, a recursive solution for sorting an array of numbers. *Hint:* First find the smallest value in the array.

★★ **R12.4** Outline, but do not implement, a recursive solution for generating all subsets of the set $\{1, 2, \ldots, n\}$.

★★★ **R12.5** Exercise P12.12 shows an iterative way of generating all permutations of the sequence $(0, 1, \ldots, n - 1)$. Explain why the algorithm produces the correct result.

★ **R12.6** Write a recursive definition of x^n, where $n \geq 0$, similar to the recursive definition of the Fibonacci numbers. *Hint:* How do you compute x^n from x^{n-1}? How does the recursion terminate?

★★ **R12.7** Improve upon Exercise R12.6 by computing x^n as $(x^{n/2})^2$ if n is even. Why is this approach significantly faster? *Hint:* Compute x^{1023} and x^{1024} both ways.

★ **R12.8** Write a recursive definition of $n! = 1 \times 2 \times \ldots \times n$, similar to the recursive definition of the Fibonacci numbers.

★★ **R12.9** Find out how often the recursive version of fib calls itself. Keep a static variable fibCount and increment it once in every call of fib. What is the relationship between fib(n) and fibCount?

★★★ **R12.10** How many moves are required in the "Towers of Hanoi" problem of Exercise P12.13 to move n disks? *Hint:* As explained in the exercise,

$$\text{moves}(1) = 1$$
$$\text{moves}(n) = 2 \cdot \text{moves}(n - 1) + 1$$

Programming Exercises

★ **P12.1** Write a recursive method void reverse() that reverses a sentence. For example:

```
Sentence greeting = new Sentence("Hello!");
greeting.reverse();
System.out.println(greeting.getText());
```

prints the string "!olleH". Implement a recursive solution by removing the first character, reversing a sentence consisting of the remaining text, and combining the two.

★★ **P12.2** Redo Exercise P12.1 with a recursive helper method that reverses a substring of the message text.

★ **P12.3** Implement the reverse method of Exercise P12.1 as an iteration.

★★ **P12.4** Use recursion to implement a method `boolean find(String t)` that tests whether a string is contained in a sentence:

```
Sentence s = new Sentence("Mississippi!");
boolean b = s.find("sip"); // Returns true
```

Hint: If the text starts with the string you want to match, then you are done. If not, consider the sentence that you obtain by removing the first character.

★★ **P12.5** Use recursion to implement a method `int indexOf(String t)` that returns the starting position of the first substring of the text that matches t. Return –1 if t is not a substring of s. For example,

```
Sentence s = new Sentence("Mississippi!");
int n = s.indexOf("sip"); // Returns 6
```

Hint: This is a bit trickier than the preceding problem, because you must keep track of how far the match is from the beginning of the sentence. Make that value a parameter of a helper method.

★ **P12.6** Using recursion, find the largest element in an array.

```
public class DataSet
{
    public DataSet(int[] values, int first, int last) { . . . }
    public int getMaximum() { . . . }
    . . .
}
```

Hint: Find the largest element in the subset containing all but the last element. Then compare that maximum to the value of the last element.

★ **P12.7** Using recursion, compute the sum of all values in an array.

```
public class DataSet
{
    public DataSet(int[] values, int first, int last) { . . . }
    public int getSum() { . . . }
    . . .
}
```

★★ **P12.8** Using recursion, compute the area of a polygon. Cut off a triangle and use the fact that a triangle with corners (x_1, y_1), (x_2, y_2), (x_3, y_3) has area

$$\frac{\left|x_1 y_2 + x_2 y_3 + x_3 y_1 - y_1 x_2 - y_2 x_3 - y_3 x_1\right|}{2}$$

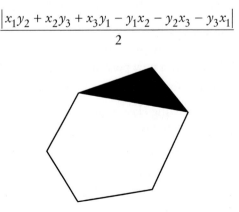

★★★ **P12.9** Implement a SubstringGenerator that generates all substrings of a string. For example, the substrings of the string "rum" are the seven strings

```
"r", "ru", "rum", "u", "um", "m", ""
```

Hint: First enumerate all substrings that start with the first character. There are *n* of them if the string has length *n*. Then enumerate the substrings of the string that you obtain by removing the first character.

★★★ **P12.10** Implement a SubsetGenerator that generates all subsets of the characters of a string. For example, the subsets of the characters of the string "rum" are the eight strings

```
"rum", "ru", "rm", "r", "um", "u", "m", ""
```

Note that the subsets don't have to be substrings—for example, "rm" isn't a substring of "rum".

★★★ **P12.11** In this exercise, you will change the PermutationGenerator of Section 12.4 (which computed all permutations at once) to a PermutationIterator (which computes them one at a time.)

```java
public class PermutationIterator
{
    public PermutationIterator(String s) { . . . }
    public String nextPermutation() { . . . }
    public boolean hasMorePermutations() { . . . }
}
```

Here is how you would print out all permutations of the string "eat":

```java
PermutationIterator iter = new PermutationIterator("eat");
while (iter.hasMorePermutations())
{
    System.out.println(iter.nextPermutation());
}
```

Now we need a way to iterate through the permutations recursively. Consider the string "eat". As before, we'll generate all permutations that start with the letter 'e', then those that start with 'a', and finally those that start with 't'. How do we generate the permutations that start with 'e'? Make another PermutationIterator object (called tailIterator) that iterates through the permutations of the substring "at". In the nextPermutation method, simply ask tailIterator what *its* next permutation is, and then add the 'e' at the front. However, there is one special case. When the tail generator runs out of permutations, all permutations that start with the current letter have been enumerated. Then

- Increment the current position.
- Compute the tail string that contains all letters except for the current one.
- Make a new permutation iterator for the tail string.

You are done when the current position has reached the end of the string.

★★★ **P12.12** The following class generates all permutations of the numbers 0, 1, 2, ..., *n* – 1, without using recursion.

```java
public class NumberPermutationIterator
{
    public NumberPermutationIterator(int n)
    {
```

```
            a = new int[n];
            done = false;
            for (int i = 0; i < n; i++) a[i] = i;
        }

        public int[] nextPermutation()
        {
            if (a.length <= 1) { return a; }

            for (int i = a.length - 1; i > 0; i--)
            {
                if (a[i - 1] < a[i])
                {
                    int j = a.length - 1;
                    while (a[i - 1] > a[j]) j--;
                    swap(i - 1, j);
                    reverse(i, a.length - 1);
                    return a;
                }
            }
            return a;
        }

        public boolean hasMorePermutations()
        {
            if (a.length <= 1) { return false; }
            for (int i = a.length - 1; i > 0; i--)
            {
                if (a[i - 1] < a[i]) { return true; }
            }
            return false;
        }

        public void swap(int i, int j)
        {
            int temp = a[i];
            a[i] = a[j];
            a[j] = temp;
        }

        public void reverse(int i, int j)
        {
            while (i < j) { swap(i, j); i++; j--; }
        }
        private int[] a;
    }
```

The algorithm uses the fact that the set to be permuted consists of distinct numbers. Thus, you cannot use the same algorithm to compute the permutations of the characters in a string. You can, however, use this class to get all permutations of the character positions and then compute a string whose ith character is word.charAt(a[i]). Use this approach to reimplement the PermutationIterator of Exercise P12.11 without recursion.

★★ **P12.13** *Towers of Hanoi.* This is a well-known puzzle. A stack of disks of decreasing size is to be transported from the leftmost peg to the rightmost peg. The middle peg can be used as temporary storage (see Figure 5). One disk can be moved at one time, from

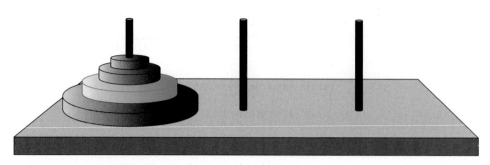

Figure 5 Towers of Hanoi

any peg to any other peg. You can place smaller disks only on top of larger ones, not the other way around.

Write a program that prints the moves necessary to solve the puzzle for *n* disks. (Ask the user for *n* at the beginning of the program.) Print moves in the form

```
Move disk from peg 1 to peg 3
```

Hint: Implement a class `DiskMover`. The constructor takes

- The source peg from which to move the disks (1, 2, or 3)
- The target peg to which to move the disks (1, 2, or 3)
- The number of disks to move

A disk mover that moves a single disk from one peg to another simply has a `nextMove` method that returns a string

```
Move disk from peg source to peg target
```

A disk mover with more than one disk to move must work harder. It needs another `DiskMover` to help it. In the constructor, construct a `DiskMover(source, other, disks - 1)` where `other` is the peg other than `from` and `target`.

The `nextMove` asks that disk mover for its next move until it is done. The effect is to move the first `disks - 1` disks to the other peg. Then the `nextMove` method issues a command to move a disk from the `from` peg to the `to` peg. Finally, it constructs another disk mover `DiskMover(other, target, disks - 1)` that generates the moves that move the disks from the other peg to the target peg.

Hint: It helps to keep track of the state of the disk mover:

- `BEFORE_LARGEST`: The helper mover moves the smaller pile to the other peg.
- `LARGEST`: Move the largest disk from the source to the destination.
- `AFTER_LARGEST`: The helper mover moves the smaller pile from the other peg to the target.
- `DONE`: All moves are done.

Test your program as follows:

```
DiskMover mover = new DiskMover(1, 3, n);
while (mover.hasMoreMoves())
{
    System.out.println(mover.nextMove());
}
```

★★★ P12.14 *Escaping a Maze.* You are currently located inside a maze. The walls of the maze are indicated by asterisks (*).

```
* *******
*     * *
* ***** *
* * *   *
* * *** *
*   *   *
*** * * *
*     * *
******* *
```

Use the following recursive approach to check whether you can escape from the maze: If you are at an exit, return true. Recursively check whether you can escape from one of the empty neighboring locations without visiting the current location. This method merely tests whether there is a path out of the maze. Extra credit if you can print out a path that leads to an exit.

★★★G P12.15 *The Koch Snowflake.* A snowflake-like shape is recursively defined as follows. Start with an equilateral triangle:

Next, increase the size by a factor of three and replace each straight line with four line segments.

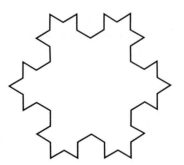

Repeat the process.

Write a program that draws the iterations of this curve. Supply a button that, when clicked, produces the next iteration.

★★ P12.16 The recursive computation of Fibonacci numbers can be speeded up significantly by keeping track of the values that have already been computed. Provide an implementation of the fib method that uses this strategy. Whenever you return a new value, also store it in an auxiliary array. However, before embarking on a computation, consult the array to find whether the result has already been computed. Compare the running time of your improved implementation with that of the original recursive implementation and the loop implementation.

Programming Projects

Project 12.1 Enhance the expression parser of Section 12.5 to handle more sophisticated expressions, such as exponents, and mathematical functions, such as sqrt or sin.

Project 12.2 Implement a graphical version of the "Towers of Hanoi" program (see Exercise P12.13). Every time the user clicks on a button labeled "Next", draw the next move.

Answers to Self-Check Questions

1. Suppose we omit the statement. When computing the area of a triangle with width 1, we compute the area of the triangle with width 0 as 0, and then add 1, to arrive at the correct area.

2. You would compute the smaller area recursively, then return
   `smallerArea + width + width - 1`.

   ```
   [][][][]
   [][][][]
   [][][][]
   [][][][]
   ```

   Of course, it would be simpler to compute the area simply as `width * width`.
   The results are identical because
   $$1 + 0 + 2 + 1 + 3 + 2 + \cdots + n + n - 1 = \frac{n(n+1)}{2} + \frac{(n-1)n}{2} = n^2.$$

3. No—the first one could be given a different name such as substringIsPalindrome.

4. When `start >= end`, that is, when the investigated string is either empty or has length 1.

5. The loop is slightly faster. Of course, it is even faster to simply compute `width * (width + 1) / 2`.

6. No, the recursive solution is about as efficient as the iterative approach. Both require $n - 1$ multiplications to compute $n!$.

7. They are b followed by the six permutations of eat, e followed by the six permutations of bat, a followed by the six permutations of bet, and t followed by the six permutations of bea.

8. Simply change `if (word.length() == 0)` to `if (word.length() <= 1)`, because a word with a single letter is also its sole permutation.

9. An iterative solution would have a loop whose body computes the next permutation from the previous ones. But there is no obvious mechanism for getting the next permutation. For example, if you already found permutations eat, eta, and aet, it is not clear how you use that information to get the next permutation. Actually, there is an ingenious mechanism for doing just that, but it is far from obvious—see Exercise P12.12.

10. Factors are combined by multiplicative operators (* and /), terms are combined by additive operators (+, -). We need both so that multiplication can bind more strongly than addition.

11. To handle parenthesized expressions, such as 2+3*(4+5). The subexpression 4+5 is handled by a recursive call to getExpressionValue.

12. The Integer.parseInt call in getFactorValue throws an exception when it is given the string ")".

Sorting and
Searching

CHAPTER GOALS

- To study several sorting and searching algorithms
- To appreciate that algorithms for the same task can differ widely in performance
- To understand the big-Oh notation
- To learn how to estimate and compare the performance of algorithms
- To learn how to measure the running time of a program

Sorting and searching are among the most common tasks in data processing. Of course, the Java library contains methods for carrying out these operations. Nevertheless, studying algorithms for sorting and searching is fruitful because you will learn how to analyze the performance of algorithms and how to choose the best algorithm for a particular task. Sorting and searching are an excellent entry point into the study of algorithm analysis because the tasks themselves are simple to understand. As you will see in this chapter, the most straightforward algorithms do not perform very well, and we can achieve dramatic improvements with more sophisticated algorithms.

CHAPTER CONTENTS

13.1 Selection Sort

In this section, we show you the first of several sorting algorithms. A *sorting algorithm* rearranges the elements of a collection so that they are stored in sorted order. To keep the examples simple, we will discuss how to sort an array of integers before going on to sorting strings or more complex data. Consider the following array a:

```
[0][1][2][3][4]
11  9  17  5  12
```

> The selection sort algorithm sorts an array by repeatedly finding the smallest element of the unsorted tail region and moving it to the front.

An obvious first step is to find the smallest element. In this case the smallest element is 5, stored in a[3]. We should move the 5 to the beginning of the array. Of course, there is already an element stored in a[0], namely 11. Therefore we cannot simply move a[3] into a[0] without moving the 11 somewhere else. We don't yet know where the 11 should end up, but we know for certain that it should not be in a[0]. We simply get it out of the way by *swapping* it with a[3].

```
[0][1][2][3][4]
 5  9  17  11  12
```

Now the first element is in the correct place. In the foregoing figure, the darker color indicates the portion of the array that is already sorted.

Next we take the minimum of the remaining entries a[1] . . . a[4]. That minimum value, 9, is already in the correct place. We don't need to do anything in this case and can simply extend the sorted area by one to the right:

```
[0][1][2][3][4]
 5  9  17  11  12
```

510

Repeat the process. The minimum value of the unsorted region is 11, which needs to be swapped with the first value of the unsorted region, 17:

Now the unsorted region is only two elements long, but we keep to the same successful strategy. The minimum value is 12, and we swap it with the first value, 17.

That leaves us with an unprocessed region of length 1, but of course a region of length 1 is always sorted. We are done.

Let's program this algorithm. For this program, as well as the other programs in this chapter, we will use a utility method to generate an array with random entries. We place it into a class ArrayUtil so that we don't have to repeat the code in every example. To show the array, we call the static toString method of the Arrays class in the Java library and print the resulting string.

This algorithm will sort any array of integers. If speed were not an issue, or if there simply were no better sorting method available, we could stop the discussion of sorting right here. As the next section shows, however, this algorithm, while entirely correct, shows disappointing performance when run on a large data set.

Special Topic 13.1 discusses insertion sort, another simple sorting algorithm.

ch13/selsort/SelectionSorter.java

```
1  /**
2     This class sorts an array, using the selection sort
3     algorithm.
4  */
5  public class SelectionSorter
6  {
7     private int[] a;
8
9     /**
10        Constructs a selection sorter.
11        @param anArray the array to sort
12     */
13     public SelectionSorter(int[] anArray)
14     {
15        a = anArray;
16     }
17
18     /**
19        Sorts the array managed by this selection sorter.
20     */
21     public void sort()
22     {
```

```
23      for (int i = 0; i < a.length - 1; i++)
24      {
25          int minPos = minimumPosition(i);
26          swap(minPos, i);
27      }
28   }
29
30   /**
31      Finds the smallest element in a tail range of the array.
32      @param from the first position in a to compare
33      @return the position of the smallest element in the
34      range a[from] . . . a[a.length - 1]
35   */
36   private int minimumPosition(int from)
37   {
38      int minPos = from;
39      for (int i = from + 1; i < a.length; i++)
40          if (a[i] < a[minPos]) minPos = i;
41      return minPos;
42   }
43
44   /**
45      Swaps two entries of the array.
46      @param i the first position to swap
47      @param j the second position to swap
48   */
49   private void swap(int i, int j)
50   {
51      int temp = a[i];
52      a[i] = a[j];
53      a[j] = temp;
54   }
55 }
```

ch13/selsort/SelectionSortDemo.java

```
1  import java.util.Arrays;
2
3  /**
4     This program demonstrates the selection sort algorithm by
5     sorting an array that is filled with random numbers.
6  */
7  public class SelectionSortDemo
8  {
9     public static void main(String[] args)
10    {
11       int[] a = ArrayUtil.randomIntArray(20, 100);
12       System.out.println(Arrays.toString(a));
13
14       SelectionSorter sorter = new SelectionSorter(a);
15       sorter.sort();
16
17       System.out.println(Arrays.toString(a));
18    }
19 }
```

ch13/selsort/ArrayUtil.java

```java
1  import java.util.Random;
2
3  /**
4     This class contains utility methods for array manipulation.
5  */
6  public class ArrayUtil
7  {
8     private static Random generator = new Random();
9
10    /**
11       Creates an array filled with random values.
12       @param length the length of the array
13       @param n the number of possible random values
14       @return an array filled with length numbers between
15       0 and n - 1
16    */
17    public static int[] randomIntArray(int length, int n)
18    {
19       int[] a = new int[length];
20       for (int i = 0; i < a.length; i++)
21          a[i] = generator.nextInt(n);
22
23       return a;
24    }
25 }
```

Typical Output

```
[65, 46, 14, 52, 38, 2, 96, 39, 14, 33, 13, 4, 24, 99, 89, 77, 73, 87, 36, 81]
[2, 4, 13, 14, 14, 24, 33, 36, 38, 39, 46, 52, 65, 73, 77, 81, 87, 89, 96, 99]
```

SELF CHECK

1. Why do we need the temp variable in the swap method? What would happen if you simply assigned a[i] to a[j] and a[j] to a[i]?

2. What steps does the selection sort algorithm go through to sort the sequence 6 5 4 3 2 1?

13.2 Profiling the Selection Sort Algorithm

To measure the performance of a program, you could simply run it and use a stop-watch to measure how long it takes. However, most of our programs run very quickly, and it is not easy to time them accurately in this way. Furthermore, when a program takes a noticeable time to run, a certain amount of that time may simply be used for loading the program from disk into memory and displaying the result (for which we should not penalize it).

In order to measure the running time of an algorithm more accurately, we will create a StopWatch class. This class works like a real stopwatch. You can start it, stop it, and read out the elapsed time. The class uses the System.currentTimeMillis method, which returns the milliseconds that have elapsed since midnight at the start of January 1, 1970. Of course, you don't care about the absolute number of seconds since this historical moment, but the *difference* of two such counts gives us the number of milliseconds of a time interval.

Here is the code for the StopWatch class:

ch13/selsort/StopWatch.java

```
1  /**
2     A stopwatch accumulates time when it is running. You can
3     repeatedly start and stop the stopwatch. You can use a
4     stopwatch to measure the running time of a program.
5  */
6  public class StopWatch
7  {
8     private long elapsedTime;
9     private long startTime;
10    private boolean isRunning;
11
12    /**
13       Constructs a stopwatch that is in the stopped state
14       and has no time accumulated.
15    */
16    public StopWatch()
17    {
18       reset();
19    }
20
21    /**
22       Starts the stopwatch. Time starts accumulating now.
23    */
24    public void start()
25    {
26       if (isRunning) return;
27       isRunning = true;
28       startTime = System.currentTimeMillis();
29    }
30
31    /**
32       Stops the stopwatch. Time stops accumulating and is
33       is added to the elapsed time.
34    */
35    public void stop()
36    {
37       if (!isRunning) return;
38       isRunning = false;
39       long endTime = System.currentTimeMillis();
40       elapsedTime = elapsedTime + endTime - startTime;
41    }
42
43    /**
44       Returns the total elapsed time.
45       @return the total elapsed time
46    */
47    public long getElapsedTime()
48    {
49       if (isRunning)
50       {
51          long endTime = System.currentTimeMillis();
52          return elapsedTime + endTime - startTime;
53       }
54       else
55          return elapsedTime;
```

```
56        }
57
58        /**
59           Stops the watch and resets the elapsed time to 0.
60        */
61        public void reset()
62        {
63           elapsedTime = 0;
64           isRunning = false;
65        }
66   }
```

Here is how we will use the stopwatch to measure the performance of the sorting algorithm:

ch13/selsort/SelectionSortTimer.java

```java
1    import java.util.Scanner;
2
3    /**
4       This program measures how long it takes to sort an
5       array of a user-specified size with the selection
6       sort algorithm.
7    */
8    public class SelectionSortTimer
9    {
10      public static void main(String[] args)
11      {
12         Scanner in = new Scanner(System.in);
13         System.out.print("Enter array size: ");
14         int n = in.nextInt();
15
16         // Construct random array
17
18         int[] a = ArrayUtil.randomIntArray(n, 100);
19         SelectionSorter sorter = new SelectionSorter(a);
20
21         // Use stopwatch to time selection sort
22
23         StopWatch timer = new StopWatch();
24
25         timer.start();
26         sorter.sort();
27         timer.stop();
28
29         System.out.println("Elapsed time: "
30               + timer.getElapsedTime() + " milliseconds");
31      }
32   }
```

Program Run

```
Enter array size: 100000
Elapsed time: 27880 milliseconds
```

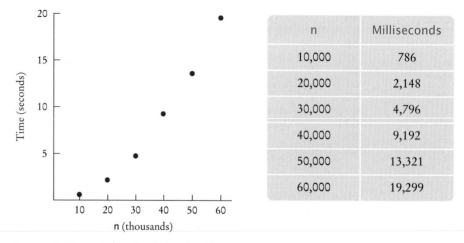

n	Milliseconds
10,000	786
20,000	2,148
30,000	4,796
40,000	9,192
50,000	13,321
60,000	19,299

Figure 1   Time Taken by Selection Sort

> To measure the running time of a method, get the current time immediately before and after the method call.

By starting to measure the time just before sorting, and stopping the stopwatch just after, you get the time required for the sorting process, without counting the time for input and output.

The table in Figure 1 shows the results of some sample runs. These measurements were obtained with a Intel processor with a clock speed of 2 GHz, running Java 6 on the Linux operating system. On another computer the actual numbers will look different, but the relationship between the numbers will be the same.

The graph in Figure 1 shows a plot of the measurements. As you can see, doubling the size of the data set more than doubles the time needed to sort it.

S E L F   C H E C K

3. Approximately how many seconds would it take to sort a data set of 80,000 values?

4. Look at the graph in Figure 1. What mathematical shape does it resemble?

13.3 Analyzing the Performance of the Selection Sort Algorithm

Let us count the number of operations that the program must carry out to sort an array with the selection sort algorithm. We don't actually know how many machine operations are generated for each Java instruction, or which of those instructions are more time-consuming than others, but we can make a simplification. We will simply count how often an array element is *visited*. Each visit requires about the same amount of work by other operations, such as incrementing subscripts and comparing values.

Let n be the size of the array. First, we must find the smallest of n numbers. To achieve that, we must visit n array elements. Then we swap the elements, which takes two visits. (You may argue that there is a certain probability that we don't need to swap the values. That is true, and one can refine the computation to reflect that observation. As we will soon see, doing so would not affect the overall conclusion.) In the next step, we need to visit only $n - 1$ elements to find the minimum. In the following step, $n - 2$ elements are visited to find the minimum. The last step visits two elements to find the minimum. Each step requires two visits to swap the elements. Therefore, the total number of visits is

$$n + 2 + (n - 1) + 2 + \cdots + 2 + 2 = n + (n - 1) + \cdots + 2 + (n - 1) \cdot 2$$
$$= 2 + \cdots + (n - 1) + n + (n - 1) \cdot 2$$
$$= \frac{n(n + 1)}{2} - 1 + (n - 1) \cdot 2$$

because

$$1 + 2 + \cdots + (n - 1) + n = \frac{n(n + 1)}{2}$$

After multiplying out and collecting terms of n, we find that the number of visits is

$$\tfrac{1}{2}n^2 + \tfrac{5}{2}n - 3$$

We obtain a quadratic equation in n. That explains why the graph of Figure 1 looks approximately like a parabola.

Now simplify the analysis further. When you plug in a large value for n (for example, 1,000 or 2,000), then $\frac{1}{2}n^2$ is 500,000 or 2,000,000. The lower term, $\frac{5}{2}n - 3$, doesn't contribute much at all; it is only 2,497 or 4,997, a drop in the bucket compared to the hundreds of thousands or even millions of comparisons specified by the $\frac{1}{2}n^2$ term. We will just ignore these lower-level terms. Next, we will ignore the constant factor $\frac{1}{2}$. We are not interested in the actual count of visits for a single n. We want to compare the ratios of counts for different values of n. For example, we can say that sorting an array of 2,000 numbers requires four times as many visits as sorting an array of 1,000 numbers:

$$\frac{\left(\frac{1}{2} \cdot 2000^2\right)}{\left(\frac{1}{2} \cdot 1000^2\right)} = 4$$

The factor $\frac{1}{2}$ cancels out in comparisons of this kind. We will simply say, "The number of visits is of order n^2". That way, we can easily see that the number of comparisons increases fourfold when the size of the array doubles: $(2n)^2 = 4n^2$.

To indicate that the number of visits is of order n^2, computer scientists often use *big-Oh notation:* The number of visits is $O(n^2)$. This is a convenient shorthand.

In general, the expression $f(n) = O(g(n))$ means that f grows no faster than g, or, more formally, that for all n larger than some threshold, the ratio $f(n)/g(n) \leq C$ for some constant value C. The function g is usually chosen to be very simple, such as n^2 in our example.

To turn an exact expression such as

$$\tfrac{1}{2}n^2 + \tfrac{5}{2}n - 3$$

into big-Oh notation, simply locate the fastest-growing term, n^2, and ignore its constant coefficient, no matter how large or small it may be.

Computer scientists use the big-Oh notation $f(n) = O(g(n))$ to express that the function f grows no faster than the function g.

We observed before that the actual number of machine operations, and the actual amount of time that the computer spends on them, is approximately proportional to the number of element visits. Maybe there are about 10 machine operations (increments, comparisons, memory loads, and stores) for every element visit. The number of machine operations is then approximately $10 \times \frac{1}{2}n^2$. As before, we aren't interested in the coefficient, so we can say that the number of machine operations, and hence the time spent on the sorting, is of the order of n^2 or $O(n^2)$.

> Selection sort is an $O(n^2)$ algorithm. Doubling the data set means a fourfold increase in processing time.

The sad fact remains that doubling the size of the array causes a fourfold increase in the time required for sorting it with selection sort. When the size of the array increases by a factor of 100, the sorting time increases by a factor of 10,000. To sort an array of a million entries, (for example, to create a telephone directory) takes 10,000 times as long as sorting 10,000 entries. If 10,000 entries can be sorted in about 1/2 of a second (as in our example), then sorting one million entries requires well over an hour. We will see in the next section how one can dramatically improve the performance of the sorting process by choosing a more sophisticated algorithm.

SELF CHECK

5. If you increase the size of a data set tenfold, how much longer does it take to sort it with the selection sort algorithm?
6. How large does n need to be so that $\frac{1}{2}n^2$ is bigger than $\frac{5}{2}n - 3$?

Special Topic 13.1

Insertion Sort

Special Topic 13.1 describes insertion sort, another simple sorting algorithm that is commonly used for small arrays. Like selection sort, its run time is $O(n^2)$.

Special Topic 13.2

Oh, Omega, and Theta

Special Topic 13.2 defines the big-Theta and big-Omega notations that describe the growth of a function more precisely than the big-Oh notation.

13.4 Merge Sort

In this section, you will learn about the merge sort algorithm, a much more efficient algorithm than selection sort. The basic idea behind merge sort is very simple.

Suppose we have an array of 10 integers. Let us engage in a bit of wishful thinking and hope that the first half of the array is already perfectly sorted, and the second half is too, like this:

Now it is simple to *merge* the two sorted arrays into one sorted array, by taking a new element from either the first or the second subarray, and choosing the smaller of the elements each time:

In fact, you may have performed this merging before if you and a friend had to sort a pile of papers. You and the friend split the pile in half, each of you sorted your half, and then you merged the results together.

That is all well and good, but it doesn't seem to solve the problem for the computer. It still must sort the first and second halves of the array, because it can't very well ask a few buddies to pitch in. As it turns out, though, if the computer keeps dividing the array into smaller and smaller subarrays, sorting each half and merging them back together, it carries out dramatically fewer steps than the selection sort requires.

Let's write a MergeSorter class that implements this idea. When the MergeSorter sorts an array, it makes two arrays, each half the size of the original, and sorts them recursively. Then it merges the two sorted arrays together:

> The merge sort algorithm sorts an array by cutting the array in half, recursively sorting each half, and then merging the sorted halves.

```java
public void sort()
{
   if (a.length <= 1) return;
   int[] first = new int[a.length / 2];
   int[] second = new int[a.length - first.length];
   // Copy the first half of a into first, the second half into second
   . . .
   MergeSorter firstSorter = new MergeSorter(first);
   MergeSorter secondSorter = new MergeSorter(second);
   firstSorter.sort();
   secondSorter.sort();
   merge(first, second);
}
```

The merge method is tedious but quite straightforward. You will find it in the code that follows.

ch13/mergesort/MergeSorter.java

```java
1  /**
2     This class sorts an array, using the merge sort algorithm.
3  */
4  public class MergeSorter
5  {
6     private int[] a;
```

```
 7
 8     /**
 9        Constructs a merge sorter.
10        @param anArray the array to sort
11     */
12     public MergeSorter(int[] anArray)
13     {
14        a = anArray;
15     }
16
17     /**
18        Sorts the array managed by this merge sorter.
19     */
20     public void sort()
21     {
22        if (a.length <= 1) return;
23        int[] first = new int[a.length / 2];
24        int[] second = new int[a.length - first.length];
25        // Copy the first half of a into first, the second half into second
26        for (int i = 0; i < first.length; i++) { first[i] = a[i]; }
27        for (int i = 0; i < second.length; i++)
28        {
29           second[i] = a[first.length + i];
30        }
31        MergeSorter firstSorter = new MergeSorter(first);
32        MergeSorter secondSorter = new MergeSorter(second);
33        firstSorter.sort();
34        secondSorter.sort();
35        merge(first, second);
36     }
37
38     /**
39        Merges two sorted arrays into the array managed by this merge sorter.
40        @param first the first sorted array
41        @param second the second sorted array
42     */
43     private void merge(int[] first, int[] second)
44     {
45        int iFirst = 0;   // Next element to consider in the first array
46        int iSecond = 0;   // Next element to consider in the second array
47        int j = 0;   // Next open position in a
48
49        // As long as neither iFirst nor iSecond past the end, move
50        // the smaller element into a
51        while (iFirst < first.length && iSecond < second.length)
52        {
53           if (first[iFirst] < second[iSecond])
54           {
55              a[j] = first[iFirst];
56              iFirst++;
57           }
58           else
59           {
60              a[j] = second[iSecond];
61              iSecond++;
62           }
63           j++;
64        }
65
```

```
66        // Note that only one of the two loops below copies entries
67        // Copy any remaining entries of the first array
68        while (iFirst < first.length)
69        {
70           a[j] = first[iFirst];
71           iFirst++; j++;
72        }
73        // Copy any remaining entries of the second half
74        while (iSecond < second.length)
75        {
76           a[j] = second[iSecond];
77           iSecond++; j++;
78        }
79     }
80  }
```

ch13/mergesort/MergeSortDemo.java

```
1  import java.util.Arrays;
2
3  /**
4     This program demonstrates the merge sort algorithm by
5     sorting an array that is filled with random numbers.
6  */
7  public class MergeSortDemo
8  {
9     public static void main(String[] args)
10    {
11       int[] a = ArrayUtil.randomIntArray(20, 100);
12       System.out.println(Arrays.toString(a));
13
14       MergeSorter sorter = new MergeSorter(a);
15       sorter.sort();
16       System.out.println(Arrays.toString(a));
17    }
18 }
```

Typical Output

```
[8, 81, 48, 53, 46, 70, 98, 42, 27, 76, 33, 24, 2, 76, 62, 89, 90, 5, 13, 21]
[2, 5, 8, 13, 21, 24, 27, 33, 42, 46, 48, 53, 62, 70, 76, 76, 81, 89, 90, 98]
```

 **SELF CHECK**

7. Why does only one of the two `while` loops at the end of the `merge` method do any work?
8. Manually run the merge sort algorithm on the array 8 7 6 5 4 3 2 1.

13.5 Analyzing the Merge Sort Algorithm

The merge sort algorithm looks a lot more complicated than the selection sort algorithm, and it appears that it may well take much longer to carry out these repeated subdivisions. However, the timing results for merge sort look much better than those for selection sort.

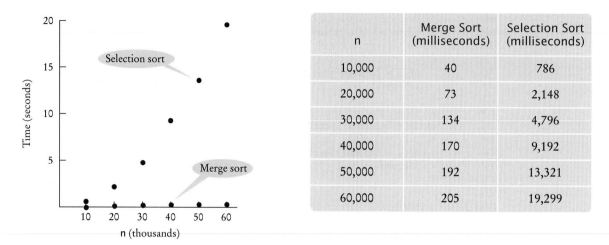

n	Merge Sort (milliseconds)	Selection Sort (milliseconds)
10,000	40	786
20,000	73	2,148
30,000	134	4,796
40,000	170	9,192
50,000	192	13,321
60,000	205	19,299

Figure 2 Merge Sort Timing versus Selection Sort

Figure 2 shows a table and a graph comparing both sets of performance data. As you can see, merge sort is a tremendous improvement. To understand why, let us estimate the number of array element visits that are required to sort an array with the merge sort algorithm. First, let us tackle the merge process that happens after the first and second halves have been sorted.

Each step in the merge process adds one more element to a. That element may come from first or second, and in most cases the elements from the two halves must be compared to see which one to take. We'll count that as 3 visits (one for a and one each for first and second) per element, or 3n visits total, where n denotes the length of a. Moreover, at the beginning, we had to copy from a to first and second, yielding another 2n visits, for a total of 5n.

If we let $T(n)$ denote the number of visits required to sort a range of n elements through the merge sort process, then we obtain

$$T(n) = T\left(\frac{n}{2}\right) + T\left(\frac{n}{2}\right) + 5n$$

because sorting each half takes $T(n/2)$ visits. Actually, if n is not even, then we have one subarray of size $(n-1)/2$ and one of size $(n+1)/2$. Although it turns out that this detail does not affect the outcome of the computation, we will nevertheless assume for now that n is a power of 2, say $n = 2^m$. That way, all subarrays can be evenly divided into two parts.

Unfortunately, the formula

$$T(n) = 2T\left(\frac{n}{2}\right) + 5n$$

does not clearly tell us the relationship between n and $T(n)$. To understand the relationship, let us evaluate $T(n/2)$, using the same formula:

$$T\left(\frac{n}{2}\right) = 2T\left(\frac{n}{4}\right) + 5\frac{n}{2}$$

Therefore

$$T(n) = 2 \times 2T\left(\frac{n}{4}\right) + 5n + 5n$$

Let us do that again:

$$T\left(\frac{n}{4}\right) = 2T\left(\frac{n}{8}\right) + 5\frac{n}{4}$$

hence

$$T(n) = 2 \times 2 \times 2T\left(\frac{n}{8}\right) + 5n + 5n + 5n$$

This generalizes from 2, 4, 8, to arbitrary powers of 2:

$$T(n) = 2^k T\left(\frac{n}{2^k}\right) + 5nk$$

Recall that we assume that $n = 2^m$; hence, for $k = m$,

$$T(n) = 2^m T\left(\frac{n}{2^m}\right) + 5nm$$

$$= nT(1) + 5nm$$

$$= n + 5n\log_2(n)$$

Because $n = 2^m$, we have $m = \log_2(n)$.

To establish the growth order, we drop the lower-order term n and are left with $5n\log_2(n)$. We drop the constant factor 5. It is also customary to drop the base of the logarithm, because all logarithms are related by a constant factor. For example,

$$\log_2(x) = \log_{10}(x)/\log_{10}(2) \approx \log_{10}(x) \times 3.32193$$

Hence we say that merge sort is an $O(n\log(n))$ algorithm.

Is the $O(n\log(n))$ merge sort algorithm better than the $O(n^2)$ selection sort algorithm? You bet it is. Recall that it took $100^2 = 10{,}000$ times as long to sort a million records as it took to sort 10,000 records with the $O(n^2)$ algorithm. With the $O(n\log(n))$ algorithm, the ratio is

> Merge sort is an $O(n\log(n))$ algorithm. The $n\log(n)$ function grows much more slowly than n^2.

$$\frac{1{,}000{,}000\log(1{,}000{,}000)}{10{,}000\log(10{,}000)} = 100\left(\frac{6}{4}\right) = 150$$

Suppose for the moment that merge sort takes the same time as selection sort to sort an array of 10,000 integers, that is, 3/4 of a second on the test machine. (Actually, it is much faster than that.) Then it would take about 0.75×150 seconds, or under 2 minutes, to sort a million integers. Contrast that with selection sort, which would take over 2 hours for the same task. As you can see, even if it takes you several hours to learn about a better algorithm, that can be time well spent.

In this chapter we have barely begun to scratch the surface of this interesting topic. There are many sorting algorithms, some with even better performance than merge sort, and the analysis of these algorithms can be quite challenging. These important issues are often revisited in later computer science courses.

9. Given the timing data for the merge sort algorithm in the table at the beginning of this section, how long would it take to sort an array of 100,000 values?

10. If you double the size of an array, how much longer will the merge sort algorithm take to sort the new array?

Special Topic 13.3

The Quicksort Algorithm

Special Topic 13.3 describes the quicksort algorithm, a commonly used algorithm that has an advantage over merge sort in that no temporary arrays are required to sort and merge the partial results. On average, the quicksort algorithm is an $O(n \log(n))$ algorithm. Because it is simpler, it runs faster than merge sort in most cases. However, its worst-case run-time behavior is $O(n^2)$.

Random Fact 13.1

The First Programmer

Random Fact 13.1 tells the story of Charles Babbage, the builder of a programmable mechanical calculator, and Ada Lovelace, his friend and sponsor. Lovelace is considered by many to be the world's first programmer.

13.6 Searching

Suppose you need to find your friend's telephone number. You look up the friend's name in the telephone book, and naturally you can find it quickly, because the telephone book is sorted alphabetically. Now suppose you have a telephone number and you must know to what party it belongs. You could of course call that number, but suppose nobody picks up on the other end. You could look through the telephone book, a number at a time, until you find the number. That would obviously be a tremendous amount of work, and you would have to be desperate to attempt it.

This thought experiment shows the difference between a search through an unsorted data set and a search through a sorted data set. The following two sections will analyze the difference formally.

> A linear search examines all values in an array until it finds a match or reaches the end.

If you want to find a number in a sequence of values that occur in arbitrary order, there is nothing you can do to speed up the search. You must simply look through all elements until you have found a match or until you reach the end. This is called a **linear** or **sequential search**.

> A linear search locates a value in an array in $O(n)$ steps.

How long does a linear search take? If we assume that the element v is present in the array a, then the average search visits $n/2$ elements, where n is the length of the array. If it is not present, then all n elements must be inspected to verify the absence. Either way, a linear search is an $O(n)$ algorithm.

Here is a class that performs linear searches through an array a of integers. When searching for the value v, the search method returns the first index of the match, or -1 if v does not occur in a.

ch13/linsearch/LinearSearcher.java

```java
1  /**
2      A class for executing linear searches through an array.
3  */
4  public class LinearSearcher
5  {
6     private int[] a;
7
8     /**
9         Constructs the LinearSearcher.
10        @param anArray an array of integers
11     */
12    public LinearSearcher(int[] anArray)
13    {
14       a = anArray;
15    }
16
17    /**
18        Finds a value in an array, using the linear search
19        algorithm.
20        @param v the value to search
21        @return the index at which the value occurs, or -1
22        if it does not occur in the array
23     */
24    public int search(int v)
25    {
26       for (int i = 0; i < a.length; i++)
27       {
28          if (a[i] == v)
29             return i;
30       }
31       return -1;
32    }
33 }
```

ch13/linsearch/LinearSearchDemo.java

```java
1  import java.util.Arrays;
2  import java.util.Scanner;
3
4  /**
5      This program demonstrates the linear search algorithm.
6  */
7  public class LinearSearchDemo
8  {
9     public static void main(String[] args)
10    {
11       int[] a = ArrayUtil.randomIntArray(20, 100);
12       System.out.println(Arrays.toString(a));
13       LinearSearcher searcher = new LinearSearcher(a);
14
15       Scanner in = new Scanner(System.in);
16
17       boolean done = false;
18       while (!done)
19       {
20          System.out.print("Enter number to search for, -1 to quit: ");
21          int n = in.nextInt();
```

```
22          if (n == -1)
23             done = true;
24          else
25          {
26             int pos = searcher.search(n);
27             System.out.println("Found in position " + pos);
28          }
29       }
30    }
31 }
```

Typical Output

```
[46, 99, 45, 57, 64, 95, 81, 69, 11, 97, 6, 85, 61, 88, 29, 65, 83, 88, 45, 88]
Enter number to search for, -1 to quit: 11
Found in position 8
```

SELF CHECK

11. Suppose you need to look through 1,000,000 records to find a telephone number. How many records do you expect to search before finding the number?

12. Why can't you use a "for each" loop for (int element : a) in the search method?

13.7 Binary Search

Now let us search for an item in a data sequence that has been previously sorted. Of course, we could still do a linear search, but it turns out we can do much better than that.

Consider the following sorted array a. The data set is:

[0][1][2][3][4][5][6][7]
1 5 8 9 12 17 20 32

We would like to see whether the value 15 is in the data set. Let's narrow our search by finding whether the value is in the first or second half of the array. The last point in the first half of the data set, a[3], is 9, which is smaller than the value we are looking for. Hence, we should look in the second half of the array for a match, that is, in the sequence:

[0][1][2][3][4][5][6][7]
1 5 8 9 **12 17 20 32**

Now the last value of the first half of this sequence is 17; hence, the value must be located in the sequence:

[0][1][2][3][4][5][6][7]
1 5 8 9 **12 17** 20 32

The last value of the first half of this very short sequence is 12, which is smaller than the value that we are searching, so we must look in the second half:

[0][1][2][3][4][5][6][7]
1 5 8 9 12 **17** 20 32

It is trivial to see that we don't have a match, because 15 ≠ 17. If we wanted to insert 15 into the sequence, we would need to insert it just before a[5].

This search process is called a **binary search**, because we cut the size of the search in half in each step. That cutting in half works only because we know that the sequence of values is sorted.

The following class implements binary searches in a sorted array of integers. The search method returns the position of the match if the search succeeds, or –1 if v is not found in a.

ch13/binsearch/BinarySearcher.java

```
1   /**
2       A class for executing binary searches through an array.
3   */
4   public class BinarySearcher
5   {
6      private int[] a;
7
8      /**
9          Constructs a BinarySearcher.
10         @param anArray a sorted array of integers
11     */
12     public BinarySearcher(int[] anArray)
13     {
14        a = anArray;
15     }
16
17     /**
18         Finds a value in a sorted array, using the binary
19         search algorithm.
20         @param v the value to search
21         @return the index at which the value occurs, or -1
22         if it does not occur in the array
23     */
24     public int search(int v)
25     {
26        int low = 0;
27        int high = a.length - 1;
28        while (low <= high)
29        {
30           int mid = (low + high) / 2;
31           int diff = a[mid] - v;
32
33           if (diff == 0) // a[mid] == v
34              return mid;
35           else if (diff < 0) // a[mid] < v
36              low = mid + 1;
37           else
38              high = mid - 1;
39        }
40        return -1;
41     }
42  }
```

Now let's determine the number of visits to array elements required to carry out a binary search. We can use the same technique as in the analysis of merge sort.

Because we look at the middle element, which counts as one visit, and then search either the left or the right subarray, we have

$$T(n) = T\left(\frac{n}{2}\right) + 1$$

Using the same equation,

$$T\left(\frac{n}{2}\right) = T\left(\frac{n}{4}\right) + 1$$

By plugging this result into the original equation, we get

$$T(n) = T\left(\frac{n}{4}\right) + 2$$

That generalizes to

$$T(n) = T\left(\frac{n}{2^k}\right) + k$$

As in the analysis of merge sort, we make the simplifying assumption that n is a power of 2, $n = 2^m$, where $m = \log_2(n)$. Then we obtain

$$T(n) = 1 + \log_2(n)$$

Therefore, binary search is an $O(\log(n))$ algorithm.

> A binary search locates a value in a sorted array in $O(\log(n))$ steps.

That result makes intuitive sense. Suppose that n is 100. Then after each search, the size of the search range is cut in half, to 50, 25, 12, 6, 3, and 1. After seven comparisons we are done. This agrees with our formula, because $\log_2(100) \approx 6.64386$, and indeed the next larger power of 2 is $2^7 = 128$.

Because a binary search is so much faster than a linear search, is it worthwhile to sort an array first and then use a binary search? It depends. If you search the array only once, then it is more efficient to pay for an $O(n)$ linear search than for an $O(n \log(n))$ sort and an $O(\log(n))$ binary search. But if you will be making many searches in the same array, then sorting it is definitely worthwhile.

The Arrays class contains a static binarySearch method that implements the binary search algorithm, but with a useful enhancement. If a value is not found in the array, then the returned value is not –1, but –k – 1, where k is the position before which the element should be inserted. For example,

```
int[] a = { 1, 4, 9 };
int v = 7;
int pos = Arrays.binarySearch(a, v);
   // Returns -3; v should be inserted before position 2
```

SELF CHECK

13. Suppose you need to look through a sorted array with 1,000,000 elements to find a value. Using the binary search algorithm, how many records do you expect to search before finding the value?

14. Why is it useful that the Arrays.binarySearch method indicates the position where a missing element should be inserted?

15. Why does Arrays.binarySearch return –k – 1 and not –k to indicate that a value is not present and should be inserted before position k?

13.8 Sorting Real Data

The Arrays class implements a sorting method that you should use for your Java programs.

When you write Java programs, you don't have to implement your own sorting algorithms. The Arrays class contains static sort methods to sort arrays of integers and floating-point numbers. For example, you can sort an array of integers simply as

```java
int[] a = . . .;
Arrays.sort(a);
```

That sort method uses the quicksort algorithm—see Special Topic 13.3 for more information about that algorithm.

Of course, in application programs, there is rarely a need to search through a collection of integers. However, it is easy to modify these techniques to search through real data.

The sort method of the Arrays class sorts objects of classes that implement the Comparable interface.

The Arrays class also supplies a static sort method for sorting arrays of objects. However, the Arrays class cannot know how to compare arbitrary objects. Suppose, for example, that you have an array of Coin objects. It is not obvious how the coins should be sorted. You could sort them by their names, or by their values. The Arrays.sort method cannot make that decision for you. Instead, it requires that the objects belong to classes that implement the Comparable interface. That interface has a single method:

```java
public interface Comparable
{
    int compareTo(Object otherObject);
}
```

The call

```java
a.compareTo(b)
```

must return a negative number if a should come before b, 0 if a and b are the same, and a positive number otherwise.

Several classes in the standard Java library, such as the String and Date classes, implement the Comparable interface.

You can implement the Comparable interface for your own classes as well. For example, to sort a collection of coins, the Coin class would need to implement this interface and declare a compareTo method:

```java
public class Coin implements Comparable
{
    . . .
    public int compareTo(Object otherObject)
    {
        Coin other = (Coin) otherObject;
        if (value < other.value) return -1;
        if (value == other.value) return 0;
        return 1;
    }
    . . .
}
```

When you implement the compareTo method of the Comparable interface, you must make sure that the method defines a **total ordering** relationship, with the following three properties:

- *Antisymmetric:* If a.compareTo(b) ≤ 0, then b.compareTo(a) ≥ 0
- *Reflexive:* a.compareTo(a) = 0
- *Transitive:* If a.compareTo(b) ≤ 0 and b.compareTo(c) ≤ 0, then a.compareTo(c) ≤ 0

Once your Coin class implements the Comparable interface, you can simply pass an array of coins to the Arrays.sort method:

```
Coin[] coins = new Coin[n];
// Add coins
. . .
Arrays.sort(coins);
```

> The Collections class contains a sort method that can sort array lists.

If the coins are stored in an ArrayList, use the Collections.sort method instead; it uses the merge sort algorithm:

```
ArrayList<Coin> coins = new ArrayList<Coin>();
// Add coins
. . .
Collections.sort(coins);
```

As a practical matter, you should use the sorting and searching methods in the Arrays and Collections classes and not those that you write yourself. The library algorithms have been fully debugged and optimized. Thus, the primary purpose of this chapter was not to teach you how to implement practical sorting and searching algorithms. Instead, you have learned something more important, namely that different algorithms can vary widely in performance, and that it is worthwhile to learn more about the design and analysis of algorithms.

SELF CHECK

16. Why can't the Arrays.sort method sort an array of Rectangle objects?
17. What steps would you need to take to sort an array of BankAccount objects by increasing balance?

Common Error 13.1

The compareTo Method Can Return Any Integer, Not Just –1, 0, and 1

The call a.compareTo(b) is allowed to return *any* negative integer to denote that a should come before b, not necessarily the value –1. That is, the test

```
if (a.compareTo(b) == -1) // ERROR!
```

is generally wrong. Instead, you should test

```
if (a.compareTo(b) < 0) // OK
```

Why would a compareTo method ever want to return a number other than –1, 0, or 1? Sometimes, it is convenient to just return the difference of two integers. For example, the compareTo method of the String class compares characters in matching positions:

```
char c1 = charAt(i);
char c2 = other.charAt(i);
```

If the characters are different, then the method simply returns their difference:

```
if (c1 != c2) return c1 - c2;
```

This difference is a negative number if c1 is less than c2, but it is not necessarily the number –1.

Special Topic 13.4

The Parameterized Comparable **Interface**

As of Java version 5, the Comparable interface is a parameterized type, similar to the ArrayList type:

```
public interface Comparable<T>
{
    int compareTo(T other)
}
```

The type parameter specifies the type of the objects that this class is willing to accept for comparison. Usually, this type is the same as the class type itself. For example, the Coin class would implement Comparable<Coin>, like this:

```
public class Coin implements Comparable<Coin>
{
    . . .
    public int compareTo(Coin other)
    {
        if (value < other.value) return -1;
        if (value == other.value) return 0;
        return 1;
    }
    . . .
}
```

The type parameter has a significant advantage: You need not use a cast to convert an Object parameter into the desired type.

Special Topic 13.5

The Comparator **Interface**

Special Topic 13.5 describes the Comparator interface. You want to use a Comparator to sort objects of classes that don't implement the compareTo method at all, or don't implement the comparison that you want to use.

Summary of Learning Objectives

Describe the selection sort algorithm.

- The selection sort algorithm sorts an array by repeatedly finding the smallest element of the unsorted tail region and moving it to the front.

Measure the running time of a method.

- To measure the running time of a method, get the current time immediately before and after the method call.

Use the big-Oh notation to describe the running time of an algorithm.

- Computer scientists use the big-Oh notation $f(n) = O(g(n))$ to express that the function f grows no faster than the function g.
- Selection sort is an $O(n^2)$ algorithm. Doubling the data set means a fourfold increase in processing time.

Describe the merge sort algorithm.

- The merge sort algorithm sorts an array by cutting the array in half, recursively sorting each half, and then merging the sorted halves.

Contrast the running times of the merge sort and selection sort algorithms.

- Merge sort is an $O(n \log(n))$ algorithm. The $n \log(n)$ function grows much more slowly than n^2.

Describe the linear search algorithm and its running time.

- A linear search examines all values in an array until it finds a match or reaches the end.
- A linear search locates a value in an array in $O(n)$ steps.

Describe the binary search algorithm and its running time.

- A binary search locates a value in a sorted array by determining whether the value occurs in the first or second half, then repeating the search in one of the halves.
- A binary search locates a value in a sorted array in $O(\log(n))$ steps.

Use the Java library methods for sorting data.

- The Arrays class implements a sorting method that you should use for your Java programs.
- The sort method of the Arrays class sorts objects of classes that implement the Comparable interface.
- The Collections class contains a sort method that can sort array lists.

Classes, Objects, and Methods Introduced in this Chapter

```
java.lang.Comparable<T>          java.util.Collections
   compareTo                        binarySearch
java.lang.System                    sort
   currentTimeMillis             java.util.Comparator<T>
java.util.Arrays                    compare
   binarySearch
   sort
   toString
```

Media Resources

WILEY
PLUS

*www.wiley.com/
go/global/
horstmann*

- Lab Exercises
- Practice Quiz
- Code Completion Exercises

Review Exercises

★   **R13.1** What is the difference between searching and sorting?

★★   **R13.2** *Checking against off-by-one errors.* When writing the selection sort algorithm of Section 13.1, a programmer must make the usual choices of < against <=, a.length against a.length - 1, and from against from + 1. This is a fertile ground for off-by-one errors. Conduct code walkthroughs of the algorithm with arrays of length 0, 1, 2, and 3 and check carefully that all index values are correct.

★★   **R13.3** For the following expressions, what is the order of the growth of each?

   a. $n^2 + 2n + 1$

   b. $n^{10} + 9n^9 + 20n^8 + 145n^7$

   c. $(n + 1)^4$

   d. $(n^2 + n)^2$

   e. $n + 0.001n^3$

   f. $n^3 - 1000n^2 + 10^9$

   g. $n + \log(n)$

   h. $n^2 + n \log(n)$

   i. $2^n + n^2$

   j. $\dfrac{n^3 + 2n}{n^2 + 0.75}$

★   **R13.4** We determined that the actual number of visits in the selection sort algorithm is

$$T(n) = \tfrac{1}{2}n^2 + \tfrac{5}{2}n - 3$$

We characterized this method as having $O(n^2)$ growth. Compute the actual ratios

$$T(2{,}000)/T(1{,}000)$$
$$T(4{,}000)/T(1{,}000)$$
$$T(10{,}000)/T(1{,}000)$$

and compare them with

$$f(2{,}000)/f(1{,}000)$$
$$f(4{,}000)/f(1{,}000)$$
$$f(10{,}000)/f(1{,}000)$$

where $f(n) = n^2$.

★   **R13.5** Suppose algorithm A takes 5 seconds to handle a data set of 1,000 records. If the algorithm A is an $O(n)$ algorithm, how long will it take to handle a data set of 2,000 records? Of 10,000 records?

★★ **R13.6** Suppose an algorithm takes 5 seconds to handle a data set of 1,000 records. Fill in the following table, which shows the approximate growth of the execution times depending on the complexity of the algorithm.

	$O(n)$	$O(n^2)$	$O(n^3)$	$O(n \log(n))$	$O(2^n)$
1,000	5	5	5	5	5
2,000					
3,000		45			
10,000					

For example, because $3,000^2 / 1,000^2 = 9$, the algorithm would take 9 times as long, or 45 seconds, to handle a data set of 3,000 records.

★★ **R13.7** Sort the following growth rates from slowest to fastest growth.

$$O(n) \qquad\qquad O(n \log(n))$$

$$O(n^3) \qquad\qquad O(2^n)$$

$$O(n^n) \qquad\qquad O(\sqrt{n})$$

$$O(\log(n)) \qquad\qquad O(n\sqrt{n})$$

$$O(n^2 \log(n)) \qquad\qquad O(n^{\log(n)})$$

★ **R13.8** What is the growth rate of the standard algorithm to find the minimum value of an array? Of finding both the minimum and the maximum?

★ **R13.9** What is the growth rate of the following method?

```java
public static int count(int[] a, int c)
{
    int count = 0;

    for (int i = 0; i < a.length; i++)
    {
        if (a[i] == c) count++;
    }
    return count;
}
```

★★ **R13.10** Your task is to remove all duplicates from an array. For example, if the array has the values

$$4\ 7\ 11\ 4\ 9\ 5\ 11\ 7\ 3\ 5$$

then the array should be changed to

$$4\ 7\ 11\ 9\ 5\ 3$$

Here is a simple algorithm. Look at a[i]. Count how many times it occurs in a. If the count is larger than 1, remove it. What is the growth rate of the time required for this algorithm?

★★ **R13.11** Consider the following algorithm to remove all duplicates from an array. Sort the array. For each element in the array, look at its next neighbor to decide whether it is present more than once. If so, remove it. Is this a faster algorithm than the one in Exercise R13.10?

★★★ **R13.12** Develop an $O(n \log (n))$ algorithm for removing duplicates from an array if the resulting array must have the same ordering as the original array.

★★★ **R13.13** Why does insertion sort perform significantly better than selection sort if an array is already sorted?

★★★ **R13.14** Consider the following speedup of the insertion sort algorithm of Special Topic 13.1. For each element, use the enhanced binary search algorithm that yields the insertion position for missing elements. Does this speedup have a significant impact on the efficiency of the algorithm?

Programming Exercises

★ **P13.1** Modify the selection sort algorithm to sort an array of integers in descending order.

★ **P13.2** Modify the selection sort algorithm to sort an array of coins by their value.

★★ **P13.3** Write a program that generates the table of sample runs of the selection sort times automatically. The program should ask for the smallest and largest value of n and the number of measurements and then make all sample runs.

★ **P13.4** Modify the merge sort algorithm to sort an array of strings in lexicographic order.

★★★ **P13.5** Write a telephone lookup program. Read a data set of 1,000 names and telephone numbers from a file that contains the numbers in random order. Handle lookups by name and also reverse lookups by phone number. Use a binary search for both lookups.

★★ **P13.6** Implement a program that measures the performance of the insertion sort algorithm described in Special Topic 13.1.

★★★ **P13.7** Write a program that sorts an `ArrayList<Coin>` in decreasing order so that the most valuable coin is at the beginning of the array. Use a `Comparator`.

★★ **P13.8** Consider the binary search algorithm in Section 13.7. If no match is found, the `search` method returns −1. Modify the method so that if a is not found, the method returns $-k - 1$, where k is the position before which the element should be inserted. (This is the same behavior as `Arrays.binarySearch`.)

★★ **P13.9** Implement the `sort` method of the merge sort algorithm without recursion, where the length of the array is a power of 2. First merge adjacent regions of size 1, then adjacent regions of size 2, then adjacent regions of size 4, and so on.

★★★ **P13.10** Implement the `sort` method of the merge sort algorithm without recursion, where the length of the array is an arbitrary number. Keep merging adjacent regions whose size is a power of 2, and pay special attention to the last area whose size is less.

★★★ **P13.11** Use insertion sort and the binary search from Exercise P13.8 to sort an array as described in Exercise R13.14. Implement this algorithm and measure its performance.

★ **P13.12** Supply a class Person that implements the Comparable interface. Compare persons by their names. Ask the user to input 10 names and generate 10 Person objects. Using the compareTo method, determine the first and last person among them and print them.

★★ **P13.13** Sort an array list of strings by increasing *length*. *Hint:* Supply a Comparator.

★★★ **P13.14** Sort an array list of strings by increasing length, and so that strings of the same length are sorted lexicographically. *Hint:* Supply a Comparator.

Programming Projects

Project 13.1 Write a program that keeps an appointment book. Make a class Appointment that stores a description of the appointment, the appointment day, the starting time, and the ending time. Your program should keep the appointments in a sorted array list. Users can add appointments and print out all appointments for a given day. When a new appointment is added, use binary search to find where it should be inserted in the array list. Do not add it if it conflicts with another appointment.

Project 13.2 Implement a *graphical animation* of sorting and searching algorithms. Fill an array with a set of random numbers between 1 and 100. Draw each array element as a bar, as in Figure 3. Whenever the algorithm changes the array, wait for the user to click the Step button, then call the repaint method. The Run button should run the animation until the animation has finished or the user clicks the Step button again.

Animate selection sort, merge sort, and binary search. In the binary search animation, highlight the currently inspected element and the current values of from and to.

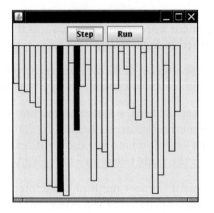

Figure 3
Graphical Animation

Answers to Self-Check Questions

1. Dropping the temp variable would not work. Then a[i] and a[j] would end up being the same value.
2. 1 | 5 4 3 2 6, 1 2 | 4 3 5 6, 1 2 3 4 5 6
3. Four times as long as 40,000 values, or about 50 seconds.
4. A parabola.
5. It takes about 100 times longer.
6. If n is 4, then $\frac{1}{2}n^2$ is 8 and $\frac{5}{2}n - 3$ is 7.
7. When the preceding while loop ends, the loop condition must be false, that is, iFirst >= first.length or iSecond >= second.length (De Morgan's Law).
8. First sort 8 7 6 5. Recursively, first sort 8 7. Recursively, first sort 8. It's sorted. Sort 7. It's sorted. Merge them: 7 8. Do the same with 6 5 to get 5 6. Merge them to 5 6 7 8. Do the same with 4 3 2 1: Sort 4 3 by sorting 4 and 3 and merging them to 3 4. Sort 2 1 by sorting 2 and 1 and merging them to 1 2. Merge 3 4 and 1 2 to 1 2 3 4. Finally, merge 5 6 7 8 and 1 2 3 4 to 1 2 3 4 5 6 7 8.
9. Approximately 100,000 · log(100,000) / 50,000 · log(50,000) = 2 · 5 / 4.7 = 2.13 times the time required for 50,000 values. That's 2.13 · 97 milliseconds or approximately 207 milliseconds.
10. $\dfrac{2n\log(2n)}{n\log(n)} = 2\dfrac{(1 + \log(2))}{\log(n)}$ For $n > 2$, that is a value < 3.
11. On average, you'd make 500,000 comparisons.
12. The search method returns the index at which the match occurs, not the data stored at that location.
13. You would search about 20. (The binary log of 1,024 is 10.)
14. Then you know where to insert it so that the array stays sorted, and you can keep using binary search.
15. Otherwise, you would not know whether a value is present when the method returns 0.
16. The Rectangle class does not implement the Comparable interface.
17. The BankAccount class would need to implement the Comparable interface. Its compareTo method must compare the bank balances.

An Introduction to Data Structures

CHAPTER GOALS

- To learn how to use the linked lists provided in the standard library
- To be able to use iterators to traverse linked lists
- To understand the implementation of linked lists
- To distinguish between abstract and concrete data types
- To know the efficiency of fundamental operations of lists and arrays
- To become familiar with the stack and queue data types

Up to this point, we have used arrays as a one-size-fits-all mechanism for collecting objects. However, computer scientists have developed many different data structures that have varying performance tradeoffs. In this chapter, you will learn about the *linked list*, a data structure that allows you to add and remove elements efficiently, without moving any existing elements. You will also learn about the distinction between concrete and abstract data types. An abstract type spells out the fundamental operations that should be supported efficiently, but it leaves the implementation unspecified. The stack and queue types, introduced at the end of this chapter, are examples of abstract types.

CHAPTER CONTENTS

14.1 Using Linked Lists

A **linked list** is a data structure used for collecting a sequence of objects that allows efficient addition and removal of elements in the middle of the sequence.

To understand the need for such a data structure, imagine a program that maintains a sequence of employee objects, sorted by the last names of the employees. When a new employee is hired, an object needs to be inserted into the sequence. Unless the company happened to hire employees in alphabetical order, the new object probably needs to be inserted somewhere near the middle of the sequence. If we use an array to store the objects, then all objects following the new hire must be moved toward the end.

Conversely, if an employee leaves the company, the object must be removed, and the hole in the sequence needs to be closed up by moving all objects that come after it. Moving a large number of values can involve a substantial amount of processing time. We would like to structure the data in a way that minimizes this cost.

> A linked list consists of a number of nodes, each of which has a reference to the next node.

Rather than storing the values in an array, a linked list uses a sequence of *nodes*. Each node stores a value and a reference to the next node in the sequence (see Figure 1). When you insert a new node into a linked list, only the neighboring node references need to be updated. The same is true when you remove a node. What's the catch? Linked lists allow speedy insertion and removal, but element access can be slow.

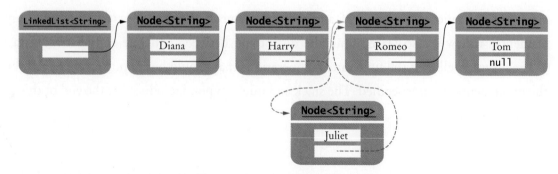

Figure 1 Inserting an Element into a Linked List

540

Adding and removing elements in the middle of a linked list is efficient.

Visiting the elements of a linked list in sequential order is efficient, but random access is not.

You use a list iterator to access elements inside a linked list.

For example, suppose you want to locate the fifth element. You must first traverse the first four. This is a problem if you need to access the elements in arbitrary order. The term "random access" is used in computer science to describe an access pattern in which elements are accessed in arbitrary (not necessarily random) order. In contrast, sequential access visits the elements in sequence. For example, a binary search requires random access, whereas a linear search requires sequential access.

Of course, if you mostly visit all elements in sequence (for example, to display or print the elements), you don't need to use random access. Use linked lists when you are concerned about the efficiency of inserting or removing elements and you rarely need element access in random order.

The Java library provides a linked list class. In this section you will learn how to use that library class. In the next section you will peek under the hood and see how some of its key methods are implemented.

The LinkedList class in the java.util package is a **generic class**, just like the Array-List class. That is, you specify the type of the list elements in angle brackets, such as LinkedList<String> or LinkedList<Product>.

The methods shown in Table 1 give you direct access to the first and the last element in the list.

How do you add and remove elements in the middle of the list? The list will not give you references to the nodes. If you had direct access to them and somehow messed them up, you would break the linked list. As you will see in the next section, when you implement some of the linked list operations yourself, keeping all links between nodes intact is not trivial.

Instead, the Java library supplies a ListIterator type. A list **iterator** describes a position anywhere inside the linked list (see Figure 2).

Table 1 LinkedList Methods

`LinkedList<String> lst = new LinkedList<String>();`	An empty list.
`lst.addLast("Harry")`	Adds an element to the end of the list. Same as add.
`lst.addFirst("Sally")`	Adds an element to the beginning of the list. lst is now [Sally, Harry].
`lst.getFirst()`	Gets the element stored at the beginning of the list; here "Sally".
`lst.getLast()`	Gets the element stored at the end of the list; here "Harry".
`String removed = lst.removeFirst();`	Removes the first element of the list and returns it. removed is "Sally" and lst is [Harry]. Use removeLast to remove the last element.
`ListIterator<String> iter = lst.listIterator()`	Provides an iterator for visiting all list elements (see Table 2 on page 544).

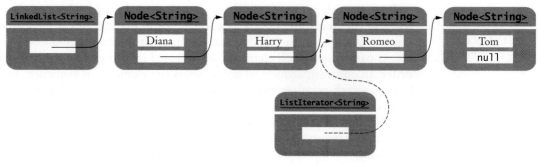

Figure 2 A List Iterator

Conceptually, you should think of the iterator as pointing between two elements, just as the cursor in a word processor points between two characters (see Figure 3). In the conceptual view, think of each element as being like a letter in a word processor, and think of the iterator as being like the blinking cursor between letters.

You obtain a list iterator with the `listIterator` method of the `LinkedList` class:

```
LinkedList<String> employeeNames = . . .;
ListIterator<String> iterator = employeeNames.listIterator();
```

Note that the iterator class is also a generic type. A `ListIterator<String>` iterates through a list of strings; a `ListIterator<Product>` visits the elements in a `LinkedList<Product>`.

Initially, the iterator points before the first element. You can move the iterator position with the `next` method:

```
iterator.next();
```

The `next` method throws a `NoSuchElementException` if you are already past the end of the list. You should always call the method `hasNext` before calling `next`—it returns true if there is a next element.

```
if (iterator.hasNext())
   iterator.next();
```

The `next` method returns the element that the iterator is passing. When you use a `ListIterator<String>`, the return type of the `next` method is `String`. In general, the return type of the `next` method matches the type parameter of the list.

You traverse all elements in a linked list of strings with the following loop:

```
while (iterator.hasNext())
{
   String name = iterator.next();
   Do something with name
}
```

As a shorthand, if your loop simply visits all elements of the linked list, you can use the "for each" loop:

```
for (String name : employeeNames)
{
   Do something with name
}
```

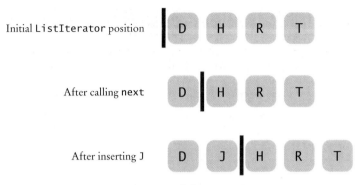

Figure 3 A Conceptual View of the List Iterator

Then you don't have to worry about iterators at all. Behind the scenes, the for loop uses an iterator to visit all list elements (see Special Topic 14.1).

The nodes of the LinkedList class store two links: one to the next element and one to the previous one. Such a list is called a **doubly linked list**. You can use the previous and hasPrevious methods of the ListIterator interface to move the iterator position backwards.

The add method adds an object after the iterator, then moves the iterator position past the new element.

```
iterator.add("Juliet");
```

You can visualize insertion to be like typing text in a word processor. Each character is inserted after the cursor, and then the cursor moves past the inserted character (see Figure 3). Most people never pay much attention to this—you may want to try it out and watch carefully how your word processor inserts characters.

The remove method removes the object that was returned by the last call to next or previous. For example, the following loop removes all names that fulfill a certain condition:

ANIMATION
List Iterators

```
while (iterator.hasNext())
{
    String name = iterator.next();
    if (name fulfills condition)
        iterator.remove();
}
```

You have to be careful when using the remove method. It can be called only once after calling next or previous. The following is an error:

```
iterator.next();
iterator.next();
iterator.remove();
iterator.remove(); // Error: You cannot call remove twice.
```

You cannot call remove immediately after a call to add:

```
iter.add("Fred");
iter.remove(); // Error: Can only call remove after calling next or previous
```

If you call the remove method improperly, it throws an IllegalStateException.

Table 2 summarizes the methods of the ListIterator interface.

Table 2	Methods of the `ListIterator` Interface
`String s = iter.next();`	Assume that `iter` points to the beginning of the list [`Sally`] before calling `next`. After the call, `s` is `"Sally"` and the iterator points to the end.
`iter.hasNext()`	Returns `false` because the iterator is at the end of the collection.

`if (iter.hasPrevious())`
`{`
   `s = iter.previous();`
`}`
	`hasPrevious` returns `true` because the iterator is not at the beginning of the list.

`iter.add("Diana");`	Adds an element before the iterator position. The list is now [`Diana, Sally`].
`iter.next();` `iter.remove();`	`remove` removes the last element returned by `next` or `previous`. The list is again [`Diana`].

Here is a sample program that inserts strings into a list and then iterates through the list, adding and removing elements. Finally, the entire list is printed. The comments indicate the iterator position.

ch14/uselist/ListTester.java

```java
 1  import java.util.LinkedList;
 2  import java.util.ListIterator;
 3
 4  /**
 5     A program that tests the LinkedList class.
 6  */
 7  public class ListTester
 8  {
 9     public static void main(String[] args)
10     {
11        LinkedList<String> staff = new LinkedList<String>();
12        staff.addLast("Diana");
13        staff.addLast("Harry");
14        staff.addLast("Romeo");
15        staff.addLast("Tom");
16
17        // | in the comments indicates the iterator position
18
19        ListIterator<String> iterator = staff.listIterator(); // |DHRT
20        iterator.next(); // D|HRT
21        iterator.next(); // DH|RT
22
23        // Add more elements after second element
24
25        iterator.add("Juliet"); // DHJ|RT
26        iterator.add("Nina"); // DHJN|RT
27
28        iterator.next(); // DHJNR|T
29
30        // Remove last traversed element
31
32        iterator.remove(); // DHJN|T
```

```
33
34        // Print all elements
35
36        for (String name : staff)
37           System.out.print(name + " ");
38        System.out.println();
39        System.out.println("Expected: Diana Harry Juliet Nina Tom");
40     }
41  }
```

Program Run

```
Diana Harry Juliet Nina Tom
Expected: Diana Harry Juliet Nina Tom
```

SELF CHECK

1. Do linked lists take more storage space than arrays of the same size?
2. Why don't we need iterators with arrays?

Special Topic 14.1

The Iterable Interface and the "For Each" Loop

Special Topic 14.1 discusses the Iterable interface. The "for each" loop can be applied to any object that implements the Iterable interface.

14.2 Implementing Linked Lists

In the last section you saw how to use the linked list class supplied by the Java library. In this section, we will look at the implementation of a simplified version of this class. This shows you how the list operations manipulate the links as the list is modified.

To keep this sample code simple, we will not implement all methods of the linked list class. We will implement only a singly linked list, and the list class will supply direct access only to the first list element, not the last one. Our list will not use a type parameter. We will simply store raw Object values and insert casts when retrieving them. The result will be a fully functional list class that shows how the links are updated in the add and remove operations and how the iterator traverses the list.

A Node object stores an object and a reference to the next node. Because the methods of both the linked list class and the iterator class have frequent access to the Node instance variables, we do not make the instance variables of the Node class private. Instead, we make Node a private inner class of the LinkedList class. Because none of the LinkedList methods returns a Node object, it is safe to leave the instance variables public.

```
public class LinkedList
{
   . . .
   class Node
   {
```

```
            public Object data;
            public Node next;
    }
}
```

Our LinkedList class holds a reference first to the first node (or null, if the list is completely empty).

```
public class LinkedList
{
    private Node first;
    . . .
    public LinkedList()
    {
        first = null;
    }

    public Object getFirst()
    {
        if (first == null)
            throw new NoSuchElementException();
        return first.data;
    }
}
```

Now let us turn to the addFirst method (see Figure 4). When a new node is added to the list, it becomes the head of the list, and the node that was the old list head becomes its next node:

```
public class LinkedList
{
    . . .
    public void addFirst(Object element)
    {
        Node newNode = new Node();  ❶
        newNode.data = element;
        newNode.next = first;  ❷
        first = newNode;  ❸
    }
    . . .
}
```

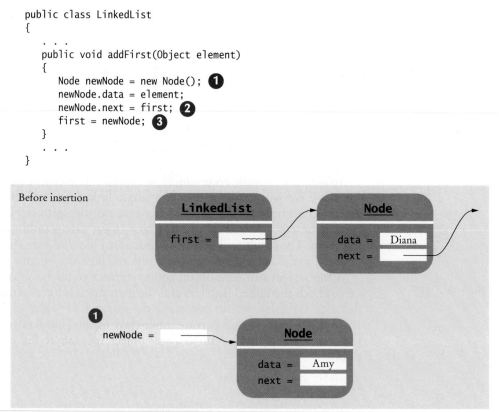

Figure 4 Adding a Node to the Head of a Linked List

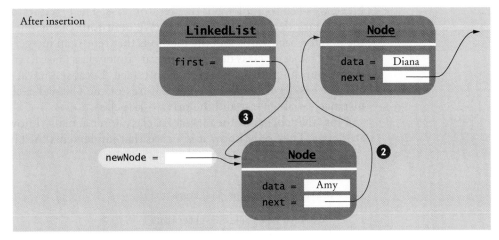

Figure 4 (continued) Adding a Node to the Head of a Linked List

Removing the first element of the list works as follows. The data of the first node are saved and later returned as the method result. The successor of the first node becomes the first node of the shorter list (see Figure 5). Then there are no further references to the old node, and the garbage collector will eventually recycle it.

```java
public class LinkedList
{
   . . .
   public Object removeFirst()
   {
      if (first == null) throw new NoSuchElementException();
      Object element = first.data;
      first = first.next; ❶
      return element;
   }
   . . .
}
```

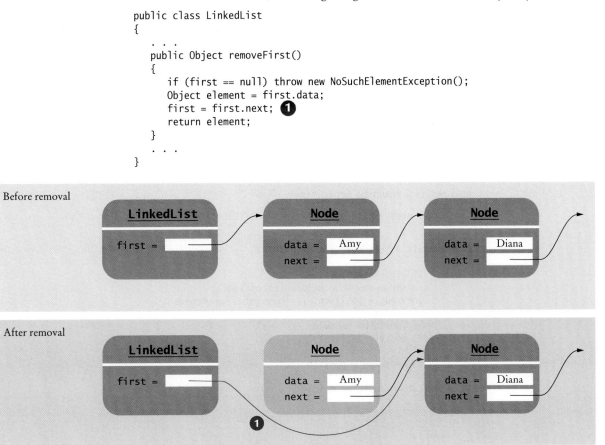

Figure 5 Removing the First Node from a Linked List

Next, we need to implement the iterator class. The `ListIterator` interface in the standard library declares nine methods. We omit four of them (the methods that move the iterator backwards and the methods that report an integer index of the iterator).

Our `LinkedList` class declares a private inner class `LinkedListIterator`, which implements our simplified `ListIterator` interface. Because `LinkedListIterator` is an inner class, it has access to the private features of the `LinkedList` class—in particular, the instance variable `first` and the private `Node` class.

Note that clients of the `LinkedList` class don't actually know the name of the iterator class. They only know it is a class that implements the `ListIterator` interface.

```
public class LinkedList
{
   . . .
   public ListIterator listIterator()
   {
      return new LinkedListIterator();
   }

   class LinkedListIterator implements ListIterator
   {
      private Node position;
      private Node previous;
      . . .
      public LinkedListIterator()
      {
         position = null;
         previous = null;
      }
   }
   . . .
}
```

A list iterator object has a reference to the last visited node.

Each iterator object has a reference, `position`, to the last visited node. We also store a reference to the last node before that, `previous`. We will need that reference to adjust the links properly in the `remove` method.

The `next` method is simple. The `position` reference is advanced to `position.next`, and the old position is remembered in `previous`. There is a special case, however—if the iterator points before the first element of the list, then the old `position` is `null`, and `position` must be set to `first`.

```
class LinkedListIterator implements ListIterator
{
   . . .
   public Object next()
   {
      if (!hasNext())
         throw new NoSuchElementException();
      previous = position; // Remember for remove

      if (position == null)
         position = first;
      else
         position = position.next;

      return position.data;
   }
   . . .
}
```

The `next` method is supposed to be called only when the iterator is not yet at the end of the list, so we declare the `hasNext` method accordingly. The iterator is at the end if the list is empty (that is, `first == null`) or if there is no element after the current position (`position.next == null`).

```
class LinkedListIterator implements ListIterator
{
    . . .
    public boolean hasNext()
    {
        if (position == null)
            return first != null;
        else
            return position.next != null;
    }
    . . .
}
```

The set method changes the data stored in the previously visited element. Its implementation is straightforward because our linked lists can be traversed in only one direction. The linked list implementation of the standard library must keep track of whether the last iterator movement was forward or backward. For that reason, the standard library forbids a call to the set method following an `add` or `remove` method. That restriction is unnecessary in our implementation, and we do not enforce it.

```
public void set(Object element)
{
    if (position == null)
        throw new NoSuchElementException();
    position.data = element;
}
```

Removing the last visited node is more involved. If the element to be removed is the first element, we just call `removeFirst`. Otherwise, an element in the middle of the list must be removed, and the node preceding it needs to have its `next` reference updated to skip the removed element (see Figure 6). If the `previous` reference equals `position`, then this call to `remove` does not immediately follow a call to `next`, and we throw an `IllegalStateException`.

According to the declaration of the `remove` method, it is illegal to call `remove` twice in a row. Therefore, the `remove` method sets the `position` reference to `previous`.

> Implementing operations that modify a linked list is challenging— you need to make sure that you update all node references correctly.

```
class LinkedListIterator implements ListIterator
{
    . . .
    public void remove()
    {
        if (previous == position)
            throw new IllegalStateException();
        if (position == first)
        {
            removeFirst();
        }
        else
        {
            previous.next = position.next;    ❶
        }
        position = previous;    ❷
    }
    . . .
}
```

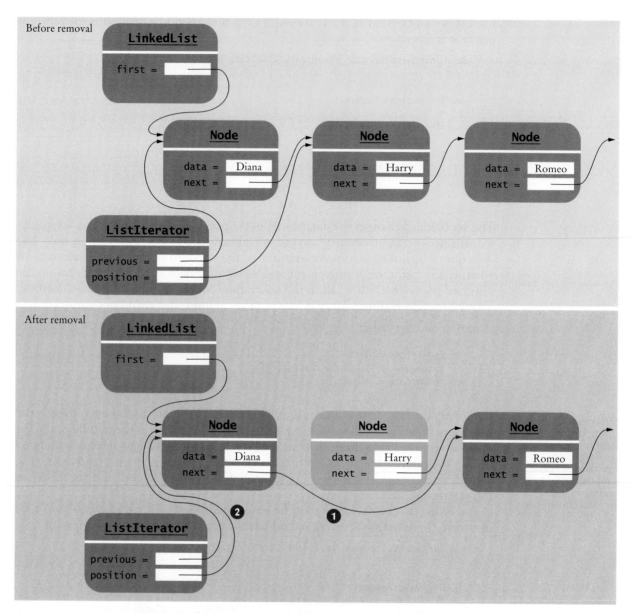

Figure 6 Removing a Node from the Middle of a Linked List

Finally, the most complex operation is the addition of a node. You insert the new node after the node last visited by the iterator (see Figure 7).

```
class LinkedListIterator implements ListIterator
{
   . . .
   public void add(Object element)
   {
      if (position == null)
      {
         addFirst(element);
         position = first;
      }
```

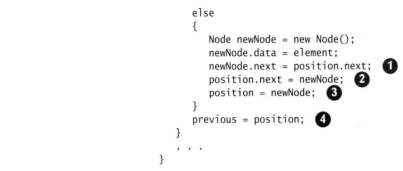

```
      else
      {
         Node newNode = new Node();
         newNode.data = element;
         newNode.next = position.next;    ❶
         position.next = newNode;    ❷
         position = newNode;    ❸
      }
      previous = position;    ❹
   }
   . . .
}
```

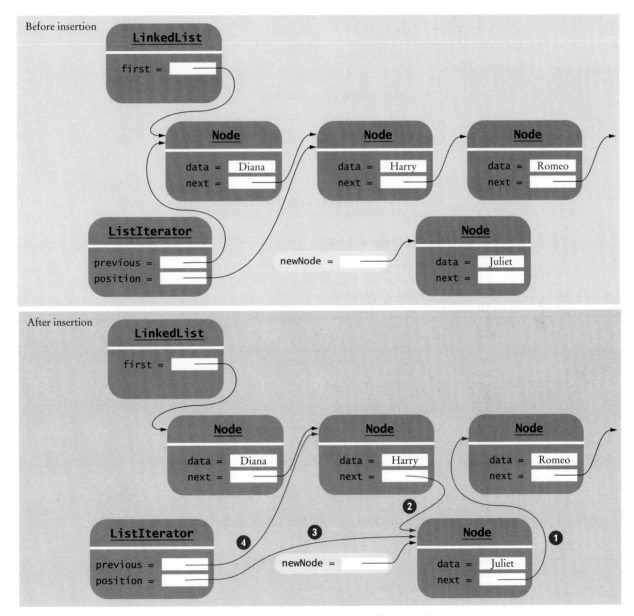

Figure 7 Adding a Node to the Middle of a Linked List

At the end of this section is the complete implementation of our `LinkedList` class.

You now know how to use the `LinkedList` class in the Java library, and you have had a peek "under the hood" to see how linked lists are implemented.

ch14/impllist/LinkedList.java

```java
1   import java.util.NoSuchElementException;
2
3   /**
4       A linked list is a sequence of nodes with efficient
5       element insertion and removal. This class
6       contains a subset of the methods of the standard
7       java.util.LinkedList class.
8   */
9   public class LinkedList
10  {
11      private Node first;
12
13      /**
14          Constructs an empty linked list.
15      */
16      public LinkedList()
17      {
18          first = null;
19      }
20
21      /**
22          Returns the first element in the linked list.
23          @return the first element in the linked list
24      */
25      public Object getFirst()
26      {
27          if (first == null)
28              throw new NoSuchElementException();
29          return first.data;
30      }
31
32      /**
33          Removes the first element in the linked list.
34          @return the removed element
35      */
36      public Object removeFirst()
37      {
38          if (first == null)
39              throw new NoSuchElementException();
40          Object element = first.data;
41          first = first.next;
42          return element;
43      }
44
45      /**
46          Adds an element to the front of the linked list.
47          @param element the element to add
48      */
49      public void addFirst(Object element)
50      {
51          Node newNode = new Node();
52          newNode.data = element;
53          newNode.next = first;
```

```
 54          first = newNode;
 55       }
 56
 57       /**
 58          Returns an iterator for iterating through this list.
 59          @return an iterator for iterating through this list
 60       */
 61       public ListIterator listIterator()
 62       {
 63          return new LinkedListIterator();
 64       }
 65
 66       class Node
 67       {
 68          public Object data;
 69          public Node next;
 70       }
 71
 72       class LinkedListIterator implements ListIterator
 73       {
 74          private Node position;
 75          private Node previous;
 76
 77          /**
 78             Constructs an iterator that points to the front
 79             of the linked list.
 80          */
 81          public LinkedListIterator()
 82          {
 83             position = null;
 84             previous = null;
 85          }
 86
 87          /**
 88             Moves the iterator past the next element.
 89             @return the traversed element
 90          */
 91          public Object next()
 92          {
 93             if (!hasNext())
 94                throw new NoSuchElementException();
 95             previous = position; // Remember for remove
 96
 97             if (position == null)
 98                position = first;
 99             else
100                position = position.next;
101
102             return position.data;
103          }
104
105          /**
106             Tests if there is an element after the iterator position.
107             @return true if there is an element after the iterator position
108          */
109          public boolean hasNext()
110          {
111             if (position == null)
112                return first != null;
```

```
113          else
114              return position.next != null;
115      }
116
117      /**
118          Adds an element before the iterator position
119          and moves the iterator past the inserted element.
120          @param element  the element to add
121      */
122      public void add(Object element)
123      {
124          if (position == null)
125          {
126              addFirst(element);
127              position = first;
128          }
129          else
130          {
131              Node newNode = new Node();
132              newNode.data = element;
133              newNode.next = position.next;
134              position.next = newNode;
135              position = newNode;
136          }
137          previous = position;
138      }
139
140      /**
141          Removes the last traversed element. This method may
142          only be called after a call to the next() method.
143      */
144      public void remove()
145      {
146          if (previous == position)
147              throw new IllegalStateException();
148
149          if (position == first)
150          {
151              removeFirst();
152          }
153          else
154          {
155              previous.next = position.next;
156          }
157          position = previous;
158      }
159
160      /**
161          Sets the last traversed element to a different value.
162          @param element  the element to set
163      */
164      public void set(Object element)
165      {
166          if (position == null)
167              throw new NoSuchElementException();
168          position.data = element;
169      }
170  }
171 }
```

ch14/impllist/ListIterator.java

```
1   /**
2       A list iterator allows access to a position in a linked list.
3       This interface contains a subset of the methods of the
4       standard java.util.ListIterator interface. The methods for
5       backward traversal are not included.
6   */
7   public interface ListIterator
8   {
9       /**
10          Moves the iterator past the next element.
11          @return the traversed element
12      */
13      Object next();
14
15      /**
16          Tests if there is an element after the iterator position.
17          @return true if there is an element after the iterator position
18      */
19      boolean hasNext();
20
21      /**
22          Adds an element before the iterator position
23          and moves the iterator past the inserted element.
24          @param element the element to add
25      */
26      void add(Object element);
27
28      /**
29          Removes the last traversed element. This method may
30          only be called after a call to the next() method.
31      */
32      void remove();
33
34      /**
35          Sets the last traversed element to a different value.
36          @param element the element to set
37      */
38      void set(Object element);
39  }
```

SELF CHECK

3. Trace through the addFirst method when adding an element to an empty list.
4. Conceptually, an iterator points between elements (see Figure 3). Does the position reference point to the element to the left or to the element to the right?
5. Why does the add method have two separate cases?

Special Topic 14.2

Static Inner Classes

Special Topic 14.2 shows how you can make the inner Node class slightly more efficient by declaring it as a static inner class.

14.3 Abstract Data Types

There are two ways of looking at a linked list. One way is to think of the concrete implementation of such a list as a sequence of node objects with links between them (see Figure 8).

On the other hand, you can think of the *abstract* concept that underlies the linked list. In the abstract, a linked list is an ordered sequence of data items that can be traversed with an iterator (see Figure 9).

Similarly, there are two ways of looking at an array list. Of course, an array list has a concrete implementation: a partially filled array of object references (see Figure 10). But you don't usually think about the concrete implementation when using an array list. You take the abstract point of view. An array list is an ordered sequence of data items, each of which can be accessed by an integer index (see Figure 11).

The concrete implementations of a linked list and an array list are quite different. The abstractions, on the other hand, seem to be similar at first glance. To see the difference, consider the public interfaces stripped down to their minimal essentials.

An array list allows *random access* to all elements. You specify an integer index, and you can get or set the corresponding element.

> An abstract data type defines the fundamental operations on the data but does not specify an implementation.

```
public class ArrayList
{
    . . .
    public Object get(int index) { . . . }
    public void set(int index, Object element) { . . . }
    . . .
}
```

With a linked list, on the other hand, element access is a bit more complex. A linked list allows *sequential access*. You need to ask the linked list for an iterator. Using that iterator, you can easily traverse the list elements one at a time. But if you want

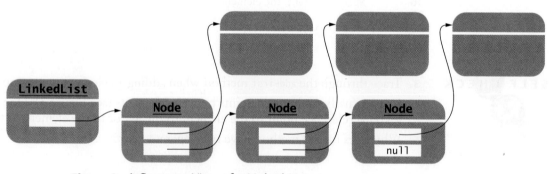

Figure 8 A Concrete View of a Linked List

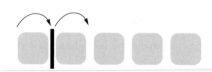

Figure 9 An Abstract View of a List

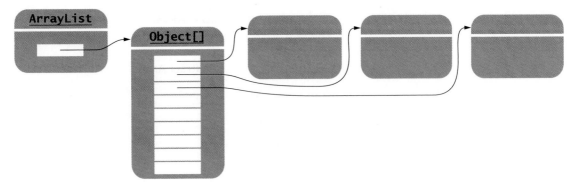

Figure 10 A Concrete View of an Array List

[0]   [1]   [2]   [3]   [4]

Figure 11 An Abstract View of an Array

to go to a particular element, say the 100th one, you first have to skip all elements before it.

```
public class LinkedList
{
    . . .
    public ListIterator listIterator() { . . . }
    . . .
}

public interface ListIterator
{
    Object next();
    boolean hasNext();
    void add(Object element);
    void remove();
    void set(Object element);
    . . .
}
```

Here we show only the *fundamental* operations on array lists and linked lists. Other operations can be composed from these fundamental operations. For example, you can add or remove an element in an array list by moving all elements beyond the insertion or removal index, calling get and set multiple times.

Of course, the ArrayList class has methods to add and remove elements in the middle, even if they are slow. Conversely, the LinkedList class has get and set methods that let you access any element in the linked list, albeit very inefficiently, by performing repeated sequential accesses.

In fact, the term ArrayList signifies that its implementors wanted to combine the interfaces of an array and a list. Somewhat confusingly, both the ArrayList and the LinkedList class implement an interface called List that declares operations both for random access and for sequential access.

That terminology is not in common use outside the Java library. Instead, let us adopt a more traditional terminology. We will call the abstract types *array* and *list*.

Table 3 Efficiency of Operations for the Abstract Array and List Types		
Operation	Abstract Array	Abstract List
Random access	$O(1)$	$O(n)$
Linear traversal step	$O(1)$	$O(1)$
Add/remove an element	$O(n)$	$O(1)$

The Java library provides concrete implementations `ArrayList` and `LinkedList` for these abstract types. Other concrete implementations are possible in other libraries. In fact, Java arrays are another implementation of the abstract array type.

To understand an abstract data type completely, you need to know not just its fundamental operations but also their relative efficiency.

> An abstract list is an ordered sequence of items that can be traversed sequentially and that allows for $O(1)$ insertion and removal of elements at any position.

In an abstract list, an element can be added or removed in constant time (assuming that the iterator is already in the right position). A fixed number of node references need to be modified to add or remove a node, regardless of the size of the list. Using the big-Oh notation, an operation that requires a bounded amount of time, regardless of the total number of elements in the structure, is denoted as $O(1)$. Random access in an abstract array also takes $O(1)$ time.

> An abstract array is an ordered sequence of items with $O(1)$ random access via an integer index.

Adding or removing an arbitrary element in an abstract array of size n takes $O(n)$ time, because on average $n/2$ elements need to be moved. Random access in an abstract list takes $O(n)$ time because on average $n/2$ elements need to be skipped.

Table 3 shows this information for abstract arrays and lists.

Why consider abstract types at all? If you implement a particular algorithm, you can tell what operations you need to carry out on the data structures that your algorithm manipulates. You can then determine the abstract type that supports those operations efficiently, without being distracted by implementation details.

For example, suppose you have a sorted collection of items and you want to locate items using the binary search algorithm (see Section 13.7). That algorithm makes a random access to the middle of the collection, followed by other random accesses. Thus, fast random access is essential for the algorithm to work correctly. Once you know that an abstract array supports fast random access and an abstract list does not, you then look for concrete implementations of the abstract array type. You won't be fooled into using a `LinkedList`, even though the `LinkedList` class actually provides `get` and `set` methods.

In the next section, you will see additional examples of abstract data types.

S E L F   C H E C K

6. What is the advantage of viewing a type abstractly?

7. How would you sketch an abstract view of a doubly linked list? A concrete view?

8. How much slower is the binary search algorithm for an abstract list compared to the linear search algorithm?

14.4 Stacks and Queues

In this section we will consider two common abstract data types that allow insertion and removal of items at the ends only, not in the middle. A **stack** lets you insert and remove elements at only one end, traditionally called the *top* of the stack. To visualize a stack, think of a stack of books (see Figure 12).

New items can be added to the top of the stack. Items are removed at the top of the stack as well. Therefore, they are removed in the order that is opposite from the order in which they have been added, called *last in, first out* or *LIFO* order. For example, if you add items A, B, and C and then remove them, you obtain C, B, and A. Traditionally, the addition and removal operations are called push and pop.

A **queue** is similar to a stack, except that you add items to one end of the queue (the *tail*) and remove them from the other end of the queue (the *head*). To visualize a queue, simply think of people lining up (see Figure 13). People join the tail of the queue and wait until they have reached the head of the queue. Queues store items in a *first in, first out* or *FIFO* fashion. Items are removed in the same order in which they have been added.

There are many uses of queues and stacks in computer science. The Java graphical user interface system keeps an event queue of all events, such as mouse and keyboard events. The events are inserted into the queue whenever the operating system notifies the application of the event. Events are removed and passed to event listeners in the order in which they were inserted. Another example is a print queue. A printer may be accessed by several applications, perhaps running on different computers. If each of the applications tried to access the printer at the same time, the printout would be garbled. Instead, each application places all bytes that need to be sent to the printer into a file and inserts that file into the print queue. When the printer is done printing one file, it retrieves the next one from the queue. Therefore,

> A stack is a collection of items with "last in, first out" retrieval.

> A queue is a collection of items with "first in, first out" retrieval.

Figure 12
A Stack of Books

Figure 13 A Queue

print jobs are printed using the "first in, first out" rule, which is a fair arrangement for users of the shared printer.

Stacks are used when a "last in, first out" rule is required. For example, consider an algorithm that attempts to find a path through a maze. When the algorithm encounters an intersection, it pushes the location on the stack, and then it explores the first branch. If that branch is a dead end, it returns to the location at the top of the stack and explores the next untried branch. If all branches are dead ends, it pops the location off the stack, revealing a previously encountered intersection. Another important example is the **run-time stack** that a processor or virtual machine keeps to organize the variables of nested methods. Whenever a new method is called, its parameters and local variables are pushed onto a stack. When the method exits, they are popped off again. This stack makes recursive method calls possible.

There is a Stack class in the Java library that implements the abstract stack type and the push and pop operations.

The Queue interface in the standard Java library has methods add to add an element to the tail of the queue, remove to remove the head of the queue, and peek to get the head element of the queue without removing it.

The standard library provides a number of queue classes for programs in which multiple activities, called threads, run in parallel. These queues are useful for sharing work between threads. We do not discuss those classes in this book. The LinkedList class also implements the Queue interface, and you can use it when a queue is required:

```
Queue<String> q = new LinkedList<String>();
```

Table 4 shows how to use the stack and queue methods in Java.

The Stack class in the Java library uses an array list to implement a stack. Exercise P14.15 shows how to use a linked list instead.

Table 4 Working with Queues and Stacks

`Queue<Integer> q = new LinkedList<Integer>();`	The `LinkedList` class implements the `Queue` interface.
`q.add(1); q.add(2); q.add(3);`	Adds to the tail of the queue; q is now [1, 2, 3].
`int head = q.remove();`	Removes the head of the queue; head is set to 1 and q is [2, 3].
`head = q.peek();`	Gets the head of the queue without removing it; head is set to 2.
`Stack<Integer> s = new Stack<Integer>();`	Constructs an empty stack.
`s.push(1); s.push(2); s.push(3);`	Adds to the top of the stack; s is now [1, 2, 3].
`int top = s.pop();`	Removes the top of the stack; top is set to 3 and s is now [1, 2].
`head = s.peek();`	Gets the top of the stack without removing it; head is set to 2.

You would definitely not want to use an array list to implement a queue. Removing the first element of an array list is inefficient—all other elements must be moved toward the beginning. A queue can be efficiently implemented as a linked list. Moreover, Exercise P14.16 shows you how to implement a queue efficiently as a "circular" array, in which all elements stay at the position at which they were inserted, but the index values that denote the head and tail of the queue change when elements are added and removed.

In this chapter, you have seen the two most fundamental abstract data types, arrays and lists, and their concrete implementations. You also learned about the stack and queue types. In the next chapter, you will see additional data types that require more sophisticated implementation techniques.

SELF CHECK

9. Draw a sketch of the abstract queue type, similar to Figures 9 and 11.

10. Why wouldn't you want to use a stack to manage print jobs?

Worked Example 14.1

A Reverse Polish Notation Calculator

Worked Example 14.1 shows how to use a stack for implementing a "Reverse Polish Notation" calculator.

Random Fact 14.2

Reverse Polish Notation

In the 1920s, the Polish mathematician Jan Łukasiewicz realized that it is possible to dispense with parentheses in arithmetic expressions, provided that you write the operators *before* their arguments, for example, + 3 4 instead of 3 + 4. Thirty years later, Australian computer scientist Charles Hamblin noted that an even better scheme would be to have the operators *follow* the operands. This was termed **reverse Polish notation** or RPN.

Reverse Polish notation might look strange to you, but that is just an accident of history. Had earlier mathematicians realized its advantages, today's schoolchildren might be using it and not worry about precedence rules and parentheses.

Standard Notation	Reverse Polish Notation
3 + 4	3 4 +
3 + 4 × 5	3 4 5 × +
3 × (4 + 5)	3 4 5 + ×
(3 + 4) × (5 + 6)	3 4 + 5 6 + ×
3 + 4 + 5	3 4 + 5 +

In 1972, Hewlett-Packard introduced the HP 35 calculator that used reverse Polish notation. The calculator had no keys labeled with parentheses or an equals symbol. There is just a key labeled ENTER to push a number onto a stack. For that reason, Hewlett-Packard's marketing department used to refer to their product as "the calculators that have no equal".

Figure 14
The Calculator with No Equal

Over time, calculator vendors have adapted to the standard algebraic notation rather than forcing its users to learn a new notation. However, those users who have made the effort to learn reverse Polish notation tend to be fanatic proponents, and to this day, some Hewlett-Packard calculator models still support it.

Summary of Learning Objectives

Describe the linked list data structure and the use of list iterators.

- A linked list consists of a number of nodes, each of which has a reference to the next node.
- Adding and removing elements in the middle of a linked list is efficient.
- Visiting the elements of a linked list in sequential order is efficient, but random access is not.
- You use a list iterator to access elements inside a linked list.

Explain how linked lists are implemented.

- A linked list object holds a reference to the first node, and each node holds a reference to the next node.
- A list iterator object has a reference to the last visited node.
- Implementing operations that modify a linked list is challenging— you need to make sure that you update all node references correctly.

Describe the notion of abstract data types and the behavior of the abstract list and array types.

- An abstract data type defines the fundamental operations on the data but does not specify an implementation.
- An abstract list is an ordered sequence of items that can be traversed sequentially and that allows for $O(1)$ insertion and removal of elements at any position.
- An abstract array is an ordered sequence of items with $O(1)$ random access via an integer index.
- A stack is a collection of items with "last in, first out" retrieval.
- A queue is a collection of items with "first in, first out" retrieval.

Classes, Objects, and Methods Introduced in this Chapter

`java.util.Collection<E>`	`java.util.LinkedList<E>`	`java.util.ListIterator<E>`
add	addFirst	add
contains	addLast	hasPrevious
iterator	getFirst	previous
remove	getLast	set
size	removeFirst	
`java.util.Iterator<E>`	removeLast	
hasNext	`java.util.List<E>`	
next	listIterator	
remove		

Media Resources

*www.wiley.com/
go/global/
horstmann*

- ***Worked Example*** A Reverse Polish Notation Calculator
- Lab Exercises
- ⊕ ***Animation*** List Iterators
- ⊕ Practice Quiz
- ⊕ Code Completion Exercises

Review Exercises

★ **R14.1** Explain what the following code prints. Draw pictures of the linked list after each step. Just draw the forward links, as in Figure 1.

```
LinkedList<String> staff = new LinkedList<String>();
staff.addFirst("Harry");
staff.addFirst("Diana");
staff.addFirst("Tom");
System.out.println(staff.removeFirst());
System.out.println(staff.removeFirst());
System.out.println(staff.removeFirst());
```

★ **R14.2** Explain what the following code prints. Draw pictures of the linked list after each step. Just draw the forward links, as in Figure 1.

```
LinkedList<String> staff = new LinkedList<String>();
staff.addFirst("Harry");
staff.addFirst("Diana");
staff.addFirst("Tom");
System.out.println(staff.removeLast());
System.out.println(staff.removeFirst());
System.out.println(staff.removeLast());
```

★ **R14.3** Explain what the following code prints. Draw pictures of the linked list after each step. Just draw the forward links, as in Figure 1.

```
LinkedList<String> staff = new LinkedList<String>();
staff.addFirst("Harry");
staff.addLast("Diana");
staff.addFirst("Tom");
System.out.println(staff.removeLast());
System.out.println(staff.removeFirst());
System.out.println(staff.removeLast());
```

★ **R14.4** Explain what the following code prints. Draw pictures of the linked list and the iterator position after each step.

```
LinkedList<String> staff = new LinkedList<String>();
ListIterator<String> iterator = staff.listIterator();
iterator.add("Tom");
iterator.add("Diana");
iterator.add("Harry");
iterator = staff.listIterator();
if (iterator.next().equals("Tom"))
    iterator.remove();
while (iterator.hasNext())
    System.out.println(iterator.next());
```

★ **R14.5** Explain what the following code prints. Draw pictures of the linked list and the iterator position after each step.

```
LinkedList<String> staff = new LinkedList<String>();
ListIterator<String> iterator = staff.listIterator();
iterator.add("Tom");
iterator.add("Diana");
iterator.add("Harry");
iterator = staff.listIterator();
iterator.next();
iterator.next();
iterator.add("Romeo");
```

```
iterator.next();
iterator.add("Juliet");
iterator = staff.listIterator();
iterator.next();
iterator.remove();
while (iterator.hasNext())
    System.out.println(iterator.next());
```

★★ **R14.6** The linked list class in the Java library supports operations addLast and removeLast. To carry out these operations efficiently, the LinkedList class has an added reference last to the last node in the linked list. Draw a "before/after" diagram of the changes of the links in a linked list under the addLast and removeLast methods.

★★ **R14.7** The linked list class in the Java library supports bidirectional iterators. To go backward efficiently, each Node has an added reference, previous, to the predecessor node in the linked list. Draw a "before/after" diagram of the changes of the links in a linked list under the addFirst and removeFirst methods that shows how the previous links need to be updated.

★★ **R14.8** What advantages do lists have over arrays? What disadvantages do they have?

★★ **R14.9** Suppose you needed to organize a collection of telephone numbers for a company division. There are currently about 6,000 employees, and you know that the phone switch can handle at most 10,000 phone numbers. You expect several hundred look-ups against the collection every day. Would you use an array or a list to store the information?

★★ **R14.10** Suppose you needed to keep a collection of appointments. Would you use a list or an array of Appointment objects?

★ **R14.11** Suppose you write a program that models a card deck. Cards are taken from the top of the deck and given out to players. As cards are returned to the deck, they are placed on the bottom of the deck. Would you store the cards in a stack or a queue?

★ **R14.12** Suppose the strings "A" . . . "Z" are pushed onto a stack. Then they are popped off the stack and pushed onto a second stack. Finally, they are all popped off the second stack and printed. In which order are the strings printed?

★ **R14.13** Consider the following algorithm for traversing a maze such as this one:

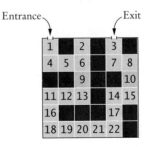

Make the cell at the entrance the current cell. Take the following actions, then repeat:
- If the current cell is adjacent to the exit, stop.
- Mark the current cell as visited.

- Add all unvisited neighbors to the north, east, south, and west to a queue.
- Remove the next element from the queue and make it the current cell.

In which order will the cells of the sample maze be visited?

★ **R14.14** Repeat Exercise R14.13, using a stack instead of a queue.

Programming Exercises

★★ **P14.1** Using only the public interface of the linked list class, write a method

```
public static void downsize(LinkedList<String> staff)
```

that removes every other employee from a linked list.

★★ **P14.2** Using only the public interface of the linked list class, write a method

```
public static void reverse(LinkedList<String> staff)
```

that reverses the entries in a linked list.

★★★ **P14.3** Add a method reverse to our implementation of the LinkedList class that reverses the links in a list. Implement this method by directly rerouting the links, not by using an iterator.

★ **P14.4** Add a method size to our implementation of the LinkedList class that computes the number of elements in the list, by following links and counting the elements until the end of the list is reached.

★ **P14.5** Add an instance variable currentSize to our implementation of the LinkedList class. Modify the add and remove methods of both the linked list and the list iterator to update the currentSize variable so that it always contains the correct size. Change the size method of the preceding exercise so that it simply returns the value of this instance variable.

★★ **P14.6** The linked list class of the standard library has an add method that allows efficient insertion at the end of the list. Implement this method for the LinkedList class in Section 14.2. Add an instance variable to the linked list class that points to the last node in the list. Make sure the other mutator methods update that variable.

★★★ **P14.7** Repeat Exercise P14.6, but use a different implementation strategy. Remove the reference to the first node in the LinkedList class, and make the next reference of the last node point to the first node, so that all nodes form a cycle. Such an implementation is called a *circular linked list*.

★★★ **P14.8** Reimplement the LinkedList class of Section 14.2 so that the Node and LinkedList-Iterator classes are not inner classes.

★★★ **P14.9** Add an instance variable previous to the Node class in Section 14.2, and supply previous and hasPrevious methods in the iterator.

★★ **P14.10** The LISP language, created in 1960, implements linked lists in a very elegant way. You will explore a Java analog in this set of exercises. The key observation is that the *tail* of an abstract list—that is, the list with its head node removed—is also a list. The tail of that list is again a list, and so on, until you reach the empty list. Here is a Java interface for such as list:

```
public interface LispList
{
   boolean isEmpty();
   Object head();
   LispList tail();
   . . .
}
```

There are two kinds of lists, empty lists and nonempty lists:

```
public class EmptyList extends LispList { ... }
public class NonEmptyList extends LispList { ... }
```

These classes are quite trivial. The EmptyList class has no instance variables. Its head and tail methods simply throw an UnsupportedOperationException, and its isEmpty method returns true. The NonEmptyList class has instance variables for the head and tail.

Here is one way of making a lisp list with three elements:

```
LispList list = new NonEmptyList("A", new NonEmptyList("B",
   new NonEmptyList("C", new EmptyList())));
```

This is a bit tedious, and it is a good idea to supply a convenience method cons that calls the constructor, as well as a static variable NIL that is an instance of an empty list. Then our list construction becomes

```
LispList list = NIL.cons("C").cons("B").cons("A");
```

Note that you need to build up the list starting from the (empty) tail.

To see the elegance of this approach, consider the implementation of a toString method that produces a string containing all list elements. The method must be implemented by both subclasses:

```
public class EmptyList
{
   ...
   public String toString() { return ""; }
}

public class NonEmptyList
{
   ...
   public String toString() { return head() + " " + tail().toString(); }
}
```

Note that no if statement is required. A list is either empty or nonempty, and the correct toString method is invoked due to polymorphism.

In this exercise, complete the LispList interface and the EmptyList and NonEmptyList classes. Write a test program that constructs a list and prints it.

★ **P14.11** Add a method length to the LispList interface of Exercise P14.10 that returns the length of the list. Implement the method in the EmptyList and NonEmptyList classes.

★★ **P14.12** Add a method

```
LispList merge(LispList other)
```

to the LispList interface of Exercise P14.10 that returns the length of the list. Implement the method in the EmptyList and NonEmptyList classes. When merging two lists, alternate between the elements, then add the remainder of the longer list. For example, merging the lists with elements 1 2 3 4 and 5 6 yields 1 5 2 6 3 4.

★ **P14.13** Add a method

```
boolean contains(Object obj)
```

to the LispList interface of Exercise P14.10 that returns true if the list contains an element that equals obj.

★★★ **P14.14** The standard Java library implements a Stack class, but in this exercise you are asked to provide your own implementation. Do not implement type parameters. Use an Object[] array to hold the stack elements. When the array fills up, allocate an array of twice the size and copy the values to the larger array.

★ **P14.15** Implement a Stack class by using a linked list to store the elements. Do not implement type parameters.

★★ **P14.16** Implement a queue as a *circular array* as follows: Use two index variables head and tail that contain the index of the next element to be removed and the next element to be added. After an element is removed or added, the index is incremented (see Figure 15).

After a while, the tail element will reach the top of the array. Then it "wraps around" and starts again at 0—see Figure 16. For that reason, the array is called "circular".

```java
public class CircularArrayQueue
{
    private int head;
    private int tail;
    private int theSize;
    private Object[] elements;

    public CircularArrayQueue(int capacity) { . . . }
    public void add(Object x) { . . . }
    public Object remove() { . . . }
    public int size() { . . . }
}
```

This implementation supplies a *bounded* queue—it can eventually fill up. See the next exercise on how to remove that limitation.

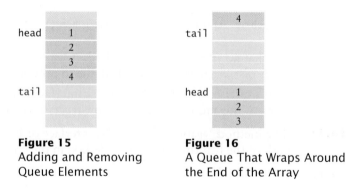

Figure 15
Adding and Removing
Queue Elements

Figure 16
A Queue That Wraps Around
the End of the Array

★★★ **P14.17** The queue in Exercise P14.16 can fill up if more elements are added than the array can hold. Improve the implementation as follows. When the array fills up, allocate a larger array, copy the values to the larger array, and assign it to the elements instance variable. *Hint:* You can't just copy the elements into the same position of the new array. Move the head element to position 0 instead.

★★ **P14.18** Modify the insertion sort algorithm of Special Topic 13.1 to sort a linked list.

★★ **P14.19** Modify the Invoice class of Chapter 11 so that it implements the Iterable<LineItem> interface. Then demonstrate how an Invoice object can be used in a "for each" loop.

★ **P14.20** In a paint program, a "flood fill" fills all empty pixels of a drawing with a given color, stopping when it reaches occupied pixels. In this exercise, you will implement a simple variation of this algorithm, flood-filling a 10 × 10 array of integers that are initially 0. Prompt for the starting row and column. Push the (row, column) pair on a stack. (You will need to provide a simple Pair class.)

Then repeat the following operations until the stack is empty.

- Pop off the (row, column) pair from the top of the stack.
- If it has not yet been filled, fill it now. (Fill in numbers 1, 2, 3, and so on, to show the order in which the square is filled.)
- Push the coordinates of any unfilled neighbors in the north, east, south, or west direction on the stack.

When you are done, print the entire array.

★ **P14.21** Repeat Exercise P14.20, but use a queue instead.

★★ **P14.22** Use a stack to enumerate all permutations of a string. Suppose you want to find all permutations of the string meat. Push the string +meat on the stack. Now repeat the following operations until the stack is empty.

- Pop off the top of the stack.
- If that string ends in a + (such as tame+), remove the + and print the string
- Otherwise, remove each letter in turn from the right of the +, insert it just before the +, and push the resulting string on the stack. For example, after popping e+mta, you push em+ta, et+ma, and ea+mt.

★★ **P14.23** Repeat Exercise P14.22, but use a queue instead.

★★G **P14.24** Write a program to display a linked list graphically. Draw each element of the list as a box, and indicate the links with line segments. Draw an iterator as in Figure 3. Supply buttons to move the iterator and to add and remove elements.

Programming Projects

Project 14.1 Implement a class Polynomial that describes a polynomial such as

$$p(x) = 5x^{10} + 9x^7 - x - 10$$

Store a polynomial as a linked list of terms. A term contains the coefficient and the power of *x*. For example, you would store *p(x)* as

$$(5, 10), (9, 7), (-1, 1), (-10, 0)$$

Supply methods to add, multiply, and print polynomials, and to compute the derivative of a polynomial.

Project 14.2 Make the list implementation of this chapter as powerful as the implementation of the Java library. (Do not implement type parameters, though.)

- Provide bidirectional iteration.
- Make `Node` a static inner class.
- Implement the standard `List` and `ListIterator` interfaces and provide the missing methods. (*Tip:* You may find it easier to extend `AbstractList` instead of implementing all `List` methods from scratch.)

Project 14.3 Implement the following algorithm for the evaluation of arithmetic expressions.

Each operator has a *precedence*. The + and - operators have the lowest precedence, * and / have a higher (and equal) precedence, and ∧ (which denotes "raising to a power" in this exercise) has the highest. For example,

```
3 * 4 ∧ 2 + 5
```

should mean the same as

```
(3 * (4 ∧ 2)) + 5
```

with a value of 53.

In your algorithm, use two stacks. One stack holds numbers, the other holds operators. When you encounter a number, push it on the number stack. When you encounter an operator, push it on the operator stack if it has higher precedence than the operator on the top of the stack. Otherwise, pop an operator off the operator stack, pop two numbers off the number stack, and push the result of the computation on the number stack. Repeat until the top of the operator stack has lower precedence. At the end of the expression, clear the stack in the same way. For example, here is how the expression 3 * 4 ∧ 2 + 5 is evaluated:

	Expression: 3 * 4 ∧ 2 + 5			
❶	Remaining expression:	* 4 ∧ 2 + 5	Number stack: 3	Operator stack
❷	Remaining expression:	4 ∧ 2 + 5	Number stack: 3	Operator stack: *
❸	Remaining expression:	∧ 2 + 5	Number stack: 4, 3	Operator stack: *
❹	Remaining expression:	2 + 5	Number stack: 4, 3	Operator stack: ∧, *
❺	Remaining expression:	+ 5	Number stack: 2, 4, 3	Operator stack: ∧, *
❻	Remaining expression:	+ 5	Number stack: 16, 3	Operator stack: *

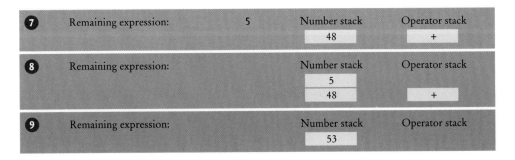

⑦	Remaining expression:	5	Number stack	Operator stack
			48	+

⑧	Remaining expression:		Number stack	Operator stack
			5	
			48	+

⑨	Remaining expression:		Number stack	Operator stack
			53	

You should enhance this algorithm to deal with parentheses. Also, make sure that subtractions and divisions are carried out in the correct order. For example, 12 - 5 - 3 should yield 4.

Answers to Self-Check Questions

1. Yes, for two reasons. You need to store the node references, and each node is a separate object. (There is a fixed overhead to store each object in the virtual machine.)
2. An integer index can be used to access any array location.
3. When the list is empty, first is null. A new Node is allocated. Its data instance variable is set to the newly inserted object. It's next instance variable is set to null because first is null. The first instance variable is set to the new node. The result is a linked list of length 1.
4. It points to the element to the left. You can see that by tracing out the first call to next. It leaves position to point to the first node.
5. If position is null, we must be at the head of the list, and inserting an element requires updating the first reference. If we are in the middle of the list, the first reference should not be changed.
6. You can focus on the essential characteristics of the data type without being distracted by implementation details.
7. The abstract view would be like Figure 9, but with arrows in both directions. The concrete view would be like Figure 8, but with references to the previous node added to each node.
8. To locate the middle element takes $n / 2$ steps. To locate the middle of the subinterval to the left or right takes another $n / 4$ steps. The next lookup takes $n / 8$ steps. Thus, we expect almost n steps to locate an element. At this point, you are better off just making a linear search that, on average, takes $n / 2$ steps.
9.
10. Stacks use a "last in, first out" discipline. If you are the first one to submit a print job and lots of people add print jobs before the printer has a chance to deal with your job, they get their printouts first, and you have to wait until all other jobs are completed.

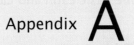

The Basic Latin and Latin-1 Subsets of Unicode

This appendix lists the Unicode characters that are most commonly used for processing Western European languages. A complete listing of Unicode characters can be found at http://unicode.org.

Table 1 Selected Control Characters			
Character	Code	Decimal	Escape Sequence
Tab	'\u0009'	9	'\t'
Newline	'\u000A'	10	'\n'
Return	'\u000D'	13	'\r'
Space	'\u0020'	32	

Table 2   The Basic Latin (ASCII) Subset of Unicode

Char.	Code	Dec.	Char.	Code	Dec.	Char.	Code	Dec.
			@	'\u0040'	64	`	'\u0060'	96
!	'\u0021'	33	A	'\u0041'	65	a	'\u0061'	97
"	'\u0022'	34	B	'\u0042'	66	b	'\u0062'	98
#	'\u0023'	35	C	'\u0043'	67	c	'\u0063'	99
$	'\u0024'	36	D	'\u0044'	68	d	'\u0064'	100
%	'\u0025'	37	E	'\u0045'	69	e	'\u0065'	101
&	'\u0026'	38	F	'\u0046'	70	f	'\u0066'	102
'	'\u0027'	39	G	'\u0047'	71	g	'\u0067'	103
(	'\u0028'	40	H	'\u0048'	72	h	'\u0068'	104
)	'\u0029'	41	I	'\u0049'	73	i	'\u0069'	105
*	'\u002A'	42	J	'\u004A'	74	j	'\u006A'	106
+	'\u002B'	43	K	'\u004B'	75	k	'\u006B'	107
,	'\u002C'	44	L	'\u004C'	76	l	'\u006C'	108
-	'\u002D'	45	M	'\u004D'	77	m	'\u006D'	109
.	'\u002E'	46	N	'\u004E'	78	n	'\u006E'	110
/	'\u002F'	47	O	'\u004F'	79	o	'\u006F'	111
0	'\u0030'	48	P	'\u0050'	80	p	'\u0070'	112
1	'\u0031'	49	Q	'\u0051'	81	q	'\u0071'	113
2	'\u0032'	50	R	'\u0052'	82	r	'\u0072'	114
3	'\u0033'	51	S	'\u0053'	83	s	'\u0073'	115
4	'\u0034'	52	T	'\u0054'	84	t	'\u0074'	116
5	'\u0035'	53	U	'\u0055'	85	u	'\u0075'	117
6	'\u0036'	54	V	'\u0056'	86	v	'\u0076'	118
7	'\u0037'	55	W	'\u0057'	87	w	'\u0077'	119
8	'\u0038'	56	X	'\u0058'	88	x	'\u0078'	120
9	'\u0039'	57	Y	'\u0059'	89	y	'\u0079'	121
:	'\u003A'	58	Z	'\u005A'	90	z	'\u007A'	122
;	'\u003B'	59	[	'\u005B'	91	{	'\u007B'	123
<	'\u003C'	60	\	'\u005C'	92	|	'\u007C'	124
=	'\u003D'	61	]	'\u005D'	93	}	'\u007D'	125
>	'\u003E'	62	^	'\u005E'	94	~	'\u007E'	126
?	'\u003F'	63	_	'\u005F'	95			

Table 3   The Latin-1 Subset of Unicode

Char.	Code	Dec.	Char.	Code	Dec.	Char.	Code	Dec.
			À	'\u00C0'	192	à	'\u00E0'	224
¡	'\u00A1'	161	Á	'\u00C1'	193	á	'\u00E1'	225
¢	'\u00A2'	162	Â	'\u00C2'	194	â	'\u00E2'	226
£	'\u00A3'	163	Ã	'\u00C3'	195	ã	'\u00E3'	227
¤	'\u00A4'	164	Ä	'\u00C4'	196	ä	'\u00E4'	228
¥	'\u00A5'	165	Å	'\u00C5'	197	å	'\u00E5'	229
¦	'\u00A6'	166	Æ	'\u00C6'	198	æ	'\u00E6'	230
§	'\u00A7'	167	Ç	'\u00C7'	199	ç	'\u00E7'	231
¨	'\u00A8'	168	È	'\u00C8'	200	è	'\u00E8'	232
©	'\u00A9'	169	É	'\u00C9'	201	é	'\u00E9'	233
ª	'\u00AA'	170	Ê	'\u00CA'	202	ê	'\u00EA'	234
«	'\u00AB'	171	Ë	'\u00CB'	203	ë	'\u00EB'	235
¬	'\u00AC'	172	Ì	'\u00CC'	204	ì	'\u00EC'	236
-	'\u00AD'	173	Í	'\u00CD'	205	í	'\u00ED'	237
®	'\u00AE'	174	Î	'\u00CE'	206	î	'\u00EE'	238
¯	'\u00AF'	175	Ï	'\u00CF'	207	ï	'\u00EF'	239
°	'\u00B0'	176	Ð	'\u00D0'	208	ð	'\u00F0'	240
±	'\u00B1'	177	Ñ	'\u00D1'	209	ñ	'\u00F1'	241
²	'\u00B2'	178	Ò	'\u00D2'	210	ò	'\u00F2'	242
³	'\u00B3'	179	Ó	'\u00D3'	211	ó	'\u00F3'	243
´	'\u00B4'	180	Ô	'\u00D4'	212	ô	'\u00F4'	244
µ	'\u00B5'	181	Õ	'\u00D5'	213	õ	'\u00F5'	245
¶	'\u00B6'	182	Ö	'\u00D6'	214	ö	'\u00F6'	246
·	'\u00B7'	183	×	'\u00D7'	215	÷	'\u00F7'	247
¸	'\u00B8'	184	Ø	'\u00D8'	216	ø	'\u00F8'	248
¹	'\u00B9'	185	Ù	'\u00D9'	217	ù	'\u00F9'	249
º	'\u00BA'	186	Ú	'\u00DA'	218	ú	'\u00FA'	250
»	'\u00BB'	187	Û	'\u00DB'	219	û	'\u00FB'	251
¼	'\u00BC'	188	Ü	'\u00DC'	220	ü	'\u00FC'	252
½	'\u00BD'	189	Ý	'\u00DD'	221	ý	'\u00FD'	253
¾	'\u00BE'	190	Þ	'\u00DE'	222	þ	'\u00FE'	254
¿	'\u00BF'	191	ß	'\u00DF'	223	ÿ	'\u00FF'	255

Java Operator Summary

The Java operators are listed in groups of decreasing precedence in the table below. The horizontal lines in the table indicate a change in operator precedence. For example, z = x - y; means z = (x - y); because = has lower precedence than -.

The prefix unary operators, conditional operator, and the assignment operators associate right-to-left. All other operators associate left-to-right.

Operator	Description	Associativity
.	Access class feature	
[]	Array subscript	Left to right
()	Function call	
++	Increment	
--	Decrement	
!	Boolean *not*	
~	Bitwise *not*	
+ *(unary)*	(Has no effect)	Right to left
- *(unary)*	Negative	
(*TypeName*)	Cast	
new	Object allocation	
*	Multiplication	
/	Division or integer division	Left to right
%	Integer remainder	
+	Addition, string concatenation	
-	Subtraction	Left to right

Operator	Description	Associativity
<<	Shift left	
>>	Right shift with sign extension	Left to right
>>>	Right shift with zero extension	
<	Less than	
<=	Less than or equal	
>	Greater than	Left to right
>=	Greater than or equal	
instanceof	Tests whether an object's type is a given type or a subtype thereof	
==	Equal	Left to right
!=	Not equal	
&	Bitwise *and*	Left to right
^	Bitwise exclusive *or*	Left to right
|	Bitwise *or*	Left to right
&&	Boolean "short circuit" *and*	Left to right
||	Boolean "short circuit" *or*	Left to right
? :	Conditional	Right to left
=	Assignment	Right to left
op=	Assignment with binary operator (*op* is one of +, -, *, /, &, |, ^, <<, >>, >>>)	

Java Reserved Word Summary

Reserved Word	Description
abstract	An abstract class or method
assert	An assertion that a condition is fulfilled
boolean	The Boolean type
break	Breaks out of the current loop or labeled statement
byte	The 8-bit signed integer type
case	A label in a switch statement
catch	The handler for an exception in a try block
char	The 16-bit Unicode character type
class	Defines a class
const	Not used
continue	Skip the remainder of a loop body
default	The default label in a switch statement
do	A loop whose body is executed at least once
double	The 64-bit double-precision floating-point type
else	The alternative clause in an if statement
enum	An enumeration type
extends	Indicates that a class is a subclass of another class
final	A value that cannot be changed after it has been initialized, a method that cannot be overridden, or a class that cannot be extended
finally	A clause of a try block that is always executed
float	The 32-bit single-precision floating-point type
for	A loop with initialization, condition, and update expressions
goto	Not used

Reserved Word	Description
if	A conditional branch statement
implements	Indicates that a class realizes an interface
import	Allows the use of class names without the package name
instanceof	Tests whether an object's type is a given type or a subtype thereof
int	The 32-bit integer type
interface	An abstract type with only abstract methods and constants
long	The 64-bit integer type
native	A method implemented in non-Java code
new	Allocates an object
package	A collection of related classes
private	A feature that is accessible only by methods of the same class
protected	A feature that is accessible only by methods of the same class, a subclass, or another class in the same package
public	A feature that is accessible by all methods
return	Returns from a method
short	The 16-bit integer type
static	A feature that is defined for a class, not for individual instances
strictfp	Use strict rules for floating-point computations
super	Invoke the superclass constructor or a superclass method
switch	A selection statement
synchronized	A block of code that is accessible to only one thread at a time
this	The implicit parameter of a method; or invocation of another constructor of the same class
throw	Throws an exception
throws	The exceptions that a method may throw
transient	Instance variables that should not be serialized
try	A block of code with exception handlers or a finally handler
void	Tags a method that doesn't return a value
volatile	A variable that may be accessed by multiple threads without synchronization
while	A loop statement

The Java Library

This appendix lists all classes and methods from the standard Java library that are used in this book.

In the following inheritance hierarchy, superclasses that are not used in this book are shown in gray type. Some classes implement interfaces not covered in this book; they are omitted. Classes are sorted first by package, then alphabetically within a package.

```
java.awt.Shape
java.lang.Cloneable
java.lang.Object
    java.awt.BorderLayout
    java.awt.Color
    java.awt.Component
        java.awt.Container
            javax.swing.JComponent
                javax.swing.AbstractButton
                    javax.swing.JButton
                    javax.swing.JMenuItem
                        javax.swing.JMenu
                    javax.swing.JToggleButton
                        javax.swing.JCheckBox
                        javax.swing.JRadioButton
                javax.swing.JComboBox
                javax.swing.JFileChooser
                javax.swing.JLabel
                javax.swing.JMenuBar
                javax.swing.JPanel
                javax.swing.JOptionPane
                javax.swing.JScrollPane
                javax.swing.JSlider
                javax.swing.text.JTextComponent
                    javax.swing.JTextArea
                    javax.swing.JTextField
            java.awt.Panel
                java.applet.Applet
                    javax.swing.JApplet
        java.awt.Window
            java.awt.Frame
                javax.swing.JFrame
    java.awt.Dimension2D
        java.awt.Dimension implements Cloneable
    java.awt.FlowLayout
    java.awt.Font
```

```
java.awt.Graphics
   java.awt.Graphics2D;
java.awt.GridLayout
java.awt.event.MouseAdapter implements MouseListener
java.awt.geom.Line2D implements Cloneable, Shape
   java.awt.geom.Line2D.Double
java.awt.geom.Point2D implements Cloneable
   java.awt.geom.Point2D.Double
java.awt.geom.RectangularShape implements Cloneable, Shape
   java.awt.geom.Rectangle2D
      java.awt.Rectangle
   java.awt.geom.Ellipse2D
      java.awt.geom.Ellipse2D.Double
java.io.File implements Comparable<File>
java.io.InputStream
   java.io.FileInputStream
   java.io.ObjectInputStream
java.io.OutputStream
   java.io.FileOutputStream
   java.io.FilterOutputStream
      java.io.PrintStream
   java.io.ObjectOutputStream
java.io.RandomAccessFile
java.io.Writer
   java.io.PrintWriter
java.lang.Boolean implements Comparable<Boolean>
java.lang.Character implements Comparable<Character>
java.lang.Math
java.lang.Number
   java.math.BigDecimal implements Comparable<BigDecimal>
   java.math.BigInteger implements Comparable<BigInteger>
   java.lang.Double implements Comparable<Double>
   java.lang.Integer implements Comparable<Integer>
java.lang.String implements Comparable<String>
java.lang.System
java.lang.Throwable
  java.lang.Error
  java.lang.Exception
     java.lang.CloneNotSupportedException
     java.io.IOException
        java.io.EOFException
        java.io.FileNotFoundException
     java.lang.RuntimeException
        java.lang.IllegalArgumentException
           java.lang.NumberFormatException
        java.lang.IllegalStateException
        java.util.NoSuchElementException
           java.util.InputMismatchException
        java.lang.NullPointerException
java.net.URL
java.util.AbstractCollection<E>
   java.util.AbstractList<E>
      java.util.AbstractSequentialList<E>
         java.util.LinkedList<E> implements Cloneable, List<E>
      java.util.ArrayList<E> implements Cloneable, List<E>
   java.util.AbstractQueue<E>
      java.util.PriorityQueue<E>
```

```
        java.util.AbstractSet<E>
            java.util.HashSet<E> implements Cloneable, Set<E>
            java.util.TreeSet<E> implements Cloneable, SortedSet<E>
    java.util.AbstractMap<K, V>
        java.util.HashMap<K, V> implements Cloneable, Map<K, V>
        java.util.TreeMap<K, V> implements Cloneable, Map<K, V>
    java.util.Arrays
    java.util.Collections
    java.util.Calendar
        java.util.GregorianCalendar
    java.util.EventObject
        java.awt.AWTEvent
            java.awt.event.ActionEvent
            java.awt.event.ComponentEvent
                java.awt.event.InputEvent
                    java.awt.event.MouseEvent
        javax.swing.event.ChangeEvent
    java.util.Random
    java.util.Scanner
    java.util.logging.Level
    java.util.logging.Logger
    javax.swing.ButtonGroup
    javax.swing.ImageIcon
    javax.swing.Timer
    javax.swing.border.AbstractBorder
        javax.swing.border.EtchedBorder
        javax.swing.border.TitledBorder
java.lang.Comparable<T>
java.util.Collection<E>
    java.util.List<E>
    java.util.Set<E>
        java.util.SortedSet<E>
java.util.Comparator<T>
java.util.EventListener
    java.awt.event.ActionListener
    java.awt.event.MouseListener
    javax.swing.event.ChangeListener
java.util.Iterator<E>
    java.util.ListIterator<E>
java.util.Map<K, V>
```

In the following descriptions, the phrase "this object" ("this component", "this container", and so forth) means the object (component, container, and so forth) on which the method is invoked (the implicit parameter, `this`).

Package `java.applet`

Class `java.applet.Applet`

- void **destroy**()
  This method is called when the applet is about to be terminated, after the last call to `stop`.
- void **init**()
  This method is called when the applet has been loaded, before the first call to `start`. Applets override this method to carry out applet-specific initialization and to read applet parameters.
- void **start**()
  This method is called after the `init` method and each time the applet is revisited.
- void **stop**()
  This method is called whenever the user has stopped watching this applet.

Package `java.awt`

Class `java.awt.BorderLayout`

- **BorderLayout**()
  This constructs a border layout. A border layout has five regions for adding components, called "North", "East", "South", "West", and "Center".
- static final int CENTER
  This value identifies the center position of a border layout.
- static final int EAST
  This value identifies the east position of a border layout.
- static final int NORTH
  This value identifies the north position of a border layout.
- static final int SOUTH
  This value identifies the south position of a border layout.
- static final int WEST
  This value identifies the west position of a border layout.

Class `java.awt.Color`

- **Color**(int red, int green, int blue)
  This creates a color with the specified red, green, and blue values between 0 and 255.
  Parameters: red The red component
   green The green component
   blue The blue component

Class java.awt.Component

- void **addMouseListener**(MouseListener listener)
  This method adds a mouse listener to the component.
  Parameters: listener The mouse listener to be added
- int **getHeight**()
  This method gets the height of this component.
  Returns: The height in pixels.
- int **getWidth**()
  This method gets the width of this component.
  Returns: The width in pixels.
- void **repaint**()
  This method repaints this component by scheduling a call to the paint method.
- void **setPreferredSize**(Dimension preferredSize)
  This method sets the preferred size of this component.
- void **setSize**(int width, int height)
  This method sets the size of this component.
  Parameters: width the component width
                  height   the component height
- void **setVisible**(boolean visible)
  This method shows or hides the component.
  Parameters: visible true to show the component, or false to hide it

Class java.awt.Container

- void **add**(Component c)
- void **add**(Component c, Object position)
  These methods add a component to the end of this container. If a position is given, the layout manager is called to position the component.
  Parameters: c The component to be added
                  position An object expressing position information for the layout manager
- void **setLayout**(LayoutManager manager)
  This method sets the layout manager for this container.
  Parameters: manager A layout manager

Class java.awt.Dimension

- **Dimension**(int width, int height)
  This constructs a Dimension object with the given width and height.
  Parameters: width The width
                  height The height

Class java.awt.FlowLayout

- FlowLayout()
  This constructs a new flow layout. A flow layout places as many components as possible in a row, without changing their size, and starts new rows when necessary.

Class java.awt.Font

- Font(String name, int style, int size)
  This constructs a font object from the specified name, style, and point size.

  Parameters: name The font name, either a font face name or a logical font name, which must be one of "Dialog", "DialogInput", "Monospaced", "Serif", or "SansSerif"

  style One of Font.PLAIN, Font.ITALIC, Font.BOLD, or Font.ITALIC+Font.BOLD

  size The point size of the font

Class java.awt.Frame

- void **setTitle**(String title)
  This method sets the frame title.

  Parameters: title The title to be displayed in the border of the frame

Class java.awt.Graphics

- void **setColor**(Color c)
  This method sets the current color. From now on, all graphics operations use this color.

  Parameters: c The new drawing color

Class java.awt.Graphics2D

- void **draw**(Shape s)
  This method draws the outline of the given shape. Many classes—among them Rectangle and Line2D.Double—implement the Shape interface.

  Parameters: s The shape to be drawn

- void **drawString**(String s, int x, int y)
- void **drawString**(String s, float x, float y)
  These methods draw a string in the current font.

  Parameters: s The string to draw

  x,y The basepoint of the first character in the string

- void **fill**(Shape s)
  This method draws the given shape and fills it with the current color.

  Parameters: s The shape to be filled

Class java.awt.GridLayout

- GridLayout(int rows, int cols)
  This constructor creates a grid layout with the specified number of rows and columns. The components in a grid layout are arranged in a grid with equal widths and heights. One, but not both, of rows and cols can be zero, in which case any number of objects can be placed in a row or in a column, respectively.

  Parameters: rows The number of rows in the grid

  cols The number of columns in the grid

Class java.awt.Rectangle

- Rectangle()
  This constructs a rectangle with a top-left corner at (0, 0) and width and height set to 0.

- `Rectangle(int x, int y, int width, int height)`
  This constructs a rectangle with given top-left corner and size.
  Parameters: x,y   The top-left corner
  width   The width
  height   The height
- `double getHeight()`
- `double getWidth()`
  These methods get the height and width of the rectangle.
- `double getX()`
- `double getY()`
  These methods get the *x*- and *y*-coordinates of the top-left corner of the rectangle.
- `void grow(int dw, int dh)`
  This method adjusts the width and height of this rectangle.
  Parameters: dw   The amount to add to the width (can be negative)
  dh   The amount to add to the height (can be negative)
- `Rectangle intersection(Rectangle other)`
  This method computes the intersection of this rectangle with the specified rectangle.
  Parameters: other   A rectangle
  Returns: The largest rectangle contained in both this and other
- `void setLocation(int x, int y)`
  This method moves this rectangle to a new location.
  Parameters: x,y   The new top-left corner
- `void setSize(int width, int height)`
  This method sets the width and height of this rectangle to new values.
  Parameters: width   The new width
  height   The new height
- `void translate(int dx, int dy)`
  This method moves this rectangle.
  Parameters: dx   The distance to move along the *x*-axis
  dy   The distance to move along the *y*-axis
- `Rectangle union(Rectangle other)`
  This method computes the union of this rectangle with the specified rectangle. This is not the set-theoretic union but the smallest rectangle that contains both this and other.
  Parameters: other   A rectangle
  Returns: The smallest rectangle containing both this and other

Interface java.awt.Shape

The Shape interface describes shapes that can be drawn and filled by a Graphics2D object.

Package java.awt.event

Interface java.awt.event.ActionListener

- `void actionPerformed(ActionEvent e)`
  The event source calls this method when an action occurs.

Class java.awt.event.MouseEvent

- int **getX**()
  This method returns the horizontal position of the mouse as of the time the event occurred.
  Returns: The *x*-position of the mouse
- int **getY**()
  This method returns the vertical position of the mouse as of the time the event occurred.
  Returns: The *y*-position of the mouse

Interface java.awt.event.MouseListener

- void **mouseClicked**(MouseEvent e)
  This method is called when the mouse has been clicked (that is, pressed and released in quick succession).
- void **mouseEntered**(MouseEvent e)
  This method is called when the mouse has entered the component to which this listener was added.
- void **mouseExited**(MouseEvent e)
  This method is called when the mouse has exited the component to which this listener was added.
- void **mousePressed**(MouseEvent e)
  This method is called when a mouse button has been pressed.
- void **mouseReleased**(MouseEvent e)
  This method is called when a mouse button has been released.

Package java.awt.geom

Class java.awt.geom.Ellipse2D.Double

- **Ellipse2D.Double**(double x, double y, double w, double h)
  This constructs an ellipse from the specified coordinates.
  Parameters: x, y The top-left corner of the bounding rectangle
  w The width of the bounding rectangle
  h The height of the bounding rectangle

Class java.awt.geom.Line2D

- double **getX1**()
- double **getX2**()
- double **getY1**()
- double **getY2**()
  These methods get the requested coordinate of an endpoint of this line.
  Returns: The *x*- or *y*-coordinate of the first or second endpoint
- void **setLine**(double x1, double y1, double x2, double y2)
  This methods sets the endpoints of this line.
  Parameters: x1, y1 A new endpoint of this line
  x2, y2 The other new endpoint

Class java.awt.geom.Line2D.Double

- **Line2D.Double**(double x1, double y1, double x2, double y2)
  This constructs a line from the specified coordinates.
  Parameters: x1, y1 One endpoint of the line
  x2, y2 The other endpoint
- **Line2D.Double**(Point2D p1, Point2D p2)
  This constructs a line from the two endpoints.
  Parameters: p1, p2 The endpoints of the line

Class java.awt.geom.Point2D

- double **getX**()
- double **getY**()
  These methods get the requested coordinates of this point.
  Returns: The x- or y-coordinate of this point
- void **setLocation**(double x, double y)
  This method sets the x- and y-coordinates of this point.
  Parameters: x, y The new location of this point

Class java.awt.geom.Point2D.Double

- **Point2D.Double**(double x, double y)
  This constructs a point with the specified coordinates.
  Parameters: x, y The coordinates of the point

Class java.awt.geom.RectangularShape

- int **getHeight**()
- int **getWidth**()
  These methods get the height or width of the bounding rectangle of this rectangular shape.
  Returns: The height or width, respectively
- double **getCenterX**()
- double **getCenterY**()
- double **getMaxX**()
- double **getMaxY**()
- double **getMinX**()
- double **getMinY**()
  These methods get the requested coordinate value of the corners or center of the bounding rectangle of this shape.
  Returns: The center, maximum, or minimum x- and y-coordinates

Package `java.io`

Class `java.io.EOFException`

- `EOFException(String message)`
  This constructs an "end of file" exception object.
  Parameters: message   The detail message

Class `java.io.File`

- `File(String name)`
  This constructs a `File` object that describes a file (which may or may not exist) with the given name.
  Parameters: name   The name of the file
- `static final String pathSeparator`
  The sytem-dependent separator between path names. A colon (:) in Linux or Mac OS X; a semicolon (;) in Windows.

Class `java.io.FileInputStream`

- `FileInputStream(File f)`
  This constructs a file input stream and opens the chosen file. If the file cannot be opened for reading, a `FileNotFoundException` is thrown.
  Parameters: f   The file to be opened for reading
- `FileInputStream(String name)`
  This constructs a file input stream and opens the named file. If the file cannot be opened for reading, a `FileNotFoundException` is thrown.
  Parameters: name   The name of the file to be opened for reading

Class `java.io.FileNotFoundException`

  This exception is thrown when a file could not be opened.

Class `java.io.FileOutputStream`

- `FileOutputStream(File f)`
  This constructs a file output stream and opens the chosen file. If the file cannot be opened for writing, a `FileNotFoundException` is thrown.
  Parameters: f   The file to be opened for writing
- `FileOutputStream(String name)`
  This constructs a file output stream and opens the named file. If the file cannot be opened for writing, a `FileNotFoundException` is thrown.
  Parameters: name   The name of the file to be opened for writing

Class `java.io.InputStream`

- `void close()`
  This method closes this input stream (such as a `FileInputStream`) and releases any system resources associated with the stream.

- `int` **`read`**`()`
  This method reads the next byte of data from this input stream.
  Returns: The next byte of data, or -1 if the end of the stream is reached.

Class `java.io.InputStreamReader`

- **`InputStreamReader`**`(InputStream in)`
  This constructs a reader from a specified input stream.
  Parameters: `in` The stream to read from

Class `java.io.IOException`

This type of exception is thrown when an input/output error is encountered.

Class `java.io.ObjectInputStream`

- **`ObjectInputStream`**`(InputStream in)`
  This constructs an object input stream.
  Parameters: `in` The stream to read from
- `Object` **`readObject`**`()`
  This method reads the next object from this object input stream.
  Returns: The next object

Class `java.io.ObjectOutputStream`

- **`ObjectOutputStream`**`(OutputStream out)`
  This constructs an object output stream.
  Parameters: `out` The stream to write to
- `Object` **`writeObject`**`(Object obj)`
  This method writes the next object to this object output stream.
  Parameters: `obj` The object to write

Class `java.io.OutputStream`

- `void` **`close`**`()`
  This method closes this output stream (such as a `FileOutputStream`) and releases any system resources associated with this stream. A closed stream cannot perform output operations and cannot be reopened.
- `void` **`write`**`(int b)`
  This method writes the lowest byte of b to this output stream.
  Parameters: `b` The integer whose lowest byte is written

Class `java.io.PrintStream`/Class `java.io.PrintWriter`

- **`PrintStream`**`(String name)`
- **`PrintWriter`**`(String name)`
  This constructs a `PrintStream` or `PrintWriter` and opens the named file. If the file cannot be opened for writing, a `FileNotFoundException` is thrown.
  Parameters: `name` The name of the file to be opened for writing
- `void` **`close`**`()`
  This method closes this stream or writer and releases any associated system resources.

- void **print**(int x)
- void **print**(double x)
- void **print**(Object x)
- void **print**(String x)
- void **println**()
- void **println**(int x)
- void **println**(double x)
- void **println**(Object x)
- void **println**(String x)

These methods print a value to this PrintStream or PrintWriter. The println methods print a newline after the value. Objects are printed by converting them to strings with their toString methods.

Parameters: x The value to be printed

- PrintStream **printf**(Sting format, Object... values)
- Printwriter **printf**(Sting format, Object... values)

This method prints the format string to this PrintStream or PrintWriter, substituting the given values for placeholders that start with %.

Parameters: format The format string
values The values to be printed. You can supply any number of values

Returns: The implicit parameter

Class java.io.RandomAccessFile

- **RandomAccessFile**(String name, String mode)
This method opens a named random access file for reading or read/write access.
Parameters: name The file name
mode "r" for reading or "rw" for read/write access
- long **getFilePointer**()
This method gets the current position in this file.
Returns: The current position for reading and writing
- long **length**()
This method gets the length of this file.
Returns: The file length
- char **readChar**()
- double **readDouble**()
- int **readInt**()
These methods read a value from the current position in this file.
Returns: The value that was read from the file
- void **seek**(long position)
This method sets the position for reading and writing in this file.
Parameters: position The new position
- void **writeChar**(int x)
- void **writeChars**(String x)
- void **writeDouble**(double x)
- void **writeInt**(int x)
These methods write a value to the current position in this file.
Parameters: x The value to be written

Package `java.lang`

Class `java.lang.Boolean`

- **`Boolean`**`(boolean value)`
  This constructs a wrapper object for a `boolean` value.
  Parameters: `value` The value to store in this object
- `boolean` **`booleanValue`**`()`
  This method returns the `boolean` value stored in this `Boolean` object.
  Returns: The Boolean value of this object

Class `java.lang.Character`

- `static boolean` **`isDigit`**`(ch)`
  This method tests whether a given character is a Unicode digit.
  Parameters: `ch` The character to test
  Returns: `true` if the character is a digit
- `static boolean` **`isLetter`**`(ch)`
  This method tests whether a given character is a Unicode letter.
  Parameters: `ch` The character to test
  Returns: `true` if the character is a letter
- `static boolean` **`isLowerCase`**`(ch)`
  This method tests whether a given character is a lowercase Unicode letter.
  Parameters: `ch` The character to test
  Returns: `true` if the character is a lowercase letter
- `static boolean` **`isUpperCase`**`(ch)`
  This method tests whether a given character is an uppercase Unicode letter.
  Parameters: `ch` The character to test
  Returns: `true` if the character is an uppercase letter

Interface `java.lang.Cloneable`

A class implements this interface to indicate that the `Object.clone` method is allowed to make a shallow copy of its instance variables.

Class `java.lang.CloneNotSupportedException`

This exception is thrown when a program tries to use `Object.clone` to make a shallow copy of an object of a class that does not implement the `Cloneable` interface.

Interface `java.lang.Comparable<T>`

- `int` **`compareTo`**`(T other)`
  This method compares this object with the `other` object.
  Parameters: `other` The object to be compared
  Returns: A negative integer if this object is less than the other, zero if they are equal, or a positive integer otherwise

Class java.lang.Double

- **Double**(double value)
  This constructs a wrapper object for a double-precision floating-point number.
  Parameters: value The value to store in this object
- double **doubleValue**()
  This method returns the floating-point value stored in this Double wrapper object.
  Returns: The value stored in the object
- static double **parseDouble**(String s)
  This method returns the floating-point number that the string represents. If the string cannot be interpreted as a number, a NumberFormatException is thrown.
  Parameters: s The string to be parsed
  Returns: The value represented by the string parameter

Class java.lang.Error

This is the superclass for all unchecked system errors.

Class java.lang.IllegalArgumentException

- **IllegalArgumentException**()
  This constructs an IllegalArgumentException with no detail message.

Class java.lang.IllegalStateException

This exception is thrown if the state of an object indicates that a method cannot currently be applied.

Class java.lang.Integer

- **Integer**(int value)
  This constructs a wrapper object for an integer.
  Parameters: value The value to store in this object
- int **intValue**()
  This method returns the integer value stored in this wrapper object.
  Returns: The value stored in the object
- static int **parseInt**(String s)
  This method returns the integer that the string represents. If the string cannot be interpreted as an integer, a NumberFormatException is thrown.
  Parameters: s The string to be parsed
  Returns: The value represented by the string parameter
- static Integer **parseInt**(String s, int base)
  This method returns the integer value that the string represents in a given number system. If the string cannot be interpreted as an integer, a NumberFormatException is thrown.
  Parameters: s The string to be parsed
  base The base of the number system (such as 2 or 16)
  Returns: The value represented by the string parameter

- static String **toString**(int i)
- static String **toString**(int i, int base)

  This method creates a string representation of an integer in a given number system. If no base is given, a decimal representation is created.

  Parameters: i An integer number

  base The base of the number system (such as 2 or 16)

  Returns: A string representation of the number parameter in the specified number system

- static final int MAX_VALUE

  This constant is the largest value of type int.

- static final int MIN_VALUE

  This constant is the smallest (negative) value of type int.

Class java.lang.Math

- static double **abs**(double x)

  This method returns the absolute value $|x|$.

  Parameters: x A floating-point value

  Returns: The absolute value of the parameter

- static double **acos**(double x)

  This method returns the angle with the given cosine, $\cos^{-1} x \in [0, \pi]$.

  Parameters: x A floating-point value between −1 and 1

  Returns: The arc cosine of the parameter, in radians

- static double **asin**(double x)

  This method returns the angle with the given sine, $\sin^{-1} x \in [-\pi/2, \pi/2]$.

  Parameters: x A floating-point value between −1 and 1

  Returns: The arc sine of the parameter, in radians

- static double **atan**(double x)

  This method returns the angle with the given tangent, $\tan^{-1} x$ $(-\pi/2, \pi/2)$.

  Parameters: x A floating-point value

  Returns: The arc tangent of the parameter, in radians

- static double **atan2**(double y, double x)

  This method returns the arc tangent, $\tan^{-1}(y/x) \in (-\pi, \pi)$. If x can equal zero, or if it is necessary to distinguish "northwest" from "southeast" and "northeast" from "southwest", use this method instead of atan(y/x).

  Parameters: y,x Two floating-point values

  Returns: The angle, in radians, between the points (0,0) and (x,y)

- static double **ceil**(double x)

  This method returns the smallest integer $\geq x$ (as a double).

  Parameters: x A floating-point value

  Returns: The "ceiling integer" of the parameter

- static double **cos**(double radians)

  This method returns the cosine of an angle given in radians.

  Parameters: radians An angle, in radians

  Returns: The cosine of the parameter

- static double **exp**(double x)

  This method returns the value e^x, where e is the base of the natural logarithms.

  Parameters: x A floating-point value

  Returns: e^x

- static double **floor**(double x)

  This method returns the largest integer ≤x (as a double).

  Parameters: x A floating-point value

  Returns: The "floor integer" of the parameter

- static double **log**(double x)
- static double **log10**(double x)

  This method returns the natural (base e) or decimal (base 10) logarithm of x, ln x.

  Parameters: x A number greater than 0.0

  Returns: The natural logarithm of the parameter

- static int **max**(int x, int y)
- static double **max**(double x, double y)

  These methods return the larger of the given parameter values.

  Parameters: x, y Two integers or floating-point values

  Returns: The maximum of the parameter values

- static int **min**(int x, int y)
- static double **min**(double x, double y)

  These methods return the smaller of the given parameter values.

  Parameters: x, y Two integers or floating-point values

  Returns: The minimum of the parameter values

- static double **pow**(double x, double y)

  This method returns the value x^y ($x > 0$, or $x = 0$ and $y > 0$, or $x < 0$ and y is an integer).

  Parameters: x, y Two floating-point values

  Returns: The value of the first parameter raised to the power of the second parameter

- static long **round**(double x)

  This method returns the closest long integer to the parameter.

  Parameters: x A floating-point value

  Returns: The value of the parameter rounded to the nearest long value

- static double **sin**(double radians)

  This method returns the sine of an angle given in radians.

  Parameters: radians An angle, in radians

  Returns: The sine of the parameter

- static double **sqrt**(double x)

  This method returns the square root of x, $\sqrt{x}$.

  Parameters: x A nonnegative floating-point value

  Returns: The square root of the parameter

- static double **tan**(double radians)

  This method returns the tangent of an angle given in radians.

  Parameters: radians An angle, in radians

  Returns: The tangent of the parameter

- static double **toDegrees**(double radian)

  This method converts radians to degrees.

  Parameters: radians An angle, in radians

  Returns: The angle in degrees

- static double **toRadians**(double degrees)

  This methods converts degrees to radians.

  Parameters: degrees An angle, in degrees

  Returns: The angle in radians

- `static final double E`
  This constant is the value of *e*, the base of the natural logarithms.
- `static final double PI`
  This constant is the value of π.

Class java.lang.NullPointerException

This exception is thrown when a program tries to use an object through a `null` reference.

Class java.lang.NumberFormatException

This exception is thrown when a program tries to parse the numerical value of a string that is not a number.

Class java.lang.Object

- `protected Object clone()`
  This constructs and returns a shallow copy of this object whose instance variables are copies of the instance variables of this object. If an instance variable of the object is an object reference itself, only the reference is copied, not the object itself. However, if the class does not implement the `Cloneable` interface, a `CloneNotSupportedException` is thrown. Subclasses should redefine this method to make a deep copy.

  Returns: A copy of this object

- `boolean equals(Object other)`
  This method tests whether `this` and the other object are equal. This method tests only whether the object references are to the same object. Subclasses should redefine this method to compare the instance variables.

  Parameters: other The object with which to compare
  Returns: `true` if the objects are equal, `false` otherwise

- `void notify()`
  This method notifies one of the threads that is currently on the wait list for the lock of this object.

- `void notifyAll()`
  This method notifies all of the threads that are currently on the wait list for the lock of this object.

- `String toString()`
  This method returns a string representation of this object. This method produces only the class name and locations of the objects. Subclasses should redefine this method to print the instance variables.

  Returns: A string describing this object

- `void wait()`
  This method blocks the currently executing thread and puts it on the wait list for the lock of this object.

Class java.lang.RuntimeException

This is the superclass for all unchecked exceptions.

Class java.lang.String

- int **compareTo**(String other)

This method compares this string and the other string lexicographically.

Parameters: other   The other string to be compared

Returns: A value less than 0 if this string is lexicographically less than the other, 0 if the strings are equal, and a value greater than 0 otherwise.

- boolean **equals**(String other)
- boolean **equalsIgnoreCase**(String other)

These methods test whether two strings are equal, or whether they are equal when letter case is ignored.

Parameters: other   The other string to be compared

Returns: true if the strings are equal

- static String **format**(String format, Object... values)

This method formats the given string by substituting placeholders that start with % with the given values.

Parameters: format   The string with the placeholders

values   The values to be substituted for the placeholders

Returns: The formatted string, with the placeholders replaced by the given values

- int **length**()

This method returns the length of this string.

Returns: The count of characters in this string

- String **replace**(String match, String replacement)

This method replaces matching substrings with a given replacement.

Parameters: match   The string whose matches are to be replaced

replacement   The string with which matching substrings are replaced

Returns: A string that is identical to this string, with all matching substrings replaced by the given replacement

- String **substring**(int begin)
- String **substring**(int begin, int pastEnd)

These methods return a new string that is a substring of this string, made up of all characters starting at position begin and up to either position pastEnd - 1, if it is given, or the end of the string.

Parameters: begin   The beginning index, inclusive

pastEnd   The ending index, exclusive

Returns: The specified substring

- String **toLowerCase**()

This method returns a new string that consists of all characters in this string converted to lowercase.

Returns: A string with all characters in this string converted to lowercase

- String **toUpperCase**()

This method returns a new string that consists of all characters in this string converted to uppercase.

Returns: A string with all characters in this string converted to uppercase

Class java.lang.System

- static void **arraycopy**(
      Object from, int fromStart, Object to, int toStart, int count)
  This method copies values from one array to the other. (The array parameters are of type Object because you can convert an array of numbers to an Object but not to an Object[].)

  Parameters: from   The source array

                     fromStart   Start position in the source array

                     to   The destination array

                     toStart   Start position in the destination data

                     count   The number of array elements to be copied

- static long **currentTimeMillis**()
  This method returns the difference, measured in milliseconds, between the current time and midnight, Universal Time, January 1, 1970.

  Returns: The current time in milliseconds

- static void **exit**(int status)
  This method terminates the program.

  Parameters: status   Exit status. A nonzero status code indicates abnormal termination

- static final InputStream in
  This object is the "standard input" stream. Reading from this stream typically reads keyboard input.

- static final PrintStream out
  This object is the "standard output" stream. Printing to this stream typically sends output to the console window.

Class java.lang.Throwable

This is the superclass of exceptions and errors.

- **Throwable**()
  This constructs a Throwable with no detail message.

- String **getMessage**()
  This method gets the message that describes the exception or error.

  Returns: The message

- void **printStackTrace**()
  This method prints a stack trace to the "standard error" stream. The stack trace contains a printout of this object and of all calls that were pending at the time it was created.

Package java.math

Class java.math.BigDecimal

- **BigDecimal**(String value)
  This constructs an arbitrary-precision floating-point number from the digits in the given string.

  Parameters: value   A string representing the floating-point number

- BigDecimal **add**(BigDecimal other)
- BigDecimal **multiply**(BigDecimal other)
- BigDecimal **subtract**(BigDecimal other)

  These methods return a BigDecimal whose value is the sum, difference, product, or quotient of this number and the other.

  Parameters: other   The other number

  Returns: The result of the arithmetic operation

Class java.math.BigInteger

- **BigInteger**(String value)

  This constructs an arbitrary-precision integer from the digits in the given string.

  Parameters: value   A string representing an arbitrary-precision integer

- BigInteger **add**(BigInteger other)
- BigInteger **divide**(BigInteger other)
- BigInteger **mod**(BigInteger other)
- BigInteger **multiply**(BigInteger other)
- BigInteger **subtract**(BigInteger other)

  These methods return a BigInteger whose value is the sum, difference, product, quotient, or remainder of this number and the other.

  Parameters: other   The other number

  Returns: The result of the arithmetic operation

Package java.net

Class java.net.URL

- **URL**(String s)

  This constructs an URL object from a string containing the URL.

  Parameters: s   The URL string, such as "http://java.sun.com/index.html"

- InputStream **openStream**()

  This method gets the input stream through which the client can read the information that the server sends.

  Returns: The input stream associated with this URL

Package java.util

Class java.util.ArrayList<E>

- **ArrayList**()

  This constructs an empty array list.

- boolean **add**(E element)

  This method appends an element to the end of this array list.

  Parameters: element   The element to add

  Returns: true (This method returns a value because it overrides a method in the List interface.)

- void **add**(int index, E element)
  This method inserts an element into this array list.
  Parameters: index   Insert position
                    element   The element to insert
- E **get**(int index)
  This method gets the element at the specified position in this array list.
  Parameters: index   Position of the element to return
  Returns: The requested element
- E **remove**(int index)
  This method removes the element at the specified position in this array list and returns it.
  Parameters: index   Position of the element to remove
  Returns: The removed element
- E **set**(int index, E element)
  This method replaces the element at a specified position in this array list.
  Parameters: index   Position of element to replace
                    element   Element to be stored at the specified position
  Returns: The element previously at the specified position
- int **size**()
  This method returns the number of elements in this array list.
  Returns: The number of elements in this array list

Class java.util.Arrays

- static int **binarySearch**(Object[] a, Object key)
  This method searches the specified array for the specified object using the binary search algorithm. The array elements must implement the Comparable interface. The array must be sorted in ascending order.
  Parameters: a   The array to be searched
                    key   The value to be searched for
  Returns: The position of the search key, if it is contained in the array; otherwise, $-index - 1$, where *index* is the position where the element may be inserted
- static T[] **copyOf**(T[] a, int newLength)
  This method copies the elements of the array a, or the first newLength elements if a.length < newLength, into an array of length newLength and returns that array. T can be a primitive type, class, or interface type.
  Parameters: a   The array to be copied
                    key   The value to be searched for
  Returns: The position of the search key, if it is contained in the array; otherwise, $-index - 1$, where *index* is the position where the element may be inserted
- static void **sort**(Object[] a)
  This method sorts the specified array of objects into ascending order. Its elements must implement the Comparable interface.
  Parameters: a   The array to be sorted
- static String **toString**(T[] a)
  This method creates and returns a string containing the array elements. T can be a primitive type, class, or interface type.
  Parameters: a   An array
  Returns: A string containing a comma-separated list of string representations of the array elements, surrounded by brackets.

Class `java.util.Calendar`

- `int` **`get`**`(int field)`
  This method returns the value of the given field.
  Parameters: One of `Calendar.YEAR`, `Calendar.MONTH`, `Calendar.DAY_OF_MONTH`, `Calendar.HOUR`, `Calendar.MINUTE`, `Calendar.SECOND`, or `Calendar.MILLISECOND`

Interface `java.util.Collection<E>`

- `boolean` **`add`**`(E element)`
  This method adds an element to this collection.
  Parameters: `element` The element to add
  Returns: `true` if adding the element changes the collection
- `boolean` **`contains`**`(E element)`
  This method tests whether an element is present in this collection.
  Parameters: `element` The element to find
  Returns: `true` if the element is contained in the collection
- `Iterator` **`iterator`**`()`
  This method returns an iterator that can be used to traverse the elements of this collection.
  Returns: An object of a class implementing the `Iterator` interface
- `boolean` **`remove`**`(E element)`
  This method removes an element from this collection.
  Parameters: `element` The element to remove
  Returns: `true` if removing the element changes the collection
- `int` **`size`**`()`
  This method returns the number of elements in this collection.
  Returns: The number of elements in this collection

Class `java.util.Collections`

- `static <T> int` **`binarySearch`**`(List<T> a, T key)`
  This method searches the specified list for the specified object using the binary search algorithm. The list elements must implement the `Comparable` interface. The list must be sorted in ascending order.
  Parameters: a The list to be searched
  key The value to be searched for
  Returns: The position of the search key, if it is contained in the list; otherwise, $-index - 1$, where *index* is the position where the element may be inserted
- `static <T> void` **`sort`**`(T[] a)`
  This method sorts the specified list of objects into ascending order. Its elements must implement the `Comparable` interface.
  Parameters: a The list to be sorted

Interface java.util.Comparator\<T>

- int **compare**(T first, T second)
  This method compares the given objects.
  Parameters: first, second The objects to be compared
  Returns: A negative integer if the first object is less than the second, zero if they are equal, or a positive integer otherwise

Class java.util.EventObject

- Object **getSource**()
  This method returns a reference to the object on which this event initially occurred.
  Returns: The source of this event

Class java.util.GregorianCalendar

- GregorianCalendar()
  This constructs a calendar object that represents the current date and time.
- GregorianCalendar(int year, int month, int day)
  This constructs a calendar object that represents the start of the given date.
  Parameters: year, month, day The given date

Class java.util.HashMap\<K, V>

- HashMap\<K, V>()
  This constructs an empty hash map.

Class java.util.HashSet\<E>

- HashSet\<E>()
  This constructs an empty hash set.

Class java.util.InputMismatchException

This exception is thrown if the next available input item does not match the type of the requested item.

Interface java.util.Iterator\<E>

- boolean **hasNext**()
  This method checks whether the iterator is past the end of the list.
  Returns: true if the iterator is not yet past the end of the list
- E **next**()
  This method moves the iterator over the next element in the linked list. This method throws an exception if the iterator is past the end of the list.
  Returns: The object that was just skipped over
- void **remove**()
  This method removes the element that was returned by the last call to next or previous. This method throws an exception if there was an add or remove operation after the last call to next or previous.

Class java.util.LinkedList<E>

- void **addFirst**(E element)
- void **addLast**(E element)

These methods add an element before the first or after the last element in this list.

Parameters: element   The element to be added

- E **getFirst**()
- E **getLast**()

These methods return a reference to the specified element from this list.

Returns: The first or last element

- E **removeFirst**()
- E **removeLast**()

These methods remove the specified element from this list.

Returns: A reference to the removed element

Interface java.util.List<E>

- ListIterator<E> **listIterator**()

This method gets an iterator to visit the elements in this list.

Returns: An iterator that points before the first element in this list

Interface java.util.ListIterator<E>

Objects implementing this interface are created by the listIterator methods of list classes.

- void **add**(E element)

This method adds an element after the iterator position and moves the iterator after the new element.

Parameters: element   The element to be added

- boolean **hasPrevious**()

This method checks whether the iterator is before the first element of the list.

Returns: true if the iterator is not before the first element of the list

- E **previous**()

This method moves the iterator over the previous element in the linked list. This method throws an exception if the iterator is before the first element of the list.

Returns: The object that was just skipped over

- void **set**(E element)

This method replaces the element that was returned by the last call to next or previous. This method throws an exception if there was an add or remove operation after the last call to next or previous.

Parameters: element   The element that replaces the old list element

Interface java.util.Map<K, V>

- V **get**(K key)

Gets the value associated with a key in this map.

Parameters: key   The key for which to find the associated value

Returns: The value associated with the key, or null if the key is not present in the table

- Set<K> **keySet**()

This method returns all keys in the table of this map.

Returns: A set of all keys in the table of this map

- V **put**(K key, V value)
  This method associates a value with a key in this map.
  Parameters: key The lookup key

  value The value to associate with the key

  Returns: The value previously associated with the key, or null if the key was not present in the table

- V **remove**(K key)
  This method removes a key and its associated value from this map.
  Parameters: key The lookup key
  Returns: The value previously associated with the key, or null if the key was not present in the table

Class java.util.NoSuchElementException

This exception is thrown if an attempt is made to retrieve a value that does not exist.

Class java.util.PriorityQueue<E>

- PriorityQueue<E>()
  This constructs an empty priority queue. The element type E must implement the Comparable interface.

- E **remove**()
  This method removes the smallest element in the priority queue.
  Returns: The removed value

Class java.util.Random

- Random()
  This constructs a new random number generator.

- double **nextDouble**()
  This method returns the next pseudorandom, uniformly distributed floating-point number between 0.0 (inclusive) and 1.0 (exclusive) from this random number generator's sequence.
  Returns: The next pseudorandom floating-point number

- int **nextInt**(int n)
  This method returns the next pseudorandom, uniformly distributed integer between 0 (inclusive) and the specified value (exclusive) drawn from this random number generator's sequence.
  Parameters: n Number of values to draw from
  Returns: The next pseudorandom integer

Class java.util.Scanner

- Scanner(File in)
- Scanner(InputStream in)
- Scanner(Reader in)
  These construct a scanner that reads from the given file, input stream, or reader.
  Parameters: in The file, input stream, or reader from which to read

- void **close**()
  This method closes this scanner and releases any associated system resources.

- boolean **hasNext**()
- boolean **hasNextDouble**()
- boolean **hasNextInt**()
- boolean **hasNextLine**()

  These methods test whether it is possible to read any non-empty string, a floating-point value, an integer, or a line, as the next item.

  Returns: true if it is possible to read an item of the requested type, false otherwise (either because the end of the file has been reached, or because a number type was tested and the next item is not a number)

- String **next**()
- double **nextDouble**()
- int **nextInt**()
- String **nextLine**()

  These methods read the next whitespace-delimited string, floating-point value, integer, or line.

  Returns: The value that was read

- Scanner **useDelimiter**(String pattern)

  Sets the pattern for the delimiters between input tokens.

  Parameters: pattern A regular expression for the delimiter pattern

  Returns: This scanner

Interface java.util.Set<E>

This interface describes a collection that contains no duplicate elements.

Class java.util.TreeMap<K, V>

- **TreeMap**<K, V>()

  This constructs an empty tree map. The TreeMap iterator visits the entries in sorted order.

Class java.util.TreeSet<E>

- **TreeSet**<E>()

  This constructs an empty tree set.

Package java.util.logging

Class java.util.logging.Level

- static final int ALL

  This value indicates logging of all messages.

- static final int INFO

  This value indicates informational logging.

- static final int NONE

  This value indicates logging of no messages.

Class java.util.logging.Logger

- static Logger **getGlobal**()

  This method gets the global logger. For Java 5 and 6, use getLogger("global") instead.

  Returns: The global logger that, by default, displays messages with level *INFO* or a higher severity on the console.

- void **info**(String message)
  This method logs an informational message.
  Parameters: message   The message to log
- void **setLevel**(Level aLevel)
  This method sets the logging level. Logging messages with a lesser severity than the current level are ignored.
  Parameters: aLevel   The minimum level for logging messages

Package javax.swing

Class javax.swing.AbstractButton

- void **addActionListener**(ActionListener listener)
  This method adds an action listener to the button.
  Parameters: listener   The action listener to be added
- boolean **isSelected**()
  This method returns the selection state of the button.
  Returns: true if the button is selected
- void **setSelected**(boolean state)
  This method sets the selection state of the button. This method updates the button but does not trigger an action event.
  Parameters: state   true to select, false to deselect

Class javax.swing.ButtonGroup

- void **add**(AbstractButton button)
  This method adds the button to the group.
  Parameters: button   The button to add

Class javax.swing.ImageIcon

- **ImageIcon**(String filename)
  This constructs an image icon from the specified graphics file.
  Parameters: filename   A string specifying a file name

Class javax.swing.JButton

- **JButton**(String label)
  This constructs a button with the given label.
  Parameters: label   The button label

Class javax.swing.JCheckBox

- **JCheckBox**(String text)
  This constructs a check box, having the given text, initially deselected. (Use the setSelected() method to make the box selected; see the javax.swing.AbstractButton class.)
  Parameters: text   The text displayed next to the check box

Class javax.swing.JComboBox

- JComboBox()
  This constructs a combo box with no items.
- void addItem(Object item)
  This method adds an item to the item list of this combo box.
  Parameters: item The item to add
- Object getSelectedItem()
  This method gets the currently selected item of this combo box.
  Returns: The currently selected item
- boolean isEditable()
  This method checks whether the combo box is editable. An editable combo box allows the user to type into the text field of the combo box.
  Returns: true if the combo box is editable
- void setEditable(boolean state)
  This method is used to make the combo box editable or not.
  Parameters: state true to make editable, false to disable editing

Class javax.swing.JComponent

- protected void paintComponent(Graphics g)
  Override this method to paint the surface of a component. Your method needs to call super.paintComponent(g).
  Parameters: g The graphics context used for drawing
- void setBorder(Border b)
  This method sets the border of this component.
  Parameters: b The border to surround this component
- void setFont(Font f)
  Sets the font used for the text in this component.
  Parameters: f A font

Class javax.swing.JFileChooser

- JFileChooser()
  This constructs a file chooser.
- File getSelectedFile()
  This method gets the selected file from this file chooser.
  Returns: The selected file
- int showOpenDialog(Component parent)
  This method displays an "Open File" file chooser dialog box.
  Parameters: parent The parent component or null
  Returns: The return state of this file chooser after it has been closed by the user: either APPROVE_OPTION or CANCEL_OPTION. If APPROVE_OPTION is returned, call getSelectedFile() on this file chooser to get the file
- int showSaveDialog(Component parent)
  This method displays a "Save File" file chooser dialog box.
  Parameters: parent The parent component or null
  Returns: The return state of the file chooser after it has been closed by the user: either APPROVE_OPTION or CANCEL_OPTION

Class javax.swing.JFrame

- void **setDefaultCloseOperation**(int operation)
  This method sets the default action for closing the frame.
  Parameters: operation   The desired close operation. Choose among
  DO_NOTHING_ON_CLOSE, HIDE_ON_CLOSE (the default), DISPOSE_ON_CLOSE, or
  EXIT_ON_CLOSE

- void **setJMenuBar**(JMenuBar mb)
  This method sets the menu bar for this frame.
  Parameters: mb   The menu bar. If mb is null, then the current menu bar is removed

- static final int EXIT_ON_CLOSE
  This value indicates that when the user closes this frame, the application is to exit.

Class javax.swing.JLabel

- **JLabel**(String text)
- **JLabel**(String text, int alignment)
  These containers create a JLabel instance with the specified text and horizontal alignment.
  Parameters: text   The label text to be displayed by the label
  alignment   One of SwingConstants.LEFT, SwingConstants.CENTER, or SwingCon-
  stants.RIGHT

Class javax.swing.JMenu

- **JMenu**()
  This constructs a menu with no items.

- JMenuItem **add**(JMenuItem menuItem)
  This method appends a menu item to the end of this menu.
  Parameters: menuItem   The menu item to be added
  Returns: The menu item that was added

Class javax.swing.JMenuBar

- **JMenuBar**()
  This constructs a menu bar with no menus.

- JMenu **add**(JMenu menu)
  This method appends a menu to the end of this menu bar.
  Parameters: menu   The menu to be added
  Returns: The menu that was added

Class javax.swing.JMenuItem

- **JMenuItem**(String text)
  This constructs a menu item.
  Parameters: text   The text to appear in the menu item

Class javax.swing.JOptionPane

- static String **showInputDialog**(Object prompt)
  This method brings up a modal input dialog box, which displays a prompt and waits for the user to enter an input in a text field, preventing the user from doing anything else in this program.
  Parameters: prompt The prompt to display
  Returns: The string that the user typed

- static void **showMessageDialog**(Component parent, Object message)
  This method brings up a confirmation dialog box that displays a message and waits for the user to confirm it.
  Parameters: parent The parent component or null
  message The message to display

Class javax.swing.JPanel

This class is a component without decorations. It can be used as an invisible container for other components.

Class javax.swing.JRadioButton

- **JRadioButton**(String text)
  This constructs a radio button having the given text that is initially deselected. (Use the setSelected() method to select it; see the javax.swing.AbstractButton class.)
  Parameters: text The string displayed next to the radio button

Class javax.swing.JScrollPane

- **JScrollPane**(Component c)
  This constructs a scroll pane around the given component.
  Parameters: c The component that is decorated with scroll bars

Class javax.swing.JSlider

- **JSlider**(int min, int max, int value)
  This constructor creates a horizontal slider using the specified minimum, maximum, and value.
  Parameters: min The smallest possible slider value
  max The largest possible slider value
  value The initial value of the slider

- void **addChangeListener**(ChangeListener listener)
  This method adds a change listener to the slider.
  Parameters: listener The change listener to add

- int **getValue**()
  This method returns the slider's value.
  Returns: The current value of the slider

Class javax.swing.JTextArea

- JTextArea()
  This constructs an empty text area.
- JTextArea(int rows, int columns)
  This constructs an empty text area with the specified number of rows and columns.
  Parameters: rows   The number of rows
  columns   The number of columns
- void **append**(String text)
  This method appends text to this text area.
  Parameters: text   The text to append

Class javax.swing.JTextField

- JTextField()
  This constructs an empty text field.
- JTextField(int columns)
  This constructs an empty text field with the specified number of columns.
  Parameters: columns   The number of columns

Class javax.swing.Timer

- Timer(int millis, ActionListener listener)
  This constructs a timer that notifies an action listener whenever a time interval has elapsed.
  Parameters: millis   The number of milliseconds between timer notifications
  listener   The object to be notified when the time interval has elapsed
- void **start**()
  This method starts the timer. Once the timer has started, it begins notifiying its listener.
- void **stop**()
  This method stops the timer. Once the timer has stopped, it no longer notifies its listener.

Package javax.swing.border

Class javax.swing.border.EtchedBorder

- EtchedBorder()
  This constructor creates a lowered etched border.

Class javax.swing.border.TitledBorder

- TitledBorder(Border b, String title)
  This constructor creates a titled border that adds a title to a given border.
  Parameters: b   The border to which the title is added
  title   The title the border should display

Package javax.swing.event

Class javax.swing.event.ChangeEvent

Components such as sliders emit change events when they are manipulated by the user.

Interface javax.swing.event.ChangeListener

- void **stateChanged**(ChangeEvent e)
  This event is called when the event source has changed its state.
  Parameters: e A change event

Package javax.swing.text

Class javax.swing.text.JTextComponent

- String **getText**()
  This method returns the text contained in this text component.
  Returns: The text
- boolean **isEditable**()
  This method checks whether this text component is editable.
  Returns: true if the component is editable
- void **setEditable**(boolean state)
  This method is used to make this text component editable or not.
  Parameters: state true to make editable, false to disable editing
- void **setText**(String text)
  This method sets the text of this text component to the specified text. If the text is empty, the old text is deleted.
  Parameters: text The new text to be set
  This method sets the validation mode for all document builders that are generated from this factory.
  Parameters: b true if documents should be validated during parsing

GLOSSARY

Abstract array   An ordered sequence of items that can be efficiently accessed at random through an integer index.

Abstract class   A class that cannot be instantiated.

Abstract list   An ordered sequence of items that can be traversed sequentially and that allows for efficient insertion and removal of elements at any position.

Abstract method   A method with a name, parameter types, and return type but without an implementation.

Abstraction   The process of finding the essential feature set for a building block of a program such as a class.

Access specifier   A reserved word that indicates the accessibility of a feature, such as private or public.

Accessor method   A method that accesses an object but does not change it.

Actual parameter   The expression supplied for a formal parameter of a method by the caller.

ADT (Abstract Data Type)   A specification of the fundamental operations that characterize a data type, without supplying an implementation.

Aggregation   The *has-a* relationship between classes.

Algorithm   An unambiguous, executable, and terminating specification of a way to solve a problem.

Anonymous class   A class that does not have a name.

Anonymous object   An object that is not stored in a named variable.

API (Application Programming Interface)   A code library for building programs.

API Documentation   Information about each class in the Java library.

Applet   A graphical Java program that executes inside a web browser or applet viewer.

Argument   An actual parameter in a method call, or one of the values combined by an operator.

Array   A collection of values of the same type stored in contiguous memory locations, each of which can be accessed by an integer index.

Array list   A Java class that implements a dynamically-growable array of objects.

Assertion   A claim that a certain condition holds in a particular program location.

Assignment   Placing a new value into a variable.

Association   A relationship between classes in which one can navigate from objects of one class to objects of the other class, usually by following object references.

Asymmetric bounds   Bounds that include the starting index but not the ending index.

Attribute   A named property that an object is responsible for maintaining.

Auto-boxing   Automatically converting a primitive type value into a wrapper type object.

Balanced tree   A tree in which each subtree has the property that the number of descendants to the left is approximately the same as the number of descendants to the right.

Big-Oh notation   The notation $g(n) = O(f(n))$, which denotes that the function g grows at a rate that is bounded by the growth rate of the function f with respect to n. For example, $10n^2 + 100n - 1000 = O(n^2)$.

Binary file   A file in which values are stored in their binary representation and cannot be read as text.

Binary operator   An operator that takes two arguments, for example $+$ in $x + y$.

Binary search   A fast algorithm for finding a value in a sorted array. It narrows the search down to half of the array in every step.

Binary search tree   A binary tree in which *each* subtree has the property that all left descendants are smaller than the value stored in the root, and all right descendants are larger.

Binary tree   A tree in which each node has at most two child nodes.

Bit   Binary digit; the smallest unit of information, having two possible values: 0 and 1. A data element consisting of n bits has 2^n possible values.

Black-box testing   Testing a method without knowing its implementation.

Block   A group of statements bracketed by {}.

Boolean operator   See **Logical operator**

Boolean type   A type with two possible values: true and false.

Border layout   A layout management scheme in which components are placed into the center or one of the four borders of their container.

Boundary test case   A test case involving values that are at the outer boundary of the set of legal values. For example, if a function is expected to work for all nonnegative integers, then 0 is a boundary test case.

Bounds error   Trying to access an array element that is outside the legal range.

Breakpoint   A point in a program, specified in a debugger, at which the debugger stops executing the program and lets the user inspect the program state.

break statement   A statement that terminates a loop or switch statement.

Bucket   In a hash table, a set of values with the same hash code.

Buffer   A temporary storage location for holding values that have been produced (for example, characters typed by the user) and are waiting to be consumed (for example, read a line at a time).

Buffered input   Input that is gathered in batches, for example, a line at a time.

Bug   A programming error.

Byte   A number made up of eight bits. Essentially all currently manufactured computers use a byte as the smallest unit of storage in memory.

Bytecode   Instructions for the Java virtual machine.

Callback   A mechanism for specifying a block of code so it can be executed at a later time.

Call by reference   A method call mechanism in which the method receives the memory location of a variable supplied as an actual parameter. Call by reference enables a method to change the contents of the original variable so that the change remains in effect after the method returns.

Call by value   A method call mechanism in which the method receives a copy of the contents of a variable supplied as an actual parameter. Java uses only call by value. If a parameter variable's type is a class, its value is an object reference, so the method can alter that object but cannot make the parameter variable refer to a different object.

Call stack   The ordered set of all methods that currently have been called but not yet terminated, starting with the current method and ending with main.

Case sensitive   Distinguishing upper- and lowercase characters.

Cast   Explicitly converting a value from one type to a different type. For example, the cast from a floating-point number x to an integer is expressed in Java by the cast notation (int) x.

catch clause   A part of a try block that is executed when a matching exception is thrown by any statement in the try block.

Central processing unit (CPU)   The part of a computer that executes the machine instructions.

Character   A single letter, digit, or symbol.

Check box   A user-interface component that can be used for a binary selection.

Checked exception   An exception that the compiler checks. All checked exceptions must be declared or caught.

Class   A programmer-defined data type.

Class method   See **Static method**

Class path   The set of directories and archives that the virtual machine searches for class files.

Client   A computer program or system that issues requests to a server and processes the server responses.

Cloning   Making a copy of an object so the copy's state can be modified independently of the original object.

Code coverage   A measure of the amount of source code that has been executed during testing.

Cohesion   A class is cohesive if its features support a single abstraction.

Collaborator   A class on which another class depends.

Combo box   A user-interface component that combines a text field with a drop-down list of selections.

Command line   The line the user types to start a program in DOS or UNIX or a command window in Windows. It consists of the program name followed by any necessary arguments.

Comment   An explanation to help the human reader understand a section of a program; ignored by the compiler.

Compiler   A program that translates code in a high-level language (such as Java) to machine instructions (such as bytecode for the Java virtual machine).

Compile-time error   An error that is detected when a program is compiled.

Component   See **User-interface component**

Compound statement   A statement such as if or while that is made up of several parts such as a condition and a body.

Concatenation   Placing one string after another to form a new string.

Concrete class   A class that can be instantiated.

Console program   A Java program that does not have a graphical window. A console program reads input from the keyboard and writes output to the terminal screen.

Constant   A value that cannot be changed by a program. In Java, constants are defined with the reserved word final.

Construction   Setting a newly allocated object to an initial state.

Constructor   A method that initializes a newly instantiated object.

Container   A user-interface component that can hold other components and present them together to the user. Also, a data structure, such as a list, that can hold a collection of objects and present them individually to a program.

Content pane   The part of a Swing frame that holds the user-interface components of the frame.

Coupling   The degree to which classes are related to each other by dependency.

CRC card   An index card representing a class that lists its responsibilities and collaborating classes.

De Morgan's Law   A law about logical operations that describes how to negate expressions formed with *and* and *or* operations.

Debugger   A program that lets a user run another program one or a few steps at a time, stop execution, and inspect the variables in order to analyze it for bugs.

Default constructor   A constructor that is invoked with no parameters.

Dependency   The *uses* relationship between classes, in which one class needs services provided by another class.

Dictionary ordering   See **Lexicographic ordering**

Directory   A structure on a disk that can hold files or other directories; also called a folder.

Documentation comment   A comment in a source file that can be automatically extracted into the program documentation by a program such as javadoc.

Dot notation   The notation *object.method(parameters)* or *object.variable* used to invoke a method or access a variable.

Doubly linked list   A linked list in which each link has a reference to both its predecessor and successor links.

Dynamic method lookup   Selecting a method to be invoked at run time. In Java, dynamic method lookup considers the class of the implicit parameter object to select the appropriate method.

Editor   A program for writing and modifying text files.

Embedded system   The processor, software, and supporting circuitry that is included in a device other than a computer.

Encapsulation   The hiding of implementation details.

End of file   The condition that is true when all characters of a file have been read. Note that there is no special "end of file character". When composing a file on the keyboard, you may need to type a special character to tell the operating system to end the file, but that character is not part of the file.

Enumeration type   A type with a finite number of values, each of which has its own symbolic name.

Escape character   A character in text that is not taken literally but has a special meaning when combined with the character or characters that follow it. The \ character is an escape character in Java strings.

Event   See **User-interface event**

Event class   A class that contains information about an event, such as its source.

Event adapter   A class that implements an event listener interface by defining all methods to do nothing.

Event handler   A method that is executed when an event occurs.

Event listener   An object that is notified by an event source when an event occurs.

Event source   An object that can notify other classes of events.

Exception   A class that signals a condition that prevents the program from continuing normally. When such a condition occurs, an object of the exception class is thrown.

Exception handler   A sequence of statements that is given control when an exception of a particular type has been thrown and caught.

Explicit parameter   A parameter of a method other than the object on which the method is invoked.

Expression   A syntactical construct that is made up of constants, variables, method calls, and operators combining them.

Extension   The last part of a file name, which specifies the file type. For example, the extension .java denotes a Java file.

Extreme Programming   A development methodology that strives for simplicity, by removing formal structure and focusing on best practices.

Fibonacci numbers   The sequence of numbers 1, 1, 2, 3, 5, 8, 13, . . ., in which every term is the sum of its two predecessors.

File   A sequence of bytes that is stored on disk.

File pointer   The position within a random-access file of the next byte to be read or written. It can be moved so as to access any byte in the file.

`finally` **clause**   A part of a try block that is executed no matter how the try block is exited.

Flag   See **Boolean type**

Floating-point number   A number that can have a fractional part.

Flow layout   A layout management scheme in which components are laid out left to right.

Flushing a stream   Sending all characters that are still held in a buffer to its destination.

Folder   See **Directory**

Font   A set of character shapes in a particular style and size.

Formal parameter   A variable in a method definition; it is initialized with an actual parameter value when the method is called.

Frame   A window with a border and a title bar.

Garbage collection   Automatic reclamation of memory occupied by objects that are no longer referenced.

Generic class   A class with one or more type parameters.

Generic method   A method with one or more type parameters.

Generic programming   Providing program components that can be reused in a wide variety of situations.

goto statement   A statement that transfers control to some other statement, which is tagged with a label. Java does not have a goto statement.

Graphics context   A class through which a programmer can cause shapes to appear on a window or off-screen bitmap.

grep   The "global regular expression print" search program, useful for finding all strings matching a pattern in a set of files.

Grid layout   A layout management scheme in which components are placed into a two-dimensional grid.

GUI (Graphical User Interface)   A user interface in which the user supplies inputs through graphical components such as buttons, menus, and text fields.

Hash code   A value that is computed by a hash function.

Hash collision   Two different objects for which a hash function computes identical values.

Hash function   A function that computes an integer value from an object in such a way that different objects are likely to yield different values.

Hash table   A data structure in which elements are mapped to array positions according to their hash function values.

Hashing   Applying a hash function to a set of objects.

Heap   A balanced binary tree that is used for implementing sorting algorithms and priority queues.

Heapsort algorithm   A sorting algorithm that inserts the values to be sorted into a heap.

HTML (Hypertext Markup Language)   The language in which web pages are described.

IDE (Integrated Development Environment)   A programming environment that includes an editor, compiler, and debugger.

Immutable class   A class without a mutator method.

Implementing an interface   Implementing a class that defines all methods specified in the interface.

Implicit parameter   The object on which a method is invoked. For example, in the call x.f(y), the object x is the implicit parameter of the method f.

Importing a class or package   Indicating the intention of referring to a class, or all classes in a package, by the simple name rather than the qualified name.

Inheritance   The *is-a* relationship between a more general superclass and a more specialized subclass.

Initialization   Setting a variable to a well-defined value when it is created.

Inner class   A class that is defined inside another class.

Instance method   A method with an implicit parameter; that is, a method that is invoked on an instance of a class.

Instance of a class   An object whose type is that class.

Instance variable   A variable defined in a class for which every object of the class has its own value.

Instantiation of a class   Construction of an object of that class.

Integer   A number that cannot have a fractional part.

Integer division   Taking the quotient of two integers and discarding the remainder. In Java the / symbol denotes integer division if both arguments are integers. For example, 11/4 is 2, not 2.75.

Interface   A type with no instance variables, only abstract methods and constants.

Internet   A worldwide collection of networks, routing equipment, and computers using a common set of protocols that define how participants interact with each other.

Interpreter   A program that reads a set of codes and carries out the commands specified by them.

Iterator   An object that can inspect all elements in a container such as a linked list.

javadoc   The documentation generator in the Java SDK. It extracts documentation comments from Java source files and produces a set of linked HTML files.

JDK   The Java software development kit that contains the Java compiler and related development tools.

JVM   The Java Virtual Machine.

Layout manager   A class that arranges user-interface components inside a container.

Lazy evaluation   Deferring the computation of a value until it is needed, thereby avoiding the computation if the value is never needed.

Legacy code   Software that has existed for a long time and that continues to operate.

Lexicographic ordering   Ordering strings in the same order as in a dictionary, by skipping all matching characters and comparing the first non matching characters of both strings. For example, "orbit" comes before "orchid" in lexicographic ordering. Note that in Java, unlike a dictionary, the ordering is case-sensitive: Z comes before a.

Library   A set of precompiled classes that can be included in programs.

Linear search   Searching a container (such as an array or list) for an object by inspecting each element in turn.

Linked list   A data structure that can hold an arbitrary number of objects, each of which is stored in a link object, which contains a pointer to the next link.

Local variable   A variable whose scope is a block.

Logging   Sending messages that trace the progress of a program to a file or window.

Logical operator   An operator that can be applied to Boolean values. Java has three logical operators: &&, ||, and !.

Logic error   An error in a syntactically correct program that causes it to act differently from its specification. (A form of run-time error.)

Loop   A sequence of instructions that is executed repeatedly.

Loop and a half   A loop whose termination decision is neither at the beginning nor at the end.

Loop invariant   A statement about the program state that is preserved when the statements in the loop are executed once.

Machine code   Instructions that can be executed directly by the CPU.

Magic number   A number that appears in a program without explanation.

main method   The method that is first called when a Java application executes.

Map A data structure that keeps associations between key and value objects.

Markup Information about data that is added as humanly readable instructions. An example is the tagging of HTML documents with elements such as <h1> or <b>.

Memory location A value that specifies the location of data in computer memory.

Merge sort A sorting algorithm that first sorts two halves of a data structure and then merges the sorted subarrays together.

Meta data Data that describe properties of a data set.

Method A sequence of statements that has a name, may have formal parameters, and may return a value. A method can be invoked any number of times, with different values for its parameters.

Method signature The name of a method and the types of its parameters.

Mock object An object that is used during program testing, replacing another object and providing similar behavior. Usually, the mock object is simpler to implement or provides better support for testing.

Mutator method A method that changes the state of an object.

Mutual recursion Cooperating methods that call each other.

Name clash Accidentally using the same name to denote two program features in a way that cannot be resolved by the compiler.

Negative test case A test case that is expected to fail. For example, when testing a root-finding program, an attempt to compute the square root of −1 is a negative test case.

Nested block A block that is contained inside another block.

Nested loop A loop that is contained in another loop.

new operator An operator that allocates new objects.

Newline The '\n' character, which indicates the end of a line.

Null reference A reference that does not refer to any object.

Number literal A constant value in a program this is explicitly written as a number, such as −2 or 6.02214115E23.

Object A value of a class type.

Object-oriented design Designing a program by discovering objects, their properties, and their relationships.

Object reference A value that denotes the location of an object in memory. In Java, a variable whose type is a class contains a reference to an object of that class.

Off-by-one error A common programming error in which a value is one larger or smaller than it should be.

Opening a file Preparing a file for reading or writing.

Operating system The software that launches application programs and provides services (such as a file system) for those programs.

Operator A symbol denoting a mathematical or logical operation, such as + or &&.

Operator associativity The rule that governs in which order operators of the same precedence are executed. For example, in Java the - operator is left-associative because a - b - c is interpreted as (a - b) - c, and = is right-associative because a = b = c is interpreted as a = (b = c).

Operator precedence   The rule that governs which operator is evaluated first. For example, in Java the && operator has a higher precedence than the || operator. Hence a || b && c is interpreted as a || (b && c). (See Appendix B.)

Oracle   A program that predicts how another program should behave.

Overloading   Giving more than one meaning to a method name.

Overriding   Redefining a method in a subclass.

Package   A collection of related classes. The import statement is used to access one or more classes in a package.

Package access   Accessibility by methods of classes in the same package.

Panel   A user-interface component with no visual appearance. It can be used to group other components.

Parallel arrays   Arrays of the same length, in which corresponding elements are logically related.

Parameter   An item of information that is specified to a method when the method is called. For example, in the call System.out.println("Hello, World!"), the parameters are the implicit parameter System.out and the explicit parameter "Hello, World!".

Parameter passing   Specifying expressions to be actual parameter values for a method when it is called.

Parameter variable   A variable of a method that is initialized with a parameter value when the method is called.

Partially filled array   An array that is not filled to capacity, together with a companion variable that indicates the number of elements actually stored.

Permutation   A rearrangement of a set of values.

Polymorphism   Selecting a method among several methods that have the same name on the basis of the actual types of the implicit parameters.

Positive test case   A test case that a method is expected to handle correctly.

Postcondition   A condition that is true after a method has been called.

Postfix operator   A unary operator that is written after its argument.

Precondition   A condition that must be true when a method is called if the method is to work correctly.

Predicate method   A method that returns a Boolean value.

Prefix operator   A unary operator that is written before its argument.

Primitive type   In Java, a number type or boolean.

Priority queue   An abstract data type that enables efficient insertion of elements and efficient removal of the smallest element.

Private feature   A feature that is accessible only by methods of the same class or an inner class.

Project   A collection of source files and their dependencies.

Prompt   A string that tells the user to provide input.

Protected feature   A feature that is accessible by a class, its inner classes, its subclasses, and the other classes in the same package.

Pseudocode A high-level description of the actions of a program or algorithm, using a mixture of English and informal programming language syntax.

Pseudorandom number A number that appears to be random but is generated by a mathematical formula.

Public feature A feature that is accessible by all classes.

Public interface The features (methods, variables, and nested types) of a class that are accessible to all clients.

Qualified name A name that is made unambiguous because it starts with the package name.

Queue A collection of items with "first in, first out" retrieval.

Quicksort A generally fast sorting algorithm that picks an element, called the pivot, partitions the sequence into the elements smaller than the pivot and those larger than the pivot, and then recursively sorts the subsequences.

Radio button A user-interface component that can be used for selecting one of several options.

RAM (random-access memory) Electronic circuits in a computer that can store code and data of running programs.

Random access The ability to access any value directly without having to read the values preceding it.

Reader In the Java input/output library, a class from which to read characters.

Recursion A method for computing a result by decomposing the inputs into simpler values and applying the same method to them.

Recursive method A method that can call itself with simpler values. It must handle the simplest values without calling itself.

Redirection Linking the input or output of a program to a file instead of the keyboard or display.

Reference See **Object reference**

Regression testing Keeping old test cases and testing every revision of a program against them.

Regular expression A string that defines a set of matching strings according to their content. Each part of a regular expression can be a specific required character; one of a set of permitted characters such as [abc], which can be a range such as [a-z]; any character not in a set of forbidden characters, such as [^0-9]; a repetition of one or more matches, such as [0-9]+, or zero or more, such as [ACGT]; one of a set of alternatives, such as and|et|und; or various other possibilities. For example, "[A-Za-z][0-9]+" matches "Cloud9" or "007" but not "Jack".

Relational operator An operator that compares two values, yielding a Boolean result.

Reserved word A word that has a special meaning in a programming language and therefore cannot be used as a name by the programmer.

Return value The value returned by a method through a return statement.

Reverse Polish notation A style of writing expressions in which the operators are written following the operands, such as 2 3 4 + for 2 + 3 4.

Roundoff error An error introduced by the fact that the computer can store only a finite number of digits of a floating-point number.

Run-time error An error in a syntactically correct program that causes it to act differently from its specification.

Run-time stack The data structure that stores the local variables of all called methods as a program runs.

Scope The part of a program in which a variable is defined.

Scripting language A programming language that favors rapid development over execution speed and code maintainability.

Selection sort A sorting algorithm in which the smallest element is repeatedly found and removed until no elements remain.

Sentinel A value in input that is not to be used as an actual input value but to signal the end of input.

Sequential access Accessing values one after another without skipping over any of them.

Sequential search See **Linear search**

Serialization The process of saving an object, and all the objects that it references, to a stream.

Server A computer program or system that receives requests from a client, obtains or computes the requested information, and sends it to the client.

Set An unordered collection that allows efficient addition, location, and removal of elements.

Shadowing Hiding a variable by defining another one with the same name.

Shallow copy Copying only the reference to an object.

Shell script A file that contains commands for running programs and manipulating files. Typing the name of the shell script file on the command line causes those commands to be executed.

Shell window A window for interacting with an operating system through textual commands.

Short circuit evaluation Evaluating only a part of an expression if the remainder cannot change the result.

Side effect An effect of a method other than returning a value.

Sign bit The bit of a binary number that indicates whether the number is positive or negative.

Signature See **Method signature**

Simple statement A statement consisting of a single expression.

Single-stepping Executing a program in the debugger one statement at a time.

Software life cycle All activities related to the creation and maintenance of the software from initial analysis until obsolescence.

Source code Instructions in a programming language that need to be translated before execution on a computer.

Source file A file containing instructions in a programming language such as Java.

Spiral model An iterative process model of software development in which design and implementation are repeated.

Stack   A data structure with "last in, first out" retrieval. Elements can be added and removed only at one position, called the top of the stack.

Stack trace   A printout of the call stack, listing all currently pending method calls.

State   The current value of an object, which is determined by the cumulative action of all methods that were invoked on it.

State diagram   A diagram that depicts state transitions and their causes.

Statement   A syntactical unit in a program. In Java a statement is either a simple statement, a compound statement, or a block.

Static method   A method with no implicit parameter.

Static variable   A variable defined in a class that has only one value for the whole class, which can be accessed and changed by any method of that class.

Stream   An abstraction for a sequence of bytes from which data can be read or to which data can be written.

String   A sequence of characters.

Stub   A method with no or minimal functionality.

Subclass   A class that inherits variables and methods from a superclass but adds instance variables, adds methods, or redefines methods.

Superclass   A general class from which a more specialized class (a subclass) inherits.

Swing   A Java toolkit for implementing graphical user interfaces.

Symmetric bounds   Bounds that include the starting index and the ending index.

Syntax   Rules that define how to form instructions in a particular programming language.

Syntax diagram   A graphical representation of grammar rules.

Syntax error   An instruction that does not follow the programming language rules and is rejected by the compiler. (A form of compile-time error.)

Tab character   The '\t' character, which advances the next character on the line to the next one of a set of fixed positions known as tab stops.

TCP/IP (Transmission Control Protocol/Internet Protocol)   The pair of communication protocols that is used to establish reliable transmission of data between two computers on the Internet.

Ternary operator   An operator with three arguments. Java has one ternary operator, a ? b : c.

Test coverage   The instructions of a program that are executed in a set of test cases.

Test harness   A program that calls a function that needs to be tested, supplying parameters and analyzing the function's return value.

Test suite   A set of test cases for a program.

Text field   A user-interface component that allows a user to provide text input.

Text file   A file in which values are stored in their text representation.

Throwing an exception   Indicating an abnormal condition by terminating the normal control flow of a program and transferring control to a matching catch clause.

throws specifier   Indicates the types of the checked exceptions that a method may throw.

Token A sequence of consecutive characters from an input source that belongs together for the purpose of analyzing the input. For example, a token can be a sequence of characters other than white space.

Total ordering An ordering relationship in which all elements can be compared to each other.

Trace message A message that is printed during a program run for debugging purposes.

Tree A data structure consisting of nodes, each of which has a list of child nodes, and one of which is distinguished as the root node.

try block A block of statements that contains exception processing clauses. A try block contains at least one catch or finally clause.

Turing machine A very simple model of computation that is used in theoretical computer science to explore computability of problems.

Two-dimensional array A tabular arrangement of elements in which an element is specified by a row and a column index.

Type A named set of values and the operations that can be carried out with them.

Type parameter A parameter in a generic class or method that can be replaced with an actual type.

Type variable A variable in the declaration of a generic type that can be instantiated with a type.

Unary operator An operator with one argument.

Unchecked exception An exception that the compiler doesn't check.

Unicode A standard code that assigns code values consisting of two bytes to characters used in scripts around the world. Java stores all characters as their Unicode values.

Unified Modeling Language (UML) A notation for specifying, visualizing, constructing, and documenting the artifacts of software systems.

Uninitialized variable A variable that has not been set to a particular value. In Java, using an uninitialized local variable is a syntax error.

Unit test A test of a method by itself, isolated from the remainder of the program.

URL (uniform resource locator) A pointer to an information resource (such as a web page or an image) on the World Wide Web.

User-interface component A building block for a graphical user interface, such as a button or a text field. User-interface components are used to present information to the user and allow the user to enter information to the program.

User-interface event A notification to a program that a user action such as a key press, mouse move, or menu selection has occurred.

Variable A symbol in a program that identifies a storage location that can hold different values.

Virtual machine A program that simulates a CPU that can be implemented efficiently on a variety of actual machines. A given program in Java bytecode can be executed by any Java virtual machine, regardless of which CPU is used to run the virtual machine itself.

Visual programming Programming by arranging graphical elements on a form, setting program behavior by selecting properties for these elements, and writing only a small amount of "glue" code linking them.

void A reserved word indicating no type or an unknown type.

Watch window A window in a debugger that shows the current values of selected variables.

Waterfall model A sequential process model of software development, consisting of analysis, design, implementation, testing, and deployment.

White-box testing Testing methods by taking their implementations into account, in contrast to black-box testing; for example, by selecting boundary test cases and ensuring that all branches of the code are covered by some test case.

White space Any sequence of only space, tab, and newline characters.

Wrapper class A class that contains a primitive type value, such as Integer.

Writer In the Java input/output library, a class to which characters are to be sent.

INDEX

Page references followed by *t* indicate material in tables. Java library classes are indexed under java, as for example "java.util.Scanner class."

ILLUSTRATION CREDITS

Chapter 1   Page 3: Copyright © 2007, Intel Corporation.
Page 4: PhotoDisc, Inc./Getty Images.
Page 5 (top): PhotoDisc, Inc./Getty Images.
Page 5 (bottom): Copyright © 2007, Intel Corporation.
➕ Courtesy of Sperry Univac, Division of Sperry Corporation.
Page 23: Robert Ban/iStockphoto.

Chapter 2   Page 45: Constance Bannister Corp/Hulton Archive/Getty Images, Inc.
Page 45: Cay Horstmann.
Page 45: Jasmin Awad/iStockphoto.
Page 58: Mark Evans/iStockphoto.
Page 80: Punchstock.

Chapter 3   ➕ Larry Hoyle, Institute for Policy & Social Research, University of Kansas.
Page 118: Holger Mette/iStockphoto.
➕ Henrik Aija/iStockphoto.
Page 124: Rich Legg/iStockphoto.

Chapter 4   Page 157: Sidney Harris/ScienceCartoonsPlus.com.
➕ Vaughn Youtz/Zuma Press.

Chapter 5   Page 202: iStockphoto.
Page 204: Cay Horstmann.
Page 211: Mark Poprocki/iStockphoto.
Page 212: Naval Surface Weapons Center, Dahlgren, VA.

Chapter 6   Page 255: Kiyoshi Takahase/iStockphoto.
➕ Ryan Ruffatti/iStockphoto.

Chapter 7   ➕ Visicalc screen capture, Copyright © IBM Corporation. Used with permission.

Chapter 8   Page 317: gregory horler/iStockphoto.
Page 323 iStockphoto.
➕ Courtesy of Satoru Satoh.
➕ Courtesy of Sun Microsystems, Inc.

Chapter 9   Page 353: Tony Tremblay/iStockphoto (vehicle); Peter Dean/iStockphoto (motorcycle); nicholas belton/iStockphoto (car); Robert Pernell/iStockphoto (truck); Clay Blackburn/iStockphoto (sedan); iStockphoto (SUV).
Page 374: Sean Locke/iStockphoto.

Chapter 10   Page 403: age fotostock/SUPERSTOCK.
➕ AP/Wide World Photos.

Chapter 11   Page 429: Booch/Jacobson/Rumbaugh, *The Unified Modeling Language Reference Manual*, pg. 41, © 1999 by Addison Wesley Longman, Inc. Reproduced by permission of Pearson Education, Inc.

Chapter 12   ➕ Science Photo Library/Photo Researchers, Inc.

Chapter 13   ➕ Topham/The Image Works.

Chapter 14   Page 560: Photodisc/Punchstock.
Page 562: Courtesy Nigel Tout.

Animation Icon   james steidl/iStockphoto.